In Context

In Context

Reading and Writing in Cultural Conversations

SECOND EDITION

Ann Merle Feldman
University of Illinois-Chicago

Ellen McManus
Dominican University

Nancy Downs
University of Illinois-Chicago

New York San Francisco Boston
London Toronto Sydney Tokyo Singapore Madrid
Mexico City Munich Paris Cape Town Hong Kong Montreal

Senior Vice President and Publisher: Joseph Opiela
Senior Acquisitions Editor: Lynn M. Huddon
Development Editor: Katharine Glynn
Senior Supplements Editor: Donna Campion
Marketing Manager: Wendy Albert
Managing Editor: Bob Ginsberg
Production Manager: Joseph Vella
Project Coordination, Text Design, and Electronic Page Makeup: Shepherd, Inc.
Senior Cover Design Manager: Nancy Danahy
Cover Design Manager: John Callahan
Cover Designer: Maria Ilardi
Cover Photos: *First Image:* Juan Munoz, *Last Conversation Piece* 1994–1995. Bronze, 66½ × 244¾ × 321⅛ inches. Hirshhorn Museum and Sculpture Garden, Smithsonian Institution, museum purchase, 1995. *Second Image:* Getty Images, Inc.
Photo Researcher: Photosearch, Inc.
Manufacturing Manager: Mary Fischer
Manufacturing Buyer: Lucy Hebard
Printer and Binder: R.R. Donnelley & Sons, Inc.
Cover Printer: The Lehigh Press

For permission to use copyrighted material, grateful acknowledgement is made to the copyright holders on pp. 586–589, which are hereby made part of this copyright page.

Library of Congress Cataloging-in-Publication Data
On file with the Library of Congress

Please visit us at http://www.ablongman.com

ISBN: 0-321-23302-6

1 2 3 4 5 6 7 8 9 10—DOH—07 06 05 04

Brief Contents

Detailed Contents vii
Readings Listed by Genre xx
Writing Projects Listed by Genre xxiii
Preface xxv

Unit I
Reading and Writing Rhetorically 1
Chapter 1 *Contexts for Reading and Writing* 5
Chapter 2 *Strategies for Writers at Work* 18

Unit II
Searching for Authenticity 39
Chapter 3 *Representing and Misrepresenting the Self* 41
Chapter 4 *Buying and Selling Authenticity* 96
Chapter 5 *Case Study: Contesting the Ownership of Music* 132

Unit III
Creating a Sense of Place 167
Chapter 6 *On the Road* 169
Chapter 7 *Making a Home* 205
Chapter 8 *Case Study: On Painting a House Purple* 263

Unit IV
Participating in Civic Conversations 287
Chapter 9 *What Makes Democracy Work?* 289
Chapter 10 *Redefining Disability* 342
Chapter 11 *Case Study: Designing Memorials* 389

Unit V
Adapting to the Changing Economy 419
Chapter 12 *Living in the Global Economy* 421
Chapter 13 *Adapting to the Changing Workplace* 470
Chapter 14 *Case Study: Advocating for Temporary Workers* 525

Genre Glossary 561
Credits 586
Index 590

Detailed Contents

Reading Listed by Genre xx
Writing Projects Listed by Genre xxiii
Preface xxv

Unit I

Reading and Writing Rhetorically 1

Chapter 1

Contexts for Reading and Writing 5

Analyzing a Feature Story: Graffiti as Art or Vandalism 5

Phat X. Chiem *Taggers Spray Over Vandal Image* 5
A newspaper article describing a community art project by graffiti artists illustrates one moment in an ongoing public conversation. Through this illustration we introduce four dimensions that shape writing and reading.

Four Ways to Look at Reading and Writing 7

Situation 7

Genre 8

Language 8

Consequences 8

Reading the Graffiti Article 9

Exploring a Writing Scenario 10

Questions to Ask as You Read and Write

A Guide to Analyzing Readings in Context 12

A Guide to Analyzing Contexts for Writing 15

Chapter 2

Strategies for Writers at Work 18

A Writer Talks about Her Work 18

A How-To List for Reading and Writing 24

Before You Read: Connecting with the Conversation 24

Consider Your Own Related Experiences 24

Pay Attention to Discussions in the Media 24

Search the Topic Online 25
Talk to People with Relevant Knowledge or Experiences 25
As You Read: Exploring Texts and Contexts 25
Understand the Writing Situation 25
Identify and Analyze the Genre of the Text 26
Analyze the Language of the Text 26
Consider the Consequences of the Text 26
Compare the Text with Other Texts 26
Search the Library and the Internet for Related Texts 27
Visit a Real or Electronic Bookstore 28
Evaluate Sources 28
Getting Down to Writing: Creating Texts 29
Identify a Situation and Purpose for Writing 29
Take Advantage of the Writing Process 29
Planning 29
Drafting 30
Revising 31
Editing 33
Writing Arguments 33
Integrating Material from Other Texts 34
Summarizing 34
Paraphrasing 34
Quoting 34
Avoiding Plagiarism 34
Creating Visual Texts 35
Collaborating with Others on the Writing of a Text 35

Unit II

Searching for Authenticity 39

Chapter 3

Representing and Misrepresenting the Self 41

Esmeralda Santiago *Skin* *43*

We represent ourselves to others when we're absent—for example in a letter or photograph—but we also represent ourselves when we're present, for example in our clothes or language. Santiago explores how our very skin can represent our lives both to others and to ourselves.

Shane Madden *A Portfolio of Self Representations 50*
We represent ourselves to others in a variety of ways, from our online chat to our job applications. Here we look at three different ways in which a college freshman represents himself to his world.

Todd Boyd *Representin' the Real 58*
Boyd explains his struggle to represent himself authentically to different people with different expectations, thus exploring the blurry line between representation and misrepresentation.

Sherry Turkle *Identity in the Age of the Internet 67*
Turkle argues that computers allow us to experience the self as multiple, and in this excerpt she explores the possibilities and dangers of this multiplicity.

Danny Santiago *Famous All Over Town 82*
When this novel was first published, its author was hailed as an authentic voice from the barrio. Revelations about its author set off a continuing debate about authenticity, misrepresentation, and the self. We also include a review of the novel by David Quammen and an article about its author by Edwin McDowell.

Chapter 4

Buying and Selling Authenticity 96

Nell Bernstein *Goin' Gangsta, Choosin' Cholita 97*
The editor of a magazine about youth culture tells the stories of young people who use fashion and music to identify themselves with ethnic groups they consider more authentic.

Marc Spiegler *Marketing Street Culture: Bringing Hip-Hop Style to the Mainstream 104*
Aimed at companies that produce clothing for young people, this piece from *American Demographics* advises marketing experts on how to "keep it real."

James Ledbetter *Imitation of Life 115*
This editorial from *Vibe* magazine challenges "wannabes" to do more than buy records. Ledbetter calls for those who identify with Black culture to "end America's political and cultural apartheid."

David Klinghoffer *The Heart of the Matter 121*
Klinghoffer traces his search for what is real through hypochondria, a desire for authentic clothing, and a quest for his birth mother but finally fulfills his need for a spiritual center by turning to Jewish orthodoxy.

Chapter 5

Case Study: Contesting the Ownership of Music 132

Popular music is the arena in which definitions of authenticity are fought over most publicly, boisterously, and expensively. Is music, or any art form, authentic only if it is individual self-expression? Do artists own their work? How has modern technology changed our ideas about both art and ownership? When the experimental rock group Negativland made a single that sampled words and music from a variety of sources, they set in motion a lawsuit and public debate about these questions of art, ownership, and authenticity. In this case study, by examining documents related to the Negativland lawsuit, you will develop your own answers to these questions.

The Case **132**

The Issues **133**

The Documents **135**

Your Role **136**

U2 *I Still Haven't Found What I'm Looking For* *137*
Negativland's sampling of this single from U2's 1987 album *The Joshua Tree* became one focus of the lawsuit.

Richard Harrington *U2's Double Trouble* *138*
The Negativland lawsuit has been analyzed and debated in a variety of media from counterculture magazines and online discussion groups to academic and legal journals. This *Washington Post* news story was one of the first pieces of coverage in the mainstream media.

Island Records/Warner-Chappell Music *Excerpts from the Island/Warner-Chappell Lawsuit* *140*
In this legal document, the plaintiffs make their case against Negativland.

Negativland *U2 Negativland: The Case from Our Side* *147*
The legal case of Negativland and its record company was made by its lawyers in court, but Negativland also took its wider argument to the public in a variety of ways, including this press release sent out soon after the case was filed.

Excerpts from Chapter 1 of the 1976 United States Copyright Act *154*
This chapter of the Copyright Act, which includes the section known as the Fair Use Clause, is commonly referred to in copyright infringement suits.

Negativland *In Fair Use Debate, Art Must Come First* *158*

Andrian Adams and Paul McKibbins *Sampling Without Permission Is Theft* *160*

Negativland lost its case in court but has continued to argue its position in public, as in this exchange of opinion pieces published in *Billboard* magazine.

Tom Samiljan *Build a Desktop Studio* *162*

Despite the outcome of the Negativland case, sampling has hardly disappeared from the music business. This software review from *Rolling Stone* magazine suggests how technology might continue to change attitudes and practices surrounding art and ownership.

RTMARK *RTMARK Finds Bucks for Beck Rip-off* *164*

Artistic subversion of the music industry did not end with the Negativland case. The musical/political action group RTMARK describes its own anticorporate activity in this 1998 online press release.

Unit III

Creating a Sense of Place 167

Chapter 6

On the Road 169

Andrea Barrett *Why We Go* *171*

How can people find adventure when there seem to be so few unexplored places left? Reflecting on her own experiences as an amateur kayaker, journalist Barrett suggests some possible answers.

Yi-Fu Tuan *Nature and Culture* *177*

We think of nature as an escape from culture and society: this is why outdoor adventure appeals to many of us. But geographer Tuan argues that, even more primally, culture is an escape from nature.

R. B. Kitaj *First Diasporist Manifesto* *189*

An American painter in London proclaims that losing one's sense of place contributes to a new style of painting, which he names Diasporist painting.

Clifton L. Taulbert *Bright Boy from the Delta* *193*

Taulbert's memoir takes us back to his childhood in a small segregated town in rural Mississippi and reveals how his early upbringing sustained him through his journey to the north and into the military.

Chapter 7

Making a Home 205

Witold Rybczynski *Comfort and Well-Being* *207*

Reflecting on the complex relationship between design, behavior, and deeply rooted cultural traditions, Rybczynski explains why we need to do more than borrow from the styles of the past to regain the sense of well-being and comfort we all seek from our homes.

Sharon Haar and Christopher Reed *Coming Home* *219*

Haar and Reed ask us to rethink our ideas about home. Do we see our homes through a nostalgic desire for comfort, or do we use home as a base for enacting social change?

Michael Pollan *The Triumph of Burbopolis* *234*

Pollan's return to the suburb of his childhood inspires a playful analysis of what the suburbs were and what they have become.

Margaret Crawford and Adobe LA *Mi Casa es Su Casa* *243*

Crawford and Adobe LA write as a collaborative team about an architectural design project that looks anew at how Mexicans migrating to East Los Angeles have personalized their dwellings.

Richard Rodriguez *Late Victorians: San Francisco, AIDS, and the Homosexual Stereotype* *249*

An essayist describes how gay men created a style of living and a community in the Castro district of San Francisco and how the coming of AIDS transformed that community.

Chapter 8

Case Study: *On Painting a* House *Purple* 263

When Sandra Cisneros, author of the acclaimed novel *The House on Mango Street,* painted her house in San Antonio a bright purple, she thought she was complying with the code stipulating that houses in historic districts must be painted "historic" colors—after all, purple is a historic color for Mexicans. But the San Antonio Historic and Design Review Commission argued that purple did not fit the criteria to preserve the historic look of the neighborhood. Cisneros, a Mexican American whose work has powerfully addressed issues of ethnicity and women's rights to self-determination, decided to fight back.

The Case 263

The Issues 264

The Documents 266

Your Role 267

City of San Antonio *Understanding the Preservation Process 269*
San Antonio distributes this brochure to help residents understand the meaning and process of historic preservation.

Susan Yerkes *King William Seeing Red over Purple 275*
San Antonio Express-News columnist explains the controversy, which many San Antonians may have been reading about for the first time.

Susan Yerkes *Now We Know Why It's Called Purple Passion 276*
In a follow-up column a few days later, Yerkes describes a variety of emotional responses to her earlier column.

Mike Greenberg *Purple Debate Reaches Commission—Cisneros Agrees to Work with City Staff on Mutually Acceptable Color Scheme 277*
When Cisneros made her case before the Historic and Design Review Commission, reporter and columnist Greenberg covered the story for the *San Antonio Express-News.*

Letters to the Editor 278
In the weeks following the first reports of the controversy, many San Antonio residents wrote to the *San Antonio Express-News,* venting strong opinions about Cisneros and her purple house.

Sandra Cisneros *Purple Politics—Our Tejano History Has Become Invisible 280*
Not long after the hearing, the *San Antonio Express-News* published opinion pieces by Cisneros and Milton Babbitt, a member of the Historic and Design Review Commission. Cisneros argues that the colors meaningful to Mexican Americans were not included in historic guidelines because they are, like much of the history of American minorities, undocumented.

Milton Babbitt *Purple Politics—Individuality Surrendered for Preservation 283*
Babbitt, a well-known composer and San Antonio resident, argues that design codes have an important community function and are meaningful only if they apply to everyone in the community.

Michele Norris and Lisa McRee *The Purple House—Coat of Paint Causes Cultural War in San Antonio 285*
About a year after the controversy first began, *Good Morning America* brought the story of the purple house to a national audience.

Unit IV

Participating in Civic Conversations 287

Chapter 9

What Makes Democracy Work? 289

Harry C. Boyte and Nancy N. Kari *The New Democracy* *291*
Boyte and Kari ask us to think differently about work and how it can contribute to the common good.

Robert D. Putnam *Toward an Agenda for Social Capitalists* *304*
In the last chapter from his book *Bowling Alone,* Putnam sets out his plan to renew civic engagement and social connectedness in the twenty-first century. In six key areas ranging from youth and schools to politics and government, he challenges individuals to restore the sense of community in America.

Patricia J. Williams *Hate Radio: Why We Need to Tune In to Limbaugh and Stern* *319*
Of the many traditional and new media through which American citizens discuss public issues, perhaps the most controversial has been not the Internet but talk radio. In this essay a law professor raises questions about the effects of talk radio on the civility of our national conversations.

Ray Suarez, Ellis Cose, Joie Chen, George de Lama, and Mark Trahant *Symposium on Minority Journalists and the Media* *327*
In a nationally broadcast radio forum, journalists and interested citizens discuss the role of minority journalists in providing balanced coverage and diverse perspectives in the media.

Chapter 10

Redefining Disability 342

Paul K. Longmore *The Second Phase: From Disability Rights to Disability Culture* *344*
In an overview of the events of the last two decades, this historian characterizes the first phase of the disability rights movement as a search for equal rights and inclusion and the second phase as the creation of a disability culture.

Simi Linton *Negotiating Disability* *353*
Linton makes a case for establishing Disability Studies as part of the liberal arts curriculum by asking us to consider how encounters with disability affect our understanding of ourselves in a variety of professional and personal situations.

Michael Bérubé ***Life as We Know It*** ***368***
The father of a child with Down syndrome, Bérubé analyzes the connection between the language we use to talk about disability and current social policies and institutional practices.

James S. Brady ***Save Money: Help the Disabled*** ***379***

New York Times **Editors** ***Blank Check for the Disabled?*** ***380***
In the days before the U.S. Senate debated the Americans with Disabilities Act, columnists and editorialists expressed their opinions, and senators paid attention. These two pieces from the *New York Times* were referred to in the debate and read into the *Congressional Record.*

Rosemarie Garland-Thomson ***The FDR Memorial: Who Speaks from the Wheelchair?*** ***382***
Ten years after the passage of the ADA, the building of the Franklin Delano Roosevelt Memorial in Washington, D.C., sparked a debate about how our society should represent disability.

Chapter 11

Case Study: Designing Memorials 389

What is the role of a memorial designed to commemorate a public tragedy? This case study examines the public conversations surrounding the development and design of two memorials: The Vietnam Veterans Memorial and the memorial designed to commemorate the fall of World Trade Center towers on September 11, 2001. Often memorials have been a target of controversy rather than a vehicle for strengthening communal ties. Debate has revolved around issues of representation, style and design, and ultimately reception.

The Case 389

The Issues 389

The Documents 392

Your Role 394

Jan C. Scruggs and Joel L. Swerdlow ***Vietnam Veterans Memorial Statement of Purpose*** ***395***
A statement written by the executive director of the Vietnam Veterans Memorial Fund was released to the public in November 1980 announcing the design competition for the memorial.

Maya Ying Lin ***Design Competition: Winning Designer's Statement*** ***396***
This statement of purpose written by Maya Lin was presented as part of her competition submission in March 1981.

Maya Ying Lin *Boundaries* *398*
As the Vietnam Veterans Memorial was being completed in 1982, Maya Lin wrote her own personal account of the how the memorial was designed and built. But it wasn't until she published her memoirs in 2000 that she was able to return to her account of those events.

Robert Ivy *Memorials, Monuments, and Meaning* *409*
Ivy's article focuses on a wide range of historical, philosophical, artistic, and religious aspects of memorial design. This article addresses how questions about human nature, attitudes toward death, and spiritual beliefs have influenced the discussions about both the Vietnam Veterans Memorial and the proposed World Trade Center Memorial.

Michael Kimmelman *The New Ground Zero: Finding Comfort in the Safety of Names* *412*
In an article published in the *New York Times* on August 31, 2003, Michael Kimmelman discusses the significance of including names of the dead on memorials even when, as with the Vietnam Veterans Memorial, the numbers are in the thousands.

Allison Keyes for the Tavis Smiley Show *Continuing Controversy over Construction of a Memorial at the World Trade Center Site* *416*
This document, a transcript of a story that aired on National Public Radio on December 5, 2003, gives a glimpse into the public debate about the emotional topic of the memorial design.

Photo of the Design for the World Trade Center Memorial *418*
The final document in the case study is a photograph of the design for the World Trade Center Memorial.

Unit V

Adapting to the Changing Economy 419

Chapter 12

Living in the Global Economy 421

Robert Wright and Robert Kaplan *Mr. Order Meets Mr. Chaos* *423*
This debate highlights two perspectives on globalization: Robert Wright, Mr. Order, claims that everyone benefits from the globalization of markets and workforce. Robert Kaplan, Mr. Chaos, isn't so sure and wants us to prepare for global disruption.

William Wolman and Anne Colamosca *A Passage to India: The Case of Bangalore* 435

This chapter from a book on work and global capital documents what can happen to a poverty-stricken third-world city when education is free and when students become knowledge workers.

Robert Reich *Becoming a Knowledge Worker* 447

Reich suggests that there are three kinds of workers in today's global economy. For two of the three—those who do routine work and those who provide in-person services—the prospects are not good. Reich believes that only the knowledge worker will thrive in the global economy.

Chan Lean Heng *Women on the Global Assembly Line* 460

The impact of the global economy has had profound consequences for Malaysian women factory workers. Heng recounts their experiences through their own voices.

Chapter 13

Adapting to the Changing Workplace 470

Robyn Meredith *For This We Sent You to College?* 472

Are new college graduates underemployed? Does college tuition pay off? Meredith profiles the starting careers of several new college graduates. And two readers respond to this article in letters to the editor.

Daniel P. Goleman *What Makes a Leader?* 484

Goleman describes "emotional intelligence" as the ability to work with others and to create change. Those who have it rise to the top, while those with only intelligence in the more traditional sense may fail.

Barbara Ehrenreich *Nickel-and-Dimed: On (Not) Getting by in America* 497

Ehrenreich goes undercover as a low-wage earner and writes about her experiences. Follow her frustration trying to support an extremely meager lifestyle.

Victoria de Grazia, Claudia Goldin, Jacqueline Jones, Juliet B. Schor, Marta Tienda, William Julius Wilson, and moderator Michael Weinstein *A Man's Place* 516

This dialogue, featuring experts from a variety of fields, traces women's economic progress over the last 100 years.

Chapter 14

Case Study: Advocating for Temporary Workers 525

As the economy changes, so does the relationship between employer and worker. One of the fastest-growing job categories is that of the contingent, or temporary, worker. Temporary employment is often touted as a creative response to the changing economy. The claim is that "economic nomads" can choose where and when to work. However, recent labor research indicates that temporary workers have few choices, low pay, and often no benefits. Recently groups have emerged to act as advocates for temporary workers, providing training, advice, and support. These advocacy groups challenge the notion that temporary work opens up career options.

The Case 525

The Issues 525

The Documents 529

Your Role 530

Merrill Goozner ***Longtime Temps Want Some Perks: Now Some Are Suing Companies for Benefits*** *532*

A *Chicago Tribune* news article explains how temporary jobs turn into long-term but not permanent jobs and how "permatemps" are denied the benefits available to other workers doing the same work.

Aaron Bernstein ***A Leg Up for the Lowly Temp: Advocates Are Lobbying for Better Benefits and an Employers' Code of Conduct*** *536*

Bernstein describes a variety of advocacy groups and how they are working to provide training, support, and benefits for temporary workers.

Barry Peterson ***The Temp Workers Alliance's Consumer Guide to "Best Practices" Temp Agencies*** *539*

This publication of the Temp Workers Alliance, a support group for New Jersey temps, offers a variety of documents to help deal with conflicts between temporary workers and employers. The following items are included:

Temp Task Force Mission Statement: Principles of the Temp Workers Alliance.

Considering the Temp Option: Guidelines for choosing temporary work.

Ethics for Temporary Workers: A list enumerating the responsibilities of temp workers.

Temp Workers—Know the Law!: Summary highlighting New Jersey and federal laws that temps should be aware of.

Share Your Temp Experiences: A survey for workers to report on their experiences with temp agencies.

Principles of Fair Conduct for Temporary Employment Agencies: A checklist for agencies to grade themselves on the support they provide for temporary workers.

Brian Hassett ***The Temp Survival Guide: How to Prosper as an Economic Nomad of the Nineties*** ***550***

This introductory chapter from a "how to" guide paints an optimistic picture of the opportunities available to the temporary worker.

Jeff Kelly ***Best of Temp Slave!*** ***556***

Best of Temp Slave! is a collection from the well-known Internet 'zine, which offered temp workers an opportunity to comment on their plight. Included here are two comics and a personal narrative.

A *Genre Glossary* 561

Academic Article/Research Paper 561

Address/Speech 563

Advice Book/Article 564

Brochure 564

Business Letter/Memo 565

Codes/Guidelines 566

Comics 567

Cover Letter/Reflective Essay 568

Dialogue/Symposium/Debate 569

Essay 570

Personal/Informal/Literary Essay 572

Argumentative/Analytical/Persuasive Essay 573

Feature Story/Profile 574

Interview 575

Letter to the Editor 576

Manifesto 577

Online Posts 578

Opinion Piece/Commentary 578

Proposal 580

Report 581

Resume/Cover Letter 582

Review 583

Web Page 584

Credits 586

Index 590

Readings Listed by Genre

The readings for *In Context* were selected to create conversations on issues and themes, as you can see in the Detailed Table of Contents. But as you can see in this listing, the readings also represent a wide range of genres. The readings are organized below according to the genres in the Genre Glossary, with some additional, more specialized genres—court document, exhibit catalogue, legislation, lyrics, mission statement, news article, press release, survey and transcript of radio and television show—represented as well. Of course the boundary lines between some genres—for example academic article, essay, feature article, and opinion piece—are not always clear. Rather than cross-listing readings, we have made the categorizations below on the basis of content, format, place of publication, and when possible the designation given to the piece in the original publication. But you might want to categorize differently.

Academic Articles (including chapters and excerpts from books for an academic audience)

Witold Rybczynski, "Comfort and Well-Being" 207

Sharon Haar and Christopher Reed, "Coming Home" 219

Robert D. Putnam, "Toward an Agenda for Social Capitalists" 304

Simi Linton, "Negotiating Disability" 353

Chan Lean Heng, "Women on the Global Assembly Line" 460

Daniel Goleman, "What Makes a Leader?" 484

Harry C. Boyte and Nancy Kari, "The New Democracy" 291

Sherry Turkle, "Identity in the Age of the Internet" 67

Advice Book/Article

Brian Hassett, "The Temp Survival Guide: How to Prosper as an Economic Nomad of the Nineties" 550

Brochure

City of San Antonio, "Understanding The Preservation Process" 269

Codes/Guidelines

"Considering the Temp Option" 540

"Ethics for Temporary Workers" 541

"Temp Workers—Know the Law!" 542

"Principles of Fair Conduct for Temporary Employment Agencies" 547

Comics

Comics from *Best of Temp Slave!* 556

Court Document

"Excerpts from the Island/Warner-Chappell Lawsuit" 140

Cover Letter/Resume

Shane Madden, Cover letter and Resume 56, 57

Dialogue/Symposium/Debate

Ray Suarez, Ellis Cose, Joie Chen, George de Lama, Mark Trahant, "Symposium on Minority Journalists and the Media" 327

Victoria De Grazia, Claudia Goldin, Jacqueline Jones, Juliet B. Schor, Marta Tienda, William Julius Wilson, and moderator Michael Weinstein, "A Man's Place" 516

Robert Wright and Robert Kaplan, "Mr. Order Meets Mr. Chaos" 423

Essays (including essay-like chapters and excerpts from books)

Esmeralda Santiago, "Skin" 43
Shane Madden, "College Application Essay" 54
Todd Boyd, "Representin the Real" 58
David Klinghoffer, "The Heart of the Matter" 121
Andrea Barrett, "Why We Go" 171
Yi-Fu Tuan, "Nature and Culture" 177
Clifton L. Taulbert, "Bright Boy from the Delta" 193
Richard Rodriguez, "Late Victorians: San Francisco, AIDS, and the Homosexual Stereotype" 241
Patricia J. Williams, "Hate Radio" 319
Paul K. Longmore, "The Second Phase: From Disability Rights to Disability Culture" 344
Michael Bérubé, "Life as We Know It" 368
Rosemarie Garland-Thomson, "The FDR Memorial: Who Speaks from the Wheelchair?" 382
William Wolman and Anne Colamosca, "A Passage to India: The Case of Bangalore" 435
Robert Reich, "Becoming a Knowledge Worker" 447
Barbara Ehrenreich, "Nickel-and-Dimed: On (Not) Getting by in America" 497
Maya Ying Lin, "Boundaries" 398
Robert Ivy, "Memorials, Monuments, and Meanings" 409

Exhibit Catalogue

Margaret Crawford and Adobe LA, "Mi Casa es Su Casa" 243

Feature Stories/Profiles

Phat X. Chiem, "Taggers Spray Over Vandal Image" 5
Edwin McDowell, "A Noted 'Hispanic' Novelist Proves to Be Someone Else" 91
Nell Bernstein, "Goin' Gangsta, Choosin' Cholita" 97
Marc Spiegler, "Marketing Street Culture: Bringing Hip-Hop Style to the Mainstream" 104
Michael Pollan, "The Triumph of Burbopolis" 234
Robyn Meredith, "For This We Sent You to College?" 472

Legislation

Excerpt from Chapter 1 of the 1976 United States Copyright Act 154

Letter to the Editor

"Letters to the Editor of *San Antonio Express-News*" 278
Peter A. Benoliel, "Education, Not Glamour" 482
Peter J. Vergano, Letter to the Editor, 482

Lyrics

U2, "I Still Haven't Found What I'm Looking For" 137

Manifesto

R. B. Kitaj "First Diasporist Manifesto" 189

Mission Statement

"Purpose of the Temp Task Force" 539

News Articles

Richard Harrington, "U2's Double Trouble" 138

Susan Yerkes, "King William Seeing Red Over Purple" 275

Susan Yerkes, "Now We Know Why It's Called Purple Passion" 276

Mike Greenberg, "Purple Debate Reaches Commission—Cisneros Agrees to Work with City Staff on Mutually Acceptable Color Scheme" 277

Merrill Goozner, "Longtime Temps Want Some Perks: Now Some Are Suing Companies for Benefits" 532

Aaron Bernstein, "A Leg Up for the Lowly Temp: Advocates Are Lobbying for Better Benefits and an Employers' Code of Conduct" 536

Novel

Danny Santiago, Chapter 1 from *Famous All Over Town* 82

Opinion Pieces/Editorials

Berenice Salas, "Delicious Culture in a Pushcart." 22

James Ledbetter, "Imitation of Life" 115

Negativland, "In Fair Use Debate, Art Must Come First" 158

Andrian Adams and Paul McKibbins, "Sampling Without Permission Is Theft" 160

Sandra Cisneros, "Purple Politics—Our Tejano History Has Become Invisible" 280

Milton Babbitt, "Purple Politics—Individuality Surrendered for Preservation" 283

Michael Kimmelman, "The New Ground Zero: Finding Comfort in the Safety of Names" 412

James S. Brady, "Save Money: Help the Disabled" 379

New York Times Editors, "Blank Check for the Disabled?" 380

Press Releases

Negativland, "U2 Negativland: The Case from Our Side" 147

RTMARK, "RTMARK Finds Bucks for Beck Rip-off" 164

Robert Doubek, "Vietnam Veterans Memorial Fund Statement of Purpose" 395

Proposal

Maya Ying Lin, "Design Competition: Winning Designer's Statement" 396

Reviews

Review of Danny Santiago's *Famous All over Town* 90

Tom Samiljan, "Build a Desktop Studio" 162

Survey

"Share Your Temp Experiences" 546

Transcripts of Radio or Television Shows

Michele Norris and Lisa McRee, "The Purple House" 162

Allison Keyes, "Continuing Controversy over Constuction of a Memorial at the World Trade Center Site" 416

Web Page

Shane Madden, Personal Home Page 52

Writing Projects Listed by Genre

Each reading in *In Context* includes at least two writing projects. Many of these are essays, the most common genre for academic discourse. But because we believe that writing in a variety of genres helps students better understand the context-dependent, consequential nature of writing, the rest of the writing projects offer opportunities to write in other genres. This comprehensive list of writing projects will allow for sequences of readings and writing projects that focus on genre.

Academic Article/Research Paper 218, 377, 516, 524, 531

Address/Speech 388, 434, 459

Advice Book/Article 204

Brochure 319, 394

Business Letter/Memo 497

Codes/Guidelines 469

Comics 50, 326, 434

Cover Letter/Reflective Essay 58, 66, 95, 103, 115, 204, 434

Dialogue/Symposium/Debate 81, 176, 242, 262, 302, 326, 340, 367, 447, 523

Review 218

Resume/Cover letter 58

Web Page 88

Essay 50, 58, 66, 81, 95, 103, 120, 131, 136, 176, 189, 193, 203, 218, 234, 242, 249, 261, 268, 302, 319, 341, 352, 368, 377, 388, 394, 447, 460, 469, 516, 532

Feature Story/Profile 66, 120, 218, 319, 483

Interview 460, 497

Letter to the Editor 249, 484

Online Post 115

Manifesto 193, 233

Opinion Piece/Commentary 103, 115, 131, 136, 189, 268

Report 352

Preface

Writing is a way of acting in the world; that is the idea that drives this textbook. *In Context* focuses on how societies and individuals, including students, use writing and reading to do things in the world. It presents a series of contexts in which people use writing to create, sustain, understand, and change their worlds.

Although organized with the flexibility of a thematic reader, *In Context* presents its reading selections as pieces of writing that emerge from specific situations. We want students to see themselves as participants in important public conversations, which means that they must see themselves as readers and writers in situations that engage their attention and response. We have chosen readings that can easily be put into conversation with each other, and we have included genres—for example academic articles, newspaper stories, and symposia of various kinds—that report on, comment on, or analyze situations, as well as genres—for example press releases, codes of conduct, legal documents, and the manifesto—that take more direct actions in situations. Similarly, the writing projects that accompany each reading invite students to reflect on issues raised in the readings, as well as to use genres that allow them to participate more directly in the situations referred to in the readings. The case studies in Chapters 5, 8, 11, and 14, consisting of documents gathered around a specific moment in a larger conversation, give students particularly vivid opportunities to see themselves as agents—readers and writers—in well-defined situations.

New Features of the Second Edition

The newly reconceptualized introductory unit, **Unit I,** provides teachers and students the support they need to do *In Context*'s situated writing projects.

Chapter 1, Reading and Writing Rhetorically, makes use of a newspaper article on graffiti to illustrate and define the key rhetorical dimensions—situation, genre, language, and consequences—that help students see themselves participating in situations that call for writing. Two guides—The Guide to Analyzing Readings in Context and The Guide to Analyzing Contexts for Writing—offer sets of questions that help students analyze reading and writing situations.

Chapter 2, Strategies for Writers at Work, illustrates how an understanding of the four rhetorical dimensions contributes to the activities of a writer as she revises an opinion piece about an ongoing issue in her neighborhood. Chapter 2 also guides writers through the many activities they will encounter in this book. Before students read a selection, we ask them to consider the larger context of the situation. We ask students as they read to look closely at the text and to think about how this text fits into larger contexts. To help students prepare to write, we offer advice on research, on the composing process, and on writing in teams and groups.

Chapter 3, Representing and Misrepresenting the Self, composed of almost entirely new pieces, helps students explore the nature of representation, the complexities of representing and misrepresenting the self, and the relationship between identity and authenticity. This chapter includes a student portfolio of self-representations and a new reading on the use of alter egos in online environments. Finally, it includes a mini case study of literary misrepresentation in which an Anglo author uses a pen name to represent himself as a Latino.

Chapter 9, What Makes Democracy Work, focuses on civic participation. A new reading offers a historical view of what the authors call "public work," in which everday life and labor contributes to the common good. This chapter examines how writing and public conversations can contribute to a contemporary attempt to reinvigorate the idea of public work.

The Case Study in **Chapter 11, Designing Memorials,** examines the public conversations leading up to the design and construction of the Vietnam Veterans Memorial and the projected memorial to the victims of the World Trade Center attacks. For this case study, students might design a brochure introducing other students to one of the memorials or write an essay in which they discuss what Americans can learn about public debate from the discussions surrounding the design and construction of each of these memorials.

Distinctive Features

Rhetorical Framework: Situation, Genre, Language, and Consequences

In Context is organized around a set of concepts—situation, genre, language, and consequences—that consolidate important rhetorical ideas. This set of concepts is powerful for several reasons. Because students can use the concepts as both readers and writers, they help students see the connections between reading and writing. They help students see the complexities of reading and writing by drawing attention to the fact that any text and any act of reading or writing has many dimensions. And because students are already familiar with the everyday meanings of these words, the terms themselves are very user-friendly.

When we use these concepts in our classrooms, we find that they help students make a variety of connections. Whether reading an essay or writing a letter to the editor, students see that they must take into account the many situations involved, consider the implications of genre, recognize the language of a text as a range of choices guided by various constraints, and focus on the consequences of what they read and write.

We have designed *In Context* so that instructors can use these concepts fully to guide the course but can also choose to make only occasional use of them for particular purposes or not use them at all. To allow for this range of choices, we use icons to highlight activities that focus on one of the concepts, but all activities can be used productively without reference to the concepts.

Situation. How histories, cultures, communities, and individual experiences influence the writing and reading of texts. This concept helps students consider the complex contexts from which a piece of writing emerges.

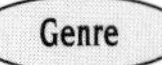

Genre. The forms—in writing, speech, or any other medium—that have evolved in response to repeated situations, needs, or desires. As readers, students learn to think about what genre a piece of writing belongs to and how that has shaped its way of representing the world. As writers, they understand that they choose and modify a genre in response to the situation they are in.

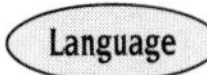

Language. The words, sentences, organization, and design of a text. Often the language of a text is considered only in terms of correctness on the one hand or as a matter of individual voice on the other hand. Our approach is to help students, as they read and write, see language issues in light of both genre and situation.

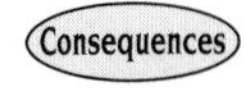

Consequences. The effects of writing in the world. Especially when writing in a classroom, it is easy to forget that writing has consequences, that this is why we write, and that these projected consequences guide our writing.

Guides to Analyzing Contexts for Writing and Analyzing Readings in Context

Perhaps the most distinctive feature of *In Context* is the set of concepts we introduce to help students think about writing from a variety of perspectives. But such concepts remain "teacher talk" unless students have ways to use them on their own and to make such concepts part of their critical vocabulary and practical strategies. The Guide to Analyzing Contexts for Writing and the Guide to Analyzing Readings in Context help students do just that. Each guide poses a series of questions to help students use these concepts as either a reader or a writer. For example, from the Situation section of the Guide to Analyzing Readings in Context, questions such as the following help students gain an in-depth understanding of the effect of context on a particular reading:

> When and where was this text published? If it wasn't published, when, where, and how was it distributed? . . . Judging by the text itself and where it was published, what can I conclude about who the intended readers are? . . . Who is the writer? What relevant credentials and expertise does the writer have, including previous publications on the topic? . . . What events in the world was this text written in response to, and how might these or other events have influenced the writer? . . . How might my background affect how I respond to this text?

Similarly, questions such as the following from the Genre section of the Guide to Analyzing Contexts for Writing remind students of the genre-related issues they need to consider as they write:

> Does this writing situation call for a particular genre? . . . If not, what genre would typically be used for the situation I am in or the purpose for which I am writing? . . . What experience do I have with the genre I am expected to use or that I have chosen? . . . What is the typical form for this genre? How can I use or adapt it to fit my purposes? What form will my readers expect? . . . What content will my readers expect?

> Do I have access to this expected content? Is the content that I do have appropriate to the genre? . . . What language choices will help me achieve my purpose? . . . Do I need to adapt my language style or the genre?

In the activities and writing assignments throughout the book, icons indicate activities that focus on a particular dimension. Thus students can, either as part of the assignment or on their own, turn to the guides for help with the reading or writing assignment in terms of that particular dimension. Used in combination with the Genre Glossary, the guides are particularly powerful tools for helping students read and write in new genres.

Headnotes. The headnotes work along with other features of the textbook to provide context for students as they connect to an ongoing conversation. Unlike headnotes that offer only biographical information about the author, our headnotes connect students to the issues under discussion.

Activities. *In Context* includes two kinds of activities that help students locate each reading in a wider social context, explore the relationship between situation and genre, and think about the consequences of writing. These activities enable the students to work both individually and collaboratively to prepare for the writing projects that follow each reading.

Preceding each reading are activities called "Connecting with the Conversation," which help students identify and create a variety of contexts in which to understand the reading. Working individually or in groups, students write about their own experiences with and knowledge of an issue; do research on an issue, author, or type of publication; and share their experiences and findings with a small group or the class as a whole. Often students use online resources to carry out these activities.

Following each reading, "Exploring Texts and Contexts" includes activities that guide students through a close examination of the language, composition, and design of a text; help students consider these textual features in terms of genre; and encourage students to make connections with other readings in the book, outside resources, and their own experiences and observations. Many of the activities ask students to reflect on one of the four rhetorical concepts and these activities are highlighted with the appropriate icon.

Writing Projects. Each reading is followed by two or three assignments that we call "Creating Texts," which are a key part of the book's overall effort to show the complexities of reading and writing in action. Many of these writing projects ask students to analyze texts, situations, and issues, often using traditional genres of academic discourse. Other writing projects ask students to use genres that intervene more directly in specific situations, for example a proposal to solve a problem, a code of conduct to shape behavior, a brochure to inform, a Web page to make connections, a speech to inspire action. Many sets of assignments invite students to reflect on the relationship between these different kinds of writing and more broadly on the many ways that we use writing to understand and do things in the world. Writing projects often ask students to draw ideas and information from other readings. Many projects involve using online resources of various kinds.

Genre Glossary

Students recognize genres much more easily than they can produce them. They easily distinguish television sitcoms, comedies, dramas, and talk shows and recognize written genres such as letters to the editor, essays, symposia, and feature articles. The "Genre Glossary" offers students a resource for producing writing in the wide variety of genres we ask for in *In Context.* This very important tool reinforces the message of *In Context* that writing emerges out of specific situations. To decide which genre, or even which aspects of a particular genre, might be appropriate, student writers must analyze possible situations and consequences as they plan and produce writing that will achieve their purposes.

The Genre Glossary contains more than twenty elaborated definitions of genres such as the dialogue, Web page, essay, manifesto, cover letter, code of conduct, and interview. Each entry describes the typical situations the genre emerges from, the form usually expected, the kinds of content typically included, and the range of language choices expected and accepted in that genre. These descriptions are meant to capture a sense of the genre, to show students where they are constrained and where they have latitude, and, most important, to show students that even within the most rule-bound genres they have decisions to make as they write.

Instructor's Manual

The instructor's manual highlights the flexibility of *In Context.* The textbook's internal apparatus allows instructors to build a course around thematic units, dimensions of writing, or cross chapter combinations of readings and assignments. The instructor's manual includes sample syllabi, additional activities and writing assignments, support for responding to and evaluating student writing, and additional research resources (0-321-25943-2).

Acknowledgments

We wish to acknowledge our debt most broadly to our colleagues in composition, English, and rhetorical studies whose theory, research, and pedagogy have informed our work. We are also indebted to the writers we include in the book, who have taught us much about writing as a social activity. We especially want to thank our colleagues at the University of Illinois at Chicago (UIC) and at Dominican University. At UIC we thank Patty Harkin, Jim Sosnoski, Marcia Farr, Ralph Cintron, Don Marshall, Walter Benn Michaels, Lennard Davis, Jerry Graff, Cathy Birkenstein-Graff, Stanley Fish, Jane Tompkins, Tom Moss, Toby Tate, Uday Sukhatme, Anne Cruz, Chris Messenger, Debra Hale, Julie Smith, Barbara Zusman, John Huntington, Gerry Sorensen, Richard Cameron, and Jessica Williams. At Dominican we thank Jeffrey Carlson; Robert Kaftan; Sister Jeanne Crapo, O.P.; Sister Mary Clemente Davlin, O.P.; Robert Greenwald; Sister Marci Hermesdorf, O.P.; Lisa Higgins; Mary Pat Radke; Chad Rohman; Donald Shaffer; Mary Scott Simpson; Mickey Sweeney; Sister Melissa Waters, O.P.; and Robbi Byrdsong-Wright. A special thanks to Barry Peterson at the Seton Hall University Institute on Work and Sharon Haar for her contributions to the section "Making a Home." Special thanks as well to Blondeen Jones, Michele Mancione, Kimberly Barba, and Lyæll Wallerstedt.

Graduate students and lecturers who help administer the UIC composition program, who have taken English 555, and who teach or have taught in the program, we thank all of you, and among you Paula Mathieu, Kelly Ritter, Bridget Harris-Tsemo, Nels Highberg, Mary Biddinger, Beth Burmeister, Sharon Palo, Tina Kazan, Daiva Markelis, Diane Chin, Margaret Gonzalez, Rebecca de Wind Mattingly, Simone Meunch, Marianne Lyons, Jackie White, Brian Sheerin, John Martin, Grace Chan, Michael Badino, Amy L. Smith, Richard Kroeger, Susan Weinstein, Wendy Maland, Margaret Boyer, Mary Kay Mulvaney, Candice Rai, and Megan Marie. We also thank students in English 402 at Dominican University; Sue Cunningham, Kate Lyon, and Edith Villarreal. We also thank the members of our writing groups: Lauri Schaafner, Irma Olmedo, Ulrike Jaeckel, Sheila Kennedy, Martha Pacelli, and Linda Vavra.

This book could not have been completed without the detailed and wise commentary shared by members of our profession. Although their comments were anonymous at the time, we are pleased to recognize their fine work here: Michael Barry, University of Detroit-Mercy; Christina Bentley, University of Kentucky; Karen Lee Boren, University of Wisconsin-Milwaukee; Craig Branham, Saint Louis University; Brenda Brueggemann, Ohio State University; Ann Ciasullo, University of Kentucky; Gina Claywell, Murray State University; Deborah Coxwell Teague, Florida State University; Laurie Delany, Kent State University; Michelle Ephraim, Worcester Polytechnic Institute; Linda Ferreira-Buckley, University of Texas at Austin; Patricia Garcia Ocañas, Our Lady of the Lake University; Paul Heilker, Virginia Technical University; Shari Horner, Shippensburg University; Thomas Huckin, University of Utah; Alan Hutchinson, Des Moines Area Community College; Megan Knight, University of Iowa; Anna Laskaya, University of Oregon; Mark Mabrito, Purdue University at Calumet; Richard Marback, Wayne State University; Dennis M. Moore, University of Iowa; Matthew Parfitt, Boston University; Joe Pellegrino, Eastern Kentucky University; Pegeen Reichert Powell, Miami University-Ohio; Colleen Reilly, Purdue University; Abigail Robin, SUNY at New Paltz; Lance Ruben, Arapahoe Community College; Carolyn Stevenson, East West University; Gary Tate, Texas Christian University; Nancy Taylor, California State University at Northridge; Richard Taylor, East Carolina University; John Wegner, Angelo State University; and Abbey Zink, Northern Illinois University.

We have worked with an impressive group of publishing professionals throughout the development of this book, and we thank; Lynn Huddon, Katharine Glynn, Wendy Albert, Donna Campion, Joseph Vella, and Esther Hollander at Longman Publishers; and Mary Grivetti and Phyllis Padula.

Our families have sustained us throughout this process. We thank them and thank them again: Lawrence Gorman and Jack Gorman; Mary McManus and Jim, Kevin, Brian, and Terry McManus; Sheila Freeman and Colleen Hein; Philip Matsuhashi and Amy Matsuhashi; Robert, Jonah, and Aaron Meyerhoff; Florence Feldman; David and Bobby Feldman; Joel and Meryl Feldman; Tom Downs, Joseph Downs, and Thomas J. Downs.

Ann Merle Feldman
Ellen McManus
Nancy Downs

UNIT I

Reading and Writing Rhetorically

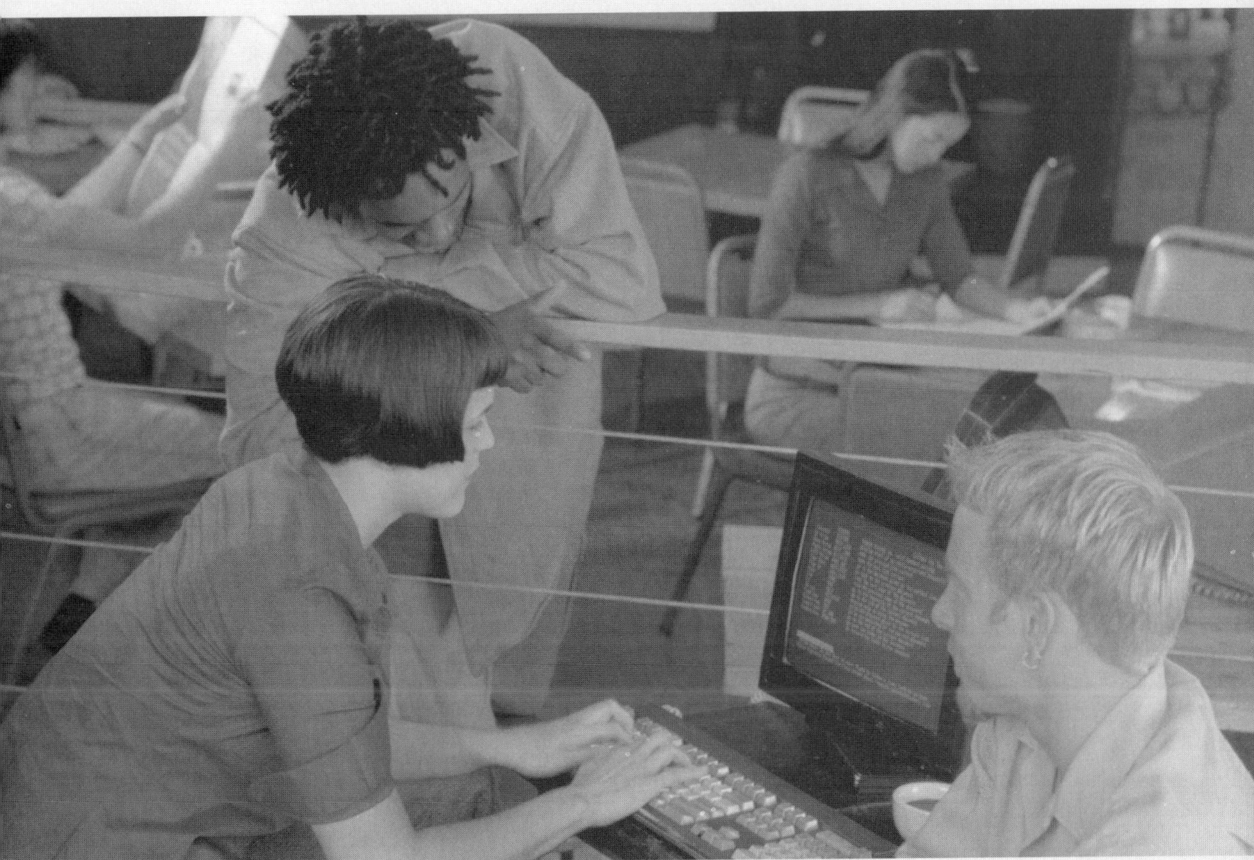

Every day we talk to each other about our common concerns and shared interests. Some conversations are as private and immediate as families talking around the dinner table, two friends exchanging e-mail messages, or a class discussing an assigned reading. Other conversations are as public and wide-ranging as an exchange of remarks by politicians through the mass media, a series of articles in a newspaper or magazine with opinion pieces and letters written in response to it, or a national "town meeting" broadcast on television.

Notice that we are using the word *conversation* here to refer to written as well as spoken communication and even to situations in which participants may not be in direct contact with each other; this is the sense with which politicians and pundits sometimes refer to "a national conversation" or your philosophy teacher might say that thinkers today are still "in conversation" with Plato and Aristotle. Often what we call a conversation is a combination of local and wide-ranging conversations.

In Context invites you to explore how such conversations get started, what keeps them going, what forms they take, who participates and who doesn't, and how they affect us and the world. We focus on four ongoing conversations that have an impact on events in the world and that affect the way we see ourselves: what it means to be authentic, how we create a sense of place, how to get people involved in civic dialogues, and how the increasingly global economy affects us as workers and consumers. The essays, dialogues, editorials, newspaper articles, and other documents included in this book reflect moments in these conversations, and the activities and assignments throughout the book invite you to join the conversations through your reading and writing.

Consider, for example, this scenario. In your composition class, you read a piece by Richard Rodriguez, an essayist and cultural commentator, and you are assigned to write an essay about the issue he discusses. In the piece included in this book, Rodriguez discusses the impact of AIDS on gay culture and the gay community. But Rodriguez has written about other controversial topics, including multiculturalism, diversity, and assimilation, arguing most recently that our celebration of multiculturalism is shallow and doesn't recognize that assimilation is the much more powerful force in American culture. As you're trying to think of how to begin your essay, you remember that in one of the online forums you sometimes visit there's an ongoing debate about Rodriguez. You didn't pay attention to this debate before because you'd never heard of Rodriguez, but now you go into the forum and reread some of those exchanges. Rodriguez, you find, has taken controversial positions that you strongly agree (or disagree) with. You post some comments in the forum, to which you get several responses, both agreeing and disagreeing, and you soon find yourself an active participant in this forum's ongoing debates about multiculturalism and assimilation.

Meanwhile, you now have a much better sense of how to write your essay. You begin by referring to the ongoing controversies about Rodriguez, and the conversations you've been having in the online forum help you develop a stronger voice and a much more detailed argument. At the next class, one of your peer group members, reading your draft, remarks that Rodriguez once spoke at the university a friend attends and that members of a Latino student group protested his visit. You do some research to check this out, and then you integrate this information into your argument, adding a couple of new paragraphs about the role of universities in civic debates and cultural change. Later in the semester, there's a discussion on your own campus about whether or not to invite a controversial politician to speak at commencement, and you use some of the ideas from your essay to write a letter to the editor supporting (or opposing) the invitation of this speaker. In reshaping the material to address a different audience and purpose, you give greater emphasis to some of the ideas you included in your essay and you leave others out, and in this process you get different insights into the issue and your own response to it.

This is a hypothetical scenario but not an unrealistic picture of how private and public conversations intersect and, more importantly, how you might get involved in them. In order to participate in the complex civic and cultural conversations that help to shape our world, you must read with alertness to context, make connections between different things that you read, pay attention to your own responses, be willing to use writing to follow through on those responses, and shape your writing to particular purposes and audiences. That is, you must read and write rhetorically, with attention to how writing grows out of and responds to particular situations. Rhetoric is the study and practice of shaping communication to particular purposes, and *In Context* invites you to read and write rhetorically in order to enter the civic and cultural conversations that are important to you.

In this opening unit, we illustrate our belief that reading and writing are multidimensional activities, and we introduce a variety of strategies to help you read and write with more complex understanding. Chapter 1 opens with a newspaper article from which we draw a set of rhetorical concepts—situation, genre, language, and consequences—that can help you read and write with more complexity and power, and we provide a set of guides that will help you use these concepts in very practical ways. In Chapter 2 we look at how one writer entered a conversation about a community issue, and then we introduce a variety of reading and writing strategies designed to help you get interested in and eventually join such conversations yourself.

Contexts for Reading and Writing

Analyzing a Feature Story: *Graffiti as* Art *or* Vandalism

This feature story from the *Chicago Tribune* illustrates how contexts influence how we read and respond to what we read.

Taggers Spray Over Vandal Image

Phat X. Chiem

Ramiro makes no excuses for how he has spent much of the last nine of his 22 years. He is a graffiti bomber, a tagger, a vandal in the eyes of police and an artist to those like him.

"I basically do it because I grew up with it, and I feel really strongly about it," he said, "I don't care about the police. That's the whole point of graffiti: bombing and getting chased. That's how we get our respect."

For Ramiro, as for many graffiti "writers," his scribbling and scrawling on city viaducts and subway lines has become less a hobby and more a way of life. The possibility of arrest only adds to the thrill, said the burly Ramiro, who has been arrested five times on vandalism charges.

Wearing his "work uniform" of denim shorts and a black T-shirt, Ramiro has come to paint two huge retaining walls on West 59th Street between Damen and Western Avenues. About 30 graffiti artists have been commissioned by two community groups, the Southwest Community Congress and the Southwest Youth Service Collaborative, to create a 12,000-square-foot mural on the pristine walls.

5 Called "Pieces of Chicago," the graffiti mural depicts the history of Chicago, with individual sections devoted to events such as the Great Chicago Fire, the civil rights movement and the Columbian Exposition. With an $8,500 grant from the Chicago Community Trust, organizers have bought over a thousand cans of paint and hope to have the piece completed by this weekend.

From the *Chicago Tribune*, September 12, 1996. Metro Section, pp. 1–2.

A 22-year-old artist called Gnome 174 works on the mural at West 59th Street between Damen and Western Avenues.

For many of these inner-city youths, graffiti represents an art form born of urban squalor and frustration. Graffiti became a part of the rap and hip-hop culture that spread across the country from cities such as New York, Philadelphia, and San Francisco during the late 1970s and early '80s.

"People who think we're vandals are ignorant of the whole hip-hop culture," said Glenn Johnson, the 18-year-old artistic director of the mural project.

Graffiti, along with rap music, breakdancing and deejaying, or spinning records, has always served as an expression of hip-hop culture, said Johnson, who has been a graffiti artist since he was 13.

"Graffiti has never been about tagging," said Johnson, a freshman at the American Academy of Art, where he hopes to major in computer animation. "Some people just want to be known as vandals. But me, I'm an artist."

10 Joe Damal, a project organizer, hopes the mural will educate the public about "one of the few indigenous forms of art for urban youth." Many graffiti artists who paint big pieces such as the one on 59th Street differentiate themselves from taggers who simply want to spray their signature across as many public surfaces as possible, he said.

"When it is completed, I will consider this mural graffiti art," Damal said. "But not all graffiti is art. There's some that's really vandalism. That's an important distinction."

Not everyone makes that distinction—certainly not the Chicago Police Department, which has committed a special tactical police unit to keep the city's walls from becoming overnight canvases. Members of the unit are derisively called the "graf squad" by the taggers.

The tension between the two groups was shown when a pair of undercover officers approached the muralists while they were working last week. After Damal refused to leave as an officer questioned one of the artists, he was arrested and charged with disorderly conduct. Later released, he faces a court date next month.

Police said they had every right to question the muralists, even though the graffiti wall had been approved by city officials and the Englewood District police had been notified.

15 "The police were there because they noticed six well-known taggers working on a wall," said Patrol Officer Patrick Camden, a police spokesman.

Police may be critics of so-called permission walls such as the South Side mural, but the concept of channeling graffiti artists' creativity has its supporters. The Chicago Transit Authority began a scholarship program four years ago for mural contest winners.

CTA spokeswoman Noelle Gaffney said the permission-wall program has saved the agency up to $20 million in cleanup costs over four years because vandals tend not to tag walls with murals. But the CTA continues to spend about $20 million annually to fight graffiti elsewhere.

The Streets and Sanitation Department spends about $4 million a year to clean up graffiti. Department spokesman Terry Levin said permission walls only deter illegal graffiti at that particular spot.

"I don't see any sign that [permission programs] are a deterrent for taggers to go somewhere else and vandalize," Levin said.

20 Allen Tyson, a West Side resident who has had his garage vandalized twice with graffiti, had stronger sentiments.

"I find it offensive to call these guys artists," Tyson said. "I don't think they deserve to be called artists when they're destroying public property."

Meanwhile, Johnson spent Tuesday afternoon at 59th Street using his Krylon paint sprays to depict a civil rights scene from the 1960s. One of his figures had one fist in the air and the other holding a sign reading "Equalitee."

"In the 1960s, there was a lot of segregation at first," Johnson said. "Then there was a lot of integration. People began to wake up and understand that, before we're white human or black human, we're human."

A few yards away, Ramiro was working on his piece, which he said pays homage to artists throughout Chicago, especially those whose outside work is removed by city crews.

25 "That's the whole basic struggle of graffiti: to keep it up," he said.

Four Ways to Look at Reading and Writing

This article, like any piece of writing, has multiple dimensions. There are, of course, the words on the page, but consider also the situations in which the article was written and will be read, the particular form or genre of this piece of writing, and the consequences this writing may have. Identifying these different dimensions of writing reveals a powerful set of rhetorical concepts with which we can think about what we read and write. These concepts help us see this piece of writing as part of a conversation, or several intersecting conversations, and help us think about what we bring to these conversations and how we might want to continue them.

Situation

The young people in the article see their work on the mural as an important form of artistic and political expression. But the city resident quoted in the article sees all graffiti as damage to property, and the police who arrest the artists working on the mural see it as a violation of laws that they must enforce. These opposing views emerge from different understandings of the situation. By **situation** we mean the immediate circumstance in which an act of reading or writing takes place, recognizing that the immediate circumstance, as well as the participants' understanding of it, is shaped by histories, cultures, communities, institutions, ideas, experiences, and other written texts. Our responses to this article will depend on the immediate circumstance in which we read the article as well as our individual histories, our social and economic background, our experiences with and ideas about graffiti, and perhaps things that we have read about graffiti, art, or vandalism.

Genre

But the controversy over the mural might also be seen as a question of **genre**. Genres are ways of doing things that, over a period of time and in response to repeated situations, needs, or desires, have evolved into recognizable forms. In this book we are concerned mainly with genres of writing and speech, but people also use the term to talk about music, art, movies, TV shows, and other forms of expression. Genres are a kind of social agreement about what forms and conventions are expected in particular situations. For example, if we want to express a strong opinion publicly, we know that one way of doing this is to write a letter to the editor and that our letter needs to follow certain rules and conventions. All genres have their own rules and conventions, but writers (or speakers, musicians, artists, etc.), depending on the situation or their particular goals, may choose to follow those rules, bend them, or break them. Using a graffiti mural to tell the history of Chicago may disrupt, and maybe eventually change, our expectations about the genres of graffiti, murals, and history writing. Similarly, in reading the newspaper article, we might be surprised if the reporter suddenly expressed a strong personal opinion about the mural or graffiti in general because we expect newspaper articles, with the exception of editorials and opinion columns, to be reasonably objective.

Language

When you look at this article, what do you see first? Even before you see the text, you notice the overall look of the article on the page, which includes its heading and byline, its overall layout and length, and the accompanying photo and caption. All of these elements contribute to the overall impact of the article. We use the term **language** to refer not only to the words and sentences but also to the organization and design of a text. In the case of a newspaper article, the reporter may not make visual design decisions, but in other kinds of texts such as brochures, comics, and graffiti murals, the same person may control all these elements. In addition to design elements, this dimension also refers to the overall organization and specific sentences and words of a text. Phat Chiem, the reporter who wrote the article, has organized it to describe the mural project first from the young people's perspective, then from an antigraffiti perspective, and again from the perspective of the mural painters. Notice also that he often describes the muralists and their work by using their own words—"writers," "work uniform"—but puts these words in quotation marks to show that they do not necessarily represent his perspective. All of a writer's choices contribute to the overall effect of a piece of writing. Individual word choices express nuances of meaning, and the combinations of words into phrases, clauses, and sentences build the complexities of meaning that create the overall impact of the work.

Consequences

A graffiti artist quoted in the article says that "the whole point of graffiti" is "bombing and getting chased." But Joe Damal, an organizer of the graffiti mural project, says that the purpose of the mural is to "educate the public about 'one of the few indigenous forms of art for urban youth.' " But whatever the goals of different graffiti artists might be, the police and property owners may see all graffiti in the same light—as vandalism—whereas other present or future readers of its messages might be affected in completely different ways. Depending on the contexts you bring to your reading of this article, you might think differently about graffiti or you might decide to take action by writing a letter to the editor or by joining your neighborhood's clean-up effort. The notion of consequences can help you think about these different intentions and results. By **consequences** we mean the effects of writing in the world. If we think of writing only in terms of school assignments, we may not take into account the important concerns about ethics and responsibility that writing can raise. Writers intend their writing to have particular effects on the world, and they work very hard to ensure that it will have those effects, but the effects of a piece of writing are not always controlled by what the writer intended.

Although each of these four dimensions—situation, genre, language, and consequences—has its own particular meaning and emphasis, they overlap and interact with each other. For example, the **situation** in which an act of writing takes place—participating in a chat room or wanting to express your opinion on a local issue—suggests which **genres** are appropriate to use, though writers might choose to use an unexpected genre or to reshape the expected genre. Genres, that is, have rules and conventions that to some extent determine the **language** choices that are acceptable. And decisions that the writer makes about genre and language, as well as the situation in which the text is ultimately read, will help determine the **consequences** of the text.

In the next two sections we look more closely at how you might use the concepts of situation, genre, language, and consequences to think in more complex ways about your own reading and writing.

Reading the Graffiti Article

Perhaps you are reading the newspaper over breakfast, and you come across Phat Chiem's article about the graffiti mural. How you read and respond to the article will depend on your own particular background and experience. Any time you read, you're already in a **situation** that influences the way you read. For instance, you may have some interest in this issue. You may be a graffiti artist yourself, a homeowner whose garage has recently been "tagged," or a student who partly admires and partly disapproves of graffiti artists.

Your reading might also be influenced by what section of the paper this article appears in. When you read a front-page article, you expect a conventional form that includes facts about a current, ongoing situation or event presented in an even-handed way. When you get to the feature section of the paper, you expect a human-interest piece that tells a story rather than just giving the facts. You bring a set of expectations to whatever you read that influences how you understand it. Although you may not be thinking of this word, the fact that you have these expectations means you are already bringing your **genre** knowledge to bear on your reading. To see this more clearly, imagine that an article about the graffiti mural had appeared on the front page of the paper. You would bring different expectations to it, and it would most likely be a different article. A front-page news article on the mural might focus on an aspect mentioned in passing in the feature article by Chiem, the arrest for vandalism of artists involved in the project. This focus would give the story a quite different meaning.

As you read the article, you will continue bringing various contexts to bear on your understanding of it. You might notice that the Chicago Community Trust is mentioned, and your knowledge of other Community Trust projects might reassure you that the mural is a worthwhile project. Or you might recall that the city has recently passed antigang and antiloitering laws, and you might hope that such laws will put a stop to things like graffiti murals. In other words, you are beginning to connect this story with the many contexts in which we find discussions of graffiti. You also bring to bear, probably unconsciously, other contexts such as your knowledge of how this newspaper has covered similar stories in the past. All these aspects of context contribute to the different **consequences** that this article might have. Did your ideas about graffiti change in any way after you read the article? Perhaps you concluded that graffiti murals are not the best choice for public art. Or did you come away with a feeling that such murals can have a positive impact on a particular community as well as the city as a whole? Was this article good publicity for the youth group? What effect do you think the story had on the neighborhood in which the mural appeared? Could the article have brought people to the neighborhood to see the mural?

The consequences of this article have to do partly with what you bring to it and partly with the social context of the article, but they also have to do with how the writer has crafted it. The **language** choices Chiem makes help us speculate on the effects he wanted the article to have. For instance, what effect is created through introducing the artist, Ramiro, by both quoting him—"I basically do it because I grew up with it, and I feel really strongly about it"—and describing him—"Wearing his 'work uniform' of denim shorts and a black T-shirt"? These choices suggest that Chiem wants the reader to see Ramiro in a sympathetic light and think about the situation from his point of view. Or consider the sentence: "For many of these inner-city youths, graffiti represents an art form born of urban squalor and frustration." By beginning the sentence with a qualifying phrase and by using the verb "represents," Chiem communicates a complex message: that he offers this description of graffiti as a potentially legitimate definition but not necessarily his own. What if the sentence had begun "Graffiti is" or "Many inner-city youths believe that graffiti is"; how would the message be different? Every decision about word choice or sentence structure can make a difference in the overall impact of a piece of writing.

We read every day in many circumstances and for many purposes. Although we don't necessarily think of what we read in terms of situation, genre, language, and consequences, we bring some awareness of all these concepts to our reading. Any act of reading, even of a newspaper article over breakfast, is far more than decoding words on a page; it is a complex activity that takes place within a variety of social contexts and involves a variety of intellectual operations.

Exploring a Writing Scenario

Chiem's article describes a series of events in which writing plays an important part. One of the most important instances of writing involved here is the grant proposal to the Chicago Community Trust that resulted in a grant of $8,500 to buy paint, which is what allowed the project to be completed. Imagine how a person writing a grant proposal—perhaps one of the organizers of the youth collaborative—might approach this task. This writing scenario is not unlike the reading and writing assignments you will encounter in this book: complex situations in which writing interacts with many other factors.

Let's imagine that the organizer has already gotten the youth collaborative interested in the project; maybe she's even contacted city officials for approval to use a specific space for the mural. But she realizes that her organization's budget cannot possibly cover the amount of paint needed for the huge surface. One way to get funding is to write a grant proposal to a foundation or agency to subsidize the project.

Our community organizer knows the proposal will be distributed to the board members of the funding agency to which she is applying. Thus she considers who these people are and what their expectations might be. She might also think about her own credentials and what she still needs to know about her project in order to write a persuasive proposal. In other words, she begins to define the immediate **situation** and its shaping contexts as she sits down to plan and draft her proposal.

While the writer is deliberating about the complex situation in which she writes, she is also aware that the situation demands a specific **genre** of writing—the grant proposal. She knows what sorts of information to include because funding agencies often give out guidelines for writing proposals. In situations in which genre guidelines do not exist, writers might look at other texts in the same genre. In this case, the agency's guidelines direct the project organizer to begin with an abstract that summarizes the project; to review the background of the situation and articulate a problem that must be solved; to offer a solution to the problem; to show how the proposed project will provide that solution; and to include a budget for the project. For all of these requirements, she has to determine whether she has the necessary information. For the most part she will probably follow the rules of the proposal genre, but she may find that in some respects her purposes don't match the expectations of the genre.

She might then need to consider whether she should change her purpose or adapt—or even break—the rules of the genre. She knows that in order to make her proposal effective, she must make careful **language** choices. In the case of a grant proposal, organization and design are usually predetermined; in fact, sometimes the writer simply fills out a form. Also, with a proposal, standard usage is expected; our project organizer knows she cannot make mistakes in grammar, punctuation, or spelling. And the proposal reviewers also expect the writer to speak in a professional voice, using precise and formal language. However, the project organizer also wants to convey how the teens think of themselves and how they describe themselves and their work. For example, should she refer to the teens as "graffiti artists," which is how the reviewers might think of them, or should she call them "writers," which is how the youths refer to themselves? How would you solve this problem? When you write, you are constantly making language decisions that determine the overall meaning and effect of what you write.

A writing project can be so absorbing that you think of little besides getting the writing finished. You may not think ahead to its **consequences**. But much writing takes its meaning from its consequences. In this situation the consequences will be very real: whether or not the money is granted will make a big difference in the lives of the teens the project organizer works with. As she writes, our organizer must remember that she needs to plan and draft her writing with its intended consequences in mind. It may seem that some writing activities—for example, journal entries—don't have significant consequences. But an idea that you write in your journal may in fact have consequences, if only for yourself and your future writing and thinking. Even if only your own mind is changed, that is a real consequence.

If you think of situation, genre, language, and consequences as conceptual tools to help you read and write with more awareness, think of the following guides as toolkits. These guides are sets of questions organized around these concepts, and they are designed to help you in both your reading and your writing. In the activities following each reading in this textbook, you will see icons that symbolize the four concepts of situation, genre, language, and consequences. When you see one of these icons, turn to the relevant section in the Guide to Analyzing Readings in Context or the Guide to Analyzing Contexts for Writing, and use the questions in that section to help you approach your reading or writing with more complexity and depth. Experienced readers and writers, mostly unconsciously, ask themselves similar kinds of questions when they read and write. As you use these guides, you'll discover which questions you find most useful, and you'll begin to ask yourself these questions whenever you read and write.

Questions to Ask as You Read and Write

A Guide to Analyzing Readings in Context

Situation

By situation we mean the immediate circumstance in which an act of reading or writing takes place, recognizing that the immediate circumstance, as well as the participants' understanding of it, is shaped by histories, cultures, communities, institutions, ideas, experiences, and other written texts.

- When and where was this text published? If it wasn't published, when, where, and how was it distributed? What costs were involved in publishing or otherwise distributing this piece of writing, and who paid those costs? What does this information suggest about the text and how I or others might respond to it?
- Judging by the text itself and where it was published, what can I conclude about who the intended readers are? What do I know about these readers, their beliefs and values, what they might know and feel about this topic, and how they might respond to this text? How might these facts have influenced the writing of the text?
- Who is the writer? What relevant credentials and expertise does the writer have, including previous publications on the topic? What other facts about

the writer's personal, cultural, social, intellectual, or political background might be relevant to understanding his or her perspective on the issue?

- What events in the world was this text written in response to, and how might these or other events have influenced the writer? What larger historical events, philosophical issues, or social concerns relate to this issue? How was this text a response to other writing or discussion of this issue?
- How might my background affect how I respond to this text? How does my background compare with what I know or infer about the backgrounds of the writer and the intended readers? How familiar am I with the issues, persuasive strategies, and vocabulary of this text? What can I do to help myself better understand this text?

Genre

Genre

Genres are ways of writing that have evolved, in response to repeated situations, needs, or desires, into recognizable forms. Genres are a kind of social agreement about what forms and conventions are expected in particular situations. Some examples are thank-you notes, short stories, graduation speeches, college essays, and rap songs. Each genre has rules—some strict, others loose—that tell what is expected and acceptable in both form and content. Writers may choose to follow the rules strictly, adapt them, or break them, possibly developing new genres. Some genres seem unchanging; others, such as electronic communications, are currently evolving.

- Do I recognize the genre of this text? If so, what do I know about this genre? How can I find out more?
- What are the purposes of texts in this genre? Does this text seem to accomplish those purposes? How does it do so? How effectively?
- In what situations do writers typically use this genre? What do I know or what can I guess about the situation in which this text was produced? Is it the appropriate genre to use in this situation? What other genre options might the writer have had?
- What is the typical overall form of texts in this genre? In what ways does this text fit or not fit the typical form?
- What is the typical content of texts in this genre? What kinds of information, arguments, or sources are included? Is the content what would be expected in texts of this genre?
- What kind of language is typically used in this genre? Is the language in this text what would be expected? Is it effective?

(*continued*)

Language

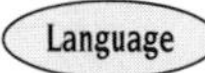

Language refers to the words, sentences, organization, and design of a text. It is thus the sum of a series of choices the writer makes that in turn may reflect many things, including the writer's personality and intentions, the subject matter, the context, the rules of the genre, and the sounds of particular words and combinations of words.

- What is the text's overall design? How does it use such features as fonts, margins, line spacing, justification, headings, lists, bullets, numbering, and white space or such visuals as charts, photos, or drawings? How does the design contribute to the overall effect? Should the design be changed in any way?
- What is the text's overall organization? What would an outline of the text look like? Do the paragraphs follow an identifiable order? Is the main point of each paragraph clear and sufficiently developed? Is it easy to follow the logic from one sentence or paragraph to another? Are there helpful transitions between sentences and paragraphs? How does the organization contribute to the overall effect? Could the organization be changed in any way to make the text more effective?
- What kinds of sentences does the writer use? Long, short, simple, complex, choppy, smooth, or a variety of types? Do they follow standard rules of grammar, are they clear, and do they have appropriate emphases? If not, does it seem that the writer has done this intentionally or has made mistakes? How does the writer use the ideas of others—direct quotes, indirect quotes, or paraphrasing—to make a point? How do the sentence structures contribute to the overall effect? Should they be changed in any way?
- What kinds of words does the writer use? Common, unusual, formal, informal, slang, or jargon? Do the words seem precise, imprecise, strong, weak, surprising, or predictable? What tone do the words create? Do the words and combinations of words sound pleasing or unpleasing? Are the words grammatically correct and spelled correctly? If they seem incorrect or inappropriate, does it seem that the writer has done this intentionally or has made mistakes? How do the word choices contribute to the overall effect? Could the words be changed in any way to make the text more effective?

Consequences

By consequences we mean the effects of writing in the world. Consequences can be intended or unintended, they can be ideas or actions, and they can be immediate and local or long-term and wide-ranging.

- What effects did this text have on me? Did it change my opinions or ideas in any way? Did it inspire me to act in any way? What specific features of the text contributed to this effect?

- Based on both the text itself and any context information I have about the text or the writer, what consequences do I think the writer intended this text to have? What specific things has the writer done to ensure these intended consequences and avoid unintended ones?
- How might this text affect other people? Could it help or hurt someone? Do you think the writer has thought about his or her responsibility to others in producing this piece of writing? How could, or did, this writing change something in the world, and would this be, or was this, a good change?
- Do I know of any other specific consequences this text has had—intended or unintended, ideas or actions, immediate and local or long-term and wide-ranging? What specific features of the text do I think contributed to these consequences?

A *Guide to Analyzing Contexts for Writing*

Situation

By situation we mean the immediate circumstance in which an act of reading or writing takes place, recognizing that the immediate circumstance, as well as the participants' understanding of it, is shaped by histories, cultures, communities, institutions, ideas, experiences, and other written texts. Situation

- Where would I want to publish/distribute this text? Could I, in reality, publish this text where I want to? How much, if anything, will it cost for me to reach the audience I want to reach? How will these factors influence my writing?
- Who are my intended readers? What are they likely to know/not know about my topic? What position are they likely to take? How might their expectations influence how I write this text?
- Do I have the credentials and/or authority to make my audience hear my message? How might I achieve these? What more do I need to know about the topic? How can I find out this additional information?
- What events in the world am I writing in response to? How have these or other events influenced my thinking about the topic? What other historical events, philosophical issues, or social concerns relate to this issue? How have I been influenced by what others have said or written about the topic?
- How does my background influence my thinking and writing about this topic? How does my background compare with that of my intended readers? What facts about my personal, cultural, social, intellectual, or political background might influence my readers' response to my text?

(*continued*)

Genre

Genres are ways of writing that have evolved, in response to repeated situations, needs, or desires, into recognizable forms. Genres are a kind of social agreement about what forms and conventions are expected in particular situations. Some examples are thank-you notes, short stories, graduation speeches, college essays, and rap songs. Each genre has rules—some strict, others loose—that tell what is expected and acceptable in both form and content. Writers may choose to follow the rules strictly, adapt them, or break them, possibly developing new genres. Some genres seem unchanging; others, such as electronic communications, are currently evolving.

- Does this writing situation call for a particular genre? If not, what genre would typically be used for the situation I am in or the purpose for which I am writing? Do I want to use this expected genre or do something else?
- What experience do I have with the genre I am expected to use or that I have chosen? Have I written or read other texts in this genre? What do I need to know before I can write effectively in this genre? Why have people written in this genre historically? What about this genre has changed over time?
- What is the typical form for this genre? How can I use or adapt it to fit my purposes?
- What content will my readers expect? Do I have access to this expected content? Is the content that I do have appropriate to the genre? Will I need to adapt the genre in response to my content?
- What language choices will help me achieve my purpose? What sort of language does the reader expect? Do I need to adapt my language style or the genre?
- See the Genre Glossary for descriptions of genres you'll be asked to produce in this textbook.

Language

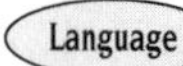

Language refers to the words, sentences, organization, and design of a text. It is thus the sum of a series of choices the writer makes that in turn may reflect many things, including the writer's personality and intentions, the subject matter, the context, the rules of the genre, and the sounds of particular words and combinations of words.

- How should I organize the text? Does the genre of the text, the subject matter I am writing about, the context in which I am writing (including audience and purpose), or my own experience suggest a particular organization? Can I make a tentative outline for the text? Does each paragraph have a clear and well-developed point? What transitions would help the reader? Does the organization contribute to the text's overall effectiveness? What organization changes might a reader suggest, and would these be helpful?

- What do I want my sentences to sound like? Fast-paced, smooth and flowing, or a mixture? Should they be long, short, simple, complex, or a variety of lengths and structures? Do my sentences follow standard rules of structure and grammar? If not, is this to achieve a desired effect, or should I make corrections? Do the sentence structures contribute to the overall effectiveness of the text? How might I use the ideas of others—direct quotes, indirect quotes, or paraphrasing—to make my point? What sentence structure changes might a reader suggest, and would these be helpful?
- What tone do I want the text to have, and what kinds of words would create that tone? Formal, informal, casual, intimate, slangy, professional, serious, or humorous? Does the genre, subject matter, context, or the persona I want to project suggest which words I should use? Do the words express my meanings precisely and effectively? Do the words and combinations of words sound pleasing? Do my word choices contribute to the overall effectiveness of the text? What word changes might a reader suggest, and would these be helpful?
- How can I use design elements to contribute to the overall meaning of the text? What do I want the text to look like, and what design elements would achieve that look? Does the situation, genre, language, or intended consequences suggest a design? How can I use such features as fonts, margins, line spacing, justification, headings, lists, bullets, numbering, and white space or such visuals as charts, photos, or drawings? Does the design contribute to the overall effectiveness of the text? What design changes might a reader suggest, and would these be helpful?

Consequences

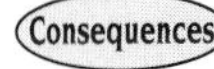

By consequences we mean the effects of writing in the world. Consequences can be intended or unintended, they can be ideas or actions, and they can be immediate and local or long-term and wide-ranging.

- What consequences do I want my text to have? Ideas or actions, immediate and local or long-term and wide-ranging? What consequences would I like to avoid?
- How might this text affect other people? Could it help or hurt someone? Have I thought about my responsibility to others in producing this piece of writing? How could my writing change something in the world, and would this be a good change?
- What specific things can I do to ensure these intended consequences and avoid unintended ones?

Strategies for Writers at Work

In Chapter 1 we saw how the grant writer for the graffiti project evaluated the situation, considered the demands of genre, looked closely at language, and anticipated the possible consequences of her writing. We also saw how she employed a variety of strategies to help her do those things. For example, she did library or online research and talked with people in order to get a fuller sense of the particular situation she was working in. She knew that in order to get a clear sense of the requirements of the grant proposal genre she would also have to study proposal guidelines from the agency she was applying to, as well as proposals for similar projects. At various times throughout the process, she jotted down ideas and drafts in a notebook, brainstormed with co-workers, engaged in e-mail discussions with people involved in the project, worked with others to draft parts of the proposal, and asked people for feedback at different stages of the writing. The procedures, resources, and people that were part of her situation all provided her with specific strategies for planning, researching, drafting, and revising the proposal.

As suggested in the introduction to Unit I, students also engage in a range of strategies to help them carry out writing projects, but students may not be aware of all the strategies available to them. In this chapter we describe a variety of strategies that will help you carry out writing projects. To help you think about how those strategies might help you, we'll look at the work of college freshman Berenice Salas and follow as she discusses how she wrote and revised an opinion piece for a first-year writing class. This mini case study will let us see the strategies used by one particular writer to complete a project. Because different strategies work for different writers in different situations, the second part of this chapter describes a wide range of such strategies, including strategies to help you connect with a context, explore a reading and the issues it raises, and tackle those issues yourself in a writing project of your own.

A Writer Talks About Her Work

Berenice Salas, a first-year student at the University of Illinois at Chicago, took a course called "Writing on Location," in which students read about home, community, and work. The class had read the article by Phat Chiem, "Taggers Spray Over Vandal Image," and talked about the ways that situation, genre, language, and consequences helped to provide new perspectives for thinking about reading and writing. Chiem's feature story reports on a conflict between graffiti artists, community residents, and city officials over a mural painted on a graffiti "permission wall." Berenice's assignment asked her to identify an unresolved community issue and write an opinion piece aimed at changing her readers' minds about the issue. Berenice chose to write in defense of the *eloteros*, neighborhood pushcart vendors who sell mangos, corn, and frozen treats on the street corners of a largely Latino neighborhood called Pilson, just west of downtown Chicago.

Let's take a "before and after" look at the first paragraph of Berenice's opinion piece to get some idea of the role played by the four dimensions—situation, genre, language, and consequences. We have included the first and final draft of her first paragraph:

First Paragraph/First Draft: Elotes!

Elote is Spanish for corn: Eloteros is Spanish for corn vendors. Eloteros are typically Mexican immigrants who sell corn, pineapple, and other types of foods in a pushcart on the street. To the Little Village neighborhood they are micro-entrepreneurs who create jobs for themselves in order to support their families. They are found everywhere in Little Village, especially in the parks during the summer. Chicago's Eloteros are a valuable part of the city's culture and street life. They are part of the ethnic mosaic that makes Chicago a great city and also provide a needed service to the community.

First Paragraph/Final Draft: Delicious Culture in a Pushcart

Elote **is** Spanish for corn; *eloteros* **is** Spanish for corn vendors. *Eloteros* are typically Mexican immigrants who sell corn, pineapple, and other foods in a pushcart on the street. They promptly **prepare** fresh foods with your choice of condiments. **I would refer to the *elotes* as culture on a stick with a pinch of authenticity**. To the Little Village neighborhood these micro-entrepreneurs **create** jobs for themselves in order to support their families. They can be **found** everywhere in Little Village, especially in the parks during the summer. Chicago's *eloteros*, a valuable part of our city's culture and street life, **contribute** to the ethnic mosaic that makes Chicago a great city. Most importantly, these food vendors **provide** a needed service to the community.

Notice that in her first draft, Berenice uses forms of the verb "to be" as the main verb in most of her sentences. By revising to include stronger verbs, Berenice strengthened the initial picture we get of the *eloteros*. Focusing on the **language** of her text also helped Berenice look more closely at the situation and think of ways to further describe the role of the *eloteros* in her community. Here's what she told us about her writing process:

My teacher asked us to circle all of our "to be" verbs and count how many we had in our papers. I think everybody had a good amount of "is" and "are" verbs in their papers. I never really noticed it before; I was surprised that I had weak verbs. I just couldn't believe I had that many. And actually, once I changed them, it made a big difference in the paper. But, I didn't change the first three because I was defining elote *and* eloteros. *I added strong verbs in the last sentence—contribute and provide. I want to be persuasive and these verbs help my audience to see how necessary* eloteros *are to our culture, that they really have a function in society.*

I also added the sentence, "I would refer to the elotes as culture on a stick with a pinch of authenticity." I used to always get elotes; *everyone from my neighborhood would run outside when they heard the horn, "Honk! Honk!" the* eloteros *are coming. It's like the ice cream truck. So it's like our culture on a stick. And then when I added a pinch of authenticity, I was thinking of the condiments we add to the corn. This helped me think of a new title, too.*[1]

Next, let's take a close look at how Berenice revised the second and third paragraphs in her opinion piece:

Second and Third Paragraphs from Berenice's First Draft:

In the late 90's Alderman Bernard Stone began banning street vendors in the 50th Ward. Alderman Burton Natarus, whose 42nd Ward now includes most of downtown, quickly followed by sponsoring a law that forbids street vending anywhere in the Loop (with the exception of city-commissioned fruit stands on State Street). The Park District added its own citywide ban that summer. Shortly after, Aldermen Mell and Burke also contributed to an ordinance against these vendors. Burke told the story of how his aid's dog getting sick and dying after eating a popsicle purchased from one of these street vendors. In support of this ordinance health inspectors went to Little Village and ticketed all street vendors: there was even a case in which the inspectors poured bleach all over the food.

First of all, why would you feed a popsicle to a dog? I have eaten food from Eloteros all of my life and have never known of anyone who had ever gotten sick from a street vendor. Furthermore, the lesson in hygiene and food preparation as the ordinance calls forth is not only insulting but illogical. When one buys from a street vendor one is seeing what is going on, however restaurants are another story.

Second and Third Paragraphs from Berenice's Final Draft:

In the late 90's Alderman Bernard Stone began banning street vendors in the 50th Ward. Alderman Burton Natarus, whose 42nd Ward now includes most of downtown, quickly followed by sponsoring a law that forbids street vending anywhere in the Loop (with the exception of city-commissioned fruit stands on State Street). The Park District added its own citywide ban that summer. Shortly after, Aldermen Mell and Burke also contributed to an ordinance against these vendors. In support of this ordinance, Burke told the story of how his aide's dog got sick and died after eating a popsicle purchased from one of these street vendors. Health inspectors went to Little Village and ticketed all street vendors. The inspectors' unjust actions included a case in which they poured bleach over a vendor's food. This unreasonable act not only cost the vendor a day's work, but also insulted the hygiene of Mexicans.

---

[1] This transcript was revised to improve clarity.

> I lived in Little Village and I have eaten food from *eloteras* all my life and have never known of anyone who ever got sick from a street vendor. If anything, *eloteras* sell the best tasting fruits and vegetables in all of Chicagoland. The variety of fruits and vegetables that the *eloteras* offer help improve my eating habits. It takes skill to prepare mouth-watering food in less than a minute. They offer a convenient service, provide nourishing snacks, and promote wholesome nutrition. When one buys from a street vendor, one sees what is going on; however restaurants are another story. I feel confident in the hygiene of the vendors, but much less confident about the hidden violations that can occur in the backrooms of many Chicago restaurants.

Berenice's revision helped strengthen her description of the challenges posed by city officials. In addition, she developed a rebuttal having to do with the healthy nature of the food served by *eloteros*. She knows that she can strengthen this particular **genre**, the opinion piece, by making an argument in which claims are supported by evidence; she also knows that she must persuade her reader if the piece is to have the **consequences** she intends. Here's what Berenice said about her revision process:

> *What I'm trying to get across in this paragraph is how this is not fair. It's an unreasonable act because it costs the vendors a day's work. And by saying that this is their work, you know, it isn't just something to take lightly, like it's a teenager's side job. Sometimes it's their second job, so it's even more important because they're sacrificing time they could have at home.*
>
> *I took out the question about feeding the popsicle to the dog because it was a little too personal. I have this anger toward these aldermen—not all of them—just about what happened here. But I should sound neutral but persuasive at the same time.*
>
> *I added the stuff about the food because this food really is nutritious. I want to bring my readers into a world they haven't been in. Some of them don't realize that this goes on because they haven't been outside of their neighborhood. After reading this I want them to say, "I want to go see these* eloteros; *why don't we go over there?"*

Berenice clearly wants her writing to have consequences; she wants her readers to understand the situation the *eloteros* find themselves in and she'd like to make things better for them. As she wrote and revised she considered both the specific situation and the larger context. She considered her own background and experience but also tried to imagine her readers' background and experiences. She already had some familiarity with an opinion piece and knew that she needed to build an argument that would persuade others. Because she was using language that might not be widely known, she took care to define *elotes* and describe the *eloteros* who sell them.

And now, we offer the final draft[2] of Berenice Salas's opinion piece. You can see how the revisions she discussed helped strengthen her argument about the important contributions that the *eloteros* make to their community and how they should be permitted to obtain licenses without being challenged by city officials.

---

2 This essay was edited to correct surface-level errors in a conference with the student during the semester following the class.

Salas 1

Berenice Salas

Writing on Location

13 February 2003

Delicious Culture in a Pushcart

Elote is Spanish for corn; *eloteros* is Spanish for corn vendors. *Eloteros* are typically Mexican immigrants who sell corn, pineapple, and other foods in a pushcart on the street. They promptly prepare fresh foods with your choice of condiments. I would refer to the *elotes* as culture on a stick with a pinch of authenticity. To the Little Village neighborhood these micro-entrepreneurs create jobs for themselves in order to support their families. They can be found everywhere in Little Village, especially in the parks during the summer. Chicago's *eloteros,* a valuable part of our city's culture and street life, contribute to the ethnic mosaic that makes Chicago a great city. Most importantly, these food vendors provide a needed service to the community.

In the late 90's Alderman Bernard Stone began banning street vendors in the 50th Ward. Alderman Burton Natarus, whose 42nd Ward now includes most of downtown, quickly followed by sponsoring a law that forbids street vending anywhere in the Loop (with the exception of city-commissioned fruit stands on State Street). The Park District added its own citywide ban that summer. Shortly after, Aldermen Mell and Burke also contributed to an ordinance against these vendors. In support of this ordinance, Burke told the story of how his aide's dog got sick and died after eating a popsicle purchased from one of these street vendors. Health inspectors went to Little Village and ticketed all street vendors. The inspectors' unjust actions included a case in which they poured bleach over a vendor's food. This unreasonable act not only cost the vendor a day's work, but also insulted the hygiene of Mexicans.

I lived in Little Village and I have eaten food from *eloteros* all my life and have never known of anyone who ever got sick from a street vendor. If anything, *eloteros* sell the best tasting fruits and vegetables in all of Chicagoland. The variety of fruits and vegetables that the *eloteros* offer help improve my eating habits. It takes skills to prepare mouth-watering food in less than a

Salas 2

minute. They offer a convenient service, provide nourishing snacks, and promote wholesome nutrition. When one buys from a street vendor, one sees what is going on; however restaurants are another story. I feel confident in the hygiene of the vendors, but much less confident about the hidden violations that occur in the backrooms of many Chicago restaurants.

So where does this ordinance leave the people of my community? Street vending is a longstanding tradition in Mexico, and the Mexicans of Little Village are expressing and sharing their culture with the city. When I observe that the city is overzealously attempting to restrict street vendors from creating legitimate means of work, my intuitive reaction is frustration. Chicago's success has come from waves of immigrants to its shores. These Mexican immigrants have to make their own jobs.

Chicago attracts tourists because of its diversity: Greektown, Little Italy, Chinatown, etc. What about Little Mexico? It is to the city's advantage to have *eloteros* add their culture to the diversity of Chicago. Mexican people come from other places because they like the corn; this is the tradition of *La Veintiseis*, of 26th Street. When my family moved from *La Villita* to my current neighborhood, I missed the *eloteros*. They have become part of my heritage and I try to travel back every weekend to eat authentic *elotes*. *Eloteros* also make people feel safe and prevent crime; they are like street police stationed on each block. Police can't be everywhere so they depend on informal social control. *Eloteros* as well as other street vendors increase safety on the street.

For many reasons, I believe that the city officials should not allow heavy-handed forces to over regulate the humble but important Mexican *eloteros*. This may be a class clash or a case of racism that has ignited from fear of a minority's success. One thing that these officials must realize is that Latinos are a part of mainstream society and should not be shunned. Perhaps some see this as one way of weeding out undesirable elements that conflict with the rapid gentrification occurring in Chicago. How can it not be? Just look at who it directly affects. This ordinance is immoral and unprincipled. It completely disregards many of those that will be affected, including customers, and is a direct attack on the Mexican and minority communities at large.

A How-To List for Reading and Writing

Identifying and shaping a specific context for her writing project helped Berenice Salas figure out what strategies she needed to complete her project. The readings in this book are designed to help you similarly identify and shape contexts for your writing, and the activities that accompany each reading suggest specific strategies to help you write. This section gives you an overview of those strategies, organized into three categories according to the sets of activities that accompany each reading. The first group helps you connect to the larger context in which your reading and writing will take place. The second group helps you look closely at the readings and make connections with other readings and related issues. The third group helps you get started with and follow through on a variety of writing projects by helping you make the best use of the stages of the writing process. The following section is designed as a reference guide to be used as you need it, but you might want to look through it now to see which kinds of strategies are covered and think about how you might use them.

Before You Read: Connecting with the Conversation

The more you bring to a reading, the better you will understand it and be able to connect with it. Thus before each reading in the textbook, we ask you to think about your own knowledge of and experiences with the situations and issues described or referred to in the reading. These connections will help you create a context as you begin to write about the issues yourself. Consider the following strategies as ways to help you approach your reading, whether it's the morning paper, assignments for another class, readings in this book, or reading that you do on your own.

Consider Your Own Related Experiences. Use your experience to help you think about the broad context of and the specific situation presented in the text. Notice differences between what an author says and what you believe to be true or likely based on your experience. Also, use your experience with different kinds of writing to think about issues related to the genre of a reading, for example its overall form and design, organization, and language.

Pay Attention to Discussions in the Media. Newspapers and magazines are important forums for detailed reports on and extended discussions of issues. You and your family may regularly read a newspaper and a few magazines, and you may be familiar with the particular interests and biases of those periodicals. Reading other newspapers and magazines can give you different perspectives on issues or introduce you to new issues and ideas.

Some assignments might ask you to look at newspapers or magazines you are already familiar with; others might ask you to explore unfamiliar newspapers and magazines. In the case of the latter, you might go to the current periodicals section of a large library, to a large newsstand, or to the periodicals section of one of the large chain bookstores. Select a few periodicals that you don't usually read, from a variety of categories—dailies, weeklies, monthlies, quarterlies, news, financial, entertainment, general interest, special interest, scholarly, or literary. Browse through your selections, making notes about the overall look of the periodical and the kinds of writing, topics, and attitudes that seem typical for each. Pay special attention to genres, topics, or ideas that are new to you. Consider what kinds of conclusions you can draw about the writing practices in the familiar or new periodicals you have looked at.

Radio and television programs and advertising can give us interesting examples of how language is used in our society. Again, some assignments ask you to listen to or watch familiar stations or programs; others ask you to explore new ones. Make notes about the kinds of programs and advertising and about topics, attitudes, and uses of language, paying special attention to those that are new to you. Review your notes and consider what conclusions you can draw about the language practices you have heard or observed.

Search the Topic Online. Searching a topic online is a wonderful way to get basic information or a quick overview, and many young people today, by the time they get to college, have already developed strategies for getting information quickly from the Internet, whether for school projects or other purposes. But as you probably learned in high school, doing a quick search just to get a preliminary picture of a topic is not the same as doing systematic research in order to write a paper or complete a project. In order to help you connect with the context of a reading or a new topic, your teacher may ask you to follow certain steps or may simply allow you to do your own search. If you do your own search, be sure to keep track of the sites from which you take information so that you can provide references later if required or return to the same site for more information.

Talk to People with Relevant Knowledge or Experiences. You can enhance your understanding of any event or issue by talking with people who know something about it. You may want to start with someone you already know, or you can call an appropriate agency or office, explain your project, and ask whether there is someone appropriate who might have time to speak with you. When you first contact your interviewee, whether by phone or in person, remember to introduce yourself and explain your project. Try to tell the person what kind of information you're looking for and what kinds of questions you might want to ask. If that person is too busy or doesn't think she will be of much help, ask if she knows anyone who might be willing to be interviewed for your project. See the Interview entry in the Genre Glossary.

As You Read: Exploring Texts and Contexts

Each of the readings in this book comes out of a specific situation, which is itself part of a larger context. Activities following each reading help you explore both the text itself and the situations and conversations that surround it, and this in turn should help you think about how you might enter one of those conversations through your own writing.

Understand the Writing Situation. The following questions will help you explore how the writer's situation shapes the meaning of the text. What is the writer's background and experience? What larger conversation is the writer responding to? Does the writer mention a specific situation that sparked the writing? How does the writer's purpose and situation influence the form of the writing?

You might be able to intuit answers to some of these questions. Answers to other questions will be found in introductory material. But for other answers you may need to do other kinds of analysis, research, and observation.

Identify and Analyze the Genre of the Text. If you are used to reading and writing mainly personal narratives or essays, you may be surprised at the range of genres included in this book. Activities that follow each reading will help you identify the genre of the reading and think about how the genre helps shape meaning. This in turn may help you think about genres that you want to use as you write about these issues.

Analyze the Language of the Text. Carefully examining the language of a text will help you think more specifically about how a piece of writing works. Here are some specific strategies.

- Think about the significance of the title.
- Identify key terms—words that the writer uses in a special way, a way not easily explained by dictionary definition alone, especially words used in ways that puzzle you.
- Notice figurative language—images, metaphors—and consider how it shapes the meaning of the text.
- The questions posed in the Guides on pages 12–17 will help you look more closely at the language of a text. As you develop into a more active reader, you will learn which questions are most useful to you, and you will also develop your own questions.

Consider the Consequences of the Text. When we write in school to fulfill assignments, the most immediate consequence we can imagine for our work is the grade assigned to our work by the teacher. But as you become an engaged reader and writer, you will begin to think about writing that has consequences beyond the classroom. The news article about graffiti artists in Chapter 1 gets us thinking about all the ways in which writing might enter a situation and helps us to imagine all the ways in which consequences might play out. The grant writer we introduce later in Chapter 1 is hoping that her proposal will be funded, but she hopes for other consequences as well. For instance, she wants the Chicago Community Trust to fund her project for what she thinks is a good reason—supporting a culturally significant form of local art. This consequence—more subtle than being given funding—involves changing the funders' minds. Perhaps they began reading the proposal thinking that the money would be useful as a deterrent, keeping graffiti artists busy and away from the alleys and garages of local citizens. The grant writer hoped to change their view of graffiti, and this too is a potential consequence.

As you probably know, writing can have unintended consequences. An editorial you write for a school newspaper might not be understood as you intended it. An assignment is returned to you for revision because, the teacher explains, you did not complete it as he or she expected. A diary you have been keeping for some time, including very personal information, is found and read by someone discussed in the diary. We leave these consequences to your imagination!

Even when you are writing just to fulfill an assignment, thinking about the potential consequences of your writing will help you see it in a more complex way.

Compare the Text with Other Texts. Any individual text is part of a situation or history that includes other texts. Thus it makes sense to ask how particular texts relate to each other. Comparing one text to another makes it possible to notice things you might not have noticed looking at it in isolation.

- How do the perspectives of different writers change the way they treat an issue?
- How do different genres change the treatment of an issue?
- How do different language choices shape what writers communicate about an issue?
- How do writers' differing purposes and goals for writing affect what they say about an issue?

Search the Library and the Internet for Related Texts. Research usually grows out of and is an extension of classroom work, but it is more open-ended in the sense that you are usually working on your own, and neither you nor the teacher may know what you are going to find. Research is a crucial part of learning because it allows you to make connections between what you have learned in the classroom and what you yourself have observed or what others have said about an issue, and it allows you to take more responsibility for your learning. The following kinds of activities will require you to do research in the library or online.

Search Reference Materials for Context Information. Some activities will ask you to look for information on the context or background of an issue or a person. Searching the Internet may produce a lot of material, but it may not be the information you need, and you'll have to evaluate it carefully. You might instead want to use library reference materials, which are materials that can't be taken out of the library, including dictionaries, encyclopedias, almanacs, resource guides, and other books in which you can "look things up." The reference librarian can help you find the most up-to-date source for the information you need.

Search Popular Magazines and Academic Journals for a Particular Topic. Some activities ask you to find out and compare what different kinds of periodicals are saying about a topic. Popular magazines are those that are read by general readers; they are usually published weekly or monthly. Academic journals are written and read by specialists in particular academic disciplines; they usually come out four times a year. Both can be searched by using either print or electronic indexes. Articles in popular magazines can be found by using general interest indexes, most of which can be found online, including FirstSearch or Wilson Select Plus. Articles in academic journals can be found by using various specialized indexes. Many electronic indexes and databases contain the full text of articles, usually more recent ones.

Search the Internet. Other assignments will ask you to do a search of a topic on the Internet. As with library research, there are tools that will help you find information, such as Yahoo and Google. Although each of these has its own procedures, which may change over time, all of them basically allow you to type in a keyword, and then they search for any documents on the Internet that contain this keyword. This usually results in a list of hundreds or thousands of documents, most of which may not be at all relevant to what you are looking for. Many handbooks on electronic research contain tips for choosing the best search tool and using it effectively to narrow or broaden your search so that you find the range of information you need. An assignment may ask you to find specific information, in which case you may want to narrow your search strategies, or to get an overview of an issue, in which case you may want to broaden your search strategies.

Explore a Web Site. Some activities ask you to go to a specific Web site to find information or to explore the site. (In these cases, the URL for the Web site will be provided, though note that URLs, like phone numbers, can become outdated.) In exploring a Web site, notice the kind of information it contains, including how up-to-date it is and whether sources for the information are provided; notice the graphics used and how they interact with the text; and check out the various links. The assignment may ask you to retrieve specific information or to analyze the composition of the site.

Visit a Real or Electronic Bookstore. An assignment may ask you to browse in a bookstore to see what is currently available on a particular topic. Many large bookstores these days—in addition to Amazon.com, which exists only online—have Web sites that allow you to shop for books online. This is a very good way to get an overview of the most recent publications on a topic. Browsing in a real bookstore will allow you to actually take the books off the shelf and look through them. Browsing in an electronic bookstore, on the other hand, allows you to see titles and descriptions of books that are too old or obscure to be given space on a shelf but which may be relevant to your topic. Thus you may want to browse in both places to get the best overview.

Evaluate Sources. Since we now use computers to search for both library materials and online materials, it's easy to confuse the two kinds of research. But it's important to understand the difference between online sources and library sources, for two reasons. First, there are differences in reliability between the two. Statements made in formally published books, periodicals, and other print documents may not always be true, and some published materials are less reliable than others, but it is usually at least possible to identify the publisher and author of such materials and take that information into account in doing your own assessment of the material's reliability. With material published on the Internet, it's often difficult to track down the source of the material, and it's easy for online materials to be misrepresented. The second reason to understand the difference is simply that there are different ways of citing print materials and online materials.

When you do online research, you will be using materials from Web sites, listservs, e-mail, and data banks of various sorts that sometimes exist only online. In all of these cases, you will have to do your best to identify the origins of the material and assess its reliability using that information and the judgment that you use in assessing the reliability of any materials. A number of recent guides and handbooks will help you find, identify, evaluate, and use these online sources. They will also explain the new and still-developing systems for documenting online sources, which are also available in most recent standard handbooks.

On the other hand, when you go online to access library catalogs, indexes, or databases of published print materials, you should think of yourself as doing library research. Thus, you should make sure that you can identify the traditional print publication information and use traditional print documentation systems when you incorporate parts of the material into your own work. On the other hand, if you use an article that you find on a Web page, you should determine whether it has only been published on that Web page or is reprinted from a print periodical; if the latter, make sure you cite the periodical. And when you use an online index such as FirstSearch, remember that the articles listed are from print periodicals and should be documented as such.

Getting Down to Writing: Creating Texts

Each reading in this book will be followed by at least two writing projects, which may include an essay as well as one of the other genres we describe in our Genre Glossary. In the following pages you will find strategies and processes that will help you complete writing projects assigned in this book as well as other writing for school or for work.

Identify a Situation and Purpose for Writing. One of the most helpful things you can do to get started writing is to think of yourself as participating in a situation and imagine how a piece of writing can have an impact on the situation. Review the Guide to Analyzing Contexts for Writing to generate new ways to think about the situation in which you are writing. Consider carefully what you bring to the situation and what you have learned from similar situations. Consider also who your readers are and what experiences they might have had in similar situations. Then think about what kind of impact you would like your writing to have and how you can help assure that it will have that impact.

Take Advantage of the Writing Process. Even though you are often by yourself when you write, the process does not take place entirely in your head. Instead, your writing emerges from interactions with other people, with readings, with the world as you experience it, and with your own previous writing. Therefore, writing well depends on seeing yourself in a particular situation that will help shape your writing process.

In the pages that follow, you will find general descriptions of the writing process—planning, drafting, revising, and editing. But keep in mind that the particular process you use will be shaped by the situation you are in, and that the four phases of the process overlap and recur. After completing a draft and even after revising it, you may need to return to the prewriting phase to reconsider an aspect of the issue you had not previously considered. Some of the strategies described here will work better than others in particular writing situations. Through practice and experience you'll learn which strategies work best for you.

Planning. Imagine that you have been reading and writing about a particular issue that interests you, and you have decided to work through one of the writing activities suggested in this textbook. Here's a list of suggestions. Choose the ones that are most effective in pushing your process forward.

- *Review the Guide to Analyzing Contexts for Writing.* What is your writing situation and how will it shape your writing? What form will your writing take? Will it be an essay, a dialogue, or a report? How does genre influence your approach? What stylistic choices do you anticipate making? How will your voice emerge in your writing? What consequences do you want your writing to have for yourself and others? Who will read your work? What kind of impact do you want it to have?
- *Review and supplement previous work.* Reread all of your journal entries. Reread, annotate, and take notes on material that you think will contribute to your writing project. Consider where you might get more information. Do you need to read more, search the Internet, or conduct interviews? Do you need to take another trip to the library to search out journals, magazines, or documents?

- *Develop your ideas.* Engage in mind-stretching activities that encourage you to consider your information in different ways. Brainstorming, listing, and diagramming are all ways to identify, organize, and reorganize ideas and information. Initially you might want to brainstorm with yourself or others to generate as many ideas as possible. A special kind of brainstorming is freewriting, in which you write without stopping for a period of time. Next you may want to organize these ideas into lists. Or you could use a diagram to explore the relationships among these ideas. These activities might help you to determine whether your topic is too broad or too narrow.
- *Reflect on your project.* A valuable technique at any point in the process is to step back and reflect on your writing project as a whole. One of the best ways to do this is to use a journal. Not only will you want to reread all the journal entries you have written up to this point, but you will also want to keep writing in your journal to reflect on your current thinking about your project. Try explaining to someone else the purpose for your writing. Try writing a memo to your teacher with key questions you have yet to answer. Or try writing a progress report and exchange it with a friend.

Drafting. Moving from notes to a complete first draft can be the most challenging aspect of a writing project. Remember that you are producing a *first* draft. It doesn't have to be perfect; it just has to emerge in some form so that you can continue working on it. The following suggestions offer a variety of approaches to crossing this bridge from notes to first draft.

- *Review the section on genre in the Guide to Analyzing Contexts for Writing.* This section of the guide encourages you to think about the relationship between the situation for writing and the typical forms that writing takes.
- *Consider your time frame.* When is this writing project due? Estimate how long it will take you to get started and complete a draft. Create a time line that includes time for prewriting, drafting, revising, and editing. If you work better doing small portions of a project on a day-by-day basis, schedule your work in this way.
- *So you have only four hours!* Here's a plan for generating a draft, developed by Peter Elbow (*Writing Without Teachers*, Oxford University Press, 1973). This plan works best for certain kinds of writing, usually writing that depends primarily on your own personal experience and not on a lot of outside research. Still, it provides a useful way to push yourself into completing a first draft.

    Divide your four hours into units of one hour each. During the first 45 minutes of the first hour do some freewriting; write everything that comes into your head; dump it out onto the page. During the last 15 minutes of the first hour read over what you have written and evaluate it. What seems important? What could you be moving toward? What big idea or ideas emerge? Sum up this idea in a sentence or two.

    This first version is your starting point for the next hour, in which you write for 45 minutes, continuing to discuss the main idea you identified in the previous version. Once again, take the last 15 minutes to reread and see what important ideas you can pull from this version. Sum up the main idea again; try to take it further than the last version suggests. Try this same process one more time during the third hour you have allotted. If you can see an organization emerging, try to use it to guide this version. Again, during the last 15 minutes ask yourself what you are trying to say. Write it as if you are telling it directly to a specific person that you imagine as part of your audience. Use the last hour to revise and shape the piece; during the last 15 minutes give the piece a final editing.

- *Develop an Outline.* An outline helps you to structure your draft, a substantially different approach from the one just described. You may find that your writing style makes one of the two approaches more comfortable for you. Or you may find that one of the approaches works better for a particular writing project.

  In developing an outline, consider what the genre section of the Guide to Analyzing Contexts for Writing suggests for your writing project. Next consider your main idea for the project. What do you intend to explain or argue in this project? How might you develop the main idea? How can you divide this project into sections? What is the relationship among the sections? When you have answered these questions, you should proceed to develop an outline.

  An outline is a hierarchical approach to organizing information. You can adopt a formal approach in which you organize your main topics and supporting details alphanumerically, labeling your main ideas with Roman numerals, letters, and numbers; or you can take a more informal approach, simply listing all main topics and supporting details. In either case, you write under each major section heading and subheading a sentence that you will include in that section and explain how it contributes to the project as a whole. When you finish your outline, share it with a partner and discuss where it works and where the organization isn't clear. Writing an outline challenges you to group your ideas in units that help you explore your topic in an interesting and compelling way.

Revising. Revising provides an opportunity to shape and refine the paper so that it says to others just what you want it to say. This is the point in the writing process when you focus on how the project hangs together. If you have time, put the project aside for a day or two in order to look at it again with fresh eyes. Often you can get the best feedback on how successful your draft is by sharing it with another writer. Here are some strategies for revising:

- *Collaborate with Others to Review Your Work.* At any point in the writing process, it helps to talk to someone else and get feedback on both your plans and your draft. Try to guide your reader's response in order to elicit the most useful response possible. A useful response will help you to understand the text as others do and decide what aspects need revision. Look on the peer review situation as a kind of interview; you need to ask questions that will give you the information you need to know. You may want to design a feedback sheet for your reader to work with. On the next page you will find an outline of a peer review worksheet that you can customize to suit your particular writing project.

Peer Review Worksheet

Writer's Name ____________________

Writer's comments: In the space below summarize the main point of your text. Comment on its purpose. Tell your reader what you think works best in the paper and what you think needs more work. Tell your reader what you would do if you had a few more days to work on the text. Finally, write down a few questions that you would like your reader to consider.

Reader's Name: ____________________

Reader's Comments:

1. **Overall response:** Summarize the text's main point. Comment on how your reading differs from or confirms the writer's comments.
2. **Consider issues of situation and genre.** What events in the world is the writer responding to? How have these events influenced the writer's work? Does the writer offer enough background information and supporting material to help the text succeed in its purpose? What genre has the writer chosen? Does the shape of the text fit its purpose? Is the writer speaking with authority? Do you believe what the writer is telling you?
3. **Consider issues of language and consequences.** Outline the text briefly. How does the organization contribute to the overall effect? Do the writer's language choices seem appropriate? Does the introduction help you get started reading the text? What effect does the text have on you? Do you think this is the intended or an unintended effect? What specific things could the writer do to avoid unintended effects?
4. **Examine the text for correctness.** Do you see any problems with sentence structure, quoting and paraphrasing, usage, or spelling? Note these for the writer.
5. **Tell the writer about one strength in the text.**
6. **Suggest ways in which the writer can improve the text.**

- *Consider your project as a whole.* Reread the Guide to Analyzing Contexts for Writing and ask yourself how your perspective shapes what you have written. Ask yourself whether you are following the conventions of a genre or changing it in some way. Are your genre choices appropriate? Ask how design, organization, sentences, and words contribute to or detract from your paper in view of its goals. Finally, consider the consequences you hope it will have. Try to determine how to avoid unintended consequences.
- *If you wrote your introduction first, take an especially hard look at it.* Sometimes when you finish your paper you end up thinking differently about your project than when you began. You might read your paper over completely, put it aside, and write a new introduction. Compare that introduction to the rest of the paper and make the appropriate changes.

- *Write an outline for your paper as it is currently organized.* Think hard about this plan. Might a different plan work better? How would moving sections around help your project succeed?
- Determine whether you have enough information to successfully complete this writing project. Do you need to gather more information to bolster a particular point you want to make?
- *Examine your language choices.* Do your stylistic choices further the points you are making? Does your personal voice come through the way you want it to? Do you use transitions appropriately to develop the path you want your project to take?
- Finally, revisit your main idea or argument and make certain that it will be clear to your readers. Is it supported fully throughout the project?

Editing. Never underestimate the impact that surface errors can have on your readers. One final step is editing your paper for style and usage, punctuation, and other mechanics. Here are some techniques for catching errors that may cause readers to undervalue your work:

- Read your essay aloud from beginning to end. Listen to the way individual sentences sound and the way paragraphs hold together.
- Did you title your work? Did you pay attention to other design issues, for example how the text is formatted on the page?
- Did you check for correct usage, paying particular attention to problems you have had in your writing before? Have you used your handbook to resolve editing questions?
- Have you documented sources correctly using the appropriate citation system? Have you correctly punctuated quotes?

In the previous sections we identified strategies that might be used in any writing project. The following sections provide information on some special strategies that you may use in particular kinds of projects: writing arguments, integrating material from other texts, creating visual texts, and collaborating with others on the writing of a text.

Writing Arguments

Whether you are writing in school or in a public context, you will often be asked to take a position, develop a thesis, and support your thesis with evidence. This thesis-driven writing underlies many of the genres we present in the Genre Glossary. Speeches, reviews, proposals, and, most obviously, the argumentative essay require you to place yourself in a context, evaluate an ongoing conversation, and develop your position within that conversation. We do this naturally as we participate in daily activities, but sometimes when asked to take a position in a classroom setting, we forget all the competencies we have developed over the years of taking positions in contexts outside of school.

You may be comfortable generating a lot of reasons for any given claim that you make, but as a writer, in school or out, you'll want to think carefully about how to support a particular position. When you gather evidence, consider its source. Consider also how reasonable it is to use that evidence in support of the particular thesis you want to support.

Integrating Material from Other Texts

Summarizing. Summarizing a text will help you understand it better and prepare you for thinking critically about it. Experienced readers go through a text several times before summarizing it. In an initial reading, focus on questions of content and meaning. Then, on a second pass, focus on the way the content is related to the structure of the text. Consider, also, the writer's goals.

Writing a summary requires that you restate the text in your own words. Remember, though, that it will not be enough to simply restate the message of the text in the order the material is presented. Consider which ideas are most important. This will help you decide what information is key and what can be left out. Consider also how the text is organized and how that influences its meaning. Most important, consider your purpose for summarizing the text. Consider these questions as you plan your summary:

- For what occasion did the writer produce this text?
- What is the purpose for writing?
- What is the genre of the text?
- What is the main point?
- Which parts develop the main point?
- Which parts provide the support and examples?
- How has the writer organized the parts?

Paraphrasing. Paraphrasing means *putting someone else's ideas or statements into your own words.* To summarize, you reduce a larger body of material to a smaller size; paraphrasing allows you to restate material fully while not quoting it exactly. Many of the same questions posed for summarizing apply to paraphrasing. Ask yourself why you need to use this information and how it contributes to your ideas. As you practice putting someone else's ideas into your own words, you'll get a better sense of what the text means and how best you can express its ideas.

Quoting. Often you will want to repeat *exactly* what another writer or speaker says, especially if the language is particularly compelling or if you cannot put the language in your own words. Be aware, however, that if you quote too often, you risk losing your own voice and your own point of view. The use of quotes requires appropriate punctuation, which will be explained in your handbook.

Avoiding Plagiarism. As you write, you may rely on the work of other writers. When you use the ideas of others, you'll want to include in-text citations to signal to your readers where the information comes from. When you work with exact language from your source, be sure to use quotation marks to set off this language. When you restate others' ideas, be sure to use your own words and syntax. If you don't give credit to other writers when you use their words and ideas, you will be accused of plagiarism. Plagiarism also includes turning in a paper that contains another's writing without acknowledging that other writer by quoting, citing, and listing the work in a reference list. This, however, does not mean that you should avoid using others' ideas and words in your own writing. But you must identify the work of those writers you are in conversation with.

Creating Visual Texts

More than ever before, we now communicate through visual texts; for this reason many projects in this book ask you to try your hand at comics, brochures, Web pages and other visual texts. Creating such texts draws on everything that you have learned about communicating a message but asks you to do so in an electronic or visual medium. Here are some things to think about as you prepare for such projects:

- Does the visual image tell a story? Will viewers be able to tell you what story they can draw from your visual text?
- If your visual text departs from viewer expectations, will viewers be able to make sense of your text in some new way?
- Can viewers interpret your visual text based on what they already know?
- Have you thought about who your audience is? Have you composed your visual text for, perhaps, fellow students, teachers, an audience with specific musical or artistic tastes, or a specific group of consumers?
- Have you represented the people in your visual text to reflect the diversity that exists in the larger society?
- Consider how realistic you want your visual text to be. You can work along a wide continuum—from close imitation of reality to imaginative representations that will ask your reader to make use of his or her interpretive powers.

Collaborating with Others on the Writing of a Text

As you use this textbook, you may be asked to write as a member of a team. A writing team may be helpful when you need to include other perspectives in your work. Sometimes a project or writing task is simply too large for one person, or you don't have enough time to complete the project on your own and you need to divide up the work. Or members of a group may have special expertise on different aspects of a topic.

There are several ways to work with a team. In a one-author team, the team discusses the project, and team members may draft portions of the document, but in the end one person writes the final document. In a multiple-author team, each team member contributes a specified portion to the project, and the pieces are then combined to create the final document. In a collaborative team, all members of the group contribute to the process and work together to produce the final product. This is one of the most challenging team situations because it may require the group to write as if one author has produced the document.

How to Handle the Writing Process

- Writing together differs from writing alone in many ways. Talk with your group about how you will divide up the work. Determine whether you will all be writing one document or whether you each will contribute parts of the final product.
- Brainstorm about ideas for your project.
- Set up a schedule and a way for the team to keep track of its progress.
- Identify ways to help each other with the writing—both finding information and reviewing drafts.
- Determine how you will evaluate the project once it is done.

How to Handle Conflict and Difference

- Sources of conflict: Personality differences, insensitivity to gender or ethnic difference, lack of clear team procedures, different ideas about the team's purpose or goal, and different ideas about how to get things done
- Conflict resolution: Determine how your team will make decisions—by consensus or by majority? Talk about the behavior in specific, concrete terms, and discuss what effect it is having on the team. Discuss possible alternative behaviors and how they might influence the team's work. Learn to use reflective listening, which means repeating to a person what that person has said so that the team has the opportunity to understand that person's position or approach. Ask enough questions so that the team can determine a way to resolve a conflict.

How to Handle Leadership and Communication Skills

- Build into your process ways to observe yourselves. For instance, set aside a portion of every meeting for discussing the group's process.
- Assign leadership roles and discuss how those roles might be carried out. Members of teams can be assigned tasks as leader, secretary, and evaluator.
- Plan to play different roles in different team situations. See whether you can discover how you function best and whether your response in some roles surprises you.

The Multiple-Author Team. Kelly Ritter, an assistant professor at Eastern Connecticut State University, used a very structured, multiple-author approach to guide her students through the process of making a group presentation on their work. Her writing class was exploring film studies, and each group of four or five students was to make a presentation and turn in a report. Students, working individually, had already identified a topic and were writing a paper on it. Ritter grouped together students who were working on similar topics. Some of the groups' presentation topics included minorities in films, praise and blame in Hollywood, film genres and society, and stars and studios. The group presentations were to take 10 to 15 minutes, and students would be graded on both their oral and written contributions. As you work in groups, consider the following guidelines for class presentations and for handouts:

Oral Class Presentation

- Each writer summarizes his or her paper.
- One group member offers an overview of how the group members' topics are related to each other and how they differ. In addition, this member explains how these topics relate to the issues discussed in the course.
- Another group member reports on the group's process: what students learned from each other, how they identified and shared resources, how they helped each other sharpen the focus of their papers, and how they solved any problems the group had.

Handouts for the Presentation

- One group member should prepare a handout listing the group members and the topics they will discuss and summarizing the relationship of the presentation to the coursework.
- Another group member should write a summary of the entire group presentation in essay form. The essay might be two to three pages in length.
- If appropriate, another group member should provide film clips or visual material. This presenter should make it clear how the visual is necessary to a discussion of the topic.

The Collaborative Team. Maya Luna Books (2000) published an erotic thriller, *The Student Body*, under the pseudonym Jane Harvard. In reality, it was written by Michael Francisco Melcher, Faith Adiele, Julia Sullivan, and Bennet Singer, four Harvard grads. In a recent feature article in the *Chicago Tribune*, writer Patrick Reardon describes how the group went about writing this novel together. Initially, the four friends thought they would get together for a weeklong vacation and start the book. Melcher, the only one of the four who was not a writer, thought the entire project could be done during that week. Adiele, who is an English professor, knew that writing a novel in a week was unrealistic but looked at the project as a way to spend time with her closest friends and, at the same time, come to closure about their Harvard experience.

Here's how Reardon described the group's process:

> They wanted to produce a book that didn't read like it was written by four people. So they made sure that no one person had responsibility for any particular character or for any particular chapter. Adiele might start to draft a chapter, but when she'd get stuck, Melcher or Sullivan would step in.
>
> On vacations—yes, there were several other working vacations—they had their computer terminals set up next to each other, and, in between times, they communicated via e-mail and conference calls. Singer, who did relatively little of the initial writing, functioned as the group's editor, carried out research, and made business contacts with agents and publishers.
>
> Finally, they completed the book they wanted to write—a book about close friends from many backgrounds who helped one another struggle through the growing pains of reaching maturity at Harvard. The prostitution ring angle was in there to give the work a commercial hook. They turned it in to their publisher.

And it was kicked back.

There was too much talking and not enough action. Not enough plot. So a heavy rewrite took place. "We cut 250 pages and added 200 pages," Melcher said.

And—voila—*The Student Body,* an erotic thriller.

—"Designed by Committee" by Patrick Reardon, *Chicago Tribune*, Friday, May 15, 1998, p.5.

What do you make of the differences between these two descriptions of writing teams? Under what circumstances would you choose the more structured approach offered first, and when might you want to follow the procedures of the group writing a novel?

In this how-to list we provide a variety of strategies to help you prepare for reading, analyze and make connections with what you read, and most importantly get down to writing. Think of it as a resource that you can return to for help with specific projects, for example visual texts or group projects. Or you may turn to this list when you are stuck at any point of a project. Browse around in the list until you find a strategy that will help you get past that particular roadblock. Eventually you will be able to use the strategies you need without consulting the list!

UNIT II

Searching for Authenticity

Source: (*left*) *Van Gogh's Chair by Vincent van Gogh*, 1888, *National Gallery, London*, NG 3862; (*right*): *The Billionaire in Vincent's Chair*, by R. B. Kitaj, 1999, Marlborough Fine Art, London.

How do these two paintings talk to each other? The one on the left, painted by Vincent van Gogh in 1888, might be considered an ironic self-portrait: The striking presence of the empty chair, the tobacco and pipe left behind, draws our attention to the absence of its owner. In the painting on the right, on the other hand, the figure in the chair is the most striking presence in the painting: It seems to fill not only the chair but the whole room as well as the painting itself. In the late 1990s, the British Museum asked a number of artists to create a work that "conversed" with any of the paintings in their collection. R. B. Kitaj painted "The Billionaire in Vincent's Chair" as a comment on the huge sums needed to purchase famous works of art. The conversation between these two paintings helps us reflect on the different meanings of authenticity. In the art world, authenticity means the certainty that a work was truly created by the artist whose name is on it. In a world of technologically produced copies, authenticity is associated with uniqueness, which makes an object or experience more valuable. But some artists have responded to our technological environment by playing with the idea of the copy, as Kitaj plays with the image of van Gogh's chair. The conversation thus set up between the earlier work and the new one becomes part of our larger cultural conversation about the meaning of authenticity.

CHAPTER 3

Representing and Misrepresenting the Self

Situation: Have you seen *Spiderman,* the movie that this photo comes from? What is the movie about? Are you familiar with the original *Spiderman* comics? Consider what this photo suggests about representing and misrepresenting the self.

Genre: What do you know about the genre of the superhero story? How would you describe the rules or conventions of movies or comics that involve a superhero who switches identities?

Language: How does this photograph represent what happens in the movie? What are the different visual elements, and how do they work together to create an overall effect?

Consequences: In any superhero story, what are the consequences of switching identities?

Have you ever described a movie to a friend who hadn't seen it? Did you focus on the plot, the theme, or the look of the movie? If you focused on the plot, did you tell the whole story or just describe a few particular scenes? If you told a different friend about the same movie, did you describe it differently? Did you ever worry that you were not describing it accurately or that you had misunderstood something about it?

If you've done any of these things, then you know what it means to represent something. To represent something means to re-present it, make it present again, or make it present in a new place or a new way. Different people can represent the same thing differently, and the same person can represent the same thing in different ways. We might tailor our representation to the audience or the situation. When we represent something, we have to make decisions about it.

Thus as soon as we begin representing, we have to think about form. The thing itself is not present, and to make it present again we have to embody it in a new way or give it a form. How will we shape our representation of a movie we've seen: a very detailed account of the plot, a description of the characters, a philosophical discussion of the theme, a dramatic recreation of a specific scene, a comparison of this movie to another of the same genre? To represent something is to make decisions about form or genre.

It follows, then, that as soon as we represent something, we also need to think about the possibility of misrepresenting it. Each decision we make has the potential to be a kind of misrepresentation. If we emphasize plot, are we misrepresenting the whole? If we describe the same movie differently to different people, is one of these descriptions a misrepresentation? Suppose you misrepresent the movie—describe it inaccurately—but in doing so you give your friend an accurate sense of what the movie is like. These complications suggest that the relationships between representing and misrepresenting, and thus between representation and authenticity, are not as clear-cut as we might think at first.

We represent things all the time: movies, books, events, experiences. But perhaps the thing that we represent most often is our self. To represent yourself is to make yourself present in a place where you are not or to make yourself present in a different form, for example when you give a picture of yourself to someone, send an e-mail, write a college application essay, or create a personal Web page. In all these cases you are representing yourself, yet each representation is different, and the difference is determined by the situation, the audience, and the form itself. Are all of these representations authentic?

In the reading and writing you do in this chapter, you will explore the complicated relationship between representation, misrepresentation, and authenticity, particularly in connection with the self and with the complicated things that we do when we represent or misrepresent ourselves.

Skin

Esmeralda Santiago

Although in this chapter we focus mainly on representation as a stand-in for something that is not present—the picture of yourself that you give to someone, the e-mail message that you send, the application essay that you write—it can be said that we represent ourselves even when we are present. That is, the ways we *present* ourselves—how we look, the things we say, the clothes we wear, the ways we behave—cause others to form impressions of us. In this sense of representation, our body plays a complicated role. Our body makes us physically present, but it also represents our self to others. In such situations of "presence," our body is usually the first thing about our selves that people encounter, and it's the most concrete possible representation of our selves, yet we all know that our body can misrepresent us in various ways.

Our skin is both the most public and one of the most private parts of both our bodies and our selves. Parts of our skin—our face, our hands—may be the first things that people notice about us, but other parts of our skin are covered up and private, and in fact the amount of skin that we show is often a significant aspect of how we represent ourselves to others. This essay by Esmeralda Santiago explores how our skin might help us represent our selves to ourselves. Santiago, the author of the novels *When I Was Puerto Rican, America's Dream,* and *Almost a Woman,* sees her skin as a form of memory, a record of significant events and experiences in her life. This record—her scars, her wrinkles—has significance mostly for Santiago herself, but she also recognizes that it is an important part of what others see and know about her, and she rejects the idea of plastic surgery because she knows that it would erase the evidence of experiences that make her who she is.

This essay appeared in a book called *Body,* a collection of personal essays about body parts written by poets, fiction writers, playwrights, essayists, and journalists. The collection's editors, Sharon Sloan Fiffer and Steve Fiffer, have edited two similar collections, *Family: American Writers Remember Their Own* and *Home: American Writers Remember Rooms of Their Own.* The assumption behind these collections is that, because it is the business of writers to perceive and record the world with clarity, they may describe our experiences even when they are writing with most intimate detail about their own. As you read Santiago's essay, consider how well she succeeds in doing this.

Connecting with the Conversation

1. English has a number of expressions that refer to skin: skin deep, thin skinned, it makes my skin crawl, and I almost jumped out of my skin. Working in small groups, think of other such expressions, and then explore what each suggests about how we see the relationship between our skin and ourselves.

2. Our skin is just another organ, like a liver or a kidney, but much more than these, and even more than our heart, we tend to identify our skin with ourselves, at least in terms of how we present ourselves and relate to the outside world. Write in your journal about how you see the relationship between your skin and yourself.

My skin is richly toned, soft brown, *trigueña* we say in Puerto Rico, wheat-colored. Not white, not black, *trigueña* is not a race. It is a blend of all the races that have contributed to my brownness. *Trigueña* is what, in the United States, makes me "Other."

There are spots on my *trigueña* skin, birthmarks and scars, blemishes, wrinkles, veins that refuse to be contained in deeper tissue and have made their way to just below the surface. I often find unexplained bruises on my limbs, dark blue, angry splotches that turn purple before they fade. Below my eye there is a red dot that appeared one day, a punctuation to something I saw, perhaps. On my neck, around my torso there are small chocolate brown tags that materialized during my first pregnancy.Or maybe they were always there and I didn't notice them before. Lately they seem to be creeping toward my face, and I imagine it is the darker me emerging, taking over the lighter skinned Esmeralda.Maybe I'm becoming other than "Other."

I need not look hard to read history etched on my skin. There, along the arch of my left foot, is the scar left when I stepped on the sharp barbs of a wire fence. On the outside of my left knee is another scar, formed when a nail that protruded from the balusters of our porch cut a deep wedge that took weeks to heal. A smile hovers over my pubic hair, the wound through which doctors delivered my two children. Right in the center of my forehead is a dash, all that remains of the bloody mess when Chago, my childhood playmate, threw a rock that found its mark. That scar has been swallowed by the deep wrinkles left by surprise and worry.

Each line, each spot, each scar is a story, forgotten by almost everyone else involved, but not by me. That scar on top of my foot? It was not an accident, as I told Mami. We were living in the city, in two rooms behind a bar. My brother Raymond's foot had been injured in an accident—my fault, I thought, because I'd been left in charge and wasn't careful enough. Raymond, then four years old, was in and out of hospitals for weeks. Nights, he cried because his foot hurt so much. Days, he limped, and whimpered pitifully with every step. Doctors thought he'd never heal and that he should be amputated.

5 Curled at the edge of my foot, my smallest toe looked silly and useless. I pinched it, stuck pins into it, placed it under the metal leg of a chair, then pressed hard with all my weight. It hurt, but not nearly as much as I thought it should, and it didn't bleed. Raymond's foot bled, and angry bubbles of pus formed around the wound the doctors cleaned again and again.

One day, while Mami was outside de-feathering a chicken, I went into the bedroom, rummaged through her sewing box, and found the heavy scissors she took to

From *Body*, Edited by Sharon Sloan Fiffer and Steve Fiffer. New York: Avon Books, 1999, pp. 61–72.

work in the bra factory. They were black and silver, weighed on my hand solid and menacing. They were very sharp, and I was certain they could slice through that useless little toe in a neat cut.

I straddled the windowsill, my left leg dangling outside, my right knee pressed up to my chest. It was mid-afternoon, and shadows crept from one end of the yard to another. I held the scissors, cool to the touch, opened and closed them a couple of times as if they were jaws. I was not afraid. I'd been cut, scraped, or bruised hundreds of times. My skin was, even then, spotted with scars on every limb. They had all been accidents, but this was the first time I deliberately hurt myself.

I placed the sharp blades of the scissors around my toe and squeezed the handle, but didn't have the strength to cut clear through. The skin opened and a bubble of blood sprouted then trickled down to my sole. It hurt, but not nearly enough. I hopped down from the windowsill, was about to put the scissors away and take care of the wound when I noticed how my bare feet provided a perfect target. I dropped the scissors, point down, an inch above my middle toe. It hurt more than I could have imagined, and I screamed and hopped around as the scissors twinked onto the cement floor. Everyone came running. Mami, her hands and hair clumped with chicken feathers. My sisters and brothers, who had been playing in the shadows under the mango tree. Even Raymond limped over, and screeched when he saw the blood spurt from my foot, the same foot that hurt him so much.

Mami took care of it right away, so the wound didn't fester, and there was no threat that my foot would be amputated. But it hurt a lot, almost as much, I thought, as Raymond's must have. The scar that was left is round, less than a quarter inch in diameter, a tiny crater where I store guilt.

10 An active child will get hurt, a competitive one will hurt others. I was both, and my skin confirms the many falls and tumbles of a childhood in motion. I never broke a bone, but scrapes, cuts, stings, and punctures have left their mark on me, and I have inflicted them on others. My ten sisters and brothers can each point to what's left of the arguments that turned into fights that drew blood.

I was eighteen when I chased my brother Héctor up the stairs. I caught up to him on the top step, reached out, grabbed a handful of his hair, and yanked. We tumbled down, causing a racket that brought my mother, stepfather, grandmother, her boyfriend, my nine other sisters and brothers, and a neighbor to the hallway, where Héctor and I lay sprawled, punching one another. Mami pulled us apart, yelled at me that as the eldest, I should stop acting like a little kid, and at Héctor that at fourteen and almost a man, he should not hit girls. I threw one last punch, and so did he, and we had to be separated again. I stumbled off, blood dribbling down my leg, a thin red ribbon from a gash below my knee.

I don't remember what Héctor said or did that made me chase him up the stairs, and probably neither does he. But I'm reminded of that humid afternoon every time I shave my legs because there is a round, flat scar on my right shin, its surface lighter than the skin around it. On that scar there is no hair, just as now, thirty-two years later, there is no hair atop Héctor's head. Within the uneven borders of the scar on my shin I hold the course of time, the physical changes it has wrought on me and my loved ones.

In my rural childhood, toys were not purchased, they were made. As children, we sought Y-shaped branches of various sizes, set them to dry and harden in the hot Puerto Rican sun. A discarded bicycle inner tube cut into strips made the perfect tensile straps and cradle for a slingshot. A battered bucket was my first target, the pings of a hit resonating with a satisfying echo that no one could argue with. As I gained skill, the targets became smaller—a bottle, a tomato sauce can, a mango still on its branch.

Not allowed to wear pants, I insisted Mami put pockets in the cotton dresses she made for me and my sisters so that I could carry pebbles in them. The sash at my waist that tied into a bow in the back of the dresses held the slingshot at my side, and I practiced drawing it out like a cowboy a six-shooter. No one could outdraw me, or outshoot me.

An iguana scurrying into the shade of the annatto bushes had no chance against me. A bird in mid-flight would plummet to the ground, stunned by a well-aimed rock. Snakes slithering under piles of kindling for the stove, lizards scuttling from branch to branch on the avocado tree, mice scampering toward the kitchen—not one reached their goal. Their death came as a soft hiss through the humid air followed by a sharp thwack to their narrow heads.

"Girls shouldn't play with slingshots," the neighbors muttered, but if I killed the rat that ate into their sack of rice, they sent Mami a bowl of candied papaya or a bagful of fresh pigeon peas.

It was a well-aimed slingshot stone that left a scar I never see. My neighbor and playmate, Chago, claimed to have seen an *ardilla,* a Puerto Rican mongoose, in the hill behind his house. We set out to hunt it, but on the way down the road we got into an argument about who was the best shot. Everyone knew I was, and I reminded him of this, but his response was to mumble "*Tu madre,*" under his breath. *Mencionar la madre,* to mention another person's mother as a curse, is a major insult in Puerto Rico, and I did what anyone would have done. I punched him in the mouth. After he recovered from the surprise of a girl striking out, he backed up, bent over, picked up a fist-size rock, and threw it at me. I fell on my face, my forehead covered in blood. As he ran off, he called out a few more specific insults about my mother. When he looked back to see if I was following him, a stone from my slingshot found its mark, square on his left eye. The scar I never see was formed when doctors sewed his eyelid shut. And while there were welts left after the beating administered by my mother, who did not care I was defending her when I shot Chago's eye out, they healed soon after we moved from the barrio. The scar Chago left on me closed into a hyphen that divides and connects the right side of my face from the left. Inside it I store power.

Another scar invisible to me was found by a hairdresser. WALK-INS WELCOME the sign on the window of Tami's Hair and Nails stated. Inside was Tami herself, redheaded, green-eyed, long orange nails in the shape of spades. She tried to talk me out of cutting my waist-length hair. "If I cut it to shoulder length," she offered, "it will be enough of a change." It had taken over seven years to grow, seven years in which I fell in love with, and was betrayed by, a man who loved my long hair. "I want it really short," I insisted. Tami gathered a long ponytail at the base of my neck, tightened a rubber band around it, and cut. The strands that were freed from the weight of the hair below the cut line came to attention into a fuzzy halo around my face. "More," I ordered. "Chop it all off."

"Boy," Tami giggled, "you must be really mad at him."

20 The more she cut, the more liberated I felt, until she stopped, gently tipped my head forward, and parted the stubble. "Oh, honey," she murmured, "this must have hurt." She traced a line from just above the nape of my neck toward the crown of my head.

That one was caused by my mother. Quique and I had been discovered behind the outhouse with our hands on each other's private parts. His mother used a switch that left puffy red stripes on his legs and back. But Mami grabbed the first thing she could get her hands on, a cast-iron frying pan. She chased me around the yard, screaming that I had no shame. Inside the scar she left on the back of my head I store desire.

The scars on my skin are only the most painful traces of my life. There are also the stamps I was born with, the freckles that dot my cheeks and nose, the birthmark shaped like the island of Hispaniola that floats just under my navel, the dark dot on the back of my neck that I thought was sexy. Those birthmarks are my disappointment. Why do I have freckles? Why did no lover ever kiss that spot on the back of my neck?

As a child fascinated with geography, I loved the fact that the middle of the Greater Antilles was represented on my belly. I searched for Cuba and Puerto Rico, but neither was visible on my skin. Superstitious enough to believe anything, I thought the birthmark meant that someday I was destined to live in Santo Domingo or Port au Prince. But when I did leave Puerto Rico, it wasn't for another island. I studied a map of the United States, wondering which had the same shape as the birthmark under my navel. None do, but I'm still superstitious enough to believe there is some significance to it, some reason why the shape of the island near my navel looks like Haiti and the Dominican Republic but not Puerto Rico. I've concluded that it is because I will die there. Within the ragged borders of that birthmark I hold fear.

My cousin Corazón has a birthmark on the inside of her right knee. It is round, chocolate brown, the size of a plain M&M. I once asked her about it, and she told me her mother wished for it when she was pregnant, and that's why Corazón was born with one. I didn't believe her, so I asked her mother.

25 "There is a reason," Titi Ana said, "that it's called a *lunar.*"

When she was pregnant with Corazón, Titi Ana confessed to her midwife that if her child were a girl, she wished she would have a birthmark near her lip, just like Maria Félix, the Mexican movie star. The midwife assured Titi Ana that the moon would not deny a pregnant woman an *antojo,* and told her what she had to do to make her wish come true. Titi Ana followed the midwife's instructions, but at the last minute, realized that the birthmark might not look as good near the lip if the child were a boy. So she wished for it where it would be invisible to everyone else. Titi Ana could not have predicted that someday Corazón would wear miniskirts and that people would compliment her on the moon-shaped dark spot near her knee.

Years later, when I became pregnant and modern medicine assured me I was having a girl, I remembered Titi Ana's story, and decided to test the moon. Would it fulfill my wish for a pretty *lunar* on my daughter? Titi Ana had died years earlier, but I'd never forgotten her soft voice repeating the midwife's instructions for ensuring a birthmark on a child.

On the seventh month of my pregnancy, I stepped outside on the first night of a full moon. "You must invite the spirit of a woman in your family to help you," Titi Ana had said, and so I closed my eyes and called upon her, until I felt her presence, cool and silent near me. My hands on my belly, I rubbed circles counterclockwise, spoke to my child until I felt her moving. "Tonight you will receive a gift," I said, "from the moon and from your Great-aunt Ana, who watch over you."

I faced the moon, opened my eyes, and was about to put my right index finger near my lip when, like Titi Ana before me, I worried that a *lunar* would not look good there. I changed my mind, but then it occurred to me that, now that I was outside, facing the full moon, having summoned both my unborn child and the ghost of Titi Ana, I had to make a wish because spirits didn't like to be disturbed for no reason at all. If I didn't make a wish, it might mean bad luck for my daughter. I pressed the tip of my index finger halfway up my left thigh, and wished for a *lunar* there, a much more intimate place than where Corazón has hers. Two months later, when Ila was born, she had a dark chocolate birthmark on the inside of her left thigh. As soon as the doctors saw it, they took a biopsy, and on subsequent exams, her doctor has studied it, measured it, scraped the center of it, concerned it might be malignant.

But it's not a precancerous lesion. It is a gift from me, Titi Ana, and the moon, a spot where Ila can gather knowledge of the mysteries of woman.

WHEN I STAND NAKED BEFORE A MIRROR, I see how skin has evolved from the tight, firm, bouncy sheath that held me in, to the looser, softer, more textured canvas on which I sketch my life. Except for the ones I was born with, there are no marks on my skin that have not come from experience. But even the birthmarks and freckles on my body have meaning, imposed on them by superstition.

Wrinkles, engraved time on my skin, reveal themselves in unexpected ways at surprising times. I noticed the lines across my forehead as a teenager, after reading an article in *Glamour* magazine. As the writer instructed, I faced the mirror to determine if I had dry, oily, or combination skin, and there they were, two faint inverted vees over my eyebrows, and one line that ran temple to temple above the scar left by Chago's rock. When I looked closer, there were more; two tiny vertical lines where my nose met my forehead, two more beside my lips.

It was the first time I realized that I was not just growing up, I was growing old. Old like my grandmother and the man who owned the candy store. Old like my social studies teacher and the school principal. Old like my uncle Chico and great-aunt Chía. The first signs of mortality were etched on my skin, faint but visible, wrinkles formed by an often too expressive face. Should I stop frowning, smiling, squinting, puckering my lips? No, the beauty magazines only advised I moisturize.

Years later, and in spite of thousands of dollars spent on beauty products that promised to keep the skin on my face looking younger, firmer, more supple, I am wrinkled. Were I to slather moisturizer on every part of my body, my skin might not reveal its fifty years. But would moisturizer keep away the wrinkles I recently noticed around my breasts? How about the folds over my knees, and over my elbows? Would several more thousand dollars have erased the deep lines around my neck? The beauty industry would say yes. Plastic surgeons would argue that a nip here, a tuck there, would accomplish more than truckloads of creams. I could look twenty years younger, they promise.

Twenty years! I can erase the wrinkles caused by the final frantic days before my wedding. The puffy folds around my eyes can be cut away, so that it looks as if I never cry. The saggy skin around my breasts can be excised, eradicating three years of nursing babies. The skin around my middle can be tucked so as to deny the pregnancies, the distention caused by too many rich meals, the aversion to sit-ups.

But what about the scars? Would they too be erased? Where would I hide despair? Would each and every birthmark locate to a different spot now that the skin has been pulled, nipped, pinched? What do I do with superstition? And if these new scars, the ones created by plastic surgery, the ones that will erase experience from my body, come to me while I'm unconscious on an operating table, what will they contain?

* * *

My skin scars easily, but it also heals fast. It has been an advantage in life, this skin that has taken such abuse but still responds to a caress. In spite of all the scars, or maybe because of them, I'm thin-skinned and sensitive. This skin that has held me in but has loosed so much it's had to fold into itself, still feels, still bleeds, still stores who I am, have been, hope to become. *Trigueña,* wrinkled, spotted, bruised, marked, and scarred, my skin is the surface on which I read sorrow, superstition, the passage of time. Its texture, color, and tone have changed over the years, but within its confines I have survived a half century of life, each moment indelibly carved into my flesh.

Exploring Texts and Contexts

For activities with icons, refer to the Guide to Analyzing Readings in Context.

1. Santiago's essay is carefully structured with an introduction and conclusion framing four sections in which she examines four different marks on her skin, and within each of these four sections she interweaves description, narration, and metaphor to help us understand what each mark means to her. See if you can divide the essay into its six main sections (some but not all of which are marked off with double spaces), and then within each of the four middle sections, see if you can identify the movements of description, narration, and metaphor.
2. Santiago identifies herself as a 50-year-old Puerto Rican woman. How might her essay have been different if she had been Caucasian, African American, Native American, Asian, a man, 20 years old, or 80 years old? 

Creating Texts

For activities with icons, refer to the Guides to Analyzing Contexts for Writing and Analyzing Readings in Context. For additional help with these writing projects, read the description of **Essay** and **Comics** in the Genre Glossary.

1. In the collection from which Santiago's essay was taken, other writers such as National Public Radio host Jacki Lyden, novelists Francine Prose and Jane Smiley, cartoonist Lynda Barry, and short-story writer Chris Offutt write about such parts of the body as the brain, the nose, the belly, the teeth, and the knee bone. Using Santiago's essay as a general model, write a personal essay that might be included in such a collection.

2. In this personal essay Santiago uses language to explore a very physical phenomenon: how marks on the skin represent life experiences. Visual artists, almost conversely, may use visual images to express ideas or concepts. In Connecting with the Conversation Activity 1 on page 43, there is a list of expressions that refer to skin: skin deep, thin skinned, it makes my skin crawl, and I almost jumped out of my skin; you may have thought of others. Choose two or three of these expressions and draw a set of comics that visually convey the meanings of these expressions.

A Portfolio of Self Representations

Shane Madden

In the last few years, you have probably created at least some of the following: a college application essay, a resume and cover letter, a profile of yourself for an online forum, a description of yourself for a yearbook, a Web page, a username, or a voice mail greeting. In all of these ways you have used language, written or spoken, to represent yourself to others. It might seem to you that what is being represented—your self—stays the same, yet each of these representations is different because each arises out of a different situation and thus takes a different form; that is, each one is a different genre.

People use a surprisingly wide array of genres to represent themselves, and in contemporary American culture, young people represent themselves in more complex ways than they themselves might be aware of. Just within the last few years, for example, Shane Madden, a college freshman, has filled out numerous college applications, most of which requested a personal statement; composed a statement about himself for his high school yearbook; submitted brief profiles of himself for some of the chat rooms and online forums that he participates in; created two different personal Web pages, one that he made with the help of some friends when he was in high school and one that he had to make for one of his fall semester college classes; written a resume and cover letter for a summer job; and recorded a voice mail greeting for the phone in his dormitory room. This is in addition to the many essays, and occasional stories and poems, that he wrote for high school and college classes; the e-mails, posts, and instant messages that he writes almost every day; the thank you notes that his mom made him write after his graduation party; and the "video letter" that he made for a friend attending a different college, all of which—although they are not "self-portraits" like a resume or a Web page—are certainly acts of self representation.

Here we include three of Madden's self representations:* parts of the Web page that he created in high school and still sporadically maintains, one of his college application essays, and the resume and cover letter that he recently wrote for a summer job. How does Madden represent himself in these different genres? What significant common ground and what interesting differences do you find between them? How do the conventions of the different genres both open up and limit possibilities for expressing himself? Do the three different self-portraits seem to be separate, different portraits or pieces of a larger whole? Does any one of them seem to be more authentic than the others? Do you think Madden would describe them as representations or misrepresentations of himself?

Connecting with the Conversation

1. Bring to class an object that you see as representing yourself and be prepared to discuss why you chose it.
2. Put together a mini portfolio of self representations—for example, your high school yearbook picture and caption, your dorm room application, your voice mail greeting, or an introduction of yourself that you had to write for a college orientation activity or for one of your classes—and discuss how you see them as representing or misrepresenting you.

---

*Details have been changed to protect the privacy of the author.

My So-Called Home Page

www.shanemadden.com/index.htm

My So-Called Home Page

If you really want to hear about it...

My name is Shane Madden, I'm fifteen years old, and I live in Chicago with my dog, my parents, my cat, and my sister, in that order. I go to Thomas Paine High School but I won't bore you with the details. Here's what I like, more or less in this order: movies, music, and politics. My favorite director is David Lynch, but I'm interested in all kinds of movies, even one or two made in Hollywood. My favorite music is punk rock, but any kind of real rock and roll is fine by me. Politically, I'm pretty leftwing, but I enjoy reading about all kinds of political perspectives; some of them are very entertaining. I could tell you what I look like, but here's a couple pictures instead. You could click to enlarge them, but why would you want to? Thanks to Sandy for both of them.

But if you want to know who I really am,
check out my favorite web sites

www.theonion.com
www.indymedia.org
www.imdf.com
www.allmusic.com
http://news.yahoo.com
www.fourthwall.org

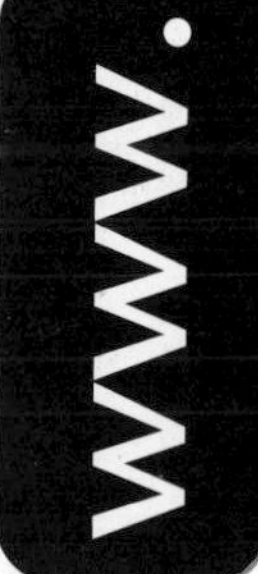

If you'd rather read about my life as it happens, click here

BLOG

My So-Called BLOG Page

www.shanemadden.com/blog.html

BLOG

February 9

Sorry its been so long again since my last post. Life still sucks of course but not as much. The show last night was awesome, and it looks like Kyle and Jorge and I are really going to get Misconduct off the ground. Maybe this time next year we'll have our own awesome show. Hey, you never know.

—1 comment

January 27

Thanks for all the calls, IMs, and general support. Not to get all sentimental, but it's good to have droogs at times like this. I'll be online again later tonight.

—3 comments

January 25

Sorry I haven't posted in so long. You know what's been going on. Or if you haven't heard the news, call me. I don't feel like saying it online, better to talk about it in person . . .

—5 comments

January 5

How's everyone's winter break been treating them? You all ready to head back to school? I know I'm not. I'd write a nice long and detailed explanation of mine, but I'm strapped for time right now. I went to see GBH. Partied at Tracy's house. Spent lots of time with many cousins. Got to hear lots of almost interesting family stories. Did some work on my room, put up some new posters. Didn't do any homework.

January 1

Well, I didn't intend for this to be a holiday blog, but happy new year. Does anyone remember Y2K? That is so last century. This has been an interesting year. Failing second-semester English and going to summer school, the play last fall, which was great, but then all that weirdness with Gina, and then the "election." Well, at least now we know why they made us learn about the electoral college in seventh grade. I remember my teacher saying that the electoral college was just a "meaningless formality." Haha, we wish. Well, maybe this will be a better year anyway.

—2 comments

December 25

Happy Holidays, kiddies. I got those Twin Peaks videos that I've been wanting, plus a book about David Lynch—it was a totally David Lynch Christmas. My parents told me that Twin Peaks was my favorite show when I was like five or something. I can't decide if that's really cool or really weird, or both.

Anyway, it's about 9:30. My parents and my grandmother, who's staying over, have already gone to bed, my sister's talking on the phone, the house is half really cleaned up and half really a mess. You know that feeling on the night of a holiday when the excitement is over but everything is still all chaotic? Nuf said. Good night.

December 17

Well I finally got this page set up. Thanks for all the help, Steve, couldn't have done it without you. Now, odds are, I'm not going to do anything productive with it, but it's going to be fun to have for a little while, until I abandon it like so many other projects.

So anyways, today I hung out with Jenna and Sam. We went to see some movie at the Davis. I can't even remember what it was, but it sucked. I'd reccommend you not to see it, but how could I without knowing it's name? Afterwards, we went down to Kyle's for dinner. Had a good time.

On a last note, does anybody know what happened to Jorge? We havn't seen him in a couple of weeks. He sick or something?

—1 comment

College Application Essay

Write an essay of about 500–750 words in which you answer this question: What idea has most influenced your life and why?

As cliched as it might sound, I think that the idea that has most influenced my life is the oft-repeated creed: question everything. In a society where public debate seems limited to a very few voices, many of which have obvious financial interests, ideas put forth in the mainstream are likely to have flaws and benefit a small minority. I feel that in order to maintain a clear mind, a mind where you have more control over your own opinions, it is necessary to look rationally at everything you're told and to examine it with extreme scrutiny.

All too often in today's world, I see people blindly swallowing any idea that is given to them. When there are incredible amounts of evidence against something, they'll believe it if it's drilled into their heads long enough. This includes everything from religion to political issues. And, often, when it comes to the most important things, things that could sway votes and change public opinion, the people who put forth the false ideas have their own interests in mind. Whether it's a pundit who tells it on a network that owns a corporation that would be affected by the issue, or it's a politician whose power is at stake, the loudest voices don't necessarily have the best interest of the public in mind. This is why I believe it's important to question everything.

But I have to say that the influence of this idea on my life has been complicated. On the one hand it sometimes means that it's not easy for me to get involved in things, even things that I believe in. For example, I am definitely and strongly anti-war. Recently I went to an anti-war rally with some friends. The speeches were great, and I pretty much agreed with everything they said. But there was a part of me that kept thinking, Okay, but what about this, or Do I really believe that statement? Then when everyone started marching and shouting slogans, I just couldn't bring myself to join in. Of course I was marching with everyone else—I couldn't help it—but I wasn't shouting slogans and getting all excited. I kept wondering what the people who disagreed with us thought about the arguments against the war, what kinds of arguments they would make in favor of it, and what kinds of questions they might ask us—especially if they also believed in "question everything"! My friends had a great time during the march, but I was a little bored by it and would rather have gotten into a discussion with the people standing on the sidewalk watching us.

So it seems as if the idea of questioning everything limits my ability to get involved. But on the other hand it makes me more interested in everything. I like reading about other perspectives and other political and religious beliefs. I probably spend as much time on Web sites that I disagree with as on the ones that I agree with. I like going to the Web sites of really fundamentalist religious organizations or the various pro-Bush Web sites. I'm usually not convinced by their arguments, but they do tend to make me more skeptical about the arguments that I thought I agreed with. Although people think of me as someone with strong opinions, I get along pretty well with people who have different beliefs because I'm interested in finding out why they believe what they do, even if I don't agree with them.

So I still think that "question everything" is one of the most important ideas in the world, even if it makes your life more complicated. Thinking for yourself and questioning things will lead to further understanding of the world around you. If you understand something because you yourself sought to educate yourself about it, then it will resonate that much more in your head, and you will understand it that much more. Besides, if you blindly accept any idea, you may become prone to accepting falsehoods, whether they're falsehoods created with malicious intentions or just false common beliefs that are rarely questioned.

I feel that I understand many more things by thinking about them myself. I feel that if I did not set about trying to understand things for myself, my understanding of the world would be much more shallow, and would be limited to the opinions of others. My vision of the world might be vulnerable to the selfish desires of others. I feel that I am all the more intelligent and better for being naturally inquisitive. I feel that I would not be the person I am if I did not realize the importance of questioning everything.

Shane Madden

Shane Madden
4625 W. Cooper
Chicago, IL 60613

March 10, 2004

Leslie Stephens
Director of Counselors
Timberland Theater Camp
Timberland Lake, WI

Dear Ms. Stephens:

I am writing to you because I heard about your camp from my teachers at The Fourth Wall Theater Ensemble. They feel that I should apply for a counselor position at your camp this summer.

I was a member for five years of the Youth and Teen Ensembles at the Fourth Wall Theater. This involved acting classes as well as taking part in two or three productions a year. I have had parts in productions ranging from *Macbeth* to plays written and staged by the ensemble members. I have also had parts in several high school productions.

For the last five years I have attended the High Tower YMCA summer camp in Chicago, and last summer I worked there as a Junior Counselor. In this position I supervised children aged 6 through 10. I initiated and taught a playwriting and acting class, and at the end of the summer the kids put on a production of a play that they had written themselves. This was a great experience, and I would very much like to do this kind of work again.

I have good skills working with children and can help them further develop their acting talent, as well as help them feel comfortable in a summer camp environment. I am also good at the other various tasks involved with being a camp counselor.

I am currently a freshman at State University, and I will be finished with my spring semester by May 15. The fall semester begins on September 4. I will be available any time between those two dates. I can be reached at 773 234-5678, and I would be able to come to Timberland for an interview any weekend. I am very much looking forward to discussing the counselor position with you.

Sincerely,

Shane Madden

Shane Madden

4625 W. Cooper
Chicago, IL 60613
773 234-5678

Objective	To obtain a counselor job at a summer theater camp.
Education	
Fall 2003 – Present	Enrolled at State University Anticipated major: Philosophy Anticipated graduation date: May 2007
Fall 1999 – Spring 2003	Thomas Paine High School Graduated June 2003 GPA: 3.2 (on a 4-point scale)
Work and Other Related Experience	
Fall 2003 – Present	Assistant in the archives at the State University library. Catalogued documents and other materials; assisted in organizing materials in a newly designed document room.
Summer 2003	Junior Counselor at the High Tower YMCA Summer Camp. Supervised children aged six to ten; initiated and taught a class in playwriting and acting; assisted the children in writing and planning the production of a play; directed the play and supervised its production as part of the end-of-summer parents weekend.
Fall 1999 – Spring 2003	Acted in several productions at Thomas Paine High School.
Fall 1998 – Spring 2003	Member of the Fourth Wall Theater's Youth and Teen Ensemble. Acted in two or three productions each year; participated in writing of several productions; and participated in the stage design of all productions.
Other Skills	Computer skills including Word, Access, and HTML. Studied French for eight years and Latin for four years. Play guitar.
References	Available upon request.

Exploring Texts and Contexts

For activities with icons, refer to the Guide to Analyzing Readings in Context.

1. Describe the conventions of each genre included in this portfolio and discuss how these conventions might have shaped Madden's self representations.
2. What were Madden's purpose and audience in each of these self representations, and how did these considerations shape the representation? How successful do you think each of these pieces is? If you were responding to any of these pieces as a peer reviewer, what suggestions for improvement would you make?
3. Discuss the different ways that Madden represents himself. What kind of person do you think he "really" is? Do you think any of these is more accurate or truthful, more authentic, than the others? Why?

Creating Texts

For activities with icons, refer to the Guides to Analyzing Contexts for Writing and Analyzing Readings in Context. For additional help with these writing projects, read the descriptions of **Personal Essay, Web Page, Resume/Cover Letter**, and **Cover Letter/Reflective Essay** in the Genre Glossary.

1. Add to the mini portfolio you put together for Connecting with the Conversation Activity 2, on page 51, a personal essay, a personal Web page, a resume and cover letter, and one or two other self representations that you choose.

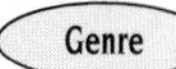

2. Write a Cover Letter/Reflective Essay in which you discuss the relationship between each of the pieces of self representation in the portfolio and what you see as your authentic self or true identity, if you think there is such a thing. Do you see some as more accurate representations than others, and why? Do the conventions of any of these genres require you to represent yourself in ways that seem like distortions? On the other hand, do the rules of any of these genres allow you to represent yourself in ways that you otherwise are not able to express? Do you feel that you learned anything about yourself by representing yourself in any of these forms?

Representin' the Real

Todd Boyd

Suppose that you represent yourself in different ways in different situations, say when you are with friends as opposed to with your parents or a teacher. Which is the real you? We tend to think that authenticity is a question of expressing our true self, finding our true voice. But what if you have more than one true self? What if your true self changes according to the context? Have you ever been in one of those situations where you had to interact with two people, or two groups of people, who knew you in different contexts and had different expectations about your behavior? How do you feel in such a situation, and how do you handle it?

Todd Boyd, an assistant professor of critical studies in the School of Cinema-Television at the University of Southern California, takes up this question in connection with writing, specifically academic writing. Boyd has written extensively about popular culture, in particular black popular culture, and he wants to make his writing accessible to ordinary people who are interested in and affected by the things he writes about. At the same time, in order to have professional credibility, he must write and publish for other experts in his field and academic readers in general. Because different audiences measure authenticity differently, Boyd has a complex sense of the hazards of trying to sound authentic to two different audiences. In this excerpt from his book *Am I Black Enough for You? Popular Culture from the 'Hood and Beyond,* Boyd both discusses and illustrates the struggle to develop an authentic style in this situation.

Connecting with the Conversation

1. In your journal, answer the questions posed in the first paragraph of the headnote above.
2. You've probably had a few occasions—for example, in writing a research paper—to read academic writing, that is, not a textbook written for students but a book or article written for other people in the field, other experts. And of course you've read popular media articles, for example in newspapers and magazines. In your journal, describe the differences between academic and popular writing. Discuss how you respond to these two kinds of writing.

One of my most vivid childhood memories is the constant presence of neatly though conservatively dressed Black men in dark suits with bow ties, sporting closely cropped hair, or a "Quo Vadis," as it was called at the time. These men were of course members of the Nation of Islam who sold *Muhammed Speaks* from the street corners of downtown Detroit. Their polite manner of speaking and dignified appearance were always interesting to me, and I looked forward to encountering them, if for no other reason than that they would often refer to me, a little boy, as "Sir" or sometimes "young brother," terms of acknowledgment and respect that had lasting meaning.

I guess in hindsight I was impressed by their pride and dignity, the fact that they looked you straight in the eye when talking, that they did not scratch when they did not itch, that they did not laugh when things were not funny, and that they seemed to

From *Am I Black Enough for You: Popular Culture from the 'Hood and Beyond.* Bloomington: Indiana University Press, 1997, pp. 1–12.

remain stoic at all times, regardless of the circumstances. They appeared fearless and the embodiment of what people now refer to as "hard."

Later on in life I began to understand why this was the case. As I learned about the Nation, or the Black Muslims as they were called in that day, it became clear that the reason for their stunning appearance was that the teachings of the Honorable Elijah Muhammed had given them the self-esteem that so many Black men are deprived of. While I have never been interested in being a Muslim, as their religious code of honor is unappealingly restrictive, the restoration of pride and dignity to their mostly male followers was laudable. Upon further investigation I discovered that many of the members of the Nation were ex-convicts or recovering substance abusers who found solace in this particular place.

Indeed, the Nation had established as its primary target for membership the neglected souls of our ghettoized society. These individuals are best summarized by Marx's description of the lumpenproletariat or, more concisely, what Frantz Fanon later described as the "wretched of the earth." Considering the fact that so few people are truly interested in assisting these depressed and deprived individuals, I have to commend the Nation for their assistance, even though I still have problems with their overall beliefs.

5 This "respect" for the Nation of Islam eventually led me to write a chapter of my doctoral dissertation on their current leader, Louis Farrakhan, and his place in popular culture and political discourse. At the time I was interested in finding a strident aesthetic of Blackness, somehow related to Black nationalism, but updated from its last incarnation in the late 1960s and early 1970s. I innocently called what I was searching for "Afrocentricity." Since that time the notion of an Afrocentric discourse has all but disappeared from my thought process. This is due to a lived politics of location that not only informs what I write but, in essence, defines the subject.

When I started the project, I was finishing my graduate studies at the University of Iowa, and upon completion I worked at my first academic job, as a professor at the University of Utah. The placement of a Black man in either one of these settings would be bad enough, but together, one behind the other, they were certainly a feat deserving of additional compensation. I have often called this my "fly in the buttermilk" tour. Nonetheless, my thoughts during that time were indicative of being marginalized in a sense that I am sure most cultural theorists have never thought of. Thus my writing was in defense, a justification for African American culture, as opposed to dealing with any substantive matter. While this process proved a good exercise, it was ultimately draining. African American culture does not need to be defended, as its impact on American culture is undeniable.

So as I began rethinking these ideas in the contested spaces of Los Angeles, I slowly realized that the battle lines were drawn somewhat differently. Here there was no doubt about the presence of African American culture; the point of reference had to do with its reception. I can vividly recall a member of the interview team at USC asking me to justify my critical inquiry into Louis Farrakhan. In the interviewer's mind, anything short of a pure dismissal was unacceptable. Not only was this attitude counterproductive in a scholarly environment, but as the public reaction after the October 1995 Million Man March would demonstrate, the refusal to treat the issue of Louis Farrakhan seriously remains a problem in American society. This dismissive attitude is still prevalent as I am writing this preface: one-time presidential hopeful Governor Pete

Wilson of California in the spring of 1995 led a vote by the University of California Board of Regents to end affirmative action. Wilson and others, including the interviewer, want to dismiss Black people in a way much more direct than a simple critical dismissal, though.

I moved to L.A. shortly after a jury in Simi Valley tried to disregard the fact that several police officers, who are charged with upholding the law, decided that they were above that law in their beating of Rodney King. I was a true resident of L.A. by the time a second jury conceded the bare minimum in sentencing two of the officers, though a judge decided that their punishment was too severe.

By then it was no longer a novelty to see members of the Nation of Islam standing on the corner of Crenshaw and Vernon selling newspapers and beanpies, nor was it a rarity to see Black men and women dressed in Afrocentric garb as I traveled around the area where USC is situated. No, these things were no longer abstract intellectual concerns, as they were in Iowa or Utah, but real live artifacts that were not as romantic or as distant as my state of denial might have made them seem before moving to L.A.

10 What was real was the way in which I often oscillated between being surrounded by the gang members of South Central and the Hollywood "niggaz" with whom most of my social time was being spent. I was constantly transposed between the "gangstaz" that Ice Cube rapped about, and the "gangstaz" themselves—or for that matter Ice Cube himself. Black men were once again real, as they had been for so much of my life. Thus I had to approach my subject with the same determination with which I would approach a real Black man. Romanticized theoretical concepts would no longer be privileged over real interaction.

In all this, my subject matter began to change. No longer was I searching for an Afrocentric position in Black popular culture. Instead I was in search of what held these competing tenets together: how Black men navigated the treacherous terrain of L.A., and how my own identity was being transformed in the process. No longer was I the novelty image; I had become real as well.

My move to L.A. also underscored another reason why Afrocentricity no longer seemed a relevant concern. This new evaluation of Afrocentricity had to do with commodification at the highest level. In Hollywood, where commercialization is so deeply ingrained, the selling out of Black political discourse in popular culture was readily evident—not only in the way that numerous individuals wore Afrocentric clothing for style, though having little knowledge of the politics, but in that the whole political process seemed empty. The media had simply found a way of co-opting everything, from the picture of Malcolm X on Roc's wall, to the emblematic X on baseball caps. Nothing appeared to be sacred.

Though Hollywood and commodity have never been enemies, there was a time when culture and politics that deviated from the mainstream were viewed as threatening. When there was a political theme that ran through popular culture, it was bounded by the real-life threat of a strong political presence. For instance, Les McCann and Eddie Harris's challenging political tune "Compared to What" was informed by the fact that the Black Panther Party was asking some of the same questions in society. Whereas politics at one time prompted popular culture, now popular culture exists in a world where politics has been completely displaced. Politics can exist only to the extent that it is replicated in the media, and even then this is short-lived.

This began to occur to me while listening to Gil Scott-Heron shortly after the riots in the spring of 1992. His tune "The Revolution Will Not Be Televised" is a concise deconstruction of the uselessness of media in a world where the people have decided to address their fate. Media, in this construction, would be obsolete. They could in no way alter the demands of history. Yet in 1992 the revolution was televised, and it proved quite entertaining at that. Not only did it displace Cosby, but the prevalence of home video cameras proved that we no longer had to be satisfied with a dominant version of the news, either. Most of the best footage came from amateur filmmakers, whose street ethnography became more valuable than the normally sophisticated news crews and their footage. The revolution was televised, and the availability of video equipment at the personal level made it that much more of a media event. Up close and personal took on an entirely different meaning.

15 So with the need for more and more authentic footage, the people in the street became simultaneously their own best friend and worst enemy. On one hand, they used the instruments of technology to momentarily halt their own materially motivated rampage through the streets, or in some cases to demonstrate it. On the other hand, they functioned as their own publicist by foregrounding their own images, totally ignoring, while ultimately falling into, the same traps that the mainstream media normally set for impoverished minorities. Is this what Buggin' Out, the character in Spike Lee's *Do the Right Thing,* meant when he said, "Put some brothers on the wall"?

What we saw in those streets was a true expression of urban politics in the postmodern world. All pretense toward social revolution was displaced by the more immediate goal of accumulating the commodities that were often advertised but normally denied to these oppressed people. Watching this and the cultural events that followed showed me that this was the state of contemporary politics for the urban poor: the imitation of crass materialism, by any means possible. This made me realize that we had entered a new day, when chaos as a way of life was forced onto the mainstream agenda for the first time. So any attempt on my part to argue about the politics of popular culture as it was linked to any overriding ideological theme, particularly Afrocentricity, would be a total waste of time.

As far as cultural representations of African Americans are concerned, we are in a seller's market. As mainstream representation requires more and more images to fill the ever-expanding visual space, it is inevitable that there will be a minority presence. Though the overall control of the media lies in the hands of the real "other," I would be remiss if I did not point out that African Americans do have some control over their image. Considering that excess sells in general, the more excessive the African American image, the stronger the likelihood that it will be accepted. The politics of negotiated conformity, focusing on excess, dominates the representation of contemporary Black popular culture. For this reason, Snoop Doggy Dogg is more relevant today than Spike Lee.

I MAKE THESE POINTS to emphasize what it means to analyze Black male culture in the context in which it is being produced. While the West Coast is not known for its intellectual acumen, it is known for the vast entertainment complex that produces the culture we all consume. "Hollywood" is the generic term that we often associate with this mode of production and the ensuing discourse that it brings. Considering all this, I am confronted with the task of being intelligent with respect to Black culture, while being an integral part of it. Those on the cultural side say that there is no meaning to what they do, that their work is often misinterpreted. They denounce both cause and effect. The academic side says that there is much meaning being produced, that cause and effect are parts of larger cultural systems, and that these cultural producers are simply agents of a much larger process. In Hollywood one has to listen to both sides. The writing in this book is a demonstration of these two approaches.

The entertainment world generally has little regard for academic pontification. The academic world, on the other hand, has much regard for entertainment, yet in such a distanced way that seldom do the twain meet. Being that I get paid for academic pontification—though some find it entertaining that a Black man could do such a thing—I will begin by explaining how I see my position in this larger arena.

20 As cultural critics, we should aim to explain the various processes of culture in relation to aesthetics, the economy, and the political systems that define the larger world around us. Our goal is much like that of the country preachers I used to hear as a child who would be encouraged by a church member to "make it plain!" In the process of making it plain, we have to evaluate and deconstruct our subjects so as to speak to others about our interpretation of the material. So often, though, we make it plain only for the already converted, the huddled masses of other academics in our respective fields. We make it plain to people who already understand. This is a problem. There are so many people outside the academy who never read our books, attend our conferences, or take our classes. Yet these people are often more interesting to talk to and learn from than those of us who are supposedly educated.

This propensity toward isolation in academia is currently being challenged by a new generation of African American scholars who have internalized the fundamentals of the academy, but have chosen to pitch their ideas to a larger audience. Unfortunately, there are still many in the academy who assume that by being accessible, one is somehow less serious. As Black intellectuals gain a stronger foothold in the marketplace, however, such pronouncements are becoming common. Often this debate is placed in the opposition between the terms "journalism" and "scholarship," the former clearly being less substantial than the latter. Thus, Black public intellectuals are considered journalists, while those intellectuals who deal in esoterica are considered scholars, and in some way use knowledge, like a country club membership, as an exclusionary resource. At the end of the day we must ask ourselves, Who does this help, and who does it hurt?

This dichotomy is similar to the old racially coded debate in sports that describes African American athletes as "natural" and white athletes as "hard-working." It is assumed that African American athletes are born with the skills to play and excel at sports, a clear reference to an assumed physical prowess that defies mental capacity, while white athletes are regarded as industrious, in keeping with the ideology of the American work ethic. In the same way, it is assumed that Black scholars are somehow less well equipped, or as former Los Angeles Dodger general manager Al Campanis once said, they do not have the "necessities" to do the job.

These concerns are representative of the racism that is operative in code words offered by liberal whites in the form of a compliment that is really defined by traditional racist tenets being expressed in a new era. African American cultural criticism has more to do with a mission of access to a large enough audience that the words can possibly mean something to the world in which we live, than with any lack of necessities. This is especially true when you consider that the academic credentials of African American cultural critics are indeed valid, if for no other reason than that they were earned according to the rules set in place by an overwhelmingly white academy.

It is my intention to fuse the formal and the vernacular in such a way that it informs both sides, as opposed to being limited to one or the other. As African American discourse has always been defined in conjunction with its audience, so too will be the scholarship that emanates from this position. Those African American scholars who are redefining the academy are like the African American musicians who constantly redefined American music throughout the twentieth century. They are forces that must be dealt with in the same way that blues, jazz, soul, and now rap must be dealt with. The key is being accessible without losing one's critical edge—to, in the immortal words of George Clinton, "dance underwater and not get wet."

If living in L.A. has taught me one thing, it is that entertainment sells, esoterica does not. Many would consider my stance to be a sellout. So as not to be misunderstood, let me say that insights on culture should be arrived at with nothing less than rigorous detail to attention. What I am suggesting, though, is that the work of scholars who make a living dealing with popular culture should in some sense be concerned with the popular in all its manifestations.

Recently the media have become interested in what are now called "public intellectuals"—all of whom, interestingly enough, have been Black. Since the beginning of 1995, several major publications have commented on the emerging Black intellectuals who seem to be taking the academy by storm. Among others, the *New Yorker, Atlantic Monthly, Village Voice,* and *Los Angeles Times Magazine* have done cover stories on the Black intellectual in the 1990s. Names which continually pop up are Henry Louis Gates Jr., Cornel West, bell hooks, Houston Baker, and Michael Eric Dyson. These names have been bandied about in both positive and negative ways in sectors normally off-limits to academics. This popularity is coupled with a rise over the last five years in the number of publications by Black authors who study popular culture. At least for the time being, Black academics are in the mix. So the path has already been trod. Now is the time to till some new ground.

One of the most prevalent themes that inform the field of cultural studies, especially popular culture, is the tendency toward politicizing the objects we study. It is as though our interest in things that other people consider frivolous is somehow justified by the political dimension that we bring to them. Yet I have long had a problem with the phrase "popular culture," as there seems to be a hierarchy with respect to those things that we choose to study. The artifacts that receive the most attention are those that carry the most obvious progressive political baggage. If ever the demands of political correctness were a factor, it is in the study of popular culture. Why have I never read an intense study of the films of Rudy Ray Moore, the novels of Iceberg Slim or Donald Goines, the music of Tyrone Davis, etc.? Why? Because they do not fit in so easily with what we consider acceptable, and because they are works of the lower class that have never transcended the world of folk culture in which they exist. In addition, their politics are a huge stumbling block in light of the resulting contradictions. Nonetheless, they still need to be studied.

This is also true of contemporary culture. Though several people make cursory mention of rap music, few fully explore its possibilities. Those who do seem interested only to the extent that they can make rap into an artifact of political discourse. I am not suggesting that rap transcends this political dimension, but rather that it is a product of political circumstances in America; it is a defense of and a response to certain historical and social conditions. It need not be defended, though it is constantly under attack; its presence signifies a defense that can come only from the product itself.

As academics, we need not defend rap, though the pressures of intellectual life and the superstructure of the university profession strongly urge us to do so. As practitioners of culture studies, we are encouraged to find the political as a way of linking us with an academic community—e.g. Marxist, poststructuralist, feminist. Without these labels we are constantly dismissed, our work disregarded. And notice that this is the reaction that we receive from the so-called left side of the academic spectrum. So the pressure is on to do a Marxist reading of Ice Cube, or a feminist reading of Salt n Pepa, so as to prove to our colleagues that we are one with them, that we are ultimately no threat. We are like Rodney King, in that we want only to get along.

Though you will find the influence of both Marxist thought and poststructuralist discourse in my work, I consider myself a follower of neither. In addition, I must constantly remind myself not to fall into the trap of articulating a Black nationalist party line. Criticism, like the best of the jazz tradition, should be an improvisation on cultural studies itself. Though I may borrow from the intellectual styles mentioned earlier, it is the context in which the thoughts arise that propels the project. The art of improvisation is informed by many components but driven by one, an abiding notion of African American oral culture and its effects. In the same way, the improvisers of jazz nuanced existing meanings, while on the bandstand their primary function was the articulation of the oral impulses that have always defined Black life in America. In this process it is the appropriation of other forms and their usefulness in furthering the African American oral project.

Thus quotations are used as just that, quotes, appropriated thoughts that strengthen my points. This is similar to rappers' use of sampling, where preexisting forms of music are incorporated into the contemporary as a way of enhancing the overall project. As with improvisation, the original is useful not as an object of sacred devotion but as a way of motivating contemporary expression. In this process, the improviser and the sampler are judged on their ability to recontextualize, not on their acumen in imitating the original.

In jazz you are required to improvise, to create your own form of expression by using other bits of information as they inspire you. The emphasis is not on the original but on one's own articulation. In this way jazz and rap are very similar. As jazz improvises, rap emphasizes the freestyle, an impromptu lyrical explosion that is defined by its spontaneity. These are the oral forms I hope to express through my writing, to improvise on the canon of popular culture and freestyle my way through the idiom of African American life in the late twentieth century, doing both at the same time, without missing a beat.

Exploring Texts and Contexts

For activities with icons, refer to the Guide to Analyzing Readings in Context.

Language

1. Working in a small group, identify the passages where you think Boyd is trying to appeal to his popular audience, where he is trying to appeal to his academic audience, and where he is trying to appeal to both. Because Boyd is a good writer who is consciously trying to create a blended style that can appeal to both audiences, you won't find obvious shifts in style; rather look for subtle shifts in content and tone. You might find these shifts between paragraphs, within paragraphs, or even within a single sentence. Discuss the different strategies that Boyd uses to appeal to his diverse audience.

Situation

2. Working with the class as a whole—and making use of online resources if they're available—try to identify all the writers, musicians, filmmakers, critics, and intellectuals that Boyd refers to, and discuss what these references tell you about the contexts in which Boyd is writing and the audiences that he is trying to speak to.
3. What is Boyd's central argument in this piece? Is it stated directly anywhere in the piece, or do you have to figure it out?

Creating Texts

For activities with icons, refer to the Guides to Analyzing Contexts for Writing and Analyzing Readings in Context. For additional help with these writing projects, read the descriptions of **Essay, Feature Article**, and **Cover Letter/Reflective Essay** in the Genre Glossary.

1. Using Boyd's piece as both a source of ideas and a model, write a personal essay about experiences you've had in which you had to behave differently or represent yourself differently to different groups. Describe your experiences in such a way that your readers can share your experiences, but also analyze the wider implications of these experiences, either in terms of the idea of authentic identity or in terms of the social consequences of different kinds of behavior. Using Boyd's piece as a model, interweave description and analysis.

Genre

2. With your teacher's guidance, find an article in an academic journal on some topic that you are interested in and/or have some knowledge about. You'll be surprised at the wide range of "popular" topics that academics have written about, from hairstyles to lowriders, from science fiction to romance novels. Identify the most important ideas and rewrite them as a feature article for a popular magazine read by nonacademic people who are interested in that topic. Then write a cover letter discussing the kinds of changes you made.

Identity in the Age of the Internet

Sherry Turkle

Technology has given us new possibilities for self representation. While e-mail, for example, is an extension of letter writing, which has been around for centuries, the personal Web page and the voice mail greeting seem to be completely new forms of self representation. In this piece, Sherry Turkle describes how people have begun to use new technology to misrepresent themselves, and she discusses the risks and possibilities of these new forms of misrepresentation.

People have always found ways to misrepresent themselves or to pretend to be someone else. Plays, games, and pageants, for example, have allowed people to pretend to be someone else for fun, while costumes, disguises, makeup, and more recently surgery have helped people carry out these socially acceptable activities as well as engage in various kinds of fraudulent activities—pretending to be someone else in order to harm someone or benefit oneself. In addition to their own bodies, people have also used writing—forgeries, for example—to misrepresent themselves. In her book *Life on the Screen: Identity in the Age of the Internet,* Turkle discusses how computers and the Internet allow people to use writing to engage in extremely complex forms of misrepresentation. She interviews a variety of people who use MUDs, Multiple User Domains, to create alter egos, alternative worlds, and whole new virtual lives for themselves online. She discusses how some are able to use these alternative realities to explore and develop aspects of themselves that they haven't been able to develop in real life (RL) but how these alternative realities can also become means of escape from and excuses for not facing RL problems. For some MUD participants, online life becomes more real than real life, and their online personae become their most authentic selves.

Turkle argues that, for good or ill, these online activities are changing the way we think of the self and identity. Whereas we once thought of the self as singular, well-integrated, and with clear boundaries, today we tend to think of the self as multiple, changing, and fluid. Perhaps most interestingly, she argues that you don't need to participate in MUDs to be involved in these changing attitudes toward identity: Simply by using Windows—which allows you to simultaneously work on a document, check your e-mail, surf the net, play a game, and engage in an instant messaging conversation—you are in a sense splitting your self into multiple selves. Thus even in our most ordinary routines, we may be participating in an extraordinary change in the human understanding of identity, and we should be alert to both the possibilities and the dangers of this change.

Sherry Turkle is Professor of the Social Studies of Science and Technology at the Massachusetts Institute of Technology and has been one of the most perceptive thinkers about how computers are changing human life and even human nature. Her 1984 book, *The Second Self: Computers and the Human Spirit,* was the first in what she calls her "computational trilogy" of books about humans' interactions with computers and other kinds of artificial intelligence and artificial life. The excerpts here are from the second book in the trilogy, the 1995 *Life on the Screen.* The first excerpt is from Chapter 7, in which she describes how a variety of people, especially people in their teens and early twenties, interact in online environments; the second excerpt is from the book's final chapter, in which she looks at the larger social implications of our involvement with computers. Turkle is currently working on the third book in her computational trilogy

Connecting with the Conversation

1. Have you ever participated in a chat room, online forum, or online game, or do you know someone who has? Do you ever do anything to disguise or change your identity online? Write in your journal about your experience or the experiences of others. What does it feel like to misrepresent yourself online?
2. American popular culture seems preoccupied, almost obsessed, with the idea of alter egos, imposters, double identities, switched identities, and assumed identities. Consider, for example, the movies *Fight Club, The Nutty Professor, The Talented Mr. Ripley, Tootsie,* and *The Bourne Identity;* the singers Eminem and Prince; the phenomenon of professional wrestling; or any movie, comic book, or TV show about superheroes. Working with a small group, choose a movie, TV show, book, singer, or other artist or form of expression that embodies or explores the phenomena of alter egos, imposters, double identities, switched identities, or assumed identities, and make a presentation to the class about how that person or form of expression explores that phenomenon.

In the early 1970s, the face-to-face role-playing game Dungeons and Dragons swept the game culture. In Dungeons and Dragons, a dungeon master creates a world in which people take on fictional personae and play out complex adventures. The game is a rule-driven world that includes charisma points, levels of magic, and rolls of the dice. The Dungeons and Dragons universe of mazes and monsters and its image of the world as a labyrinth whose secrets could be unlocked held a particular fascination for many members of the nascent computer culture. The computer game Adventure captured some of the same aesthetic. There, players proceeded through a maze of rooms presented to them through text description on a computer screen.

The term "dungeon" persisted in the high-tech culture to connote a virtual place. So when virtual spaces were created that many computer users could share and collaborate within, they were deemed Multi-User Dungeons or MUDs, a new kind of social virtual reality. Although some games use software that make them technically such things as MUSHes or MOOs, the term MUD and the verb MUDding have come to refer to all of the multi-user environments. As more and more players have come to them who do not have a history with Dungeons and Dragons, some people have begun to refer to MUDs as Multi-User Domains or Multi-User Dimensions.

From *Life on the Screen: Identity in the Age of the Internet.* New York: Simon & Schuster, 1995, pp. 180–186 and 255–269.

Some MUDs use screen graphics or icons to communicate place, character, and action. The MUDs I am writing about here do not. They rely entirely on plain text. All users are browsing and manipulating the same database. They can encounter other users or players as well as objects that have been built for the virtual environment. MUD players can also communicate with each other directly in real time, by typing messages that are seen by other players. Some of these messages are seen by all players in the same "room," but messages can also be designated to flash on the screen of only one specific player.

The term "virtual reality" is often used to denote metaphorical spaces that arise only through interaction with the computer, which people navigate by using special hardware—specially designed helmets, body suits, goggles, and data gloves. The hardware turns the body or parts of the body into pointing devices. For example, a hand inside a data glove can point to where you want to go within virtual space; a helmet can track motion so that the scene shifts depending on how you move your head. In MUDs, instead of using computer hardware to immerse themselves in a vivid world of sensation, users immerse themselves in a world of words. MUDs are a text-based, social virtual reality.

5 Two basic types of MUDs can now be accessed on the Internet. The adventure type, most reminiscent of the games' Dungeons and Dragons heritage, is built around a medieval fantasy landscape. In these, affectionately known by their participants as "hack and slay," the object of the game is to gain experience points by killing monsters and dragons and finding gold coins, amulets, and other treasure. Experience points translate into increased power. A second type consists of relatively open spaces in which you can play at whatever captures your imagination. In these MUDs, usually called social MUDs, the point is to interact with other players and, on some MUDs, to help build the virtual world by creating one's own objects and architecture. "Building" on MUDs is something of a hybrid between computer programming and writing fiction. One describes a hot tub and deck in a MUD with words, but some formal coded description is required for the deck to exist in the MUD as an extension of the adjacent living room and for characters to be able to "turn the hot tub on" by pushing a specially marked "button." In some MUDs, all players are allowed to build; sometimes the privilege is reserved to master players, or wizards. Building is made particularly easy on a class of MUDs known as "MOOs" (MUDs of the Object Oriented variety).

In practice, adventure-type MUDs and social MUDs have much in common. In both, what really seems to hold players' interest is operating their character or characters and interacting with other characters. Even in an adventure-type MUD, a player can be an elf, a warrior, a prostitute, a politician, a healer, a seer, or several of these at the same time. As this character or set of characters, a player evolves relationships with other players, also in character. For most players these relationships quickly become central to the MUDding experience. As one player on an adventure-type MUD put it, "I began with an interest in 'hack and slay,' but then I stayed to chat."

The characters one creates for a MUD are referred to as one's personae. This is from the Latin *per sonae* which means "that through which the sound comes," in other words, an actor's mask. Interestingly, this is also the root of "person" and "personality." The derivation implies that one is identified by means of a public face distinct from some deeper essence or essences.

All MUDs are organized around the metaphor of physical space. When you first enter a MUD you may find yourself in a medieval church from which you can step out into the town square, or you may find yourself in the coat closet of a large, rambling house. For example, when you first log on to LambdaMOO, one of the most popular MUDs on the Internet, you see the following description:

> The Coat Closet. The Closet is a dark, cramped space. It appears to be very crowded in here; you keep bumping into what feels like coats, boots and other people (apparently sleeping). One useful thing that you've discovered in your bumbling about is a metal doorknob set at waist level into what might be a door. There's a new edition of the newspaper. Type "news" to see it.

Typing "out" gets you to the living room:

> The Living Room. It is very bright, open, and airy here, with large plate-glass windows looking southward over the pool to the gardens beyond. On the north wall, there is a rough stonework fireplace, complete with roaring fire. The east and west walls are almost completely covered with large, well-stocked bookcases. An exit in the northwest corner leads to the kitchen and, in a more northerly direction, to the entrance hall. The door into the coat closet is at the north end of the east wall, and at the south end is a sliding glass door leading out onto a wooden deck. There are two sets of couches, one clustered around the fireplace and one with a view out the windows.

This description is followed by a list of objects and characters present in the living room. You are free to examine and try out the objects, examine the descriptions of the characters, and introduce yourself to them. The social conventions of different MUDs determine how strictly one is expected to stay in character. Some encourage all players to be in character at all times. Most are more relaxed. Some ritualize stepping out of character by asking players to talk to each other in specially noted "out of character" (OOC) asides.

On MUDs, characters communicate by invoking commands that cause text to appear on each other's screens. If I log onto LambdaMOO as a male character named Turk and strike up a conversation with a character named Dimitri, the setting for our conversation will be a MUD room in which a variety of other characters might be present. If I type, "Say hi," my screen will flash, "You say hi," and the screens of the other players in the room (including Dimitri) will flash, "Turk says 'hi.'" If I type "Emote whistles happily," all the players' screens will flash, "Turk whistles happily." Or I can address Dimitri alone by typing, "Whisper to Dimitri Glad to see you," and only Dimitri's screen will show, "Turk whispers 'Glad to see you.'" People's impressions of Turk will be formed by the description I will have written for him (this description will be available to all players on command), as well as by the nature of his conversation.

In the MUDs, virtual characters converse with each other, exchange gestures, express emotions, win and lose virtual money, and rise and fall in social status. A virtual character can also die. Some die of "natural" causes (a player decides to close them down) or they can have their virtual lives snuffed out. This is all achieved through writing, and this in a culture that had apparently fallen asleep in the audiovisual arms of television. Yet this new writing is a kind of hybrid: speech momentarily frozen into artifact, but curiously ephemeral artifact. In this new writing, unless it is printed out on paper, a screenful of flickers soon replaces the previous screen. In MUDs as in other forms of electronic communication, typographic conventions known as emoticons replace physical gestures and facial expressions. For example, :–) indicates a smiling face and :–(indicates an unhappy face. Onomatopoeic expletives and a relaxed attitude toward sentence fragments and typographic errors suggest that the new writing is somewhere in between traditional written and oral communication.

15 MUDs provide worlds for anonymous social interaction in which you can play a role as close to or as far away from your real self as you choose. For many game participants, playing one's character(s) and living in the MUD(s) becomes an important part of daily life. Since much of the excitement of the game depends on having personal relationships and being part of a MUD community's developing politics and projects, it is hard to participate just a little. In fact, addiction is a frequently discussed subject among MUD players. A *Newsweek* article described how "some players attempt to go cold turkey. One method is to randomly change your password by banging your head against the keyboard, making it impossible to log back on."[1] It is not unusual for players to be logged on to a MUD for six hours a day. Twelve hours a day is common if players work with computers at school or at a job and use systems with multiple windows. Then they can jump among windows in order to intersperse real-world activities on their computers with their games. They jump from Lotus 1-2-3 to LambdaMOO, from Wordperfect to DragonMUD. "You can't really be part of the action unless you are there every day. Things happen quickly. To get the thrill of MUDs you have to be part of what makes the story unfold," says a regular on DuneMUSH, a MUD based on the world of Frank Herbert's science fiction classic.[2]

In MUDs, each player makes scenes unfold and dramas come to life. Playing in MUDs is thus both similar to and different from reading or watching television. As with reading, there is text, but on MUDs it unfolds in real time and you become an author of the story. As with television, you are engaged with the screen, but MUDs are interactive, and you can take control of the action. As in acting, the explicit task is to construct a viable mask or persona. Yet on MUDs, that persona can be as close to your real self as you choose, so MUDs have much in common with psychodrama. And since many people simply choose to play aspects of themselves, MUDs can also seem like real life.

Play has always been an important aspect of our individual efforts to build identity. The psychoanalyst Erik Erikson called play a "toy situation" that allows us to "reveal and commit" ourselves "in its unreality."[3] While MUDs are not the only "places" on the Internet in which to play with identity, they provide an unparalleled opportunity for such play. On a MUD one actually gets to build character and environment and then to live within the toy situation. A MUD can become a context for discovering who one is and wishes to be. In this way, the games are laboratories for the construction of identity, an idea that is well captured by the player who said:

> You can be whoever you want to be. You can completely redefine yourself if you want. You can be the opposite sex. You can be more talkative. You can be less talkative. Whatever. You can just be whoever you want, really, whoever you have the capacity to be. You don't have to worry about the slots other people put you in as much. It's easier to change the way people perceive you, because all they've got is what you show them. They don't look at your body and make assumptions. They don't hear your accent and make assumptions. All they see is your words. And it's always there. Twenty-four hours a day you can walk down to the street corner and there's gonna be a few people there who are interesting to talk to, if you've found the right MUD for you.

The anonymity of most MUDs (you are known only by the name you give your characters) provides ample room for individuals to express unexplored parts of themselves. A twenty-one-year-old college senior defends his violent characters as "something in me; but quite frankly I'd rather rape on MUDs where no harm is done." A twenty-six-year-old clerical worker says, "I'm not one thing, I'm many things. Each part gets to be more fully expressed in MUDs than in the real world. So even though I play more than one self on MUDs, I feel more like 'myself' when I'm MUDding." In real life, this woman sees her world as too narrow to allow her to manifest certain aspects of the person she feels herself to be. Creating screen personae is thus an opportunity for self-expression, leading to her feeling more like her true self when decked out in an array of virtual masks.

20 MUDs imply difference, multiplicity, heterogeneity, and fragmentation. Such an experience of identity contradicts the Latin root of the word, *idem,* meaning "the same." But this contradiction increasingly defines the conditions of our lives beyond the virtual world. MUDs thus become objects-to-think-with for thinking about postmodern selves. Indeed, the unfolding of all MUD action takes place in a resolutely postmodern context. There are parallel narratives in the different rooms of a MUD. The cultures of Tolkien, Gibson, and Madonna coexist and interact. Since MUDs are authored by their players, thousands of people in all, often hundreds at a time, are all logged on from different places; the solitary author is displaced and distributed. Traditional ideas about identity have been tied to a notion of authenticity that such virtual experiences actively subvert. When each player can create many characters and participate in many games, the self is not only decentered but multiplied without limit.

Sometimes such experiences can facilitate self-knowledge and personal growth, and sometimes not. MUDs can be places where people blossom or places where they get stuck, caught in self-contained worlds where things are simpler than in real life, and where, if all else fails, you can retire your character and simply start a new life with another.

As a new social experience, MUDs pose many psychological questions: If a persona in a role-playing game drops defenses that the player in real life has been unable to abandon, what effect does this have? What if a persona enjoys success in some area (say, flirting) that the player has not been able to achieve? In this, chapter and the next I will examine these kinds of questions from a viewpoint that assumes a conventional distinction between a constructed persona and the real self. But we shall soon encounter slippages—places where persona and self merge, places where the multiple personae join to comprise what the individual thinks of as his or her authentic self.

These slippages are common on MUDs, but as I discuss MUDs, it is important to keep in mind that they more generally characterize identity play in cyberspace. One Internet Relay Chat (IRC) enthusiast writes to an online discussion group, "People on [this mailing list] tell me that they make mistakes about what's happening on cyberspace and what's happening on RL. Did I really type what's happening *ON* Real Life?" (Surrounding a word with asterisks is the net version of italicizing it.) He had indeed. And then he jokingly referred to real life as though it, too, were an IRC channel: "Can anyone tell me how to/join #real.life?"[4]

* * *

Identity Crisis

Every era constructs its own metaphors for psychological well-being. Not so long ago, stability was socially valued and culturally reinforced. Rigid gender roles, repetitive labor, the expectation of being in one kind of job or remaining in one town over a lifetime, all of these made consistency central to definitions of health. But these stable social worlds have broken down. In our time, health is described in terms of fluidity rather than stability. What matters most now is the ability to adapt and change—to new jobs, new career directions, new gender roles, new technologies.

25 In *Flexible Bodies,* the anthropologist Emily Martin argues that the language of the immune system provides us with metaphors for the self and its boundaries.[5] In the past, the immune system was described as a private fortress, a firm, stable wall that protected within from without. Now we talk about the immune system as flexible and permeable. It can only be healthy if adaptable.

The new metaphors of health as flexibility apply not only to human mental and physical spheres, but also to the bodies of corporations, governments, and businesses. These institutions function in rapidly changing circumstances; they too are coming to view their fitness in terms of their flexibility. Martin describes the cultural spaces where we learn the new virtues of change over solidity. In addition to advertising, entertainment, and education, her examples include corporate workshops where people learn wilderness camping, high-wire walking, and zip-line jumping. She refers to all of these as flexibility practicums.

In her study of the culture of flexibility, Martin does not discuss virtual communities, but these provide excellent examples of what she is talking about. In these environments, people either explicitly play roles (as in MUDs) or more subtly shape their online selves. Adults learn about being multiple and fluid—and so do children. "I don't play so many different people online—only three," says June, an eleven-year-old who uses her mother's Internet account to play in MUDs. During our conversation, I learn that in the course of a year in RL, she moves among three households—that of her biological mother and stepfather, her biological father and stepmother, and a much-loved "first stepfather," her mother's second husband. She refers to her mother's third and current husband as "second stepfather." June recounts that in each of these three households the rules are somewhat different and so is she. Online switches among personae seem quite natural. Indeed, for her, they are a kind of practice. Martin would call them practicums.

"Logins R Us"

On a WELL discussion group about online personae (subtitled "boon or bête-noire") participants shared a sense that their virtual identities were evocative objects for thinking about the self. For several, experiences in virtual space compelled them to pay greater attention to what they take for granted in the real. "The persona thing intrigues me," said one. "It's a chance for all of us who aren't actors to play [with] masks. And think about the masks we wear every day."[6]

In this way, online personae have something in common with the self that emerges in a psychoanalytic encounter. It, too, is significantly virtual, constructed within the space of the analysis, where its slightest shifts can come under the most intense scrutiny.[7]

30 What most characterized the WELL discussion about online personae was the way many of the participants expressed the belief that life on the WELL introduced them to the many within themselves. One person wrote that through participating in an electronic bulletin board and letting the many sides of ourselves show, "We start to resemble little corporations, 'Logins R Us,' and like any company, we each have within us the bean-counter, the visionary, the heart-throb, the fundamentalist, and the wild child. Long may they wave."[8] Other participants responded to this comment with enthusiasm. One, echoing the social psychologist Kenneth Gergen,[9] described identity as a "pastiche of personalities" in which "the test of competence is not so much the integrity of the whole but the apparent correct representation appearing at the right time, in the right context, not to the detriment of the rest of the internal 'collective.' "[10] Another said that he thought of his ego "as a hollow tube, through which, one at a time, the 'many' speak through at the appropriate moment. . . . I'd like to hear more . . . about the possibilities surrounding the notion that what we perceive as 'one' in any context is, perhaps, a conglomerate of 'ones.'" This writer went on:

> Hindu culture is rooted in the "many" as the root of spiritual experience. A person's momentary behavior reflects some influence from one of hundreds of gods and/or goddesses. I am interested in . . . how this natural assumption of the "many" creates an alternative psychology.[11]

Another writer concurred:

> Did you ever see that cartoon by R. Crumb about "Which is the real R. Crumb?" He goes through four pages of incarnations, from successful businessman to street beggar, from media celebrity to gut-gnawing recluse, etc. etc. Then at the end he says, "Which is the real one?" . . . "It all depends on what mood I'm in!"
>
> We're all like that online.[12]

35 Howard Rheingold, the member of the WELL who began the discussion topic, also referred to Gergen's notion of a "saturated self," the idea that communication technologies have caused us to "colonize each other's brains." Gergen describes us as saturated with the many "voices of humankind—both harmonious and alien." He believes that as "we absorb their varied rhymes and reasons, they become part of us and we of them.

Social saturation furnishes us with a multiplicity of incoherent and unrelated languages of the self." With our relationships spread across the globe and our knowledge of other cultures relativizing our attitudes and depriving us of any norm, we "exist in a state of continuous construction and reconstruction; it is a world where anything goes that can be negotiated. Each reality of self gives way to reflexive questioning, irony, and ultimately the playful probing of yet another reality. The center fails to hold."[13]

Although people may at first feel anguish at what they sense as a breakdown of identity, Gergen believes they may come to embrace the new possibilities. Individual notions of self vanish "into a stage of relatedness. One ceases to believe in a self independent of the relations in which he or she is embedded."[14] "We live in each other's brains, as voices, images, words on screens," said Rheingold in the online discussion. "We are multiple personalities and we include each other."[15]

Rheingold's evocation of what Gergen calls the "raptures of multiplicitous being" met with support on the WELL. One participant insisted that all pejorative associations be removed from the notion of a saturated self. "Howard, I *like* being a saturated self, in a community of similarly saturated selves. I grew up on TV and pop music, but it just ain't enough. Virtual communities are, among other things, the co-saturation of selves who have been, all their lives, saturated in isolation."[16] To which Rheingold could only reply, "I like being a saturated self too."[17] The cybersociety of the WELL is an object-to-think-with for reflecting on the positive aspects of identity as multiplicity.

Identity and Multiplicity

Without any principle of coherence, the self spins off in all directions. Multiplicity is not viable if it means shifting among personalities that cannot communicate. Multiplicity is not acceptable if it means being confused to a point of immobility.[18] How can we be multiple and coherent at the same time? In *The Protean Self,* Robert Jay Lifton tries to resolve this seeming contradiction. He begins by assuming that a unitary view of self corresponded to a traditional culture with stable symbols, institutions, and relationships. He finds the old unitary notion no longer viable because traditional culture has broken down and identifies a range of responses. One is a dogmatic insistence on unity. Another is to return to systems of belief, such as religious fundamentalism, that enforce conformity. A third is to embrace the idea of a fragmented self.[19] Lifton says this is a dangerous option that may result in a "fluidity lacking in moral content and sustainable inner form." But Lifton sees another possibility, a healthy protean self. It is capable, like Proteus, of fluid transformations but is grounded in coherence and a moral outlook. It is multiple but integrated.[20] You can have a sense of self without being one self.

Lifton's language is theoretical. Experiences in MUDs, on the WELL, on local bulletin boards, on commercial network services, and on the World Wide Web are bringing his theory down to earth. On the Web, the idiom for constructing a "home" identity is to assemble a "home page" of virtual objects that correspond to one's interests. One constructs a home page by composing or "pasting" on it words, images, and sounds, and by making connections between it and other sites on the Internet or the Web. Like the agents in emergent AI, one's identity emerges from whom one knows, one's associations and connections. People link their home page to pages about such things as music, paintings, television shows, cities, books, photographs, comic strips, and fashion models. As I write this book I am in the process of constructing my own home page. It now contains links to the text of my curriculum vitae, to drafts of recent papers (one about MUDs, one about French psychoanalysis), and to the reading lists for the two courses I shall teach next fall. A "visitor" to my home page can also click a highlighted word and watch images of Michel Foucault and Power Rangers "morph," one into the other, a visual play on my contention that children's toys bring postmodernism down to earth. This display, affectionately referred to as "The Mighty Morphin' Michel Foucault," was a present from my assistant at MIT, Cynthia Col. A virtual home, like a real one, is furnished with objects you buy, build, or receive as gifts.

My future plans for my home page include linking to Paris (the city has a home page), the bot Julia, resources on women's studies, Imari china, and recent research on migraines. I am not limited in the number of links I can create. If we take the home page as a real estate metaphor for the self, its decor is postmodern. Its different rooms with different styles are located on computers all over the world. But through one's efforts, they are brought together to be of a piece.

Within the psychoanalytic tradition, there have been schools that departed from the standard unitary view of identity. As we have seen, the object-relations theorists invented a language for talking about the many voices that we bring inside ourselves in the course of development. Jungian psychology encouraged the individual to become acquainted with a whole range of personae and to understand them as manifestations of universal archetypes, such as innocent virgins, mothers and crones, eternal youths and old men.[21] Jung believed that for each of us, it is potentially most liberating to become acquainted with our dark side, as well as the other-gendered self called anima in men and animus in women. Jung was banished from the ranks of orthodox Freudians for such suggestions. The object-relations school, too, was relegated to the margins. As America became the center of psychoanalytic politics in the mid-twentieth century, ideas about a robust executive ego became the psychoanalytic mainstream.

Through the fragmented selves presented by patients and through theories that stress the decentered subject, contemporary psychology confronts what is left out of theories of the unitary self. Now it must ask, What is the self when it functions as a society?[22] What is the self when it divides its labors among its constituent "alters"?[23] Those burdened by post traumatic dissociative disorders suffer these questions; here I have suggested that inhabitants of virtual communities play with them.

Ideas about mind can become a vital cultural presence when they are carried by evocative objects-to-think-with.[24] I said earlier that these objects need not be material. For example, dreams and slips of the tongue were objects-to-think-with that brought psychoanalytic ideas into everyday life. People could play with their own and others' dreams and slips. Today, people are being helped to develop ideas about identity as multiplicity by a new practice of identity as multiplicity in online life. Virtual personae are objects-to-think-with.

When people adopt an online persona they cross a boundary into highly charged territory. Some feel an uncomfortable sense of fragmentation, some a sense of relief. Some sense the possibilities for self-discovery, even self-transformation. Serena, a twenty-six-year-old graduate student in history, says, "When I log on to a new MUD and I create a character and know I have to start typing my description, I always feel a sense of panic. Like I could find out something I don't want to know." Arlie, a twenty-year-old undergraduate, says, "I am always very self-conscious when I create a new character. Usually, I end up creating someone I wouldn't want my parents to know about. It takes me, like, three hours. But that someone is part of me." In these ways and others, many more of us are experimenting with multiplicity than ever before.

45 With this last comment, I am not implying that MUDs or computer bulletin boards are causally implicated in the dramatic increase of people who exhibit symptoms of multiple personality disorder (MPD), or that people on MUDs have MPD, or that MUDding is like having MPD. What I am saying is that the many manifestations of multiplicity in our culture, including the adoption of online personae, are contributing to a general reconsideration of traditional, unitary notions of identity.

The history of a psychiatric symptom is inextricably tied up with the history of the culture that surrounds it. When I was in graduate school in psychology in the 1970s, clinical psychology texts regarded multiple personality as so rare (perhaps one in a million) as to be barely worthy of mention. In these rare cases, there was typically one alter personality in addition to the host personality.[25] Today, cases of multiple personality are much more frequent and typically involve up to sixteen alters of different ages, races, genders, and sexual orientations.[26] In multiple personality disorder, it is widely believed that traumatic events have caused various aspects of the self to congeal into virtual personalities, the "ones" often hiding from the "others" and hiding too from that special alter, the host personality. Sometimes, the alters are known to each other and to the host; some alters may see their roles as actively helping others. Such differences led the philosopher Ian Hacking to write about a "continuum of dissociation."[27] These differences also suggest a way of thinking about the self in terms of a continuum of how accessible its parts are to each other.

At one extreme, the unitary self maintains its oneness by repressing all that does not fit. Thus censored, the illegitimate parts of the self are not accessible. This model would of course function best within a fairly rigid social structure with clearly defined rules and roles. At the other extreme is the MPD sufferer whose multiplicity exists in the context of an equally repressive rigidity. The parts of the self are not in easy communication. Communication is highly stylized; one personality must speak to another personality. In fact, the term "multiple personality" is misleading, because the different parts of the self are not full personalities. They are split-off, disconnected fragments. But if the disorder in multiple personality disorder is the need for the rigid walls between the selves (blocking the secrets those selves protect), then the study of MPD may begin to furnish ways of thinking about healthy selves as nonunitary but with fluid access among their many aspects. Thus, in addition to the extremes of unitary self and MPD, we can imagine a flexible self.

The essence of this self is not unitary, nor are its parts stable entities. It is easy to cycle through its aspects, and these are themselves changing through constant communication with each other. The philosopher Daniel Dennett speaks to the flexible self in his multiple drafts theory of consciousness.[28] Dennett's notion of multiple drafts is analogous to the experience of having several versions of a document open on a computer screen where the user is able to move between them at will. The presence of the drafts encourages a respect for the many different versions while it imposes a certain distance from them. No one aspect can be claimed as the absolute, true self. When I got to know French Sherry I no longer saw the less confident English-speaking Sherry as my one authentic self. What most characterizes the model of a flexible self is that the lines of communication between its various aspects are open. The open communication encourages an attitude of respect for the many within us and the many within others.

As we sense our inner diversity we come to know our limitations. We understand that we do not and cannot know things completely, not the outside world and not ourselves. Today's heightened consciousness of incompleteness may predispose us to join with others. The historian of science Donna Haraway equates a "split and contradictory self" with a "knowing self." She is optimistic about its possibilities: "The knowing self is partial in all its guises, never finished, whole, simply there and original; it is always constructed and stitched together imperfectly; and *therefore* able to join with another, to see together without claiming to be another."[29]

When identity was defined as unitary and solid it was relatively easy to recognize and censure deviation from a norm. A more fluid sense of self allows a greater capacity for acknowledging diversity. It makes it easier to accept the array of our (and others') inconsistent personae—perhaps with humor, perhaps with irony. We do not feel compelled to rank or judge the elements of our multiplicity. We do not feel compelled to exclude what does not fit.

* * *

As we stand on the boundary between the real and the virtual, our experience recalls what the anthropologist Victor Turner termed a liminal moment, a moment of passage when new cultural symbols and meanings can emerge.[30] Liminal moments are times of tension, extreme reactions, and great opportunity. In our time, we are simultaneously flooded with predictions of doom and predictions of imminent utopia. We live in a crucible of contradictory experience. When Turner talked about liminality, he understood it as a transitional state—but living with flux may no longer be temporary. Donna Haraway's characterization of irony illuminates our situation: "Irony is about contradictions that do not resolve into larger wholes . . . about the tension of holding incompatible things together because both or all are necessary and true.[31] It is fitting that the story of the technology that is bringing postmodernism down to earth itself refuses modernist resolutions and requires an openness to multiple viewpoints.

Multiple viewpoints call forth a new moral discourse. I have said that the culture of simulation may help us achieve a vision of a multiple but integrated identity whose flexibility, resilience, and capacity for joy comes from having access to our many selves. But if we have lost reality in the process, we shall have struck a poor bargain. In Wim Wenders's film *Until the End of the World,* a scientist develops a device that translates the electrochemical activity of the brain into digital images. He gives this technology to his family and closest friends, who are now able to hold small battery-driven monitors and watch their dreams. At first, they are charmed. They see their treasured fantasies, their secret selves. They see the images they otherwise would forget, the scenes they otherwise would repress. As with the personae one can play in a MUD, watching dreams on a screen opens up new aspects of the self.

However, the story soon turns dark. The images seduce. They are richer and more compelling than the real life around them. Wenders's characters fall in love with their dreams, become addicted to them. People wander about with blankets over their heads the better to see the monitors from which they cannot bear to be parted. They are imprisoned by the screens, imprisoned by the keys to their past that the screens seem to hold.

We, too, are vulnerable to using our screens in these ways. People can get lost in virtual worlds. Some are tempted to think of life in cyberspace as insignificant, as escape or meaningless diversion. It is not. Our experiences there are serious play. We belittle them at our risk. We must understand the dynamics of virtual experience both to foresee who might be in danger and to put these experiences to best use. Without a deep understanding of the many selves that we express in the virtual, we cannot use our experiences there to enrich the real. If we cultivate our awareness of what stands behind our screen personae, we are more likely to succeed in using virtual experience for personal transformation.

55 The imperative to self-knowledge has always been at the heart of philosophical inquiry. In the twentieth century, it found expression in the psychoanalytic culture as well. One might say that it constitutes the ethic of psychoanalysis. From the perspective of this ethic, we work to know ourselves in order to improve not only our own lives, but those of our families and society. I have said that psychoanalysis is a survivor discourse. Born of a modernist worldview, it has evolved into forms relevant to postmodern times. With mechanistic roots in the culture of calculation, psychoanalytic ideas become newly relevant in the culture of simulation. Some believe that we are at the end of the Freudian century. But the reality is more complex. Our need for a practical philosophy of self-knowledge has never been greater as we struggle to make meaning from our lives on the screen.

Notes

1. Katie Hafner, "Get in the MOOd," *Newsweek,* 7 November 1994.
2. Frank Herbert, *Dune* (Philadelphia: Chilton Books, 1965).
3. Erik Erikson, *Childhood and Society,* 2nd rev. ed. (New York: Norton, 1963 [1950]), p. 52.
4. This communication was signed "The Picklingly herbatious one."
5. Emily Martin, *Flexible Bodies* (Boston: Beacon Press, 1994), pp. 161–225.
6. mcdee, The WELL, conference on virtual communities (vc.20.17), 18 April 1992.
7. The sentiment that life online could provide a different experience of self was seconded by a participant who described himself as a man whose conversational abilities as an adult were impaired by having been a stutterer as a child. Online he was able to discover the experience of participating in the flow of a conversation.

    I echo [the previous contributor] in feeling that my online persona differs greatly from my persona offline. And, in many ways, my online persona is more "me." I feel a lot more freedom to speak here. Growing up, I had a severe stuttering problem. I couldn't speak a word without stuttering, so I spoke only when absolutely necessary. I worked through it in my early 20s and you wouldn't even notice it now (except when I'm stressed out), but at

> 37 I'm still shy to speak. I'm a lot more comfortable with listening than with talking. And when I do speak I usually feel out of sync: I'll inadvertently step on other people's words, or lose people's attention, or talk through instead of to. I didn't learn the dynamic of conversation that most people take for granted, I think. Here, though, it's completely different: I have a feel for the flow of the "conversations," have the time to measure my response, don't have to worry about the balance of conversational space—we all make as much space as we want just by pressing "r" to respond. It's been a wonderfully liberating experience for me. (Anonymous)

8. spoonman, The WELL, conference on virtual communities (vc.20.65), 11 June 1992.
9. Kenneth Gergen, *The Saturated Self: Dilemmas of Identity in Contemporary Life* (New York: Basic Books, 1991).
10. bluefire (Bob Jacobson), The WELL, conference on virtual reality (vr.85.146), 15 August 1993.
11. The WELL, conference on virtual reality (vr.85.148), 17 August 1993.
12. Art Kleiner, The WELL, conference on virtual reality (vr.47.41), 2 October 1990.
13. Gergen, *The Saturated Self,* p. 6.
14. Gergen, *The Saturated Self,* p. 17.
15. hlr (Howard Rheingold), The WELL, conference on virtual reality (vr.47.351), 2 February 1993.
16. McKenzie Wark, The WELL, conference on virtual reality (vr.47.361), 3 February 1993.
17. hlr (Howard Rheingold), The WELL, conference on virtual reality (vr.47.362), 3 February 1993.
18. James M. Glass, *Shattered Selves: Multiple Personality in a Postmodern World* (Ithaca, N.Y.: Cornell University Press, 1993).
19. Robert Jay Lifton, *The Protean Self: Human Resilience in an Age of Fragmentation* (New York: Basic Books, 1993), p. 192.
20. Lifton, *The Protean Self,* pp. 229–32.
21. See, for example, "Aion: Phenomenology of the Self" in *The Portable Jung,* ed. Joseph Campbell, trans. R. F. C. Hull (New York: Penguin, 1971).
22. See, for example, Marvin Minsky, *The Society of Mind* (New York: Simon & Schuster, 1985).
23. See, for example, Colin Ross, *Multiple Personality Disorder: Diagnosis, Clinical Features, and Treatment* (New York: John Wiley & Sons, 1989).
24. Claude Lévi-Strauss, *The Savage Mind* (Chicago: University of Chicago Press, 1960).
25. Ian Hacking, *Rewriting the Soul: Multiple Personality and the Sciences of Memory* (Princeton, N.J.: Princeton University Press, 1995), p. 21.
26. Hacking, *Rewriting the Soul,* p. 29.
27. See Hacking, *Rewriting the Soul,* pp. 96ff.
28. Daniel C. Dennett, *Consciousness Explained* (Boston: Little, Brown and Company, 1991).
29. Donna Haraway, "The Actors Are Cyborg, Nature Is Coyote, and the Geography Is Elsewhere: Postscript to 'Cyborgs at Large'" in *Technoculture,* eds. Constance Penley and Andrew Ross (Minneapolis: University of Minnesota Press, 1991), p. 22.
30. Victor Turner, *The Ritual Process: Structure and Antistructure* (Chicago: Aldine, 1966).
31. Donna Haraway, "A Cyborg Manifesto," p. 148.

Exploring Texts and Contexts

For activities with icons, refer to the Guide to Analyzing Readings in Context.

1. Throughout this excerpt, Turkle use the words "persona," "self," and "identity." How does she define or seem to be defining these terms and what is the relationship between them? Turkle also sets up a dialectic between the terms "multiplicity" and "unity" or "multiple" and "unitary." What's the relationship between these words and between these words and Turkle's overall argument? 
2. What is Turkle's overall argument? Does she state her thesis anywhere in this excerpt? If not, can you sum it up in a sentence or two?
3. Turkle sees moral implications for the phenomena she discusses in this excerpt. What does she see as the possible consequences, and how would she like her book to influence these consequences? 

Creating Texts

For activities with icons, refer to the Guides to Analyzing Contexts for Writing and Analyzing Readings in Context. For additional help with these writing projects, read the descriptions of **Dialogue** and **Essay** in the Genre Glossary.

1. This is a group project with several stages. It involves creating a fictional character, or persona, using that persona to interact with others in an online environment, and then analyzing the interactions. Write a description of a persona that you would be interested in exploring. It might be simply a projection of yourself into the future or past, or it might be a persona that is very different from you in gender, ethnicity, or background. With your teacher's help, use the chat feature of an online course platform to set up a discussion topic or activity that everyone in the class will participate in as their personae. This works best if the group is given a task to carry out, for example deciding on the rules for an online game or the features of an online environment. This activity should be carried out over the course of several class meetings so that everyone gets a chance to "perform" his or her persona. The purpose of this activity is to give you a sense of what it might be like to participate in an online forum using a persona. Please remember, though, that this is a classroom activity, and the rules of civility and respect that are otherwise observed in your classroom should be observed in this activity as well. Print out the transcripts of these chat sessions so that the class can discuss the activity as it unfolded.
2. Write an essay in which you discuss your experiences in the activity described in Activity 1. You might begin by describing your persona and why you chose it. Then describe some of the significant interactions in the activity and your 

persona's participation, and discuss what these interactions felt like to you. What was it like to participate in this activity as your persona? In what ways was your persona's "behavior" different from and similar to what would have been your own behavior in these situations, and what do you see as the significance of these differences and similarities? To what extent did it feel as if you had actually "become" your persona? Did the activity feel risky or liberating, and in what way? Did you feel that you learned anything from this experience about yourself or the nature of representation and misrepresentation? Discuss also what you see as the larger implications of this experience for our understanding of identity, the self, authenticity, and the possibilities and dangers of the Internet.

Famous All Over Town

Danny Santiago

In 1983, the novel *Famous All Over Town* was published to modest commercial success and great critical acclaim. It was the story of a 14-year-old boy, Rudy Medina, also known as Chato, growing up in a Mexican-American neighborhood of Los Angeles. The novel was hailed as a kind of barrio *Catcher in the Rye,* a coming-of-age story that also gave readers a glimpse into an ethnic American experience. A reviewer in the *Pittsburgh Press* said, "The 14-year-old Mexican-American point of view is authentic, funny, and tragic." A *New York Times* reviewer said, "*Famous All Over Town* is a classic of Chicano urban experience. And Danny Santiago is good news." But Danny Santiago, the author, remained somewhat of a mystery. There was no picture of him on the book jacket, and the brief biography simply said that he "grew up in Los Angeles."

Why the mystery? To find out, read the three pieces included here. The first piece is the first chapter of the novel. It will give you a good sense of the novel's narrative voice and a glimpse of the main characters and setting, though it won't convey the scope and narrative arc of the plot or the complex interactions of the characters; if you enjoy the first chapter, try to get a copy of the book and finish the novel. The chapter is followed by the *New York Times* review quoted here and then by an article about Danny Santiago published in the *Times* a little over a year later.

Connecting with the Conversation

1. Many first novels, especially if they are written in the first person, are assumed to be autobiographical at least to some extent. Have you read any of the following: *I Know Why the Caged Bird Sings,* by Maya Angelou; *The House on Mango Street,* by Sandra Cisneros; *Invisible Man,* by Ralph Ellison; *To Kill a Mockingbird,* by Harper Lee; *The Bell Jar,* by Sylvia Plath; *The Catcher in the Rye,* by J. D. Salinger; or *The Joy*

Luck Club, by Amy Tan? Did you wonder about the relationship between the author and the first-person narrator?

2. Many writers, for a variety of reasons, use pseudonyms or pen names: Mark Twain for Samuel Clemens, Lewis Carroll for Charles Dodgson, O. Henry for William Sydney Porter, George Eliot for Mary Ann Evans, Jules Verne for M. Olchewitz, for example. What are some of the reasons a writer might use a pen name, and how do you think the use of a pen name changes the relationship between a writer and his or her readers? Does it make a difference to you as a reader if a writer has used a pseudonym?

Slow, law-abiding and drunk, I cruised down North Main Street toward the river. It was way past the middle of the night. Frankie Martin's bar was dark, the last drinker long gone home. I passed by old familiar Eastside Brewery, took a left into Shamrock Street and switched off my headlights. I planned to dig up various long-buried corpses and didn't care for company.

Up ahead, one long block ahead were the S.P. tracks. I watched the signal tower blink red and green as it angled south toward skyscraping City Hall beyond. When the two of them lined up just right, I coasted to the curb. This would be the place exactly. I got out and looked and listened. Not a truck, not a car, not a sound. My patriotic bumper was the loudest noise in sight

"CHICANO POWER," it yelled. "BROWN IS BEAUTIFUL. FULANO FOR SHERIFF."

"Shut up," I told my bumper. "Be quiet."

5 I stood face to face with the enemy, a long line of trailers boxcar size with S.P. Railroad on their rumps. Nothing between me and them except a 10-foot chainlink fence with two strands of friendly barbwire at the top. I planted my feet and spoke the magic word.

"114."

Trailers and chainlink went up in flames. In their place a certain saggy picket fence sprouted from the ground, a certain squeaky front porch rose up behind, and the skinny little house where I lived half my life. Down the block up popped number 112 and 110 and all their brothers. Old Shamrock lived again and I was home.

Before the S.P. rolled us under asphalt we were the best street in all L.A. with cozy little homes on both sides solid. Maybe they weren't too new or too fresh-painted but they were warm and lively, and when the trains passed by, how those little houses used to shake, rattle and roll. Strangers would ask, How can you stand it? But to tell the truth, we barely noticed. It was like rocking a baby and very good for the circulation of the blood, people used to claim.

"Gimme the pelota, Stupid." "Pítchala, pendejo!" "Enrique, vente p'acá or else you're really gonna get it." My ears tuned in ghost voices and murdered Spanish and my father's well-known whistle that used to bring me running home.

From *Famous All Over Town,* by Danny Santiago (second edition). New York: Penguin Books, 1984, pp. 7–17.

10 One hour I stood there listening to the dead and gone. It was a bad time in my life. I couldn't see my next step, should it be Left or Right, or Up or Down? Maybe if I relived my yesterdays I could be surer of my tomorrows. So I spread out old memories like hopscotch on the sidewalk, took a running jump and landed in the square of my fourteenth birthday, which was the last I spent on Shamrock Street, and that's where let's begin.

It took place on a hot Saturday in September.

"Here's your present."

My father slapped his chicken-killer knife into my hand. It was ground down thin as a needle and had a razor edge. Nobody but him was allowed to touch it.

"Huh?" I asked.

15 "Fourteen years makes a man, so prove yourself."

"Me?" I asked.

"Why not?" he said. "You seen me do it often enough."

"When?" I asked.

"When I tell you to," he told me crossly, "and quit looking so green in the face."

20 My father was quite famous for his chicken killing. People came from up and down the street to watch. He made a regular rodeo of it, jumping up and down like a cowboy with chickens running every which way. He'd grab and miss in a dozen comical ways till his watchers ran out of laughs, then he'd make one quick snatch and there was his chicken-of-the-week scooped up in his arms with a cord whipped tight around her legs. Next my father would make love to that chicken, whispering in her ear, and she'd arch her neck and wink at him as flirty as any senorita while he waltzed her round the yard singing. Then the music would stop.

"Buenas noches, mi amor," he'd say. "Go to sleep, little chickie dear."

The American Way of twisting necks off or chopping heads never pleased my father. It left the meat tough and angry, he claimed. So, Mexican style, he hung his chicken from her feet and slipped the blade into her neck so nice and easy she never felt it. She'd flop her wings once or twice and her eyes would blank out very peaceful while she bled to death with a pan underneath to catch the blood.

That was my father's style and I only hoped I could do as well. In one way I was proud he trusted me, but in another way, Who knows? So then the mailman came with the insurance check for his shortened pinkie finger. That cheered my father up and he slapped me on the shoulder.

"Let's go cash it," he suggested, which was a wonder because my father always preferred to cash his checks in private. So we climbed into our famous '55 low-mileage Buick and away we went to García's Short-Change Department Store to check on the merchandise.

25 "You call these things boots?" he hollered in that bull-voice of his. My father is very loud in stores when speaking Spanish but in English you can barely hear him. "What you make them of, worm skin?" he asked and the clerk ran to bring the best boots money could buy, and triple-soled. My father dropped them on the floor. They hit like sledgehammers and he was more or less content.

"Fit my Junior here," he ordered. "Good heavy boots will put meat on those matchstick legs of yours," he preached for all who cared to listen, "only don't leave them around where your mother will trip on them in her condition."

"Si, señor," I said and stomped my boots around the store. I was crazy to wear them home but my father said, No, put neat's-foot oil first, and peeled off a 20. As usual they tried to short him a dollar, my father's arithmetic is not the best, but I caught them at it. So from there we stopped by the Brewery for a keg and rolled home at five miles an hour to keep the foam from rising.

What followed was a little argument. My sister started throwing little indirectos like "What a thoughtful present for a fourteen-year-old and will you invite his hoodlum friends?" And, "How charming for our mother to have a gang of drunkards in the house with the baby due any minute now." Her smart remarks failed to please my father. In our house it was the pants that ruled so when Lena said Shit right out loud in English, my father hit her. In the right way of course. He never closed his fist on any girl or woman, like some, or slapped in dirty places. But even so he had a heavy hand and Lena marched out swearing she would never enter my father's door again. Personally, I expected her back for dinner. She had the biggest appetite in the family but on her it didn't show. My sister was as skinny as me except here and there, but what a temper.

On Shamrock, like most other places, people drank privately in backyards, not my father. He set up his beer on the front porch for all the world to come help him drink it. He stood the keg in a tub with ice around and threw an old rug over for shade, then he shoved in the tapper. It stuck up shiny as a sword.

"Free blood," my father shouted to various passing friends and slipped off the bandage for all to admire his stump. Myself; I didn't care to look at it.

"How much they pay you?" was asked.

"Hundred-fifty," my father said, which was not bad for one tiny knuckle on his pinkie finger's end.

"What's your fat finger worth?" they inquired.

"The S.P. Railroad don't have that kind of money," my father bragged. Quite some crowd soon collected. Virgie's Arturo and various others from S.P. and of course Chuchu Madrigal that was in Construction. My father settled his big piledriver butt onto his Superchief silver train step which he bought it for twenty-five cents. There are always good bargains on Shamrock if you don't ask too many questions. He sat there solid as a fireplug with little brown eggs of flesh poking out through the holes in his famous air-condition T-shirt, enjoying his beer and king of everybody.

Up and down the street the paychecks had been cashed. Saturday night lay ahead, and after, Lazy Sunday. My father and his friends were in the mood to laugh at everything and I was proud to laugh along with them while I sat sunning on the steps. They were soft to sit on, spongy and not like new lumber, only you had to drive the nails back in once a week which was my regular job. So I sat there working the neat's-foot oil into my new boots. My fingers slided slick and smooth over the leather and deep into the creases till I found myself wondering if a girl or woman might feel like that.

"What you dreaming there boy?" my father asked. Maybe I jumped because the men couldn't quit laughing. "You got a little window in your head," my father told me, "and oh what I can see in there. You keep your hands out of your pockets, hear? or else we'll see hair growing on your palms."

I was ready for the subject to get changed.

"Still," my father said, "this Junior of mine, he's a pretty good boy, smart too, his teachers claim, with prizes for his handwriting. So stand up, son, and let's drink him a toast on his fourteenth birthday."

"Hey, look where he's taller than his dad," Chuchu pointed out.

40 My father doubted it so they stood us back to back. I had an easy quarter-inch on him, so Chuchu gave me a dollar, and everybody cheered except my father. "It's all in that skinny goose neck," he complained and gave my head a friendly shove that nearly tore it off, then preached barbells for my self-improvement while he went back to sharpening up the chicken-killer knife.

Out on the street my friends were busy shoving Fat Manuel's car in hopes to get it started, Gorilla, Hungryman, Pelón and a couple others. Los Jesters de Shamrock was our name and in those days we were Kings in Eastside, nobody cared to mess with us.

"Esé, Chato," they called, which was my street name, from being flat-nose like a cat. "Give us a hand, man," they hollered but I shook my finger No.

"What's this 'Chato'?" my father scolded. He hated that name. "You're Rudy M. Medina, Junior, and be proud of it."

"Sí, señor," I quickly told him and hoped to be forgotten, but Pelón was a genius for trouble and here he comes with his decoráted shoeshine box, all silver stars and red reflectors.

45 "Buenos días, Padrino," he tells my father. "No quieres un free shoeshine?"

I sweated. Of all my friends Pelón was my father's least favorite. Three years back when the guy was orphaned, my father took him into our house and slept him on the couch with me like twins. Till that bad day when my father caught us doing something.

"Come on, Godfather," Pelón begged, on the sarcastic side, "I'll give you a real fine shine and you could lay back and tell us all about your cowboy days in Mexico when you were captain of one hundred horses."

"Get out of my nose, mocoso," my father shouted and started down the steps.

"Oh, indubitably," said Pelón, which was his favorite word, and off he went like a rabbit. My father knew better than to try and catch him.

50 "No-good hoodlums," he complained. "Where's Respect? Fight, steal, rob, make trouble, that's all those rat-packers know to do, light their pimpy cigarettes and blow the smoke in their fathers' face. When I was their age I was already doing a man's work down there in mi pueblo. And any time I came in the house I kissed my father's hand and any time I went out too. But when I come home these days who kisses my hand? Not even a dog or cat."

"They're all too educated," Arturo agreed, "with their twelve years in school and their television. But down there in my village we had our advantages. We were poor as dirt but there used to be a certain little dark-skin girl, a fine plump little morenita she was. We all went to school on her and nobody whined about their homework."

To hear my father's friends tell it, there was a girl like that in every village and always she seemed to be dark-skinned and generous. And while my father's knife sang on the stone, his friends' Spanish words came rolling out like on rubber tires and they all turned patriotic Mejicanos. Yes, they admitted, there was hunger down there but the food had such a taste on it. The beans themselves were better than the best prime steaks of the USA. And yes, maybe it was chilly sleeping nights on those little mats of straw, but the mornings, hombre, when you stood outside shivering against the adobe wall and then the big round Mexican sun came up to warm you. It was the blanket of the poor, they all agreed, and tequila was the other poor man's blanket. To hear them talk, you wondered why they ever left the place.

And the snakes, man, those snakes of Mexico which always raised their head by beer number 5, snakes that whipped you to death with their tails, and others that rolled after you like wheels, tail tucked into mouth. And still others, nighttime snakes that came sliding down out of the grass roof while your compadre's mother's cousin's wife was sleeping, and sucked her nipples till her baby pined away to skin and bones, but that snake grew fat as a fire hose and over 12 feet long. I found myself especially interested in that nighttime snake and its strange way of life, while I sat there on the steps working on my new boots. By now they had soaked up all the oil they could hold so I put them on and laced them up very carefully to keep the tongues from wrinkling.

"Stand up, son," my father told me.

My time had come. Everybody had their eyes on me. I was the Main Event.

"You're fourteen years today," my father said. "And old enough to be my right hand. Now for once don't mess up. And be sure you catch all the blood." He slapped the chicken-killer knife into my hand. I gripped it tight.

"Con permiso?" I asked.

"Pass," they told me in a chorus.

My new boots marched me like an army round the corner of the house, along the side fence and up the back steps to the kitchen. My mother with her swollen belly stood leaning on the stove. Her braids hung tired and heavy down her back and she didn't notice when I came in. Since last month she'd been like half-asleep with her eyes turned inside out to watch the baby grow inside her.

"Hey, where's the pan at?" I asked her.

"What pan?" she wanted to know.

"The one for the blood naturally," I told her and flashed my knife. She looked at it and looked at me.

"You?" she said.

"Why not?" I told her.

My mother groaned when she bended down to rattle the pan out from under the sink. What if she should die? flashed through my head. What if this giant baby killed her while my father and his friends sat drinking on the front porch?

"See you don't cut yourself," she said and tuned me out.

Our backest yard was where the chickens lived. We had nopales solid along the fence reaching up their prickly paws higher than your shoulders. Our tumbledown shed took up one corner. I stood by the gate, knife in hand and watched the stupid chickens peck-peck-pecking through the gravel and complaining about the hard life they had. It was our old red hen I wanted. She used to be a steady layer but now only gave eggs when in the mood.

"Hey Junior, you gonna kill the chickie?"

"Make a circus like your daddy, Junior, huh?"

70 It was those pesty little kids from next door. I ignored them. My plan was to imitate my father exactly. I opened the gate and started clowning but those dumb kids never laughed even one time. So then I got disgusted and went after that old hen for real, but she turned track star on me. Twice I missed her and fell against the nopale cactuses and tore my shirt.

"Should I call your daddy, Junior?"

Junior this and Junior that. "Shut up," I told those snotnose kids. Maybe I even threw my knife at them, I don't remember, anyway they left there running. Then I really grabbed that chicken and hit her a good one too, to learn her a lesson. The rope kept tangling. It took three tries to get her legs tied up. Next, I hung her upside down where my father always did and put the blood pan under. With my left hand I stretched her neck out long for the knife, but it felt very funny to me, like something I had possibly felt before, only with feathers on it.

I creeped the knife in till it just barely touched skin. Only one inch more, a half-inch even. But my muscles froze on me. My hand started in to shake. Out front the men were waiting. Out front my father trusted me. He had generously put his own special knife into my hand. There was no way in all this would I could possibly go back to the front porch with that chicken still alive.

We hung there, me and that old red hen, how long—who knows? Till suddenly it came to me: What's so great about my father's crazy Mexican way of chicken killing? Why not try something new for a change, something more up-to-date? In his closet, in a shoe box, my father had a revolver which he kept loaded just in case. It was another one of those Shamrock Street bargains and he paid $10 for it. For years my father always warned me, "Don't you ever touch that thing," but today I was fourteen years old which was a man, so I went for it.

75 God was good to me. My mother didn't notice when I sneaked through the kitchen with the .45 under my T-shirt. It seemed heavier than I remembered, and wanted to wave around when I took aim. So I steadied the barrel on the trash can just 6 inches away from that old chicken's throat. It was quite important not to miss. I might be criticized.

"SSAAAAHHHHSSS!"

It turned out to be the Shot Heard Round The World.

On Shamrock people can tell pistols from firecrackers any day, having heard plenty of both from time to time. No doubt they asked each other, "Did she finally shoot him? Or him her?" There were several well-known trouble spots. So they all came running to see the corpse. But of course it was my father that got to me first.

"Here's your chicken," I told him and held it up.

80 Nothing in this world was ever deader than that old red hen. It was a perfect shot, just one tiny thread of neck left and the head hanging down. I expected my father to be quite pleased with me. Instead he yelled. He grabbed the pistol. He slammed the chicken in the dirt. He slapped for my face but I ducked under.

"Hey," I told him, "what's wrong with you?"

"You wait!" he shouted and slung me into the shed and banged the door.

"What happened?" somebody outside asked. "Who's dead?"

"Medina's kid just shot a chicken."

"With a GUN?"

Then somebody hollered, "Yaaay, chicken-shooter!" It sounded like Pelón that used to be my friend. Others took it up. I heard that ugly word race up and down the block like a fire engine. But I ask you, "What's the difference how you kill a chicken as long as that chicken gets dead?" Possibly I was the first in history to use a gun. But that's people for you, try anything new and different and they're sure to criticize, my father especially. You had to do every least thing exactly his way or he blamed you for it.

I laid there in the dirt. The sun was shooting blades of light between the boards. There was a big new hole where the .45 blasted through. My hands were all over dirt and blood. My boots were bloody too. Who cared? Let it rot there. From outside I heard my father chasing people from the yard. I heard Chuchu arguing with him till my father ordered him out too. It got quite quiet. I heard the noise leather makes when you slap it on a wall. And then my father pulled the shed door open. His well-known belt squirmed in his hands like a snake.

Let him kill me. I'll never make a sound.

But behind him, through the door I saw my mother. She came waddling down the back steps. If she argued with him it would only make things worse. She didn't. Instead, she grabbed her belly and screamed a scream like no scream I ever heard before. My father dropped his belt and ran to catch her. I ran too, but it turned out to be a false alarm. The baby took two more days in coming. And I could almost swear I saw my mother wink at me while my father carried her inside.

Exploring Texts *and* Contexts

For activities with icons, refer to the Guide to Analyzing Readings in Context.

1. What do we know about Chato or Rudy, the narrator of the novel? For example, how old is he when the events of the novel take place and how old is the narrator when he is telling the story? How do we know? What else do we know about him?
2. One of the great mysteries of literature is how a writer is able to use words on the page, ink on paper, to create a character that can seem like a real person, that can seem alive. How does this writer use language to create Chato? Which descriptions particularly help us to imagine Chato? How does the writer to create a "voice" for Chato? What are some of the distinctive characteristics of this voice? (Language)
3. A concept that critics use to discuss how fiction works is the "reliability" of the narrator. Is the reader meant to believe the narrator and accept the narrator's judgments and values? Does the narrator represent the values of the author? How reliable a narrator is Chato?

Review of Famous All Over Town

David Quammen

Few things are more cheering than to pick up a first novel by an unknown author and see immediately, after only a dozen pages, that the new novelist is a natural. A writer endowed as though genetically with the sure, pure sense of how to shape his material, just where to expand and where to elide, when to maintain pace and when to change it, how to select rather than merely amass details. A writer with the delicate, precious trick of keeping a reader off balance yet engaged, with not just a keen eye but a keen ear, a keen wit and a feel for those narrative contours that make a good novel quite different from a padded short story or a veiled diary. That may not sound like much to ask but, among first novelists, it is surprisingly uncommon. So it is cheering to be able to report that Danny Santiago is a natural.

His book is "Famous All Over Town" and very simple in program: It chronicles the 15th year in the life of Rudy Medina Jr., a.k.a. "Chato," a street-wise Chicano kid trying to live long enough to look back someday and say he grew up in the tough Eastside neighborhood of Los Angeles. Chato measures out on the school tests with a brilliant I.Q. but he nevertheless gets himself in enough idiotic and punk-daring trouble to make that 15th year a lively one. Besides being bright and warmhearted he is also a born comic, which to readers may be his greatest charm but to himself (in dealing with all levels of authority) is often his worst liability.

Chato's life as a schoolboy, his neighborhood and gang of friends, his immediate family and even the familial house itself all collapse during the course of this novel, yet Chato floats on through the flotsam, buoyed up only by a manic appetite for experience and his own detached humor. "Famous All Over Town" is full of poverty, violence, emotional injury, and other forms of major disaster, all vividly and realistically portrayed, yet, like a spring feast-day in a barrio, it is nevertheless relentlessly joyous. Best of all is its language; narrated by Chato, the novel employs a rich street Chicano English that pleases the ear like sly and cheerful Mejicana music.

"Famous All Over Town" is an honest, steady novel that presents some hard cultural realities while not for a paragraph failing to entertain. I am totally ignorant of the Chicano urban experience but I have to believe this book is, on that subject, a minor classic. And Danny Santiago is good news.

From *The New York Times Book Review* by David Quammen, April 24, 1983, section 7, page 12.

A Noted "Hispanic" Novelist Proves to Be Someone Else

Edwin McDowell

At the annual meeting of the American Academy and Institute of Arts and Letters last May, John Kenneth Galbraith presented a $5,000 award for an outstanding work of fiction published during the preceding 12 months.

The winner was "Famous All Over Town," a novel about a Mexican-American family in the Los Angeles neighborhood of Eastside. The dust jacket of the book described the author, Danny Santiago, as having grown up in Los Angeles.

But Mr. Santiago did not show up to receive the award. To this day, neither his agent nor his editor has ever seen him. In fact, hardly anyone else has ever seen Danny Santiago. For the author of "Famous All Over Town" is not a Hispanic American, as many critics assumed, but Daniel James, 73 years old, who grew up in Kansas City, Mo., graduated from Andover and says he was the only member of the Yale Class of 1933 to major in classical Greek.

"We figured there was something strange going on, having to write to him in care of a post office box and his saying he did not have a telephone," said Bob Bender, Mr. James's editor at Simon & Schuster. "But we figured he was probably in prison and didn't want anybody to know."

5 Mr. James said he never told the publisher that he grew up in Los Angeles. "In my letter I said 'Danny Santiago was a product of Los Angeles,' " he recalled in a telephone conversation from his home in Carmel, Calif. He described his name change as only a "mild deception" for which he feels no qualms, in part because he and his wife spent 20 years in the Los Angeles barrio as volunteer workers. In addition, Mr. James believed he might still have been blacklisted. In 1951 before a Congressional committee he was named as a member of the Communist Party.

The fact that Mr. James used the pen name of Danny Santiago has evoked mixed reactions from writers of Hispanic origin, some of whom regard the deception as serious.

Prof. R. W. B. Lewis of Yale University, chairman of the seven-member American Academy committee that voted the award, said the new information about Danny Santiago casts a different light on the matter.

"We were considering the ethnic dimension," he said. But he added that the prize, called the Richard and Hinda Rosenthal Foundation Award, "was given for its literary quality."

"I don't think when I was reading it I was too much concerned with whether the author was Chicano or not," he said, "but now that I know, I think I admire the novel all the more. But I would have to say that if we had known, it would have given us pause. We would not necessarily have rejected it, but we would have had to talk a little more about it. It does raise all kinds of interesting questions."

From *The New York Times,* article by Edwin McDowell, July 22, 1984, section 1, page 1.

10 Mr. James said in the telephone interview that a number of his friends had warned him against publishing as Danny Santiago.

"They said this can be very touchy, it could hurt a lot of feelings and you shouldn't do it," he recalled. "But I said the pen name is pretty well established, with Mark Twain, Rabelais, and so many others. I said nobody's going to be hurt if the book's any good."

One of the friends who warned Mr. James against using a Hispanic name was the writer John Gregory Dunne, who met Mr. James in 1966. Mr. Dunne has written an article, for the Aug. 16 issue of *The New York Review of Books,* about Mr. James and his use of the pseudonym.

What complicates matters among Hispanic Americans is that some of them think the book, which evolved from a collection of short stories, is quite good.

"I read one of the short stories Danny Santiago wrote about a part of town I grew up in, right on the same street, and I thought the characterizations were right on target," said Felix Gutierrez, chairman of graduate studies at the University of Southern California school of journalism. But Mr. Gutierrez added, "I think Dan James should write as Dan James, because a piece should stand on the merit of the writing, not the author's name."

15 To illustrate how sensitive the issue is, he said that last year his cousin, Ricardo Munoz, telephoned and excitedly told him to read "Famous All Over Town" because it was an authentic account of growing up Mexican-American in their old neighborhood.

"The very next day a friend of ours telephoned and I told him what my cousin said," Mr. Gutierrez said. "My friend said, 'You know what? It was written by an Anglo who used a pen name,' and so I never read it."

But Mr. Gutierrez added, "You don't have to be a Latino to write on the Latino experience, and Latinos should not write only on that. There's nothing to stop an Anglo from writing authentically about it if he spends the time. That's the key, get to know us."

Philip Herrera, executive editor of *Connoisseur,* a monthly magazine of culture and the arts, said, "It is possible for Anglos to write as Hispanics and vice versa." What offended him, he said, was that one of Danny Santiago's short stories—ironically, the one Mr. Gutierrez liked so much—appeared in *Nuestro,* a magazine founded by Mr. Herrera and Jose M. Ferrer 3d, who had been at *Time* magazine."

"We were taken," Mr. Herrera said, when told of Danny Santiago's identity. "We were trying to present the best image of Hispanics we could. We were not trying to publish Anglo writers with Spanish surnames."

20 Mr. Ferrer, now a senior editor at *Time,* also expressed mild annoyance. "Our magazine was intended as an outlet for Latin voices," he said.

But he added that there were two different issues – "the longstanding question for the philosophers to settle, about whether somebody who has not lived the experience of another can write accurately about it; and whether the motive in choosing the name Danny Santiago had to do with cachet, with trying to get onto the bandwagon of minority writers who might be more publishable these days. In other words, can you gain an advantage by changing your name?"

Thomas Sanchez, the author of "Rabbit Boss" and "Zoot-Suit Murders," the latter novel set in the Los Angeles barrio in the 1940's, is quoted approvingly on the jacket of

"Famous All Over Town." In a recent conversation he said he had heard a rumor "that Danny Santiago was an Anglo."

He added: "But you have to ask, was this intentional deceit? And it doesn't appear to be that, since he chose the Spanish equivalent of his name rather than going out of his way to call himself Raul Alameda, for example."

Besides, what matters, Mr. Sanchez said, is not the author but the art.

25 "A work must be judged by the work itself, not the political or ethnic orientation of the author," he said. "A lot of professional Chicanos, professional blacks, professional Jews, professional Anglo-Saxons say no one else can cut into their territory. I don't believe in terms of the human race there is any such thing as territory. What creativity and art are all about are the absolute freedom to cross all those lines and go into any point of view in terms of the context of the work."

Mr. James based the novel on people and places that he and his wife, Lilith, experienced in the 20 years they spent as volunteer workers in the Eastside neighborhood depicted in the book. That neighborhood forms the world of Chato Medina, the book's sensitive, 14-year-old protagonist, who becomes famous all over town because he spray-paints his name everywhere. "We went down to the barrio at the invitation of a social worker for the Los Angeles Church Federation," Mr. James said. Mr. James soon began writing short stories based on that experience. His reason for choosing a pen name was not to deceive, he said, but in part because he believed that he had been blacklisted after he was named before the House Committee on Un-American Activities in 1951 as having been a member of the Communist Party.

Mr. James and his wife were party members for 10 years, but quit in 1948, according to Mr. Dunne's article. In the war years, the article says, one of Mr. James's contributions to the Communist cause was a 1942 play called "Winter Soldiers," which played 25 performances at the New School for Social Research. It won a $1,500 prize given to a promising young playwright. Mr. Dunne said in a telephone conversation that it was pure propaganda. "It was a true Stalinist play," he said. "People actually say in it, 'That's what my tractor said to me.'"

Mr. and Mrs. James collaborated on a play that, after various revisions, became the libretto for "Bloomer Girl," a musical that opened on Broadway on Oct. 5, 1944, and ran for 654 performances. "When it was later done as a two-hour television spectacular," Mr. James said, "they removed our credits, apparently to protect the morals of the American people. But we still collected royalties."

Those royalties helped pay the bills. So did his work on the scripts of two monster movies, "The Giant Behemoth" and "Gorgo," written under a family name, Daniel Hyatt. The movies were a far cry from Charlie Chaplin's "The Great Dictator," on which he had worked for two years in the 1930s and for which he received a screen credit as an assistant director.

30 In 1966, Mr. Dunne, his wife, Joan Didion, and their daughter moved into the house in Hollywood owned by Mr. and Mrs. James. Eventually, Mr. James showed Mr. Dunne some short stories he had written in the 1950s under the name of Danny Santiago but had been unable to sell.

"I had published a book about Cesar Chavez and the grape strike," Mr. Dunne said, "and he knew I was interested in the Chicanos. He had also helped me by giving me some names when I wanted to see if the strike had any impact on urban Chicanos."

Mr. Dunne liked the stories but said he was troubled by the idea of the author presenting himself as a Chicano. But Mr. James said that he had been unable to write under his own name for nearly 20 years, because of the blacklist and because he had lost confidence in his own ability. In a letter to Mr. Dunne, written from Carmel, he said, "In any event, unless you feel too guilty about this mild little deception of mine, I'd like you to send on the stories to Brandt."

He referred to Carl Brandt, the New York literary agent for Mr. Dunne and other writers. Mr. Brandt placed the stories in various magazines, including *Playboy* and *Redbook,* but in all those years he neither saw nor spoke to his reclusive client.

"The first time he heard my voice was earlier this month," Mr. James said, "when I told him that I had agreed to let John Dunne write about my secret. All he could say was 'Oh my God, oh my God.'"

The book jacket's description of the author said: "Danny Santiago grew up in Los Angeles. He is the author of short stories published in *Playboy, Redbook,* and *Nuestro.* One of his stories, 'The Somebody,' was chosen for Martha Foley's annual collection The Best American Short Stories and has been widely anthologized. 'Famous All Over Town' is Danny Santiago's first novel." The book was issued in paperback last April by New American Library.

Mr. James said he had "one day of misgivings" that his identity was about to be disclosed. "I wondered if it was going to hurt my writing," he said. "And while I was happy with Danny Santiago, it was getting a little claustrophobic never being able to meet my agent or editor or people who wrote to me."

He is working on another book with a Mexican-American theme, also set in Los Angeles. It too will appear under the name of Danny Santiago.

"Dan James couldn't ever write that book," he said. "Besides, I now realize that I enjoy my hours as Danny Santiago more than I enjoy my hours as Dan James."

Exploring Texts and Contexts

1. In David Quammen's review of *Famous All Over Town,* written soon after the book was published, what assumptions does the writer make about the author of the novel? Did you share these assumptions?
2. (Consequences) In the article written by Edwin McDowell a year or so after the novel was published, what does McDowell reveal about the author of *Famous*? Were you surprised by this revelation?
3. (Consequences) According to McDowell, on what grounds has Daniel James been criticized on the one hand and defended on the other hand?
4. (Consequences) What do we know about Daniel James's motivation? Are you sympathetic or unsympathetic with what he did and his motivation for doing it?

Creating Texts

For activities with icons, refer to the Guides to Analyzing Contexts for Writing and Analyzing Readings in Context. For additional help with these writing projects, read the description of **Cover Letter/Reflective Essay** and **Essay**.

1. Try your hand at writing a short story about a character who is very different from you in some way. You might, if you like, write about the persona that you created for the Creating Texts Activity 1 on page 81. This character should be the first-person narrator of the story and can be a reliable or unreliable narrator. Use description and dialogue to make the character as realistic, believable, and interesting as possible. After writing the story, or a portion of it, write a cover letter in which you discuss how you chose the character and how you tried to make that character come alive.
2. Write an essay in which you take and defend a position on the ethics, social implications, and artistic validity of Daniel James's authorship of *Famous All Over Town*. Should he have written the novel, and should he have published it under the name Danny Santiago? In developing your position on this issue, you should consider the following questions: Can writers create works of fiction about people who are different from them and whose experiences are different? Do such works of fiction have artistic validity and social value? Can they be considered authentic representations of the experiences they describe? Can readers learn anything from reading such works of fiction? What are the social and ethical implications of publishing works of fiction under a pseudonym that leads readers to believe one belongs to a different social or ethnic group or is a different gender? What are the social implications of imagining and writing about the experiences of others? If you know of other instances of impostorship that would illuminate this discussion, feel free to bring them in.

CHAPTER 4

Buying and Selling Authenticity

Situation: What aspects of contemporary culture does this photograph seem to refer to or draw on?

Genre: What kind of photograph is this? What clues help you decide?

Language: How does the angle the photograph was taken from affect its composition and impact? Describe the attitude of the three people in the photograph; which visual elements lead you to that description—pose, facial expression, clothes?

Consequences: If this picture were part of an ad in a magazine, how might you respond to it?

No true artist wants to sell out, but most artists would at least like to have the opportunity to resist selling out, because having that opportunity also means that you have reached an audience. There is a real tension for artists who would like to reach an audience—whether the art is folk craft or music or fashion—but remain true to their creative process. Is it possible for something to have mass appeal and still be genuine? What happens to the authenticity of art when it becomes a commodity?

The story of mediagossip.com—a personal Web site created by Jim Romenesko, a once-obscure journalist—raises questions about the nature of the creative process, the role of the artist, and the function of art in an increasingly commercialized culture. In 1999, Romenesko's work became the subject of feature stories and columns in national papers such as the *New York Times* and the *Wall Street Journal.* He was the focus of a panel discussion on new media at the University of California at Berkeley media conference and was interviewed for the Internet magazine Salon.com. Why all the attention?

At that time, mediagossip.com was one of the most popular of a new kind of Web site, which later became known as weblogs or blogs. At the time the most creative area of the Internet, such sites provided links to other stories and places on the Web that the blog's creator found interesting. The designers of these sites interspersed information with commentary and personal asides. Because they bore the personal stamp of their creators, they were unlike other lists of links. Part online journal, part referrer site, they were a wholly new form of expression, the products of irreverent writers whose independent spirit and subversive nature drew people who were looking for an authentic voice.

Romenesko's site recorded anywhere from 5,000 to 7,000 hits a day, a fact that drew the attention of businesses and corporations. If Romenesko linked a story to his site, it had the potential to reach thousands of new readers. But partly because of the increasing popularity of the site, Romenesko eventually decided to relinquish independence and agreed to have his site sponsored. Mediagossip.com is now Jim Romenesko's MediaNews, sponsored by the Poynter Institute, a nonprofit journalism education foundation.

The deal immediately inspired talk about the dangers of being co-opted. Most sponsored sites are not as popular as the independent sites, in part because they lack the strong personal voice and subversive element of many independent sites. Much of what they publish can be found in other sources such as the evening news and the mainstream press. In any case, Romenesko's creative process might already have been affected by all the attention he had been attracting and the knowledge that large numbers of people were viewing his site. What will happen to this new form of discourse, the weblog, as the original creators succumb to pressure to give up their independence? Can these sites keep their edge and their authenticity under corporate or more benign forms of sponsorship?

The tug-of-war between authenticity and commercial success, exemplified by the creation and subsequent development of weblogs, is played out in many forms of art, commerce, and self-expression, as we will see in this chapter.

Goin' Gangsta, Choosin' Cholita

Nell Bernstein

In "Goin' Gangsta, Choosin' Cholita," Nell Bernstein tells the stories of young people who use fashion and music to identify with a particular ethnic group. Bernstein's feature story grows out of her work with teens in the San Francisco Bay area. She edits a publication called *YO!* (an acronym for "youth outlook" and the Spanish word for "I"), a bimonthly news journal of youth culture produced by young people in the Bay Area. The young people profiled here are bored because they see their lives as conventional and "too bland," and they are attracted to lifestyles and cultures they perceive as more authentic than their own.

Whether exposed to ethnic difference in their own schools and neighborhood or through the media, these teens believe in their ability to identify with other lifestyles by listening to alternative music or wearing the clothes promoted by famous rap artists. Published in the mid-nineties, Bernstein's article was one of the first to document our growing fascination with the cultural phenomenon of the wannabe. Other newspapers, magazines, and radio and TV talk shows were also running stories featuring "wiggers," white youth who want to be black, and other teens searching for an authentic identity. Is this behavior merely rebellion for its own sake, or are these young people a vision of the future?

Connecting with the Conversation

For activities with icons, refer to the Guide to Analyzing Readings in Context.

1. Map out the cafeteria or hangout at your college or the high school you graduated from. In a journal entry, describe the seating arrangements. Who sits where, and how do clothing, hairstyles, and taste in music help identify the different groups?
2. What words do you and your peers use to describe people that you consider fake or phony? Do you also have words for people you consider genuine or sincere? In a small group, compare notes. Discuss how young people use language, including slang, to express their values and make judgments.

Her lipstick is dark, the lip liner even darker, nearly black. In baggy pants, a blue plaid Pendleton, her bangs pulled back tight off her forehead, 15-year-old April is a perfect cholita, a Mexican gangsta girl.

But April Miller is Anglo. "And I don't like it!" she complains. "I'd rather be Mexican."

April's father wanders into the family room of their home in San Leandro, California, a suburb near Oakland. "Hey, cholita," he teases. "Go get a suntan. We'll put you in a barrio and see how much you like it."

A large, sandy-haired man with "April" tattooed on one arm and "Kelly"—the name of his older daughter—on the other, Miller spent 21 years working in a San Leandro glass factory that shut down and moved to Mexico a couple of years ago. He recently got a job in another factory, but he expects NAFTA to swallow that one, too.

5 "Sooner or later we'll all get nailed," he says. "Just another stab in the back of the American middle class."

Later, April gets her revenge: "Hey, Mr. White Man's Last Stand," she teases. "Wait till you see how well I manage my welfare check. You'll be asking me for money."

From *San Jose Mercury News,* November 13, 1994. Reprinted in the *Utne Reader,* March–April 1995.

A once almost exclusively white, now increasingly Latin and black working-class suburb, San Leandro borders on predominantly black East Oakland. For decades, the boundary was strictly policed and practically impermeable. In 1970 April Miller's hometown was 97 percent white. By 1990 San Leandro was 65 percent white, 6 percent black, 15 percent Hispanic, and 13 percent Asian or Pacific Islander. With minorities moving into suburbs in growing numbers and cities becoming ever more diverse, the boundary between city and suburb is dissolving, and suburban teenagers are changing with the times.

In April's bedroom, her past and present selves lie in layers, the pink walls of girlhood almost obscured, Guns N' Roses and Pearl Jam posters overlaid by rappers Paris and Ice Cube. "I don't have a big enough attitude to be a black girl," says April, explaining her current choice of ethnic identification.

What matters is that she thinks the choice is hers. For April and her friends, identity is not a matter of where you come from, what you were born into, what color your skin is. It's what you wear, the music you listen to, the words you use—everything to which you pledge allegiance, no matter how fleetingly.

10 The hybridization of American teens has become talk show fodder, with "wiggers"—white kids who dress and talk "black"—appearing on TV in full gangsta regalia. In Indiana a group of white high school girls raised a national stir when they triggered an imitation race war at their virtually all-white high school last fall simply by dressing "black."

In many parts of the country, it's television and radio, not neighbors, that introduce teens to the allure of ethnic difference. But in California, which demographers predict will be the first state with no racial majority by the year 2000, the influences are more immediate. The California public schools are the most diverse in the country: 42 percent white, 36 percent Hispanic, 9 percent black, 8 percent Asian.

Sometimes young people fight over their differences. Students at virtually any school in the Bay Area can recount the details of at least one "race riot" in which a conflict between individuals escalated into a battle between their clans. More often, though, teens would rather join than fight. Adolescence, after all, is the period when you're most inclined to mimic the power closest at hand, from stealing your older sister's clothes to copying the ruling clique at school.

White skaters and Mexican would-be gangbangers listen to gangsta rap and call each other "nigga" as a term of endearment; white girls sometimes affect Spanish accents; blond cheerleaders claim Cherokee ancestors.

"Claiming" is the central concept here. A Vietnamese teen in Hayward, another Oakland suburb, "claims" Oakland—and by implication blackness—because he lived there as a child. A law-abiding white kid "claims" a Mexican gang he says he hangs with. A brown-skinned girl with a Mexican father and a white mother "claims" her Mexican side, while her fair-skinned sister "claims" white. The word comes up over and over, as if identity were territory, the self a kind of turf.

15 At a restaurant in a minimall in Hayward, Nicole Huffstutler, 13, sits with her friends and describes herself as "Indian, German, French, Welsh, and, um . . . American": "If somebody says anything like 'Yeah, you're just a peckerwood,' I'll walk up and I'll say 'white pride!' 'Cause I'm proud of my race, and I wouldn't wanna be any other race."

"Claiming" white has become a matter of principle for Heather, too, who says she's "sick of the majority looking at us like we're less than them." (Hayward schools were

51 percent white in 1990, down from 77 percent in 1980, and whites are now the minority in many schools.)

Asked if she knows that nonwhites have not traditionally been referred to as "the majority" in America, Heather gets exasperated: "I hear that all the time, every day. They say, 'Well, you guys controlled us for many years, and it's time for us to control you.' Every day."

When Jennifer Vargas—a small, brown-skinned girl in purple jeans who quietly eats her salad while Heather talks—softly announces that she's "mostly Mexican," she gets in trouble with her friends.

"No, you're not!" scolds Heather.

20 "I'm mostly Indian and Mexican," Jennifer continues flatly. "I'm very little . . . I'm mostly . . . "

"Your mom's white!" Nicole reminds her sharply. "She has blond hair."

"That's what I mean," Nicole adds. "People think that white is a bad thing. They think that white is a bad race. So she's trying to claim more Mexican than white."

"I have very little white in me," Jennifer repeats. "I have mostly my dad's side, 'cause I look like him and stuff. And most of my friends think that me and my brother and sister aren't related, 'cause they look more like my mom."

"But you guys are all the same race, you just look different," Nicole insists. She stops eating and frowns. "OK, you're half and half each what your parents have. So you're equal as your brother and sister, you just look different. And you should be proud of what you are—every little piece and bit of what you are. Even if you were Afghan or whatever, you should be proud of it."

25 WILL MOSLEY, HEATHER'S 17-year-old brother, says he and his friends listen to rap groups like Compton's Most Wanted, NWA, and Above the Law because they "sing about life"—that is, what happens in Oakland, Los Angeles, anyplace but where Will is sitting today, an empty Round Table Pizza in a minimall.

"No matter what race you are," Will says, "if you live like we do, then that's the kind of music you like."

And how do they live?

"We don't live bad or anything," Will admits. "We live in a pretty good neighborhood, there's no violence or crime. I was just . . . we're just city people, I guess."

Will and his friend Adolfo Garcia, 16, say they've outgrown trying to be something they're not. "When I was 11 or 12," Will says, "I thought I was becoming a big gangsta and stuff. Because I liked that music, and thought it was the coolest, I wanted to become that, I wore big clothes, like you wear in jail. But then I kind of woke up. I looked at myself and thought, 'Who am I trying to be?' "

30 They may have outgrown blatant mimicry, but Will and his friends remain convinced that they can live in a suburban tract house with a well-kept lawn on a tree-lined street in "not a bad neighborhood" and still call themselves "city" people on the basis of musical tastes. "City" for these young people means crime, graffiti, drugs. The kids are law-abiding, but these activities connote what Will admiringly calls "action." With pride in his voice, Will predicts that "in a couple of years, Hayward will be like Oakland. It's starting to get more known, because of crime and things. I think it'll be bigger, more things happening, more crime, more graffiti, stealing cars."

"That's good," chimes in 15-year-old Matt Jenkins, whose new beeper—an item that once connoted gangsta chic but now means little more than an active social life—goes off periodically. "More fun."

The three young men imagine with disdain life in a gangsta-free zone. "Too bland, too boring," Adolfo says. "You have to have something going on. You can't just have everyday life."

"Mowing your lawn," Matt sneers.

"Like Beaver Cleaver's house," Adolfo adds. "It's too clean out here."

35 Not only white kids believe that identity is a matter of choice or taste, or that the power of "claiming" can transcend ethnicity. The Manor Park Locos—a group of mostly Mexican-Americans who hang out in San Leandro's Manor Park—say they descend from the Manor Lords, tough white guys who ruled the neighborhood a generation ago.

They "are like our . . . uncles and dads, the older generation," says Jesse Martinez, 14. "We're what they were when they were around, except we're Mexican."

"There's three generations," says Oso, Jesse's younger brother. "There's Manor Lords, Manor Park Locos, and Manor Park Pee Wees." The Pee Wees consist mainly of the Locos' younger brothers, eager kids who circle the older boys on bikes and brag about "punking people."

Unlike Will Mosley, the Locos find little glamour in city life. They survey the changing suburban landscape and see not "action" or "more fun" but frightening decline. Though most of them are not yet 18, the Locos are already nostalgic, longing for a Beaver Cleaver past that white kids who mimic them would scoff at.

Walking through nearly empty Manor Park, with its eucalyptus stands, its softball diamond and tennis courts, Jesse's friend Alex, the only Asian in the group, waves his arms in a gesture of futility. "A few years ago, every bench was filled," he says. "Now no one comes here. I guess it's because of everything that's going on. My parents paid a lot for this house, and I want it to be nice for them. I just hope this doesn't turn into Oakland."

40 Glancing across the park at April Miller's street, Jesse says he knows what the white cholitas are about. "It's not a racial thing," he explains. "It's just all the most popular people out here are Mexican. We're just the gangstas that everyone knows. I guess those girls wanna be known."

Not every young Californian embraces the new racial hybridism. Andrea Jones, 20, an African-American who grew up in the Bay Area suburbs of Union City and Hayward, is unimpressed by what she sees mainly as shallow mimicry. "It's full of posers out here," she says. "When *Boyz N the Hood* came out on video, it was sold out for weeks. The boys all wanna be black, the girls all wanna be Mexican. It's the glamour."

Driving down the quiet, shaded streets of her old neighborhood in Union City, Andrea spots two white preteen boys in Raiders jackets and hugely baggy pants strutting erratically down the empty sidewalk. "Look at them," she says. "Dislocated."

She knows why. "In a lot of these schools out here, it's hard being white," she says. "I don't think these kids were prepared for the backlash that is going on, all the pride now in people of color's ethnicity, and our boldness with it. They have nothing like that, no identity, nothing they can say they're proud of.

"So they latch onto their great-grandmother who's a Cherokee, or they take on the most stereotypical aspects of being black or Mexican. It's beautiful to appreciate different aspects of other people's culture—that's like the dream of what the 21st century should be. But to garnish yourself with pop culture stereotypes just to blend—that's really sad."

45 Roland Krevocheza, 18, graduated last year from Arroyo High School in San Leandro. He is Mexican on his mother's side, Eastern European on his father's. In the new hierarchies, it may be mixed kids like Roland who have the hardest time finding their place, even as their numbers grow. (One in five marriages in California is between people of different races.) They can always be called "wannabes," no matter what they claim.

"I'll state all my nationalities," Roland says. But he takes a greater interest in his father's side, his Ukrainian, Romanian, and Czech ancestors. "It's more unique," he explains. "Mexican culture is all around me. We eat Mexican food all the time, I hear stories from my grandmother. I see the low-riders and stuff. I'm already part of it. I'm not trying to be; I am."

His darker-skinned brother "says he's not proud to be white," Roland adds. "He calls me 'Mr. Nazi.' " In the room the two share, the American flags and the reproduction of the Bill of Rights are Roland's; the Public Enemy poster belongs to his brother.

Roland has good reason to mistrust gangsta attitudes. In his junior year in high school, he was one of several Arroyo students who were beaten up outside the school at lunchtime by a group of Samoans who came in cars from Oakland. Roland wound up with a split lip, a concussion, and a broken tailbone. Later he was told that the assault was "gang-related"—that the Samoans were beating up anyone wearing red.

"Rappers, I don't like them," Roland says. "I think they're a bad influence on kids. It makes kids think they're all tough and bad."

50 Those who, like Roland, dismiss the gangsta and cholo styles as affectations can point to the fact that several companies market overpriced knockoffs of "ghetto wear" targeted at teens.

But there's also something going on out here that transcends adolescent faddishness and pop culture exoticism. When white kids call their parents "racist" for nagging them about their baggy pants; when they learn Spanish to talk to their boyfriends; when Mexican-American boys feel themselves descended in spirit from white "uncles"; when children of mixed marriages insist that they are whatever race they say they are, all of them are more than just confused.

They're inching toward what Andrea Jones calls "the dream of what the 21st century should be." In the ever more diverse communities of Northern California, they're also facing the complicated reality of what their 21st century will be.

Meanwhile, in the living room of the Miller family's San Leandro home, the argument continues unabated. "You don't know what you are," April's father has told her more than once. But she just keeps on telling him he doesn't know what time it is.

Exploring Texts and Contexts

For activities with icons, refer to the Guide to Analyzing Readings in Context.

1. Add your own voice to those in Bernstein's article. Andrea Jones, a young woman quoted in the article, sees the other young people in the article as

posers and their behavior as shallow mimicry. Do you agree? Or do you think that they are genuinely trying to create a new identity for themselves? Do you see the situation as yet one more attempt by companies to market overpriced reproductions of urban wear to adolescents? Or can you offer some other explanation?

2. Look closely at the last three paragraphs of Bernstein's article. Who is being addressed here? "Goin' Gangsta, Choosin' Cholita" was originally published in the Sunday supplement magazine of the *San Jose Mercury News*. Speculate on how the type of publication and its audience may have influenced Bernstein's conclusion to this article. Situation

Creating Texts

For activities with icons, refer to the Guides to Analyzing Contexts for Writing and Analyzing Readings in Context. For additional help with these writing projects, read the descriptions of **Essay, Opinion Piece,** and **Cover Letter/Reflective Essay** in the Genre Glossary.

1. In an essay, explore how three different writers portray young people who try to create an identity by adopting a particular look and attitude. Bernstein, as well as other writers in this unit such as Marc Spiegler and James Ledbetter, all discuss teens who make lifestyle choices to attain authenticity, but each author writes about this phenomenon within a different context. What conclusions can you draw about the connection between the author's context and his or her portrayal of young people? Situation
2. The opinion piece is a familiar genre that appears in the editorial section of newspapers and journals. Typically, writers concerned about a particular social issue use opinion pieces to persuade readers to adopt a specific plan or idea. Feature articles like this one by Bernstein may also discuss larger social issues, but they are very different from opinion pieces. For one thing, because these feature articles often appear in Sunday papers, the writers have the space to use vivid descriptions, anecdotes, and pictures. What are some other similarities and differences between feature articles and opinion pieces? Rewrite Bernstein's feature article as an opinion piece. Then, in a cover letter to your teacher, discuss how genre influences the meaning and impact of a piece of writing. Genre

Marketing Street Culture

Bringing Hip-Hop Style to the Mainstream

Marc Spiegler

When a company attempts to design clothes that appeal to a specific group of consumers, they conduct what is called *market research*. You may have participated in such research if you have answered questions on the telephone about your interests or filled out a survey in your local mall. It is in this transaction between your desires as a consumer and a company's desire to sell its product that authenticity finds itself being stretched and pulled almost beyond recognition. Corporations recognize that if their product is not seen as authentic, consumers will not buy it. Yet artists as well as consumers would like to believe that authenticity is not a commodity that can be sold.

In his article, "Marketing Street Culture: Bringing Hip-Hop Style to the Mainstream," Marc Spiegler explores the possibility that corporations can identify and sell authenticity if they have a more sophisticated understanding of the social processes involved in achieving authenticity. He relies primarily on survey data gathered by marketing or trendwatching firms and on observers of the hip-hop scene such as Upski Wimsatt to analyze what makes white surburban youth willing consumers. Spiegler has even produced a hip-hop quiz for you to determine for yourself how much you know. For instance, what does the term "sampling" mean in the context of hip-hop culture? Or "bombing trains"? How about "freestyling"? Understanding the inner circle of hard-core hip-hop culture, according to Spiegler, will allow corporations to design and market authentic products attractive to teens who want to identify with rappers.

Connecting with the Conversation

1. Visit two or three of the stores you usually shop at and ask to interview the manager or the buyer. Ask how that company or franchise makes decisions about what clothes to feature. What sorts of information do they need to make those decisions? How do they get that information? Write up what you find out and report to the class.
2. Go to your library and browse through several issues of *American Demographics* or look at the journal online at www.demographics.com. Look over at least two other articles that attempt to explain a trend or offer information on a cultural phenomenon. What are some common characteristics of this genre? Write a brief report and share it with the class.

The Scene: Martha's Vineyard, Massachusetts, a bastion of the white East Coast establishment. A teenaged boy saunters down the street, his gait and attitude embodying adolescent rebellion. Baggy jeans sag atop over-designed sneakers, gold hoops adorn both ears, and a baseball cap shields his eyes. On his chest, a Tommy Hilfiger shirt sports the designer's distinctive pairing of blue and red rectangles.

Once, this outfit would have been unimaginable to this cool teen: only his clean-cut, country-club peers sported Hilfiger clothes. What linked the previously preppy Hilfiger to jeans so low-slung they seem to defy gravity? To a large extent, the answer lay 200 miles southwest, in the oversized personage of Brooklyn's Biggie Smalls, an admitted ex-drug dealer turned rapper, who was killed in 1997.

During the mid '90s, Smalls and other hip-hop stars became a crucial part of Hilfiger's open attempt to tap into the urban youth market. In exchange for giving artists free wardrobes, Hilfiger found its name mentioned in both the rhyming verses of rap songs and their "shout-out" lyrics, in which rap artists chant out thanks to friends and sponsors for their support.

For Tommy Hilfiger and other brands, the result is *de facto* product placement. The September 1996 issue of *Rolling Stone* magazine featured the rap group The Fugees, with the men prominently sporting the Tommy Hilfiger logo. In February 1996, Hilfiger even used a pair of rap stars as runway models: horror-core rapper Method Man and muscular bad-boy Treach of Naughty by Nature.

5 Threatened by Hilfiger in a market he had profited from but never embraced, it hardly seems coincidental that Ralph Lauren signed black male super-model Beckford Tyson to an exclusive contract. Even the patrician perfumier Esteé Lauder jumped on the Hilfiger bandwagon, launching a new cross-promotion series with the clothing company. The name of one of Lauder's new perfumes said it all. "Tommy Girl" plays on both Tommy Hilfiger's name and the seminal New York hip-hop record label Tommy Boy. Hilfiger also launched a clothing line for teenaged girls in fall 1996, projected by the company to gross $100 million in its first year on retail racks.

On the surface, it seems Hilfiger and others are courting a market too small and poor to matter. The majority of true hip-hoppers live in inner cities, although not all urban youths embrace the culture. About 5 million U.S. teens aged 15 to 19 lived in central cities in 1994, or 28 percent of all people that age. Inner-city blacks aged 15 to 19 are an even smaller group. At 1.4 million, they are only 8 percent of all teens. They also have significantly lower incomes than their white suburban counterparts. The numbers of 20-to-24-year-olds and black 20-to-24-year-olds in central cities are also small, at 6.5 million and 1.6 million, respectively.

So why are companies pitching products to the hip-hop crowd? Because for most of the 1990s, hordes of suburban kids—both black and white—have followed inner-city idols in adopting everything from music to clothing to language. The most prominent examples are in evidence at suburban shopping malls across the country: licensed sports apparel, baseball caps, oversized jeans, and gangster rap music.

Scoring a hit with inner-city youths can make a product hot with the much larger and affluent white suburban market. But to take advantage of this phenomenon, you

---

From *American Demographics*, November 1996, pp. 29–34. Updated by the author, November 2000.

have to dig into how hip-hop culture spreads from housing projects to rural environs, understand why hip-hop is so attractive to suburban whites, and discern the process by which hip-hoppers embrace products.

Hip Hop Hits the Mainstream

In its early years, MTV drew jeers for being too "white," for shying away even from vanilla-flavored black pop stars such as Michael Jackson. Yet most pop-culture watchers agree that the cable channel's launching "Yo! MTV Raps" in 1992 was the pivotal event in the spread of hip-hop culture. Running in a prime after-school spot, and initially hosted by graffiti artist and rapper Fab Five Freddy, the show beamed two daily hours of inner-city attitude at adolescent eyeballs in even the most remote Iowa corn country.

10 "There's no question—'Yo! MTV Raps' was the window into that world for Middle America," says Janine Misdom of Sputnik, a Manhattan-based firm that tracks youth trends for clients such as Levi-Strauss, Reebok, and Pepsi. Other video-oriented media soon followed. Within a few years, an all-day viewer-controlled channel called The Box supplied a steady stream of harder-edged hip-hop to any kid within the viewing area of a major metropolis. In 1993, about a year after "Yo! MTV Raps" hit cable, more than six in ten teens aged 12 to 19 rated hip-hop music as "in," according to Teenage Research Unlimited (TRU) of Northbrook, Illinois.

Music and fashion went hand in hand, as teens adopted the looks sported by rappers. Most Americans first saw baggy jeans in music videos sagging around the hips of white rap star Marky Mark (now known as *Perfect Storm* film star Mark Wahlberg). Teens also got an eyeful of Mark's boxers-exposed backside in his beefcake ads for Calvin Klein jeans. By spring 1993, 80 percent of teens favored the style, up from two-thirds six months earlier. And the look has staying power. Seventy-eight percent of teens still say baggy clothes are "in," according to TRU's Spring 1996 survey, although the style's popularity may be waning slightly.

Today, elements of hip-hop culture appear in the mainstream media, from commercials using rapped slogans to hit films such as *Menace II Society* and *Boyz N the Hood*. Suburban record stores stock relatively extensive hip-hop sections, and with good reason. Among consumers aged 12 to 17, almost three in five (58 percent) either "like" or "strongly like" rap, according to SounData of Hartsdale, New York, which tracks sales and other trends for the music industry. The 1996 figure is equally high among 18-to-20-year-olds. And even among the solidly adult 21-to-24-year-old age group, almost two-fifths favor the genre. Not surprisingly, it has now become a music-industry maxim that for a rap record to go platinum, it must sell strongly among white youths.

What draws white teens to a culture with origins so strongly linked to the inner city, and so distant from their suburbia's sylvan lawns? Clearly, rebellion is a big factor. "People resonate with the strong anti-oppression messages of rap, and the alienation of blacks," says Ivan Juzang of Motivational Educational Entertainment, a six-year-old Philadelphia firm specializing in targeting urban youth. "All young people buy into rebellion in general, as part of rebelling against parental authority."

Embracing Fear

Gangster rap artists such as the late Tupac Shakur and Dr. Dre represent only the latest link in a long chain of anti-establishment American icons (Shakur was wounded in a drive-by shooting in Las Vegas in September 1996 and died a week later). American teens have always been fascinated with outsider heroes, who score money and fame without being cowed by societal strictures. Such idols run from John Dillinger and Dennis Rodman, to Marlon Brando's fictional biker in *The Wild One* to James Dean's *Rebel Without a Cause.*

Yet many argue that hip-hop's attractiveness transcends mere rebellion, placing it in a different category from past teen trends. For instance, punk, with its body piercing and mohawked heads, was often rebellion for rebellion's sake. Based on the urge to shock, it constructed a new reality for its adherents outside of societal norms. In contrast, hip-hop springs from the experiences of young blacks living in cities. It's based on a real culture, giving it more permanence than earlier teen trends. People who want a part of hip-hop culture always have something new to latch onto, because the culture is always evolving.

But perhaps more important to white teens, embracing hip-hop fashion, language, and music lets them claim to be part of black, inner-city culture. "By entering into the

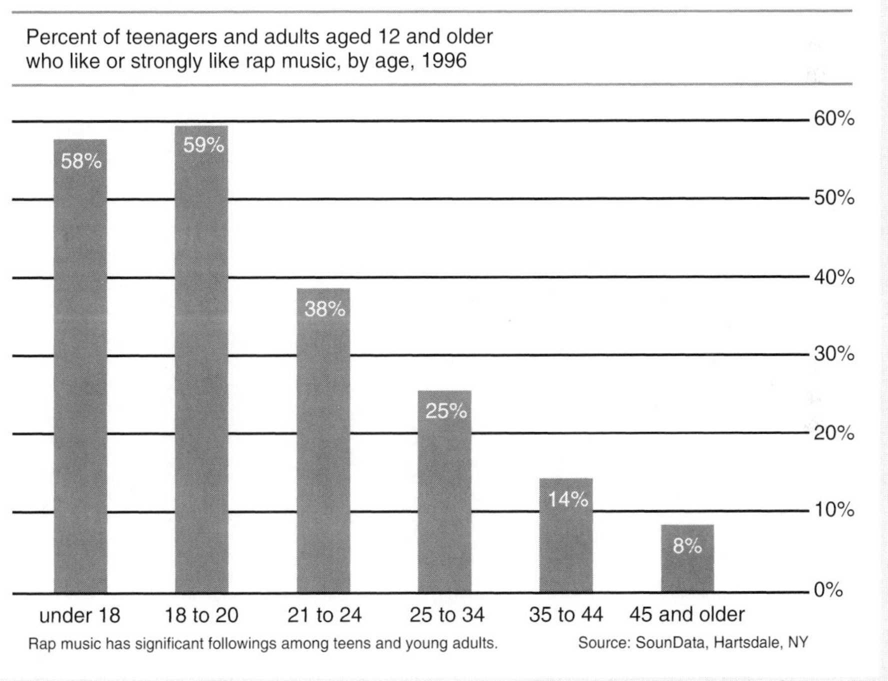

Rap music has significant followings among teens and young adults.

hip-hop sphere, I felt like I was opening a whole world that was closed to me before—it gave me a basis to meet all these people I had been scared of, whose main context for me was that they stole my bikes," says white 23-year-old William "Upski" Wimsatt, author of the memoir *Bomb the Suburbs*. The book in part details his trajectory from University of Chicago faculty brat to graffiti artist and journalist covering the rap music scene.

The attraction, he says, is part admiration, part fascination, and part fear. "A lot of white kids suspect they wouldn't make it through what inner-city blacks do, so there's an embedded admiration that's almost visceral," Wimsatt says. "Fear is one of our strongest impulses, and poor black men are the greatest embodiment of that fear."

Skateboarders, snowboarders, and other practitioners of nontraditional sports were among the first white teens to adopt the accouterments of hip-hop culture. Yet they are also some of the culture's least devoted adherents. "Most of them don't really understand hip-hop," says Chicagoan Tim Haley, a Midwest sales representative for snowboarding gear. "They want to come off as being bad ass, pumping their stereo around town," he says. "So you'll see a bunch of white kids in Podunk, Michigan, trying to dress 'hip-hop,' but really they're just jocks with rich parents."

Got to Be Real

Turning teens like these on to hip-hop styles begins with a much smaller group—hard-core hip-hoppers. "If we develop the hardest core element, we reach middle-class blacks, and then there's a ripple effect," says Juzang of Motivational Educational Entertainment. "If you don't target the hard-core, you don't get the suburbs." For example, marketers for the 1995 Mario Van Peebles film *Panther* misfired by casting it "as *JFK* for African Americans," Juzang says. The flick bombed. Soon after, the comedy *Friday* came out, pitched as a straight-up ghetto laugh-fest, and scored big both inside and outside

Music Video Generation

Percent of hip-hoppers* and all blacks aged 16 and older who watch selected types of television programs at least once a week, 1995

	Hip-hoppers	Bourgeois/Mercantile
Game Shows	44%	40%
Music Video Shows	42	34
Weekday Morning News	37	37
Dramas	36	40
Award Shows	35	29
Nighttime Comedies	31	32
Late-night Entertainment	29	24

*Hip-hoppers are young, urban blacks as defined by Yankelovich Partners.
Source: Yankelovich Partners Inc. Norwalk, CT.

city borders. The lesson here: core hip-hoppers display an almost fanatical obsession with authenticity. Sanitizing any element of hip-hop culture to make it more palatable for middle-class suburban whites is likely to result in failure, because the core hip-hop audience will reject it. And other groups look to this core for their cues. This wasn't always the case. The pop-music audience was responsible for the commercial success of artists such as faux rapper Vanilla Ice and thinly disguised pop star MC Hammer. Both scored major hits by unimaginatively sampling 1980s pop songs and rapping bland rhymes over them. Some critics would argue that Puff Daddy did the same thing only a few years later. But now, even peripheral hip-hop consumers have grasped the difference between real and rip-off. If white kids realize a product has been toned down in a bid to make it "cross over," they'll avoid it. Instead they go for music with a blunt, urban sensibility—the harder-edged stuff Chuck D of the rap group Public Enemy once described as "CNN for black America." Soundscan sales statistics bear this out. In 1994, three-quarters of hard-core rap albums were sold to white consumers.

The Inner and Outer Circles

20 The hip-hop market encompasses consumers with varying levels of commitment to the culture. Millions of people buy rap records, but can hardly be called hard-core. Strictly speaking, a person must do at least one of three things to qualify: rap or be a disc jockey; breakdance; or paint graffiti.

Few white teenagers meet these criteria. Some are afraid to venture into inner cities or cities at all, many are restricted by their parents, and others are content to absorb hip-hop culture through television and other media. "Lots of kids' parents won't let them cross certain borders. So they're watching videos to see how to dress, how to look, how to talk," says black urban-sportswear designer Maurice Malone. "They can visualize the inner city. But they don't go there, so they can't fully communicate with the heart of the hip-hop movement."

Wimsatt, the Chicago hip-hop writer, sees the white parts of the "hip-hop nation" as a series of concentric attitudinal rings. At the center lie those who actually know blacks and study the intricacies of hip-hop's culture. "These people tend to consider themselves the racial exception," says Wimsatt. "They have a very regimented idea of what's cool and what's not."

Next is a group that has peripheral contact with the culture through friends or relatives, but doesn't actively seek "true hip-hopper" status. They go to shows, but don't rap, spray-paint, or breakdance. "After that, you have people who play hip-hop between other types of music," Wimsatt says. "They're sort of free-floating fans." Most white suburban teens probably fall into this category, listening to accessible acts such as A Tribe Called Quest and De La Soul.

Finally, the people in the outermost circle are those Wimsatt documented in a controversial 1993 article for hip-hop's *Source* magazine. Touring America, he met rural "wiggers" who avoided cities, thought blacks complained too much about their societal lot, and spouted phrases such as, "We wear a lot of pro-black clothes." To Wimsatt, such kids "are pure consumers—they're really into rap, but don't know much, so they're easily manipulated."

Unlocking the Door

25 As hip-hop has made its mark on the mainstream, all but the most gullible fans have spotted a flurry of laughable bids to capitalize on the trend. Anybody with a drum machine and a rhyming dictionary, it seemed, could be presented as a true hip-hopper. "The history of semi-insiders trying to exploit hip-hop is an incredible comedy of errors," Wimsatt says. "I've seen so many commercials with some sort of hip-hop theme that are just transparent. You can almost see the creatives looking around the office and saying, 'Hmm . . . who do we know who's black and has a teenage cousin? Maybe that cousin raps . . . ' " If you're trying to reach the hip-hop crowd, he says, take the time to find and hire legitimate hip-hop players. Good places to start tracking down insiders include record stores, music venues, and recording studios. National magazines such as *Vibe, RapPages*, and *The Source* may also mention local players on their pages.

Sprite evidently did its homework. For a series of NBA-game commercials, Coca-Cola Company (makers of Sprite) hired two of hip-hop's legendary "MCs," wordsmiths KRS-One and MC Shan. Even better they had them face off in the sort of extemporaneous "freestyle battle" seen as any rapper's truest test of verbal skills and mental agility. The spot was roundly acclaimed, both inside and outside the rap world.

In the clothing arena, it's the same game. Mainstream designers such as Hilfiger and Lauren have scored. But smaller "underground" lines can also flourish in both city and suburb, says Misdom of Sputnik. "Even in places like [Minnesota's] Mall of America, you'll see kids who dress 'hip-hop' wearing grass-roots brands like Mecca,

Rappin' on the Web

Hip-hop enthusiasts maintain dozens of Internet Web sites. These are good sources of information on language, art, music, and figures in hip-hop. The following is a sampling. Most have links to other rap and hip-hop sites.

Gossip, commentary, insider news:
www.urbanexpose.com/

Vibe magazine
www.vibe.com

The Source magazine
www.thesource.com/

The Original Hip-Hop Lyrics Archive
www.ohhla.com

All purpose commercial hip-hop site
www.360hiphop.com

The Rap Dictionary
www.rapdict.org

Boss Jeans, and Phat Farm," she says. "They are embracing these brands because they are seen as 'true.' "

Not every company that wants to sell to the inner-city crowd has grasped this wisdom. Malone cites two design prototypes making the rounds recently. Both try to emulate the boxers-exposed-by-sagging-jeans look. One pair of pants sports an underwear-like band of cloth sewn directly into the jeans waist, to peek out in a risk-free risqué style. Another features two waists—the first hangs at pelvis height giving the impression of disdain for belts, the second sitting traditionally on the hips. Both models have yet to make any splash. As Malone points out mockingly, "The most successful crossovers don't try. People will cross over to you if you don't try to play to them."

An Ever-Changing Scene

There's another reason the phony jeans may have failed. In hip-hop, the baggy jeans look has started to fade, following the lead of the skate-boarding subculture that abandoned drowning in denim for a "cleaner," tighter look in 1995. Baggy clothes of all kinds reached their peak in popularity in Fall 1993 and Spring 1994, when 82 percent of teens aged 12 to 19 said baggy clothes were in. That share slipped to 78 percent in spring 1996, according to Teenage Research Unlimited.

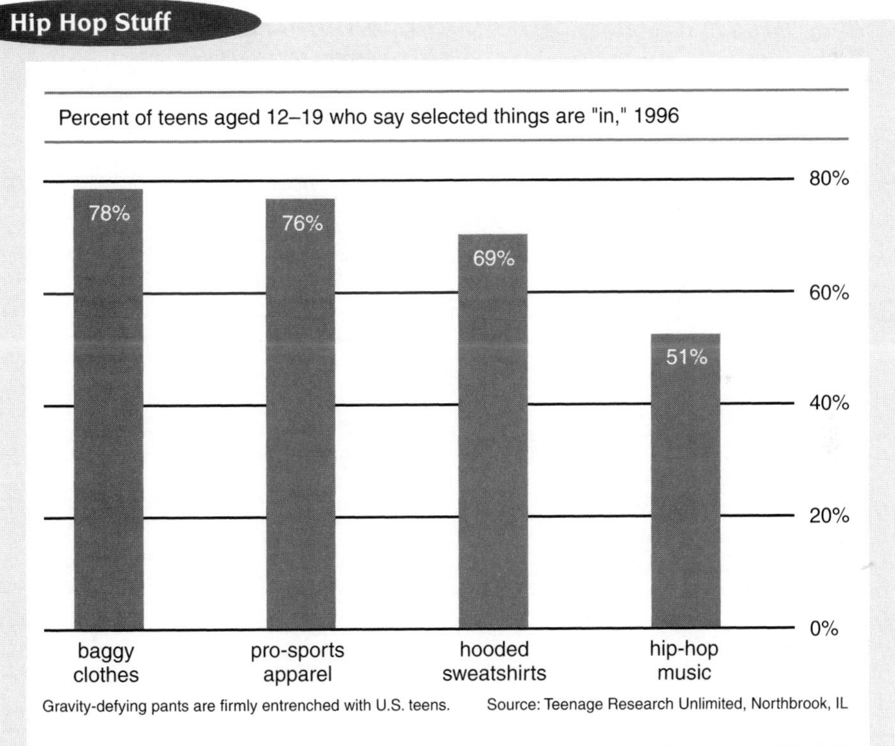

Gravity-defying pants are firmly entrenched with U.S. teens. Source: Teenage Research Unlimited, Northbrook, IL

Hip-Hop 101: The Placement Test

Although hip-hop's media prominence has risen, the culture's slang, dress, and music evolve so quickly that it's hard to track. Below, a little test of how much hip-hop knowledge has come your way over the years, broken down into three levels of difficulty.

Easy

1. When Will Smith was "The Fresh Prince," who was his partner?
   A. Jazzy Jeff
   B. Schooly D
   C. Big Daddy Kane
   D. Queen Latifah
2. Which of the following terms used to mean "cool" in hip-hop slang?
   A. "Dope"
   B. "Fat"
   C. "Stupid"
   D. All of the above
3. For hip-hop fans, the term "sampling" refers to:
   A. Any poll-taking method
   B. Reusing sections of an older song
   C. Shoplifting "gear" from malls
   D. Using rhymes from other artists
4. Deliberately "scratching" a record yields:
   A. An angry record owner
   B. A broken record needle
   C. New sounds for a musical mix
5. Run-DMC's lyrics promoted which shoe company?
   A. Nike
   B. Adidas
   C. Pony
   D. Converse

Moderate

6. The Beastie Boys started as:
   A. A breakdancing group
   B. Art-school students
   C. A 3-on-3 basketball team
   D. A hardcore-punk band
7. Two of the following pairs were partners. Two had famous feuds. Which are which?
   A. Scott LaRock and Kris Parker
   B. Canibus and LL Cool J
   C. Puff Daddy and Suge Knight
   D. Q-Tip and Phife
8. Which of the following white rappers are generally considered "legit" by their black peers?
   A. Eminem
   B. Marky Mark
   C. Vanilla Ice
   D. Everlast
9. "Freestyling" refers to:
   A. Impromptu breakdancing
   B. Spontaneous rapping
   C. Drawing graffiti without stencils
10. For the late Tupac Shakur, conviction and imprisonment on sexual-assault charges meant:
   A. The end of a budding career
   B. A temporary hiatus
   C. A huge boost in popularity
   D. A religious conversion
11. In 2000, which NBA team had two players who are rap recording artists?
   A. The L.A. Lakers
   B. Chicago Bulls
   C. The New York Knicks
   D. The Boston Celtics

12. In hip-hop slang, the term "bombing" refers to:
    A. Artistry
    B. Terrorism
    C. Insect extermination
13. Doctor Dre is:
    A. The ex-NWA member who scored a huge hit with "the Chronic"
    B. A movie actor and MTV VJ
    C. The man charged with recruiting dancers for Sisqo videos
14. A "B-Boy":
    A. Plays basketball well
    B. Wears baseball caps
    C. Breakdances
    D. Works as a bouncer at rap shows
15. Which of the following brands has never been embraced by hip-hop's fashion mavens? No partial credit will be awarded.
    A. Brooks
    B. Puma
    C. Timberland
    D. Bass
    E. Polo
    F. North Face
    G. Stetson
    H. Kangol
    I. Gucci
    J. Ferragamo

Answers:

1. A
2. D
3. B
4. C
5. B. The 1986 song "My Adidas" counts among the earliest of rap's frequent product "shout-outs."
6. D. (Kate Schellenbach, of Luscious Jackson, was their drummer)
7. The allies: A, as Boogie Down Productions; and D, in A Tribe Called Quest. The enemies: B and C.
8. A, D, though some will debate this. Our case: In 1999, mythic producer Dr. Dre oversaw production on Eminem's hit record "Slim Shady." And Everlast was featured on Prince Paul's critically acclaimed "Prince Among Thieves."
9. B
10. C, Shakur scored a No. 1 song, "Dear Mama," while behind bars in New York.
11. A. Center Shaquille O'Neal has cut several records, while guard Kobe Bryant rapped on R&B star Brian McKnight's 1998 single "Hold Me."
12. A. The "bomb" involved is an aerosol can used by graffiti artists
13. B. The DJ and producer is *Dr.* Dre, not *Doctor* Dre. And, yes, it's a trick question.
14. C
15. A, D, G, J

30 Hip-hop culture is constantly evolving, partly because of the commercial success of some of its elements. As Don DeLillo wrote in his novel *America*, "as soon as Madison Avenue breaks the code, Harlem devises a new one." But hip-hop music, language, and fashion also change because looking good and sporting the latest styles are very important to core members of the culture.

The 1995 Yankelovich African-American Monitor clusters black consumers into six segments based on attitudes and income. Its "hip-hopper" segment includes 27 percent of U.S. blacks. These single, urban blacks probably include members who are not authentic hip-hoppers. But their attitudes are telling, nonetheless. More than half of Yankelovich's hip-hoppers strongly agree that they feel the need to be fashionably dressed, compared with only 33 percent of all blacks aged 16 and older. These hip-hoppers are twice as likely as all blacks to strongly feel the need to keep up with new styles, at 42 percent.

To Sputnik's Misdom, hip-hop culture's emphasis on innovative fashion counts among its strongest selling points for teens, who demand a never-ending slew of status symbols to define them against both their peers and parents. "All the rock and grunge styles have stayed the same," she says. "But hip-hop always has a lot of styles coming out." Already her studies project a shift away from the preppier Hilfiger style toward "uptown," high-end designer labels such as DKNY, Versace, and Dolce & Gabana. Garments bearing these labels have a sleeker, more European look than brands such as Hilfiger. They also have higher price tags.

Recent rap videos support her observations. "Roughneck" styles featuring hunting and fishing apparel are on the wane. Another emerging hot style uses high-tech fabrics and styles that resemble those worn by scientists at the South Pole and by mountain climbers. Last summer, designer Donna Karan dressed many of New York City's fashionable young in DKNY Tech. This lower-priced line of clothing featuring high-tech fabrics represents the designer's nod to the trendsetting power of urban teens.

Hip-hop culture is in some ways the next page in the decades-long book of teenagers embracing the forbidden. Yet it's also more lasting, because it is based on the day-to-day experiences of millions of inner-city teens. Targeting this relatively small group of teens may open the door to the larger, more affluent, white, suburban market. But the niche has countless pitfalls. Companies that have successfully negotiated them know a fundamental truth of hip-hop culture: For a product to appeal to a rapper in south central L.A. or a white mall crawler in Des Moines, it's got to be real.

Exploring Texts and Contexts

For activities with icons, refer to the Guide to Analyzing Readings in Context.

Genre

1. Consider what you know about the genre of quizzes like the one that appears in this article. Why do you suppose quizzes like this commonly appear in popular magazines? Take Spiegler's hip-hop placement quiz and compare your answers with his guide. Write about your experience taking this quiz and how it affected your attitudes and understanding of hip-hop. Why do you suppose Spiegler included this quiz in his article?
2. Spiegler explains that "Scoring a hit with inner-city youths can make a product hot with the much larger and affluent white suburban market." What does he think corporations need to know to take advantage of that process? What kinds of explanations and information does he rely on to guide those who want to market hip-hop fashions? How does he use the data from trendwatching firms to support his argument?

Language

3. Examine the language of Spiegler's article. Are there any terms you are not familiar with? What words or phrases does he use frequently? How has he made lan-

guage choices to fit the needs of his corporate readers? How does Spiegler's use of language differ from that of James Ledbetter in "Imitation of Life"?

4. In his article, Spiegler says, "If white kids realize a product has been toned down in a bid to make it 'cross over,' they'll avoid it" (page 109). The term *cross over* refers to the phenomenon in which a product or performer shifts from one category or market niche to another. What does Spiegler mean by the term? How has this term been used in discussions of authenticity? What are the broader implications of this term?

Creating Texts

For activities with icons, refer to the Guides to Analyzing Contexts for Writing and Analyzing Readings in Context. For additional help with these writing projects, read the descriptions of **Opinion Piece, Cover Letter/Reflective Essay**, and **Online Posts** in the Genre Glossary.

1. Write an opinion piece in which you respond critically to Spiegler's position on educating corporations to improve their marketing know-how. Imagine that you disagree with his approach. Consider who your audience will be and in what magazine or journal your opinion piece will appear. Choose one particularly strong area of disagreement with Spiegler and share it with your readers. After writing your opinion piece, write a cover letter discussing what you learned about genre in completing this project. Genre
2. Divide into several small groups. One group should use the dictionary, thesaurus, and a book of quotations to explore the definitions that are offered for the term "authenticity." Another group should look at the section of Spiegler's article subtitled "Got To Be Real" (pp. 108–109). What does Spiegler mean by "authenticity"? A third group should examine Ledbetter's "Imitation of Life." How does Ledbetter discuss the notion of authenticity? Each group should post the results of its work on the class listserv or message board, and then members of the class should respond to each other, contributing to a conversation about how a writer's context influences the way he or she defines authenticity. Situation

Imitation of Life

James Ledbetter

In "Imitation of Life," James Ledbetter articulates the deep ambivalence Americans feel about race relations and particularly about the cultural expression of ethnicity through music. The cultural schism between blacks and whites has recently been explored by white youth who wish to connect to the African American cultural experience through rap and hip-hop in an attempt to empathize with the experience of racism. When Janis Joplin and Madonna announced their desire to be black, they identified themselves with the longstanding oppression of African Americans. On the other hand, the fact that Madonna, Joplin, and others have not personally experienced this oppression raises questions about their authenticity. Is this expression of solidarity productive, or is it just a commercial move? Ledbetter focuses on "wiggers," white youth who talk and dress black, and how their behavior emerges from a complex historical scenario that includes African American musicians, white musicians with "soul," the media, and the market.

In an earlier period, when whites embraced black music, they were considered to be "hip" and their crossover was, if not a compliment to the authentic music, at least not considered a blatant rip-off. However, today, according to Ledbetter, America's powerful culture industry has created enormous incentives for promoting the African American cultural experience, and when wiggers participate, they are doing so more with their wallets than with their conscience. Ledbetter wants wannabes to do more than buy records; he wants them to understand the history and current marketing efforts that fuel their desire and then to act out of a more critical understanding of the context.

Connecting with the Conversation

1. Gather some popular fashion or music magazines and examine how issues concerning race and culture are written about. In particular look at *Vibe* magazine in hard copy or online at www.vibe.com. Report to the class what you find.
2. Crossover behavior is common among young people. Write in your journal about crossover situations you may have observed or participated in.

In 1989, Madonna gushed to an interviewer: "When I was a little girl, I wished I was black. . . . If being black is synonymous with having soul, then, yes, I feel that I am." In concert, the Beastie Boys strut around the stage in an exaggerated "black" walk and chant a street dialect somewhere between an imitation of black speech and a bad translation of it. Radio clown Howard Stern has said of his childhood: "I remember for the longest time wanting to be black." A 16-year-old white Pennsylvanian says his high school is full of "wiggers," whites so desperate to adopt black modes of dress and conduct that they end up being parodies. Call 'em wannabes, call 'em rip-offs, call 'em suckers, but they're everywhere—white folks who think they're black, or wish they were.

The arrival of hip-hop as a leading musico-cultural force has created an entire subclass of these wannabes. Following the Beasties' lead, there was 3rd Bass, white rappers who, until their recent breakup, expressed an almost painful identification with New York blacks. Then came House of Pain, an Irish-American rap group whose video cuts from black-styled hip-hop dancing to marching bagpipe players. Now there's

From *Vibe* magazine, September, 1992, pp. 113–116.

A.D.O.R., a hard-core white rapper whose name means Against Discrimination of Race and a Definition of Real. Perhaps most extreme are Young Black Teenagers, an all-white and not very good rap group whose strut and postures are "blacker" than most of their fans, even more so than most blacks. What's more, millions of white fans of black rappers have adopted modes of dress, speech, and style that they consider black.

The phenomenon isn't new. American writers, sociologists, and armchair sociologists have long spotlighted black wannabes, arguing that their desire to be black has some tenuous connection to African-American social oppression. Norman Mailer, in his prescient, bizarre, and overwritten 1957 essay "The White Negro" asserted that "it is no accident that the source of Hip is the Negro for he has been living on the margin between totalitarianism and democracy for two centuries." Nor is it new that attempted race bending expresses itself musically, with earlier examples ranging from minstrel shows, a dominant Southern entertainment form through the mid-20th century, to Janis Joplin, who a generation ago told a reporter: "Being black for a while will make me a better white."

It's a curious spectacle, and one that pisses off a lot of people, both black and white. Americans take their segregation very seriously, and not just the de facto racial separation of housing, education, and income, but our cultural apartheid as well. America reacts dramatically, even violently, to cultural expressions that suggest racial admixture—the original 1952 rock 'n' roll riot in Cleveland was due not only to an oversold show, but also, some say, to the fact that inside the Cleveland Arena ballroom, blacks and whites were dancing together to the same music.

5 In part, the disgust with wannabes comes from the sheer vulgarity of the white who cavalierly adopts the black mantle without having to experience life-long racism, restricted economic opportunity, or any of the thousand insults that characterize black American life. (Similar ridicule was aimed at an earlier generation's purveyors of radical chic.) And, as depicted in Lou Reed's outrageous lyrics, whites' interpretation of what it means "to be black," even when they're attempting to "understand" or "empathize with" victims of racism, often results in a version that looks an awful lot like racism itself. Finally, whites have been riffing off—or ripping off—black cultural forms for more than a century and making a lot more money from them. Whether it's Al Jolson, Elvis, the Rolling Stones, Blues Brothers, Commitments, New Kids, or Beasties, it's impossible to deny that, as a rule, the market responds much better to a black sound with a white face.

There are two crucial factors separating the minstrel of past generations from today's racial flaneurs. The first is easily identified: the market. In Mailer's essay, for example, the white hipster was necessarily on the margins; Mailer even identified him with the psychopath. The white Negro, with his lust for jazz and grass, was a threat to the American way of life, a figure whose existential insight was contingent on his isolation from society. Today, the inverse is true: There are a number of intersecting multibillion-dollar American industries (music, advertising, television, sports) whose survival at current profit levels depends on the existence of a massive audience of white Negroes.

Take *Saturday Night Live*'s fall 1991 premiere, hosted by Michael Jordan, with musical guest Public Enemy and cameo appearances by Spike Lee and Jesse Jackson. It was punctuated by Gatorade ads featuring white and black kids singing "If I

Could Be Like Mike." Coincidentally, it aired the night Miles Davis died and thus the live program carried several allusions to the jazz legend. The resulting episode was the highest-rated *SNL* season opener ever. It wasn't just black viewers who made those Nielsens jump, but whites who, as fans of basketball, hip-hop, jazz, and Lee's movies, have become more or less integrated into a black ethos. Rap music may be, as Chuck D says, black people's CNN, but there are a lot of white folks tuning into that signal too.

And where such black-oriented whites do not exist, they must—through advertising, fashion, MTV, and magazines such as this one—be created. Somewhere in the mid-Black Power period, America's culture industry discovered that, instead of being polarizing and threatening, black slang, music, and energy could be harnessed for immense profits. (My earliest memory of this co-optation was the slogan "Write on, Bros., write on," used to sell 19-cent Write Bros. pens.) Just as on the record charts, hip-hop and its derivatives have taken over this promotional agenda; its beat and style are today used to hype not just hip-hop artists, but also television shows, children's clothing, bubble gum—even hair-care products for whites. This guarantees thousands, even millions more hipsters than Mailer could ever have imagined, but their value is accordingly debased. If a white can become "hip" simply by buying the right shampoo or CD, then the control of "hip" has been passed from society's rebels to its representatives.

The second factor differentiating the contemporary wannabe is more obscure, and not as powerful as the market, though its rise also corresponds to the development, beginning in the mid-1960s, of a more militant black agenda. There exists today a limited (but nonetheless quasi-institutionalized) school of music critics, artists, record industry honchos, intellectuals, and activists whose tolerance for the white Negro has more or less expired. This isn't to say that, in the past, white beatniks or hippies were universally embraced by the blacks they emulated. But there has been a shift in the balance of power. Whereas black jazz musicians in the 1940s had to shrug (or innovate further) when whites copied their musical styles, today the more exploitative wannabes—Vanilla Ice is the best example—are called out as the frauds they are. Armed with a body of criticism that extends from LeRoi Jones through Greg Tate, and with an ideology that draws strength from Afrocentrism (even while rejecting portions of it), rappers and writers today regularly dis wannabes in public as opportunists or racists or both. One of the more extraordinary developments is that even the contemporary white hipster must go through this ritual of denouncing a fellow wannabe as somehow being less authentic. Both 3rd Bass albums, for example, seem almost obsessed with denouncing Vanilla Ice, as if his downfall would inflate their "genuine" attachment to blacks and to rap.

10 The authenticity argument gets even blurrier when rappers rank on Hammer, thus far their most commercially successful colleague. To say, as so many have, that Hammer can't rap or has sold out introduces the idea of the Oreo, the inauthentic black, cousin to the wannabe (and a target of equally vehement criticism from many black artists and critics, notably Ice Cube in "True to the Game" on *Death Certificate*). It also breaks down the simple dichotomy under which both wannabes and some black artists and critics operate; it admits the possibility that blackness is a quality other than pigmentation, even other than a social condition, since Hammer's upbringing wasn't

radically different from those considered true black rappers. This is the direction in which a number of intellectuals, notably Stuart Hall and Paul Giroy, have been heading, insisting that "blackness" is too complex, too amorphous a code to be reduced to a simple question of color or even class.

In a way, the very existence of the wannabe implies this complexity. Because while the Vanilla Ices of the world can be explained as mere economic exploiters, the 1990s white suburbanite gets no money from listening to Public Enemy. And at least he or she gets out of it some exposure to a black urban reality—which is more than Beaver Cleaver ever got. Janis Joplin's comment, sincere as it was naïve, speaks to the multiple motivations behind youth's racial switcheroo—it's intended to resolve a racial gap that the white kid doesn't feel responsible for. Lou Reed's offensive, funny lyrics are a frank expression of the self-emptiness that makes some renegade whites want to be "black" (and, at the same time, a vicious parody of that desire). Later in the song, Reed sings of wanting to be shot like Martin Luther King and wanting to be like Malcolm X. Those lyrics, as nasty as they are, speak to a genuine yearning: There is, for young American whites, no white leader in recent memory who invokes such a powerful self-identity and moral force. The closest for them may be artists and rock stars (including Reed), but they never achieved anything approaching the status and power those men had. That both were gunned down only enhances, for black and whites, their embodiment of authenticity and unapologetic rebellion.

By listening to rap and tapping into it as extramusical expressions, then, whites are attempting to bear witness to—even correct—their own often sterile, oppressive culture. Cornel West has referred to this as the Afro-Americanization of American youth, a potent thought since this country is fast headed toward a non-white majority for the first time since its colonization. If current population growth trends hold, with Asian, Latino, black, and other nonwhite segments growing at much higher rates than white, the U.S. will be a "minority majority" nation within the next century. Wannabes, in that sense, are harbingers of America's multicultural future.

Intentions, though, aren't enough, today or ever. The most difficult (and almost always unasked) question for wannabes, particularly those with access to airwaves and media, is: Does their identification with what they view as black culture extend to taking concrete steps to end America's political and cultural apartheid? Are they at the very least willing to renounce, up front, the systemic abuses of the white order, from which, regardless of their implicit dissent, they have doubtlessly benefited? It accomplishes nothing to play at being black and ignore the society that made you want to do it. Indeed, the wannabe is at great risk of using black posturing solely as a way to assuage his or her conscience.

The challenge for the wannabe is to make the critique of America more explicit. There are very clear analogies in politics. Whites would find themselves on the defensive a lot less if they stopped ignoring those political causes that seem to affect blacks almost exclusively. For example, where are the white political leaders willing to put themselves on the line to oppose the Bush administration's unconscionable wholesale repatriation of Haitian refugees, announced not coincidentally in an election year? More shocking is that even after a willingly slumbering nation was awakened by the videotape of white cops bashing Rodney King, no prominent white leader has announced that police brutality against people of color is an outrage that must be stopped. If America's wannabes wanna be taken seriously, they ought to be adopting such issues. For white hip-hop artists, this means using the music as a vehicle to discuss segregation and economic blight, rather than simply as a way to provide one more commercial distraction. For the far more numerous white fans, it means screaming out that you accept the criticism of the American system offered by the likes of Ice Cube and Public Enemy, and you want the society to do something more than buy and sell their records.

Exploring Texts and Contexts

For activities with icons, refer to the Guide to Analyzing Readings in Context.

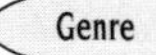

1. In this opinion piece, Ledbetter attempts to persuade his readers to reconsider their assumptions. Bring in an opinion piece from a daily newspaper, and exchange copies with other members of a small group. Work with this group to create a list of guidelines for writing in this genre as though you were going to teach others how to do so. Present these guidelines to the class with examples from the clippings you brought in.
2. Ledbetter's piece is a carefully constructed argument, in which he presents several premises about authenticity and wannabes, and then builds on those premises an argument that takes a couple of interesting turns, leading to a final call to action. With your teacher's help, identify the stages of Ledbetter's argument and discuss how they work together.

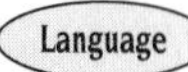

3. Ledbetter's language choices create shifts in tone as he moves through the different stages of his argument. Identify those shifts in tone and discuss specific language choices that create those different tones.

Creating Texts

For activities with icons, refer to the Guides to Analyzing Contexts for Writing and Analyzing Readings in Context. For additional help with these writing projects, read the descriptions of **Feature Story/Article** and **Essay** in the Genre Glossary.

1. Ledbetter and Marc Spiegler, another writer in this chapter, write from very different perspectives about the phenomenon of white kids dressing like black rap stars and buying their music. Drawing ideas from both of these writers as well as your own observations, and using Nell Bernstein's article as one possible model, develop a feature story or profile of someone who attempts to "cross over" from one group to another. Remember that while a feature story presents a broad view of a situation, it explores that situation through very specific details. Your profile may include descriptions, stories, quotes, information, and commentary, all woven together to create a picture of the person and an analysis of the situation.

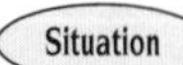

2. Ledbetter refers to an essay written in 1957 by Norman Mailer called "The White Negro," in which he describes the beginnings of the idea of "hip." With your teacher's help, find a copy of that essay, read it, and write an essay in which you critique and update Mailer's essay.

The Heart of the Matter

David Klinghoffer

In the realm of pop music and fashion, authenticity might be associated with a certain kind of experience, an experience outside of and even opposed to the mainstream, the traditional. In the realm of fine art or cooking, authenticity has the almost opposite meaning of "traceable to a particular origin"; the word "authenticated" means that something has been proven to have the origins it claims to have. But even the idea of origins is complicated. What do we mean by origins, and who determines what something's or someone's true origins are?

Journalist David Klinghoffer explores these complicated questions in his book *The Lord Will Gather Me In: My Journey to Jewish Orthodoxy*. The title of the chapter included here is telling. It has a very literal meaning, as you'll see, as well as a metaphorical one having to do with coming to a realization after a long search. But the metaphor may also refer to the question about authenticity we've just raised. Even if we agree on defining authenticity in terms of origins, we still have to ask *which* origins we mean, and the answer to that, the heart of the matter, may change from person to person, from case to case, even according to the perspective from which we're looking.

Connecting with the Conversation

1. Do you know much about your ancestors? Have you ever been interested in tracing your family tree, or do you know someone who has done this? Discuss in your journal what you think the attraction of this kind of activity is.
2. Do you know anyone who has converted from one religion to another or who has returned to a religion he or she once practiced but lapsed from? Explore in your journal what you know or can infer about the spiritual, psychological, or social processes that accompany such a change.
3. When you shop for clothes, are you more interested in finding clothes that express "the real you" regardless of fashion or accepted taste; clothes that suggest a certain kind of "class," preferring, say, clothes made from natural rather than synthetic fibers; or clothes that suggest a certain kind of authentic experience, say, a black leather jacket or hiking boots? Compare your answers within a small group, and report your findings to the class.

If this were a novel, I would be at fault for neglecting to clarify the motivation of the main character. Because we read novels and see movies, we become accustomed to thinking in terms of this concept, motivation. We take it to mean that any course of

From *The Lord Will Gather Me In: My Journey to Jewish Orthodoxy*. New York: The Free Press, 1999, pp. 125–139.

action will be executed with the intention of bringing about certain results. But the return of an individual to God does not necessarily submit to that sort of analysis.

Judaism asserts that man possesses a free will, that, in the words of the Talmud, "Everything is the hand of Heaven except the fear [that hard-to-translate *yirah*] of Heaven." In other words, God controls the world, but we have it in our power to decide whether we will acknowledge His control and act accordingly. This suggests that had someone asked why, in fits and starts, I had undertaken part of a commandment here, another part of a different commandment there, I should have been able to give a coherent answer. But I could not have done so. Sometimes the power of *yirah* acts on us without our knowing it.

When I graduated from Brown and drove to New York to work as an editorial assistant at *National Review*, the conservative opinion magazine, I was still keeping kosher, in my way. Once in a while I would put on tefillin. But otherwise my spiritual life was submerged under the cares of my daily life. I had other things on my mind, which I would have said were independent of my relationship, or lack of a relationship, with God. But they were not independent.

What was on my mind? I mention the following absurd episode only because it was the start of a growing intuition I had, in that first year out of college, that I was dying.

5 I was not one of those kids at Miraleste who experimented with drugs or alcohol. In college I tried marijuana only once. After college, during the Christmas break we took at *National Review* the first year I was there, I went home to California for a week. A college classmate, living in Los Angeles, had discovered that he enjoyed cocaine, and one night in his apartment we sniffed a lot of it. It was my first and last cocaine high. No one could have failed to enjoy the first few hours, the sensation that you are the most fascinating person in the world, that you possess many brilliant insights that pour forth with breaks only to half listen to your companion, who is under the identical impression about himself. The hard part is coming down. For me it was simply terror. The basketball player Len Bias had died of cocaine intoxication the previous year, and for seven hours I lay on a couch, expecting that any moment the same thing would happen to me.

How I wished I had never sniffed that cocaine. My vacation was scheduled to end the next day. I took an overnight flight into Kennedy Airport and was at my desk the next morning, but I wasn't the same calm person I had been when I'd sat there a week earlier. Anxiety had descended on me as never before. I kept expecting my pulse to shoot back up to whatever rate it had reached under the influence of the drug.

It was "Magazine Monday" at *NR*, the day every other week when the magazine's editor, William F. Buckley Jr., led the editorial meeting. At the end of the day, he and the senior editors would walk to a grottolike Italian restaurant, Nicola Paone's. By the end of this particular Monday, I was eager to go home to my apartment in Brooklyn. But at four P.M. the executive editor cheerfully poked her head through my office door to invite me to dinner with the senior editors: a treat.

Throughout the meal I had my hands under the table, taking my pulse, waiting for it to shoot up. *NR*'s publisher, William Rusher, described a fatal heart attack that had befallen a contributor to the magazine at a surprisingly early age. Bill Buckley must have noticed me go pale, because he kindly asked if I was jet-lagged and suggested that jet-lag remedies, pep pills, could be bought over the counter. The mere idea of such a thing made my pulse race with fear. I had to get out of there.

"Actually," I said, "I'd better go home and go to sleep. Right now." I got up and left.

10 For weeks my heart was continually on my mind. I went to a cardiologist, who told me I had higher blood pressure than a young man should have. On his recommendation I took hypertension medicine for several years, until another doctor guessed that my blood pressure at the time had something to do with my anxiety at the possibility of having high blood pressure. At Brown I had become a regular at University Health Services, mainly in connection with assorted skin complaints. Now I began to visit the doctors of New York City. Two cardiologists. Two neurologists, when I started getting headaches in the morning. A dermatologist, when blue patches began to appear on my fingers at night. (Dr. Stein was puzzled, until it occurred to me that the patches came from the ink in a cheaply printed novel I was reading.)

Gradually the headaches went away. My pulse seemed normal. And I began to accept that there was nothing seriously wrong with me.

Meanwhile I had moved to Manhattan. As I will explain later, where I chose to live says as much about my motivation as a *ba'al teshuvah* as does my hypochondria. I wanted to live in an old building.

My fondness for anything antique had persisted after high school. In Providence I got to know the used-clothing shops along Thayer Street and bought large quantities of new clothes that looked old: wrinkled cotton Oxford shirts of the kind that became chic five years later and baggy cardigan sweaters and baggy khaki pants, likewise ahead of their time, which friends said reminded them of their grandfathers. It was my great hope, realized when I was a senior, to live in Brown's second-oldest dormitory, Slater Hall, on the college green next to the pre–Revolutionary War administration building, University Hall. When my classmate David Lipsky and I decided to find a place together in Manhattan, I sought out the most antique building we could afford and found it on 19th Street in Chelsea: a sepulchral tenement blackened with soot.

But despite my pleasure at these physical surroundings, my fear of death by sudden heart attack returned in a fury. I do not blame William Buckley for the coincidence of his being present at both the apparent beginning and the true beginning of my years of hypochondria.

15 Another treat: Bill Buckley had invited me and another assistant editor for an overnight trip on his sailboat, out across the Long Island Sound from the Buckleys' home in Connecticut. We anchored in a little indentation on the north coast of Long Island—after which, really living it up, the other editorial assistant and I did more drinking and cigar smoking than was prudent. Though I learned how to drink liquor at *National Review*, at this point I had not yet learned. Then we all went to sleep. At about four A.M. the liquor woke me up. Something was wrong, I could tell, and what it was occurred to me in a moment: my heart was beating as fast as it had the night I took that cocaine. I walked out on the deck of the boat and imagined myself waking Bill Buckley to tell him I was having a heart attack. I waited for the chest pains signaling cardiac arrest, but they didn't come. As I had the night at Paone's, I felt a strong desire to get out of there and retreat to my apartment, but this time I couldn't. Finally I calmed down.

In weeks to come I found myself persistently waking up, night after night around four A.M., with an odd, anxious feeling. I would take my pulse, which of course was racing. It was another "night panic," as I came to think of these experiences.

Back I went to the cardiologist, Dr. Robbins, who fitted me with a Holter Monitor, a device somewhat larger than a Sony Walkman that automatically measured my heart's activities over twenty-four hours. But the doctor could find no abnormalities. I would call him at his home at ten or eleven at night.

"My heart's really beating fast. Maybe a hundred beats per minute."

"Why don't you have a drink and relax?" he would say.

By this time I had purchased a sphygmomanometer (a blood pressure pump and cuff), and David Lipsky would come home after a date and find me at the kitchen table with a stethoscope in my ears and the sphygmomanometer before me, measuring my blood pressure. "Shhh, I can't hear," I would tell him if he tried to talk too loudly as I was doing this. At *National Review* I would close the door to my office and, while puzzled co-workers wondered what I could be up to, take the sphygmomanometer out of a desk drawer and measure my blood pressure. When the subscription clerk mentioned he had heard that pain in the left arm could signal the onset of cardiac arrest, that very night I began to feel twinges in my left arm.

Finally Dr. Robbins gently asked if I had considered seeking professional assistance from a doctor other than a cardiologist, neurologist, or dermatologist. I took his advice and began seeing a psychiatrist named Dr. O'Brien. At first this helped a lot, and I continued to see a psychiatrist or psychologist, in whatever city I lived in, for the next seven years, longer than I had worn braces in high school: an achievement.

SEEKING THE ASSURANCE of one doctor after another that I was healthy, chasing after antique authenticity, I was suffering from a definite restlessness of the soul. Soon my hunger for security and roots found a new object. The idea struck me that, if I wanted, I could find my birth mother.

In the beginning this was pretty much all I did: I was visiting my father in California, and he had taken my brother and me for brunch in nearby San Pedro. "Dad," I found myself saying over plates of Belgian waffles, "I was wondering. Do you know anything about the woman who gave birth to me?" The question had just come out, before I had a chance to feel any nervousness about asking. I was surprised to hear myself say it, because the truth is I had not been wondering about my birth mother. But I was suddenly glad I had asked and excited to hear his answer.

That I had asked did not appear to surprise my father; from his reaction, you might have thought I was asking what he knew about the man who did his taxes. It was the first time I heard her name. "Well, she was called Harriet Lund. She was from Sweden. Your mother and I met her a couple of times for lunch at the Hamburger Hamlet in Westwood," he said, naming a restaurant I had been to many times in high school. "But we didn't know her too well. I think she had a master's degree in child psychology or something like that. She worked at—I think it was called the Kennedy Child Study Center at St. John's Hospital up in Santa Monica." She had been about twenty-seven at the time, unmarried, and had come to the United States from Sweden a few years earlier. He remembered hearing that she had gone back there.

25 Trying to conceal my excitement at this sudden, unexpected venting of information, I pressed for details. She was a "very attractive" woman, he thought. He and my mother had met Harriet Lund for lunch in order to size each other up, the meeting having been arranged by a Beverly Hills attorney named Anthony Carsola, who specialized in adoption.

"What about," I began hesitantly, "the man who got her pregnant?"

"Well, we didn't meet him," said my father. "I think he worked with Harriet, there at the Kennedy Child Study Center." Swedish too? I asked. Or Irish American, as I thought my mother had mentioned? No, said my father, he had understood that the man was an American of German descent. And that was all. My father had told me everything he knew, or remembered, or wished to remember.

I will not say I was transformed by this conversation. When we got back to the house I wrote the name of my birth mother on a slip of paper, so as not to forget it. And I walked down Palos Verdes Drive to see Bennett Schneir, who was visiting his own parents for a day or two. I immediately told him what I had learned and wondered aloud whether I might call this Kennedy Child Study Center and find out if she still worked there or, if not, where she had gone after 1965. I could then travel to wherever she was and just *look* at her. Maybe, I imagined, I would knock on her door, say my car had broken down, and ask to use her phone to call the Triple A.

Shortly afterward I went back to the East Coast and forgot all about calling the Kennedy Child Study Center.

30 IT REMAINS TO MAKE clear what any of these matters—heart fears, old things, the idea of learning about my birth mother—has to do with the others.

At the time these subjects were on my mind, I was not alone in pondering them. This is not to say that other people were concerned about my personal history or about my birth mother; they were concerned about their own. In my old preoccupation with authenticity I had company. A professor in England, David Lowenthal, recently published a book whose title summarizes a trend in global culture: *Possessed by the Past.* As Lowenthal argues, people the world over have become obsessed with what he calls "heritage" but can also be called authenticity: not history, exactly, but the past in such manifestations as can be put to use fulfilling very present-day needs.

Authenticity and heritage can take the form of the sublime or the ridiculous, but they gravitate to the ridiculous. Shoppers in the late eighties and early nineties constantly came across articles of clothing or other personal or household items marketed as "authentic." This meant new items that had been designed to look either ragged and old or like items sold decades ago but preserved in mint condition: "fossil authentic" wristwatches, old-fashioned "authentic chinos" from Dockers based on a model worn by soldiers in World War Two, Ralph Lauren khaki pants labeled "Authentic Dry Goods," J. Crew denim shirts described in the catalog as "like shirts from old photos," clothing from the Gap in "classic" styles labeled "Authentic" and "Traditional," "distressed" blue jeans simulating years of wear, "distressed" jewelry from Donna Karan intended to look like military dog tags that survived World War One, and other miscellaneous stuff like copper candle sticks from the Pottery Barn patinaed in green as if from decades of use.

In film, the mid-1990s were notable for the popularity of precisely researched costume dramas—Merchant-Ivory knockoffs, multiple renditions of Jane Austen novels,

Little Women, Restoration, Jane Eyre, and so on—in which, a *New York Times* critic noted, "grand homes, furnishings, costumes, and hair styles take leading roles. . . . You don't doubt for an instant that each place setting is correct to the decade, if not the year." In the performance of classical music, a movement toward the use of original instruments has been in force for thirty years or so. In architecture and building design, new is out and old is decidedly in. The latest sky scraper to be built in Manhattan, the Four Seasons Hotel, gives the impression of an art deco tomb. Meanwhile actual old buildings, which in previous decades had been modernized, were being restored to their original appearance, sometimes with lovely results, such as the dinosaur galleries at New York's American Museum of Natural History, in which all the architectural details of the elaborate original design were revealed after being hidden for decades under plaster walls and lowered ceilings. Old buildings that have not been tampered with have lately come under the stewardship of conservationists determined to see that the structures never will be altered or, heaven forbid, torn down. Those seeking to fill new or old buildings with new furniture increasingly turn to copying styles of a century ago, as in the revival of the Arts and Crafts style that flourished originally at the turn of the century.

We are like Major-General Stanley in *The Pirates of Penzance*, a social climber who bought an ancient estate, including a chapel with tombs. Showing off the "family" chapel, he boasts: "In this chapel are ancestors: you cannot deny that. With the estate, I bought the chapel and its contents. I don't know whose ancestors they *were*, but I know whose ancestors they *are*." He is, he asserts, their "descendant by purchase."

It is not only other people's history that we have been seeking. It is also our own history. By 1988, the year I am writing about now, I had made only minimal attempts to find out about my biological heritage. Compared with a lot of other people, I was behind the curve. Authenticity has to do not only with jeans, but with genes.

As David Lowenthal notes, in previous decades and centuries the interest in discovering and documenting one's ancestors was confined to elderly aunts and blue-blooded aristocrats. Since the 1970s, that interest has been democratized. Visit your local branch of the National Archives, where microfilmed U.S. Census documents are kept, and you will see microfilm machines crowded with men and women of all ages, races, and ethnicities. Online bulletin boards devoted to genealogy likewise overflow with folks seeking the history of their blood. "All at once heritage is everywhere," writes Lowenthal. "Millions now hunt their roots, protect beloved scenes, cherish mementos, and generally dote on the past."

The 1970s also saw the beginning of another back-to-roots movement: among adults who as children had been adopted by families unrelated to them by blood. My blossoming interest in finding my birth mother was an interest shared by thousands of other adoptees. According to Betty Jean Lifton, a writer and an adoptee, before 1975 there was no history of "reunions" between birth parents and adopted children. Today, David Lowenthal estimates, almost half of adoptees attempt to locate their natural parents. He quotes one twenty-eight-year-old: "To feel that I'm *authentic*, I need to be like every other human being who knows where he came from and where he belongs." Recently the adoptee-return phenomenon has spun off a movement among people who grew up knowing their birth mother but not their birth father, the latter having merely donated his sperm through a sperm bank or other anonymous medium. *The*

New York Times Magazine devoted a cover story to sperm donors who are being tracked down by their biological children.

CLEARLY SOMETHING HAS changed in the atmosphere of American life to cause so many of us to long for "heritage" and "authenticity," but what? An answer is hinted at by a verse in Psalms. The concept of heritage entered Western thinking in the Bible. In Psalm 16 it is understood as a gift from God: the "goodly heritage" for which David thanked the Lord. Of course, other ancient peoples were familiar with the idea of a heritage in the sense of an inheritance of material goods left by a father ordinarily to his sons. However, the heritage that was most important to the Jews of the Bible consisted not of gold and silver, but of something metaphysical: namely the Covenant between God and the Jews. Knowledge of this Covenant was passed from parents to children. Parents taught Torah to their children, who taught it to their children. Both parents participated in this act of intergenerational transmission; but as in many other areas, Judaism assumes a division of labor.

Traditional Jews lay great stress on the idea that the status of a Jew as a Jew is passed from mother to children; but the father has an equally important role. In the Pentateuch, God instructs Moses to conduct censuses of the Israelites "according to their fathers' household." These were censuses by tribe, and tribal status was determined by a child's father. Commenting on Numbers 26:2 and citing the Talmud, Rashi states that "by the tribe of their father they shall trace their genealogy, and not by [that of] the mother." In the wilderness, the Jews encamped according to which of the tribes of Israel they belonged to. When they entered the Land of Israel, each tribe was assigned to a portion of it. So tribal membership was significant, but what does it mean?

As Rabbi Daniel Lapin points out, the Hebrew word for male, *zachor*, shares a root with the Hebrew word for memory, *zachar*. Whereas the nation of Israel as a whole is defined by race, the tribe signifies culture and, more important, history. A mother conveys race; and for reasons of His own, God determined that a father should convey history, memory. In *Mishneh Torah*, his codification of Jewish law, Maimonides considers this idea important enough to allude to it in the first chapter, second sentence, of his division "Torah Study": "A father is obligated to teach his son Torah. . . . A woman is not obligated to teach her son." The principal content of Jewish memory is the Covenant, standing at Mt. Sinai and receiving the two Torahs from God. When a Jew compiles his genealogy, he counts the links in the chain connecting him to Sinai.

The relationship between all this and the authenticity/heritage movement should be coming clear. Obviously most of the hundreds of thousands of roots seekers in America are gentiles, but the underlying principles of Torah do not apply only to Jews. When the Torah establishes the connection of genealogy, especially patrilineal genealogy, to the memory of revelation, this has a universal significance. All people receive their knowledge of God from their parents, who received it from their parents, who received it from their parents. It may sound like a stretch to say that those of us who have lately found ourselves with a craving for roots are really in search of something else: namely, God. Surely, though, the hunger for authenticity, like a hunger for food or water, arises from a lack of *something*. What do we lack that our great-grandparents possessed in abundance?

When we recall the past thirty or forty years under the perspective of world history, it becomes apparent that we have experienced no truly unprecedented changes—except for one. Since the 1950s God has been banished from public life. In the United States the change has been vivid. By Supreme Court fiat, children may not pray in public schools. Crèches are forbidden on public land. In many places landlords are forbidden to bring their religious convictions to bear in choosing tenants and must rent to anyone who can pay regardless of the sexual lifestyle he intends to carry on in the rented apartment. Employees are fired for displaying pictures of Jesus or quotations from the Bible above their desks at work.

Such legal reformations, or deformations, mirror an evolution in the rules of polite public discourse. God and religion are rarely depicted in the news and entertainment media except as objects of doubt and scorn. In other areas, such as politics and academia, public figures who purport to be sympathetic to religion often refer to it as if it were merely a useful fiction rather than the expression of God's relationship with humanity. Republicans like Bob Dole and Dan Quayle, linked in the media with the nefarious forces of the Christian Right, praise religion as a helpful force in subjugating the evil impulse of their fellow citizens, but in public they rarely speak of God Himself as a Living Being. Even the Christian Right itself has been secularized, its legislative priorities consisting mainly of practical issues like tax reform and school vouchers.

If our Father in heaven does indeed live, then this is not a natural situation, any more than it is natural for a child to be out of contact with his mortal parents. Freud wrote of the tendency of repressed instincts to express themselves under the cloak of a disguise. Just as my interest in knowing something about my birth mother could not be suppressed forever, neither can the spiritual hunger of men and women be denied without some consequence. For the past few years feature reporters in newspapers and magazines have reported, half in wonder and half in horror, the stirrings of a religious revival in the United States; and though this revival remains inchoate, mixing elements of traditional faith with flakier New Age notions, it would be hard to deny that it is under way. What's less certain is that the desire to know God only recently began to move itself in American hearts. More likely the spiritual instinct has been stirring among secularized Americans for decades. Possibly it has been doing so in the form of the movement toward heritage and authenticity.

45 HERE IS ANOTHER REASON to link the past with God. Most of us sense that reliable knowledge about the transcendent force in the universe cannot be arrived at in our spare time by speculation or meditation. Rabbi Abraham Joshua Heschel drew a distinction between mystical knowledge of God and prophetic knowledge. In one, knowledge of God is sought by man; in the other, God seeks out man. In the Jewish tradition there is an ancient belief in knowledge through mystical practices. These are said to have been passed down from the first human, Adam, who received them from God. Two thousand years ago in Palestine and a thousand years later in Babylon, Jewish scholars employed the system called "Chariot" mysticism to experience an ascent through the seven palaces of heaven. In thirteenth-century Spain the practice was to enter a darkened room lit only by candles, don tefillin and tallit, and contemplate the

letters in the esoteric Name of God. If the disciple was worthy, he could experience the Divine Light, and mysteries of God and His Kingdom would reveal themselves.

Jews continue to practice mysticism and seek out firsthand knowledge of God. But so do a lot of other people, as they have for millennia, and the awkward thing about mystical knowledge is that mystics have discovered widely divergent spiritual "facts" about God. Nothing, for instance, could be farther from Judaism than New Age mystical pantheism, with its belief that divinity is in everything except maybe in God.

If reliable knowledge of Him is what we want, then we must look elsewhere, and as Heschel argued, the prophetic tradition is the only conceivable source. In prophecy, God made it his custom to descend suddenly on the soul of a man, unexpected and unsought after, in a moment of terror and anguish, and communicate through him to the rest of humanity. Beginning with Moses at Sinai, that tradition speaks in one voice. Or rather the tradition *spoke*, for Jews and Christians agree that it has ceased temporarily. Prophecy is of the past. The prophet Malachi assures us that God will eventually send the prophet Elijah "before the coming of the great and dreadful day of the Lord," when prophecy will resume. Meanwhile it should come as no surprise if in our era the repressed longing for God roused itself and sought expression, disguised as a longing for the past.

That is, I believe, what lay behind my own preoccupation with old things and my new interest in knowing about my birth mother. The first preoccupation I mentioned in this chapter, my hypochondria, tends to confirms that.

The first time I feared mortal illness was in the middle of my mother's sickness. It was halfway through my senior year at Miraleste when I suddenly found it difficult to walk. My legs felt stiff all the time, and I worried that my mother's bone cancer had leaped across the house into my own bones. A few years later, at Brown, I began to worry about throat cancer. For a while I worried about brain tumors. Then came my heart and the concern that it wasn't working right.

I have forgotten my several psychotherapists' explanations of this, the relation they posited between my health fears and my mother's illness and death. But a rabbi's explanation stuck with me. I was visiting Rabbi Daniel Lapin at his home near Seattle in 1996, and one morning we got onto the subject of hypochondria. He opened a Bible to Deuteronomy, in which (7:12–15) Moses prophesies about the blessings the Israelites will receive if they hearken to the Torah and its commandments. One blessing is bodily health: "The Lord will remove from you every illness; and all the evil maladies of Egypt that you knew. He will not set them upon you, but will set them upon your foes."

In fact Moses was speaking not of the world we live in today, but of the redeemed world we will inherit after Elijah returns. Even so, Rabbi Lapin explained, a connection exists between Torah in our time and the *perception* of health. He next opened the Talmud's tractate Eruvin to a puzzling statement from Rabbi Joshua ben Levi: "When a man fears [illness] because of [a pain in] his head, let him occupy himself with Torah. . . . When a man fears because of his throat, let him occupy himself with Torah. . . . When he fears because of his innards, let him occupy himself with Torah." This rabbi from the second century C.E. was not anticipating Christian Science, the view that bodily ills can be cured through faith alone. A better way to understand the teaching, said Rabbi Lapin, is this: If a man is sick, let him go to a doctor. But if he is merely *worried* about his head, *worried* about his throat, *worried* about his innards, *then* "let him occupy himself with Torah."

"If you were fixing a hole in your wall," said Rabbi Lapin, "you would call in some workmen. They would spend hours working on the problem, and they would create a huge mess in the meantime. You might wander into the room where the hole was, see the dollar signs flashing before your eyes, and wish you'd never hired them in the first place. You brought them into your home to fix a problem, and here they are, turning a little hole into an enormous mess! Spiritual growth works in much the same way."

When did you first begin to worry that you were going to die from some terrible disease? he asked. My senior year in high school, I said. And when did you "convert" yourself? (He knew that story.) Around the same time, I said.

At that moment the clouds parted a little for me. It was true that my hypochondria ran a course parallel to my growing interest in Judaism. Rabbi Joshua had anticipated not Christian Science, but rather my own peculiar symptoms and very likely the symptoms of a lot of other people. Spiritual growth, he was saying, brings with it what you might call growing pains.

The Torah is God's plan for the Jews. The realization that God has a plan for you, and that you do not know what it is, produces a kind of distress that can manifest itself in any number of ways, including somatic distress. What is the solution? "Occupy yourself with Torah."

Today I still don't know enough Torah. But I have some idea of how much I do not know. In 1988 I had no such idea. Like the many other seekers of authenticity and heritage, I had no sense of what it was that would satisfy the hunger I felt. I didn't know I was hungry for God. It would take a Christian to tell me that.

Exploring Text and Contexts

For activities with icons, refer to the Guide to Analyzing Readings in Context.

1. This chapter from Klinghoffer's book falls into four fairly distinct sections. In a small group, identify and briefly describe each section, focusing in particular on the different perspective each part offers on the nature of authenticity. Then discuss how the different parts relate to each other and how they work together to make a coherent whole. Does this piece have a single unifying thesis? If so, what is it, and how do the four parts work in different ways to develop that thesis?

Situation

2. The four sections of the chapter all draw on very different aspects of Klinghoffer's background and experiences—the contexts out of which he wrote this essay—and the references and vocabulary change accordingly, especially in the first and last sections. Write in your journal about the different kinds of knowledge and experience that Klinghoffer draws upon in these different sections. Then think about the different kinds of knowledge and experience that you might draw upon in writing an essay on authenticity.

Creating Texts

For activities with icons, refer to Guides to Analyzing Contexts for Writing and Analyzing Readings in Context. For additional help with these writing projects, read the descriptions of **Opinion Piece** and **Personal Essay** in the Genre Glossary.

1. Klinghoffer's comment that "Authenticity has to do not only with jeans, but with genes" (page 126) might be taken as a comment on the phenomenon described in Nell Bernstein's "Goin' Gangsta, Choosin' Cholita" or in Marc Spiegler's "Marketing Street Culture." Imagine that Klinghoffer reads one of these articles and decides to write an opinion piece for the *National Review* about the phenomenon described in the article. What would Klinghoffer say? In addition to rereading the chapter from Klinghoffer's book, you might want to do some research on the *National Review*. What kinds of issues does the magazine typically address, and what kind of perspective does it usually take? Be careful, though; don't jump too quickly to conclusions about the perspective Klinghoffer might take. Remember that he doesn't say, "Authenticity has to do with genes, not jeans" and that he himself is very interested in the relationship between fashion and authenticity. Situation
2. This chapter from Klinghoffer's book in many ways exemplifies what we often call the personal essay, in that it intricately interweaves personal narrative/description and general commentary about an issue. Drawing upon the notes from your group discussion in Exploring Texts and Contexts Activity 1, for ideas about organization, and your journal entry in Exploring Texts and Contexts Activity 2, for ideas about content, write an essay in which you relate your own experiences with and questions about authenticity to some of the larger social issues raised in this reading and throughout this chapter. Genre

CHAPTER 5

CASE STUDY

Contesting the Ownership of Music

The Case

If you're a college student, listen to music, and have a computer, you probably remember the controversies over Napster and Kazaa, the programs that allow users to download music for free from the Internet and that were challenged in court by musicians and record companies who argued that their music was being stolen. You probably also know that these programs were not the first technological innovation to cause controversy over the ownership of music. The practice of sampling—incorporating bits of recorded music by other musicians into one's own songs—has also been the subject of legal challenges, most famously in the 2 Live Crew case, in which the Supreme Court ruled in 1994 that the sampling was legal under the Fair Use clause of the U.S. Copyright Act. But you might not be aware that others have contested the ownership of music not just to make money but to make an artistic and political point. Here we look at the Negativland/U2 case in order to raise questions about art, ownership, and authenticity.

Negativland is a group of musicians who create works of art that make extensive use of already-recorded words and music from songs, advertisements, radio and television broadcasts, and other sources. Their work usually comments in some way on technology, the media, business, and mass consumer culture. In 1990 Negativland created a 13-minute single that included, among other things, computer-modified segments of the song "I Still Haven't Found What I'm Looking For," by the Irish rock group U2, and other sampled bits related to the song and the music industry in general. Negativland did not obtain permission to use any of this material, and in August 1991—a few months before the real U2 was expected to release its album *Achtung Baby*—they released the single under the title "U2," in packaging that featured a picture of a U2 spy plane superimposed over a large letter U and number 2, and with their name, Negativland, printed across the bottom. Almost immediately, the record company and publishers of the band U2, Island Records and Warner-Chappell Music, filed a suit against Negativland and its record company, SST Records. A judge issued a restraining order requiring SST to recall and turn over all copies of the single and the original tapes and artwork, pay damages and legal costs, and publish explanations and apologies. A se-

ries of complex legal maneuvers followed in the next few years, but Negativland has never been able to recover and release the copies of the single.

The Issues

The two central legal issues here are the concepts of copyright and fair use. Island Records/Warner Chappell base their legal arguments on the principle of copyright. One purpose of copyright laws is to protect the creative work of writers, composers, and other artists from intellectual and commercial exploitation by giving them exclusive control over their work for a specified period. To use all or a part of a copyrighted work, one must obtain permission from the holder of the copyright and often pay a fee. But the concept of copyright creates a tension. While the purpose of copyright laws is to protect writers, composers, and other artists, a very strict interpretation of the laws puts severe restrictions on anyone who wants to use copyrighted material. The concept of fair use, on which Negativland based its arguments, was developed to balance the needs of copyright holders against the needs of members of the public, in particular critics, reporters, researchers, scholars, and teachers, as well as other writers and artists. The fair use clause of the 1976 United States Copyright Act stipulates that in certain situations copyrighted material can be used without permission or fees. But, like most legal concepts and most laws, the fair use clause and the Copyright Act itself contain ambiguities, places where the law is open to different interpretations, thus requiring lawsuits and trials to clarify how the law should be applied.

The Negativland case illustrates the complexities involved in discussing authenticity in contemporary art and entertainment, especially popular music. Some critics of contemporary culture have suggested that traditional ideas about art and authenticity are no longer applicable when words, images, and sounds can be almost endlessly reproduced and distributed. This problem was noticed as far back as the 1930s in a famous essay, "The Work of Art in the Age of Mechanical Reproduction," which asked what would happen to the "aura" of unique works of art when photography and other techniques could make unlimited copies of an image.[1] In our time, digital technology has multiplied this copying ability so vastly and complexly that the very idea of originality is thrown into question; as cultural critic Mary Poovey says of the rock concert experience,

> [T]he familiarity of the art object [the album, album art, or music video] so completely anticipates the experience that the "event" as such only exists as a repetition, and there is never an "original," not even in the moment of supreme presence, the moment of performance itself.[2]

But what if we redefine both art and authenticity to fit with the technological conditions of our age? Rap music, with its use of sampling, might be considered one such redefinition. But this redefinition still leaves many questions about art, ownership, and technology unanswered. The case of *Island Records/Warner-Chappell Music vs. Negativland* allows us to explore some of these questions.

At the heart of the Negativland case, under layers of legal principles and arguments, is a set of claims and counterclaims about authenticity. One of the arguments against Negativland was that their work was not authentic art because it was not an original creation but rather a pastiche of things, some of them created by other, "authentic" artists. In their analysis of the case, cultural critics Andrew Herman and John Sloop argue that Negativland built their defense by redefining authenticity as "free appropriation" rather than individual expression:

> While Negativland initially attempted to defend itself using the logic of romantic authenticity (the artist as free-standing author of his/her own ideas, created solely by him or her), this logic was certain to fail as it could—and was—effectively deployed against the band's own practices, given that their performances are reassemblages of fragmented discourses.[3]

We can see this defense in Negativland's claim that

> Our work is an authentic and original "whole," being much more than the sum of its samples. This is not a form of "bootlegging" intending to profit from the commercial potential of the subjects appropriated. The law must come to terms with distinguishing the difference between economic intent and artistic intent.[4]

Herman and Sloop argue further that Negativland sees this new definition of authenticity as a necessary response to the problems caused by the "postmodern landscape" of unlimited reproduction and circulation of images.

---

[1]Walter Benjamin. *Illuminations.* Edited by Hannah Arendt. New York: Schocken Books, 1969, pp. 217–251.

[2]Mary Poovey. "Cultural Criticism: Past and Present." *College English* 52, p. 615.

[3]Andrew Herman and John Sloop. "The Politics of Authenticity in Postmodern Rock Culture: The Case of Negativland and The Letter 'U' and the Numeral '2'." *Critical Studies in Mass Communication* 15 (March 1998), p. 5.

[4]Negativland. "Tenets of Free Appropriation." *Fair Use: The Story of the Letter U and the Numeral 2.* Concord, CA: Seeland, 1995, p. 251.

The Documents

- The first document in the case study is the **lyrics of U2's "I Still Haven't Found What I'm Looking For"** from the 1987 album *The Joshua Tree.*
- Periodicals in the music industry and counterculture began covering the Negativland story in September 1991, just after the lawsuit was filed, but by December the mainstream press also picked up the story nationally. This ***Washington Post* article, "U2's Double Trouble" by Richard Harrington,** explains the case and the issues involved. Note which passages it quotes from the two documents that follow. After reading the next two documents, think about how you would have presented the story and the issues. What passages would you have chosen to quote?
- The next document is an **excerpt from the Island/Warner-Chappell Lawsuit** requesting a restraining order that would require SST Records to recall all copies of the single and turn them over to Island Records and Warner-Chappell Music. As you read the excerpts from this legal document, note how the lawyers build their argument and how they explicitly or implicitly define art in the process of making their case. How does the style of legal writing shape the way the case is made?
- Negativland and its record company were represented by lawyers in court, but Negativland also took its wider argument to the public in a variety of ways, for example in **"U2 Negativland: The Case from Our Side,"** a press release sent out soon after the case was filed. Compare Negativland's style of argument and implied definition of art with those in the Island Records/Warner-Chappell legal brief. What similarities and differences do you see?
- Both the Island Records/Warner-Chappell legal brief and the Negativland press release refer to the U.S. Copyright Act of 1976. Negativland makes particular reference to the fair use clause of the Copyright Act, included in the excerpt. As you read this **excerpt of the Copyright Act,** in particular the fair use clause, consider which parts of it seem ambiguous—open to different interpretations—and how these ambiguities might turn on assumptions about art and ownership.
- Since the court did not accept Negativland's underlying interpretation of fair use, Negativland took its argument directly to the public. In December 1993, they published a statement of their position in a guest commentary in *Billboard Magazine.* The following March, two music business executives published a response. This exchange of commentaries, **"In Fair Use Debate, Art Must Come First"** and Andrian Adams and Paul McKibbins' **"Sampling Without Permission Is Theft,"** presents two very different perspectives on art, ownership, and, by implication, authenticity. As you reach this point in the case study, you should be developing your own perspective on these questions. Where do you stand in relation to the positions presented by Negativland on the one hand and Adams and McKibbins on the other?
- Keep in mind that this case unfolded in 1993. Much has happened in the world of music and technology since then—for example the development of MP3 technology and the controversies over Napster and Kazaa—and your perspective is probably influenced by these developments. A software review in *Rolling Stone* magazine, **"Build a**

Desktop Studio," describes just one of these developments. **"RTMARK Finds Bucks for Beck Rip-off,"** a press release from the group ®RTMARK, suggests that the Negativland tradition of musical subversion continues. What other developments along these lines do you know of, and how do these developments influence your own ideas about art, ownership, and authenticity?

YOUR ROLE

The following writing projects are designed to help you think through the issues raised by the Negativland case, using writing both as a form of action and as a means of reflection. On the one hand we ask you to imagine yourself participating as someone who is immediately and actively affected by these issues, which some of you may indeed be. For example, you may be sampling some other Web pages in order to build your own home page. What kinds of artistic, ethical, and legal questions would you have to confront? In the first activity that follows, you write about the practical implications of these issues on your own campus. Another way of participating is as a critic or other thoughtful observer. In the second activity you analyze the larger issues suggested by this case study.

1. Your college probably has policies and codes of conduct related to the legal and ethical issues raised by the Negativland case, for example policies on downloading music and codes of conduct regarding plagiarism, the unacknowledged use of someone else's ideas or words. Do some research on those policies and on students' observation of and attitudes toward these policies, and write an opinion piece for your campus paper in which you express an opinion on those policies, students' observation of them, and your school's enforcement of them. As part of your argument, discuss what you see as the similarities and differences between sampling and other copyright violations, the illegal downloading of music, and academic plagiarism, perhaps in particular plagiarism involving online resources. (See **Opinion Piece** in the Genre Glossary.)
2. Write an essay exploring the nature of art, ownership, and authenticity, drawing upon the case study, as well as any other events, phenomena, or materials you find useful. Use the documents in the case study to help you think carefully about the relationship between ownership and authenticity in the context of art. You might consider how these terms have been traditionally defined and how this case study does or does not change your own definitions of these terms. Remember that you must consider the concepts of ownership and authenticity from the perspectives of both art and law. Working closely with the case study documents, consider how these perspectives influence, conflict with, or help define each other. (See **Essay** in the Genre Glossary.)

The Joshua Tree

I Still Haven't Found What I'm Looking For

I have climbed the highest mountains
I have run through the fields
Only to be with you
Only to be with you

I have run I have crawled
I have scaled these city walls
Only to be with you

But I still haven't found what I'm looking for
But I still haven't found what I'm looking for

I have kissed honey lips
Felt the healing in her fingertips
It burned like fire
This burning desire
I have spoke with the tongue of angels
I have held the hand of a devil
It was warm in the night
I was cold as a stone

But I still haven't found what I'm looking for
But I still haven't found what I'm looking for

I believe in the Kingdom Come
Then all the colours will bleed into one
But yes I'm still running

You broke the bonds
You loosed the chains
You carried the cross
And my shame
And my shame
You know I believe it

But I still haven't found what I'm looking for
But I still haven't found what I'm looking for

From U2, *The Joshua Tree.* Island Records, Ltd., 1987.

U2's Double Trouble

Richard Harrington, Washington Post Staff Writer

U2, whose new "Achtung, Baby" opened at the top of Billboard's album chart, has stomped down hard on California agitpopsters Negativland, which in September released a single titled "U2" that incorporated smidgens of the Irish group's hit "I Still Haven't Found What I'm Looking For." Island Records, to which U2 is signed, and Warner-Chappell Music, U2's publisher, filed suit against Negativland and SST Records, charging deceptive advertising, copyright infringement and "image defamation." Island and SST settled last month.

Indeed, Negativland's 12-inch single features a huge letter "U" and numeral "2" occupying 90 percent of its cover; there's also the shadow of the famous spy plane. "Negativland" is printed at the bottom. Indeed, the group, which has been in existence almost as long as U2, did not get (or seek) permission to sample the original. Indeed, U2's lyrics are drolly recited, the melody is solemnly hummed by a male chorus, and both elements are incorporated into the kind of socially sharp sound collage Negativland is know for (albeit in very small circles). Anybody but U2 and its lackeys would have a hard time not laughing at what Negativland calls "a work of art . . . created as parody, satire, social commentary and cultural criticism."

Right now, though, Negativland and SST are not laughing. The settlement requires all distributors that received the record be notified to return it; if they don't, or engage in "selling, advertising, promoting or otherwise exploiting" the record, they are subject to penalties, "which may include imprisonment and fines."

Once all copies are returned, SST must deliver them to Island, which will destroy them along with all of SST's on-hand stock. All artwork is also to be turned over to Island, which has been assigned the copyright to the song "U2" (with Warner- Chappell). SST also had to fork over $25,000 and half the wholesale proceeds from copies sold or not returned—SST estimates the settlement's total cost at $70,000, "more money than we've made in our 10 years of existence," the label said in a statement. SST said it settled the suit because it feared "the tremendous costs in fighting for our rights in court."

Eric Levine, senior director of business affairs for Island, said: "Record companies' primary assets are rights—copyrights, exclusive rights for recording services, names, trademarks etc. When certain of those rights were violated, we felt we had no choice but to act swiftly and, apparently, successfully."

One of the complaints in Island's original suit was that U2 fans might confuse Negativland's "U2" with "Achtung, Baby" and that SST would "be free to flood the shelves of record stores . . . creating massive confusion among the record-buying public." In fact, SST had shipped out 7,643 copies of "U2," and none of the five Negativland albums has sold more than 15,000 copies ("Achtung, Baby" sold 295,000 copies in its first week on the market).

"Our single deals, in part, with our perception of the group U2 as an international cultural phenomenon, and therefore particularly worthy

(continued)

From *The Washington Post,* December 18, 1991, Style section p. B7.

of artistic comment and criticism," the band noted in a statement. "Island's legal action thoroughly ignores the possibility that any such artistic rights or inclination might exist. Apparently Island's sole concern in this act of censorship is their determination to control the marketplace, as if the only reason to make records is to make money."

The Negativland/SST statement also insists that claiming economic gain as the sole criterion for legal deliberation "is to admit that music itself is not to be taken seriously. Culture is more than commerce. It may actually have something to say about commerce. It may even use examples of commerce to comment upon it."

The four members of Negativland explain their approach as "recontextualizing captured fragments to create something entirely new—a psychological impact based on a new juxtaposition of diverse elements, ripped from their usual context."

In terms of sampling, which remains one of pop culture's great unresolved issues, Negativland claims "fair use . . . as it was used for purposes of fair comment, parody and cultural criticism, which the copyright law specifically allows." As for the cover art, "Island's inference that U2 fans might actually assume that we are them upon hearing our record is simply ridiculous on the face of it, and another indication of their lack of respect for their own audience."

The original Island complaint also noted that U2 "has cultivated a clean-cut image, and its recordings never include expletives, curses and scatological language"—a reference to a bootlegged comment about U2 by Casey Kasem that can be heard on the Negativland single—"which will undoubtedly anger and upset parents of youngsters who purchase the 'U2 Negativland' record." Ironically, the back cover of "Achtung, Baby's" CD booklet had to be censored because it contained a frontal nude photo of bassist Adam Clayton. A discreet X was added.

Excerpts from the Island/Warner-Chappell Lawsuit

MILGRIM THOMAJAN & LEE
DANIAEL H. WILLICK, ESQ. (Cal. State Bar No. 58643)
2049 Century Park East, Suite 3350
Los Angeles, California 90067
(213) 282-0899

MILGRIM THOMAJAN & LEE P.C.
CHARLES B. ORTNER, ESQ.
53 Wall Street
New York, New York 10005-2815
(212) 858-5300

Attorneys for Plaintiffs

UNITES STATES DISTRICT COURT

CENTRAL DISTRICT OF CALIFORNIA

ISLAND RECORDS LTD. (a United Kingdom Corporation), ISLAND RECORDS, INC. (a New York corporation), WARNER CHAPPELL MUSIC INTERNATIONAL LTD., (a United Kingdom corporation), and WARNER/CHAPPELL MUSIC, INC. (a California corporation), Plaintiffs, vs.	Case No. CV 91-4735AAH (GHKx) DECLARATION OF ERIC LEVINE IN SUPPORT OF ORDER TO SHOW CAUSE, RE PRELIMINARY INJUNCTION, TEMPORARY RESTRAINING ORDER AND EXPEDITED DISCOVERY
SST RECORDS (an entity), SEELAND MEDIA-MEDIA (an entity), NEGATIVLAND (an entity), Gregory Ginn (an individual), Chris Grigg (an individual), Mark Hosler (an individual), Don Joyce (an individual), and David Wills (an individual), Defendants.	DATE: September ____, 1991 TIME: PLACE: Courtroom (Judge ____________________) Andrew A. Hauk

I.

PRELIMINARY STATEMENT

This Application seeks an *ex parte* temporary restraining order, preliminary injunction and related relief in order to halt the defendants' unlawful exploitation of a record entitled "U2 Negativland" by using deceptive and misleading packaging in violation of the plaintiffs' rights under Section 43(a) of the Lanham Trademark Act, 15 U.S.C. §1125(a), and by making unauthorized use of a sound recording and musical composition in violation of the rights of certain plaintiffs under the Copyright Act of 1976, as amended (the "Copyright Act"), 17 U.S.C. §101, *et. seq.*

The plaintiffs include (a) the affiliated record companies (Island Records Ltd. and Island Records, Inc.) which have the exclusive rights throughout the world to manufacture, distribute and sell (either directly or through authorized licensees) sound

(continued)

Excerpts from *Island/Warner-Chappell (Plaintiffs) vs. SST/Seeland/Negativland et al.* lawsuit, Sept. 3, 1991. Reprinted in Negativland, *Fair Use: The Story of the Letter U and the Numeral 2.* Concord, CA: Seeland, 1995, pp. 4–20.

recordings embodying the performances by the renowned musical group known as "U2," and (b) the affiliated publishing companies (Warner Chappell Music International Ltd. and Warner/Chappell Music, Inc.) which, directly or through affiliated corporations and licensees, have the exclusive rights to publish and administer the copyrights in U2's musical compositions. Plaintiffs are exclusively entitled to use the band's well-known name and mark "U2" in connection with the exploitation of those rights.

The defendants are violating the plaintiffs' rights by selling or otherwise exploiting the "U2 Negativland" recording in interstate commerce using cover artwork, packaging and labelling which is so deceptive as to create the false impression that the recording is a genuine U2 record album. This unlawful conduct—which will deceive consumers into believing that when they purchase "U2 Negativland" they are buying an album by U2—constitutes a violation of Section 43(a) of the Lanham Trademark Act, which prohibits the use of false and misleading packaging which may tend to deceive consumers.

Plaintiffs Island Records Ltd. and Island Records, Inc. have publicized the imminent release of U2's next record album. The defendants' "U2 Negativland" recording constitutes a transparent use of deceptive packaging designed to dupe U2's millions of fans throughout the United States into believing that this "new record" is the widely-anticipated new album by U2. It is not. "U2 Negativland" is nothing less than a consumer fraud, and a blatantly unlawful attempt to usurp the anticipated profits and goodwill to which plaintiffs are entitled from the exploitation of recordings and musical compositions by U2.

Moreover, one of the two songs contained in the "U2 Negativland" recording incorporates an unauthorized copy of a portion of U2's recording of the song "I Still Haven't Found What I'm Looking For," which is part of U2's hit album entitled "The Joshua Tree," released in 1987. The second song contains an unauthorized and mutilated instrumental version of "I Still Haven't Found What I'm Looking For" performed by persons other than U2. As discussed below, defendants' unauthorized use of the foregoing U2 recording and musical composition constitutes infringement of the rights of two of the plaintiffs (as evidenced by Certificates of Copyright Registration issued by the United States Copyright Office) in violation of the Copyright Act.

To prevent the irreparable harm which plaintiffs will suffer from the violation of their rights under the Lanham Trademark Act and the Copyright Act, the defendants should be immediately restrained and enjoined from manufacturing, distributing, selling or otherwise exploiting "U2 Negativland." And, defendants should be required to immediately disclose certain information, discussed below, pertaining to the extent of their infringing activities (and the involvement, if any, by others), and to submit to expedited discovery to permit plaintiffs to prepare for a preliminary injunction hearing without delay.

I, Eric Levine, hereby declare and say as follows:

1. I am the Senior Director of Business Affairs of Island Records, Inc., one of the plaintiffs in this action. I submit this declaration on personal knowledge in support of the motion by plaintiffs, brought on by Order to Show Cause, for a Temporary Restraining Order and Preliminary Injunction to prohibit the defendants from manufacturing, copying, marketing, advertising, promoting, distributing, selling or otherwise exploiting a sound recording entitled "U2 Negativland" (or derivatives thereof) on the grounds that defendants' conduct constitutes a violation of the plaintiffs' rights under, among other things, Section 43(a) of the Lanham Act and the Copyright Act. Plaintiffs also seek certain other relief, including expedited discovery, described below.

2. As set forth in the Complaint (a copy of which is annexed hereto as Exhibit A), and as discussed below in greater detail, since 1980 Island Records, Inc. and its affiliate Island Records Ltd. (and their authorized licensees) have been manufacturing, marketing, promoting, advertising and selling millions of records by the enormously popular recording group known as "U2" in the United States and abroad. The U2 band's name and trademark, "U2," have been prominently displayed on all album packaging, artwork and labels. The public has thus come to recognize and associate the name and

(continued)

mark "U2" with the band and its recordings released by Island Records, Inc., Island Records Ltd. and their authorized licensees.

3. Recently, plaintiffs learned that defendants* released a recording which, on the cover artwork packaging and record label (Exhibit B), is prominently labeled "U2 Negativland." "U2" is the dominant feature of the cover and label.** Defendants have falsely created the impression that "U2 Negativland" is a record album embodying performances by U2. On the face of the cover packaging artwork and labelling, it would appear to any consumer that "U2 Negativland" is a U2 recording, and nothing contained on the cover artwork or label indicates that it is not.

4. Such false and deceptive packaging and labelling is a clear violation of Section 43(a) of the Lanham Act, and the defendants should be restrained for that reason alone. However, as discussed below, the "U2 Negativland" recording also infringes the plaintiffs' copyrights, providing additional grounds upon which to restrain defendants from continued exploitation of "U2 Negativland."

BACKGROUND FACTS

5. Plaintiffs Island Records, Inc. (based in New York) and Island Records Ltd. (based in London) are affiliated companies. For ease of expression, both corporations and their authorized licensees will sometimes be referred to herein collectively as "Island Records."

6. Island Records has long been closely associated with the U2 band. Between 1980 and 1986, Island Records manufactured and distributed in the United States and abroad four long-playing albums, so-called "single" records, and two "extended play" recordings, prominently displaying the name and trademark "U2" on packaging, artwork and labels to denote that the recordings embodied the performances of the particular band known as "U2."

7. In 1987, Island Records released the band's album entitled "The Joshua Tree."*** That album—which was clearly labelled with the "U2" name and mark (see Exhibit C hereto, which is a copy of the compact disc packaging)—was released and distributed by Island Records throughout the world under a master sales agreement which granted Island Records the exclusive worldwide rights to U2's recordings, including the copyright and the exclusive right to use the band's name "U2" in connection with the exploitation of sound recordings.

8. "The Joshua Tree" album was an enormous artistic and commercial success. Island Records, Inc. sold over 5 million copies of that album in the United States alone, all clearly labelled "U2." Indeed, that was the first album in history to have been certified by the Record Industry Association of America as having sold at least one million copies in the "compact disc," or "CD," format.

9. The band's success was enhanced by the release of a single of U2's recording of one of "The Joshua Tree" album's songs—"I Still Haven't Found What I'm Looking For"—which was sold throughout the United States and abroad, and received widespread air-play on radio stations and television stations (including MTV).

10. The success of U2's "The Joshua Tree" album and U2's recording of "I Still Haven't Found What I'm Looking For" was highlighted when U2 was awarded a Grammy award on a nationwide award telecast in February 1989.

---

* Apparently, SST is a proprietorship owned by defendant Gregory Ginn, and affiliated with defendants Seeland MediaMedia and Negativland.

** The "U2 Negativland" recording is being distributed in interstate commerce. The copy obtained by plaintiffs, which alerted them to defendants' unlawful conduct, was purchased at a record store in Athens, Georgia.

*** As discussed below, SST (and apparently the other defendants) has recently unlawfully copied a portion of U2's recording of the song entitled "I Still Haven't Found What I'm Looking For" from "The Joshua Tree" album, and incorporated that unlawful and unauthorized copy into the "U2 Negativland" recording in violation of the Copyright Act.

(continued)

11. Thereafter, Island Records released throughout the world U2's next album, entitled "Rattle and Hum." That enormously successful album was also clearly labelled as a U2 recording (see copy of packaging for that album annexed hereto as Exhibit D).

12. Recently, numerous publications read by U2's fans, and the music industry trade press, have reported that U2 has completed a new album which will soon be released by Island Records. Annexed hereto as Exhibits E, F and G are copies of a few of the articles that have been published about the anticipated new U2 album. Given U2's enormous popularity, it is inescapable that U2's fans are anxiously awaiting the day when they will find U2's new album in record stores.

DEFENDANTS' INFRINGING ACTS

13. Island Records recently learned that the defendants, under the names SST Records and Seeland MediaMedia, have released a recording entitled "U2 Negativland." It is apparent that defendants are unlawfully seeking to capitalize upon U2's popularity and the anticipation by U2's fans of the release of U2's new album, by packaging and labelling the "U2 Negativland" recording in such a false, misleading and deceptive manner as to confuse consumers into believing that the defendants' recording is a "U2" album, which it is not.

14. As discussed above, Exhibit B hereto is a copy of the cover artwork for the "U2 Negativland" recording in the CD format, and the CD label itself.

15. On the face of the packaging artwork, it appears that the recording is an album by U2. Indeed, the name "U2" is displayed prominently on the cover, and nearly takes up the entire cover artwork. The cover clearly would lead any unsuspecting consumer into believing that SST's recording is a "U2" album, and nothing contained anywhere on the cover artwork or the CD label would disabuse a consumer of that erroneous belief.

16. Indeed, the artwork which appears on the reverse side of the cover, and the label on the CD itself, also fosters the false impression that "U2 Negativland" is a recording by U2 in at least two ways:

(a) First, the artwork identifies the song on the recording as "I Still Haven't Found What I'm Looking For"—the same title as one of the songs recorded by U2 on the band's "The Joshua Tree" album.

(b) Second, the inside packaging artwork and the CD label lists in two places the names of the members of U2—Paul Hewson, David Evans, Lawrence Mullen and Adam Clayton—falsely implying that the recording is by U2.

17. There can be no doubt that consumers will be deceived by the "U2 Negativland" artwork into falsely believing that it is a U2 album. Such false and deceptive packaging is precisely the kind of unfair and unlawful competition that Section 43(a) of the Lanham Act was designed to prohibit. Unless SST is immediately restrained and enjoined from further exploitation of "U2 Negativland," unwitting consumers will be duped into purchasing that record in the mistaken belief that it is the new U2 album.

18. The egregious nature of this consumer fraud is underscored by the content of the record itself, which contains only two songs (although the CD is deceptively packaged as an album, which in the popular record industry ordinarily contains approximately ten songs).

19. The first song is over seven minutes long. It contains approximately one minute's worth of portions of U2's recording of "I Still Haven't Found What I'm Looking For," unlawfully copied from "The Joshua Tree" album and incorporated into the "U2 Negativland" recording without the authorization or consent of Island Records.

20. In that regard, it should be emphasized that Island Records Ltd. is the proprietor throughout the world of the copyright in and to "The Joshua Tree" album, including U2's recording of "I Still Haven't Found What I'm Looking For." Accordingly, Island Records Ltd. obtained a Copyright Registration from the United States Copyright Office for the entire "The Joshua Tree" album. Annexed hereto as Exhibit H is a copy of the Certificate of Copyright Registration for the entire "The Joshua Tree" album as

(continued)

performed by U2—SR 78-949. This Certificate establishes, *prima facie,* that Island Records Ltd. is the copyright proprietor of U2's recordings contained in "The Joshua Tree" album, including U2's recording of the song entitled "I Still Haven't Found What I'm Looking For."

21. The unauthorized copying of a portion of U2's recording of "I Still Haven't Found What I'm Looking For," and incorporation of that recording into "U2 Negativland," constitutes a blatant case of copyright infringement. Under the Copyright Act, 17 U.S.C. § 101 *et seq.,* such infringement entitles Island Records to, among other things, a restraining order and injunction.

22. Equally outrageous is the content of the second song on the "U2 Negativland" recording. It is replete with expletives, curses and scatological language which many consumers will likely find offensive, and which will undoubtedly anger and upset parents of youngsters who purchase the "U2 Negativland" record.

23. It must be emphasized that U2 has cultivated a clean-cut image, and its recordings never include such language. The band's image will be tarnished, and the name and mark "U2" and the goodwill associated with it, will be substantially harmed as a result of defendants' deception which will lead consumers to purchase what they believe to be a U2 album, only to find a recording containing such lyrics.

24. "U2 Negativland" gives every indication that it is a U2 album, and there is nothing in the artwork or otherwise which indicates that that is not the case. Thus, some unwitting consumers, upon purchasing and listening to the "U2 Negativland" recording, might well conclude that U2 has made a poor quality and offensive recording, thus further unlawfully tarnishing the band's reputation and image, and the enormously valuable "U2" name and mark. This would undoubtedly diminish future sales of U2 recordings, to the detriment of both U2 and Island Records.

The Requested Relief

25. Plaintiffs have demonstrated a clear right to the injunctive relief which they seek in this action. There can be no doubt that the packaging, artwork, labeling and text employed by the defendants create the overwhelming impression that "U2 Negativland" is a recording by U2. There also can be no doubt that consumers will be confused by the prominent use of the name and mark "U2" on "U2 Negativland," and that the confusion and deception will be enhanced by defendants' use of the names of the members of U2 and the title of their hit song "I Still Haven't Found What I'm Looking For."

26. This strong showing of deceptive labeling and likelihood of confusion, compounded by a clear case of copyright infringement, establishes that plaintiffs will likely prevail on the merits.

27. Moreover, the balance of hardships tips decidedly in favor of the plaintiffs and against the defendants. If the requested injunctive relief is not granted, the defendants will be free to flood the shelves of record stores with the infringing recording on the eve of the release by Island Records of the new U2 album, thereby creating massive confusion among the record-buying public. Once the "horses" are out of the "barn door," the harm to Island Records will be done, and will be irreparable.

WHEREFORE, plaintiffs demand judgment against defendants, jointly and severally, as follows:

(1) Preliminarily and permanently enjoining and restraining the defendants, their officers, directors, agents, servants, employees, subsidiaries, affiliates, assigns, licensees, distributees, attorneys and all persons in active concert or participation with them or in privity with them from (a) manufacturing, distributing, promoting, advertising, marketing, selling or otherwise exploiting the sound recording entitled and labelled "U2 Negativland" or any derivatives thereof, or otherwise affixing or utilizing the name and mark "U2" in connection with any goods or services furnished by or on

(continued)

behalf of defendants or any of them; (b) suggesting or implying that any of defendants' goods or services are associated with, sponsored by or otherwise authorized by plaintiffs and/or the performing group known as U2; and (c) manufacturing, copying, recording, distributing, promoting, selling or otherwise exploiting the sound recording and musical composition entitled "U2 Negativland," or any derivatives thereof, or any other sound recording or musical composition embodying any portion of the sound recording by U2 and musical composition entitled "The Joshua Tree," including "I Still Haven't Found What I'm Looking For," or otherwise infringing the respective copyrights of Island Records Ltd. and Warner/Chappell.

(2) Awarding damages to plaintiffs due to defendants' violation of Section 43(a) of the Lanham Trademark Act in such amounts as may be determined by the Court, the amounts to be trebled in accordance with 15 U.S.C. § 1117, together with such punitive damages and trebled damages where authorized under applicable state law;

(3) Statutory damages under the Copyright Act of 1976, as amended, 17 U.S.C. § 504, for defendants' willful copyright infringement.

(4) Requiring defendants to account for all copies of "U2 Negativland" and all derivatives thereof manufactured, distributed, sold and/or otherwise exploited by or on behalf of defendants, their officers, directors, agents, servants, employees, subsidiaries, affiliates, assigns, licensees, distributees and all persons in active concert or participation with them or in privity with them;

(5) Requiring defendants to account for and pay over to plaintiffs all revenues derived from defendants' activities set forth above, received by or payable to defendants, their officers, directors, agents, servants, employees, subsidiaries, affiliates, assigns, licensees, distributees, and all persons in active concert or participation with them or in privity with them, the amounts thereof pertaining to violations of Section 43(a) of the Lanham Trademark Act to be trebled in accordance with 15 U.S.C. § 1117;

(6) Directing defendants to recall and withdraw "U2 Negativland" and all derivatives thereof from all radio stations and clubs, and from sale or distribution, and to deliver to the plaintiffs to be impounded during the pendency of this action, and for destruction thereafter, all copies of "U2 Negativland" and all derivatives thereof in all formats;

(7) Directing defendants to deliver to plaintiffs to be impounded during the pendency of this action, and for destruction thereafter: (a) all inventory of "U2 Negativland" and all derivatives thereof in all formats; (b) all advertising, sales, promotional packaging, labelling, and other materials, in connection with the distribution, sale or other exploitation of "U2 Negativland" in any media; and (c) all devices for manufacturing copies of "U2 Negativland" and all derivatives thereof, including, without limitation, all lacquers, plates, molds, masters, stampers and tapes in defendants' possession, custody or control;

(8) Directing defendants to publish in *Billboard Magazine* and other trade publications to be determined by the Court, a prominent announcement that it has withdrawn and recalled "U2 Negativland" and all derivatives thereof, and requesting the withdrawal of all copies of "U2 Negativland" and all derivatives thereof from play lists and store shelves;

(9) Awarding plaintiffs the costs of this action and reasonable attorneys' fees under the Lanham Trademark Act, the Copyright Act of 1976, as amended, and other applicable laws and rules; and

(10) Awarding plaintiffs such other and further relief as the Court deems just and proper.

(continued)

Dated: Los Angeles, California
September 3, 1991

MILGRIM THOMAJAN & LEE

By: *Daniel H. Willick*
Daniel H. Willick
Attorneys for Plaintiffs
2049 Century Park East
Suite 3350
Los Angeles, CA 90067
(213) 282-0899

Dated: Los Angeles, California
September 3, 1991

MILGRIM THOMAJAN & LEE P.C.

By: *Charles B. Ortner*
Charles B. Ortner
Attorneys for Plaintiffs
53 Wall Street
New York, NY 10005
(212) 858-5300

NEGATIVLAND'S FIRST PRESS RELEASE, NOVEMBER 10, 1991

U2 Negativland

The Case from Our Side

Negativland is a small, dedicated group of musicians who, since 1980, have released 5 albums, 4 cassette-only releases, 1 video, and now a single. This single, which is entitled "U2," was created as parody, satire, social commentary, and cultural criticism. As a work of art, it is consistent with, and a continuation of, the artistic viewpoint we have been espousing toward the world of media for the last ten years.

Island Records and music publisher Warner-Chappell Music, presumably acting on behalf of their group U2, have instigated legal action against our single and have succeeded not only in removing it from circulation, but ensuring that it cannot ever be released again. It is clear that their preference is that the record never even be heard again. The terms of the settlement that was forced on us include:

- Everyone who received a copy of the record—record distributors and stores (6951 copies), and radio stations, writers, etc. (692 copies)—is being notified to return it, and that if they don't do so, or if they engage in "distributing, selling, advertising, promoting, or otherwise exploiting" the record, they may be subject to penalties "which may include imprisonment and fines." Once returned, the records will be forwarded to Island for destruction.
- All of SST's on-hand stock of the record, in vinyl, cassette, and CD (5357 copies total), is to be delivered to Island, where it will be destroyed.
- All mechanical parts used to prepare and manufacture the record are to be delivered to Island, presumably also for destruction. This includes "all tapes, stampers, molds, lacquers and other parts used in the manufacturing," and "all artwork, labels, packaging, promotional, marketing, and advertising or similar material."

(continued)

From Negativland, *Fair Use: The Story of the Letter U and the Numeral 2.* Concord, CA: Seeland, 1995, pp. 21–25.

- Our copyrights in the recordings themselves have been assigned to Island and Warner-Chappell. This means we no longer own two of our better works.
- Payment of $25,000 and half the wholesale proceeds from the copies of the record that were sold and not returned. We estimate the total cost to us, including legal fees and the cost of the destroyed records, cassettes, and CDs, at $70,000—more money than we've made in our twelve years of existence.

Our single deals, in part, with our perception of the group U2 as an international cultural phenomenon, and therefore particularly worthy of artistic comment and criticism. Island's legal action thoroughly ignores the possibility that any such artistic right or inclination might exist. Apparently Island's sole concern in this act of censorship is their determination to control the marketplace, as if the only reason to make records is to make money.

This issue is not a contest among equals. U2 records are among the most popular in history: *The Joshua Tree* sold over 14,000,000 copies. Negativland releases usually sell about 10,000 to 15,000 copies each. Our label, SST Records, is a relatively small, independent label interested in alternative music. Neither of us could afford the tremendous costs involved in fighting for our rights in court. Island could. What we *can* do is try to bring as much publicity and attention to Island's actions as possible. This statement, we hope, is a more humane attempt at reasonable discourse about artistic integrity and the artless, humorless legalism that controls corporate music today.

We've included a small sampling (excuse the expression) from the large stack of legal documents that arrived from Island's attorneys dripping with the unyielding intimidation of money and power. That preliminary stack of documents, 180 pages in all, cost Island approximately $10,000 to produce (they ultimately spent over $55,000 to stop us). Preferring retreat to total annihilation, Negativland and SST had no choice but to agree to comply completely with these demands.

Companies like Island depend on this kind of economic inevitability to bully their way over all lesser forms of opposition. Thus, Island easily wipes us off the face of their earth purely on the basis of how much more money they can afford to waste than we can. We think there are

(continued)

issues to stand up for here, but Island can spend their way out of ever having to face them in a court of law. So some important ideas about what constitutes art, and whether those ideas can supersede product constraints, will not reach a forum of precedent. In this culture, the market rules and money *is* power. They own the law, and no one who is still interested in the supremacy of a vital and freewheeling art can afford to challenge this aspect of our decline. It is a telling tribute to this culture corporation's crass obsessions that Island's whole approach to our work automatically assumed its goal was to siphon off their rightful profits. These people lost their ability to appreciate the very nature of what they're selling a long time ago.

As you will notice from the accompanying legal documents, Island is able to bring certain existing laws to bear against our work under the assumption that any infringement of those laws is done for purposes of diverting their monetary return. Our question is: how and why should these laws apply when the infringement is not done for economic gain? For the law to claim that this alleged motive is the sole criterion for legal deliberation is to admit that music, itself, is not to be taken seriously. Culture is more than commerce. It may actually have something to say about commerce. It may even use examples of commerce to comment upon it. We suggest that the law should begin to acknowledge the artistic domain of various creative techniques which may actually conflict with what others claim to be their economic domain. Any serious observer of modern music can cite a multitude of examples, from Buchanan and Goodman's humorous collages of song fragments in the 50's to today's canonization of James Brown samples, wherein artists have incorporated the actual property of others into their own unique creations. This is a 20th century mode of artistic operation that is now nothing short of dramatic in its proliferation, in spite of all the marketplace laws designed to prohibit it. We believe that art is what artists do. We hope for laws that recognize this, just as the dictionary recognizes new words (even slang) that come into common usage.

At this late date in the mass distribution of capturing technology (audio tape recorders, samplers, xerox machines, camcorders, VCRs, computers, etc.) there should be no need to prove the cultural legitimacy of what we do with sound. And this is even more obvious when you look further back. We pursue audio works in the tradition of found-image collage which originated in the visual arts—from Schwitters and Braque to Rauschenberg and Warhol. In music, we

(continued)

refer you to the whole histories of folk music and the blues, both of which have always had creative theft as their modus operandi. Jazz and rock are full of this too. The music business can try to reach the end of this century pretending that there is something wrong with this, or they can begin to acknowledge the truth and make way for reality.

Perceptually and philosophically, it is an uncomfortable wrenching of common sense to deny that once something hits the airwaves, it is literally in the public domain. The fact that the owners of culture and its material distribution are able to claim this isn't true belies their total immersion in a reality-on-paper. Artists have always approached the entire world around them as both inspiration to act and as raw material to mold and remold. Other art is just more raw material to us and to many, many others we could point to. When it comes to cultural influences, ownership is the point of fools. Copycats will shrink in the light of comparison. Bootlegging exact duplicates of another's product should be prosecuted, but we see no significant harm in anything else artists care to do with anything available to them in our "free" marketplace. We claim the right to create with mirrors. This is our working philosophy.

Negativland occupies itself with recontextualizing captured fragments to create something entirely new—a psychological impact based on a new juxtaposition of diverse elements, ripped from their usual context, chewed up, and spit out as a new form of hearing the world around us. One of Negativland's artistic obsessions involves the media, itself, as source and subject for much of our work. We respond (as artists always have) to our environment. An environment increasingly filled with artificial ideas, images, and sounds. Television, billboards, newspapers, advertisements, and music/muzak being blasted at us everywhere we go (and that background hum of everyday life certainly includes top forty bands like U2). We follow our working philosophy as best we can amid the proprietary restrictions of a self-serving marketing system that has imposed itself on culture. In reality, that system of ownership is today's emperor's clothes, now casually subverted by every kid with a tape recorder. However, it is crucial to note that, as we plunder the ocean of media we all swim in, we believe in artistic responsibility. We do not duplicate existing work or bootleg others' products. We believe every artist is due whatever rewards he or she can reap from his or her own products. The question that must rise to the surface of legal consciousness now is: at what point in the process of found sound

(continued)

incorporation does the new creation possess its own unique identity which supersedes the sum of its parts, thus gaining artistic license?

One of Island's objections to our record is the unauthorized use of a sample from the U2 song that formed the basis for both of our pieces: *I Still Haven't Found What I'm Looking For.* We believe that what we did is legally protected fair use of the segment, as it was used for purposes of fair comment, parody, and cultural criticism, which the copyright law specifically allows. A relevant precedent was set earlier this year in 2 Live Crew's *Pretty Woman* case. The fact is that today there is no operationally workable way to reuse existing sound recordings in collage-based work and see that the original artists are paid for the use of their work. Those artists who only use a few samples and have the time, money, and inclination can have their record companies negotiate payments for "sampling clearances" to the labels that originally released the records containing the desired snippets. But this is cumbersome, arbitrary, and expensive enough to discourage advanced sound collage work where there might be anywhere from one to a dozen found sound elements present at any instant, dozens or hundreds over the duration of a record.

So much for content. It is clear that the more significant objection to our single was Island's concern about our cover graphics, which they claimed would cause "massive confusion," resulting in millions of U2 fans buying the wrong record. Does our packaging look like a new release by the group U2? *Yes, of course it does . . .* at first. But upon closer inspection it reveals itself to be something else. Closer inspection is one of the things we like to promote, while Island appears resigned to the entrenchment of stupidity and the inability of their audience to notice subtle cues such as our name on the cover or our label's logo on the back.

Further, the context in which any potential confusion would take place is a retail record store. The first clue to record store employees would be that our single arrives from SST, not Island, and in small quantities, not the hundreds Island would send. Ours would be located in the "Indies" bins common to most outlets, not the general "Rock" bins where U2 records are found. Ours would be filed under "N," not "U." These logistics aside, let's assume someone does buy our record thinking it's theirs. Does Island really believe that the U2 fan will be satisfied with such a mistake and, returning ours or not, not proceed to buy U2's new record? Accusing

(continued)

us of trying to make money off their name is one thing, but claiming that the money we would make would be money they would not make is not very realistic. Island's inference that U2 fans might actually assume that we are them upon hearing our record is simply ridiculous on the face of it, and another indication of their lack of respect for their own audience.

As to Island's point about scheduling our single to coincide with U2's new release, we must plead to interesting coincidence. Island should come to grips with the fact that not everybody in the world avidly soaks up every promo blurb that Island feeds to the mainstream rock press. We don't generally read that press and neither knew nor cared that U2 was about to release another chart-busting epic. Our single was scheduled for fall release because our market stems primarily from college radio airplay, and that's when school resumes and the listening population is largest. Fall is also a prime time to release throughout the record industry, which is probably why U2's new record was also scheduled for fall. It seems clear that both Island and SST were attempting to take advantage of the same situation, not each other.

So why would we want to simulate a U2 cover if not to swipe some of the big money that this big band attracts? Our real reasons are actually so reflective that they would never cross the corporate legal mind. The image on our cover was U2's namesake, the U-2: a high-altitude espionage plane which, prophetically enough, was shot down over the now-defunct Soviet Union in 1960 causing a huge, meaningless international flap. The only point of light in those dark days was that it gave a self-righteous and complacent America its first clear photo opportunity to catch its own president telling a blatant lie which the CIA assured him was plausible deniability. Our U2 was a spy full of secrets intruding into the self-righteous and complacent image-world of polite pop. We did it as an example of something not being what it seems to be. We did it because we're all subject to too much media image mongering. We did it because tricksters and jesters are the last best hope against the corporate music bureaucracies of good grooming that have all but killed the most interesting thing in popular music—grassroots inspiration. We did it for laughs—listen to it and try not to. We did it so you could read this. The fact that Island Records can't understand all this, or if they can understand it they can't appreciate it, or if they can appreciate it they can't allow themselves to acknowledge it, is precisely why they should not have the right to control the life of other people's art.

(continued)

One basic failing of the U.S. legal system is that it treats the plaintiff and the defendant as though they are equally powerful entities, regardless of the actual resources each may have. Further, it disregards the fact that the cost of preparing a legal defense for a trial is prohibitively high—unthinkable for any entity other than a wealthy individual or a good-sized corporation. Thus, when a corporation goes after a small business or low-income individuals, the conflict automatically rolls outside of the court system because of the defendant's inability to pay the costs of mounting a proper defense. The matter is resolved by the more powerful organization threatening to press the suit back into the courts unless the smaller party agrees to their terms unconditionally. The powerful crush the weak. Note that all of this is purely a *power* relationship, essentially without regard to the legality of the issue, let alone the morality.

What would be the solution to prevent the cruel squashing of interesting jokes such as ours? How about a thorough revamping of the antique copyright, publishing, and cultural property laws to bring them into comfortable accord with modern technology and a healthy respect for the artist's impulse to incorporate public influences? Marketer's constraints should be restrained in cases of valid artistic commentary. This is a huge and complex Congressional undertaking and would inevitably result in sticky legal decisions akin to deciding whether or not a particular work of art is pornographic. So be it.

Art needs to begin to acquire an equal footing with marketers in court. We can even imagine such changes extending all the way to recording contracts which, strange as it may seem, might actually be written so as to allow the artist, rather than the marketer, to own and control his or her own work. You might as well start thinking about these problems now because they're not going to go away.

Excerpts from Chapter 1 of the 1976 United States Copyright Act

PUBLIC LAW 94-553—OCT. 19, 1976 90 STAT. 2541

Public Law 94-553
94th Congress

An Act

For the general revision of the Copyright Law, title 17 of the United States Code, and for other purposes.

Oct. 19, 1976
[S. 22]

Be it enacted by the Senate and House of Representatives of the United States of America in Congress assembled,

Title 17, USC, copyrights.

TITLE I—GENERAL REVISION OF COPYRIGHT LAW

Sec. 101. Title 17 of the United States Code, entitled "Copyrights," is hereby amended in its entirety to read as follows:

TITLE 17—COPYRIGHTS

Chapter 1.—SUBJECT MATTER AND SCOPE OF COPYRIGHT
§ 101. Definitions

As used in this title, the following terms and their variant forms mean the following:

A "compilation" is a work formed by the collection and assembling of preexisting materials or of data that are selected, coordinated, or arranged in such a way that the resulting work as a whole constitutes an original work of authorship. The term "compilation" includes collective works.

"Copies" are material objects, other than phonorecords, in which a work is fixed by any method now known or later developed, and from which the work can be perceived, reproduced, or otherwise communicated, either directly or with the aid of a machine or device. The term "copies" includes the material object, other than a phonorecord, in which the work is first fixed.

"Copyright owner," with respect to any one of the exclusive rights comprised in a copyright, refers to the owner of that particular right.

A work is "created" when it is fixed in a copy or phonorecord for the first time; where a work is prepared over a period of time, the portion of it that has been fixed at any particular time constitutes the work as of that time, and where the work has been prepared in different versions, each version constitutes a separate work.

A "derivative work" is a work based upon one or more preexisting works, such as a translation, musical arrangement, dramatization, fictionalization, mo-

(continued)

From 1976 United States Copyright Act, Public Law 94-553, Oct. 19, 1976.

tion picture version, sound recording, art reproduction, abridgment, condensation, or any other form in which a work may be recast, transformed, or adapted. A work consisting of editorial revisions, annotations, elaborations, or other modifications which, as a whole, represent an original work of authorship, is a "derivative work."

A "device," "machine," or "process" is one now known or later developed. To "display" a work means to show a copy of it, either directly or by means of a film, slide, television image, or any other device or process or, in the case of a motion picture or other audiovisual work, to show individual images nonsequentially.

A work is "fixed" in a tangible medium of expression when its embodiment in a copy or phonorecord, by or under the authority of the author, is sufficiently permanent or stable to permit it to be perceived, reproduced, or otherwise communicated for a period of more than transitory duration. A work consisting of sounds, images, or both, that are being transmitted, is "fixed" for purposes of this title if a fixation of the work is being made simultaneously with its transmission.

"Phonorecords" are material objects in which sounds, other than those accompanying a motion picture or other audiovisual work, are fixed by any method now known or later developed, and from which the sounds can be perceived, reproduced, or otherwise communicated, either directly or with the aid of a machine or device. The term "phonorecords" includes the material object in which the sounds are first fixed.

"Publication" is the distribution of copies or phonorecords of a work to the public by sale or other transfer of ownership, or by rental, lease, or lending. The offering to distribute copies or phonorecords to a group of persons for purposes of further distribution, public performance, or public display, constitutes publication. A public performance or display of a work does not of itself constitute publication.

To perform or display a work "publicly" means—

(1) to perform or display it at a place open to the public or at any place where a substantial number of persons outside of a normal circle of a family and its social acquaintances is gathered; or

(2) to transmit or otherwise communicate a performance or display of the work to a place specified by clause (1) or to the public, by means of any device or processs, whether the members of the public capable of receiving the performance or display receive it in the same place or in separate places and at the same time or at different times.

"Sound recordings" are works that result from the fixation of a series of musical, spoken, or other sounds, but not including the sounds accompanying a motion picture or other audiovisual work, regardless of the nature of the material objects, such as disks, tapes, or other phonorecords, in which they are embodied.

(continued)

17 USC 102. **§ 102. Subject matter of copyright: In general**

(a) Copyright protection subsists, in accordance with this title, in original works of authorship fixed in any tangible medium of expression, now known or later developed, from which they can be perceived, reproduced, or otherwise communicated, either directly or with the aid of a machine or device.

Works of authorship. Works of authorship include the following categories:

(1) literary works;

(2) musical works, including any accompanying words;

(3) dramatic works, including any accompanying music;

(4) pantomimes and choreographic works;

(5) pictorial, graphic, and sculptural works;

(6) motion pictures and other audiovisual works; and

(7) sound recordings.

(b) In no case does copyright protection for an original work of authorship extend to any idea, procedure, process, system, method of operation, concept, principle, or discovery, regardless of the form in which it is described, explained, illustrated, or embodied in such work.

17 USC 103. **§ 103. Subject matter of copyright: Compilations and derivative works**

(a) The subject matter of copyright as specified by section 102 includes compilations and derivative works, but protection for a work employing preexisting material in which copyright subsists does not extend to any part of the work in which such material has been used unlawfully.

(b) The copyright in a compilation or derivative work extends only to the material contributed by the author of such work, as distinguished from the preexisting material employed in the work, and does not imply any exclusive right in the preexisting material. The copyright in such work is independent of, and does not affect or enlarge the scope, duration, ownership, or subsistence of, any copyright protection in the preexisting material.

17 USC 106. **§ 106. Exclusive rights in copyrighted works**

Subject to sections 107 through 118, the owner of copyright under this title has the exclusive rights to do and to authorize any of the following:

(1) to reproduce the copyrighted work in copies or phonorecords;

(2) to prepare derivative works based upon the copyrighted work;

(3) to distribute copies or phonorecords of the copyrighted work to the public by sale or other transfer of ownership, or by rental, lease, or lending;

(4) in the case of literary, musical, dramatic, and choreographic works, pantomimes, and motion pictures and other audiovisual works, to perform the copyrighted work publicly; and

(5) in the case of literary, musical, dramatic, and choreographic works, pantomimes, and pictorial, graphic, or sculptural works, including the individual images

(continued)

of a motion picture or other audiovisual work, to display the copyrighted work publicly.

17 USC 107. **§ 107. Limitations on exclusive rights: Fair use**

Notwithstanding the provisions of section 106, the fair use of a copyrighted work, including such use by reproduction in copies or phonorecords or by any other means specified by that section, for purposes such as criticism, comment, news reporting, teaching (including multiple copies for classroom use), scholarship, or research, is not an infringement of copyright. In determining whether the use made of a work in any particular case is a fair use the factors to be considered shall include—

(1) the purpose and character of the use, including whether such use is of a commercial nature or is for nonprofit educational purposes;

(2) the nature of the copyrighted work;

(3) the amount and substantiality of the portion used in relation to the copyrighted work as a whole; and

(4) the effect of the use upon the potential market for or value of the copyrighted work.

17 USC 114. **§ 114. Scope of exclusive rights in sound recordings**

(a) The exclusive rights of the owner of copyright in a sound recording are limited to the rights specified by clauses (1), (2), and (3) of section 106, and do not include any right of performance under section 106(4).

(b) The exclusive right of the owner of copyright in a sound recording under clause (1) of section 106 is limited to the right to duplicate the sound recording in the form of phonorecords, or of copies of motion pictures and other audiovisual works, that directly or indirectly recapture the actual sounds fixed in the recording. The exclusive right of the owner of copyright in a sound recording under clause (2) of section 106 is limited to the right to prepare a derivative work in which the actual sounds fixed in the sound recording are rearranged, remixed, or otherwise altered in sequence or quality. The exclusive rights of the owner of copyright in a sound recording under clauses (1) and (2) of section 106 do not extend to the making or duplication of another sound recording that consists entirely of an independent fixation of other sounds, even though such sounds imitate or simulate those in the copyrighted sound recording. The exclusive rights of the owner of copyright in a sound recording under clauses (1), (2), and (3) of section 106 do not apply to sound recordings included in educational television and radio programs (as defined in
47 USC 397. section 397 of title 47) distributed or transmitted by or through public broadcasting entities (as defined by section 118(g)): *Provided,* That copies or phonorecords of said programs are not commercially distributed by or through public broadcasting entities to the general public.

(c) This section does not limit or impair the exclusive right to perform publicly, by means of a phonorecord, any of the works specified by section 106(4).

In Fair Use Debate, Art Must Come First

By Negativland

As Duchamp pointed out many decades ago, the act of selection can be a form of inspiration as original and significant as any other. Throughout our various mass media, we now find many artists who work by "selecting" existing cultural material to collage with, to create with, and to comment upon. In general, this continues to be a method that both "serious" and "popular" arts incorporate. But is it theft? Do artists, for profit or not, have the right to "sample" freely from the already-"created" electronic environment that surrounds them?

The psychology of art has always favored fragmentary "theft" in a way that does not engender a "loss" to the owner. Call this "being influenced" if you want to sound legitimate. But some will say there is a big difference between stealing ideas, techniques, and styles that are not easily copyrighted, and stealing actual material that is easily copyrighted. However, aside from the copyright-deterrence factor prevalent throughout our law-bound art industries, we can find nothing intrinsically wrong with an artist deciding to incorporate existing art "samples" into their own work. The fact that we have economically motivated laws against it does not necessarily make it an undesirable artistic move.

All of music history has involved the fragmentary appropriation of existing works within "new" creations. Even material "theft" has a well-respected tradition in the arts, dating back to the Industrial Revolution. It first flowered in Cubist collages, then became blatant in Dada's found objects and concept of "detournment," and finally peaked in mid-Century with Pop Art's appropriation of mass-culture icons and mass-media imagery. Techniques of material appropriation bear a direct relationship to this century's *invention* of mass culture and the technologically-based barrage of information, imagery, and communication directed at the masses. Now, at the end of this century, it is in music where we find appropriation raging anew as a major creative method and legal controversy.

It's about time that the obvious aesthetic validity of appropriation begins to be raised in opposition to the assumed preeminence of historically recent copyright laws prohibiting the free reuse of cultural material. The prevailing assumption—that our culture, and all its cultural artifacts, should be privately controlled and locked away from any and all further creative uses by the audience they are directed at—is both undesirable and unworkable. Uninvited appropriation is inevitable when a population bombarded with electronic media meets the hardware that encourages people to capture those media. However, laws devised to protect the "ownership" of transmittable information have, for example, resulted in a music industry in which the very *idea* of collage is a dangerous one, and artists inspired by "direct reference" forms of creation do not have the "right" to decide what their own art will consist of. Has it occurred to anyone that the private ownership of mass culture is a bit of a contradiction in terms?

The urge to make one thing out of other things is an entirely traditional, socially healthy, and artistically valued impulse that only recently has been criminalized in order to force private tolls on the practice, or else prohibit it to escape embarrassment. Artists continue to employ appropriation because it's just plain interesting, and no law can keep artists from being interesting.

(continued)

From *Billboard,* December 25, 1993. Reprinted in Negativland, *Fair Use: The Story of the Letter U and the Numeral 2.* Concord, CA: Seeland, 1995, p. 154.

How many artistic prerogatives should we be willing to give up in order to maintain our owner-regulated culture? The directions artists want to take may sometimes be dangerous—that's the risk of democracy—but they certainly should not be dictated by what business wants to allow. Look it up in the dictionary: Art is not defined as a business! Is it a healthy state of affairs when laws of commerce get to lock in the boundaries of experimentation for artists, or is this a recipe for cultural stagnation?

Today, in a culture thoroughly colonized by private "property rights," the only solution for artists who appropriate other works rests with the legal concept of "Fair Use," which already exists within copyright law. The Fair Use statutes are intended to allow for free appropriation in certain cases of parody or commentary, and are the sole acknowledgement within copyright law of a possible need for artistic freedom and free speech. Unfortunately, the Fair Use Doctrine is now being interpreted conservatively and is being withheld from many "infringers." However, the beauty of Fair Use is that it is capable of overriding all the other restrictions.

Those of us who still value art over profit are now focusing on how to release the Fair Use Doctrine from its present commercial handcuffs. Both courts and Congress await the powerful suggestion that Fair Use issues are not about who is going to profit, but about who is going to determine what art might consist of. Until this adjustment in basic legal presumptions occurs, modern societies will find the corporate stranglehold on cultural "properties" continuously at war with the common sense and natural inclinations of their "user" populations.

Here is our main suggestion for updating the concept of Fair Use in order to accommodate the realities of recent technology, and to promote, rather than inhibit, "direct reference" art forms. Clear all restrictions—including requirements for payment and permission—on any practice of *fragmentary* appropriation. We would retain the present protections and fees for artists and their administrators only in uses of their *entire* works (cover versions) or for any form of usage at all by commercial advertisers. The test of whether a "fragment" is too close to the whole should be an artistic definition, not a commercial one. Namely: Is the material used superseded by a *new nature* of the usage itself—is the whole more than the sum of its parts? When faced with actual examples, this is not difficult to evaluate.

This one alteration in the Fair Use Doctrine would (for a change) serve to balance the will of commerce to monopolize its products with the socially desirable urge of artists to remix culture. If this occurred, the rest of copyright law might stay as it is (if that's what we want) and continue to apply in all cases of "whole" theft for commercial gain (bootlegging entire works).

The law *must* come to terms with the difference between artistic intent and economic intent. We believe that artistic freedom for all is more important to the health of society than the supplemental and extraneous incomes derived from private copyright tariffs that create a climate of art control and Art Police. No matter how valid the original intent of our copyright laws may have been, they are now clearly being subverted to censor resented works, to suppress the public's need to reuse and reshape information, and to garner purely opportunistic incomes. The U.S. Constitution clearly shows that the reason for copyright law was to promote a *public* good, not a private one. No one should be allowed to claim a private control over the creative process itself. Make no mistake: This is essentially a struggle of art against commerce, and ultimately about which one must make way for the other.

Sampling Without Permission Is Theft

By Andrian Adams and Paul McKibbins

A chill crawled up our spines upon reading the commentary on fair use by self-described "noisemakers" Negativland (*Billboard,* Dec. 25, 1993).

Through a series of wildly specious arguments, Negativland seeks to promote the idea that they should be able—through the technique of "sampling"—to use others' creative and interpretive work for their own commercial gain without the inconvenience of payment or permission. To those who put in the time, energy, creative effort, and money necessary to create their music in its original form, this is intellectual and physical theft.

The Supreme Court is considering the definitions of "fair use" and "parody" as they apply to the 2 Live Crew's use of the Acuff-Rose-owned song "Oh, Pretty Woman" on their album "As Clean As They Wanna Be." If the Court rules in favor of the publishers, some argue that it could have a dampening effect on other artists that employ parody (*Billboard,* Nov. 20, 1993). The ruling is expected this spring, and the case has spurred some artists, like Negativland, to call for dramatic alteration of the Copyright Act.

Negativland's position—"We believe that artistic freedom for all is more important to the health of society than the supplemental and extraneous incomes derived from private copyright tariffs"—actually negates the whole concept of music as a business. In Negativland's world, "art" and commerce are completely distinct entities. However, in our world of realism and logic, there is no distinction between art and commerce once the art is offered for sale. To insist otherwise is naive.

We feel compelled to address the other sides of the sampling issue. However, before we clean up the minefield of negativism and reseed it with positivism, let us state our view on sampling: If you use copyright-protected music for commercial gain, you must pay. Period.

In very practical terms—in fact, the Constitution guarantees it—intellectual property is no different than physical property regarding ownership. Just as one cannot take another's car without permission, one cannot take or use another's copyrighted creation without permission. Taking this one step further, no one, except a thief, would take another person's car and sell it without the proper, formal, legal arrangements. But this is exactly what happens when an artist appropriates a musical fragment and then profits from its use and sale. It's taking without permission.

Although Negativland justifies "fragmentary theft" (read: sampling) as an inescapable part of the artistic process, they defend this view *vis à vis* music with a historical reference linking Cubist collages to Dada and, finally, to Pop Art's use of mass-culture icons, i.e., Andy Warhol's Campbell's Soup can. Historical borrowing, says Negativland, supersedes modern copyright law.

But beyond the issue of art as commerce also lie the intrinsic moral and ethical responsibilities that come with the privilege of participating in a free-market system. In more colloquial terms, "doing the right thing."

With regard to music, the "right thing" is for users to pay the people who own the prop-

(continued)

From *Billboard,* March 5, 1994. Reprinted in Negativland, *Fair Use: The Story of the Letter U and the Numeral 2.* Concord, CA: Seeland, 1995.

erty, i.e., the copyright holders. In a civilized society, the rule of law, through legislation, rightfully plays an important role in codifying moral and ethical behavior. It also dictates the practical elements of the free market: The law defines who gets what and who has "the right to copy." Without laws to help guide a nation's citizens, there would be anarchy, although this seems to be the direction in which Negativland wants our nation to head.

Interestingly, Negativland claims that our "owner-regulated culture" prevents artists from partaking in their instinctive "urge" to create musical "collages" should they so desire. Furthermore, according to Negativland, "uninvited appropriation is inevitable" since our population is "bombarded with electronic media."

If the real issue is only that artists have the right to sample, we completely agree with Negativland's, and their "artist" friends', desire to sample. You may sample *anything,* as long as it is not for commercial gain. Since Negativland values "art over profit" and embraces a definition that "art is not a business," why should they care about selling their creations? Therefore, the point is moot. Sample away!

While determined to justify the appropriation of others' creative sweat, Negativland devises a bizarre interpretation of the "Fair Use" statute contained in current copyright law, which allows for free appropriation in instances that include parody, education, and commentary. Negativland benignly views these exceptions as a window for an "artistic freedom" and "free speech" interpretation of the Fair Use statute that would allow stealing for personal gain.

We believe that Negativland's position that "the private ownership of mass culture is a contradiction in terms" is nonsense. Mass culture is made up of an infinite number of distinct parts. It's the protection of those parts—that is, the copyrights—that continually stimulates creators to work in the arts. Without the stimulus of financial gain, how will artists survive? This brings us back to the idea of laws, morals, and ethical values.

While it is unlikely that Negativland's ideas will ever be implemented by Congress or the courts, we in the music business must be vigilant in protecting the copyrights we control. It is sad that there are growing numbers of Negativlands in our midst, people who want to steal from us in the name of "art." Like Negativland, these people want to "clear all restrictions—including payment and permission—on any practice of fragmentary appropriation." Whether it's one James Brown shout or the whole "hook" of a song, Negativland wants the right to have it in *their* music without paying the rightful owners of that music.

Make no mistake. This is not a struggle of art against commerce. It is about honest, hard-working people being compensated for the music they create and rightfully own.

Build a Desktop Studio

By Tom Samiljan

Previously the exclusive realm of professional studio musicians, music-creation software has become so simple that any amateur with a decent computer can start making noise. Two of the following programs—Acid and Mixman—are powerful enough to be used by professional DJs and musicians; Sounder is a Web-based diversion that lets duffers remix for free.

Mixman Studio Pro
(Windows and Mac, $90)

If you want to be making music within minutes of installing your software, try Mixman Studio Pro, a user-friendly suite of professional quality mixing tools. Mixman has more than 300 offerings in its library of presupplied tracks—everything from deep-house loops to funky guitar licks to classic-rock drumbeats. (You can make your own tracks as well.) Each selected track is assigned a different button on the keyboard; you can, say, lock in a salsa groove by triggering the correct track and holding down the space bar, then tap in little guitar flourishes wherever you please. You can port your remixes over to MP3 or WAV formats, or burn them onto a CD. Besides Mixman's ease of use, its other great advantage is its library of D-plates, which are Mixman-compatible songs by Luscious Jackson, Moby and others.

Acid 2.0
Sonicfoundry.com

Acid comes in three flavors: Acid Pro (for professionals), Acid Music (the intermediate-level software, for something called "prosumers") and Acid Style (for armchair DJs). Getting started is more difficult than with Mixman; Acid's interface, a huge grid in which each cell holds a different sound, looks more like a professional mixing program. First you preview loops of sounds (samples of drums, keyboards, bass, whatever). When you have enough sounds in your track list to make a song, you just drag sounds into the spreadsheet-like grid (each sound is color-coded so you can keep track). Prerecorded loops (which you can play and remix) can be gathered from a separate CD that comes with the program—choices vary from generic rock beats to jungle and house rhythms. If you want to focus on a particular kind of music, you can buy specialized versions of Acid in genres such as hip-hop, rock and dance ($60 each) or download loops off Sonic Foundry's site (individual loops can be purchased for $1 each). Of course, you can record and manipulate your own loops, too. Like Mixman, Acid makes it easy to use seemingly disparate samples: Place a rock & roll beat in the same song as a house beat and the software will automatically make it work, with no change in pitch. In addition, you can burn your tracks onto a CD or create MP3 and streamable tracks with simple mouse commands. Some major names (including Beck) have provided original loops from their songs for Acid users, but the program doesn't have the deep lineup of Mixman's D-plates.

Sounder
Sounder.com

A true original in the music-creation space, Sounder presents you with graphic animations-spheres, stars, rocks—that move around windows (called Sounder Spaces) on your desktop.

(continued)

From *Rolling Stone,* June 8, 2000, p. 529.

Each time an object hits the wall of a window, it plays a preassigned note. You can also assign different notes (A, B, C) and timbres (telephone ring, drum, wood block) to each object. To change the music, grab Sounder objects with your cursor and throw them around the window so that they move in different ways and at different speeds, creating the same sounds at different tempos. The result is usually something that resembles an ambient, abstract composition by the likes of Brian Eno or Aphex Twin - Sounder is half desktop diversion, half genius ambient-music generator.

RTMARK Finds Bucks for Beck Rip-Off

FOR IMMEDIATE RELEASE

February 17, 1998

Contacts: *info@rtmark.com* (http://www.rtmark.com/)
illegalart@detritus.net
(*http://www.detritus.net/illegalart*)

RTMARK FINDS BUCKS FOR BECK RIP-OFF

Group channels money for subversion, hopes to spark dialogue on corporate wrongs

RTMARK is pleased to announce the February 17 release of a new Beck CD: *Deconstructing Beck.*

Recording artist Beck might be less pleased. Why? Because it isn't really his work. *Deconstructing Beck* is a collection of brilliant but allegedly illegal resamplings of Beck, produced by Illegal Art with the help of $5,000 gathered by RTMARK from anonymous donors.

Deconstructing Beck is the latest of more than twenty successful sabotage projects made possible by RTMARK since its beginnings in 1991. RTMARK's aim is to further anti-corporate activism by channelling funds from donors to workers. Other recent and upcoming acts of RTMARK-aided subversion are documented on RTMARK's web site, http://www.rtmark.com/.

According to an anonymous RTMARK spokesperson, RTMARK was first approached by Illegal Art last November. "Using artwork illegally helps fight the stranglehold that corporations have on our lives, and that's what we're all about," the spokesperson said. "We weren't sure about this project at first, since RTMARK usually targets the crassest of mass-produced items. But while Beck may be a superb artist, his lucrative persona remains just another product that others get rich from, and one that we need to subvert."

Philo T. Farnsworth, the pseudonymous main force behind Illegal Art, says his label exists to provide "an outlet for artists interested in exploring an illegal palette. Corporations invade our lives with product but forbid us to use it—in our art, or in any way they don't want. This just doesn't make sense."

(continued)

RTMARK, Deconstructing Beck Press Release, Feb. 17, 1998, http://www.rtmark.com.

What does makes sense, given the corporate climate, is that record stores won't touch this CD. It is available only from Illegal Art (*illegalart@detritus.net*), and costs just $5, including US postage. Illegal Art was able to keep production costs low by packaging the CD in a plain white box and putting its liner notes on their web site. Even more importantly, the cost of the CD reflects a markup of only 100%, instead of the industry-standard 800%. (The page with the liner notes, *http://www.detritus.net/illegalart/beck/*, also features 30-second RealAudio(tm) clips of each track.)

Illegal Art's email and web service, incidentally, is provided by *detritus.net,* an Internet site dedicated to the artistic reuse of pre-existing culture. "We're happy to be helping out with the Beck project," said Steev Hise, Detritus webmaster. "Copyright laws are too restrictive, and they're counterintuitive. These laws in their present form are there just to funnel money to corporations, not to protect artists. As artists we need to fight that."

UNIT III

Creating a Sense of Place

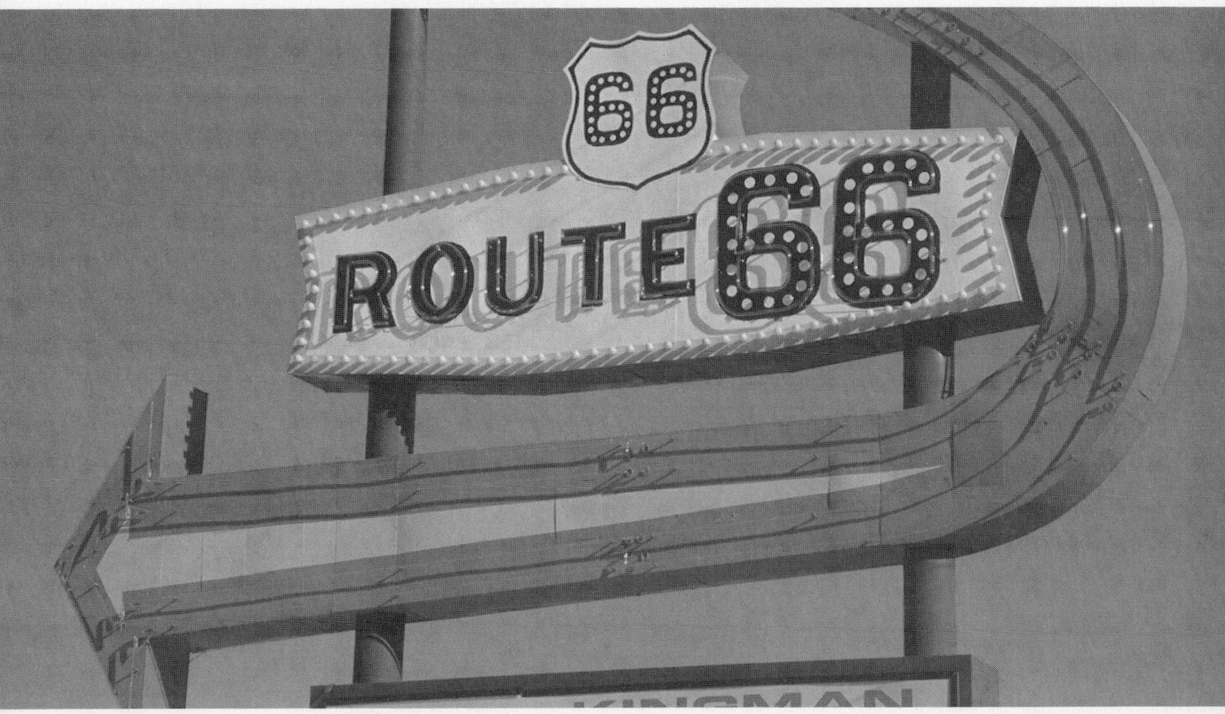

Route 66 was commissioned in 1926 to connect existing local roads into a single roadway between Chicago and Los Angeles. By the 1960s, partly because of movies, songs, and a TV series that celebrated it, Route 66 had become a symbol of freedom and adventure. But by the 1980s, the narrow, meandering road had been almost completely replaced by multilane expressways. Recently, though, the remnants of Route 66 have been rediscovered as a culturally richer alternative to the impersonal interstates. Route 66 has now come to symbolize a longing for the local sense of place that the interstates and fast food franchises seem to have taken away. For many people, photographs like this one of the motels, restaurants, gas stations, and tourist attractions along Route 66 are visual expressions of a dialogue between the local and the exotic. We go on the road to escape the familiar and find adventure, but travel is an adventure only if the places we travel to have retained their own local sense of place, the things that make them home to others. These are some of the complexities of creating a sense of place that you will explore in this unit. But before you turn the page, pause to read some of the meanings in this photograph. How do you "read" the sign on a motel to decide if you want to stay in that particular home on the road? How would you judge this motel if all you had to go on was this sign?

On the Road

Situation: Can you visualize where the area represented by this map is located?

Genre: What are maps used for? How have maps changed over time? What different kinds of maps are there? How would you compare this map with other maps you've seen?

Language: How do maps combine visual language with the language of words? What do you do when you "read" a map? Have you ever drawn a map? What kinds of "language" did you use?

Consequences: Have you ever tried to get somewhere using an inaccurate map? How have maps changed the way we see the world?

When Audubon Naturalist Society guide Mark Garland published his book *Watching Nature, Washington Post* reporter Kevin McManus called him for an interview. Garland, characteristically, asked the reporter to meet him "in the field," in this case on the trail along the C&O Canal, rather than at his Chevy Chase office. Reflecting on the interview later, McManus wrote,

> I'm struck by how different our powers of perception are, out here on the trail. My brain has been registering much bird chirping, leafy trees and shrubs, many flowers, some frogs nearby. When I ask Garland what he's seeing and hearing, he says: "There's a pair of yellow-throated vireos, first ones I've heard today, calling on either side. Toads are still singing to the left—I just love that long, monotonous trill of theirs. Lots of other birds: There was a chestnut-sided warbler that just sang on the other side. You try and filter out some of the resident birds that you hear all the time—there's a tufted titmouse singing like crazy off to the right. Little buzzy notes of the blue-gray gnatcatcher.
>
> "So my ears are picking all of this up while my eyes are noticing things. Like there've been a couple of catbirds jumping in the bushes on the side. And I'm just marveling at the dogwood flowers on the other side. They're in full bloom right now . . ." (The *Washington Post,* July 4, 1997)

This short anecdote suggests a number of things about why we like to move about, take to the road, go into the field, return to nature, or otherwise change our perspective.

First, it suggests how much perspective influences perception. What we are able to see and hear depends on both who we are and where we are. When we change our situation—move to a different place, look from a different angle—we see the world anew, and this in turn changes us, renews us. Literary critics have a term for a related phenomenon: *defamiliarization* or *making strange,* the process by which art renews our perception of a world grown so familiar that we can no longer truly see it. This renewal of perception is one of the functions of art, but it can also happen through unaccustomed experiences, which is why we seek out these experiences, even though they can be frightening or dangerous.

The anecdote also points to the fact that many of us look for a renewal of perception in nature. There is an otherness in the natural world, an estrangement from human life that can shock us into seeing the world differently. But many travelers have found that visiting a strange culture can have a similar effect. Notice, in fact, that what challenges the reporter's perceptions is not simply an encounter with nature but a simultaneous encounter with the culture of the naturalist. Garland's skill at identifying many different sights and sounds depends not just on his ability to see and hear more but also on his knowledge of distinguishing names—yellow-throated vireo, chestnut-sided warbler, blue-gray gnatcatcher—and these names of course belong to culture, not nature. In fact, some philosophers argue that our encounters with nature are always "cultural" because we can see nature only through our culturally determined ideas about it.

But this is not to say that nature is just an extension of culture or that when we travel to new places we see only what we project there. Both nature and culture, both the new experience and our perception of it are real. Geographer Yi-Fu Tuan suggests that what we find at the intersection of nature and culture, or at the conjunction of a new experience and our existing structures of perception, is lucidity, a state of clarity and understanding that requires both a new experience and a perceptive faculty that is capable of change. Our encounters with the strange, whether in art, nature, or different cultures, can clarify both what we perceive and our own structures of perception: We see the world anew and are ourselves renewed.

We leave our accustomed places for many reasons—maybe just for fun, relaxation, a change of scenery, or, as with the reporter in the anecdote, as part of our job—but if we allow for an interaction between the strangeness of the new place and the insistence of our old ways of perceiving, we may bring back home with us a kind of lucidity. And if, as the reporter does, we can write about our experience, we can share that lucidity with others. This is one of the reasons why, even though it's easier and usually safer to stay put, we so often want to take to the road.

Why We Go

Andrea Barrett

Andrea Barrett is best known for her fiction and poetry. She is the author of *The Voyage of the Narwhal* and *Ship Fever,* which won her the National Book Award in 1996. Her stories deal with the nature of adventure and the scientific mind. She studied science and history before turning to writing and, during an interview, once confessed she thought of herself as "Darwin in a skirt" wandering around the Galapagos Islands and the Amazon naming birds and trees. Now she uses fiction to weave together her interest in science and history and her love of telling stories.

The essay included here was written for a special millennium issue of *The New York Times Magazine* that reflected on human exploration into the unknown. Barrett investigates the complex set of internal and external forces that drive the search for adventure. Her particular sense of adventure is informed by "the discovery men," the naturalists and explorers of the nineteenth century, men such as Elisha Kent Kane, Sir Earnest Shackleton, Sir Joseph Dalton Hooker, and William Bartram, whose travels took them into uncharted territory and often ended in disaster. Barrett's own adventures are tame, she tells us, mere "imitative gestures" undertaken to create a bond with these figures from the past. Their exploits changed forever the way we see the world.

Driven by the search for new sights and experiences, the naturalists of the nineteenth century set out to make their mark by discovering all the birds, plants, animals, and geographic formations that existed in the world. For them nature meant the physical features of the landscape. The maps, charts, and catalogs they used to bring control and order into an unstable, violent, and constantly changing world still determine the way we understand nature and our relationship to the natural world. As a consequence, adventure has come to be associated with travel into uncharted territory and with a certain element of danger. Barrett explores what this legacy means for contemporary adventurers who are left with virtually no unknown physical landscapes, who can travel in modern gear, and who can buy new experiences.

Connecting with the Conversation

1. Think about times in your life that you felt challenged or were required to do something that was just beyond the boundary of what you could do easily. Jot down a brief description in your journal. Are these times associated with physical challenges or intellectual and mental challenges?
2. Make a brief list of any new discoveries that have been reported in the news or talked about in your classes at school. Include discoveries in science, technology, and medicine but also think of innovation in other areas, such as architecture. Share your list with people in your small group.

When I was just beginning to write, my husband and I lived in Philadelphia. Summers were hot there. We wished we were cool. A friend offered to teach us to kayak. Once he'd hooked us on the pleasures of slipping along the water's surface, steering with a flick of the double-bladed paddle, he began to prepare us for bigger rivers and wilder rapids.

Kayaks tip over easily, but are just as easily righted; a kayak hugs the hips, fusing body and boat into a centaurlike hybrid. When the whole arrangement tips upside down, a combination of underwater paddle gestures and an insouciant snap of the hips and shoulders can spin you back to the surface. I showed no aptitude for this particular trick, despite the best efforts of our patient friend, who stood beside me in shoulder-high water on a smooth patch of the Delaware River for hours.

I mimicked the sequence of movements he showed me—but movements that seemed perfectly clear when I was sitting upright, in air, sealed into my *Fiberglass* boat, were completely confusing when I had to perform them upside down and underwater. Again and again my friend tipped me over. My head brushed the river bottom, but gently, the way willow branches brush the ground. For however long I could hold my breath, I tried the gestures meant to pop me through the boundary between the water and the air.

During my 20's and 30's, I skied and climbed and sailed and hiked as well as kayaked; I was good at some of these, bad at others, passionate about all of them. But not athletic, or coordinated, or courageous, or strong. Nor adventurous, except in spirit. Five or six hours of strenuous effort and what I longed for was coffee, dinner, bed. I thought of these things I was trying to learn not as sports, but as tools to move me through secret parts of the world.

5 I've never engaged in the mildest adventure without a sense of echoing a larger narrative; my pale, imitative gestures give substance to my imaginings, bearing me back into history and into the lives of the naturalists and explorers who have long obsessed me. On a sailboat, in a storm, I've imagined Elisha Kent Kane sailing north toward his vision of an Open Polar Sea in 1853, or Shackleton in 1914 pushing the Endurance toward the coast of Antarctica. Hiking up Algonquin Mountain, in the

---

From *The New York Times Magazine,* June 6, 1999, pp. 77–79.

startling cold of an Adirondack January, I've felt a bond to Sir Joseph Dalton Hooker botanizing in the Himalayas in the 1840s. While walking through perfectly tame parts of Florida I've considered the naturalist William Bartram's late-18th-century encounters with alligators and Audubon's meetings, a few decades later, with pelicans and herons.

"Tell me a story," demands Robert Penn Warren's lovely poem about Audubon. "Tell me a story of deep delight." A story, a poem, inspired by someone else's adventure. If I learned to roll I could paddle down larger rivers, toward other stories. Down and up and down and up I went, on the day I finally got it; water and sky, water and sky; brightness and darkness and brightness again. The essence of repetition.

These days adventure always has this element of quotation—of repeating, retracing, rethinking the acts of others. "Oh," we think, "it felt like this." In the physical experience of storms and mosquitoes, hunger and exhaustion, loneliness, yearning for home, abstractions once only read about are converted to concrete reality. Shadowing that understanding is the gap that suddenly yawns between a place as it once was, and is now—it looks like this? Around the pond behind my mother-in-law's Florida condominium live descendants of the herons and cormorants Audubon drew. But the place where I reimagine his adventures is on the edge of a golf course.

During the two summers after I learned to roll, I spent almost every weekend with a group of kayakers strong and skilled and experienced enough to save me from the consequences of my beginner's mistakes. Most often we paddled the Youghiogheny, a medium-size river except in flood; simple for my companions but trickier for me. The rapids were predictable hazards. They had names and could be read, like a book. The cliffs unrolling in parallel, the talkative currents, the sense of being part of the water: no matter how many times I repeated the journey, it was always thrilling.

Occasionally, in a cycle of repetitions, a singular event occurs. An anomaly. We seek these, consciously or unconsciously, for they're at the heart of our drive toward adventure. Even when we retrace the adventures of others—following in the footsteps of Lewis and Clark, say, or St. Francis of Assisi—we seek not simply to replicate the journey but also to create the context in which something unexpected will happen. During a hot July day when the Youghiogheny was low and the rocks more exposed than usual, I tipped over. My paddle popped above the water, making the requisite sweeping motion. As it banged against a rock my head banged, not gently this time, along the river bottom. Again and again I repeated my practiced motions, but I remained resolutely upside down. This was what my friends called a bagel: a roll with a hole. Adventure reduced to domestic analogy.

10 The solution to a bagel is simple, if undignified: claw at the spray-skirt, snap the neoprene off the coaming and slither out. The boat drifts off in one direction and the person in another; irritating, but no worse. This time my boat refused to release me. Later I learned that the bow had caught on a rock, which was squeezing the hollow shell down on my legs.

Those moments, when I could neither roll nor escape, when I went from calmness to curiosity to worry to panic (I have always feared drowning): those moments. Why seek them? Perhaps not only to have stories to tell, but also to make sense of the stories we already know. On the Youghiogheny my friend spotted my stilled, inverted boat, and although he couldn't see the guilty rock, he grasped the situation. Like an archangel he swept his boat downriver toward mine, purposefully crashed into the stern and knocked me free. I haven't kayaked since.

What happened to me was nothing. These things happen all the time. In the preceding months my kayaking husband had been driven over by a raft, spun like laundry in the drop below a big rock, speared in the ribs by another boat. Cheerfully, he kept paddling. One person's epic (I've been telling the story of my close call for years) is another's swiftly forgotten anecdote. The story has stayed with me because I got frightened; I got frightened because I am naturally timid. Adventure depends not only on context, but on character too.

Are those people who go back to the river, and back and back, and up mountains and into the harshest environments, simply fearless in a way I am not? They don't believe they can be hurt or killed, they don't care, they do care but are willing to take the risk because the rewards are so great? Until we feel those questions—it feels like this?—we can't begin to answer them. Maybe adventure exists just beyond the boundary, different for each of us, of what we can do with assurance. On the river, contemplating the line I wouldn't cross, I learned something about the courage and disregard for self it might take to keep going. The world we inhabit has been defined, for better or worse, by a millennium's worth of adventurers who were willing to cross that boundary.

If part of adventure is the refusal to be dissuaded by the thought of one's own demise, another part is defined by the boundaries of the adventurer's culture and time. In the Arctic in the 19th century, whalers whose work took them routinely into unknown waters sneered at the nattily outfitted officers who commanded British exploring expeditions and claimed sites that the whalers had known for years. The whalers called them, not kindly, "discovery men." Eyeing both groups were Inuit on their own routine business, slipping by in kayaks made of sealskins stretched over wood or whalebone frames. Out on a wild ocean, carrying harpoons with detachable ivory points, they hunted for food, not thrills, and rolled when dumped by a walrus or a whale. Inspired by such sights, American and European visitors to the Arctic quoted the original kayaks successively in oiled cloth, Fiberglass and, these days, a bouncy tough plastic that old-timers call, sarcastically, Tupperware.

15 I still admire the bright-colored bubbles suspended midair in the stores, but these days my chief mode of adventure is to write things beyond the boundaries of what I can easily do. Reading accounts of expeditions, I imagine how they felt to the people involved; I invent variations on old ones, and characters who set off on new ones. Like everyone else addicted to armchair adventure, I experience vicariously what I no longer have the desire, or the stamina, to experience physically. "Experience," Elizabeth Bowen says in "The Death of the Heart," her wonderful novel, "isn't interesting till it begins to repeat itself—in fact, till it does that, it hardly *is* experience."

I was 26 that day on the Youghiogheny, too young to have any context for my experience. When you're young, it's possible not to know about all those who have preceded your every aspiration and attempt. It's possible not to know about a place's previous inhabitants, or the evolving history of successive cultures and communities, or the crisscrossing web of paths laid down by itinerant peddlers and missionaries and botanists and explorers and charlatans. It's possible not to know that, even in the deepest woods or the wildest stream, someone has passed before.

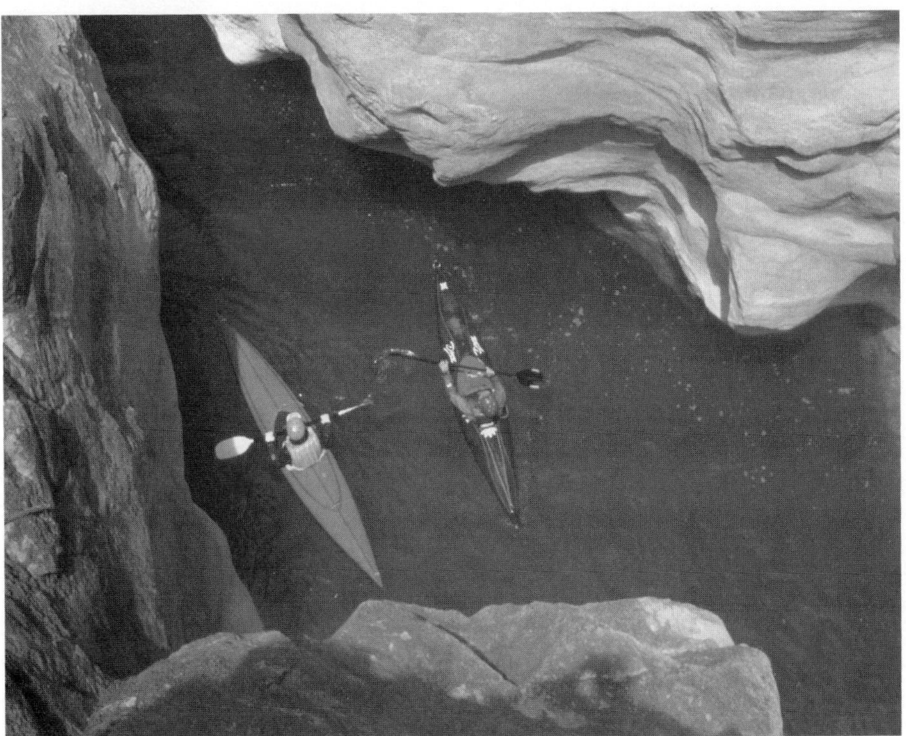

When you're older, you know. Then the adventures of inner space can seem more compelling. Art, science, the journeys of the imagination—these can seem fresher, cleaner in some sense, than the repetitions and replications involved in climbing Mount Rainier in the company of a satellite phone and a guide. Heading toward territory unknown to us, if not absolutely unknown, still offers a sense of discovery. But once adventure becomes a commodity, it is altered in some essential way. Those people pushing up mountains and down rivers centuries ago, in search of a leaf or the bones of a mastodon or a passage to China, played for different stakes, driven by outward goals as well as personal imperatives.

Whatever else they were doing, they were also mapping the world—and, with the completion of that map, changing forever the context of our adventures. The maps I consider now, when planning a trip, are dense with information. I choose among places already named. I choose known routes between them. I can choose to be lost, now, only by willfully leaving my maps behind or by ignoring a modern map in favor of an antique version. I've lost my maps of the Youghiogheny, but the old maps that litter my office all center on rivers—the Mississippi, the Missouri, the Delaware, veins leading into the heart. On one, drawn in 1825, the Ohio River is broad and dark. Each tributary and village along its route is marked but the rest is blank space. The states—Virginia, Kentucky, Ohio—are simply gestured at; the crucial news is the stream connecting one place to the next. It isn't news anymore.

So why don't we all just stay home? Part of me thinks, huffily, that we should. The trouble is that the rest of me still dreams that dream of a virgin world. A few nights ago

I met a couple who recounted with glee a dog-sledding trip they'd taken deep in the Canadian Rockies. Someone else trained the dogs and guided the visitors who came seeking new sights and experiences. My acquaintances got tossed from their sleds and trampled by dogs, froze their hands and slept outside, ate peculiar food and missed their children. They had a wonderful time. They learned something; their lives were changed. And as I listened to both of them talking at once, stories crossing, words tumbling into the air, I wanted to go.

Exploring Texts and Contexts

For activities with icons, refer to the Guide to Analyzing Readings in Context.

1. Barrett writes, "Adventure depends not only on context, but on character too" (174). How does Barrett use the idea of context—the specific situation but also the wider culture and time period—to talk about what adventure means? How is Barrett's notion of adventure shaped by her own context?

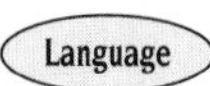

2. Barrett compares writing to the excitement of scientific discovery. Review her essay to find specific examples of references to writing as a way to fulfill her desire to discover new things. How does this metaphor provide new ways to think about writing? In what ways does her metaphor help you understand what writing means to her?

3. Referring to the explorations of nineteenth-century naturalists and historians, Barrett says, "These days adventure always has this element of quotation—of repeating, retracing, rethinking the acts of others" (173). Do you agree with her that there is nowhere left for the explorer to go to make discoveries? Drawing from your personal experiences or your study of some field of knowledge, name new frontiers or unknown territories still to be explored.

Creating Texts

For activities with icons, refer to the Guides to Analyzing Contexts for Writing and Analyzing Readings in Context. For additional help with these writing projects, read the descriptions of **Essay** and **Dialogue/Symposium** in the Genre Glossary.

1. According to Barrett, the adventures of what she calls "inner space"—the arts, science, fiction—can seem "fresher, cleaner" than other types of adventures. Reread her essay carefully to understand how and why she arrives at this conclusion. Do you agree with her that a person's age or circumstances of modern life make expeditions into the unknown less compelling? Write a personal essay either using your experience in "inner space" as an example of adventure or arguing that it is still possible to have authentic physical adventures.

Situation

2. Barrett observes, "Heading toward territory unknown to us, if not absolutely unknown, still offers a sense of discovery. But once adventure becomes a commod-

ity, it is altered in some essential way" (175). Witold Rybczynski explores both the positive and negative effects of industrialization and mass production on comfort and home design. Margaret Crawford talks about what happens to the real estate industry when the residents of East L.A. "decommodify" their houses. Write a dialogue in which these writers address this question; how does commodification affect modern life?

Nature and Culture

Yi-Fu Tuan

If you studied geography in grade school, you might think of it as just a matter of maps, capital cities, major products, and so forth. But geographers study a surprisingly wide range of phenomena and, perhaps not surprisingly, bring a broad perspective to their subjects. The academic study of geography is divided into two main branches: physical geography, which studies the kinds of things we might remember from grade school, such as land forms, terrain, climate, and natural resources; and human geography, which studies human activities as they are distributed in space, including where people live, how they sustain themselves there, why they leave, and where they go. Yi-Fu Tuan, a professor of geography at the University of Wisconsin, has moved back and forth between these branches, often combining them, in books such as *The Hydrologic Cycle and the Wisdom of God* and *Cosmos and Hearth: A Cosmopolite's Viewpoint,* and always bringing a philosophical perspective to the phenomena he studies.

This reading is an excerpt from the first chapter of Tuan's 1998 book *Escapism.* In this book Tuan discusses how humans around the world and throughout history have created their cultures as a way of escaping the dangers, uncertainties, and nonhuman strangeness of nature; but, he points out, when weary of the stresses of culture, they seek to renew themselves by escaping back into the strangeness of nature. Tuan has called *Escapism* probably his last academic work—he retired in 1998, after 40 years of teaching—and perhaps for this reason has included in it much discussion and speculation on the "big questions"—what does it mean to be human, what are the extremes of human experience, and what is the balance that we long for and then long to escape? He interweaves in this discussion ideas and information from a variety of fields and cultures. Tuan was born and raised in China but has spent most of his adult life in the United States, and he believes that this dual background may be one reason for his broad interests and tendency to compare phenomena that on the surface appear to be unrelated or very different. He is interested in both the vast differences between human cultures and the natural forces that are our common heritage and experience.

Connecting with the Conversation

1. Did you study a subject called "geography" in school? What kinds of things did you study? How has the study of geography changed recently? Compare your experiences with those of the other members of a small group.
2. What do the words *nature* and *culture* mean to you? Without consulting a dictionary, write brief definitions of these words.
3. Have you ever wanted to "get away from it all"? What did you want to get away from, and where did you want to go? Write in your journal about your thoughts and experiences.

"Escapism" has a somewhat negative meaning in our society and perhaps in all societies. It suggests an inability to face facts—the real world. We speak of escapist literature, for instance, and we tend to judge as escapist places such as mega-shopping malls, fancy resorts, theme parks, or even picture-perfect suburbs. They all lack—in a single word—weight.[1]

Suspicion of escapism has many causes. The most obvious is that no animal can survive unless it perceives its environment as it really is. Daydreaming or wishful thinking would not answer. The hard facts cannot be made to go away by shutting one's eyes. But so far as we know, only humans may withdraw, eyes shut, to ponder the nature of a threat rather than confront it directly, muscles tense, eyes open; only they daydream and engage in wishful thinking. Significantly, only humans have culture. By culture I mean not just certain acquired habits, the manufacture and use of certain tools, but a whole world of thought and belief, habits and customs, skills and artifacts. Culture is more closely linked to the human tendency not to face facts, our ability to escape by one means or another, than we are accustomed to believe. Indeed, I should like to add another definition of what it is to be human to the many that already exist: A human being is an animal who is congenitally indisposed to accept reality as it is. Humans not only submit and adapt, as all animals do; they transform in accordance with a preconceived plan. That is, before transforming, they do something extraordinary, namely, "see" what is not there. Seeing what is not there lies at the foundation of all human culture.

Reality and the Real

What do the words "reality" and "real" mean? Although philosophers do not find it easy to agree on an answer, ordinary thinking people have little difficulty using these words in everyday talk, often in conjunction with their opposites, "fantasy" and "unreal." Such talk, when looked at closely, shows how the meaning of "real" shifts, even radically, as the context changes. A common meaning draws on the model of animal life. The idea is

---

From *Escapism.* Baltimore: The Johns Hopkins University Press, 1998, pp. xi–xvii, 5–11, 13–27.

that animals live in the real world, respond as best they can to outside forces and their own nature, free of unsettling images and aspirations. Humans can approach that state of existence by also living close to nature, curbing the imagination and jettisoning excess cultural baggage. Nature itself is real. It is indubitably real to humans when they feel it as a blast of cold wind, a sudden shower, or the skin rash caused by contact with poison ivy. So another meaning of "real" emerges: the real as impact. It is not just nature; it is whatever in nature or in society imposes itself on a human being or group, doing so either suddenly or as a consistently felt pressure. "Reality" in this sense is intractable, and it is indifferent to the needs and desires of particular individuals and groups. Facing reality, then, implies accepting one's essential powerlessness, yielding or adjusting to circumambient forces, taking solace in some local pattern or order that one has created and to which one has become habituated. This "local pattern or order" points to another sense of the real: a small and thoroughly humanized world. Far from being shock or impact, the real is the familiar, the predictable, the nurturing and all-enveloping. Home is the prime example. Home is a place to which one is attached by myriad habits of thought and behavior—culturally acquired, of course, yet in time they become so intimately woven into everyday existence that they seem primordial and the essense of one's being. Moving out of home and the familiar, even when this is voluntary and of short duration, can feel like escapism, sojourn in a fantasy world, less real because less dense and all-encompassing.

Does this conclude the list of commonly accepted meanings of "real"? No. For completion, at least one more sense of the word demands to be added. Disconcertingly, it is the opposite of the one I have just given. In this usage, it is daily life, with its messy details and frustrating lack of definition and completion—its many inconclusive moves and projects twisting and turning as in a fitful dream—that is unreal. Real, by contrast, is the well-told story, the clear image, the well-defined architectural space, the sacred ritual, all of which give a heightened sense of self—a feeling of aliveness.

The Earth

5 The earth is our home. Trips to the moon, another planet, a distant star, have haunted the human imagination and may even become a commonplace reality one day. But they nevertheless have an aura of fantasy about them. Real life is life on earth; it is here that we have our roots and our being. Geographers study the earth as human habitat or home. Interestingly, they discover that the earth is never quite the home humans want it to be; hence the dreams of flying and of a paradise located elsewhere that are common to many cultures. Most people, when they think of the earth, think not of the entire planet but of a part of it—the part they live in. Wherever they happen to be, provided they have been settled there for some time, they consider home. Yet this is not quite the case either, if only because if it were, there would be no story, no *human* story, to tell; people, like other animals, will be "immersed in nature," as G.W. F. Hegel put it. It is the restless activity that produces the story line. Human beings have been and continue to be profoundly restless. For one reason or another, they are not content with being where they are. They move, or if they stay in place, they seek to rearrange that place. Migration and the in situ transformation of the environment are two major themes—*the* two major

themes—in human geography. They both reveal a discontent with the status quo, a desire to escape. Geographers have written voluminously on these themes without using "escape" or "escapism" as a guiding concept. What is to be gained by using it now? The gain is that it forces us to reconsider nature and culture, and thereby who we are and what we aspire to, in productive tandem with "real and imagined," "reality and fantasy"—ideas that traditionally are at the core of humanist scholarship and thinking.

Migration

Migration is clearly a type of escape. Animals move out when their home ground starts to deteriorate. Humans have done so since the earliest times; and it now appears that as they acquired certain critical marks of culture—outstandingly, language around sixty thousand years ago—they became better able to organize themselves in complex ways and meet the challenges of the environment by migrating, sometimes over great distances. To overcome great distance, our remote ancestors must have had not only organizational ability, enormously enhanced by language, but also new technical means at their disposal—seaworthy craft, for example. Such people must have been of lively mind and were, I will assume, quite capable of envisaging "greener pastures" elsewhere and making plans as to how best to reach their destination.[2] By the end of the Ice Age, some twelve thousand years ago, human beings had spread into every kind of natural environment, from the Tropics to the Arctic, the major exceptions being ice sheets and the highest mountains.

Much of the human story can be told as one of migration. People move a short distance to a better hunting ground, richer soil, better economic opportunity, greater cultural stimulus. Short-distance movements are likely to be periodic, their paths winding back on themselves with changing circumstance. Over the years such movements become habit, their circuits habitat. Long-distance migrations, by contrast, are likely to be in one direction and permanent. A certain epic grandeur attaches to them, for migrants must be willing to take steps that make life even more difficult than it already is in the hope of future felicity. Before people make a risky move, they must have information about their destination point. What kinds of information are available? To what extent does the need to believe in a better world at the horizon overrule or distort the "hard facts" that people know? Is reality so constraining and unbearable at home that it becomes the seedbed for wild longings and images? And do these images, by virtue of their simplicity and vividness, seem not a dream but more "real" than the familiar world? A great modern epic of migration is the spread of Europeans to the New World. The United States of America proclaims itself a land of immigrants. It would not want to be known as a "land of escapists," yet many did just that: escape from the intolerable conditions of the Old World for the promises of the New.[3]

Nature and Society

Human restlessness finds release in geographical mobility. It also finds release (and relief) in bringing about local change. The circumstance one wishes to change—to escape from—can be social, political, or economic; it can be a run-down urban neighborhood or a ravaged countryside. And it can be nature. In telling a human story, we may start at any point in time, but if we go back far enough we necessarily have nature, untouched nature, as stage: first the swamp, forest, bush, or desert, then . . . then what? Then humans enter, and our story begins.

In the long run, humans everywhere experience, if not forthrightly recognize, nature as home and tomb, Eden and jungle, mother and ogre, a responsive "thou" and an indifferent "it." Our attitude to nature was and is understandably ambivalent. Culture reflects this ambivalence; it compensates for nature's defects yet fears the consequences of overcompensation. A major defect is nature's undependability and violence. The familiar story of people altering nature can thus be understood as their effort to distance themselves from it by establishing a mediating, more constant world of their own making. The story has many versions. Almost all are anguish-ridden, especially early on, when pioneers had to battle nature for a precarious toehold.[4]

10 A natural environment can itself seem both nourishing and stable to its human habitants. A tropical forest, for example, provides for the modest needs of hunter-gatherers throughout the year, year after year. However, once a people start to change the forest, even if it is only the making of a modest clearing for crops and a village, the forest can seem to turn into a malevolent force that relentlessly threatens to move in and take over the cleared space.[5] Some such experience of harassment is known to villagers all over the world, though perhaps not to the same degree as in the humid Tropics. Villagers are therefore inclined to see nature in a suspicious light. Of course they know that it provides for their needs and are grateful—a gratitude expressed by gestures and stories of respect. But they also know from hard experience that nature provides grudgingly, and that from time to time it acts with the utmost indifference to human works and lives.

Carving a space out of nature, then, does not ensure stability and ease. To the contrary, it can make people feel more than ever vulnerable. What to do? Lacking physical power, the most basic step they can take is to rope nature into the human world so that it will be responsive—as difficult people are—to social pressures and sanctions. If these don't work, they try placatory ritual, and if this in turn fails, they appeal to the higher authority of heaven or its human regents on earth. By one means or another they seek control, with at best only tenuous success. What appears stable to the visiting ecologist, whose discipline predisposes him to focus on long-range people-environment interactions, may be not stable at all but rather full of uncertainty to the local inhabitants struggling to survive from day to day, week to week, one season to another.

Escape to Nature

I have given a brief and sweeping account of "escape from nature." The escape is made possible by different kinds of power: the power of humans working cooperatively and deliberatively together, the power of technology, and, underlying them, the power of images and ideas. The realities thus created do not, however, necessarily produce contentment. They may, on the contrary, generate frustration and restlessness. Again people seek to escape—this time "back to nature."

Escaping or returning to nature is a well-worn theme. I mention it to provide a counterpoint to the story of escaping *from* nature, but also to draw attention to certain facets of the "back to nature" sentiment that have not yet entered the common lore.

* * *

One is the antiquity of this sentiment. A yearning for the natural and the wild goes back almost to the beginning of city building in ancient Sumer. A hint of it can already be found in the epic of Gilgamesh, which tells of the natural man Enkidu, who was seduced by gradual steps to embrace the refinements of civilization, only to regret on his deathbed what he had left behind: a free life cavorting with gazelles.[13]

15 The second point I wish to underline is this: Although a warm sentiment for nature is common among urban sophisticates, as we know from well-documented European and East Asian history, it is not confined to them. The extreme artificiality of a built environment is not itself an essential cause or inducement. Consider the Lele of Kasai in tropical Africa. They do not have cities, yet they know what it is like to yearn for nature. What they wish to escape from is the modestly humanized landscape they have made from the savanna next to the Kasai River, for to keep everything there in good order—from social relations to huts and groundnut plots—they must be constantly vigilant, and that proves burdensome. To find relief, the Lele men periodically leave behind the glare and heat of the savanna, with its interminable chores and obligations, to plunge into the dark, cool, and nurturing rain forest on the other side of the river, which to them is the source of all good things, a gift of God.[14]

The third point is that "back to nature" varies enormously in scale. At one end of the scale are such familiar and minor undertakings as the weekend camping trip to the forest and, more permanently, the return to a rural commune way of life. At the other end of the scale is the European settlement of North America itself. It too might be considered a type of "escape to nature." Old Europe was the city; the New World was nature. True, many settlers came from Europe's rural towns and villages rather than from its large cities. Nevertheless, they were escaping from a reality that seemed too firmly set and densely packed to the spaces and simpler ways of life in the New World.[15]

My final point is this: Back-to-nature movements at all scales, including the epic scale of transatlantic migration, have seldom resulted in the abandonment, or even serious depletion, of populations in the home bases—the major cities and metropolitan fields, which over time have continued to gain inhabitants and to further distance themselves from nature.

This last point serves to remind us that "escape to nature" is dependent on "escaped *from* nature." The latter is primary and inexorable. It is so because pressures of population and social constraint must build up first before the desire to escape from them can arise; and I have already urged that these pressures are themselves a consequence of culture—of our desire and ability to escape from nature. "Escape from nature" is primary for another reason, namely, that the nature one escapes to, because it is the target of desire rather than a vague "out there" to which one is unhappily thrust, must have been culturally delineated and endowed with value. What we wish to escape to is not "nature" but an alluring conception of it, and this conception is necessarily a product of a people's experience and history—their culture. Paradoxical as it may sound, "escape to nature" is a cultural undertaking, a covered-up attempt to "escape from nature."

Nature and Culture

Nature is culturally defined, a point of view that is by now widely accepted among environmental theorists.[16] Culturally defined? Humanly constituted? Is this the latest eruption of hubris in the Western world? Not necessarily, for the idea can reasonably be coupled with another one, inspired by Wittgenstein, namely this: That which is defined and definable, that which can be encompassed by language or image, may be just a small part of all there is—Nature with a capital *N*.[17] Now, in this chapter I myself have been using the word "nature" in a restricted sense—nature with a small *n*. What do I mean by it? What is the culture that has influenced me? It is the culture of academic geography. The meaning that I give the word is traditional among geographers: Nature is that layer of the earth's surface and the air above it that have been unaffected, or minimally affected, by humans; hence, the farther back we reach in time, the greater will be the extent of nature. Another way of putting it is this: Nature is what remains or what can recuperate over time when all humans and their works are removed.

These ideas of nature are a commonplace in today's world, thanks in part to their popularization in the environmental movement. They seem nonarbitrary, an accurate reflection of a common type of human experience and not just the fantasy of a particular people and time. But is this true? I believe it is. The nature/culture distinction, far from being an academic artifact, is recognized, though in variant forms, in all civilized societies—"civilized" itself being a self-conscious self-designation that postulates an opposite that is either raw and crude or pure and blissful. More generally, the distinction is present—in the subtext, if not the text—whenever and wherever humans have managed to create a material world of their own, even if this be no more than a rough clearing in which are located a few untidy fields and huts. I have already referred to the Lele in Africa. Their appreciation of a pure nature away from womenfolk, society, and culture is as romantic (and sexist) as that of modern American males. Thousands of miles away live the Gimi of New Guinea, another people of simple material means, whose bipolar *kore/dusa* is roughly equivalent to our "nature/culture." *Dusa* is the cultural and social world, opposed to *kore,* which means "wild"—the rain forest with forms of life, plant and animal, that occur spontaneously and hence are "pure."[18]

What about hunter-gatherers, who live off nature and have not carved a permanent cultural space from it? "Nature/culture" is unlikely to be a part of their vocabulary; they don't need it in their intimate, personal, and constant involvement with the individualized, all-encompassing natural elements. But since they undoubtedly feel at home in the midst of these elements, what an outsider calls wild and natural is to them not that at all; rather, it is a world acculturated by naming, storytelling, rituals, personal experience. This familiar world is bounded. Hunter-gatherers are aware that it ends somewhere—at this cliff or that river.[19] Beyond is the Unknown, which, however, is not "nature" as understood by other peoples. It is too underdefined, too far beyond language and experience, to be that.

A current trend in anthropological thinking is to wonder whether the nature/culture dichotomy is not more an eighteenth-century European invention than anything fundamental to human experience.[20] The binary in Western usage has fallen into disfavor because it is considered too categorical or abstract, and because it almost invariably sets up a rank order with women somehow ending at the bottom, whether they be identified with nature or with culture. One may also raise the linguistic conundrum of how far meanings must overlap to justify the use of European-language terms for non-European ones. I now offer one more reason for the declining popularity of the nature/culture binary. It is that one of the two terms has come to be dominant. In our time, culture seems to have taken over nature. Hardly any place on earth is without some human imprint. True, nature in the large sense includes the molten interior of the earth and the distant stars, and these we have not touched. But even they bear our mental imprint. Our minds have played over them; they are, as it were, our mental/cultural constructs. The ubiquity of culture in the life experience of modern people is surprisingly like that of hunter-gatherers, who, as I have indicated, live almost wholly in a cultural world with no nature, separate and equal, to act as a counterweight. There remains what I have called Nature with the capital *N*. But it, like the Unknown of hunter-gatherers, is beyond thought, words, and pictures. Whatever we touch and modify, whatever we see or even think about, falls into the cultural side of the ledger, leaving the other side devoid of content. Culture is, in this sense, everywhere. But far from feeling triumphant, modern men and women feel "orphaned." A reality that is merely a world ("world" derives from *wer* = man) can seem curiously unreal, even if that world is functional and harmonious, which is far from being always the case. The possibility that everywhere we look we see only our own faces is not reassuring; indeed, it is a symptom of madness. In order to feel real, sane, and anchored, we need nature as impact—the "bites and blows [of wind] upon my body . . . that feelingly persuade me what I am" (Shakespeare, *As You Like It* 2.I.8, II); and we may even need nature as that which forever eludes the human mind.

But this hardly exhausts the twists and turns in meaning of nature/culture, real/imaginary. So the real is impact—the unassimilable and natural. But, as I have noted earlier, the opposite can seem more true. The real is the cultural. The cultural trumps the natural by appearing not so much humanmade as spiritual or divine. Thus, the cosmic city is more real than wilderness. The poem is more real than vague feeling. The ritual is more real than everyday life. In all of them there is a psychological factor that enhances the sense of the real and couples it with the divine, namely, lucidity. My own exposition of nature and culture, to the extent that it seems to me lucidly revelatory, is more real to me than whatever confused experiences I have of both. When I am thinking and writing well, I feel I have escaped to the real.

Escape to the Real and the Lucid

I began this chapter by noting that escapism has a somewhat negative meaning because of the common notion that what one escapes from is reality and what one escapes to is fantasy. People say, "I am fed up with snow and slush and the hassles of my job, so I am going to Hawaii." Hawaii here stands for paradise and hence the unreal. In place of Hawaii, one can substitute any number of other things: from a good book and the movies to a tastefully decorated shopping mall and Disneyland, from a spell in the suburbs or the countryside to a weekend at a first-rate hotel in Manhattan or Paris. In other societies and times, the escape might be to a storyteller's world, a communal feast, a village fair, a ritual.[21] What one escapes to is culture—not culture that has become daily life, not culture as a dense and inchoate environment and way of coping, but culture that exhibits lucidity, a quality that often comes out of a process of simplification. Lucidity, I maintain, is almost always desirable. About simplification, however, one can feel ambivalent. If, for example, a people's experience of a place or event is one of simplification, they may soon feel bored and dismiss it—in retrospect, if not at that time—as a thinly constructed fantasy of no lasting significance. Escape into it from time to time, though understandable, is suspect. If, however, their experience has more the feel of clarity than of simplification, they may well regard it as an encounter with the real. Escape into a good book is escape into the real, as the late French president François Mitterrand insisted. Participation in a ritual is participation in something serious and real; it is escape from the banality and opaqueness of life into an event that clarifies life and yet preserves a sense of mystery.[22]

To illustrate the wide acceptance of the idea that whatever is lucid feels real, consider two worlds of experience that superficially have nothing in common: academia and wild nature. Society at large has often called academia "an ivory tower," implying that life there is not quite real. Academics themselves see otherwise; it is their view that if they escape from certain entanglements of "real life," it is only so that they may better engage with the real, and it is this engagement with the real that makes what they do so deeply rewarding. And how do they engage with the real? The short answer is, Through processes and procedures of simplification that produce clarity and a quasi-aesthetic sense of having got the matter under study right. Now, consider wild nature. A sojourn in its midst may well be regarded as an escape into fantasy, far from the frustrations and shocks of social life. Yet nature lovers see otherwise. For them, the escape into nature is an escape into the real. One reason for this feeling certainly does not apply to academia. It is that the real *is* the natural, the fundament that has not been disturbed or covered up by human excrescences. What academia and nature share—perhaps the only outstanding characteristic that they share—is simplicity. Academic life is self-evidently a simpler organization than the greater society in which it is embedded. As for nature, in what sense is it simple or simpler—and simpler than what? However the answer is given, one thing is certain: People of urban background—and increasingly people are of such background—know little about plants and animals, soils and rock, even if they now live in exurbia or have a home in rural Idaho. Other than the few trained naturalists among them, their images of nature tend to be highly selective and schematic; indeed, for lack of both knowledge and experience, they may well carry reductionism further in the imaging of nature than in the imaging of social life, with the result that nature becomes the more clearly delineated of the two, more comprehensible, and therefore more real.

Middle Landscapes as Ideal and Real

Between the big artificial city at one extreme and wild nature at the other, humans have created "middle landscapes" that, at various times and in different parts of the world, have been acclaimed the model human habitat. They are, of course, all works of culture, but not conspicuously or arrogantly so. They show how humans can escape nature's rawness without moving so far from it as to appear to deny roots in the organic world.[23] The middle landscape also earns laurels because it can seem more real—more what life is or ought to be like—compared with the extremes of nature and city, both of which can seem unreal for contradictory reasons of thinness and inchoateness. Thinness occurs when nature is reduced to pretty image and city is reduced to geometric streets and high-rises; inchoateness occurs when nature and city have become a jungle, confused and disorienting. Historically, however, the middle landscape has its problems serving as ideal habitat. One problem is that it is not one, but many. Many kinds of landscape qualify as "middle"—for example, farmland, suburbia, garden city and garden, model town, and theme parks that emphasize the good life. They all distance themselves from wild nature and the big city but otherwise have different values. The second problem is that the middle landscape, whatever the kind, proves unstable. It reverts to nature, or, more often, it moves step by step toward the artifices of the city even as it strives to maintain its position in the middle.

Of the different kinds of middle landscape, the most important by far, economically, is the land given over to agriculture. People who live on and off the land are rooted in place. Peasant farmers all over the world—the mass of human population until well into the twentieth century—live, work, and die in the confines of their village and its adjoining fields. So the label "escapist" has the least application to them. Indeed, they and their way of life can so blend into nature that to visitors from the city they are nature—elements of a natural scene. That merging into nature is enhanced by another common perception of peasant life: its quality of "timelessness." Culture there is visibly a conservative force. To locals and outsiders alike, its past as a succession of goals, repeatedly met or—for lack of power—renounced, is lost to consciousness. Yet farmers, like everybody else, make improvements whenever they can and with whatever means they have. Their culture has taken cumulative steps forward, though these are normally too gradual to be noticed. Of course, one can find exceptions in the better endowed and politically more sophisticated parts of the world—Western Europe in the eighteenth century, for example. There, science in the broad sense of the systematic application of useful knowledge enabled agriculture to move from triumph to triumph in the next two hundred years, with far-ranging consequences, including one of psychological unease. An "unbearable lightness of being" was eventually to insinuate itself into the one area of human activity where people have felt—and many still feel—that they ought to be more bound than free. Nostalgia for traditional ways of making a living on the family farm is at least in part a wish to regain a sense of weight and necessity, of being subjected to demands of nature that allow little or no room for fanciful choice.

The garden is another middle landscape between wild nature and the city. Although the word evokes the natural, the garden itself is manifestly an artifact. In China one speaks of "building" a garden, whereas in Europe one may speak of "planting" a garden. The difference suggests that the Chinese, unlike Europeans, are more ready to admit the garden's artifactual character. Because artifice connotes civilization to the Chinese elite, it doesn't have quite the negative meaning it has for Europeans brought up on stories of prelapsarian Eden and on Romantic conceptions of nature.

European gardens were originally planted to meet certain basic needs around the house: food, medicinal herbs, and such-like. In early medieval times they were an indiscriminate mixture of the useful and the beautiful, as much horticulture as art. Progressively, however, the gardens of the potentates moved in the direction of aesthetics and architecture. From the sixteenth century onward, first in Renaissance Italy, then in Baroque France, gardens were proudly built to project an air of power and artifice. The technical prowess that made playful fountains and mechanical animals possible, together with the garden's traditional link to the phantasms of theater, resulted in the creation of an illusionary world remote indeed from its humble beginnings close to the soil and livelihood.[24]

A striking example of the pleasure garden in our century is the Disney theme park—a unique American creation that, thanks to modern technology, is able to produce wonder and illusion far beyond that which could be achieved in earlier times. Unique too is the theme park's erasure of the present in favor of not only a mythic past but also a starry future—in favor, moreover, of a frankly designed Fantasyland peopled by characters from fairy tales and from Disney's own fertile imagination. What is more escapist than that? In the spectrum of middle landscapes, a countryside of villages and fields stands at the opposite pole to a Disney park. The one lies closest to nature; the other is as far removed from it as possible without becoming "city."[25] Disney's carefully designed and controlled world has often been criticized for encouraging a childish and irresponsible frame of mind. But again my question is, What if culture *is,* in a fundamental sense, a mechanism of escape? To see culture as escape or escapism is to share a disposition common to all who have had some experience in exercising power—a disposition that is unwilling to accept "what is the case" (reality) when it seems to them unjust or too severely constraining. Of course, their efforts at escaping, whether purely in imagination or by taking tangible steps, may fail—may end in disaster for themselves, for other people, for nature. The human species uniquely confronts the dilemma of a powerful imagination that, while it makes escape to a better life possible, also makes possible lies and deception, solipsistic fantasy, madness, unspeakable cruelty, violence, and destructiveness—evil.

Notes

1. An earlier version of this chapter appeared as "Escapism: Another Key to Cultural-Historical Geography," *Historical Geography* 25 (1997): 10–24. I thank editors Steven Hoelscher and Karen Till for permission to use it.
2. Christopher Stinger and Clive Gamble, *In Search of the Neanderthals: Solving the Puzzle of Human Origins* (New York: Thames and Hudson, 1993).
3. Albert Hirschman, *Exit, Voice, and Loyalty* (Cambridge: Harvard University Press, 1970).
4. "Every beginning is difficult," says Goethe. An Australian historian applies this dictum to his own country: "In Australia, every beginning has not only been difficult, but scarred with human agony and squalor." In C. M. H. Clark, *Select Documents in Australian History, 1851–1900* (Sydney: Augus and Robertson, 1955), 94. For a grim account of frontier life in the United States, see Everett Dick, *The Lure of the Land: A Social History of the Public Lands from the Articles of Confederation to the New Deal* (Lincoln: University of Nebraska Press, 1970).

5. Colin Turnbull, *Wayward Servants* (London: Eyre and Spottiswode, 1965), 20–21.

. . .

13. N. K. Sandars, *The Epic of Gilgamesh* (Harmondsworth, Middlesex: Penguin, 1964), 30–31.
14. Mary Douglas, "The Lele of Kasai," in *African Worlds,* ed. Daryll Forde (London: Oxford University Press, 1963), 1–26.
15. Robert C. Ostergren, *A Community Transplanted: The Trans-Atlantic Experience of a Swedish Immigrant Settlement in the Upper Middle West* (Madison: University of Wisconsin Press, 1988).
16. William Cronon, ed., *Uncommon Ground: Toward Reinventing Nature* (New York: Norton, 1995); Neil Evernden, *The Social Creation of Nature* (Baltimore: Johns Hopkins University Press, 1992).
17. Paul Engelmann, ed., *Letters from Ludwig Wittgenstein, with a Memoir* (Oxford: Blackwell, 1967), 97–99.
18. Gillian Gillison, "Images of Nature in Gimi Thought," in *Nature, Culture, and Gender,* ed. Carol MacCormack and Marilyn Strathern (Cambridge: Cambridge University Press, 1980), 144.
19. For the concept of boundary among the Mbuti Pygmies of the Congo (Zaire) forest, see Colin Turnbull, *The Mbuti Pygmies: An Ethnographic Survey,* Anthropological Papers of the American Museum of Natural History, vol. 50, pt. 3 (New York: American Museum of Natural History, 1965), 165.
20. Marilyn Strathern, "No Nature, No Culture: The Hagen Case," in *Nature, Culture, and Gender,* ed. MacCormack and Strathern, 174–222; see also J. R. Goody, *The Domestication of the Savage Mind* (Cambridge: Cambridge University Press, 1977).
21. Victor Turner, *The Ritual Process: Structure and Anti-Structure* (Ithaca: Cornell University Press, 1969).
22. Mircea Eliade, *The Sacred and the Profane: The Nature of Religion* (New York: Harper Torchbooks, 1961).
23. "Middle landscape" is an eighteenth-century idea that became a powerful tool for understanding the people-environment relationship in the second half of the twentieth century, thanks to Leo Marx. See his *The Machine in the Garden: Technology and the Pastoral Ideal in America* (New York: Oxford University Press, 1964), 100–103.
24. Yi-Fu Tuan, "Gardens of Power and Caprice," in *Dominance and Affection: The Making of Pets* (New Haven: Yale University Press, 1984), 18–36.
25. John M. Findlay, "Disneyland: The Happiest Place on Earth," in *Magic Lands: Western Cityscapes and American Culture after 1940* (Berkeley: University of California Press, 1992), 56–116.

Exploring Texts and Contexts

For activities with icons, refer to the Guide to Analyzing Readings in Context.

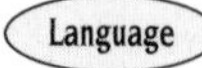

1. This excerpt from Tuan's first chapter is divided into sections with headings. Working in small groups, each group should take one or more sections and discuss how the heading does or does not sum up what the section is about. Would a different heading provide readers a better clue to what the section is about? Share your findings with the class. Then discuss with the class as a whole how the sections relate to each other and to the overall topic of the chapter.

Consequences

2. Go back to the definitions of nature and culture that you developed in response to Connecting with the Conversation Activity 2. Revise or expand your definitions

in light of Tuan's discussion. As you read the other pieces in this unit, in particular those by Andrea Barrett and Richard Rodriguez, continue expanding and refining your definitions.

Creating Texts

For assignments with icons, refer to the Guides to Analyzing Contexts for Writing and Analyzing Readings in Context. For additional help with these writing projects, read the descriptions of **Essay** and **Opinion Piece** in the Genre Glossary.

1. Tuan's overarching term to explore how humans interact with nature is *escapism,* but toward the end of this excerpt he introduces the term *lucidity* to discuss what humans can take away from their interactions with nature. Write an essay in which you discuss the relationship between escapism and lucidity. Use examples from your own life and from other readings to illustrate these terms.

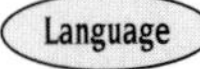

2. Tuan begins the preface to his book by describing a visit to Disneyland, saying at the end of this description,

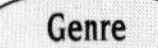

> to my surprise, I found Disneyland itself delightful. I say "to my surprise" because well-educated people, among whom I count myself, are taught to dismiss the theme park as an unreal, fantasy world supported by hidden—and therefore somewhat sinister—forces. . . . Granted that theme parks are escapist fantasies, suitable only for the immature, what human works aren't? (12)

Criticisms of Disneyland and theme parks in general are common both in academia and in the popular media. You may have read some yourself, either in your other classes or in newspapers or magazines. Tuan does not explicitly elaborate his defense of theme parks—he returns to this question only briefly at the end of the excerpt included here (187)—but much of his discussion implies this defense. Drawing on Tuan's ideas about escapism, nature and culture, and the middle landscape, write an opinion piece in which you defend theme parks against the kinds of criticisms that Tuan refers to.

First Diasporist Manifesto

R. B. Kitaj

If you turn to page 39 you'll see the painting *The Billionaire in Vincent's Chair,* by R. B. Kitaj (pronounced Kit-eye) alongside the classic painting by Vincent van Gogh, *Van Gogh's Chair.* Kitaj's painting resulted from an assignment of sorts. London's National Gallery invited several artists to choose a classic painting in their collection and redo it. An invitation was issued to R. B. Kitaj, who chose to redo van Gogh's classic because he felt a kinship with van Gogh—both painters lived away from their birth places. Van Gogh felt himself an outsider in Auvers, on the outskirts of Paris, and dreamed of returning to the comfort of his hometown in Holland. Kitaj, an expatriate and a Jew, living, teaching, and painting in London, never felt quite at home.

Kitaj adopted the term *diasporist painter* to characterize this feeling of being "not-at-home" in London. According to the Merriam Webster Collegiate Dictionary, the word *diaspora* comes from the Greek word *diaspeirein,* which means to scatter. When you hear of people living in the diaspora, it means that they are living far from their ancestral homeland. For instance, African Americans descended from the slaves who were brought over from Africa might consider their life in America as diasporic.

For Kitaj—who was born in Ohio in 1932 but moved to London at age 27 and stayed there for much of his career—living in a diaspora not only meant that he missed the United States, but as a Jew, he also felt that he was far from his spiritual homeland. Thinking about the idea of a diaspora in this way can spark our imagination as we think about the nature of home and travel away from home. The excerpt we include in this chapter comes from a short book Kitaj published in 1989 called the *First Diasporist Manifesto,* in which he announces his artistic agenda. He chose the genre of a manifesto, which as we say in the Genre Glossary on page 576, offers "a public declaration aimed at changing a social situation." Kitaj uses this form to explore what it means to be an artist who always feels, as he says, like a "dislocated pretender." The manifesto allows him to proclaim, and not just explain, that feeling as if you're on the road or not at home has a profound effect on the art you produce. As you read portions from Kitaj's manifesto, consider how his feeling of not being at home might influence his artwork.

Connecting with the Conversation

1. Look up R. B. Kitaj on the Internet and find out what you can about him; search for galleries that have his work in their collections. Check an encyclopedia for a brief biography. Search your college library's subject guide on art for articles about Kitaj's work and reviews of his shows. Find a piece of artwork by Kitaj and read about what Kitaj or others have said about it.
2. Kitaj contributed to the Pop Art movement and to Abstract Expressionism as well. Search online for information about art movements of the 1960s. What sort of art was being produced in London during the 1960s and in the decades following, while Kitaj was there? What other key artists participated in the Pop Art movement? (Hint: Who is David Hockney?) What familiar logos or artwork had their beginnings in the art of the sixties and seventies? Bring printouts of these sorts of art to class. What other artists would have been painting at the same time as Kitaj?

Painting is not my life. My life is my life. Painting is a great idea I carry from place to place. It is an idea full of ideas, like a refugee's suitcase, a portable Ark of the Covenant. Before I run for my train, spilling a few of these painting ideas, I just want to stand still on the platform and announce some of my credentials (more later): I am a dislocated pretender. I play at being a refugee, at studying, at painting. All this is pretence in the sense Picasso meant when he said: "The artist must know the manner whereby to convince others of the truthfulness of his lies."

* * *

Diasporist painting, which I just made up, is enacted under peculiar historical and personal freedoms, stresses, dislocation, rupture and momentum. The Diasporist lives and paints in two or more societies at once. Diasporism, as I wish to write about it, is as old as the hills (or caves) but new enough to react to today's newspaper or last week's aesthetic musing or tomorrow's terror. I don't know if people will liken it to a School of painting or attribute certain characteristics or even Style to it. Many will oppose the very idea, and that is the way of the world.

* * *

Since this is a manifesto, albeit not a very aggressive one (I haven't read Breton or Lewis or Marinetti and such since I was eighteen), I want it to be somewhat declarative because I think art and life are fairly married and I think I owe it to my pictures to put their stressful birth with some idiosyncratic precision.

* * *

In my time, half the painters of the great Schools of Paris, New York and London were not born in their host countries. If there is nothing which people in dispersion share in common, then my Diasporist tendency rests in my mind only and maybe in my pictures . . . but consider: every grain of common ground will firm the halting step of people in dispersion as surely as every proof of welcome has encouraged emigrés before in cosmopolitan centers. Rootedness has played its intrinsic and subtle part in the national art modes of Egypt, Japan, England, Holland and the high Mediterranean cultures and city-states. I want to suggest and manifest a commonality (for painting) in dispersion which has mainly been seen before only in fixed places; but, not unlike painters who leave those centers or those modes, such as Cézanne, who left Paris behind for his epochal old-age style at home, or Picasso who left (classical) Cubism in the lurch, Diasporists also exchange their colors, for instance, to the extent that they begin to really feel at home somewhere, or practice within a School, or indeed, refuse what I say here. . . .

5 Diasporist painting is the other side of the coin of Intimist painting. The coin itself is a Symbolist heir. The clever Intimist observes what he wants to see in his room, before the world outside his room begins; the Diasporist betrays art in his anxiety to depart from his lodgings or to return from the world.

* * *

Aside from the always still endangered Jews (in a Masadic Israel and in Diaspora), there are other resounding Diasporists—Palestinians prominent and suffering among them. Israel Zangwill (1864–1926) placed the Armenians at "the pit of Hell," and in

---

From: *First Diasporist Manifesto.* London: Thames and Hudson, 1989.

1920 bowed before their "higher majesty of sorrow." There is a Black African Disapora as terrible and outstanding as any other, which has disturbed my thoughts since early boyhood. Murderous Stalinism and Pol Potism must have all but unsung Diaspora trails of their bloody own. If the art of these Diasporists, as they emerge from historical fog, is not touched by their separate destinies, God help them. He has so often not.

* * *

I paint pictures in a Diasporist mode possible only now, after all that's happened and before all that may happen. That could be why it's appropriate that I'm so disliked by those who think I've bitten off more than I can chew. I intend to keep chewing all the new food that didn't exist for me when I was a young painter.

The Diasporist in me is impatient with host-art. I feel like a guest in the house of art, guilty if I don't perform up to snuff, anxious to leave the table (and table talk) as early and politely as I can. That's really how I make my pictures, Diasporist pictures—feigned *politesse,* anxious resolve barely revealed. The older I get, closer to the end, I look to more candid, x-rated designs upon painting.

After black slavery (its trail still unwinding), and this totalitarian century (not yet done), it is the very frailty of the human enterprise and the pathos, as an example, of painting quietly through one's days, which assume resonances, some of which I can state unequivocally: I would urge Diasporist painting to a less frail passage, as it tries to read and translate those forces which would deny it life. In this respect, I try to be, along with many artists, forward-looking—in fact, a Messianist.

Exploring Texts and Contexts

For activities with icons, refer to the Guide to Analyzing Readings in Context.

1. The word *diaspora* is a complex one with many shades of meaning. Read through this portion of the manifesto again and jot down brief notes about all the ways that Kitaj uses the tem *diaspora* and how he explores it. After compiling your notes, write about how you think Kitaj would define the term *diaspora* to someone interviewing him about his art.

2. A hallmark of the manifesto is its use to change some aspect of society. Reread the description of the manifesto on page 576 of the Genre Glossary, then reread Kitaj's manifesto and find places where he seems to want to change something. Also reread the section on consequences in the Guide to Analyzing Contexts for Writing. Imagine that you are Kitaj writing in his journal; in his voice, write about the sorts of changes you would like this manifesto to initiate.
3. Find someone who paints, sketches, draws, or does graffiti and interview that person about his or her art. Ask questions that consider the relationship between the idea of artistic creativity and a sense of place. Specifically, you might consider what issues Kitaj's manifesto raises for an artist: How does a sense of being at home or not being at home influence one's work? Or, more generally, you might consider the broader issues raised by readings in this unit about the strangeness of new places and the comforts of home. For help planning an interview, see the Genre Glossary.

Creating Texts

For activities with icons, refer to the Guides to Analyzing Contexts for Writing and Analyzing Readings in Context. For additional help with these writing projects, read the descriptions of **Essay** and **Manifesto** in the Genre Glossary.

1. Both Kitaj, in the excerpt from the *First Diasporist Manifesto,* and Tuan, in the excerpt from *Escapism,* try to locate the person in a context. Kitaj takes a personal, historical view while Tuan examines the problem with a longer lens, situating the person in contexts such as nature and the earth. Each writer makes an argument about what he thinks is most important and chooses a particular genre to develop his claim: Tuan writes an essay; Kitaj writes a manifesto. Write an essay in which you take a position on how you see individuals in their contexts. Use the very different perspectives of these two writers as well as your own experiences. As you write, take note of how Tuan and Kitaj's choice of genre helps them shape their message. Consider your own genre-related choices as you write and include some discussion of this issue in your essay. Genre
2. Kitaj announces in the second paragraph of the excerpt, "Diasporist painting, which I just made up, is enacted under peculiar historical and personal freedoms, stresses, dislocation, rupture and momentum. The Diasporist lives and paints in two or more societies at once." Write a manifesto for the diasporist writer. As a diasporist, you might be living away from your homeland. Or you might imagine a homeland far away. For instance, if your parents were born in Vietnam and you were born in the United States, you might feel that Vietnam is your homeland even if you have never been there. What difference does a sense of place make as you work and write? What sort of change will you call for in your manifesto?

Bright Boy from the Delta

Clifton L. Taulbert

Watching Our Crops Come In is the third of Clifton Taulbert's memoirs chronicling his personal journey from his boyhood in the segregated Mississippi town of Glen Allen to the completion of his military tour as a classified airman with the Eighty-Ninth Presidential Wing. Earlier memoirs included *The Last Train North* and *When We Were Colored,* which was made into an independent film directed by Tim Reid and starring Felicia Rashad, Isaac Hayes, and Richard Roundtree.

"Bright Boy from the Delta" is the first chapter of *Watching Our Crops Come In* and finds Taulbert, in 1967, at Dow Air Force Base in Bangor, Maine. In Maine's blustery cold winters, Taulbert could not be much farther from the warm winds of the Mississippi Delta where he grew up. Of Glen Allen, even though Taulbert spent long, hard hours picking cotton and had to travel to another town to attend a segregated

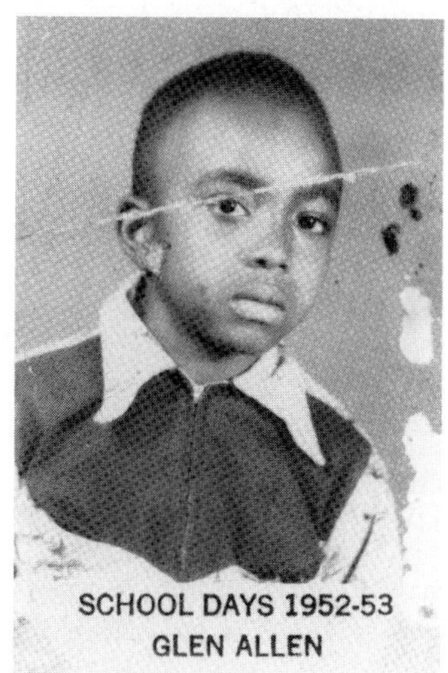

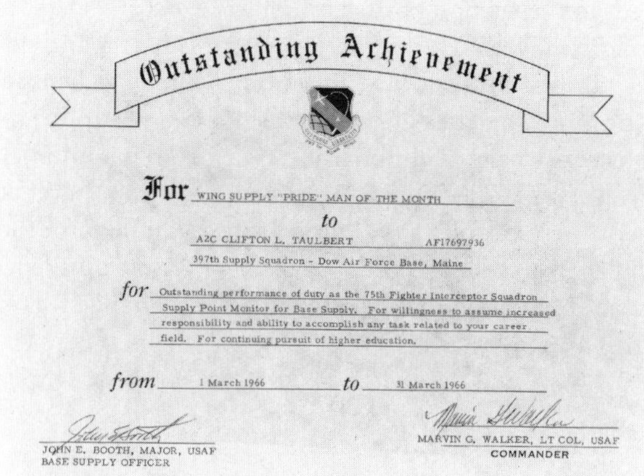

Outstanding Achievement

For WING SUPPLY "PRIDE" MAN OF THE MONTH

to

A2C CLIFTON L. TAULBERT AF17697936

397th Supply Squadron - Dow Air Force Base, Maine

for Outstanding performance of duty as the 75th Fighter Interceptor Squadron Supply Point Monitor for Base Supply. For willingness to assume increased responsibility and ability to accomplish any task related to your career field. For continuing pursuit of higher education.

from 1 March 1966 to 31 March 1966

JOHN E. BOOTH, MAJOR, USAF
BASE SUPPLY OFFICER

MARVIN G. WALKER, LT COL, USAF
COMMANDER

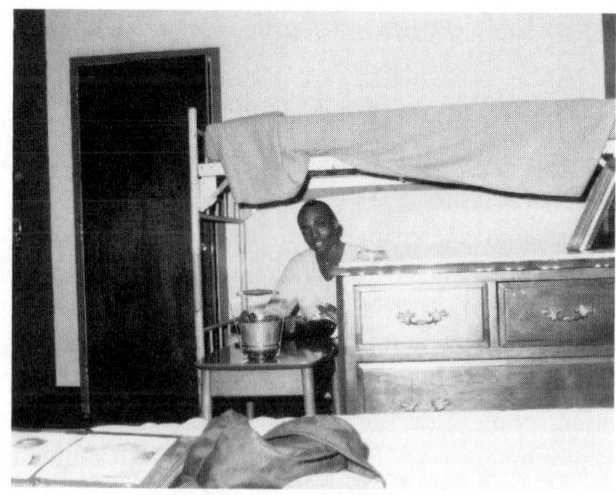

school, he has only warm memories of the times spent sitting on porch steps with his neighborhood's elders learning about trust and community. Cold winters or not, Taulbert tells us that he would rather be in Maine than in Vietnam, where young men one after another were being sent to fight for their country. This series of relocations encourages Taulbert to recall his upbringing in Glen Allen and how it had prepared him for his present challenges.

Taulbert, who consults and speaks internationally, has written a book, *The Eight Habits of the Heart: Embracing the Values that Build Strong Families and Communities,* which translates what he learned on the front-porch steps to lessons for getting along in a diverse society. These lessons form the basis for the consulting work that Taulbert does regularly with businesses and civic groups to help their members live and work together successfully.

Connecting with the Conversation

1. Whom do you get advice from? Consider the people you accept advice from and the places you receive it. Do you accept advice from people who are your elders or your contemporaries? Consider generally the giving of advice: How is it portrayed on TV, in books and stories you have read, in movies? Write in your journal about what you have observed.
2. Consider how you would tell the story of your life up to this point. What key people and events contributed to who you are today? Write in your journal about key memories that you might include in an autobiography.

It was winter, 1967, early in the year. Like thousands of other soldiers, I had lived for months with the fear that I would one day receive orders that would carry me far from home, into the random terrors of the war in Vietnam, which we witnessed daily on TV. None of this had been my plan. In August of 1964, to circumvent the draft, I had joined the air force. After basic training at Lackland Air Force Base and technical school in Amarillo, Texas, I was assigned to Dow Air Force Base in Bangor, Maine, a place I had barely heard of and knew little about. By now, I had seen two hard northeastern winters and I wanted to see no more. But I wanted Vietnam even less.

However, on this midwinter day, I could hardly believe my good fortune. Standing outside the post office in the cold, bright air, I read again and again a letter that informed me that I had been selected to serve in a classified position at Andrews Air Force Base in Washington, D.C. "Congratulations," it said. Congratulations! All I could see was that word. I had survived an extensive background check, and now I could tell my great news to everyone except my best friend, Paul Demuniz, who had already shipped out for Vietnam. I was sad for Paul, but elated for myself. This was not a pipe dream. It was a real assignment, one that would make any airman proud. But it wasn't "any

From *Watching Our Crops Come In.* New York: Viking Press, 1997, pp. 1–19.

airman," it was me, Cliff, the little boy who had grown up in the village of Glen Allen, in the Mississippi Delta, living first with Poppa, my great-grandfather, and later with Ma Ponk, my great-aunt, under whose stern but loving eye I spent my high school years.

It was a long walk but a good one back to the barracks from the post office. As I moved along the quiet path, alone except for an occasional passing car, I recalled how badly as a child I had wanted to go north and how much I hated picking and chopping cotton. But as long as I was in Ma Ponk's care, I knew I had to work and be ready every morning to catch Mr. Walter's truck, which never broke down, no matter how much I prayed.

With the letter of my good news safely put away in my satchel, I walked and whistled as I thought about Ma Ponk and my childhood dreaming. "Boy, git off them steps, wash yore hands, and git back here to dis kitchen," I could still hear her yelling from the back of her small frame house. "You know we got to git up early to catch that darn field truck."

5 Thus she would catch me resting on the front porch steps, still wet from the day's sweat but enjoying any breeze the evening swept my way, and I would hurry back to the kitchen so that I could eat, get the chickens in, and get ready for bed. Some nights, the sun would leave a trail of colors as it moved across the sky and would look as if it was going to fall right on top of our neighbor Miss Elsie's house. I dreamed of the day that I'd no longer have to eat fast, go to bed early, and get up before the roosters. I dreamed of going north, where there were no cotton fields, just good jobs.

Good jobs, I thought, as I walked up the small paved sidewalk to my barracks. I wanted to run into the building shouting the news of my good job, but instead I entered the back door by the fire escape, the one that was hardly used except as our weekend gathering place. Weekdays, our barracks were tense with the fear of impending orders. Most of the guys just went about their routine, watching the news, reading the bulletin board, and waiting for the weekend to arrive, when the mental war we waged could be put on hold. Since this was not the weekend, I hesitated to blurt out my news. I just walked up the inside stairs to the second floor and quietly approached the room that I shared with Airman Robuck from New Jersey.

Robuck was fearful of the war, but he had managed to adopt a "so what" attitude. If he had to go, I expected he would go and do what he was supposed to do. I wanted to talk to Robuck, but I hoped now to find the room empty. I needed time to reflect on this new assignment and what it could mean. In our hall, one guy stood talking on a pay phone, but everything else was quiet. I nodded at him as I got out my key to unlock my door.

When I opened the door, only the heavy smell of furniture oil and wax greeted me. Robuck wasn't back from work. I sat down in the green vinyl chair that was equally spaced between the single bed and the bunk beds, pulled the letter out of my satchel, and looked at it again. Only a few of my close friends knew how fearful I had been about the prospect of Vietnam. We seldom discussed fear, perhaps because refraining from such discussions seemed to be part of the rite of becoming a man. I just knew that I wanted to live to become a man, and I kept quiet when members of the group loudly discussed how they would handle a deadly situation. I would watch in silence as they pretended to crouch in foxholes, crawl through jungle brush, or wade through rice paddies with their imaginary weapons held high above their heads. Even though I was part of them, I never felt as "ready" for battle as they appeared to be. And I never felt I had the character and skills required to be the kind of soldier who could kill so as not to be killed. Fear had caused me to enlist to escape the draft, and I surprised myself when I not only made it through basic training but also made it with honors. However, once in, I still lived with the prospect of my being reassigned to a remote supply post in Southeast Asia. Now that prospect had itself become remote with this new assignment—an assignment I almost hadn't applied for.

Like the rest of the guys, I daily watched the bulletin board, praying not to see my name. I never dreamed that I would find there a notice that would save my life. The bulletin board was always surrounded at the end of the day, and Orell Clay, an airman from New York, was always there, his body blocking our view. Since he was big and mouthy, I felt it best to give him room, although some of the guys would elbow him aside. On the day I found my notice, I waited while Orell and Fred Crowly, his white roommate from Rhode Island, looked at every piece of posted information. When at last they left, I moved to the spot they had vacated and was relieved to see that there was no word of any need for additional troops in Vietnam. Just as I was about to walk away and join my friends at the mess hall, a small bulletin from Strategic Air Command (SAC) headquarters in Nebraska caught my eye. A new slot, a classified position, had opened at Andrews Air Force Base in Washington, D.C. Reading more closely, I realized that the job description fell under my air force classification. AF 17697936 was administrative supply, and they needed someone with my skills. For a brief moment, I fantasized that I could win this post, but I was also sure that I had no chance. Although the military was more integrated than any place I had ever seen, I somehow felt that this job would go to a white airman. I didn't want to apply only to be disappointed, but I wrote down the information anyway, and tucked it in my pocket as I walked from the barracks to the mess hall.

10 That night, I reconsidered. Maybe I did have a chance. After all, back home in Glen Allen I had applied and had been hired for a job in Mr. Hilton's grocery store that had historically been reserved for white boys. Believing that just maybe I could do it again, I completed the form requested and mailed it in. I told no one, not even my closest friends. I then planned to forget the exercise. I knew that thousands of airmen just like me would have read the same announcement and would be thinking, as I was, that this assignment could limit their chances of being shipped off to Vietnam. I returned to my routine of shipping aircraft parts from base to base and to my continuing fear of Vietnam. Days stretched into weeks, and weeks into months, and Dow Air Force Base was beginning to feel more like home than I wanted.

Home for me would always be Glen Allen, and it felt strange to find myself becoming comfortable in a place where the snow fell as frequently as rain. The Mississippi Delta was my home, and I wanted to live so that I could return to the house built by my great-grandfather Sidney Peter. Grandpa had come from Demopolis, Alabama, to the Delta, where he encountered other "colored" who had migrated from Natchez, from Louisiana, and from as far away as South Carolina. Only one generation removed from slavery, these people had held on to their dreams and had built their homes to give place to them. The front porches became the place where visiting relatives from up north would sit and spin their intoxicating tales of northern life. And as long as I can remember, the tales were told each summer. And I remembered them all.

Legal segregation kept the wonderful older people, on whose porches we sat, from using official meeting places such as the library and the community room at the town's clinic, but they seemed not to have cared. Their front porches became their centers of command, from which they welcomed us into a world and a life that had barely changed since the early days of Jim Crow, the system that evolved once slavery stopped.

Like many small towns throughout the south, ours was a cotton community whose social order set the course for both white and colored babies. Miss Lottie, the town's colored midwife, brought me into the world, a world that had already relegated me to an inferior position, but one that could not negate the welcome I felt as a child growing up in the big house with the long front porch. During my years in this rambling wooden house infused with hopes, I started school and began my youthful dreaming.

Glen Allen was a safe place to dream. Although we lived day to day with the harshness of the Jim Crow laws and the limitations imposed by legal segregation, the elders in our community still managed to instill in us the will to live, work hard, and study long because they believed that tomorrow was always the brightest day. They understood the necessity to leave home and do well, but they expected you to return. This safe, predictable world would one day pass into history. But as I grew, I had the benefit of three generations of wisdom, wisdom that years later would serve me well as I was finding my own way.

As I approached my seventeenth birthday in 1963, I found myself preparing to leave for my first train ride and my journey north. St. Louis was my destination. I would live there, get a job, go to school, and return home to Glen Allen every summer, just as my idols, Uncle William Henry and Aunt Dora, from Chicago, and other relatives had done before me. It was a grand plan: the train ride north, the colored porter, and the bright city lights and paved streets. But it was not to be. Immersed in my own dreaming, I hadn't paid close attention to the outside world and the changes taking place. At home in the Delta, I was insulated by fields of cotton and by those who picked it, by lakes of brim and catfish and those who caught them. No one had pulled me aside to tell me about the civil rights movement or the other delta, so far away in Vietnam. They left me to my chopping and picking cotton and dreaming on my own. Little did I know that the fantasy world up north I had created in my mind while working Miss Jefferson's fields would one day be derailed by the reality of war and a social revolution.

The unraveling began after I arrived in St. Louis, where I lived in a small room over a small store, in a city I had dreamed about but barely knew. Suddenly I found myself on my own, hundreds of miles away from the people who knew me best. Even though my natural father had paid for my ticket to St. Louis, I really did not know him. He had left the Delta as a young man, gone north, and created a new life for himself. I had been excited over the prospect of a relationship with him, but it never materialized as I had hoped. I don't question his joy in seeing me, but I soon learned that his life in St. Louis had little room for me. He had arranged for me to stay with relatives I had never met. For the first time in my life I found myself acting, thinking, and doing on my own.

At night, while sharing my small room with a younger cousin, I tried to sort out my feelings. Would I be able to find a good job? I had been led to believe that color was not a factor here, only skills, and I knew that I was skilled. After all, I had been given a white boy's job back home and had graduated as valedictorian of my small high school class. But the long-promised good life with the good job, where whites and blacks lived and worked together, was fraught with complexities that I hadn't understood. Still, I was determined to press forward in spite of all that wasn't there, to dig deep beneath that reality and to find a way to make my dreams come true.

For about a year, things went well enough. I was becoming a northerner. I had started school at the St. Louis branch of the American Institute of Banking and had almost lost my southern accent, a sure sign that I was becoming one of those who would one day return south to visit in the summer. However, as I moved toward social acculturation, the reality of a military conflict expanding into war invaded the world I knew. America was sending thousands of young men, mostly black, to Vietnam. I watched them leave St. Louis in the prime of their life, never to return. As the war wore on, I was sure that one day I would be drafted, too, and I was scared. Having just begun to live, I didn't want to die. But I was black, and it seemed as if black soldiers formed the ranks of the front line in Vietnam.

Although I had friends, I had no one to counsel me, not even my father, but I had grown up more than I realized as I faced the prospect of being drafted. In the quietness of my heart, a heart shaped in the Delta, I decided to enlist in the air force to escape an army draft and possible death in Vietnam. No one knew better than I that I was not guntoting soldier material. Though handling guns was a way of life in the South, I couldn't shoot straight and had never killed, bagged, or skinned anything. In light of what I knew, the air force seemed like the best place for me. And it was. Again, I boarded a train, this time the Texas Lone Star to San Antonio, where I started basic training. With a shaved head, five sets of white boxer shorts, and uniforms that didn't fit properly, I became an airman in August 1964.

20 Basic training was different. Unlike Glen Allen and even St. Louis, there were no nurturing front porches and caring people to hold my hand, just a stranger neatly dressed in a starched uniform and dark glasses, a drill sergeant who asked no questions and expected none. He only barked orders. However, with the help of such friends as Jerry Williams, James Rinderknect, and Airman Canty, I actually managed to adapt to the new and challenging world of "orders." We learned to march to them all. Too afraid to mess up, I did my best in basic training and even later became a junior barracks leader while in technical school in Amarillo, Texas. Still young and afraid, I was slowly becoming a soldier. Most of the men were as apprehensive as I was, although we all tried not to show it. We had started to learn that the military was there to make men out of us, not to deal with our idealistic views and youthful fears.

Amarillo was indeed a detour for me. I had dreamed only of going north to live, not of becoming a soldier in Texas, sitting in a barracks worrying about my orders. When my permanent orders came, I was relieved. My fate was not as bad as I had imagined. Some of the guys who seemed to have connections had found themselves with orders to Florida, but for Kenneth Cone, James Rinderknect, and me, it was the cold Northeast, a cause for sober thankfulness, if not for jubilation. We were going not to Vietnam but to Dow Air Force Base in Maine.

At first I dreaded the assignment, the remoteness of it and the chilling prospect that I could still be sent at any time to Vietnam. As the war continued and the numbers of dead and wounded increased, I began to accept that being cold and isolated was better than being warm and wounded. After making up my mind to give Dow my best shot, it wasn't long before I began to feel like the others, just doing my job, biding my time, and waiting for orders that I hoped would never come.

SOMETIME AFTER I APPLIED FOR THE CLASSIFIED POSITION, a letter came, telling me that I was among the ones selected for a background investigation. If it proved positive, I would be given orders for reassignment to Washington, D.C. I had never been investigated before and had no idea what it entailed. The letter contained a questionnaire. I was to provide information about the people I knew and the places I had lived. I carefully answered each question, wondering all the time if this was really happening to me. Maybe my porch people were right, and tomorrow was the brightest day. I didn't want to tell my friends until the investigation was complete and I had an official answer. My heart held a secret that I wanted to share, but I kept it close to me.

Without being specific, I asked Sgt. Brown, a seasoned airman, to explain to me what a classified background investigation included. When he asked why, I held him off, but I was still able to get him to tell me what I needed to know. As he talked, I realized that investigators would go to both Glen Allen and St. Louis. What a stir this would be for Glen Allen. It was so small that all news traveled fast, and this type of news would travel even faster than most.

The investigators would get all the information needed and then some if they happened to run into Miss Doll, our lady who everyone agreed was "tetched" in the head. She always seemed to intercept strangers who came looking for information from the colored side of the town. I had written down the names of my mother, Mary Taulbert, my aunt, Elna Boose, and Rev. McBeth, the colored principal. But if Miss Doll saw a strange car driving slowly, she would walk right up as close as she could and lean in the window. "I'm Louise Morris, pleased to make your acquaintance. New in town, I s'pose." I dreaded to think what she might dream up to tell them in her odd, rambling way. In St. Louis, I had provided the names of Madison Brazier and Oscar Guyton Sr., in whose homes I had stayed during my short time there.

In Glen Allen, the investigators would hear the story of my birth and meet the people who had welcomed me into the world. They would see that I had been among the fortunate ones to have been born in a town where caring had long been a way of life. Despite all hardships, I grew up being loved and learning from those who loved me, people who took their leisure on front porches, where they entertained us, nurtured us, and spoke the secrets of their hearts.

The investigators would learn all of this and more. They would learn about my aptitude as a student, which led to my being named valedictorian of my class. They would learn about my hard work not only in the fields but also in the local hardware store, owned by Mr. Freid, who had me assist him with his yearly inventory, and later in Mr. Hilton's grocery store. And they would learn about the life dreams that brought me to St. Louis and the confectionery at 2629 North Spring Avenue, where Uncle Madison ruled and reigned.

Uncle Madison and Mr. Guyton would tell them about my life in St. Louis, how I took on extra responsibility in my work at the confectionery, and how Jefferson Bank hired me at a time when there were no blacks in meaningful positions. They would learn how the civil rights activists protested the bank's hiring practices and how, after many demonstrations by young black St. Louisians, I was the one who was hired. Both men were proud of that and shared the story as if it were their own.

Dow Air Force Base was a long way from either Glen Allen or St. Louis, but in those two places lived the people who would help determine my chances to get that classified assignment. And now all I had to do was wait.

30 AFTER THE LAST WEEKS OF FALL HAD FADED and the new year had begun, the private wait was over. I held the official letter that said "Congratulations," and now I could tell my friends. I was going to Washington, D.C., to work in the Eighty-ninth Presidential Wing at Andrews Air Force Base. The people at SAC headquarters had called me a "bright boy," which I took to be a compliment. Of course it could also have been military code suggesting that I was a good risk for this new assignment because the investigation into my past had turned up no evidence of past activities that would have proven to be an embarrassment to the government. But I would never know if their meaning was different from what I took it to be. I had always been told by the old people back home that I had "mother wit," by which they meant the natural ability to make a path for myself, and an old preacher from the colony, the all-black settlement just south of Glen Allen, had once told Poppa that I was marked for good. Thus I assumed that in calling me a "bright boy" the background investigators had made a similar determination about me.

Delighted as I was, I now began to think about the challenges I would face as a new airman. I wanted the job, but because I hadn't thought I'd get it, I had paid very little attention to the skill requirements. I was now apprehensive about my technical ability to do the job. Still, no matter my feelings, I had my orders. They were expecting me at the Eighty-ninth.

While I embraced my new assignment, I also felt a bit of remorse knowing that I'd be leaving Dow. During my last few weeks, as I walked to and from my barracks, a fading green cinderblock two-story building, I fixed in my mind a picture I didn't want to forget. Amid the weekday quiet, I stood at the foot of the fire escape, our entry to the barracks. On weekends in good weather, that fire escape came to life. It was our gathering place, where we yelled at each other, cut hair, and forgot the war. Like the stoops of New York, the verandahs of New Orleans, and even the porches of the Mississippi Delta, it was a small reminder of home, where we were welcomed and visited with friends. There, dates were made and broken, cars were borrowed, and the war was put on hold. In warm weather, we dressed in jeans, cut-offs, and white tee-shirts, our dog tags the only reminders of our military life. As I stood there in the quiet, I pictured all my friends, those of different races and from vastly different social backgrounds, gathering, leaning over the railings, sitting on the steps with the end doors of the barracks propped open wide so that we could all hear the music, our voices mingling in the air like a well-cooked gumbo.

Even though most of us were thankful that we had not been sent to Vietnam, on nights when we sat on the fire escape, we also wished that we were somewhere else, preferably in a city. Getting a good assignment at a base that was close to a city with a great night life was the dream of all the airmen I had come to know, but for most of us, those bases and their cities would always be somewhere else. When the word of my new assignment got around, they were all delighted for me. I was lucky, they said. I had my orders, and they wished me well.

I had only a few weeks left, but for the most part I was gone. My room on the second floor of the barracks would soon house another guy. I hoped that he would appreciate how well I had kept his side. I had put so much wax on the floor that all my replacement would have to do was just hit it softly with a buffer and the barracks sergeant would be pleased. Although our world was focused on the war, we still had to polish those floors, tighten those green blankets, and spit shine everything that didn't move. Often I felt this was a waste of time, but I was assured that obedience to such orders was essential preparation for combat, where commands had to be followed without question if you wanted to stay alive.

35 Excitement and apprehension about my Washington assignment pulled me on. I had never been to the District of Columbia, but the media had brought Washington to me. I was a little fearful of going there, yet I wanted to experience all it had to offer a young man not long removed from the Delta, where life, it had seemed, would never change. Now, as I readied myself for my new life, I knew that the South was changing as well, as the civil rights movement penetrated ever more deeply the world behind the cotton curtains.

When the day to leave Dow came, I was packed and ready early. Since I didn't have a car, I asked John Palozzi to drive me to the airport. We had become good friends, sharing great conversations and good Italian food. John lived in a barracks close to mine. When he arrived, with a little help from my roommate, we got my duffel bag and suitcases down the hall and down the fire escape.

Although we arrived at the Bangor airport early, the waiting room was full. I knew some of the airmen, and I could tell by their faces and snatches of their conversations that they had not been as lucky as I had been. We didn't talk. There was little to say. During those days, airports were not always the places of pleasure travel that we wanted them to be; they took us to our duty, a duty that we knew could claim our lives. John waited with me until it was time to check in, and seemingly within minutes I found myself on board, buckled in, and flying into my future.

While sitting quietly in the plane, I found myself both looking out and looking back. Much had happened in my life since I left the Mississippi Delta. I was no longer the innocent, dreaming boy who loved his great-grandfather's 1949 Buick, frozen custard ice cream, and hot French bread. The reality of becoming a soldier was maturing me, and my fear of Vietnam made me value the life I had. While stationed at Dow, I had seen scores of airmen shipped off to a war they barely understood, to fight a people they hardly knew. We had been told that they were going to ensure democracy, even though it was not fully realized here at home. As a child, I hadn't had to worry about such issues as democracy denied, because Poppa and my family had protected me as long as they could, but now I was out and on my own.

As my plane approached Washington National Airport, I could see the Potomac shining below. I also caught my first glimpses of monuments I had only read about or seen in pictures. It was as though they were moving up to greet me. The plane moved in closer, and people all around me exclaimed at the sight of the Pentagon and the Washington Monument. Fathers and mothers pointed out the sights to their children, and I eagerly listened and craned my neck to see what they were seeing. I really was in Washington, and I tried desperately to catch sight of the Lincoln Memorial and the reflecting pool, which, after Dr. King's historic 1963 march, had come to symbolize the freedom that my people cherished.

40 Years earlier, I had left Glen Allen, Mississippi, loaded with dreams, my family's, our friends', and my own. Fueled by those innocent dreams, I went north, where reality led me into the military. Although I had not anticipated taking that path, I ac-

cepted the challenges of military life. The small fears that fluttered in my stomach would fade. Tomorrow would be all right. Poppa had always promised me that. In spite of the struggles that Poppa and his friends endured, they always looked forward to the next day. They had experienced more fear and anxiety than I had ever known and still managed to nurture and shield us. They didn't become selfish or cease their dreaming. They embraced the future, and so would I. And if my background had caused me to be classified as a "bright boy," I knew it was because of them.

Exploring Texts and Contexts

For activities with icons, refer to the Guide to Analyzing Readings in Context.

1. Consider the title of this chapter of Taulbert's memoir, "Bright Boy from the Delta." Also consider the title of the memoir as a whole, *Watching Our Crops Come In*. What do these titles tell you about how the author has shaped his memoir? How do they help focus your reading and understanding of the material? If you were to choose different titles, what would they be? Language
2. Taulbert never mentions the raging protests about Vietnam but focuses instead on his personal fear of war and his desire to stay alive. Neither does he say very much about the civil rights movement. Consider how Taulbert defines the contexts that shaped him. How does Taulbert see himself in relation to others? How does he respond to the larger social currents he finds himself in? (For more information about the Vietnam War and the public debate around it and a monument dedicated to the soldiers who lost their lives, see the case study in Chapter 11, "Designing Memorials.") Situation
3. Throughout this chapter of Taulbert's memoir, he moves back and forth between the ever-present possibility of being sent to Vietnam and his memories of his upbringing in Glen Allen. Trace this process and think about how it works to create a picture of the present shaped by the past.

Creating Texts

For activities with icons, refer to the Guides to Analyzing Contexts for Writing and Analyzing Readings in Context. For additional help with these writing projects, read the descriptions of **Essay, Cover Letter/Reflective Essay,** and **Advice Book/Article** in the Genre Glossary.

1. Taulbert's personal story has particular impact and significance because of the background of the civil rights movement and the Vietnam War against which the events of his life took place. Think of an event or set of events from your own life that took place against the background of an important historical event, for example the attack on the World Trade Center and Pentagon or the war in Iraq. Using Taulbert's excerpt as a model, write an essay in which you set a narrative

about your own life against the background of larger historical events and discuss how your life reflected or was influenced by them.

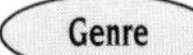

2. Taulbert concludes this first chapter of his memoir by looking to the past as well as the future, "Tomorrow would be all right. Poppa had always promised me that. In spite of the struggles that Poppa and his friends endured, they always looked forward to the next day" (203). Taulbert claims that the lessons he learned in Glen Allen offer a key to living in a diverse world. Consider your own experiences and write a section of an advice book in which you tell your audience what lessons you have learned and how they can be used in today's diverse communities. In addition, write a cover letter about your experience of writing in this genre and what you learned from it.

CHAPTER 7

Making a Home

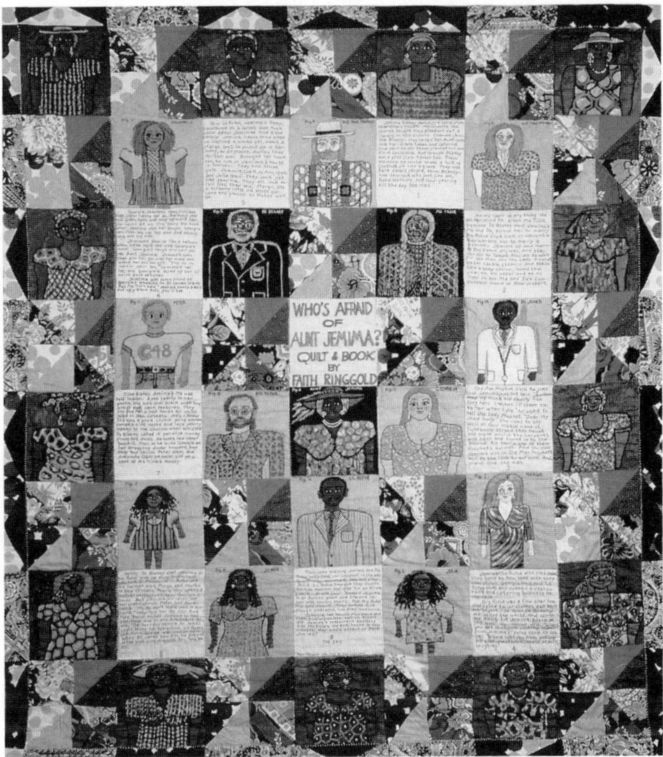

Situation: Where are quilts usually found? Have you ever seen a quilt displayed in an exhibit?

Genre: Do you think of quilting as a handicraft or an art? Are you familiar with any other uses of quilts? How can a quilt send a message or tell a story?

Language: Why do you think the artist chose to combine pictures with text? What is the title of the quilt? Does the title bring to mind any other stories or images? Why do you think the artist chose to use this title?

Consequences: What effect did the quilt have on you? Consider the title of the quilt in the context of the images; what consequences do you think the artist intended?

289,000, 3 bedrooms, 1 bathroom; estimated monthly mortgage payment, 1716.65. Charm abounds in this country Colonial. Updated kitchen with ash cabinets and ceramic floor, tiled upstairs bath w/Jado fixtures. Gleaming hardwood floors and oak doors. 3rd floor finished loft and new basement bath and family room. Professionally landscaped English garden and brick patio. Loads of expansion potential in this wonderful home in Highland Park.

Rogers Park. Spac. 2.5br., dec, LR, DR, new kit. New winds. $735 +

Fabulous gated community of condominiums and townhomes on the river in magnificent garden-like setting. Now under construction. $340,000–$1,350,000.

Hotel Covent, 2653 N. Clark $90wk, $350 mo. TVrm, a/c. Men's residence. Prkg.

A memorable image in a 1960s show like "Leave it to Beaver," "Father Knows Best," and even in the more recent movie "Home Alone" is the home that provides the backdrop for the show's action. Often it is a white frame dwelling, perhaps an imposing two-story brick affair with columns, but it always has a front yard, landscaped with bushes, flowers, and a substantial tree suggesting an established dwelling. In these sitcoms and comedies, this home offers an image—an icon—of the American Dream. By owning this home, we have made it, perhaps on our own or with a little help from others; we have the family, the house, the job, and the car. But the image of the detached suburban house and all that it symbolizes marks only one moment in an ongoing conversation about how the buildings we create say something about who we are.

The origins of the suburban home are usually traced to a Long Island development known as Levittown, named for the father and son team who, in the late 1940s, built over 17,000 two-bedroom homes with highly sought-after "built-in" kitchen appliances. In the aftermath of World War II, the homes of Levittown appealed to the American family's desire for a dream home—a modern space with picture windows, air-conditioning, and a sliding glass door opening onto a backyard in which to barbecue, play, and relax. This stand-alone suburban dwelling suggests a particular kind of family life and economic status—a father (usually the breadwinner), a mother (who may or may not work), and children. The suburbs offered economically sound, growing families an opportunity to leave the city and all of its challenges. The suburbs grew in part because of a desire to raise children in healthful surroundings, but few who moved there anticipated the pressures to conform and the isolation of the suburbs. For example, in the fifties, singles, divorced mothers, people of color, and gays and lesbians may not have found suburban life congenial.

As the children of the suburbs matured, many returned to the city, and cities experienced a renaissance. The diversity of ethnic neighborhoods, cultural resources, and public transportation kept people in the city, often throwing together the very rich and the very poor while the middle class had escaped to the suburbs. Over the last half century, then, we have seen an ebb and flow of residential change moving away from the city and back to it, and increasingly we see a complexity that mixes city and suburb into an entirely new residential formation sometimes called exurbia.

But our architectural and social history includes more than the tension between life in the city and life in the suburbs. To learn about how Americans have struggled to create a sense of place, we can look at other ways and other times in which the architecture of a home or community helped define us. Highly independent homesteaders in the early 1800s quickly put up functional wooden dwellings that suited their needs as they headed west. In the cities of the early 1800s, most Americans lived in wood-frame or brick row houses. At this same time the burgeoning population of slaves was housed in log cabins and barracks, located strategically on the plantation so that owners could maintain control.

As the country's industries grew in the early 1900s, large numbers of employees needed housing. Sometimes a company provided boardinghouses or tenements. Some industrialists who developed plants in rural areas built small cottages for employees, but these were often overcrowded and unsanitary. Sometimes industrialists built entire towns to create efficient and highly controlled living situations. In cities, government programs and urban planners contributed to the building of high-rise dwellings aimed at helping the poor become middle class but which have failed miserably at this task. Others attempted to establish homes by living together communally, sometimes for very different reasons. Currently shelters provide temporary homes for battered women or the homeless while others live together in gated communities to preserve their homogeneity and privacy. Some—such as the Sikhs who live together in ashrams or groups who support a vegetarian lifestyle—choose to live in group homes to support a particular political or religious agenda. In this unit we ask you to contemplate what is involved in making a home. Architecture is far more than designing and building residential units. It makes statements about who we are and who we hope to be. This unit asks us how architecture can embody those dreams.

Comfort and Well-Being

Witold Rybczynski

Witold Rybczynski begins his book-length exploration of comfort in *Home: A Short History of an Idea* with this brief explanation:

> During the six years of my architectural education the subject of comfort was mentioned only once. It was by a mechanical engineer whose job it was to initiate my classmates and me into the mysteries of air conditioning and heating. He described something called the "comfort zone," which, as far as I can remember, was a kidney-shaped, cross hatched area on a graph that showed the relationship between temperature and humidity. Comfort was inside the kidney, discomfort was everywhere else. This, apparently, was all that we needed

> to know about the subject. It was a curious omission from an otherwise rigorous curriculum; one would have though that comfort was a crucial issue in preparing for the architectural profession, like justice in law or health in medicine. (vii)

These observations about comfort refer to the time Rybczynski was studying architecture in school; his recognition of the relationship between comfort and lived experience didn't come until he began to design a house of his own and noticed the difference between a design and a design for living. At different points in his writing, comfort is defined as a "sense of domesticity," "feeling of privacy," "atmosphere of coziness," or "intimacy and hominess"; comfort as a concept is not easy to nail down.

Rybczynski belongs to a group of architects reacting to modernism, the prevailing building design. It is interesting to note that he writes about *home,* not *house;* house is a word associated almost exclusively with the dwelling. Home, on the other hand, connotes "refuge" as well as a "sense of ownership and affection." Home includes everything in and around a house but also the well-being of the people who live there. Modernism as an architectural movement spanned the late nineteenth century to the twentieth and encompassed a variety of styles both in Europe and the United States, but Rybczynski's critique of modernism refers specifically to home and furniture design that favors aesthetics over function. He is critical of the emphasis on form, the use of concrete, steel, and glass building materials, and efficiency—the hallmarks of the modern movement—that deemphasize comfort and domestic well-being. He understands architecture as a complex, dynamic relationship between image, behavior, and long-standing cultural traditions. In this excerpt from his book, he explains why postmodern solutions to the lack of comfort in our lives are not effective.

Rybczynski is a professor of urban studies at the University of Pennsylvania and author of numerous books including *Looking Around: A Journey Through Architecture, City Life: Urban Expectations in a New World,* and most recently, *A Clearing in the Distance: Frederich Law Olmstead and America in the 19th Century.*

Connecting with the Conversation

1. Would you describe your home as comfortable? Think about the arrangements in your house. What would you say drives decisions about choosing furniture and decorating: architectural design, the room's actual use, or comfort? Write your views in your journal.
2. Are you familiar with the architectural terms *modern* and *postmodern?* Do a Web search to familiarize yourself with these terms. Look at the pictures in architectural and design books. What architectural styles were popular before the modern era? Identify some buildings as either modern or postmodern. Share with your group what you know or what you have been able to find.

. . . lately I have been thinking how comfort
is perhaps the ultimate luxury.

—Billy Baldwin
as quoted in *The New York Times*

Domestic well-being is a fundamental human need that is deeply rooted in us, and that must be satisfied. If this need is not met in the present, it is not unnatural to look for comfort in tradition. In doing so, however, we should not confuse the idea of comfort with decor—the external appearance of rooms—nor with behavior—how these rooms were used. Decor is primarily a product of fashion, and its longevity is measured in decades or less. A decorating style like Queen Anne lasted at the most thirty years; Art Nouveau barely more than a decade; Art Deco even less than that. Social behavior, which is a function of habits and customs, is more durable. The male practice of withdrawing to a special room to smoke, for example, began in the mid-nineteenth century and continued well into the twentieth. As late as 1935, the steamship *Normandie* was provided with a smoking room, although by then women were beginning to smoke in public. Public smoking has lasted about forty years, but it is likely that before long it will cease altogether, and we will return to the time when it was considered impolite to smoke in the company of others. Cultural ideas like comfort, on the other hand, have a life that is measured in centuries. Domesticity, for example, has existed for more than three hundred years. During that time the "density" of interior decoration has varied, rooms have changed in size and function and have been more or less crowded with furniture, but the domestic interior has always demonstrated a feeling of intimacy and hominess.

Changes in fashion occur more frequently than changes in behavior; cultural ideas, because they last so long, are more resistant to change, and consequently tend to constrain both behavior and decor. Although new fashions are often called revolutionary, they are rarely that, for they can only alter social customs slightly, and traditional culture not at all. Long hair, that symbol of 1960s rebellion, was heralded as a major cultural shift; it turned out to be what we should have known it was all the time—a short-lived fashion. When fashion does attempt to change social behavior, it does so at its peril. Paper clothing, for example, another fad of the 1960s, could not satisfy people's traditional use of dress as status symbol, and did not last long. The power of culture to constrain behavior is evident when foreign customs are borrowed from abroad. The Japanese hot tub, for example, is currently an American fashion—it may eventually become a custom—but the traditions of bathing in Japan and America are tremendously different. The hot tub has consequently been turned from an oriental semireligious, contemplative ritual to a western social recreation. This adaptation occurs in both directions, and just as the hot tub has been westernized, the Japanese have altered our domestic customs to suit their own habits and culture.[1]

From *Home: A Short History of an Idea.* New York: Viking, 1986, pp. 217–232 and notes on p. 244.

Borrowing from the past must similarly accommodate itself to contemporary customs. That is why period revivals, even when they were not outright inventions, were never intended to be authentic recreations of the past; they were always, in the strict sense of the word, "superficial." When the Gothic style returned to favor in the eighteenth century it affected room decoration, but it was not meant to revive the "big house," or the medieval lack of privacy—the basic arrangement of the Victorian house remained intact. When Renaissance interiors became fashionable in America in the 1880s, there was no attempt to turn back the clock; the style was always used selectively, and only in specific rooms. There were no Renaissance kitchens, for example—the idea of convenient and efficiently planned work areas was by then too strong a part of domestic culture.

One cannot recapture the comfort of the past by copying its decor. The way that rooms looked made sense because they were a setting for a particular type of behavior, which in turn was conditioned by the way that people thought about comfort. Reproducing the former without the latter would be like putting on a play and only building the stage set, but forgetting the actors and script. It would be a hollow and unsatisfying experience. We can appreciate the interiors of the past, but if we try to copy them we will find that too much has changed. What has changed the most is the reality of physical comfort—the standard of living—largely as the result of advances in technology. Technological changes have affected the evolution of comfort throughout history, of course, but ours is a special position. The evolution of domestic technology that has been traced in the preceding chapters demonstrates that the history of physical amenities can be divided into two major phases: all the years leading up to 1890, and the three following decades. If this sounds outlandish, it is worth reminding ourselves that all the "modern" devices that contribute to our domestic comfort—central heating, indoor plumbing, running hot and cold water, electric light and power and elevators—were unavailable before 1890, and were well known by 1920. We live, like it or not, on the far side of a great technological divide. As John Lukacs reminds us, although the home of 1930 would be familiar to us, it would have been unrecognizable to the citizen of 1885.[2] Until then, recreating the past was plausible—even if it was rare—after 1920 it became an eccentricity.

5 Comfort has changed not only qualitatively, but also quantitatively—it has become a mass commodity. After 1920, especially in America (somewhat later in Europe), physical comfort in the home was no longer the privilege of a part of society, it was accessible to all. This democratization of comfort has been due to mass production and industrialization. But industrialization has had other effects—it has made handwork a luxury (in that regard Le Corbusier's analysis was correct). This, too, separates us from the past. As the Art Deco designers discovered, a reliance on craftsmanship was expensive and meant an extremely limited clientele. We can admire Mrs. Lauder's Louis XV office, but how many could afford even good reproductions, let alone authentic antiques? If we insist on Rococo we must be content with ersatz—a poor imitation that is neither commodious nor delightful. Only the wealthy or the very poor can live in the past; only the former do so by choice. If one has enough money—and enough servants—a Georgian country home is just the ticket. But the reality of small, servantless households makes it impossible for most people to undertake such wholesale restorations: who will dust all those pretty moldings, who will shake the carpets and polish the brass?

The current fashion for decorating interiors with bits and pieces of traditional-looking ornament, without adhering to any particular historical style, seems, at least on the surface—and it is mostly surface—to be an acceptable alternative. It is an inexpensive if halfhearted compromise—neither outright revivalism nor unadulterated modernism. But so-called postmodernism has missed the point; putting in a stylized strip of molding or a symbolic classical column is not really the issue. It is not watered-down historical references that are missing from people's homes. What is needed is a sense of domesticity, not more dadoes; a feeling of privacy, not neo-Palladian windows; an atmosphere of coziness, not plaster capitals. Postmodernism is more interested in (mostly obscure) architectural history than in the evolution of the cultural ideas that history represents. Moreover, it is reluctant to question any of the basic principles of modernism—it is aptly named, for it is almost never antimodern. Despite its visual wit and fashionable insouciance, it fails to address the basic problem.

What is needed is a reexamination not of bourgeois styles, but of bourgeois traditions. We should look at the past not from a stylistic point of view, but regarding the idea itself of comfort. The seventeenth-century Dutch bourgeois interior, for example, has much to teach us about living in small spaces. It suggests how simple materials, appropriately sized and placed windows, and built-in furniture can create an atmosphere of cozy domesticity. The way that Dutch homes opened up onto the street, the careful variety of types of windows, the planned gradient of increasingly private rooms, and the sequence of small sitting places are architectural devices that are applicable still.[3] The Queen Anne house offers similar lessons in informal planning. The Victorians were faced with technical devices more innovative than our own, and the ease with which they incorporated new technology into their homes without sacrificing traditional comforts is instructive. The American home of 1900 to 1920 shows that convenience and efficiency can be dealt with effectively without in any way creating a cold or machinelike atmosphere.

Reexamining bourgeois traditions means returning to house layouts that offer more privacy and intimacy than the so-called open plan, in which space is allowed to "flow" from one room to another. This produces interiors of great visual interest, but there is a price to be paid for this excitement. The space flows, but so also does sight and sound—not since the Middle Ages have homes offered as little personal privacy to their inhabitants. It is difficult for even small families to live in such open interiors, especially if they are using the large variety of home entertainment devices that have become popular—televisions, video recorders, audio equipment, electronic games, and so on. What is needed are many more small rooms—some need not be larger than alcoves—to conform to the range and variety of leisure activities in the modern home.

It also means a return to furniture that is accommodating and comfortable; not chairs that make an artistic statement, but chairs that are a pleasure to sit in. This will involve going both forward and backward—backward, to recover the eighteenth century's knowledge of ergonomics, and forward to devise furniture which can be adjusted and modified to suit different individuals. It means returning to the idea of furniture as practical rather than aesthetic object, and as something enduring rather than a passing novelty.

10 Another tradition that should be reexamined is that of convenience. In many parts of the house, the pragmatism of the early domestic engineers has been lost in the emphasis

on visual appearance. Aesthetics, not practicality, predominate. The modern kitchen, in which everything is hidden in artfully designed cabinets, looks well organized, like a bank office. But a kitchen does not function like an office; if anything, it is more like a workshop. Tools should be out in the open where they are accessible, near those places where the work is done, not secreted below counters or in deep, difficult-to-reach cupboards. The need for different work-surface heights was identified a long time ago, but kitchens continue to have uniform counters, of standardized height and width, finished in the same material. This neatness and uniformity follow the modern dictum requiring lack of clutter and visual simplicity, but they do little to improve working comfort.

The small standardized bathroom (whose layout is unchanged since the 1850s) looks efficient, but it is ill suited to the modern home. The combination of tub and shower is awkward, the fixtures are neither particularly comfortable nor safe nor even easy to clean. For functional and hygienic reasons the water closet would be better separated, as it is in Europe. When houses contained many more rooms, bathrooms could be small. Today, the bathroom must accommodate activities which previously took place in dressing rooms, nurseries, and boudoirs (even washing machines are now located in bathrooms). In small houses, the bathroom may be the only totally private room, and although bathing may not be a ritual in America as it is in Japan, it is certainly a form of relaxation, and yet this activity takes place in a room that is devoid of both charm and commodity. The modern kitchen is also too small. Early studies of kitchen efficiency focused on reducing the amount of walking done during food preparation. This has produced the tiny, so-called efficient kitchen—often without windows—in which there is little countertop area, but where one can work almost without moving. If such an arrangement was ever convenient, which is arguable, it has outlived its usefulness. There is not enough space for the large number of appliances—mixers, blenders, pasta makers, and coffee grinders—required by the time-conscious housekeeper.

Ever since the seventeenth century, when privacy was introduced into the home, the role of women in defining comfort has been paramount. The Dutch interior, the Rococo salon, the servantless household—all were the result of women's invention. One could argue, with only slight exaggeration, that the idea of domesticity was principally a feminine idea. So was the idea of efficiency. When Lillian Gilbreth and Christine Frederick introduced management and efficiency to the home, they took it for granted that this work would be done by a woman whose main occupation would be taking care of the family. Domestic management may have been more efficient, but housework was still a full-time job—the woman's place was in the home. The desire of women for careers—and not just for economic reasons—has changed all that. This does not mean that domesticity will disappear, although it may mean that the home will cease to be "the woman's place." The scarcity of servants in the early 1900s prompted an interest in machines that would help the homemaker and reduce the tedium of housework; the reduced presence of women in the home requires machines that can do chores on their own. Most recently developed home appliances, such as automatic clothes washers, ice-cube makers, self-cleaning ovens, and frost-free refrigerators, are intended to replace manual operations with self-regulating mechanical ones—they are all partially automated. This development—from tools to machines to automatons—is a characteristic of all technologies, in the home no less than in the workplace.[4] The drying rack leads to the manual- and then the machine-driven wringer, which is replaced by the automatic dryer. The availability of inexpensive microchips is hastening the day when full-scale automation will enter the home in the form of domestic robots—mechanical servants.

A reexamination of the bourgeois tradition of comfort is an implicit criticism of modernity, but it is not a rejection of change. Indeed, the evolution of comfort will continue. For the moment, this evolution is dominated by technology, though to a lesser degree than in the past. This need not dehumanize the home, any more than effective fireplaces or electricity did in the past. Can we really have coziness and robots? That will depend on how successful we are in turning away from modernism's shallow enthusiasms, and developing a deeper and more genuine understanding of domestic comfort.

WHAT IS COMFORT? Perhaps the question should have been asked earlier, but without a review of the long evolution of this complex and profound subject the answer would almost certainly have been wrong, or at least incomplete. The simplest response would be that comfort concerns only human physiology—feeling good. Nothing mysterious about that. But this would not explain why, although the human body has not changed, our idea of what is comfortable differs from that of a hundred years ago. Nor is the answer that comfort is a subjective experience of satisfaction. If comfort were subjective, one would expect a greater variety of attitudes toward it; instead, at any particular historical period there has always been a demonstrable consensus about what is comfortable and what is not. Although comfort is experienced personally, the individual judges comfort according to broader norms, indicating that comfort may be an objective experience.

15 If comfort is objective, it should be possible to measure it. This is more difficult than it sounds. It is easier to know when we are comfortable than why, or to what degree. It would be possible to identify comfort by recording the personal reactions of large numbers of people, but this would be more like a marketing or opinion survey than a scientific study; a scientist prefers to study things one at a time, and especially to measure them. It turns out that in practice it is much easier to measure *dis*comfort than comfort. To establish a thermal "comfort zone," for example, one ascertains at which temperatures most people are either too cold or too hot, and whatever is in between automatically becomes "comfortable." Or if one is trying to identify the appropriate angle for the back of a chair, one can subject people to angles that are too steep and too flat, and between the points where they express discomfort lies the "correct" angle. Similar experiments have been carried out concerning the intensity of lighting and noise, the size of room dimensions, the hardness and softness of sitting and lying furniture, and so on. In all these cases, the range of comfort is discovered by measuring the limits at which people begin to experience discomfort. When the interior of the Space Shuttle was being designed, a cardboard mock-up of the cabin was built. The astronauts were required to move around in this full-size model, miming their daily activities, and every time they knocked against a corner or a projection, a technician would cut away the offending piece. At the end of the process, when there were no more obstructions left, the cabin was judged to be "comfortable." The scientific definition of comfort would be something like "Comfort is that condition in which discomfort has been avoided."

Most of the scientific research that has been carried out on terrestrial comfort has concerned the workplace, since it has been found that comfortable surroundings will affect the morale, and hence the productivity, of workers. Just how much comfort can affect economic performance is indicated by a recent estimate that backaches—the result of poor working posture—account for over ninety-three million lost workdays, a loss of nine billion dollars to the American economy.[5] The modern office interior reflects the scientific definition of comfort. Lighting levels have been carefully controlled to fall within an acceptable level for optimal reading convenience. The finishes of walls and floors are restful; there are no garish or gaudy colors. Desks and chairs are planned to avoid fatigue.

But how comfortable do the people feel who work in such surroundings? As part of an effort to improve its facilities, one large pharmaceutical corporation, Merck & Company, surveyed two thousand of its office staff regarding their attitudes to their place of work—an attractive modern commercial interior.[6] The survey team prepared a questionnaire that listed various aspects of the workplace. These included factors affecting appearance, safety, work efficiency, convenience, comfort, and so on. Employees were asked to express their satisfaction, or dissatisfaction, with different aspects, and also to indicate those aspects that they personally considered to be the most important. The majority distinguished between the visual qualities of their surroundings—decoration, color scheme, carpeting, wall covering, desk appearance—and the physical aspects—lighting, ventilation, privacy, and chair comfort. The latter group were all included in a list of the ten most important factors, together with size of work area, safety, and personal storage space. Interestingly, none of the purely visual factors was felt to be of major importance, indicating just how mistaken is the notion that comfort is solely a function of appearance or style.

What is most revealing is that the Merck employees expressed some degree of dissatisfaction with *two-thirds* of the almost thirty different aspects of the workplace. Among those about which there was the strongest negative feelings were the lack of conversational privacy, the air quality, the lack of visual privacy, and the level of lighting. When they were asked what aspects of the office interior they would like to have individual control over, most people identified room temperature, degree of privacy, choice of chair and desk, and lighting intensity. Control over decor was accorded the lowest priority. This would seem to indicate that although there is wide agreement about the importance of lighting or temperature, there is a good deal of difference of opinion about exactly how much light or heat feels comfortable to different individuals; comfort is obviously both objective and subjective.

The Merck offices had been designed to eliminate discomfort, yet the survey showed that many of the employees did not experience well-being in their workplace—an inability to concentrate was the common complaint. Despite the restful colors and the attractive furnishings (which everyone appreciated), something was missing. The scientific approach assumes that if background noises are muffled and direct view controlled, the office worker will feel comfortable. But working comfort depends on many more factors than these. There must also be a sense of intimacy and privacy, which is produced by a balance between isolation and publicness; too much of one or the other will produce discomfort. A group of architects in California recently identified as many as nine different aspects of workplace enclosure that must be met in order to create this feeling.[7] These included the presence of walls behind and beside the worker, the amount of open space in front of the desk, the area of the workspace, the amount of enclosure, a view to the outside, the distance to the nearest person, the number of people in the immediate vicinity, and the level and type of noise. Since most office layouts do not address these concerns directly, it is not surprising that people have difficulty concentrating on their work.

20 The fallacy of the scientific definition of comfort is that it considers only those aspects of comfort that are measurable, and with not untypical arrogance denies the existence of the rest—many behavioral scientists have concluded that because people experience only discomfort, comfort as a physical phenomenon does not really exist at all.[8] It is hardly surprising that genuine intimacy, which is impossible to measure, is absent in most planned office environments. Intimacy in the office, or in the home, is not unusual in this respect; there are many complicated experiences that resist measurement. It is impossible, for example, to describe scientifically what distinguishes a great wine from a mediocre one, although a group of wine experts would have no difficulty establishing which was which. The wine industry, like manufacturers of tea and coffee, continues to rely on nontechnical testing—the "nose" of an experienced taster—rather than on objective standards alone. It might be possible to measure a threshold below which wine would taste "bad"—acidity, alcohol content, sweetness, and so on—but no one would suggest that simply avoiding these deficiencies would result in a good wine. A room may feel uncomfortable—it may be too bright for intimate conversation, or too dark for reading—but avoiding such irritations will not automatically produce a feeling of well-being. Dullness is not annoying enough to be disturbing, but it is not stimulating either. On the other hand, when we open a door and think, "What a comfortable room," we are reacting positively to something special, or rather to a series of special things.

Here are two descriptions of comfort. The first is by a well-known interior decorator, Billy Baldwin: "Comfort to me is a room that works for you and your guests. It's deep upholstered furniture. It's having a table handy to put down a drink or a book. It's also knowing that if someone pulls up a chair for a talk, the whole room doesn't fall apart. I'm tired of contrived decorating."[9] The second is by an architect, Christopher Alexander: "Imagine yourself on a winter afternoon with a pot of tea, a book, a reading light, and two or three huge pillows to lean back against. Now make yourself comfortable. Not in some way which you can show to other people, and say how much you like it. I mean so that you *really* like it, for *yourself.* You put the tea where you can reach it: but in a place where you can't possibly knock it over. You pull the light down, to shine on the book, but not too brightly, and so that you can't see the naked bulb. You put the cushions behind you, and place them, carefully, one by one, just where you want them, to support your back, your neck, your arm: so that you are supported just comfortably, just as you want to sip your tea, and read, and dream."[10] Baldwin's description was the result of sixty years of decorating fashionable homes; Alexander's was based on the observation of ordinary people and ordinary places.[11] Yet they both seem to have converged in the depiction of a domestic atmosphere that is instantly recognizable for its ordinary, human qualities.

These qualities are something that science has failed to come to grips with, although to the layman a picture, or a written description, is evidence enough. "Comfort is simply a verbal invention," writes one engineer despairingly.[12] Of course, that is precisely what comfort is. It is an invention—a cultural artifice. Like all cultural ideas—childhood, family, gender—it has a past, and it cannot be understood without reference to its specific history. One-dimensional, technical definitions of comfort, which ignore history, are bound to be unsatisfactory. How rich, by comparison, are Baldwin's and Alexander's descriptions of comfort. They include convenience (a handy table), efficiency (a modulated light source), domesticity (a cup of tea), physical ease (deep chairs and cushions), and privacy (reading a book, having a talk). Intimacy is also present in these descriptions. All these characteristics together contribute to the atmosphere of interior calm that is a part of comfort.

This is the problem with understanding comfort and with finding a simple definition. It is like trying to describe an onion. It appears simple on the outside, just a spheroidal shape. But this is deceptive, for an onion also has many layers. If we cut it apart, we are left with a pile of onion skins, but the original form has disappeared; if we describe each layer separately, we lose sight of the whole. To complicate matters further, the layers are transparent, so that when we look at the whole onion we see not just the surface but also something of the interior. Similarly, comfort is both something simple and complicated. It incorporates many transparent layers of meaning—privacy, ease, convenience—some of which are buried deeper than others.

The onion simile suggests not only that comfort has several layers of meaning, but also that the idea of comfort has developed historically. It is an idea that has meant different things at different times. In the seventeenth century, comfort meant privacy, which lead to intimacy and, in turn, to domesticity. The eighteenth century shifted the emphasis to leisure and ease, the nineteenth to mechanically aided comforts—light, heat, and ventilation. The twentieth-century domestic engineers stressed efficiency and convenience. At various times, and in response to various outside forces—social, economic, and technological—the idea of comfort has changed, sometimes drastically. There was nothing foreordained or inevitable about the changes. If seventeenth-century Holland had been less egalitarian and its women less independent, domesticity would have arrived later than it did. If eighteenth-century England had been aristocratic rather than bourgeois, comfort would have taken a different turn. If servants had not been scarce in our century, it is unlikely that anyone would have listened to Beecher and Frederick. But what is striking is that the idea of comfort, even as it has changed, has preserved most of its earlier meanings. The evolution of comfort should not be confused with the evolution of technology. New technical devices usually—not always—rendered older ones obsolete. The electric lamp replaced the gasolier, which replaced the oil lamp, which replaced candles, and so on. But new ideas about how to achieve comfort did not displace fundamental notions of domestic well-being. Each new meaning added a layer to the previous meanings, which were preserved beneath. At any particular time, comfort consists of *all* the layers, not only the most recent.

25 So there it is, the Onion Theory of Comfort—hardly a definition at all, but a more precise explanation may be unnecessary. It may be enough to realize that domestic

comfort involves a range of attributes—convenience, efficiency, leisure, ease, pleasure, domesticity, intimacy, and privacy—all of which contribute to the experience; common sense will do the rest. Most people—"I may not know why I like it, but I know what I like"—recognize comfort when they experience it. This recognition involves a combination of sensations—many of them subconscious—and not only physical, but also emotional as well as intellectual, which makes comfort difficult to explain and impossible to measure. But it does not make it any less real. We should resist the inadequate definitions that engineers and architects have offered us. Domestic well-being is too important to be left to experts; it is, as it has always been, the business of the family and the individual. We must rediscover for ourselves the mystery of comfort, for without it, our dwellings will indeed be machines instead of homes.

Notes

1. According to George Fields, an Australian marketing consultant, appliances such as washing machines and refrigerators have a higher "psychological positioning" for the Japanese, who attach the same importance to these utilitarian devices as Americans do to furniture; in a Japanese home, the refrigerator is just as likely to be placed in the living room as in the kitchen.

   George Fields, *From Bonsai to Levi's: When West Meets East, an Insider's Surprising Account of How the Japanese Live* (New York: Macmillan, 1983), pp. 25–26.
2. John Lukacs, *Outgrowing Democracy: A History of the United States in the Twentieth Century* (Garden City, N. Y.: Doubleday, 1984), p. 170.
3. Many of the patterns described in Christopher Alexander et al., *A Pattern Language: Towns, Buildings, Construction.* (New York: Oxford University Press, 1977), are derived from seventeenth-century interiors.
4. See the author's *Taming the Tiger: The Struggle to Control Technology* (New York: Viking, 1983), p. 25.
5. J. Douglas Phillips, "Establishing and Managing Advance Office Technology: A Holistic Approach Focusing on People," paper presented to the annual meeting of the Society of Manufacturing Engineers, Montreal, September 16–19, 1984, p. 3.
6. S. George Walters, "Merck and Co., Inc. Office Design Study, Final Plans Board," unpublished report (Newark, N.J.: Rutgers Graduate School of Management, August 24, 1982).
7. Alexander, *Pattern Language,* pp. 847–52.
8. Henry McIlvaine Parsons, "Comfort and Convenience: How Much?" paper presented to the annual meeting of the American Association for the Advancement of Science, New York, January 30, 1975, p. 1.
9. Quoted in George O'Brien, "An American Decorator Emeritus," *New York Times Magazine: Home Design,* April 17, 1983, p. 33.
10. Christopher Alexander, *The Timeless Way of Building* (New York: Oxford University Press, 1979), pp. 32–33.
11. Baldwin, until his death in 1983, was generally considered to be the foremost high-society decorator; his clients included Cole Porter and Jacqueline Kennedy. Alexander is the author of the iconoclastic *A Pattern Language,* a critique of modern architecture.
12. Parsons, "Comfort and Convenience," p. 1.

Exploring Texts and Contexts

For activities with icons, refer to the Guide to Analyzing Readings in Context.

1. According to Rybczynski, what is the relationship between fashion, behavior, and cultural beliefs and traditions?

Situation

2. Rybczynski points out that Dutch bourgeois architectural tradition has a lot to teach us about comfort. He says, "It suggests how simple materials, appropriately sized and placed windows, and built-in furniture can create an atmosphere of cozy domesticity. The way that Dutch homes opened up onto the street, the careful variety of types of windows, the planned gradient of increasingly private rooms, and the sequence of small sitting places are architectural devices that are applicable still" (211). How would this style suit your way of life and that of your family? How would an academic like Margaret Crawford, whose work appears in this unit, respond to this plan?
3. In the next reading, written almost ten years after Rybczynski, Sharon Haar and Christopher Reed address some of the same issues of domesticity and architectural design. In what ways do they sympathize with his work? In what ways do they challenge it? How does their approach to this subject differ from Rybczynski's? What social changes have taken place in the years since Rybczynski wrote his book that might affect the discussion?

Creating Texts

For activities with icons, refer to the Guides to Analyzing Contexts for Writing and Analyzing Readings in Context. For additional help with these writing projects, read the descriptions of **Review, Feature Story/Article, Academic Article/Research Paper,** and **Essay** in the Genre Glossary.

1. Write a review of Rybczynski's chapter about the home for students in an introduction to architecture class. In critiquing Rybczynski's discussion, consider not only your personal experience but also what other writers in this unit have contributed to the conversation about making a home. For example, you might think about the feminist issues raised by Sharon Haar and Christopher Reed, or you might look at the issues of ethnicity and class raised by Margaret Crawford. How well do you think Rybczynski makes his point? In addition to assessing his argument, be sure to evaluate the effectiveness of his language and style of writing.

Language

2. A number of writers in this book try to define "big ideas" like comfort and domesticity, respect, and community. Although we all know what these ideas mean, we don't often think about them until they are missing from our lives and we encounter disrespect, incivility, or discomfort. These words may be difficult to define, but it's important to understand what they mean in our culture. Robert Putnam (Chapter 9) cites academic studies on civic participation in past eras.

Rybczynski—rejecting academic studies—uses the "onion theory" to think about how past notions of comfort color our understanding of it. Choose a word denoting a big idea such as comfort or respect and explore it using one of these genres: feature story, academic article, or an essay. You might use profiles of particular people to explore various facets of your topic. Or you might use academic research to show how the meaning of this concept has changed over time.

Coming Home

Sharon Haar and Christopher Reed

When Dorothy in the *Wizard of Oz* cries, "There's no place like home," she articulates a nostalgic desire for home as a place from the past where we are safe and comfortable. Sharon Haar and Christopher Reed want us to rethink the usefulness of a nostalgic vision of home and ask ourselves what we can do to create homes that respond to our changing needs and contexts. In this essay they discuss how feminist and gay artists and architects have characterized domestic life and space. Traditionally, when architects think of women's relationship to the home, it is as homemakers who create a domestic environment through the daily care and maintenance of the home. But Haar and Reed want us to recognize the many other roles women play at home and at work. They have been activists and reformers, seeking to disrupt our comfortable assumptions and build new possibilities for thinking about family and community life.

Haar is an architect and a faculty member at the University of Illinois at Chicago, where she has directed the undergraduate program at the School of Architecture. Most recently she led a conference in which mayors of major cities discussed how the architecture of schools could influence community development. As a teacher and feminist, she wants architecture to be taught in ways that help students think about the built environment in a global information economy. She also wants women to find their place in the profession and architects to advocate for a more accessible and egalitarian built environment. Reed teaches art history at Lake Forest College in Lake Forest, Illinois. He both coauthored this chapter and edited the anthology in which it appeared. Many chapters in the anthology discuss how issues of home and domesticity have been ignored by artists and architects of the modernist tradition, for whom form and efficiency are paramount.

Connecting with the Conversation

1. Visit an art museum and look for pictures that illustrate domestic settings. Ask yourself who is in the picture, what scene it portrays, and what story it tells. Consider, too, what stories the pictures might not be telling.

2. Several feminist artists are mentioned in the following piece. Search the Web and see what you can find about their work. Here are some places to start: Judy Chicago, Yong Soon Min, and Betye Saar.

In contrast to the ambivalent—even antagonistic—relationship between domesticity and modernism, the postmodern era has witnessed a kind of homecoming in high culture, as artists and designers have (re)turned their attention to domesticity. It would be naïve, however, to hail this evolution as a simple solution to the complex problems of modernism. Homes are as often sites of repression and stasis as they are cradles of empowerment and change. This essay charts the place of domesticity in American[1] art and architecture since the 1960s, emphasizing important differences among phenomena often bundled together under the rubric of postmodernism. Specifically, the idea of home today is caught between the stasis of nostalgic historical fantasy and the dynamism of activist engagement with the future; on one hand, the home functions as a potent image or symbol, on the other it exists in all the complexity of daily experience in a three-dimensional world. All history is written with a purpose. Our analysis is frank in its commitment to an idea of the home, not as a symbol of an idealized past, but as a space in which to enact a better future.

The tensions in postmodern invocations of the home may be traced to the 1960s, when two independent movements—Pop and feminism—made domesticity a central element in their defiance of modernism, though with very different motives and effects. The Pop artists' use of domestic imagery finds its architectural counterpart in the work of Robert Venturi, whose 1962 house for his mother deployed, in his words, "the vivid lessons of Pop Art" to challenge "the puritanically moral language of orthodox Modern architecture." Here the anti-functionalist organization of the interior announced an antipathy to modernism reiterated in the exaggerated quotations of exterior elements associated with conventional domesticity. The now famous image of Vanna Venturi sitting on her stoop beneath the oversized split gable roof and gigantic chimney came to exemplify Venturi's goal of "creat[ing] an almost symbolic image of a house."[2]

* * *

For feminists, rebellion was not an avant-garde strategy. They aimed to undo the conventions that neglected or disparaged categories of culture associated with women—prime among these, the home. The link between feminism and domesticity was explicit in the catalog for the landmark 1977 exhibition, *Women in American Architecture,* curated by Susana Torre. The show began from the premise, "the dominant element in women's relationship to architecture has been, since the obscure beginnings of humankind, the relationship to the domestic, including everyday caretaking and maintenance labor."[5] *Women in American Architecture* showcased a range of feminist approaches to architecture, offering a rich overview of histories of women reformers and builders, theoretical propositions about the relationship of gender to design, and current work by women architects. At the same time, it disputed the ideologies

---

From *Not at Home: The Suppression of Domesticity in Modern Art and Architecture,* edited by Christopher Reed. London: Thames and Hudson, 1996, pp. 253–293.

Venturi and Rauch, Venturi House, Chestnut Hill, PA, 1964.

that confined women to a domestic sphere conceived as subordinate or marginal to the public realm. Just as the feminist dictum "the personal is political" propelled women's issues into public discourse, so for feminists in architecture, the domestic was not a retreat from the world but the arena where social forces interact with daily life.

By the early 1980s, feminist studies in architecture had produced an important body of literature. Pioneering books by Gwendolyn Wright and Dolores Hayden—original contributors to *Women in American Architecture*—chronicled the history of American domestic architecture, charting connections between the design of the home and the changing image of the American dream; exploring turn-of-the-century efforts by women activists to link home, labor, and urban design; and advocating the restructuring of family and community life through a redesign of housing and cities. . . . Linking the historical and current projects was a rejection of the modernist stress on standardization, efficiency, and style; in its place, feminists emphasized flexibility, individuality, and the social and physical organization of living space. These emphases reflect two currents in this generation of feminist thought: a widespread fascination with tactility and interiority as "women's ways of knowing" (in contrast to supposedly masculine reliance on vision and projection), and an activist commitment to social change. Both tendencies are present in the work that epitomizes early feminist engagement with domesticity: *Womanhouse*.

5 *Womanhouse* was the project of twenty-three women in Judy Chicago and Miriam Schapiro's Feminist Art Program at the California Institute of the Arts in the winter of 1971–72. According to Schapiro, their question was, "What would art look like if made in the image of domesticity by a group of women artists?" Their answer turned an abandoned mansion into a walk-in rumination on the condition of women's lives. Included were elaborate doll houses; a "Womb Room" encased in a web of crochet; a

nursery where giant furniture reduced adults to the scale of toddlers; a dining-room with a sumptuous meal displayed as art, the food rendered in fabrics, vinyl and petrified bread dough; a pantry with a numbingly repetitious array of breakfasts, lunches, and dinners; and a "Nurturant Kitchen" where fleshly-pink cabinets and appliances stood out against walls studded with breasts that echoed the forms of fried eggs stuck on the ceiling. Two "woman-nequins" enacted a deeply ambivalent relationship to the home: one, nude, was embedded in the tidy linen closet, surrounded by stacks of clean sheets, her body sliced through by the shelves; the other was a beautifully arrayed bride on the staircase with her white train trailing into the kitchen as it turned gradually gray. The most private of domestic spaces became in *Womanhouse* powerful public statements as visitors encountered a "Lipstick Bathroom" painted entirely in red; a "Fear Bathroom" where a bathing female figure made of sand dissolved in a tub; and a "Menstruation Bathroom" set up like a shrine where viewers peered through a veil of gauze to see that, in its maker's words, "under a shelf full of all the paraphernalia with which this culture 'cleans up' menstruation was a garbage can filled with the unmistakable marks of our animality." In addition to these installations, a program of performances during the month *Womanhouse* was open to the public choreographed such domestic rituals as scrubbing floors, ironing sheets, applying and removing make-up, or simply waiting.[6]

Like the uncanny domestic architecture proposed by the Surrealists (described in this volume by Anthony Vidler), *Womanhouse* aimed to disrupt conventions that rendered the home familiar and banal. The feminists' motive, however, was practical and political. As it was summed up by Arlene Raven, "*Womanhouse* turned the house inside out. The isolation and anger that many women felt in the single-nuclear-family dwelling in every suburb of America were flung out at the public who came to see the environment and performances . . . exposing a sadness which had been covered by the roofs of many in their own private homes."[7]

Although *Womanhouse* was created in just six weeks and open to the public for only four, it was seen by almost 10,000 visitors. Paradoxically, however, *Womanhouse* has gone unexamined—and barely acknowledged—by art historians, despite its anticipation of the themes and strategies for much subsequent feminist art. Both Chicago and Schapiro sustained its domestic focus through well-known later work. Chicago's *Dinner Party* installation involved over 400 craftspeople in setting a banquet table for women excluded from history. Schapiro's paintings, collaged with swatches of fabric in a technique she called "femmage", brought quilting and the domestic arts into galleries and museums.[8] Nor was *Womanhouse* the only manifestation of feminist artists' domestic orientation. Indeed, it was just the first example cited in an article on women artists working with domestic themes that Lucy Lippard published in *Ms.* in 1973. By the early 1980s, museums across America were mounting exhibitions on domesticity and art in recognition of the substantial body of recent work challenging the modernist indifference to the home.[9] For Donna Dennis, whose giant doll houses (or are they miniature buildings?) were featured in a number of these exhibitions around 1980, "Focusing on these humble structures is for me very much like the feminist movement focusing on the lives of women and discovering there a whole world that was previously overlooked." And twenty years after *Womanhouse,* Portia Munson's massive displays of scavenged pink plastic objects—everything from toilet brushes, shower caps, and curlers to Barbie dolls and sex toys—sustained the half-furious, half-exultant energy of early feminist explorations of the domestic.[10]

* * *

In the 1980s, widespread disillusionment with modernism's promises of a utopian future was expressed as nostalgic fascination with an idealized past, especially with the years around mid-century that comprised the childhood of most adults.[13] Ronald Reagan's politics of nostalgia and the renewed popularity of television comedies from the 1950s and 1960s (particularly those featuring children) attest to a yearning for the imagined simplicity of an idealized childhood, while panic over child kidnapping and satanistic day-care workers, along with pop-psychology schemes for unhappy adults to reconstitute their "inner child," register concomitant anxieties over the inevitable corruption of impossibly nostalgic fantasies. Whether footnoted to phenomenology or absorbed from popular culture, the perspective of the grown-up child pervades the art and exhibitions that, during the 1980s, focused on the home. A good deal of popular recent art uses conventional—and even archaic—media to create nostalgic visions of the home. A related phenomenon is the rise in art dealing with the inevitably broken promises of this simplistic domestic ideal.

One of the most prominent young artists of the 1980s was Eric Fischl, whose stylistically conservative paintings of unhappy suburban families deal with the theme of domestic corruption. For Fischl, "privacy"—a cardinal component of domesticity—is "what you do when you're not supposed to do something . . . Privacy is—you're playing with yourself, you're stealing, you're having sex with your neighbor, whatever, you're not supposed to be doing it." Similar associations between domesticity and secrecy animated the much publicized 1991 photography exhibition at the Museum of Modern Art, *Pleasures and Terrors of Domestic Comfort,* which documented the focus of recent photography on what it called "the *terra incognita* of the domestic scene."[14]

10 Despite their superficially similar evocations of the domestic uncanny, significant differences separate this perspective of disappointed nostalgia from feminist projects like *Womanhouse.* Though both defamiliarize the home, feminist work is informed by political analysis and oriented toward the possibility of change. In contrast, Fischl acknowledges, "There's no specific doctrine I am pushing to change things. There is criticism and a kind of analysis, but no proposal for an alternative. I don't know any." Likewise, the MoMA show—both the selection of images and the catalog essay—depoliticizes domestic imagery, allying it all with Fischl's celebrated "psycho-theater of domestic drama." Reasserting the modernist myth of the isolated figure of the artist-hero, the catalog disavows the kind of solidarity that brought women together under the banner of feminism, insisting that "the photographers represented here have worked not as . . . [a] team but as independent artists, most of them unaware of most of the others."

* * *

This dynamic of discouraged nostalgia was registered, not just in the thriving art market of the 1980s, but also in the decade's real-estate boom. Exemplary of the architects who came to prominence in the 1980s were Robert Stern, Witold Rybczynski, and the team of Andres Duany and Elizabeth Plater-Zyberk, all of whom looked to the past for the house of the future. Stern's writings promoting a return to the "bourgeois virtues" enshrined in turn-of-the-century suburbs and "shingle style" houses made him a leading designer of the revival-style suburban house and condominium developments built during the 1980s. His self-styled "modern traditionalist" practice is epitomized by his "Dream House," created for a *Life* magazine cover story in June of 1994. This relatively large (2100 square feet) and expensive ($150,000 at Midwestern prices, not counting the land) house, available in a variety of tacked-on styles and centered on a large family room, reiterates the forms of conventional up-scale suburban development, inscribing them as the appropriate "dream" solution to the needs of *Life*'s middle-class readers.[16]

More imaginative among the beneficiaries of the building boom of the 1980s were those who shared with earlier feminists a recognition that domesticity as lived experience is more complicated—both historically and socially—than an expensive image. Rybczynski's 1986 best-seller, *Home: A Short History of an Idea,* chronicled the development of the concept of domestic comfort in order to challenge both the modernist "machine for living" and grandiose postmodern reincarnations of historical styles. As an alternative, Rybczynski attempted to isolate the quality of domesticity—defined as "a feeling of privacy," "an atmosphere of coziness," and a manifestation of "bourgeois traditions"—which his later designs aim to recreate on a small scale. . . .

Despite their successes, however, what these back-to-the-future solutions illuminate most clearly is the failure of the modern home and suburb. Yet simply to return to the turn of the century for viable models of domesticity ignores what has changed in our ways of life since then. On a practical level, the interests of ethnic and religious minorities and dual-career couples, for instance, go unacknowledged in a nostalgic return to villages clustered around one or two places of worship and a single business district. Likewise, rebuilding Victorian houses reinscribes Victorian notions of family structure and divisions of public/private without taking into account widespread changes in the family or the impact of communication technologies that permeate the home with twenty-four-hour access to and from the outside world.

* * *

In contrast to such nostalgic visions, it has been widely argued that a defining characteristic of "resistant" postmodernism is its acknowledgement of difference, often phrased in terms of "multiculturalism," "diversity," and "identity."[20] Applied to domesticity, this argument implies a different reading of Dorothy's famous cry. It's true: there is no (single) place *like* home. There are multiple places that *are* home for different kinds of people. So domestic typologies founded on myths of a universal childhood experience set in an ideal past necessarily offer only partial solutions to the housing needs of the increasingly diverse populations of the present and future. In its activist orientation, "resistant" postmodernism is very much the heir to earlier feminist engagement with the home, though its focus has expanded beyond the articulation of gender differences to include perspectives differentiated by race, ethnicity, sexuality, and other forms of identity.

15 Two strategies characterize the domestically focused art associated with this "resistant" form of postmodernism. The first seeks to problematize the nostalgia surrounding the home; the second articulates varieties of identity by exploring the differences in the ways different communities live. Exemplary of the first strategy is Alice Adams, a painter and weaver who, self-taught as a carpenter, during the 1970s produced a series

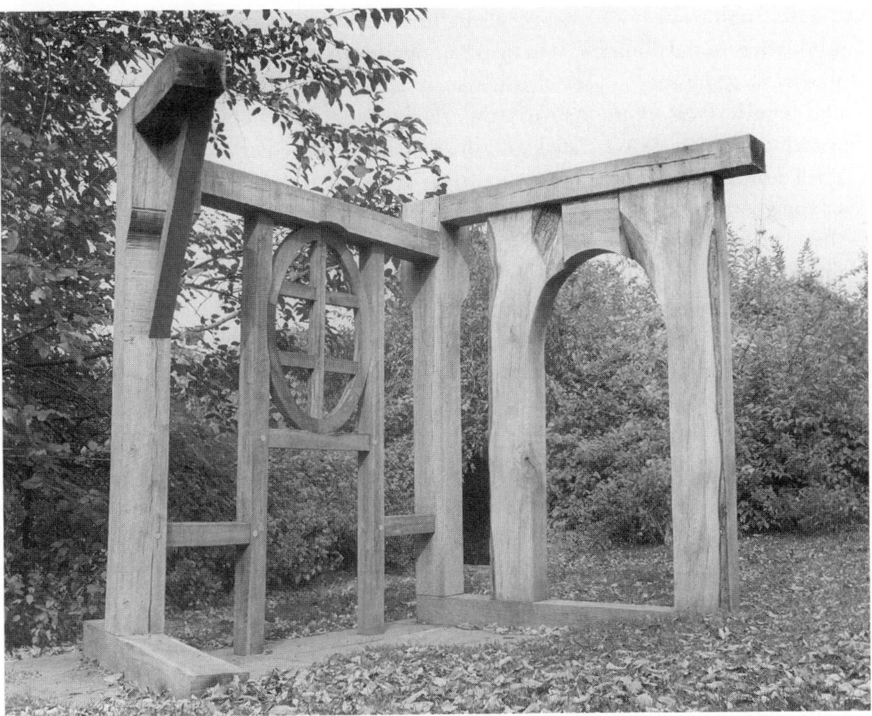

Alice Adams, The Lost House, 1979.

of sculptures dealing with the materials of home construction: first latex casts of plaster walls, then more complicated intersections of walls and vaults and constructions of lathing. From the beginning, Adams confessed her nostalgia, not just for her childhood home in the suburbs, but also for her father's print shop in a Manhattan factory loft, a space she describes as "in a way homier, closer than a house." Despite their nostalgic impulse, however, Adams's work does not so much idealize the house as demystify it, revealing its physical framework and making explicit what is taken for granted. . . .

Adams's investigation of domesticity culminated in a series of massive outdoor sculptures: *Adams' House* of 1977, *Three Structures on a Slope* of 1978, and *Lost House* of 1979. The first evoked the house she grew up in, and Adams presented it as an attempt "to possess in my art some part of my past that is really gone," though its skewed proportions and permanently unfinished status questioned the practicality of such memories of childhood perspective. *Three Structures* is even less coherent as a domestic space: just a ramp, a porch, and a flat platform are uneasily juxtaposed on a hill. Comparing the first and last of these works, Adams said "*Adams' House* was the container of my childhood and gave me the chance to go home again," while *The Lost House* "is all about NOT being able to go home again."[21] As a series and individually, Adams's domestic pieces confront the inevitable gap between the ideal and the specific, between fantasy and practice, between memory of the past and practical engagement with the here and now.

A second strategy of artists challenging the homogenizing nostalgia of mainstream approaches to the domestic is to insist on the diversity of domestic experience. Some of this work addresses . . . social issues such as domestic violence, divorce, child abuse, and homelessness. A number of exhibitions in the late 1980s collected work dealing with social problems associated with the home, including Peggy Diggs's powerful sculptures dealing with domestic violence, such as her 1991 *Objects of Abuse,* an assemblage of apparently innocuous domestic objects (a boot, a pillow, a coffee pot, a candle stick) that turn out to be weapons in domestic abuse cases. Diggs may be best known for her imaginative efforts to use art to interrupt cycles of domestic violence by designing posters and, most imaginatively, milk cartons that carry anti-violence information into the daily lives of people who may never visit a museum or gallery. Diggs's "domestication of activist art" has been interestingly analyzed as a reflection of the collapse of the boundaries between public and private at a time when the electronic media bring formerly public institutions—the theatre, for instance, or the legislature—into the home.[22]

While the public penetrates the private realm, for many Americans homelessness brings the private into the streets. Addressing this issue, Martha Rosler's 1989 *Home Front* installation used a domestic setting to document the causes and consequences of homelessness, and Krzysztof Wodiczko invented a "Homeless Vehicle" that distills the essential requirements for urban life into a compact, mobile unit that makes a powerful political point in the gallery or on the streets.[23]

For other artists, invoking the domestic is a way of foregrounding issues of "difference," an abstraction concretely embodied in variations of everyday life. Throughout long careers, Betye Saar and Faith Ringgold have used the bric-à-brac of daily life—dolls, quilts, and cookie jars—to describe the experience of black American women. Both, for instance, have invoked the ambivalent legacy of Aunt Jemima, the stereotypical "mammy" whose image is embedded in the fabric of American domestic life through the packaging of a popular brand of breakfast food. Throughout the 1970s, Saar collaged sculptures juxtaposing this familiar icon of domesticity with records of more obvious forms of racism. Ringgold's 1983 story-quilt, *Who's Afraid of Aunt Jemima,* like her other quilt pieces, exploits old techniques to weave myths appropriate for black women today; in this version of the story, Aunt Jemima comes north and gets rich running a restaurant in New York. Appropriating craft techniques and domestic objects, the work of both artists brings home issues of race.[24]

* * *

20 Artists exploring other ethnic and racial identities have also turned to images of domesticity. Angelica Pozo thematizes her identity as a black Cuban émigrée in her installations of furniture and dishes decorated with images and statistics about her homeland. The Korean-American artist Yong Soon Min often blends domestic imagery with traditional Korean clothing: in a 1991 piece, a poem entitled "Home" is painted on a diaphanous robe in English on one side and in Korean on the other; in the 1994 version of *Dwelling,* a similar dress becomes a container for personal memorabilia and is suspended over a stack of books topped with a volume open to mutilated pages on his-

Angelica Pozo, Puerto Rico
Five Differing Areas of Natural Vegetation, 1991.

tory and capped with a tiny house—in a later version of this piece, the house disappeared and the books were charred. . . .

Nor are race and ethnicity the only forms of difference enacted in the realm of the domestic. In an era when "lifestyle" became a euphemism for sexual orientation, images of daily life were often used by artists interested in alternatives to the conventional nuclear family. Kenneth Silver, in this book, describes the range of gay domestic spaces from David Hockney's "normativized" idylls of gay couples at home to Robert Mapplethorpe's insistence on "the 'queerness' of homosexuality" as it is lived out in the daily experience of (some) men. Silver's analysis of the challenge to modernist machismo posed by a gay domestic sensibility is paralleled by the art of Stuart Netsky. Reworking Impressionist paintings in sequins and geometric Abstract Expressionist compositions in textiles, Netsky blurs the contentious boundaries between art and decoration, gallery and home, masculine and feminine. In the 1993 installation, *Time Flies,* Netsky creates a corner of gay domesticity very different from Mapplethorpe's S-and-M theatrics, but nevertheless unmistakably gay. Around a carpet of grass and rose petals are strewn the fabulous accoutrements of drag: gilt furniture, an embarrassment of shoes and accessories, televisions constantly screening old "camp" movies and more recent (but equally campy) celebrity exercise programs. At one point, an elaborate vanity strewn with toiletries faces a chair displaying a cushion embroidered, in place of any conventional aphorisms of homey virtue or heterosexual bliss, with a quotation of a famous (or notorious) queen: "When Quentin Crisp was asked how he was going to spend his day he replied, 'I believe I'll try a new eye shadow.' "[27]

* * *

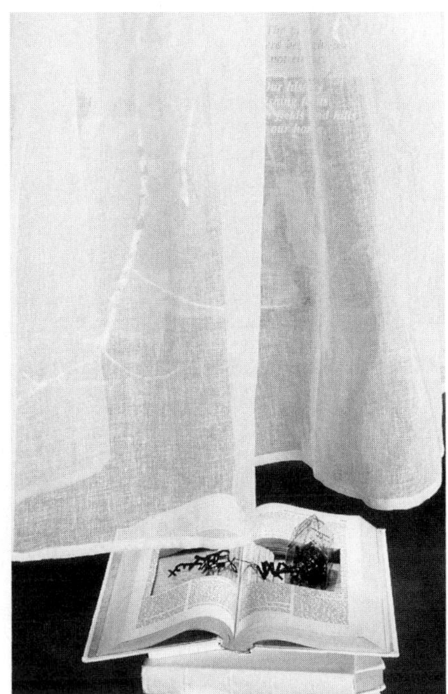

Yong Soon Min, Dwelling, 1994. Right, detail.

Architecture—far more reliant on patronage and subject to legislative surveillance than the visual arts—is among the most conservative and homogeneous cultural fields. Nevertheless, the 1980s witnessed a substantial rise in architectural awareness of the diversity of domestic experience, especially as expressed in building function and program. This shift was registered in the mid-1980s by a number of competitions soliciting, as alternatives to the highly standardized housing projects of the previous three decades, domestic designs that acknowledged, rather than suppressed, differences in ways of living.

Entrants to the 1984 "New American Home" competition in Minneapolis, for example, were asked to design small urban houses that combined work and domestic space for households of "single-parent families, two-income families, unrelated young adults sharing a single residence, adults without children at home, and retired, active adults . . . which are emerging to replace the traditional nuclear family." The winning entry by Jacqueline Leavitt and Troy West was a "kit of parts" that included in each residence a work area that could be converted to a rental unit.[29]

The 1987 *Vacant Lots* project, sponsored by the Architectural League of New York, focused on small city-owned lots that "could be developed by small scale contractors or community based development groups, [and] could be the basis of a new strategy for reweaving the fabric of neighborhoods." Emerging from this series of public programs and exhibitions were a number of projects addressing the needs of non-

Stuart Netsky, Time Flies, 1993.

nuclear families, day-care and vocational training facilities, and constituencies such as people with AIDS.[30]

* * *

25 It is symptomatic of the conservatism of the architectural profession that not until the mid-1990s did architects begin to engage the issues of identity that were central to postmodernism in the broader culture. High-profile architectural theorists reinvigorated discussions of domesticity through their use of feminist psychoanalytic and critical theory, though without engaging the more politically oriented work of 1970s' feminists.[34] The 1994 *House Rules* exhibition, curated by Mark Robbins at the Wexner Center, attempted to incorporate highly theoretical forms of analysis with political forms of identity, exploring the implications of both for "the design of a single-family home in a suburban setting." Ten "theorists"—many representing a marginalized racial, ethnic, gendered and/or sexual identity—were paired with architects to design suburban homes on individual lots, questioning the implications of conventional building codes, materials, floor plans, and marketing.

In some of the *House Rules* projects, unconventional attacks on the spatial configuration of the house symbolized challenges to conventional family structures. In other projects, the emphasis was on the diversity already present in American housing. Architectural historian Margaret Crawford, for instance, teamed up with ADOBE LA, a collaborative group of Hispanic artists and architects, to document the distinctive decoration of yards and walls in Latino neighborhoods of East Los Angeles. In contrast to this ebullient architectural expression of identity, the project "Queers in (Single-Family) Space" explored the extent to which conventional houses already both contain and mask diverse living arrangements. Emphasizing that "queerness"—a term understood to incorporate a broad range of departures from the nuclear family norm—will be defined and lived by the inhabitants rather than "staged by the architect," designers Benjamin Gianni and Scott Weir proposed what looked like a typical suburban house that "can be easily altered to accommodate a range of living situations . . . without breaching the social contract of community consensus." An example of "playing it straight"—"the suburban strategy par excellence"—the designers use careful room layout, sound-baffling walls, and multiple entrances to ensure maximum flexibility for the various inhabitants over the life of the house.[35] This project follows Robbins and Gianni's proposal for the *Queer Space* show in New York earlier that year. There they displayed a matrix of captioned snapshots of gay households solicited through ads in gay papers that asked readers to send pictures of the inside and outside of their homes. In answer to the questions, "Who are we? Where are we? How do we live?" Gianni and Robbins answered, "In gay ghettos, it is apparent, but the majority of gay people live among their heterosexual neighbors. Some of us react against normative symbols of domesticity, others of us embrace them."[36] This imbeddedness of identity within normative structures of home and community is at the core of the later proposal for *House Rules*. . . .

This approach is not without its costs, however. Design that refrains from imposing a patriarchal family structure on its inhabitants is not the same thing as architecture that articulates specific alternatives. Lost in this vision of the house as a neutral vessel for any family group is the earlier feminists' insistence on change, whether within families or in the relation of individuals to communities and houses to neighborhoods. The activist legacy of feminism was neglected in the 1980s, however. The era's nostalgia did not extend to the turn-of-the-century feminist housing projects documented by Dolores Hayden, nor was the work of feminists in the 1970s incorporated into the postmodern architectural theory that informed the participants in *House Rules,* where the acceptance of a suburban setting predicated on the single family home discouraged considerations of community. Describing the cycles of oblivion and re-invention that characterize feminist art in general, *Womanhouse* co-creator Miriam Schapiro says, "Each generation opens the wounds, which close in the night behind them."[37]

Breaking this cycle is the challenge of future efforts to re-imagine domesticity. Postmodernism has returned our culture's attention to the home, challenging the modernist antagonism toward the domestic with a new interest in the history and variety of home life. For those of us unwilling simply to fall back on nostalgic formations of domesticity, the effort now is to bring the legacy of feminism—the activist commitment to specific social change, the anger that eschews the innocuous and safe—into productive combination with current concerns for critical theory and multiculturalism. We offer the history sketched in this essay as a foundation for that work.

Notes

1. In the interests of (relative) brevity, we have confined our discussion of domesticity and postmodernism to North America, although we believe the issues we raise are applicable to other contexts. For interested readers, a provocative overview of the history of domesticity was offered by the exhibition associated with the 17th Milan Triennale, curated by Georges Teyssot: *Il prog-*

etto domestico; La casa dell'nomo, archetipi e (Milan: Palazzo della Triennake, 1986), and the installation exhibitions *Chambres d'Amis* (Ghent, 1986) and *Chambre 763* (Paris, 1994) showcased a wide range of contemporary artists' responses to the interior. In England, debates over the relationship of art and domesticity crystalized around the sculptor Rachel Whiteread, who won the 1993 Turner Prize at the same time as her controversial *House* sculpture was slated for destruction. Challenges to modernist architecture and planning similar to those described in this essay have been articulated since the early 1950s by English designers Alison and Peter Smithson, and by the Italian architect Aldo Rossi (see his *The Architecture of the City,* 1966, trans. Diane Ghirardo and Joan Ockman, Cambridge: MIT Press, 1982). In England, the more nostalgic version of postmodernism is associated with Rob and Leon Krier (see especially Demetri Porphyrios, ed., *Leon Krier: Houses, Palaces, Cities,* London: Architectural Design, 1984), though it found its most prominent spokesman in the Prince of Wales.

2. Robert Venturi, *Complexity and Contradiction in Architecture* 1966 (repr. New York: Museum of Modern Art, 1977), 104, 16, 118. See also Venturi's *Mother's House: The Evolution of Vanna Venturi's House in Chestnut Hill* (New York: Rizzoli, 1992).

. . .

5. Susana Torre, ed., *Women in American Architecture: A Historic and Contemporary Perspective* (New York: Whitney Library of Design, 1977), 11.
6. Miriam Schapiro, *Femmages 1971–1981* (St. Louis: Brentwood Gallery, 1985), n.pag.; and in *Womanhouse* catalog (Valencia, CA: California Institute of the Arts, 1972), n.pag.; Judy Chicago, *Through the Flower: My Struggle as a Woman Artist* (Garden City, NY: Doubleday, 1975), 103–32. On *Womanhouse* and related projects, see Faith Wilding. *By Our Own Hands: The Women Artist's Movement, Southern California, 1970–76* (Santa Monica, CA: Double X, 1977); see also Faith Wilding, "The Feminist Art Programs at Fresno and CalArts," and Arlene Raven, "Womanhouse," both in Norma Broude and Mary D. Garrard, eds. *The Power of Feminist Art: The American Movement of the 1970s, History and Impact* (New York: Abrams, 1994), 32–65. Portions of *Womanhouse* were recreated for the exhibition, *Division of Labor: "Women's Work" in Contemporary Art,* (New York: Bronx Museum of the Arts, 1995).
7. Arlene Raven, *At Home* (Long Beach, CA: Long Beach Museum of Art, 1983), 5.
8. Judy Chicago, *Embroidering Our Heritage: The Dinner Party Needlework* (Garden City, NY: Anchor/Doubleday, 1980). Norma Broude, "Miriam Schapiro and "Femmage": Reflections on the Conflict Between Decoration and Abstraction in Twentieth Century Art," *Arts* (February 1980), 83–87.
9. In 1978, the Institute of Contemporary Art in Philadelphia mounted *Dwellings* and the downtown branch of New York's Whitney Museum showed *Out of the House.* These were followed in 1981 by *The Image of the House in Contemporary Art* in Houston and by *House Work,* curated by the sculptor Harmony Hammond for the National Women's Hall of Fame in Seneca, New York. Two 1983 exhibitions continued the trend: *The House that Art Built* and *At Home,* curated by Arlene Raven. The following year in Massachusetts, *Domestic Tales* presented a selection of recent women's art dealing with the home.
10. Donna Dennis, in *The House that Art Built* (Fullerton, CA: California State University Main Art Gallery, 1983), 43. See Munson's work in The New Museum of Contemporary Art, *Bad Girls* (Cambridge, MA: MIT Press, 1994), 86–87.

. . .

13. Our analysis is paralleled by the discussion of the "nostalgia film" in Frederic Jameson, "Postmodernism and Consumer Society," 1982, repr. Foster, 111–25; see especially his discussion of the small-town setting of *Body Heat.*

14. Eric Fischl in Nancy Grimes, "Eric Fischl's Naked Truths," *Art News* (September 1986), 70. Peter Galassi, *Pleasures and Terrors of Domestic Comfort* (New York: Museum of Modern Art, 1991), 7.

. . .

16. Robert A. M. Stern and John M. Massengale, *The Anglo-American Suburb* (London: Academy Editions, 1981); Luis F. Rueda, ed., *Robert A. M. Stern: Buildings and Projects 1981–1985* (New York: Rizzoli 1986), 174–83, 86–93, 120–23, 156–59, 170–73, 174–83, 234, 235, 258–61, 276–79, 280–83; Stephen Petranek and Jennifer Allen, "A House For All America," *Life* (June 1994), 82–92.

. . .

20. See Christopher Reed, "Postmodernism and the Art of Identity," in Nikos Stangos, ed., *Concepts of Modern Art,* 3rd ed. (London: Thames and Hudson, 1994), 271–93. See also Abigail Solomon-Godeau and Constance Lewallen, *Mistaken Identities* (Seattle: University of Washington Press, 1993).

21. Alice Adams, quoted in Lucy Lippard, "The Abstract Realism of Alice Adams," *Art in America* (September 1976), 72–76; and in *The House that Art Built,* 25.

22. In addition to the 1992 exhibition, *Good-bye to Apple Pie,* a number of exhibits on social issues associated with the home are described in Phyllis Rosser, "There's No Place Like Home," in Joanna Frueh, Cassandra Langer, Arlene Raven, eds., *New Feminist Criticism* (New York: Harper Collins, 1994), 73–76. On Diggs, see Patricia C. Phillips, "Peggy Diggs: Private Acts and Public Art" in Nina Felshin, ed., *But Is It Art?: The Spirit of Art as Activism* (Seattle: Bay Press, 1995), 283–308.

23. Rosler's *Home Front,* along with related installations and programming, is documented in Brian Wallis, ed., *If You Lived Here: The City in Art, Theory, and Social Activism, A Project by Martha Rosler* (Seattle: Bay Press, 1991). See also *Public Address: Krzysztof Wodiczko* (Minneapolis: Walker Arts Center, 1992).

24. On the Aunt Jemima image, see Lucy Lippard, *Mixed Blessings: New Art in a Multicultural America* (New York: Pantheon, 1990), 234–36. On Saar, see Elizabeth Shepherd, ed., *Secrets, Dialogues, Revelations: The Art of Betye and Alison Saar* (Los Angeles: Wight Art Gallery, University of California, 1990). On Ringgold, see Eleanor Flomenhaft, *Faith Ringgold: A 25 Year Survey* (Hempstead, NY: Fine Arts Museum of Long Island, 1990).

. . .

27. On Netsky, see Judith Tannenbaum, *Time Flies Stuart Netsky* (Philadelphia: Institute of Contemporary Art, 1994). Other photographers dealing with lesbian and gay domesticity include Deborah Coitto and Doug Ischar, both featured in *Disclosing the Myth of Family* (exh. flyer, Betty Rymer Gallery at the School of the Art Institute of Chicago, 1991).

. . .

29. Competition brief quoted in Jacqueline Leavitt, "Two Prototypical Designs for Single Parents: The Congregate House and the New American House," in Karen A. Franck and Sherry Ahrentzen, eds., *New Households New Housing* (New York: Van Nostrand Reinhold, 1991), 161–86. This book includes several projects addressing similar concerns.

30. Carol Willis and Rosalie Genevro, eds., *Vacant Lots* (New York: Princeton Architectural Press and the Architectural League of New York, 1989), 7.

. . .

34. See essays by Beatriz Colomina, Mark Wigley, and Elizabeth Grosz in Beatriz Colomina, ed., *Sexuality & Space* (New York: Princeton Architectural Press, 1992). See also Anthony Vidler,

The Architectural Uncanny: Essays in the Modern Unhomely (Cambridge, MA: MIT Press, 1992), including "Homes for Cyborgs," reprinted in this volume.

35. Michael Moon, Eve Kosofsky Sedgwick, Benjamin Gianni, and Scott Weir, "Queers in (Single-Family) Space," *House Rules,* exh. cat. published as special issue of *Assemblage,* no. 24 (August 1994), 30–37. Additional quotations from Benjamin Gianni, "Queering (Single-Family) Space," *Sites,* no. 26 (1995), 69–77.

36. Mark Robbins and Benjamin Gianni, exhibition leaflet from *Queer Space* (New York: Storefront for Art and Architecture, 1994).

37. Miriam Schapiro, in *The Power of Feminist Art,* 83. A similar critique of the neglect of feminist forerunners in discussions of women artists and gender in the 1980s is offered in Mira Schor, "Patrilineage," in *New Feminist Criticism* (cited above), 42–59. Especially troubling is *Architecture and the Feminine: Mop-up Work* conference proceedings published in *ANY,* vol. 4 (January–February 1994), which is an analysis of the "feminine" in architecture without any acknowledgment of the feminist.

Exploring Texts and Contexts

For activities with icons, refer to the Guide to Analyzing Readings in Context.

1. Haar and Reed refer to two other readings included in this unit: Rybczynski's "Comfort and Well-Being" and Crawford's "Mi Casa es Su Casa." Read what Haar and Reed say about each and consider why they refer to these other works. Reread the section on Situation in the Guide to Analyzing Readings in Context, and observe how Haar and Reed use these other authors to establish a context. Situation

2. Look closely at the photos of sculpture and art included with this essay and read the authors' discussion of these works. How does the written discussion influence the way you see the works of art? Conversely, how does the art influence the way you read the text?

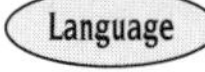

3. Why do you think Haar and Reed titled this piece the way they did? Why do you think they contrast nostalgic views of home, as in Dorothy's cry, "There's no place like home," and disrupted views of home, in which our assumptions about a comfortable home are turned upside down? What are Haar and Reed arguing for in this essay?

Creating Texts

For activities with icons, refer to the Guides to Analyzing Contexts for Writing and Analyzing Readings in Context. For additional help with these writing projects, read the descriptions of **Manifesto** and **Essay** in the Genre Glossary.

1. Haar and Reed want to upset what they call the "stasis of nostalgic historical fantasy" and imagine the home as a "space in which to enact a better future" (220). Write a manifesto in which you set out your basic ideas and requirements

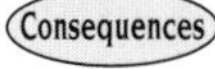

with respect to homes and housing. What would you want to change about the way we see the home? How would this change society? Consider, too, where you could publish your manifesto and what consequences it might have. Remember that a manifesto uses strong and direct language and is crafted to make demands while articulating the premises on which those demands are based.

2. Create a piece of artwork that reflects your sense of coming home. You may want to group found objects together to create a shadowbox, assemble images on a web page, create a pencil sketch, or use some other form of artistic representation. Write an essay explaining your work of art. Refer to your personal history as well as the works of art discussed in Haar and Reed and connect them to your own artwork.

The Triumph of Burbopolis

Michael Pollan

Michael Pollan writes of his return to the Long Island suburb of his childhood, wistfully taking us down memory lane to find his old house at the intersection of Juneau and Fairbanks Boulevards. He ruefully pokes fun at his younger self—his yearning to be anywhere but in the suburbs, his desire to solo on the Long Island Railroad, and his petty larceny in the pumpkin fields—all the while subtly drawing us into an analysis of how the suburbs have changed over the last 30 years. Lives are no longer centripetal, he explains, drawn to Manhattan's light and energy. But how this energy has changed is not quite clear. Searching for words, Pollan comes up with the attention-getting "Burbopolis" to signal the intermingling of suburb and city, but he only hints at what this will mean for our lifestyles, our jobs, our friends, and our connection with the places we live.

For Pollan, a sense of place is paramount. His recent book, *A Place of My Own: The Education of an Amateur Builder,* published in 1998, chronicles his attempt, having never fixed or built anything in his life, to construct with his own hands a writing hut on the grounds behind his home. Rather than observing residential change from the outside, he contemplates architecture from the inside out with hammer and nails and a first-aid kit at the ready. Pollan has for many years, even before he had a room of his own, written on gardening, nature, and the environment for a wide variety of periodicals including *House and Garden, The New York Times Magazine,* and *Harper's Magazine.*

Connecting with the Conversation

1. If you moved during your childhood and can return to your past residence, visit it and see whether it has changed in any way. Or ask relatives, parents, or older friends about places they've lived before, whether they've been back for any rea-

son, and what they found or would expect to find. Or consider where you might like to live if the usual obstacles to moving did not exist. Write in your journal about these real or imagined changes of residence.

2. Watch reruns of family sitcoms set in the suburban fifties, such as "Leave it to Beaver" or "Father Knows Best" or recent movies, such as *American Beauty,* that use suburbia as a backdrop. What generalizations run through these representations of life in the suburbs? Which seem accurate and which seem exaggerated? Write in your journal about what you have observed.

I grew up in a pretty nice subdivision on Long Island, but try as I might to kindle some spark of nostalgia for "the Gates of Woodbury," the gravitational pull of the place is almost nil. It has been nearly 30 years since I left, and at least until a couple of months ago, I could think of no reason to go back: no people to see (everybody I knew had also left), no curiosity to satisfy. In my imagination Juneau Boulevard is the same as it ever was, except maybe for the cars and the people, which I assume have been regularly updated. Isn't that the way it has always been in the burbs—change without history? More of the same?

A *lot* more of the same, it's true: since I left Long Island in the '70s, resolving henceforth to live somewhere more in the middle of things, more real, the suburbs have quietly and steadily expanded. And then the day came, a few years ago, when I read in the paper that for the first time in history a majority of Americans now lived in the suburbs. America had officially become "a suburban nation"—which sounded to me like one of those utterly weightless demographic truths, empirically verifiable, but without any real echo in experience. For wasn't this really just a change in quantity, not kind? The relative size of middle and fringe may have shifted, but surely not their relative weight.

At least this is what I assumed. It's only recently that I've felt any compulsion to go back to Woodbury to test my assumptions, and that was mostly because I needed a place to set this essay. What I found when I got there was a good bit more than that. What I found looks a lot like a whole new country—or at least a place for which "suburb" is no longer quite the right word.

FROM THE TIME I WAS 5 UNTIL I GOT OUT OF high school I lived in the Gates near the corner of Juneau and Fairbanks Boulevards. In all that time, I never really noticed just how goofily dissonant those names are, with their improbable conjunction of Yukon pluck and Old World prissiness. Yet these place names, and the conflicting dreams they embody, tell you just about all you need to know about the place and the time.

5 The development went in on the site of an old North Shore estate that had been subdivided into acre lots during the Suburban Revolution; the developer decided to preserve the wrought-iron entrance gates to give a bit of aristocratic tone to his shiny middle-class development. As for the whole Yukon theme, ground was broken in 1960, soon after Alaska had become a state, and the Gates fashioned itself a forward-looking, even pioneerish kind of place. At the time Woodbury was on the suburban

---

From *The New York Times Magazine,* April 9, 2000, pp. 51–55.

frontier, still mostly farm fields and forest, and the Gates aimed to distinguish itself from the cookie-cutter subdivisions then spreading out across Long Island.

In the same way the suburbs began as a reaction against city life, each new incarnation of suburbia has defined itself in opposition to some earlier, superseded ideal: middle-class utopias keeping one step ahead of history. In the beginning the suburban frontier stood in places like Brooklyn Heights, first made accessible by steam ferry in 1814, but the city quickly followed, folding Brooklyn's row houses into its expanding grid. To prevent that kind of thing from happening again, the next new place (epitomized by Llewellyn Park, built in New Jersey in 1853, and Riverside, built near Chicago in 1868) was carefully planned to keep the city permanently at bay. It would be an ungridded community of free-standing houses in a park, linked to the distant city by trolley or train. Then, beginning in the 1920's, the 19th-century railroad suburb was superseded by more far-flung subdivisions organized around the automobile and, after the war, the mass-production house pioneered by the Levitts.

By 1960, when my parents went house hunting on Long Island, Levittown was passé, and the next new place—the un-Levittown—promised to be the Gates of Woodbury, where the lots were generally a sprawling acre. Instead of identical houses lined up like sparrows on a wire, the developer offered three up-to-date models (ranch, split-level, and colonial), laid out his roads in sweeping, pointless curves and sited the houses so far back on their wooded acres that each appeared lost in a reverie of being a mansion. (Sometimes I think this is what is really meant by a "dream house": the recumbent ranches dreaming of California, the colonnaded white colonials dreaming of Tara.) But if the Alaska angle implied the pastless potential of the next great American place, what was with those prissy "boulevards" and "drives," all those "ways" and "terraces" and, for the cul-de-sacs, "courts"? Understand that in the suburbs a developer will go to heroic lengths not to call a street a street. Street says city, and city is precisely the last thing you want to say. Whereas boulevard said fancy, said *sophisticated,* and if this effeteness jangled alongside muscular Alaska, that evidently didn't bother the developer or his buyers.

FINDING YOUR WAY BACK TO YOUR SUBURBAN CHILDHOOD HOME is harder than you might think. I didn't know anyone who still lived in the Gates—my folks moved out in 1972, and most of their neighbors had headed down to Florida the minute the kids left for college, there to recreate a grayer, warmer Gates in Boca Raton. (One thing the burbs have done to America is to recast its geography along purely demographic lines.) To find out who lived in my old house, I had to send it a letter, addressed to "current resident." (In quotes, to make sure it didn't get tossed.) "Current resident" turned out to be Stephen and Jena Hall, and they graciously invited me to visit. Since I didn't know anybody to stay with, "going home" to Woodbury meant spending the night in a $79 room in the Executive Inn on Jericho Turnpike, the main commercial strip.

My first impression of Woodbury, after rolling off the expressway onto Jericho Turnpike, was disorientation. Every landmark on my mental map of the area had been stripped and replaced by a big-box retailer, such that it took me the better part of two days to locate my junior high school, its unmarked turn off Jericho having been swallowed up by superstores. I noticed that the brands were all high-end, the kind my mother had had to drive all the way to Manhattan for.

10 Actually the brands should have been my tip-off that this was not the same place I left, that it had a completely different relationship to Manhattan. But I didn't put that together until I turned onto Woodbury Road, passed a bunch of newer developments (including the Woodbury Estates and the almost completely flat Rolling Hills) and made the left onto Froehlich Farm Boulevard. Whenever "farm" (or "forest," or "fairground" or anything venerably rural) is honored in a suburban place name, you can bet the thing is history, and such was emphatically the case with the old Froehlich farm.

The pumpkin field to which Charlie DeSalvo and I used to drag our wagons each fall for the purpose of committing petty larceny had sprouted a half-dozen smoked-glass office buildings, blocky islands in a glittering sea of really nice cars. Gateways Executive Mall, the sign said (I half-expected to see "of Froehlich Farm"), and it listed a phalanx of law firms, insurance companies, medical practices, banks and high-tech firms. Each of those really nice cars represented at least one really good white-collar job, and there must have been a thousand of them right here, smack in the middle of the pumpkin field that backed up against Fairbanks Boulevard.

"THE CITY": WE LED CENTRIPETAL LIVES IN those days, our heads bent toward Manhattan as if it were the sun. Which in some sense it was, the city being the source not only of all money but also of entertainment and information and—what was especially important to us as teenagers—*authenticity.* The suburbs, we believed, were fake; after all, we had watched them rise like stage sets on the farm fields, seen the instantaneous lawns rolled out over the raw dirt like new linoleum. This creation of a new life ex nihilo was of course exactly what our parents liked about the place, but what was to them a blank canvas was to us an existential void. Nothing was original except, well, except us and these childhoods we were having—a thought disturbing enough to make us wonder if those were somehow fake, too, "sub" to something realer.

Like lots of other dads in the Gates, mine commuted to a job in the real world every day, leaving the house before I woke up and rarely getting home before the dinner dishes had been cleared. Only a few of the moms had jobs, but they'd dress up and drive in a couple of times a month, to shop, catch a matinee, meet the dads for a fancy dinner and a "first run" movie.

Even before kids were old enough to solo on the L.I.R.R., we looked to the city as the source of our styles and shows and news, an all-powerful broadcast antenna to whose frequency we always tried to stay tuned. Tuesday nights Cousin Brucie handed down the Top 40 from Midtown Manhattan, and by Wednesday morning the Sam Goody at the Walt Whitman Mall would have rearranged its shelves accordingly. Later on, the more time you spent in the city, the cooler you were, because you had personally bathed in coolness's headwaters, at the Fillmore East, say, or the Thalia, or the Eighth Street Bookshop.

15 It doesn't seem as though Long Island's cultural and economic antennas point west in quite the same way anymore. Oh, sure, the Long Island Expressway still creeps every morning, but often now it's creeping in both directions, and a lot of those cars are heading to places like the Gateways Executive Mall (Exit 45), rather than to Manhattan. The retail, which once helped light up the city in suburban eyes, is no

longer any different: the Walt Whitman shopping area is now basically Lexington Avenue and 59th Street—Gap, Banana Republic, Nine West, Barnes & Noble, J. Crew and Tower Records, all anchored by a Bloomingdale's. But whether this represents the colonization of the suburbs by the city or the opposite is a question.

Radio and network TV still originate in Manhattan, but the newer media have traded broadcasting's radiating waves for centerless webs of wire. Who can say where in the world cable TV comes from? (A lot of it from Long Island, actually: Cablevision's headquarters happen to be in Bethpage.) And the Internet? America Online, perhaps the first great suburban medium, originates somewhere in suburban Virginia, though like the rest of the Web it might as well be anywhere.

One way to tell the story of the American suburbs is as a story of new technologies recasting the relationship of city and countryside. Electric power, trains, automobiles and broadcast television propelled successive waves of decentralization, each along slightly different lines. Until now, however, the pattern those lines formed always resembled the spokes of a wheel, with the city firmly in the center. Radiating highways and radio waves used to reinforce the gravitational pull of cities. But cable and computer networks are forming different patterns now, ones that mirror and speed the emergence of the burbs as free-floating entities with their own overlapping gravitational fields.

TIME HAS BEEN KIND TO MANY OF THE SUBURBS, and Juneau Boulevard is much prettier than I remember it. The conehead evergreens and midget rhododendrons, the paper birches and forsythia—all that dinky nursery stock plunked into backfill by landscapers—have put down roots and grown up to reclaim half-forgotten woodland identities, picturesquely blurring the new developments' blunter edges. By now many of the trees have grown tall enough to cast interesting shadows. The American suburb was conceived in the 19th century by visionary designers like Frederick Law Olmsted, Calvert Vaux and Andrew Jackson Downing to offer Americans a kind of democratically subdivided park, and the nicer ones are actually beginning to look that way.

Modest by comparison to what's built today, the '60s ranches and split-levels in the Gates have mellowed into period pieces: this is the architecture of postwar dreams that, at least from the vantage of a new century, no longer seem grasping or pretentious so much as sweet, even poignant. For this they probably have the newer houses to thank: the fat, bombastic three-story mini-mansions that now dot the Gates, many of them rising from the foundations of tear-downs.

20 Happily, the ranch on Juneau Boulevard hasn't been a tear-down—though I was astonished to find at the far end of the driveway a hulking two-story post-modern building, a design studio perched atop a three-car garage. Jena Hall is a successful home-furnishings designer, and she has employed as many as eight people at a time here. On the exact spot where Binker, my problematic English bulldog, snored her days away in a chain-link dog run, people now come to work.

Jena Hall's home business helped me see that the suburbs have proved to be rather more adaptable to changing lives and times than people once thought. The whole idea behind the suburbs was to draw bright lines and make separations: between city and country, obviously, but also between work and home, public and private. But it turns out we overestimated the power of architectural determinism. The suburbs have proved flexible enough to accommodate working mothers (though not without difficulty: Jena Hall's studio was usually crawling with toddlers, hers and her employees') as well as a great many different kinds of families and lifestyles. Since I left the Gates, its white nuclear families have been joined by singles and gays, Asians and African-Americans, people operating home businesses and empty-nesters. The houses themselves—light, wood-frame—turned out to be as easy to remodel as they had been to build. The world that built the postwar suburbs has passed away, and yet those suburbs still stand, remodeled by the press of history. What they haven't been is reimagined or renamed, at least not yet.

When I was growing up in the Gates, suburban legend had it that one of the big white colonials on Bering Court had served as the model for Ward and June Cleaver's house on TV. They showed the façade at the beginning of every episode, and it certainly looked right. Whether this was true or not (for all I know, every suburb in America nursed the same legend), we all wanted to believe it. Sometimes we regarded Hollywood's notice as flattery, since being on TV made the Gates seem more real and substantial (fiction will do that); other times the fame seemed like the grimmest of jokes, weekly proof of the empty pretensions of the place.

Cleaverism—the sitcom image of suburbia—loomed large in our suburban lives, though its meanings were always complex and unstable. The Cleavers, Ozzie and Harriet, Donna Reed and all the rest proposed an ideal of suburban life that everyone knew was unrealistic and silly; and yet even as we made fun of it, we allowed the stereotype to exert a kind of normative hold on us. Your own family might be hopelessly dysfunctional, but maybe the Grables next door were getting it right. TV was happy to promote the Cleaver ideal because TV (alone among the arts) loved the burbs, and was eager to flatter what was, naturally, its ideal audience. Here were people marooned at home for much of the day, affluent and consumerist by inclination (having already purchased a new lifestyle), and at least at the start, insecure enough about the conduct of their new lifestyles to welcome the guidance of advertisers.

But what's remarkable is how Cleaverism continues to organize so much of our thinking about suburbia. Now, though, it's the lie of Cleaverism—call it Cheeverism—that dominates the popular image, offering writers and moviemakers a cheap way to construct a gothic version of suburbia, to throw its dark side into sharp relief. Now behind every smiling lawn is a dysfunctional family: Donna Reed's sleeping with the woman next door and Eddie Haskell's got a gun.

25 Yet the façade remains the organizing principle; in defiance of everything we know, we can't seem to see the suburbs without it. Without the ghosts of the Cleavers hovering over them, the families in "American Beauty," say, or of any number of recent suburban-gothic productions, just don't make a whole lot of sense.

Before I left the Gates I drove into Bering Court to see if I could find the Beav's old place. If I had the right one, the house has had a complete face lift since the '60s. The stately white faux-colonial now has diagonal siding painted an unfortunate shade of puce, lots of opaque glass bricks and, out front, a berm thickly planted with shrubs to hide the facade. Very '80s, it seemed, but for the life of me I could not name the dream behind this house.

IT'S HARD TO SPEND TIME DRIVING AROUND Long Island today without a gathering sense of cognitive dissonance. So many of our generalizations about the burbs no longer stick, which almost seems a shame, since generalization was one of the things that we liked best about them. Is it even right to call a place like Woodbury—no longer "sub" to any "urb"—a "suburb" any more? "Urban sprawl" might be a better term. Certainly "sprawl" hints at the centerlessness of it, "urban" at the fact there's nothing in the city you can't find here. And maybe, as some have suggested, that is what I'm looking at but can't quite yet see: a new kind of city, one we still don't have the words or name for. "Edge City" is one proposal, though that still implies a center. "Technoburb," another, hints at the role technology has played in freeing these place from their urban orbits, but it's awfully cold. How about something more floppy-effervescent, like "burbopolis"?

Whatever it ultimately gets called, the horizontal city that is now Nassau County, Long Island, is fast acquiring a city's jangly diversity, though, being horizontal, it takes a car to really see it. Freeport has its African-American neighborhoods and Great Neck a community of Persians, and even in my very white elementary school you see Indian and Asian faces now. Street culture, of all things, has come to certain suburban lanes: in Glen Cove, Central American immigrants collect on corners and in front yards, talking and playing music as if they were still in Guatemala City. (The village issued a flier gently instructing them in suburban custom.) The new city has city problems too: housing shortages, crime waves, pollution; dilapidated "first ring" suburbs are said to be in the throes of a full-fledged "urban crisis."

Though even here the generalizations don't hold. Before I left Long Island I took a long walk through Levittown, where the suburban history of Long Island got its start half a century ago. A first-ring suburb built fast and on the cheap, Levittown by all rights should be crumbling by now. Yet the place I visited appeared to be doing just fine, in defiance of every stereotype that has been thrown at it. Held up as an example of conformity and monotony, Levittown's 17,000 identical capes have mutated into an exuberant architectural Babel: the sparrows on a wire have each grown their own distinctive plumage.

30 Yet this free-for-all of Home Depot fantasy is held together nicely by the steady setback line of the houses and the mature shade trees marching down the gridded streets. Even more surprising, though, was the sidewalk scene, which even in late winter was about as lively as a New Urbanist could wish for, the young mothers out with their strollers, the kids biking home from school, the gray-haired joggers doing the loop in slo-mo. By the time I got back in my car, I felt completely confused about where, exactly, it was I'd been.

The monolith that was supposed to be suburban America—middle class, homogenous, white—has become just one of a great many neighborhoods in a larger and more complicated mosaic. So why is this new suburbia so hard to see plain, without the filter of suburban cliché? Maybe it's because we've lost our old vantage point.

When my parents moved to the Gates in 1960, one-third of America was suburb, one-third city, one-third rural. Even those of us who lived in the first third tended to look at it from the perspective of the second. The city still held what amounted to a monopoly on descriptions and, for obvious reasons, the city didn't much like what it saw rising up around it.

Forty years later, the suburbs—or whatever they are—have grown up and taken over: more people now live in suburban American than rural and urban America combined. Suburbia *is* America, and not just demographically. Today our politics are ruled by the suburbs; suburbia's agenda—that is, issues bearing on the well-being of families with children, around which the suburbs still revolve—is now America's. (Even the erstwhile party of the city has moved to the burbs, with Bill Clinton doing the driving.) Suburbia's cultural power is harder to see, but that may be because it's everywhere, indistinguishable from the air we breathe.

On the drive back to the country, where I live now, or where at least I *think* I live, I thought about the various ways suburban qualities have seeped beyond the burbs themselves. I thought about the suburbanization of the city, manifest in freshly themed neighborhoods and malled retailing, and I thought about Silicon Valley, which in some ways represents the apotheosis of suburbia: the first time in history an important economic, technological and cultural revolution has its roots in a suburb.

I also thought about manners. Ever since Levittown was built America has become a progressively more informal place, one where social distinctions get played down, where even the rich and famous feel compelled at least to act like normal suburbanites, and where hierarchical distinctions like high- and low-brow—which are fundamentally urban distinctions—come to seem quaint. Suburbia's too horizontal a place for all that.

I thought about clothes too. I usually wear a tie and sport jacket when I'm reporting, but not on this trip. Suburbanites dress up only to go to the city, a place where the presentation of self is far more serious business. That's probably because all you really have to present in the city is yourself in public, dressed this way or that. In the burbs you've got the house and the car and the lawn all working overtime to tell the world who you are, and this leaves you free to dress down. Nowadays everybody dresses down; on Fridays, even the starchiest urban offices go suburban.

I wondered too if what we used to think of as the fakeness of the suburbs hasn't also left its mark on the broader culture. To grow up on a "boulevard" conjured in a field is to be at home with the façade and the themed environment, with the quick-change and the quotation marks, not to mention the willing suspension of disbelief. It may be that ironic detachment is a mental habit we children of the burbs have come by naturally.

Anyway, these were my desultory highway thoughts, entertained on the long drive home from suburbia. The funny thing is, the closer to home I got, the more omnipresent the place I'd been began to feel. Suburbia, I realized, is no longer somewhere you go, or leave. Wherever we live now, it's where we live.

Exploring Texts and Contexts

For activities with icons, refer to the Guide to Analyzing Readings in Context.

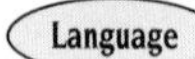

1. Pollan places much emphasis on names, for instance of the streets he grew up on, but he is also concerned with finding a name for what the suburbs have become. Reread Pollan's essay and consider how his focus on language helps him develop his essay. Consider, too, how the activity of naming helps Pollan characterize changes in demographics and lifestyle.

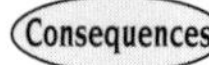

2. Pollan describes a stark contrast between the "then" of his childhood and the Gates of Woodbury today. What changes does he see and what does he see as the causes of these changes? Do you think Pollan intended his article to have any impact on the phenomena he describes? What consquences might an article like Pollan's have?
3. Pollan mentions that new technologies have contributed to the changes he sees occurring in the suburbs. Explain what he means, and consider how technological changes might continue to influence the suburbs.

Creating Texts

For activities with icons, refer to the Guides to Analyzing Contexts for Writing and Analyzing Readings in Context. For additional help with these writing projects, read the descriptions of **Dialogue/Symposium** and **Essay** in the Genre Glossary.

1. Several authors in this unit have considered the importance of establishinga sense of place in creating a home. Pollan considers the suburbs and their initial development as "a place apart," Witold Rybczynski talks about the home as a refuge, and Richard Rodriguez writes about renovating Victorian homes to create a community feeling among gays in San Francisco. Create a dialogue among these three authors in which they discuss the necessary components of making a home.

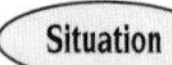

2. Pollan remembers the newness, and to some extent the inauthenticity, of the suburbs: "after all, we had watched them rise like stage sets on the farm fields, seen the instantaneous lawns rolled out over the raw dirt like new linoleum" (237). Clifton Taulbert, on the other hand, remembers how his home connected him to both the past and the future: "The Mississippi Delta was my home and I wanted to . . . return to the house built by my great-grandfather Sidney Peter. . . . The front porches became the place where visiting relatives from up north would sit and spin their intoxicating tales of northern life" (197). Write an essay in which you discuss how time-honored traditions on the one hand and change on the other hand contribute to establishing a sense of place.

Mi Casa es Su Casa

Margaret Crawford and Adobe LA

My house is your house. "Mi casa es su casa" says you are welcome, make yourself at home. Many people have given up on the idea that there is a typical family and thus a typical house, but how do we negotiate between the typical standards for home architecture and a personal place that we can call home? In 1994, the Wexner Center for the Arts, located at Ohio State University in Columbus, Ohio, presented an unusual exhibit called "House Rules." Curated by Mark Robbins, the exhibit offered teams of architects and cultural critics the opportunity to explore how a variety of individuals, families, and communities might reevaluate the single-family suburban home that, for many, has come to symbolize the American dream. The architecture journal *Assemblage: A Critical Journal of Architecture and Design Culture* published reports of many of these team projects.

Each team was given the same design specifications, based on the four-room homes built for Levittown, one of the first suburban developments, built in the early fifties, which mass-produced similar homes laid out to create a ready-made community. Working with the basic plans for this sort of house, each team was to think through and redesign the homes to respond to the needs of the people who would live in them. The Mi Casa team consisted of Margaret Crawford, an academic at the Southern California Institute for Architecture, who has written about company towns, and a collaborative group of architects and artists interested in how issues of identity, urban planning, and architecture affect the Latino community. The collaborative, Adobe LA, which stands for Architects and Designers Opening the Border Edge of Los Angeles, along with Crawford, used this project to illustrate how Latino communities have integrated culture and design in modifying the housing available to them in East Los Angeles.

Connecting with the Conversation

1. Visit the Web site for the Wexner Museum at http://www.wexarts.org. Read its mission statement and look at some of the recent exhibits. Comment on how the design of the Web site enhances its mission. Prepare to share with the class information about a particular exhibit that you would like to see.
2. Write in your journal about your idea of what makes a home comfortable and particularly suited to your needs. Next, list the various places you have lived thus far. Evaluate each for how close it comes to your ideal of home. Consider how you decorated, remodeled, or altered the places you lived in to make them feel more comfortable and more like home.

The Politics of Everyday Life in East Los Angeles

1 Even the briefest encounter with East Los Angeles reveals a landscape of heroic bricolage, a triumph of what Michel De Certeau calls "making do."[1] These lived spaces, exuberant but overlooked, pose an alternative to the middle-class American house, actual or imagined. Taking control of ordinary personal and social spaces, residents have transformed a stock of modest single-family houses into a distinctive domestic landscape. Extending their presence beyond their property lines to the sidewalk and street, they construct community solidarity from the inside out, house by house, street by street. Through personal and cultural alterations to their houses, the residents of East L.A. reenact, in innumerable individual versions, the social drama of Mexican migration to Los Angeles, invoking memories that are both unique and collective. The house and yard are sites of ambiguous signification, revealing the complex tensions between culture and personality, memory and innovation, Chicano and Mexican, Mexico and America. Charged with human expression, these houses reestablish use and meaning as their primary definition. By investing their dwellings with the personal values contained in their interests, competence, and originality, the residents remove them from the context of mass-market values, and thereby decommodify them.[2] Their pleasure in transformation and self-expression reclaims a central aspect of homeownership that many other Angelenos, obsessed with property values, have forgotten.

These activities appear to exemplify what De Certeau identifies as "tactics," the opportunistic maneuverings utilized by those without power. De Certeau's description of tactical operations emphasizes their momentary and circumstantial qualities, privileging fleeting experience over fixed and constructed space. Comparing tactics to the meandering foot-steps of thousands of ordinary pedestrians in the city, De Certeau celebrates their creativity and their meaninglessness. Since they evaporate in an infinity of personal trajectories, no order or pattern can ever emerge. Seen on the run, the quotidian transformations of East L.A. support De Certeau's conclusions. In contrast to the solidity projected by most suburban houses, these dwellings, shaped and given meaning by occupation and use, convey a provisional quality. Their occupants allow time and memory to control space.

Yet these apparently ephemeral uses and alterations, repeated countless times over the course of several generations on adjacent lots and streets enclosed within the cultural and spatial borders of East L.A., come together, not only forming a distinctive pattern but suggesting a direction. Asserting more than just personal and social autonomy, they have acquired the potential for political significance. In its decommodified form, the house becomes a vehicle for mobilizing social identity, making a publicly legible statement that provides residents with a new sense of agency. Thus redefining the political field to include issues clustered around the home, daily life, and urban residential space offers the residents of East L.A., massively underrepresented in official political channels, new venues for collective activity. As a form of social action, their continuing use and transformation of existing houses questions both the need for architectural intervention and the need for reinventing the house.

From *Assemblage: A Critical Journal of Architecture and Design Culture* 24, August 1994, pp. 12–19.

The Border

Any discussion of East Los Angeles must begin across the Mexican border, one hundred forty miles to the south, a line crossed by successive waves of immigrants drawn to the region's economic power. Mexican immigrants provided low-wage labor for the city's phenomenal industrial growth, but early in the century, Americans, intent on expanding the commercial district, building a civic center, and segregating their neighborhoods, pushed them across another border, the Los Angeles River. By 1930 the east side of the river was solidly Mexican. Currently, with more than three hundred thousand residents, the eastside is the largest concentration of Mexicans and Mexican-Americans in the United States, a Mexican city in the heart of Los Angeles. Beginning in the 1940s, thirty years of freeway construction imposed new borders. The incisions made by the San Bernadino and Santa Ana freeways on the north and south created barriers not links, separating East L.A. even further from the rest of the city. Finally, the Long Beach and Pomona freeways carved an X through the community's heart, erasing it from the view of anyone passing through.

5 Today, for most Angelenos, the eastside is both terra incognita and a zone of radical alterity. Its invisibility encourages outsiders to construct other, imaginary, borders. Is it dangerous or merely exotic, occupied by drug dealers, cholo gangs, or anonymous hordes of illegal aliens? Newspaper and television reports further demonize the eastside, providing additional ammunition for the police and sheriff 's departments that control the area like occupying armies. In fact, the eastside's crime rates are no higher than those on the westside. Seen from within, along narrow streets lined with working-class bungalows, the myths of East L.A.'s mean streets melt away. Here, unnoticed by the city and hidden from professional architectural culture, its residents have created a new hybrid form of dwelling. Negotiating between the circumstances of life in Los Angeles and the customs, rituals, and traditions brought from Mexico, they define a new border condition, no longer a line of exclusion but a cultural free trade zone, accessible to continuous movement back and forth.

The Fence

The fence is the initial gesture that defines East L.A.'s domestic landscape, a method of staking claim to the barrio for as long as Mexicans have lived here.[3] Chain link is common and acceptable but residents prefer elaborate constructions of block and wrought iron. Refusing the amorphous and impersonal suburban front lawn, they use the fence to delineate the front yard as an enclosure. This moves the domain of the house forward to the street, extending its domestic space to the corners of the lot. A permeable border, protective but inviting interaction, the fence enables each family to define their own environment while maintaining contact with the activities of the sidewalk and street. In East L.A. every street presents a characteristic topography of fences; some are patrolled by dogs, others are hung with homemade signs advertising nopales or discount diapers, others support brightly colored brooms for sale. As innovation has encouraged imitation, fence styles have become increasingly complex, spurring the rapidly evolving craft of wrought iron, one of East L.A.'s largest homegrown industries.

The Yarda

Fully occupied, the enclosed yard encapsulates the functions of the plaza, courtyard, front yard, and street. It is simultaneously an arena of sociability, a site of control, an outdoor work area, and a stage for symbolic elaboration. Both public and private, the *yarda* welcomes engagement with neighbors and passersby but can also shelter intimate discussions and family celebrations. Its nuanced space structures social encounters: strangers are met at the gate, friends invited onto the porch. By providing a vantage point onto the street, it allows residents to supervise adjacent territory. Owners and renters customize their yards by occupation and design. Busy with mundane tasks or artfully arranging plants or statuary, they expose their daily lives and deeply personal preferences to anyone passing by. Infinitely flexible and always in flux, the *yarda* can accommodate special events, from a garage sale to a *quinceanera.* It can become a lush jungle of plants or, paved over, a playground or car-repair shop. A driveway can serve as a dance floor, an outdoor hallway, or a space to display goods for sale.

Alterations

"Mexicanization" is a recognizable yet versatile idiom, a mutable aesthetic adaptable to many conditions. Immediate changes are easily accomplished with yellow, mango, or peach paint, strings of Christmas lights, and attention to intricate detail. Other alterations require more time and money: replacing wood surfaces with textured stucco or columns with ornamental wrought iron or stuccoed arches. Still others derive from family needs: garages remodeled as rental units, extra bedrooms, or small businesses. In addition porches are often added, expanded, or covered, furnished with tables, chairs, or couches and decorated with wrought iron, paint, or potted plants. Whether the product of the owner's weekend labor or that of unlicensed neighborhood contractors, most alterations are constructed without working drawings, building codes, or permits.

Plants

Apart from the ubiquity of rose bushes—collective remembrances, perhaps, of the roses miraculously transformed into an image of the Virgin of Guadeloupe—gardens in East L.A. are primarily lovingly tended personal statements. As visions of paradise, they demonstrate the many varieties of metamorphosis, blurring the distinctions between agriculture and ornament, artificial and natural, sacred and mundane. Neat rows of corn and nopales appear among the standard Southern California cypresses, fruit trees, and bougainvillea, traces, along with illegally kept chickens, of a rural past. Eno, a variety of Spanish moss used to decorate Christmas crèches, hangs from tree branches. On any street you might find container gardens in recycled washtubs set on concrete slabs, complex compositions of flowers and paving, with fountain and birdbath centerpieces, comic assemblages of plants, plaster yard ornaments, found objects, toys, and solemnly pretty shrines elaborated around statues of Christ or the Virgin Mary, all vying for attention.

The House

10 The interior of the house is the center of the family's power. Since the *yarda* is the primary site of social life, casual guests rarely enter the house. Although large extended families live in these small spaces, they rarely alter the arrangement of rooms. Instead, parents, grandmothers, and children crowd in together. With children sharing tiny bedrooms and everyone sharing the single bathroom, privacy is rare, but not particularly valued. Living rooms overflow with plastic-covered furniture, photographs of birthdays, graduations, and weddings, and carefully ordered collections of "beautiful little things," religious mementos, and family souvenirs. The television is here, imposing its schedule on the room: Spanish-language soap operas from 4 to 7 p.m., followed by American situation comedies, and, on weekends, Dodgers games and soccer matches. Still, the heart of family life remains the kitchen, the only room that might be enlarged. Focused on cooking, eating, and household chores, this is the territory of the mother and the female members of the family. Fathers, working outside the house all day, appear in the evening, to watch TV, water the plants, or putter in the yard.[4]

The activities that take place in these houses and yards unfold over time, producing the distinctive rhythm of East Los Angeles. On weekends the enclosed household routines spill out into the yard's extroverted space. On Saturday the tempo intensifies, as men gather to work on cars, friends and relatives drop by, tables and chairs are set out for parties and barbecues, vendors offer their wares, and teenagers cruise by in minitrucks or low riders. By Sunday the pace slows. Families, dressed up, leave for church, neighbors chat over the fence, and children play in the yard. Family time is measured in even slower cycles; renters move to other houses, relatives arrive from Mexico, children grow up, and a new generation moves east to suburbs in the San Gabriel Valley or San Bernadino County. Yet throughout these changes, threads of memory persist, to be rewoven into surprising new combinations. The polyglot sounds overheard from car stereos or boom boxes on Spanish-language KLAX (Southern California's most listened-to radio station) or such popular shows as *Alma del Barrio* or *Voices of Aztlan,* demonstrate this process of transformation. Segueing from norteño ballads to rhythm and blues oldies, banda to Led Zeppelin, they mix old and new, English and Spanish, nostalgia and rebellion in complex combinations that, like East L.A. itself, defy interpretation.

The Politics of Everyday Space

The cultural and political weight of these continuous transformations render speculative housing development, architectural intervention, and traditional real estate practices almost completely irrelevant in East Los Angeles. Since poor or working-class Mexicans and Mexican-Americans rarely purchase new houses, market-oriented designers and builders do not take their tastes or preferences into account when selecting spas or improving master bedroom suites for new subdivisions. In this world of hand-me-down housing, the professional services and specialized culture of architects are even more remote. When architects choose to donate their services, the results have often been inappropriate or demeaning. Contemporary architectural styles, whether postmodern or abstract formalist, hold little interest for a culture already rich in visual imagery, expression, and meaning.

Ironically, these identifiably "Mexican" qualities have contributed to low prices and stability in East L.A.'s housing market. Almost entirely Mexican, it is an unlikely target for gentrification. In other parts of the city, however, the quotidian house transformations tolerated in the East L.A. barrio are under attack. Class and ethnic struggles over space disguise themselves as struggles over architectural values. Preservationists in Pasadena, horrified by "Mexicanized" Craftsman bungalows, have issued Spanish-language pamphlets that attempt to convince homeowners not to alter their houses. In response to their arguments for the social and financial rewards of maintaining a house's original historical and cultural character, East L.A.'s lived politics of the everyday poses the questions: whose history, whose culture, whose house, whose space?

Notes

1. Michel De Certeau, *The Practice of Everyday Life* (Berkeley: University of California Press, 1984), 29–42.
2. See David Harvey, "Accumulation Through Urbanization," *Antipode* 19, no. 3 (1987): 269–71. James Holston describes the processes that Harvey outlines in his work on Brazilian self-building, "Autoconstruction in Working-Class Brazil," *Cultural Anthropology* 6, no. 4 (1991): 464–65.
3. This discussion is indebted to James Rojas's pioneering work on East L.A., "The Enacted Environment: The Creation of 'Place' by Mexicans and Mexican Americans in East Los Angeles," Master's thesis, Department of Architecture, Massachusetts Institute of Technology, 1991.
4. Ibid., 80–82.

Exploring Texts and Contexts

For activities with icons, refer to the Guide to Analyzing Readings in Context.

1. Compare the populations and economies described in Crawford's piece with Michael Pollan's description of the suburbs outside New York City. The two communities look quite different, yet both provide home and community to their residents. Discuss the ways in which communities evolve in response to economic and political circumstances.
2. Crawford uses the work of a cultural theorist named Michel de Certeau to help explain the way residents have changed the standard housing stock of East Los Angeles. She says, "In contrast to the solidity projected by most suburban houses, these dwellings, shaped and given meaning by occupation and use, convey a provisional quality. Their occupants allow time and memory to control space" (244). Explain what de Certeau means by "tactics" and how his theory about the use of tactics helps us to understand Crawford's statement.
3. As you read the case study in Chapter 8, consider how Crawford's analysis would provide additional insight into the debate over Cisneros's purple house.

Creating Texts

For activities with icons, refer to the Guides to Analyzing Contexts for Writing and Analyzing Readings in Context. For additional help with these writing projects, read the descriptions of **Letter to the Editor** and **Essay** in the Genre Glossary.

1. Crawford explains that the area she focuses on in East Los Angeles is nearly entirely Mexican and the decorative changes made to homes are encouraged and well accepted within that community. However, she says, "Preservationists in Pasadena, horrified by 'Mexicanized' Craftsman bungalows, have issued Spanish-language pamphlets that attempt to convince homeowners not to alter their houses" (248). Write a letter to the editor arguing for or against standards for exterior decoration in your neighborhood. 
2. Write an essay in which you explore, as Crawford puts it, what it means to take "control of ordinary personal and social spaces" and how one might do this. Consider her brief mention of de Certeau and his description of this process as "making do." Also, take into account Witold Rybcznski's injunction that we not leave decisions about comfort to others. Consider any other appropriate readings from this unit, and, most important, consider your experience and your family's with taking control of your own space.

Late Victorians

San Francisco, AIDS, and the Homosexual Stereotype

Richard Rodriguez

In the 1980s, when educators began to be more sensitive to the need for diversity in curricula and textbooks, excerpts from Richard Rodriguez's 1982 memoir, *Hunger of Memory,* began to appear in many high school and college reading anthologies. The excerpts usually included Rodriguez's beautifully written, painful description of being the only non-English-speaking child on his first day of school in Sacramento, California. But to the consternation of many who championed more diverse representation in education, the excerpts also included Rodriguez's passionate criticism of bilingual education, and in the next few years, Rodriguez became a hero to those who opposed bilingual education. Rodriguez was not particularly comfortable in this role, since he did not agree with all the positions taken by the opponents of bilingual education. But throughout his life as a writer and public figure, Rodriguez has resisted being categorized. Indeed, at the very beginning of his career, he turned down a number of university teaching jobs because of his sense that they'd been offered because of his ethnic background. And he has continued to go his own way since, working primarily as a freelance essayist and commentator, offering thoughtful, nuanced observations on many aspects of American life.

In 1990 Rodriguez published an essay in *Harper's Magazine* that for many of his readers constituted his coming out as a gay man. The essay was a complex analysis of the effect of the AIDS epidemic on the gay community, particularly in the Castro district of San Francisco. But as with his earlier writing, readers were not quite sure how to respond: Was the essay a celebration of the gay lifestyle or a criticism of it? It is, certainly, a complex discussion that draws together many themes related not only to the gay community and lifestyle but to American life in general.

Connecting with the Conversation

1. What do you think of when you hear the word *Victorian*? Why does the word have these connotations for you? Share your observations with the class, and then discuss in particular the associations that you have with Victorian architecture. If someone says that a building is Victorian, what images and associations come to your mind?
2. In the late 1990s gay characters became more common on network television and in mainstream movies. Discuss with a small group whether you think that these portrayals have tended to promote or challenge homosexual stereotypes.
3. When Rodriguez wrote this essay in 1990, AIDS was still thought of by many as a "gay disease." To what extent have our ideas about AIDS changed, or not changed, in the twenty-first century?

St. Augustine writes from his cope of dust that we are restless hearts, for earth is not our true home. Human unhappiness is evidence of our immortality. Intuition tells us we are meant for some other city.

Elizabeth Taylor, quoted in a magazine article of twenty years ago, spoke of cerulean Richard Burton days on her yacht, days that were nevertheless undermined by the elemental private reflection: This must end.

ON A SUNDAY IN SUMMER, TEN YEARS AGO, I was walking home from the Latin Mass at St. Patrick's, the old Irish parish downtown, when I saw thousands of people on Market Street. It was San Francisco's Gay Freedom Day parade—not the first, but the first I ever saw. Private lives were becoming public. There were marching bands. There were floats. Banners blocked single lives thematically into a processional mass, not unlike the consortiums of the blessed in Renaissance paintings, each saint cherishing the apparatus of his martyrdom: GAY DENTISTS. BLACK AND WHITE LOVERS. GAYS FROM BAKERSFIELD. LATINA LESBIANS. From the foot of Market Street they marched, east to west, following the mythic American path toward optimism.

From *Harper's Magazine*, October 1990, pp. 57–66.

I followed the parade to Civic Center Plaza, where flags of routine nations yielded sovereignty to a multitude. Pastel billows flowed over all.

5 Five years later, another parade. Politicians waved from white convertibles. Dykes on Bikes revved up, thumbs upped. But now banners bore the acronyms of death. AIDS. ARC. Drums were muffled as passing, plum-spotted young men slid by on motorized cable cars.

Though I am alive now, I do not believe that an old man's pessimism is truer than a young man's optimism simply because it comes after. There are things a young man knows that are true and are not yet in the old man's power to recollect. Spring has its sappy wisdom. Lonely teenagers still arrive in San Francisco aboard Greyhound buses. The city can still seem, I imagine, by comparison to where they came from, paradise.

FOUR YEARS AGO ON A SUNDAY IN WINTER—a brilliant spring afternoon—I was jogging near Fort Point while overhead a young woman was, with difficulty, climbing over the railing of the Golden Gate Bridge. Holding down her skirt with one hand, with the other she waved to a startled spectator (the newspaper next day quoted a workman who was painting the bridge) before she stepped onto the sky.

To land like a spilled purse at my feet.

Serendipity has an eschatological tang here. Always has. Few American cities have had the experience, as we have had, of watching the civic body burn even as we stood, out of body, on a hillside, in a movie theater. Jeanette MacDonald's loony scatting of "San Francisco" has become our go-to-hell anthem. San Francisco has taken some heightened pleasure from the circus of final things. To Atlantis, to Pompeii, to the Pillar of Salt, we add the Golden Gate Bridge, not golden at all but rust red. San Francisco toys with the tragic conclusion.

10 For most of its brief life, San Francisco has entertained an idea of itself as heaven on earth, whether as Gold Town or City Beautiful or Treasure Island or Haight-Ashbury.

San Francisco can support both comic and tragic conclusions because the city is geographically *in extremis,* a metaphor for the farthest-flung possibility, a metaphor for the end of the line. Land's end.

To speak of San Francisco as land's end is to read the map from one direction only—as Europeans would read or as the East Coast has always read it. In my lifetime, San Francisco has become an Asian city. To speak, therefore, of San Francisco as land's end is to betray parochialism. Before my parents came to California from Mexico, they saw San Francisco as the North. The West was not west for them.

I cannot claim for myself the memory of a skyline such as the one César saw. César came to San Francisco in middle age; César came here as to some final place. He was born in South America; he had grown up in Paris; he had been everywhere, done everything; he assumed the world. Yet César was not condescending toward San Francisco, not at all. Here César saw revolution, and he embraced it.

Whereas I live here because I was born here. I grew up ninety miles away, in Sacramento. San Francisco was the nearest, the easiest, the inevitable city, since I needed a city. And yet I live here surrounded by people for whom San Francisco is a quest.

15 I have never looked for utopia on a map. Of course, I believe in human advancement. I believe in medicine, in astrophysics, in washing machines. But my compass

takes its cardinal point from tragedy. If I respond to the metaphor of spring, I nevertheless learned, years ago, from my Mexican parents, from my Irish nuns, to count on winter. The point of Eden for me, for us, is not approach but expulsion.

After I met César in 1984, our friendly debate concerning the halcyon properties of San Francisco ranged from restaurant to restaurant. I spoke of limits. César boasted of freedoms.

It was César's conceit to add to the gates of Jerusalem, to add to the soccer fields of Tijuana, one other dreamscape hoped for the world over. It was the view from a hill, through a mesh of electrical tram wires, of an urban neighborhood in a valley. The vision took its name from the protruding wedge of a theater marquee. Here César raised his glass without discretion: To the Castro.

THERE WERE TIMES, DEAR CÉSAR, when you tried to switch sides if only to scorn American optimism, which, I remind you, had already become your own. At the high school where César taught, teachers and parents had organized a campaign to keep kids from driving themselves to the junior prom in an attempt to forestall liquor and death. Such a scheme momentarily reawakened César's Latin skepticism.

Didn't the Americans know? (His tone exaggerated incredulity.) Teenagers will crash into lampposts on their way home from proms, and there is nothing to be done about it. You cannot forbid tragedy.

20 BY CALIFORNIA STANDARDS I LIVE IN AN OLD HOUSE. But not haunted. There are too many tall windows, there is too much salty light, especially in winter, though the windows rattle, rattle in summer when the fog flies overhead, and the house creaks and prowls at night. I feel myself immune to any confidence it seeks to tell.

To grow up homosexual is to live with secrets and within secrets. In no other place are those secrets more closely guarded than within the family home. The grammar of the gay city borrows metaphors from the nineteenth-century house. "Coming out of the closet" is predicated upon family laundry, dirty linen, skeletons.

I live in a tall Victorian house that has been converted to four apartments; four single men.

Neighborhood streets are named to honor nineteenth-century men of action, men of distant fame. Clay. Jackson. Scott. Pierce. Many Victorians in the neighborhood date from before the 1906 earthquake and fire.

Architectural historians credit the gay movement of the 1970s with the urban restoration of San Francisco. Twenty years ago this was a borderline neighborhood. This room, like all the rooms of the house, was painted headache green, apple green, boardinghouse green. In the 1970s homosexuals moved into black and working-class parts of the city, where they were perceived as pioneers or as blockbusters, depending.

25 Two decades ago some of the least expensive sections of San Francisco were wooden Victorian sections. It was thus a coincidence of the market that gay men found themselves living with the architectural metaphor for family. No other architecture in the American imagination is more evocative of family than the Victorian house. In those same years—the 1970s—and within those same Victorian houses, homosexuals were living rebellious lives to challenge the foundations of domesticity.

Was "queer-bashing" as much a manifestation of homophobia as a reaction against gentrification? One heard the complaint, often enough, that gay men were as promiscuous with their capital as otherwise, buying, fixing up, then selling and moving on. Two incomes, no children, described an unfair advantage. No sooner would flower boxes begin to appear than an anonymous reply was smeared on the sidewalk out front: kill faggots.

The three- or four-story Victorian house, like the Victorian novel, was built to contain several generations and several classes under one roof, behind a single oaken door. What strikes me is the confidence of Victorian architecture. Stairs, connecting one story with another, describe the confidence that bound generations together through time—confidence that the family would inherit the earth.

If Victorian houses exude a sturdy optimism by day, they are also associated in our imaginations with the Gothic—with shadows and cobwebby gimcrack, long corridors. The nineteenth century was remarkable for escalating optimism even as it excavated the backstairs, the descending architecture of nightmare—Freud's labor and Engels's.

I live on the second story, in rooms that have been rendered as empty as Yorick's skull—gutted, unrattled, in various ways unlocked, added skylights and new windows, new doors. The hallway remains the darkest part of the house.

30 This winter the hallway and lobby are being repainted to resemble an eighteenth-century French foyer. Of late we had walls and carpet of Sienese red; a baroque mirror hung in an alcove by the stairwell. Now we are to have enlightened austerity of an expensive sort—black-and-white marble floors and faux masonry. A man comes in the afternoons to texture the walls with a sponge and a rag and to paint white mortar lines that create an illusion of permanence, of stone.

The renovation of Victorian San Francisco into dollhouses for libertines may have seemed, in the 1970s, an evasion of what the city was actually becoming. San Francisco's rows of storied houses proclaimed a multigenerational orthodoxy, all the while masking the city's unconventional soul. Elsewhere, meanwhile, domestic America was coming undone.

Suburban Los Angeles, the prototype for a new America, was characterized by a more apparently radical residential architecture. There was, for example, the work of Frank Gehry. In the 1970s Gehry exploded the nuclear-family house, turning it inside out intellectually and in fact. Though, in a way, Gehry merely completed the logic of the postwar suburban tract house—with its one story, its sliding glass doors, Formica kitchen, two-car garage. The tract house exchanged privacy for mobility. Heterosexuals opted for the one-lifetime house, the freeway, the birth-control pill, minimalist fiction.

THE AGE-OLD DESCRIPTION OF HOMOSEXUALITY is of a sin against nature. Moralistic society has always judged emotion literally. The homosexual was sinful because he had no kosher place to stick it. In attempting to drape the architecture of sodomy with art, homosexuals have lived for thousands of years against the expectations of nature. Barren as Shakers and, interestingly, as concerned with the small effect, homosexuals have made a covenant against nature. Homosexual survival lay in artifice, in plumage, in lampshades, sonnets, musical comedy, couture, syntax, religious ceremony, opera, lacquer, irony.

I once asked Enrique, an interior decorator, if he had many homosexual clients. *"Mais non,"* said he, flexing his eyelids. "Queers don't need decorators. They were born knowing how. All this A.S.I.D. stuff—tests and regulations—as if you can confer a homosexual diploma on a suburban housewife by granting her a discount card."

35 A knack? The genius, we are beginning to fear in an age of AIDS, is irreplaceable—but does it exist? The question is whether the darling affinities are innate to homosexuality or whether they are compensatory. Why have so many homosexuals retired into the small effect, the ineffectual career, the stereotype, the card shop, the florist? *Be gentle with me?* Or do homosexuals know things others do not?

This way power lay: Once upon a time the homosexual appropriated to himself a mystical province, that of taste. Taste, which is, after all, the insecurity of the middle class, became the homosexual's licentiate to challenge the rule of nature. (The fairy in his blood, he intimated.)

Deciding how best to stick it may be only an architectural problem or a question of physics or of engineering or of cabinetry. Nevertheless, society's condemnation forced the homosexual to find his redemption outside nature. *We'll put a little skirt here.* The impulse is not to create but to re-create, to sham, to convert, to sauce, to rouge, to fragrance, to prettify. No effect is too small or too ephemeral to be snatched away from nature, to be ushered toward the perfection of artificiality. *We'll bring out the highlights there.* The homosexual has marshaled the architecture of the straight world to the very gates of Versailles—that great Vatican of fairyland—beyond which power is converted to leisure.

In San Francisco in the 1980s the highest form of art became interior decoration. The glory hole was thus converted to an eighteenth-century French foyer.

I LIVE AWAY FROM THE STREET, in a back apartment, in two rooms. I use my bedroom as a visitor's room—the sleigh bed tricked up with shams into a sofa—whereas I rarely invite anyone into my library, the public room, where I write, the public gesture.

40 I read in my bedroom in the afternoon because the light is good there, especially now, in winter, when the sun recedes from the earth.

There is a door in the south wall that leads to a balcony. The door was once a window. Inside the door, inside my bedroom, are twin green shutters. They are false shutters, of no function beyond wit. The shutters open into the room; they have the effect of turning my apartment inside out.

A few months ago I hired a man to paint the shutters green. I wanted the green shutters of Manet—you know the ones I mean—I wanted a weathered look, as of verdigris. For several days the painter labored, rubbing his paints into the wood and then wiping them off again. In this way he rehearsed for me decades of the ravages of weather. Yellow enough? Black?

The painter left one afternoon, saying he would return the next day, leaving behind his tubes, his brushes, his sponges and rags. He never returned. Someone told me he has AIDS.

REPAINTED FACADES EXTEND NOW FROM JACKSON STREET south into what was once the heart of the black "Mo"—black Fillmore Street. Today there are watercress sandwiches at three o'clock where recently there had been loudmouthed kids, hole-in-the-wall bars, pimps. Now there are tweeds and perambulators, matrons and nannies. Yuppies. And gays.

45 The gay male revolution had greater influence on San Francisco in the 1970s than did the feminist revolution. Feminists, with whom I include lesbians—such was the inclusiveness of the feminist movement—were preoccupied with career, with escape from the house in order to create a sexually democratic city. Homosexual men sought to reclaim the house, the house that traditionally had been the reward for heterosexuality, with all its selfless tasks and burdens.

Leisure defined the gay male revolution. The gay political movement began, by most accounts, in 1969, with the Stonewall riots in New York City, whereby gay men fought to defend the nonconformity of their leisure.

It was no coincidence that homosexuals migrated to San Francisco in the 1970s, for the city was famed as a playful place, more Catholic than Protestant in its eschatological intuition. In 1975 the state of California legalized consensual homosexuality, and about that same time Castro Street, southwest of downtown, began to eclipse Polk Street as the homosexual address in San Francisco. Polk Street was a string of bars. The Castro was an entire district. The Castro had Victorian houses and churches, bookstores and restaurants, gyms, dry cleaners, supermarkets, and an elected member of the Board of Supervisors. The Castro supported baths and bars, but there was nothing furtive about them. On Castro Street the light of day penetrated gay life through clear plate-glass windows. The light of day discovered a new confidence, a new politics. Also a new look—a noncosmopolitan, Burt Reynolds, butch-kid style: beer, ball games, Levi's, short hair, muscles.

Gay men who lived elsewhere in the city, in Pacific Heights or in the Richmond, often spoke with derision of "Castro Street clones," describing the look, or scorned what they called the ghettoization of homosexuality. To an older generation of homosexuals, the blatancy of sexuality on Castro Street threatened the discreet compromise they had negotiated with a tolerant city.

As the Castro district thrived, Folsom Street, south of Market, also began to thrive, as if in counterdistinction to the utopian Castro. The Folsom Street area was a warehouse district of puddled alleys and deserted streets. Folsom Street offered an assortment of leather bars, an evening's regress to the outlaw sexuality of the Fifties, the Forties, the nineteenth century, and so on—an eroticism of the dark, of the Reeperbahn, or of the guardsman's barracks.

50 The Castro district implied that sexuality was more crucial, that homosexuality was the central fact of identity. The Castro district, with its ice-cream parlors and hardware stores, was the revolutionary place.

Into which carloads of vacant-eyed teenagers from other districts or from middle-class suburbs would drive after dark, cruising the neighborhood for solitary victims.

The ultimate gay basher was a city supervisor named Dan White, ex-cop, ex-boxer, ex-fireman, ex-altar boy. Dan White had grown up in the Castro district; he recognized the Castro revolution for what it was. Gays had achieved power over him. He murdered the mayor and he murdered the homosexual member of the Board of Supervisors.

KATHERINE, A SOPHISTICATE IF EVER THERE WAS ONE, nevertheless dismisses the two men descending the aisle at the Opera House: "All so sleek and smooth-jowled and silver-haired—they don't seem real, poor darlings. It must be because they don't have children."

Lodged within Katherine's complaint is the perennial heterosexual annoyance with the homosexual's freedom from child-rearing, which places the homosexual not so much beyond the pale as it relegates the homosexual outside "responsible" life.

55 It was the glamour of gay life, after all, as much as it was the feminist call to career, that encouraged heterosexuals in the 1970s to excuse themselves from nature, to swallow the birth-control pill. Who needs children? The gay bar became the paradigm for the single's bar. The gay couple became the paradigm for the selfish couple—all dressed up and everywhere to go. And there was the example of the gay house in illustrated life-style magazines. At the same time that suburban housewives were looking outside the home for fulfillment, gay men were reintroducing a new generation in the city—heterosexual men and women—to the complacencies of the barren house.

Puritanical America dismissed gay camp followers as Yuppies; the term means to suggest infantility. Yuppies were obsessive and awkward in their materialism. Whereas gays arranged a decorative life against a barren state, Yuppies sought early returns—lives that were not to be all toil and spin. Yuppies, trained to careerism from the cradle, wavered in their pursuit of the northern European ethic—indeed, we might now call it the pan-Pacific ethic—in favor of the Mediterranean, the Latin, the Catholic, the Castro, the Gay.

The international architectural idioms of Skidmore, Owings & Merrill, which defined the city's skyline in the 1970s, betrayed no awareness of any street-level debate concerning the primacy of play in San Francisco nor of any human dramas resulting from urban redevelopment. The repellent office tower was a fortress raised against the sky, against the street, against the idea of a city. Offices were hives where money was made, and damn all.

In the 1970s San Francisco was divided between the interests of downtown and the pleasures of the neighborhoods. Neighborhoods asserted idiosyncrasy, human scale, light. San Francisco neighborhoods perceived downtown as working against their influence in determining what the city should be. Thus neighborhoods seceded from the idea of a city.

The gay movement rejected downtown as representing "straight" conformity. But was it possible that heterosexual Union Street was related to Castro Street? Was it possible that either was related to the Latino Mission district? Or to the Sino-Russian Richmond? San Francisco, though complimented worldwide for holding its center, was in fact without a vision of itself entire.

60 In the 1980s, in deference to the neighborhoods, City Hall would attempt a counterreformation of downtown, forbidding "Manhattanization." Shadows were legislated away from parks and playgrounds. Height restrictions were lowered beneath an existing skyline. Design, too, fell under the retrojurisdiction of the city planner's office. The Victorian house was presented to architects as a model of what the city wanted to uphold and to become. In heterosexual neighborhoods, one saw newly built Victorians. Downtown, postmodernist prescriptions for playfulness advised skyscrapers to wear party hats, buttons, comic mustaches. Philip Johnson yielded to the dollhouse impulse to perch angels atop one of his skyscrapers.

IN THE 1970S, LIKE A LOT OF MEN AND WOMEN in this city, I joined a gym. My club, I've even caught myself calling it.

In the gay city of the 1970s, bodybuilding became an architectural preoccupation of the upper middle class. Bodybuilding is a parody of labor, a useless accumulation of the laborer's bulk and strength. No useful task is accomplished. And yet there is something businesslike about the habitués, and the gym is filled with the punch-clock logic of the workplace. Machines clank and hum. Needles on gauges toll spent calories.

The gym is at once a closet of privacy and an exhibition gallery. All four walls are mirrored.

I study my body in the mirror. Physical revelation—nakedness—is no longer possible, cannot be desired, for the body is shrouded in meat and wears itself.

65 The intent is some merciless press of body against a standard, perfect mold. Bodies are "cut" or "pumped" or "buffed" as on an assembly line in Turin. A body becomes so many extrovert parts. Delts, pecs, lats.

I harness myself in a Nautilus cage.

Lats become wings. For the gym is nothing if not the occasion for transcendence. From homosexual to autosexual . . .

I lift weights over my head, baring my teeth like an animal with the strain.

. . . to nonsexual. The effect of the overdeveloped body is the miniaturization of the sexual organs—of no function beyond wit. Behold the ape become Blakean angel, revolving in an empyrean of mirrors.

70 THE NINETEENTH-CENTURY MIRROR OVER THE FIREPLACE in my bedroom was purchased by a decorator from the estate of a man who died last year of AIDS. It is a top-heavy piece, confusing styles. Two ebony-painted columns support a frieze of painted glass above the mirror. The frieze depicts three bourgeois Graces and a couple of free-range cherubs. The lake of the mirror has formed a cataract, and at its edges it is beginning to corrode.

Thus the mirror that now draws upon my room owns some bright curse, maybe—some memory not mine.

As I regard this mirror, I imagine St. Augustine's meditation slowly hardening into syllogism, passing down through centuries to confound us: Evil is the absence of good.

We have become accustomed to figures disappearing from our landscape. Does this not lead us to interrogate the landscape?

With reason do we invest mirrors with the superstition of memory, for they, though glass, though liquid captured in a bay, are so often less fragile than we are. They—bright ovals or rectangles or rounds—bump down unscathed, unspilled through centuries, whereas we . . .

75 The man in the red baseball cap used to jog so religiously on Marina Green. By the time it occurs to me that I have not seen him for months, I realize he may be dead—not lapsed, not moved away. People come and go in the city, it's true. But in San Francisco in 1990, death has become as routine an explanation for disappearance as Allied Van Lines.

AIDS, it has been discovered, is a plague of absence. Absence opened in the blood. Absence condensed into the fluid of passing emotion. Absence shot through opalescent tugs of semen to deflower the city.

And then AIDS, it was discovered, is a non-metaphorical disease, a disease like any other. Absence sprang from substance—a virus, a hairy bubble perched upon a needle, a platter of no intention served round: fever, blisters, a death sentence.

AT FIRST I HEARD ONLY A FEW NAMES—NAMES CONNECTED, perhaps, with the right faces, perhaps not. People vaguely remembered, as through the cataract of this mirror, from dinner parties or from intermissions. A few articles in the press. The rumored celebrities. But within months the slow beating of the blood had found its bay.

One of San Francisco's gay newspapers, the *Bay Area Reporter,* began to accept advertisements from funeral parlors and casket makers, inserting them between the randy ads for leather bars and tanning salons. The *Reporter* invited homemade obituaries—lovers writing of lovers, friends remembering friends and the blessings of unexceptional life.

Peter. Carlos. Gary. Asel. Perry. Nikos.

Healthy snapshots accompany each annal. At the Russian River. By the Christmas tree. Lifting a beer. In uniform. A dinner jacket. A satin gown.

He was born in Puerto La Libertad, El Salvador.

He attended Apple Valley High School, where he was their first male cheerleader.

From El Paso. From Medford. From Germany. From Long Island.

I moved back to San Francisco in 1979. Oh, I had had some salad days elsewhere, but by 1979 I was a wintry man. I came here in order not to be distracted by the ambitions or, for that matter, the pleasures of others but to pursue my own ambition. Once here, though, I found the company of men who pursued an earthly paradise charming. Skepticism became my demeanor toward them—I was the dinner-party skeptic, a firm believer in Original Sin and in the limits of possibility.

Which charmed them.

He was a dancer.

He settled into the interior-design department of Gump's, where he worked until his illness.

He was a teacher.

César, for example.

César could shave the rind from any assertion to expose its pulp and jelly. But César was otherwise ruled by pulp. César loved everything that ripened in time. Freshmen. Bordeaux. César could fashion liturgy from an artichoke. Yesterday it was not ready (cocking his head, rotating the artichoke in his hand over a pot of cold water). Tomorrow will be too late (Yorick's skull). Today it is perfect (as he lit the fire beneath the pot). We will eat it now.

If he's lucky, he's got a year, a doctor told me. If not, he's got two.

The phone rang. AIDS had tagged a friend. And then the phone rang again. And then the phone rang again. Michael had tested positive. Adrian, well, what he had assumed were shingles . . . Paul was back in the hospital. And César, dammit, César, even César, especially César.

That winter before his death César traveled back to South America. On his return to San Francisco he described to me how he had walked with his mother in her garden—his mother chafing her hands as if she were cold. But it was not cold, he said. They moved slowly. Her summer garden was prolonging itself this year, she said. The cicadas will not stop singing.

95 When he lay on his deathbed, César said everyone else he knew might get AIDS and die. He said I would be the only one spared—"spared" was supposed to have been chased with irony, I knew, but his voice was too weak to do the job. "You are too circumspect," he said then, wagging his finger upon the coverlet.

So I was going to live to see that the garden of earthly delights was, after all, only wallpaper—was that it, César? Hadn't I always said so? It was then I saw that the greater sin against heaven was my unwillingness to embrace life.

IT WAS NOT AS IN SOME VICTORIAN NOVEL—THE CURTAINS DRAWN, the pillows plumped, the streets strewn with sawdust. It was not to be a matter of custards in covered dishes, steaming possets, *Try a little of this, my dear.* Or gathering up the issues of *Architectural Digest* strewn about the bed. Closing the biography of Diana Cooper and marking its place. Or the unfolding of discretionary screens, morphine, parrots, pavilions.

César experienced agony.

Four of his high school students sawed through a Vivaldi quartet in the corridor outside his hospital room, prolonging the hideous garden.

100 *In the presence of his lover Gregory and friends, Scott passed from this life . . .*

He died peacefully at home in his lover Ron's arms.

Immediately after a friend led a prayer for him to be taken home and while his dear mother was reciting the Twenty-third Psalm, Bill peacefully took his last breath.

I stood aloof at César's memorial, the kind of party he would enjoy, everyone said. And so for a time César lay improperly buried, unconvincingly resurrected in the conditional: would enjoy. What else could they say? César had no religion beyond aesthetic bravery.

Sunlight remains. Traffic remains. Nocturnal chic attaches to some discovered restaurant. A new novel is reviewed in the *New York Times.* And the mirror rasps on its hook. The mirror is lifted down.

105 A priest friend, a good friend, who out of naïveté plays the cynic, tells me—this is on a bright, billowy day; we are standing outside—"It's not as sad as you may think. There is at least spectacle in the death of the young. Come to the funeral of an old lady sometime if you want to feel an empty church."

I will grant my priest friend this much: that it is easier, easier on me, to sit with gay men in hospitals than with the staring old. Young men talk as much as they are able.

But those who gather around the young man's bed do not see spectacle. This doll is Death. I have seen people caressing it, staring Death down. I have seen people wipe its tears, wipe its ass; I have seen people kiss Death on his lips, where once there were lips.

Chris was inspired after his own diagnosis in July 1987 with the truth and reality of how such a terrible disease could bring out the love, warmth, and support of so many friends and family.

Sometimes no family came. If there was family, it was usually mother. Mom. With her suitcase and with the torn flap of an envelope in her hand.

110 *Brenda. Pat. Connie. Toni. Soledad.*

Or parents came but then left without reconciliation, some preferring to say cancer.

But others came. Sissies were not, after all, afraid of Death. They walked his dog. They washed his dishes. They bought his groceries. They massaged his poor back. They changed his bandages. They emptied his bedpan.

Men who sought the aesthetic ordering of existence were recalled to nature. Men who aspired to the mock-angelic settled for the shirt of hair. The gay community of San Francisco, having found freedom, consented to necessity—to all that the proud world had for so long held up to them, withheld from them, as "real humanity."

And if gays took care of their own, they were not alone. AIDS was a disease of the entire city; its victims were as often black, Hispanic, straight. Neither were Charity and Mercy only white, only male, only gay. Others came. There were nurses and nuns and the couple from next door, co-workers, strangers, teenagers, corporations, pensioners. A community was forming over the city.

115 *Cary and Rick's friends and family wish to thank the many people who provided both small and great kindnesses.*

He was attended to and lovingly cared for by the staff at Coming Home Hospice.

And the saints of this city have names listed in the phone book, names I heard called through a microphone one cold Sunday in Advent as I sat in Most Holy Redeemer Church. It might have been any of the churches or community centers in the Castro district, but it happened at Most Holy Redeemer at a time in the history of the world when the Roman Catholic Church still pronounced the homosexual a sinner.

A woman at the microphone called upon volunteers from the AIDS Support Group to come forward. One by one, in twos and threes, throughout the church, people stood up, young men and women, and middle-aged and old, straight, gay, and all of them shy at being called. Yet they came forward and assembled in the sanctuary, facing the congregation, grinning self-consciously at one another, their hands hidden behind them.

I am preoccupied by the fussing of a man sitting in the pew directly in front of me—in his seventies, frail, his iodine-colored hair combed forward and pasted upon his forehead. Fingers of porcelain clutch the pearly beads of what must have been his mother's rosary. He is not the sort of man any gay man would have chosen to become in the 1970s. He is probably not what he himself expected to become. Something of the old dear about him, wizened butterfly, powdered old pouf. Certainly he is what I fear becoming. And then he rises, this old monkey, with the most beatific dignity, in answer to the microphone, and he strides into the sanctuary to take his place in the company of the Blessed.

120 So this is it—this, what looks like a Christmas party in an insurance office and not as in Renaissance paintings, and not as we had always thought, not some flower-strewn, some sequined curtain call of grease-painted heroes gesturing to the stalls. A lady with a plastic candy cane pinned to her lapel. A Castro clone with a red bandanna exploding from his hip pocket. A perfume-counter lady with an Hermès scarf mantled upon her left shoulder. A black man in a checkered sports coat. The pink-haired punkess with a jewel in her nose. Here, too, is the gay couple in middle age, wearing interchangeable plaid shirts and corduroy pants. Blood and shit and Mr. Happy Face. These know the weight of bodies.

Bill died.

. . . *Passed on to heaven.*

. . . *Turning over in his bed one night and then gone.*

These learned to love what is corruptible, while I, barren skeptic, reader of St. Augustine, curator of the earthly paradise, inheritor of the empty mirror, I shift my tailbone upon the cold, hard pew.

Exploring Texts and Contexts

For activities with icons, refer to the Guide to Analyzing Readings in Context.

1. In the section that begins just after the break on page 258, Rodriguez carefully uses the rhythms of sentence and paragraph structure to convey the growing impact and awareness of AIDS in the gay community. Identify some of the stylistic devices that he uses to convey this. What impact did these devices have on you as a reader? Did you notice them on first reading? 
2. While some personal essays, like Esmeralda Santiago's (Chapter 3), refer mainly to the personal experiences of the writer, others, like Patricia Williams's "Hate Radio," begin with the personal but refer mainly to public issues and history, giving us easily accessible information about these issues and events. Rodriguez takes a kind of middle tack; his essay is intensely personal in many ways, yet it also refers to public issues. But it does this not so much through detailed explanation, as Williams's essay does, but through *allusions,* references to people, events, and ideas that are not always defined or explained. If we're not familiar with these people, events, or ideas, the essay can be difficult to read. Working with a small group, identify allusions that members of the group are not familiar with, see whether you can share information that would clarify these allusions, or examine the context of the allusion to decide whether its meaning is clarified. Consider also what these allusions tell us about the various contexts that Rodriguez brings to the essay. 
3. Why do you think Rodriguez called this essay "Late Victorians"?

Creating Texts

For activities with icons, refer to the Guides to Analyzing Contexts for Writing and Analyzing Readings in Context. For additional help with these writing projects, read the descriptions of **Essay** and **Dialogue/Symposium** in the Genre Glossary.

1. Rodriguez uses the concepts of *nature* and *artifice,* which is connected with culture, to discuss gay experience and lifestyle and ultimately to illuminate the impact of AIDS on gay men and their response to it. This adds another angle to the discussions of nature and culture in the articles by Andrea Barrett and Yi-Fu Tuan in this unit. Write an essay in which you discuss how Rodriguez's piece has expanded and/or complicated your understanding of these concepts. 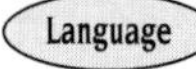

2. All of the writers in this chapter discuss how architecture both expresses and defines our attitudes about how to live as individuals, families, and communities. Construct a hypothetical dialogue that would allow at least three or four writers in this chapter to share perspectives and confront their disagreements about the relationships between architecture, values, and politics. You might begin, for example, by contrasting what Rodriguez says about architecture, feminism, and the family with what Sharon Haar and Christopher Reed say on these subjects, taking into account Witold Rybczynski's and Michael Pollan's discussions of domesticity and the home. Whatever approach and whichever writers you choose, construct your hypothetical dialogue so that it takes into account the broader social issues involved but doesn't lose sight of the very concrete questions of architecture and living space that the writers take as their starting points. By the way, don't necessarily look for direct conflicts or outright disagreements between writers; the disagreement may be more a matter of emphasis or perspective—where a writer is "coming from."

CASE STUDY

On Painting a House Purple

The Case

In the mid-1990s, Sandra Cisneros, author of the acclaimed and widely read novel *The House on Mango Street* and recipient of a MacArthur Foundation genius grant, bought a house in the King William neighborhood of San Antonio, Texas, a district whose residents must agree to abide by design guidelines developed to preserve the neighborhood's historic look. As one of a number of renovations that she made to the almost 100-year-old house, she decided to paint it a bright purple and, because of a series of miscommunications, thought that she had received approval from the San Antonio Historic and Design Review Commission (HDRC) when in fact she had not. The HDRC subsequently told Cisneros that she must either repaint the house in an approved color or demonstrate that the color she had chosen was historically appropriate.

On August 6, 1997, Cisneros presented her case to the HDRC, arguing that although bright purple might not be a historically documented color for houses in that neighborhood—primarily mansions built by wealthy German Americans at the turn of the century—bright colors like the one she had chosen were commonly used in the nearby Mexican neighborhood where Cisneros's house had originally stood; built in 1903, it had been moved to the King William neighborhood in 1913. But the HDRC did not accept that argument, sticking to their stated guidelines that house colors must be either the original color of the house, a color used on other houses in the neighborhood, or a color available in the period of the home's construction, as documented for example by paint company records of the period. Cisneros responded that the colors of houses in poor neighborhoods, like much else about the lives of the poor and members of minority groups, simply had not been documented in written records, but she also pointed to research supporting her claim that bright colors had long been common in the Mexican-American neighborhoods of San Antonio.

There is some disagreement about who agreed to what at this point, but a final decision was deferred to a later meeting to give the two sides a chance to work out a compromise. In the meantime, the controversy had received extensive local and even some national press coverage and was the subject of much heated discussion in the San Antonio community. People saw it either as a matter of recognizing the historical significance of

Sandra Cisneros's home in the King William neighborhood of San Antonio. To see its controversial color, go to http://www.accd.edu/sac/english/mcquien/htmlfils/kingwill.htm

"undocumented" groups, believing the HDRC had a narrow and biased view of history, or as a matter of everyone equally abiding by established community standards, believing that Cisneros had used her celebrity status to force the board to make an exception in her case. But in the end it was Mother Nature who resolved the stand-off: By the fall of 1998, the vibrant purple of Cisneros's house had faded to more of a lavender, and lavender is listed as one of the fourteen paint colors for sale in the Sears catalogue of 1903. Thus the HDRC agreed that, with a few minor touch-ups, Cisneros's house could stay as it was. This compromise, though in some ways satisfactory to everyone, ironically also managed to avoid taking a stand on either of the principles invoked by the two sides: inclusion of minority experience and values in historic guidelines or the necessity to apply the same rules to all. Thus the matter of Cisneros's purple house is officially settled, but the questions it raised about self-expression, community values, minority inclusion, and fairness to all continue to be hotly debated.

The Issues

Almost everyone who has written about the purple house has noted how Cisneros's fictional themes seem to eerily foreshadow the controversy. In *The House on Mango Street* and *Woman Hollering Creek,* her collection of short stories, Cisneros writes powerfully about the experiences of the poor and about self-determination for women. Two passages in particular from *The House on Mango Street* are often referred to, for example this passage from the section "Bums in the Attic":

> I want a house on a hill like the ones with the gardens where Papa works. . . .
>
> People who live on hills sleep so close to the stars they forget those of us who live too much on earth. They don't look down at all except to be content to live on hills. They have nothing to do with last week's garbage or fear of rats. Night comes. Nothing wakes them but the wind.
>
> One day I'll own my own house, but I won't forget who I am or where I came from.

Or the second-to-last section of the book, "A House of My Own":

> Not a flat. Not an apartment in back. Not a man's house. Not a daddy's. A house all my own. With my porch and my pillow, my pretty purple petunias. My books and my stories. My two shoes waiting beside the bed. Nobody to shake a stick at. Nobody's garbage to pick up after.
>
> Only a house quiet as snow, a place for myself to go, clean as paper before the poem.[1]

These passages have complex meanings within the context of the novel, and for the many participants in and observers of the controversy who had read the novel, these meanings gave resonance to an otherwise rather mundane disagreement over paint colors and historic guidelines.

But historic guidelines, if somewhat mundane, have their own complexities. The creation of historic districts in the United States has long been a popular way of preserving buildings considered to have aesthetic or historical significance, of raising property values in neighborhoods that were often falling into disrepair, and of teaching citizens about the past. But each of these goals, though laudable in itself, raises complicated questions. Who decides which buildings and neighborhoods have historic or aesthetic value, and what are the criteria for making those decisions? And raising property values in a neighborhood, while necessary to ensure that privately owned buildings are kept in good repair, often also means that the people who have been living in the neighborhood are squeezed out to make room for people who can afford to buy and maintain the now more expensive buildings. Finally, whose version of history do we teach in preserving these areas? Many of these difficult and emotional questions came into play in the debates over the purple house. Thus what might have seemed a fairly clear-cut issue—the periwinkle paint color of Cisneros's house did not exist when the house was built and was not currently used on any other houses in the neighborhood: case closed—became much more complicated when Cisneros introduced the issue of minority inclusion in standard histories and historical documents.

Whatever side they might take on these issues, most Americans have a strong belief in the democratic principle that rules must be applied equally and fairly for everyone. Although everyone knows that the world, even the American system, doesn't always work

[1]Sandra Cisneros, *The House on Mango Street.* New York: Vintage Books, 1989, pp. 86–87, 108.

this way, most people believe that it should and are resentful when it doesn't. Thus many people felt that the issue was less a question of whose history was being recognized than a question of a celebrity getting special treatment because her lawyers, fans, press coverage, and savvy enabled her to pressure the HDRC into a stand-off and then into a compromise. One board member was quoted as saying, "It's not about ethnicity. It's about eccentricity."[2] Others wondered whether Cisneros's painting of her house might have been just a publicity stunt to garner attention, or even an effort to generate material, for her next book. Suspicions and resentments over the celebrity issue were exacerbated by a related controversy over Cisneros's demand that, if a powerful local magazine wanted to interview her, they must send a Latina reporter—a demand that ultimately resulted in that magazine's hiring more Hispanic reporters.

This development, in turn, throws a different light on the "special treatment" issue. Is Cisneros a celebrity exploiting her clout to get special personal treatment or an artist using her creative gifts to make social changes? Is she using her art to transform the world or manipulating real people and situations to benefit her art? These questions return us to the broad themes of this unit: the need for individuals to challenge or transcend their environment through self-discovery and self-expression and the need for self-discovery and self-expression to be regulated or contained by community values and practices that protect and benefit everyone. As you read the documents in the case study, consider how they help us think about these different needs.

The Documents

- The **City of San Antonio** distributes a brochure, **"Historic Districts of San Antonio: Neighbors in History,"** with pictures from San Antonio's historic districts and various descriptions and guidelines related to historic preservation. The section "Understanding the Preservation Process" and the description of the King William neighborhood from the section "Neighborhoods Preserving San Antonio's Past" will give you a sense of how San Antonio residents learn about the meaning and process of historic preservation and the historic significance of the King William neighborhood.
- On Saturday, July 26, 1997, on the front page of the Metro Section of the *San Antonio Express-News,* a brief news article describes the controversy and refers readers to a column by **Susan Yerkes, "King William Seeing Red over Purple,"** which tells the story in greater detail. Yerkes's column may have been the first that many San Antonians had read about the issue, and a few days later Yerkes wrote a follow-up column, **"Now We Know Why It's Called Purple Passion,"** in which she describes a variety of emotional responses to her earlier column.
- On August 6, Cisneros made her case before the San Antonio Historic and Design Review Commission, and in the following few days a number of newspapers covered

[2]Sara Rimer, "Novelist's Purple Palette Is Not to Everyone's Taste," *New York Times,* July 13, 1998, section A.

the story, including the *San Antonio Express-News,* in an article headlined **"Purple Debate Reaches Commission—Cisneros Agrees to Work with City Staff on Mutually Acceptable Color Scheme"** by reporter and columnist **Mike Greenberg.**

- In the weeks following the first reports of the controversy, many San Antonio residents wrote **letters to the editor** of the *San Antonio Express-News.* These signed, published letters are in general much more reasonable and temperate in tone than the anonymous voicemail messages that Yerkes quotes in her July 30 column—though some make use of the sarcasm that often characterizes this genre, in which writers must catch an editor's attention and make their point in relatively few words—but they do reveal the strong personal responses that San Antonians were having to this issue.
- Not long after the August 6 hearing, the *San Antonio Express-News* published opinion pieces by Cisneros and a member of the HDRC, which elaborated the positions briefly reported in the news articles on the hearing. In **"Purple Politics—Our Tejano History Has Become Invisible," Cisneros** uses a more personal approach but combines this with references to research on the house colors of Mexican American neighborhoods and also appeals directly to the community for support. In **"Purple Politics: Individuality Surrendered for Preservation,"** HDRC member **Milton Babbitt,** himself a well-known member of the arts community, builds his argument through a series of carefully enumerated points and takes care to establish that he is writing as a commissioner, not a private citizen; the position he takes as a commissioner does not, he says, necessarily reflect his personal opinion. Notice how these two pieces, so different from each other in tone, are similar in scope in ways that distinguish them from the letters to the editor and even Yerkes's opinion columns.
- Although the purple house controversy was covered by some of the larger newspapers in the Southwest, it remained essentially a local story through the summer and early fall of 1997. But in November **Michele Norris** did a story on it for *World News Tonight,* and the following summer, on July 15, 1998, about a year after the story first broke, she did a longer piece for *Good Morning America.* People who have been involved in or closely following a local news story are often startled to see how it is represented to a larger audience: Facts that seem crucial are left out or distorted, aspects that seem peripheral are emphasized as if they are central, and the coverage often seems superficial. Consider that this may be the only coverage of the story that most people outside Texas will be exposed to; how will they understand the issue? What does this piece focus on, what does it add to our understanding of the story, and what does it leave out?

YOUR ROLE

The case of the purple house has been resolved, but the issues it raises about individual expression and community values continue to be sources of conflict. Indeed, as more people choose to live in communities that have guidelines for home design and individual behavior, such issues may be more relevant today and in the future. Thus the writing assignments for this case study ask you first to identify and research a more recent situation in which an individual and a community have come into conflict and write an opinion piece about it; and then to write an essay examining the larger principles and contexts involved in such cases.

1. Identify a recent—ideally ongoing—situation in which an individual has come into conflict with community standards or guidelines. It might be a situation in your hometown or neighborhood or in your college dormitory. If you don't know of any local situations, do some research online or in your library's newspaper and article databases, using keywords such as "homeowner association guidelines" and "conflict" or "controversy." Several recent cases have involved conflicts over flags and flagpoles, so you might try using these as keywords as well. By reading news reports and documents related to the case and, if possible, interviewing people who are part of the situation, find out as much as you can about the facts, rules, principles, and arguments involved. Using as models the opinion pieces by Sandra Cisneros and Milton Babbitt included in the case study, write an opinion piece, for the local newspaper, in which you take a stand on the issue. (See **Opinion Piece/Commentary** in the Genre Glossary.)
2. Drawing on the purple house case study and the cases that you and your classmates researched for assignment 1, write an essay in which you explore how these cases were influenced by the larger social issues that surround them. For example, in the purple house case, the larger social issues included the history of Mexicans and Americans in Texas and the inclusion of minority experiences and perspectives in official community histories. Most of the controversies over flags and flagpoles have happened since 2001, in the context of the renewed feelings of patriotism following September 11. And the overall issue of individual rights and community standards has assumed more importance as more people choose to live in gated communities in which, surrounded by people like themselves, they feel safe. How have these larger social contexts helped to create and/or influenced the debates about conflicts between individuals and communities? (See **Essay** in the Genre Glossary.)

Understanding the Preservation Process

Why Is Preservation Important?

In its City Code, San Antonio recognizes the vital importance of preservation. By ordinance, we maintain the city's unique cultural heritage by preserving our buildings, monuments, missions, acequias, and the San Antonio River. By setting aside historically valuable buildings, landmarks and areas by specific historic designation, the city actively participates in the preservation of cultural and neighborhood identity.

Examples of San Antonio's Historic Districts

Downtown	Alamo Plaza Main Plaza Military Plaza
Residential	King William Dignowity Hill Monte Vista
Largest Single-use Clusters	Mission Old Ursuline Academy *(Southwest Craft Center)* Old Lone Star Brewery *(S. A. Museum of Art)*
Commercial	Cattleman Square St. Paul Square La Villita

Historic Exceptional Landmarks are those considered most unique in terms of historic, cultural, archaeological, or architectural significance. Demolition would mean an irreplaceable loss to the quality and character of the city.

Examples: *The Alamo, Municipal Auditorium*

Historic Significant Landmarks are those considered to be important and their demolition would mean a serious loss to the character of the city.

Example: *Irish Flats houses neighborhood near Ave. E*

Designation Process

Receiving Historic Designation does not affect the use of a property. Land use is regulated by Zoning. It does, however, affect the aesthetics of any exterior changes made to the landmarks or property within the district.

What Is a Certificate of Appropriateness?

To make any exterior changes to a property with historic designation, you will need a **Certificate of Appropriateness.** *With the exception of painting,* you will also need a building permit. To obtain a permit from the Building Inspection Department, you must first present a Certificate of Appropriateness issued by the Historic Preservation Office. It will show that all proposed changes have met the aesthetic and preservation guidelines and design considerations

How owners (or the City) request designation of property as an Historic District or Landmark:

Historic Preservation Officer recommends nomination to Historic and Design Review Commission. . .

↓

HDRC approves nomination, recommends to Zoning Commission. . .

↓

Zoning Commission recommends historic designation to City Council (as an overlay to existing zoning district). . .

↓

City Council designates the historic landmark or district by ordinance.

(continued)

This brochure was funded in part through a Certified Local Government Grant from the National Park Service, U.S. Department of the Interior, as administered by the Texas Historical Commission and the City of San Antonio.

of the Historic and Design Review Commission (HDRC). Changes can be defined as, but are not limited to:

- Additions (construction or reconstruction)
- Rehabilitation and restoration
- Stabilization
- Landscaping
- Signage
- Demolition

The "Short Form" for Ordinary Repair and Maintenance

You may be eligible to complete the Certificate of Appropriateness "Short Form" if your proposed work to a structure of Historic Designation is **ordinary repair and maintenance,** defined as follows:

- Repair using same materials and design as original
- Re-painting with existing colors
- Re-roofing using same type and color of materials
- Repair of sidewalks and driveways using same type and color of materials

The Certificate of Appropriateness is issued by the Historic Preservation Officer and may be available the same day that you submit your application. You will be required to present it to the Building Inspections Department when requesting a permit.

The "Short Form" Application Requires:

- Photos of structure
- Brief written description of proposed work
- Samples of replacement materials or paint chips
- Legal description of property from Building Inspections Department

To Apply for a Certificate of Appropriateness:

Application forms are available through the Historic Preservation Office (HPO) at Municipal Plaza Building, 114 W. Commerce, or by calling 207-7900. Return completed application to the HPO. HPO staff will review it over a two-week period, and will make a recommendation to the HDRC. The Commission holds its public meeting on the first and third Wednesdays of each month. If your project is presented, the HDRC will act to *approve, approve with modifications,* or *deny* your application.

What Information Will You Be Asked to Provide for a Certificate of Appropriateness?

For proposed work which is not considered to be ordinary repair and maintenance, include with your application:

- Detailed, written description of proposed work with square footage, materials list, location, etc.
- Plans, Elevations, Sections and Details of proposed exterior changes
- Photos of existing site and/or structure
- Legal description of property, obtained through the Building Inspections Department / 9th floor 114 W. Commerce / San Antonio, TX 78205
- Samples of materials you want to use (paint swatches, roof shingles)
- Site Plan or Plot Plan that defines the structure's location or landscape on the site.

What If Your Application Is Denied?

The HDRC will make recommendations for changes to your proposed project to bring it into compliance with its guidelines as defined by ordinance. You may then modify your proposed project to incorporate these recommendations and resubmit your application, or you may appeal the HDRC's decision to City Council.

Design Considerations

If you anticipate presenting a project to the HDRC, be prepared to discuss the following design considerations:

Additions

- Should be compatible in size, materials, and style of original
- Should not radically change, obscure, damage, or destroy original or character-defining features

  Example: the Fairmount Hotel restoration uses original features of the old building; the addition (behind lighter area of brick) is distinct from *the original building* but relates well *in use of materials, colors, and "rhythm" of elements on the façade.*

New Construction

New construction in a Historic District requires careful consideration to ascertain that the "infill construction" is in harmony with the existing buildings. Fundamental criteria include:

- Height and width in proportion to surrounding buildings
- Set-back from the street consistent with adjacent structures
- Roof shape and form similar to those nearby
- Composition, rhythm, and proportion of façade
- Compatible materials

Colors

- Use no more than three colors to highlight a façade:
  1. **Base Color** (walls)
  2. **Major Trim** (windows, columns, cornice)
  3. **Minor Trim** (doors, bulkheads, window mullions, small details)

Thinking About Working on an Old House?

Some Tips Before You Start

Research

Architecture, History, Previous Owners, Builder, Architect, Neighborhood

Plan Properly and On Paper

- Take "before" photos.
- Inspect structure's original interior and exterior materials and finishes; hire professional help if needed.
- Research local sources for replacement materials.

Set Goals

- Do you plan to *Preserve? Rehabilitate? Restore?*
- Set realistic cost and time goals.

Make Sure You Can Reverse Anything You Do

Examples:

- **Don't** tear out old woodwork and discard it.
- **Don't** install aluminum or perma-stone siding, which can irreparably damage façade.
- **Repair and restore** rather than remove and replace.
- **Save** as much of original structure as possible.

Be In Control of the Project

- Make sure contractors are aware of the sensitive nature of your project, and are qualified to do the work.

From "How to Love An Old House (In 10 Easy Lessons)," *The Old House Journal Catalog, The Old Journal Corporation,* 1984.

(continued)

What Are the Secretary of the Interior's Standards?

1 — A property shall be used for its historic purpose or be placed in a new use that requires minimal change to the defining characteristics of the building and its site and environment.	2 — The historic character of a property shall be retained and preserved.
3 — Each property shall be recognized as a physical record of its time, place, and use.	4 — Most properties change over time; the changes have acquired historical significance.
5 — Distinctive features, finishes, and construction techniques or examples of craftsmanship unique to a property shall be preserved.	6 — Deteriorated historic features shall be repaired rather than replaced.
7 — Chemical or physical treatments such as sandblasting shall not be used.	8 — Significant archaeological resources affected by a project shall be protected and preserved.
9 — New additions or exterior alterations shall not destroy historic materials that characterize the property.	10 — Changes shall not permanently alter the essential form and integrity of the historic property.

(*Standards are abbreviated*)

- Use original colors of paint and materials as guidelines for new colors.
- Use paint to minimize problems in façade, if necessary.

Landscaping

- Use a variety of native plants.
- Group plants for a more natural look.
- Determine soil pH and make adjustments.
- Consider plant colors (leaves and blooms) when making selections.
- Consider plant's purpose (ornament, shade, color, wind break).
- Consider maintenance/water required.

Signs

- Effective signs are legible; contain a simple message; are attractive and durable.
- Unobtrusive, yet noticeable signs can be placed within the architectural framework of the building. Signs should not obscure or cover architectural features. They can be attached to a board placed on the upper façade, or painted on the doors, windows, or awnings.
- Color coordination with the building is important.
- Design signage in accordance with the type and quality of merchandise or service offered, as well as the architectural character of the building.

Terms Defined: National Register of Historic Places

District
Geographically definable area, urban or rural, with a significant concentration linkage, or continuity of sites, building, structures, or objects that are related historically or aesthetically.

Site
Past location of a significant event, activity, building, or structure, usually of substantial archaologi-cal interest. Example: Black Swan Battle site

Building
House, church, barn, store, or hotel that shelters any form of human activity.

Structure
Man-made construction of interdependent and interrelated parts, organized in a definite pattern. Often a large-scale railroad engineering project. Locally this includes Crockett Street Bridge, the Hayes St. Bridge and the Tower of the Americas.

Object
Material thing of functional, aesthetic, cultural, historic, or scientific value. May be movable by nature or design, yet related to a specific setting or environment. Objects listed in San Antonio include Lady Bird Fountain, (behind the Alamo), and the Madero Bust (100 Block, Concho St.)

Reconstruction
Using new construction to reproduce the form, design, and detail of a structure or object, complete or in part, as it once appeared.

Rehabilitation
(Adaptive Reuse) Repairing or upgrading a structure or property for contemporary use (such as converting a warehouse into an art gallery), while preserving its historical, architectural, and culturally important features.

Renovation
Changing and improving an old or historic structure in a way that should not duplicate its original appearance.

Restoration
Returning a building or property to its former look by removing later additions or replacing earlier features that are now missing.

This brochure was funded in part through a Certified Local Government grant from the National Park Service, U. S. Department of the Interior, as administered by the Texas Historical Commission and the City of San Antonio.

(continued)

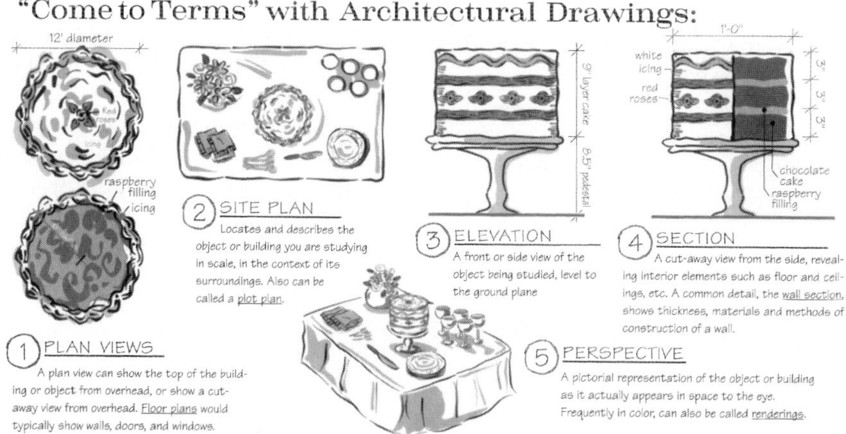

"Come to Terms" with Architectural Drawings:
12' diameter
raspberry filling
icing
1 PLAN VIEWS
A plan view can show the top of the building or object from overhead, or show a cut-away view from overhead. Floor plans would typically show walls, doors, and windows.
2 SITE PLAN
Locates and describes the object or building you are studying in scale, in the context of its surroundings. Also can be called a plot plan.
9" layer cake
8.5" pedestal
3 ELEVATION
A front or side view of the object being studied, level to the ground plane
1'-0"
white icing
red roses
3"
3"
3"
chocolate cake
raspberry filling
4 SECTION
A cut-away view from the side, revealing interior elements such as floor and ceilings, etc. A common detail, the wall section, shows thickness, materials and methods of construction of a wall.
5 PERSPECTIVE
A pictorial representation of the object or building as it actually appears in space to the eye. Frequently in color, can also be called renderings.

King William

Canals flowing from the San Antonio River and farmland belonging to the 1731 mission of Nuestra Señora de la Purísma Concepción de Acuna originally comprised the King William Historic District. By the beginning of the 19th century, the San Antonio missions were fully secularized, and the land belonging to the Mission Concepción was divided into tracts. Thomas Jefferson Devine, a lawyer and land speculator, bought the tracts in the 1840s and sold them to others who continued to divide and sell the property for residences.

One of the earliest to settle here was Carl Guenther, a German immigrant who had built a mill near Fredericksburg, Texas. Purchasing a tract of land on the lower bend of the San Antonio River in 1859, he constructed a second mill, which became Pioneer Flour Mills, and a stone cottage, which is now part of the present Guenther house at the mills. This served as the southern anchor for the King William neighborhood.

A number of other successful and influential German immigrants also began building residences in the King William area, using Greek Revival, Victorian, and Italianate architectural styles for their mansions. Ernst Altgelt, builder of the first house on King William, is credited with naming his street after King Wilhelm I of Prussia.

When San Antonio's fashionable neighborhoods to the north such as Terrell Hills and Alamo Heights began attracting King William residents in the 1920s, the grand mansions of the "Sauerkraut Bend" neighborhood were sold or turned into apartments. For more than 30 years, the district declined, until a group of creative young professionals took an interest in living and working there. At the same time, the San Antonio Conservation Society acquired the Eduard Steves house at 509 King William, leading the way for a period of revival. In 1967, the neighborhood became the King William Historic District, the first Historic District in Texas. The district was expanded in 1984 to include a more eclectic neighborhood of cottages South of Alamo Street-affectionately known as "Baja King William."

King William Seeing Red over Purple

Susan Yerkes

Purple ribbons tied to gates and trees in King William aren't there to welcome The Artist Formerly Known As Prince, who's coming to the Alamodome Aug. 8.

They're there for nationally acclaimed author and current King William housing cause célèbre Sandra Cisneros, whose home is rousing purple passions in the historic district.

The house is purple. Not a shrinking violet purple. A pulsating, passionate "periwinkle," Cisneros calls it.

And the paint job has some of her neighbors seeing red.

King William, you see, is a microcosm of S.A. life—and strife.

The picturesque area around Kaiser Wilhelm Street, where monied German burghers once built mansions, has been regentrified recently, sending housing prices soaring and creating schisms over issues from zoning to tour buses.

The dynamic King William Association takes some strong stands. But Cisneros' purple home is not one of them, association president Sarida Bradley stresses. At its last meeting, the group voted not to take sides.

"We do not endorse or condemn the color of her house," she says. "We don't want neighbors pitted against neighbors. Personally," she adds, "I don't think color is that important. It's transitory."

Some neighbors, however, do think it's important and have complained to the city's Historic Preservation Office.

Cisneros had her own historic perspective in mind when she chose the purple hue, she says. She wanted to reflect the passionate, colorful spirit of South Texas and Mexico.

"Everything I've done, from changing the concrete walks to limestone to having special wooden porch pillars made, has been to keep the integrity of spirit here."

Cisneros was commuting to Chicago as her father neared death this spring and summer, and the contractor who was painting her house met with the city's design review committee on her behalf.

Although the committee recommended muting the purples after seeing the back of the house painted, the deep shade tints the whole house.

"I started getting calls from King William," says S.A. Historic Preservation Office head Ann McGlone. And they were not pro-purple.

McGlone notified Cisneros that her color scheme violated city historic district requirements.

"It's very appealing," McGlone says. "But it's not appropriate to history. This isn't about taste; it's about historical context."

But Cisneros hasn't given up. And if she can justify the color scheme historically, McGlone says, the purple paint may stay.

Meanwhile, supportive neighbors started the purple-ribbon campaign. And in what some see as a strike against the anti-tour bus residents of the neighborhood, artist Terry Ybanez designed a purple "I (heart) (trolleys)" pictograph plaque for Cisneros' front yard—another flip in the faces of some neighbors.

Architect Ron Bechtol, who chose the more conservative color scheme that Cisneros' house sported before she bought it, has gone to bat for purple, too.

"Though the colors themselves may not be typical of local tradition," he wrote to McGlone, "they are harmonious within their distinctive vocabulary—much more so, in my opinion, than many neighborhood examples pairing yellow and green, green and red, red and yellow."

Cisneros will defend her case at the city committee's Aug. 6 meeting.

"I hope my periwinkle house will encourage baja and Lavaca residents to be even more colorful," she says.

Now We Know Why It's Called Purple Passion

Susan Yerkes

Since Saturday's column about author Sandra Cisneros and her controversial "periwinkle" purple house in S.A.'s historic King William district, the phones and computer modem have been lit up like Fourth of July fireworks.

Some folks say "right on!" to Sandra's quest to keep the deep purple her house was painted, against the behest of the city's historic review board.

A number of others—even Alaskan Dan Flanders, a regular poster on my EN-Connect forum who once worked with architect O'Neil Ford—point out Cisneros chose to live in a historic district with tight architectural rules.

But what makes the flap so interesting is the purple passion Cisneros and her bright berry of a house have generated.

Passion such as the venom of the anonymous women with condescending voices on my ExpressLine.

"The reason we're seeing red over her purple color, honey, is not the color, but because she's such a b——," one said acidly.

"She has a bad attitude, and we've just had enough of her b———. Have a nice day."

The feisty Cisneros, who contends that the deep purple expresses the passionate spiritual palate of Mexico, leaps on personal attacks as proof "how deep-seated, how much more complex this is than simply a capricious color choice."

And indeed, ExpressLine callers provide plenty of insight into attitudes that inflame the story of the purple place on Guenther Street.

"As a U.S. citizen, I'm getting real tired of these people that want to bring Mexico to the United States," a caller typical of this school harumphed.

"If they want to live in Mexico, why in the hell don't they, ah, she, go back where she came from?"

(Cisneros came from Chicago. Who'd go back there from here?)

That kind of response, which Cisneros says she often gets, is part of the city's darkest side.

But many King William folks are flat distressed that the purple-house flap has come to this.

"When you say 'King William is seeing red,' " asks Penny Wiederhold, "who is King William? It's unfair to damn the whole neighborhood because of a few people."

In fact, the King William Association voted not to take a stand on the purple cottage.

"We believe in the process," noted association vice prez Jim Johnson, whose wife is another well-known writer, Paulette Giles.

"It seems like when we get in arguments it's when the process hasn't been fully exercised. I think the historic review board is doing what it's supposed to do—protect the historic district."

On Aug. 6, the city's design review commission will hear Cisneros' appeal to keep her purple house. She's not optimistic.

"This is a part of the world where there's been such a long history of conflict, it's too bad this house issue can't be seen as opportunity for harmony among different cultures," she muses.

Attorney and King William neighbor Nancy Shivers echoes the sentiment, from a slightly different slant: "It's just sad to me to see what little we gain from this," she says. "How is it helping us make a better neighborhood?"

Stay tuned.

Purple Debate Reaches Commission—Cisneros Agrees to Work with City Staff on Mutually Acceptable Color Scheme

Mike Greenberg

Novelist Sandra Cisneros' tale of the purple house is to be continued.

Cisneros appeared Wednesday before the Historic and Design Review Commission, five TV cameras and about 30 supporters—many wearing garments in various shades of purple—to request after-the-fact approval for the predominantly purple palette of her King William Historic District House.

No vote was taken, and the case was continued to a future meeting. Cisneros agreed to work with city staff to seek a mutually acceptable paint scheme for the house on Guenther Street and return to the commission for approval.

But she reserved the right "to defend my colors" if agreement isn't reached.

Decisions by the commission, which is an advisory body, may be appealed to the City Council.

History was pitted against history in Cisneros' exchange with the commission and historic preservation officer Ann McGlone.

McGlone had recommended denial of the color scheme "because there is no evidence or documentation that these colors were ever used in the King William area."

To be deemed acceptable, McGlone said, the color scheme would have to be "appropriate to the house, the neighborhood or the era" in which the house was built.

The house, a folk Victorian cottage, was built in 1903, and according to McGlone the deep purple hue that dominates the house was not manufactured until much later.

Couching the issue as being about "historical inclusion" for the Tejano people, Cisneros countered: "According to my history, purple is a historical color. . . . This was Mexico, and the Mexican color palette isn't being allowed."

Cisneros admitted her error in beginning the paint job last year without seeking commission approval. The rear of the house already had been painted when Cisneros sought approval in October.

The commission's architectural review committee met with her painting contractor and advised muting or eliminating some paint colors and painting a test sample prior to final approval.

But Cisneros said her contractor didn't communicate that advice to her, and the color scheme was continued to the front of the house.

She told the commission she was willing to change the colors if she and staff could find a mutually agreeable scheme.

"But I still think we need to change the vision of the people on this board," she said.

Fourteen residents, including several of Cisneros' immediate neighbors, spoke in support of her color scheme. One, Emily Brace, began by singing, "for purple mountains' majesty. . . ."

Letters to the Editor

Viva el Color!

re: the Purple House of Sandra Cisneros.

The King William area is a beautiful part of our city. I appreciate the entrepreneurial spirit, creativity, and individuality of those who turned a decaying area of San Antonio into a thing of beauty and joy for us all.

Can we not also be grateful for the individuality and creativity of Sandra Cisneros? I went by to see her home for myself after reading the article in Saturday's paper. The workmanship appeared to be of excellent quality, and the finishing touches were added with artistry. I found the whole effect to be aesthetically stimulating and delightful. (Then, who am I to say since I also immediately loved "The Big Enchilada"?)

In a city which benefits immeasurably from its Hispanic roots and the colorful fiesta culture which is San Antonio's trademark, wouldn't a distaste for "periwinkle" be a little on the stuffy side?

Viva el color!

Mary Lil Chappell
August 10, 1997
San Antonio Express-News

Real Issue Behind Purple House Is Tolerance

I find the purple controversy over Sandra Cisneros' house in the King William neighborhood to be shocking and offensive.

So far, I have yet to hear anyone discuss the moral and ethical issue of the city government having the authority to harass and intimidate people about the personal choices they have regarding their own property.

What makes city government think it knows what's best for us?

We pay for our homes, pay taxes, make repairs, maintain our yards and live with all of the problems that go along with living in older, inner-city neighborhoods.

For me, a neighborhood is first and foremost a community of people living and working in harmony and mutual respect.

As a designer and lover of antiques and architecture, I appreciate many of the benefits of having our historic buildings protected, especially against demolition or poor renovation, but legislating color choice is absurd.

I also appreciate the value of color as a form of self-expression and cultural evolution.

The real issue here is tolerance. Most people conform by nature. When one individual attempts to express a different point of view, the city design authorities whip out their big paintbrush and wipe out those poisonous colors before they spread.

Scary, isn't it?

Martha Durke
August 12, 1997
San Antonio Express-News

Cisneros Put Cart before the Horse

I've got to hand it to San Antonio author Sandra Cisneros. She certainly used the media to bring notoriety to herself and her house. However, what is the true agenda?

A search for historical truth or a colorful plotline for her next book?

I have never read Cisneros' work, nor do I live in the King William neighborhood, but I would venture to guess that she is not the only person of Mexican-American origin who works hard and lives well in this wonderful neighborhood.

Perhaps someone should ask the residents of the

neighborhood if they are not annoyed by the unwarranted publicity this gives their community, as well as bothered by someone who doesn't see fit to follow the rules they all abide by.

It's OK to try to change the way others think, but didn't Cisneros put the cart before the horse by painting her house before doing her research? I don't find the color purple at all offensive, but I find Cisneros' behavior less palatable than her palette.

Nancy de Wied
August 23, 1997
San Antonio Express-News

Go Ahead and Name Paper after Purple House

It might be time to consider changing the masthead of the *Express-News* to read "San Antonio Express-Purple House" to more accurately reflect your interests.

Hayden Freeman
August 23, 1997
San Antonio Express-News

Reader Overdosed on 'Cisneros Edition'

Re: the Saturday, Nov. 15, issue of the "Sandra Cisneros Express-News":

Having been inundated in one issue with three articles and two pictures of San Antonio's favorite part-time house painter and full-time self-promoter, it occurs to me that your readership might be better served if you just go ahead and include a separate "Sandra Says" section several times a week. Her adoring fans can more easily access your relentless coverage of her, and those of us who find same to be an annoyance and perhaps just a tad redundant, can remove it easily.

If the "Sandra Says" section is still not enough for you, I certainly wouldn't mind articles about her in the only sections that were Sandra-free in Saturday's issue, i.e., the classified ads, the business section and sports. Indeed, I look forward to seeing her name in an ad under "seeking employment," a business story on how she gets daily free advertising.

Charles Stallcup
November 23, 1997
San Antonio Express-News

Purple Politics—Our Tejano History Has Become Invisible

Sandra Cisneros

Ay que telenovela mi vida! What a telenovela my life! One day I painted my house Tejano colors, and the next day my house is in all the news, cars swarming by, families having their photos taken in front of my purple casita as if it was the Alamo. The neighbors put up an iced tea stand and made $10.

All this happened because I choose to live where I do. I live in San Antonio because I'm not a minority here. I live in the King William neighborhood because I love old houses.

Since my neighborhood is historic, there are certain code restrictions that apply. Any house alteration plans have got to be approved by the Historic Design and Review Committee. This is to preserve the neighborhood's historic character, and that's fine by me.

Because I thought I had permission, I gave the go-ahead to have my house painted colors I considered regional, but, as it turned out, hadn't been approved. However, I was given the chance to prove them historically appropriate. So I did my research, and what I found is this.

We don't exist.

My history is made up of a community whose homes were so poor and unimportant as to be considered unworthy of historic preservation. No famous architect designed the houses of the Tejanos, and there are no books in the San Antonio Conservation Society library about the houses of the working-class community, no photos romanticizing their poverty, no ladies auxiliary working toward preserving their presence. Their homes are gone, their history is invisible.

The few historic homes that have survived have access to them cut off by freeways because city planners did not judge them important (i.e. Casa Ximenes and the Little Chapel of Miracles.) Or they are buildings fenced in by the Plaza Hotel; I wasn't even aware they were part of Tejano history until I began my research into my house colors even though I walk past them almost every day.

Our history is in the neighborhoods like the famous Laredito barrio, heart of the old Tejano community and just a block from City Hall; it proved so "historically valuable" it was demolished and converted into a jail, parking lot and downtown police station with only the casa of Tejano statesman Jos Angel Navarro as evidence Laredito was ever there.

Our past is present only in the churches or missions glorifying a Spanish colonial past. But I'm not talking about the Spaniards here. My question is where is the visual record of the Tejanos?

The issue is bigger than my house. The issue is about historical inclusion. I want to paint my house a traditional color. But I don't think it unreasonable to include the traditions of los Tejanos who had a great deal to do with creating the city of San Antonio we know today.

I wouldn't mind painting my house a historical color, but please give me a broader palette than surrey beige, sevres blue, hawthorne green, frontier days brown, and Plymouth Rock grey.

These colors are fine for some houses, and I think they look handsome on the dignified mansions on King William Street. But look at my casita, it's not a mansion. It's a late Victorian rental cottage, built circa 1903. (My house was originally located on South Saint Mary's, then known as Garden Street, just off Alamo, on the corner where the Babylon Restaurant now sits. In 1913 my house was sawed in two like a Houdini magic act and wheeled to its present location. This accounts for its architectural affinity with the houses in the Baja and Lavaca communities.)

Frankly, I don't understand what all the fuss is about. I thought I painted my house a historic color. Purple is historic to us. It only goes back a thousand years or so to the pyramids. It is present in the Nahua codices, book of the Aztecs, as is turquoise, the color I used for my house trim; the former color signifying royalty, the latter, water and rain. We don't have papers. Our books were burned in the conquest, and ever since then we have learned to keep quiet, to keep our history to ourselves, to keep it alive generation to generation by word of mouth, perhaps because we feared it would be taken away from us again. Too late; it has been taken from us.

In San Antonio when we say historic preservation we don't mean everyone's history, even though the historic review office is paid for by everybody's taxes. When they ask me to prove my colors historically appropriate to King William they don't mean Tejano colors. But I am certain Tejanos lived in this neighborhood too. That's what my neighbors have told me. Mr. Chavana, who lives across the street, says his family has been living in this downtown area since the 1830s, and I know he's not lying; he's not allowed to, he's a reverend.

Color is a language. In essence, I am being asked to translate this language. For some who enter my home, these colors need no translation. However, why am I translating to the historical professionals? If they're not visually bilingual what are they doing holding a historical post in a city with San Antonio's demographics? It shouldn't even be an issue.

Color is a story. It tells the history of a people. We don't have beautiful showcase houses that tell the story of the class of people I come from. But our inheritance is our sense of color. And it's been something that has withstood conquests, plagues, genocide, hatred, defeat. Our colors have survived. That's why you all love fiesta so much, because we know how to have a good time. We know how to laugh, we know a color like bougainvillea pink is important because it will lift your spirits and make your heart pirouette.

We have a tradition of bright colors. Dr. Daniel Arreola, of Texas A&M University, has written that in a survey of 1,065 houses in a Mexican-American district in San Antonio, 50 percent showed evidence of brightly painted exteriors, even if only evidenced in the bright trim. From the Arab influence of elaborate paint exteriors carried over to the Iberian peninsula, as well as to the use of intense pigment in the pre-Colombian structures, our people have always decorated their exterior walls brightly. In some pre-Colombian centers there is not only evidence of a love of color, but a love of vivid visual effects; in Teotihuacan it is the drama of red contrasted with blue. That passion for color is seen even now in our buildings on both sides of the border. Mango yellow, papaya orange, Frida Kahlo cobalt, Rufino Tamayo periwinkle, rosa mexicana and,

(continued)

yes, even enchilada red! King William architecture has been influenced by European, Greek Revival, Victorian, and Neoclassical styles. Why is it so difficult to concede a Mexican influence, especially when so many people of Mexican descent lived in the city?

This issue is not about personal taste, but about historical context. It is about the HDRC serving all of the community, not the personal interests of some. And history belongs not only to the architecturally elite, but also to los Tejanos, as well as the Germans, the African Americans, Poles, Czechs, Italians, Jews, Lebanese, Greeks, Irish, French, Native Americans, and yes, even the poor. History belongs to us all.

My purple house colors are not deemed historically appropriate because "there is no evidence or documentation these colors were ever used in King William." But if the HDRC is true to their word, oral testimonies should count as evidence. I am inviting the community to assist me. I invite Brackenridge High School especially; I'm told they've adopted my purple house because it's their school color, so why not an oral history project they could get credit for? Why not a documentation of our ancestors? It's about time we had our history count on paper.

If you know someone who lived in San Antonio at the turn of the century who remembers the colors of the Tejanos who lived in the King William/La Vaca community, document their story on paper. What block did they live on? What kind of house? What color was the main body? The trim? Do you have an old house that you could scrape to see what layers lie underneath? Would you like to be part of a collection of Tejano oral histories? If so, tell me your story. I would love to collect them and publish them in a book we could gift to the San Antonio Conservation Society, the San Antonio Public Library, the King William Association, the Historic Review Office, the city of San Antonio. After all, maybe someone else will be inspired and follow my example and paint their house a beautiful South Texas color too and nobody would raise a fuss. Now wouldn't that be something!

Purple Politics—Individuality Surrendered for Preservation

Milton Babbitt

There are three important issues to be taken into account in the case of Sandra Cisneros and the color of her house. These are the nature and importance of historic districts, guidelines for development within historic districts and the process for ensuring that these guidelines are respected.

One of the tasks of the Historic and Design Review Commission, or HDRC, working with the staff of the city's Office of Historic Preservation, is to provide oversight of development in the city's historic districts. Presently, there are five primarily residential historic districts and they represent but a tiny fraction of the residential land area in the city.

Why, then, do we have historic districts?

The importance of sustainability in development practices and design is becoming more widely understood. The ultimate in construction recycling is the rehabilitation of existing structures, and historic district designation provides an incentive for stability and neighborhood revitalization. Historic districts protect property values.

Many suburban developments safeguard values and exclude inappropriate development with restrictive covenants and subdivision regulations. These are unavailable to urban dwellers in older neighborhoods and historic designation can offer protection in much the same way.

Historic districts attract tourists—sometimes too many, as parts of the King William district can attest. Our suburban neighborhoods look like their counterparts anywhere, but our historic districts are unique and people enjoy visiting them.

Finally, historic districts educate by giving a very real link to the past, bringing meaning to history.

Historic district designation is initiated by the citizenry, not the city. Fifty-one percent of the property owners in the area must endorse the concept before the legal process of designation begins. As might be expected, some owners will be unhappy with the designation. However, in the public hearings that preceded designation of the newest district, Monticello Park, all of the speakers appearing before the HDRC spoke in support of historic designation.

Once a historic distict is created, exterior alterations to any structure are subject to review by the Office of Historic Preservation and the HDRC. With the benefits provided by district designation comes responsibility as well. A bit of individual freedom is surrendered in that owners are no longer free to do whatever they want to the exterior of their property.

We review landscape development, fencing, driveway design, new construction, building additions and alterations such as re-roofing, window replacement, porch reconstruction and repainting—yes, color. Major color issues are unusual, though color, being highly subjective, is a sensitive issue. It's far easier to deal with a homeowner who somehow feels compelled to pave his or her entire front yard with concrete.

There are no "approved" colors despite what you may have heard or read, even in this newspaper, but there are

(continued)

guidelines which establish a very broad palette of historically acceptable colors. First, a thorough paint analysis can be performed to ascertain what the original colors were. This is rarely done for homes, primarily because of the cost but also because the homeowner might not like what is found, even though they would be under no obligation to replicate the original scheme.

Second, colors which are appropriate to the neighborhood may be sought. Since historical color photographs do not exist, the tools for finding appropriate schemes are limited, consisting of reports on houses where the colors have actually been analyzed and documented or oral neighborhood histories.

Third, colors that were in use in the era of original construction can be sought. The major paint companies have histories extending well back into the 19th century and retain records of available products by time period. For example, the Sears Roebuck catalog of 1902 lists its available colors of house paint - all 16 of them! One of these was lavender. Lavender would be an appropriate color for a house built in the first decade of this century.

There is a process for securing approval and, in the vast majority of situations, the process works well. Some color changes are so minor that they don't make the HDRC agenda; the staff approves them.

Another large group of cases involving color appear on the consent agenda with a recommendation for approval by staff, pulled for individual consideration only when a commission member has a concern about some element of the case.

A third group represents color changes which are substantial or controversial enough to warrant review by the entire commission. Typically, after an initial presentation to the commission, these cases are referred to the architecture committee, generally composed of commission members who are architects. An on-site meeting is held with the owner, committee and staff. The owner's rationale for the proposed selections are heard, suggestions for changes made and common ground sought—and usually found. The committee reports the results of its meeting at the next commission meeting and the commission almost always approves a motion based on the committee recommendation.

In the Cisneros case, the process was followed up to a point. The committee met with the owner's designated representative to review a sample of the color scheme painted on the back of the house. He was informed that the colors applied in the sample were not acceptable in a historic district. Subsequently, the owner painted the remainder of the house in the same colors.

Historic preservation is not anti-color nor is the HDRC the color police. In approving colors, we do not act arbitrarily nor do we make judgments based on personal preference. Our determinations are made using the above-stated guidelines. The results are hardly timid, as the King William district has many houses with vivid color schemes—more than any other local historic district. This is primarily because the exuberant Victorian architecture of the neighborhoods suggests it and because, at least in some documented instances, it is historically accurate. I have said publicly that the color scheme which Cisneros has used is exquisite. I believe it. It is the carefully concocted product of someone who knows a great deal about color. But the fact that I like it can have no effect on my opinion as a commissioner, and my opinion is that it is wrong for the house, wrong for the neighborhood and wrong for the district. The colors chosen by Ms. Cisneros fail when held up to any guideline for historic preservation.

The Purple House

Coat of Paint Causes Cultural War in San Antonio

Michele Norris and Lisa McRee

LISA McREE, Host: The issue of color is once again dividing a community, but not in the way you might think. When noted Mexican-American author Sandra Cisneros chose to paint her historic San Antonio home, it was the color purple that landed her in trouble. ABC's Michele Norris joins us from Washington this morning with the details. Michele?

MICHELE NORRIS, ABC News:
Good morning, Lisa.

LISA McREE:
Good morning.

MICHELE NORRIS:
This is a story about color and culture and history, but the question is, whose history? And it's hard to believe that a simple coat of paint could cause a cultural war, but that's exactly what happened in San Antonio.

SANDRA CISNEROS:
"A house all my own, with my porch and my pillow, my pretty purple petunias."

MICHELE NORRIS:
(voice-over) Sandra Cisneros is the author of "The House on Mango Street," a story about a poor Latina girl who yearns for a house of her own.

SANDRA CISNEROS:
Now I see, I'm living what I wrote.

MICHELE NORRIS:
(voice-over) Cisneros grew up poor. Now she lives in one of the most prestigious neighborhoods in San Antonio, the King William Historic District, a collection of graceful homes built by wealthy German merchants almost 100 years ago.

But the Cisneros house is quite like no other. It's a bright shade of purple, a neon hue called periwinkle, and it's attracting quite a bit of attention.

DAVID NEWBERN:
There aren't any other houses dominantly painted that fluorescent purple in the area.

MICHAEL GREENBERG:
A lot of people have been driving by and looking at it. Everybody had to find out what it really looks like.

MICHELE NORRIS:
(voice-over) Cisneros says the attention-getting color pays tribute to her Mexican-American heritage.

SANDRA CISNEROS:
This is my first home. I was just trying to make it look like my home. And all the things that are in my house are—many things point to my Mexican culture.

MICHELE NORRIS:
(voice-over) But making such a vivid cultural declaration has split this city along color lines. On one side, pro-purple supporters display ribbons in their yards.

ADREN PRYOR:
It adds interest, that's what's neat about this whole neighborhood.

MICHELE NORRIS:
(voice-over) On the other side, this purple house has the Historic Design and Review Board seeing red.

MILTON BABBITT,
Historic Commission: This is more a fashion statement, I think, than it is an architectural statement.

MICHELE NORRIS:
Living in this historic district comes with certain requirements.

(continued)

From *ABC Good Morning America,* July 15, 1998.

When residents want to paint their homes, they must meet at least one of three conditions, that the proposed color was used on the home at least some point in the past, that it was used in the era when the home was built, or that it can now be found on other houses in the neighborhood.

ANN BENSON McGLONE, Historic Preservation Officer:
This is about the process of—and responsibility of—living in a historic district, and how you try to make personal taste mesh with the responsibility in the process of living in a historic district.

MICHELE NORRIS:
You moved into a historic district. You know the rules.

SANDRA CISNEROS:
The rules are very racist. All you have to do is look and see what colors they're espousing, what palettes they're espousing, and look and see how they're defining what's historically accurate.

MICHELE NORRIS:
(voice-over) Supporters argue that purple has its place in Mexican-American history.

MAN IN BLACK T-SHIRT:
It's larger than just the color of paint on a house. Is our aesthetic valid? Is our history valid? Does our history even exist?

MICHELE NORRIS:
(voice-over) San Antonians do celebrate the color and culture of Mexico in festivals like this Day of the Dead procession, in tourist attractions, and in the modern enchilada-red library, a building approved by the same commission that has rejected the purple house.

SANDRA CISNEROS:
And that's supposed to be avocado?

MICHELE NORRIS:
(voice-over) For now, Cisneros is working with the city to find an acceptable paint scheme.

(on camera) Now, what do you think of these colors?

SANDRA CISNEROS:
Pretty sad.

MICHELE NORRIS:
(voice-over) Don't expect this outspoken writer to settle on quiet colors for her home. This is Michele Norris for Good Morning America.

LISA McREE:
So Michele, how—where do the negotiations stand today?

MICHELE NORRIS:
Well, the two sides were supposed to come together and decide on a mutually acceptable palette, something might—a color scheme that might speak of her Mexican heritage without shouting. But so far, the two sides are in limbo. They haven't come together, they've scheduled meetings, they've canceled meetings. And all this means that the purple house is still there.

LISA McREE:
How does it look in person?

MICHELE NORRIS:
One person described it as a California swimsuit color. It literally vibrates. It's got this sort of neon undertone. And the camera doesn't really capture it.

LISA McREE:
All right. Thanks so much, Michele Norris, keep us in touch with what's going on in San Antone.

UNIT IV

Participating in Civic Conversations

This photograph of a sculpture called "Conversation Piece," by Juan Muñoz, taken in the sculpture garden of the Hirshhorn Museum in Washington D.C., illustrates the power and limitations of both sculpture and photography. By choosing the angle from which to take the picture, the photographer controls how we see the sculpture. This is especially significant with this sculpture, for it is about the relationship between the different figures. But the photograph thus fixes that relationship. When we view the sculpture in person, we can see the figures from many different angles and thus see different possible relationships between them. That is why this sculpture appealed to us so powerfully as an illustration for this unit. In a democracy, it is crucial for citizens to talk to each other about important public issues, but in a democracy as large and diverse as ours, it can be difficult to include everyone in these conversations. Because these conversations take place through many different channels, it can be difficult even to know who is participating. It may require a change of perspective to know whose voices have been heard.

CHAPTER 9

What Makes Democracy Work?

Situation: What larger situation do you think this scene is a part of? Use your imagination to speculate, but also use specific clues from the photo to support your speculations.

Genre: Compare this photograph with the one on page 287 and then with the one on page 470. What different stories do these pictures tell on the one hand about civic participation and on the other hand about work?

Language: The amount of detail in this photo can make it confusing at first. What specific details and patterns help you begin to make sense of it?

Consequences: Do you think this photograph was meant to communicate a message of some sort? What impact did it have on you?

Waupun, Wisconsin: small-town rural America. The well-manicured lawns and shaded streets lead you through a downtown lined by a library, churches, and small shops. While the town is too big for everyone to know everyone else, ordinary people take part in governing it; the mayor, for instance, also teaches sixth-grade math. Even small towns like this one experience vandalism, domestic violence, crime, and, perhaps most importantly, the steadily increasing isolation that some say tears at the fabric of our society. Last fall, a group of about thirty students—some quiet, some known as troublemakers, others new to the town—met one evening to decide what projects they would do over the course of the school year. They hit on the idea of a bike path into Pine Street Park, which was accessible only by a fast-moving, two-lane road. This group, Waupun Do Something, assisted only by an adult coach who kept a low profile, worked with the city council to design the path, to obtain grants to fund the project, and to get permission from property owners for the bike path to cross their land.[1]

Newark, New Jersey: Urban and diverse, this city of more than a quarter of a million people is a short drive from New York City. Newark is home to Rutgers and Seton Hall Universities and home as well to Newark Do Something, a chapter of the national youth-led organization that mobilizes students to become local leaders. Hundreds of students met here last fall for a Speak Out meeting to determine their work for the coming year. The previous year they had registered over four hundred people to vote and this year they decided to honor Martin Luther King's birthday by designating a two-week period during which they would commit acts of kindness and justice.

These two locations couldn't be more different, but the challenge is the same. The national organization Do Something recognizes that if youth from all parts of the country don't develop a sense of civic commitment, the social ills that plague us will only become worse. Research tells us that the number of young voters, those below the age of 25, has dropped by about 15 percent since 1972.[2] Do Something aims at young people because its founders, Andrew Shue and Michael Sanchez, who grew up together in New Jersey and who wanted to make a difference, realized that a commitment to community building must start no later than junior high. Do Something leader Anthony Welch worries that, "If people are not involved by fourteen, you've lost them. Twenty-five is too late."[3] Not only has voting decreased, but in many more ways we are becoming a nation of isolated individuals consumed by self-interest. Robert Putnam's 2000 book, *Bowling Alone,* traces how, over the past 60 years, we as a people not only vote less, but talk less to each other, and rarely connect the way we used to by sitting on our front stoop, by seeing each other at the market, or by meeting up to work on community projects. (See our excerpt from *Bowling Alone* in this unit.) Getting people to become involved in the day-to-day life of a democracy and getting them to participate in sustaining our democracy remains one of our most intractable social problems.

As we see in the readings in this chapter, conversations about becoming actors rather than spectators in our ongoing civic drama are conducted in a variety of contexts: Some look to historical patterns and events for clues about how work can contribute to the public good. Others propose that organizations such as Do Something are building an asset called *social capital,* a term that refers to the networks and connections that are constructed to help communities cohere. Part of our problem in building community lies in the inflammatory talk that pervades our media. Journalists struggle with ways to present the news that will encourage citizens to participate in public life. As you read the selections in this chapter and write about these issues, keep these underlying perspectives in mind.

Notes

1. Robert D. Putnam and Lewis M. Feldstein. *Better Together: Restoring the American Community,* New York: Simon & Schuster, 2003. pp. 142–165.
2. Peter Levine and Mark Hugo Lopez. "Youth Voter Turnout has Declined, by Any Measure" September 2002. *Circle: The Center for Information & Research on Civic Learning and Engagement.* University of Maryland's School of Public Affairs. http://www.civicyouth.org/research/products/fact_sheets_outside.htm
3. *Better Together,* pp. 147–148.

The New Democracy

Harry C. Boyte and Nancy N. Kari

Most of us think of work as something we have to do to earn money and pay the bills. Whatever we do—fix things, wait on customers, program computers, or manage other workers—we often consider work as part of our private lives and separate from our role as citizens. In this excerpt from *Building America: The Democratic Promise of Public Work,* Harry Boyte and Nancy Kari explain that Americans have not always separated work and citizenship the way we do today. During colonial times, work provided many opportunities to participate in public life. The early settlers knew that they would prosper only if they worked together to keep homes, churches, pastures, and roads functional. This notion of working for the common good soon extended to a concern for solving social problems. In fact, Boyte and Kari argue, work was valued differently than it is today because the work that one did to sustain one's community helped define that person's identity.

Not only have we lost our sense of working for the public good, but we are fed up with politicians and with a political system that seems to have lost its sense of responsibility towards its citizens. By restoring the idea of public work, Boyte and Kari chart a path for a renewed sense of citizenship that grows from the efforts of everyday people, not elected officials. This excerpt traces the beginnings of public work during the nineteenth century and then brings us up to date with a case study that illustrates how public work by a group of concerned citizens both saved their unlikely homesteads—houseboats on Seattle's Lake Union—and improved life for the entire city as well.

This case study, which highlights public work, illustrates the critical importance of speaking and writing to change things for the better. The community activists, whose houseboats were seen as contributing to pollution and impeding real estate developments on the lake's shores, relied on communicating a broad vision that could benefit all of Seattle and not just the owners of houseboats. Making that vision come alive depended on talk, public activities, and writing. As in this case, writing lies behind many civic successes—everyday people using writing to create change. This was true during the great depression of the 1930s when over fifteen million people had lost their jobs. President Franklin Roosevelt's New Deal program created a "portable democracy" in which our respect for work and its contribution to democracy was heightened. The New Deal also provided opportunities for the public production of art and writing through the Federal Writers' Project. Many of our best known writers were employed at an hourly wage to compile oral histories, conduct research, and write guidebooks to regions and cities. Studs Terkel, Ralph Ellison, Richard Wright, Saul Bellow, and Margaret Walker all worked as federal employees, using their writing skills to contribute to this democratic effort that combined providing work for the unemployed with building a public sense of our culture. As you read this excerpt, notice how writing and speaking in public contexts helps to redefine public work.

Connecting with the Conversation

1. Boyte and Kari want to reconnect public work with citizenship. Frequently high schools and colleges have programs that attempt to make that connection. Have you ever participated in a service-learning project for school or as part of a volunteer organization? If you have not, talk to some friends who have had such experiences. Such projects typically aim to combine some form of service with some kind of learning. Think back to your experiences and describe them first from the perspective of service and then from the perspective of learning. Are the two perspectives very different or did they come together in interesting ways?
2. Visit the National Service-Learning Clearinghouse on the Web at www.servicelearning.org. Click on "Welcome to Service Learning" and skim the sections titled Service Learning is . . . , History, and Glossary. Prepare to explain to others how this Web site characterizes service learning. How does this movement get students involved in building and strengthening communities?

> *Experience proves that the very men whom you entrust with the support and defense of your most sacred liberties are frequently corrupt . . . if ever therefore your rights are preserved, it must be through the virtue and integrity of the middling sort, as farmers, tradesmen, & c. who despise venality and best know the sweets of liberty.*
>
> "Publius," for Philadelphia artisans, 1772.[1]

" 'The Working People's Social Science Club' was organized at Hull House in the spring of 1890 by an English workingman," writes Jane Addams in her autobiographical account of the famous settlement house. "For seven years it held a weekly meeting." The evenings were highly charged with intense conversation. "The enthusiasm of this club seldom lagged," Addams writes. "Its zest for discussion was unceasing." Participants insisted on questions of the most substantial and serious nature.

From: *Building America: The Democratic Promise of Public Work.* Philadelphia: Temple University Press, 1996. pp. 33–55.

"Everything was thrown back upon general principles and all discussion save that which 'went to the root of things' was impatiently discarded as an unworthy, halfway measure." With such spirit, the group's intent remained clear throughout. "Any attempt to turn it into a study or reading club always met with the strong disapprobation of the members."[2]

Nineteenth-century America created forums for public talk and work like this in a myriad of settings and cultures. These served as schools for citizenship. Ordinary people developed in them an assertiveness and self-confidence, as well as skills.

Americans' challenge to custom and hierarchy left foreign visitors aghast. White "lower classes . . . have a tendency to be saucy and insolent," said one. Charles Augustus Murray observed that there was no proper sense of title at all. Upon first acquaintance, "farm-assistants and labourers called me 'Charlie,'" whereas the tavern owner expected to be called "General" and a local handyman "Colonel." "Everybody talks to you," complained Charles Dickens. Commonly, Europeans described the penchant of Americans to talk to strangers. "Wherever you go, you are surrounded by men (who never saw you before in their lives) who immediately have a thousand questions," said one newcomer. "Diffidence," said another, "is scarcely to be met with in the United States." The country, he groused, "greatly promotes fluency of speech."[3] Accounts like these give us a glimpse of the great democratic conversation that filled the nineteenth century.

American democracy gave its distinctive stamp to an ancient tradition. Democracy acquired an indelible connection to work and was expressed in many forms of public life, from economic associations to public debating clubs, from voluntary organizations to groups that agitated for moral renewal and education reform. These created an historical legacy of democracy of larger meaning than we have today. The wider aims of public work were especially described by the language of the commonwealth.

* * *

5 The uniqueness of nineteenth-century American democracy was especially its tie to work. Democratic ideas of freedom and independence were made practical through the notion that citizens (free white men) owned their own labor. Most were self-employed farmers and artisans. They owned their own tools. They could determine what they produced. Strong individualistic identities developed around their craft as a result. Growing from such experiences of self-direction, working men also made collective decisions about their lives. Thus American democracy, acquired a practical, down-to-earth quality. Through a language of the commonwealth it also conveyed larger, even luminous dimensions when people were able to connect their daily labor to building America.

* * *

Civic Virtue

The argument that work can be for the public good gave visibility to the civic contributions of many. . . . Figures such as Benjamin Franklin—inventor, printer, editor, as well as public statesman—became the archetypal example of civic "hero." Indeed, in America public service and profit making were not necessarily mutually exclusive. In fact, the linkage was often valued. Only in the United States, argued Francis Grund, a

European observer, had labor become fully respectable; only here was "industry an honor, and idleness a disgrace." Similarly the Frenchman Michel Chevalier observed that in England, businessmen worked only in the mornings. The rest of the day they posed as gentlemen. In contrast, "the American of the North and the Northwest whose character sets the tone in the United States is permanently a man of business, he is always the Englishman of the morning." Alexis de Tocqueville found it amazing that not only was work itself "honorable," but "work specifically to gain money" was honorable. In Europe, he wrote, there were "hardly any public officials who do not claim to serve the state without interested motives. Their salary is a detail to which sometimes they give a little thought and to which they always pretend to give none."[16]

Thus, by the early decades of the nineteenth century, the broad array of those who linked "productive labor" to democracy had carried the day, at least in rhetoric. Elites that did not spend time in gainful employment did not advertise the fact. Even southern plantation owners heralded their hard work—though their aristocratic pretensions also fueled conflict.

Yet American democracy, like the Greek *polis,* existed in the midst of a surrounding environment of exclusions and inequalities, the consequences of which we still struggle with. A focus on work brings with it, in fact, possibilities for new exclusions. Full citizens are those whose work is visible, valued, and self-directed. The exclusions from a democracy based on work, as well as its inclusions, are useful in highlighting the meanings and implications of "public work."

In starkest terms, the story of African American slaves illustrates the importance of some significant measure of self-direction and autonomy in public work. Slaves did not own their own labor. Black men and women also did not have access to the formal political world of white men. Thus they lacked the ability to negotiate democratic rights. Their roles in the more general public arena were brutally circumscribed—they appeared in the balconies and on the margins, in subservient roles.

10 Slaves were far from being simply victims, but their own work life and social activities were largely invisible. Only in subterranean places, on the margins of plantations and after hours, did blacks engage in self-directed work. There, in a sense, they created alternative public arenas where they were visible to each other, if not to dominant whites. John Vlach describes the free spaces created within the rigid confines of plantation life. "Slaves did not move through the plantation in the same way as whites, nor were they expected to." Slaves were not expected to conform to the manners and customs of white society—they escaped, in a fashion, the formality that so defined southern civility. Slaves gardened and planted crops, created their own handicrafts, tools, buildings, and other products. And they found spaces for their own worship: From Christianity which was taught to them as an effort to break blacks from African cultural traditions, they forged their own distinctive language of religion, aimed at freedom. "Understood to be a servant people, their place was defined as both away from and outside of . . . the formality that planters had so carefully laid out. They were under control but they were not totally coerced by that control," says Vlach.[17]

Women constituted a second exclusion from American democracy, in a way that illustrates the importance of public spaces for public work. Women's work, although valued, was not the same as men's self-directed work, precisely because it occurred in the private sphere, and thus was far less visible. Their world of work was largely defined by boundaries of household and family relations, or at least by domestic identities. European visitors, especially women, often remarked on the sharp divisions between the sexes and the relative exclusion of women from formal public life.

Yet as with blacks the patterns were complex. Though excluded from formal politics and defined in subordinate ways in many public arenas, women also created out of their domestic roles and identities distinctive public spaces of their own. These included wide-ranging networks of religious associations, voluntary groups, moral reform efforts, and education campaigns. There was constant argument and conflict across the whole society over women's public activities. As one minister put it in 1859, seeking (unsuccessfully) to prohibit women from forming a women's prayer group, "who knows what they would pray for if they did it by themselves?"[18]

In nineteenth-century America the fusion of democracy and work was a radical conceptual change. This was the first time people's everyday lives, once thought private affairs, were connected to the public realm in ways that generated a wide sense of participation and stake in public life. At the same time, such a tie was fraught with complexities. Work-centered democracy, in sum, raised new questions of power. It put on the public table new topics and concerns. Work also made connections between individuals and small groups and larger communities and the nation as a whole. These issues, in turn, were expressed and argued out in the language of the commonwealth.

Taking Care of the Commons

Today *commonwealth* is a musty, forgotten term. It brings to mind the old governments of the British empire, perhaps, or the states of Massachusetts, Virginia, Kentucky, and Pennsylvania, all of which are called "commonwealths." But in the eighteenth and nineteenth centuries and through the 1930s in America, the term *commonwealth* had vibrant power. It was both a description of what American democracy *was* and, simultaneously, it was a dramatic, compelling vision of what it could be and should become. The commonwealth was created by public work, and thus popular and lower-class groups could claim central standing and authority.

Commonwealth, like democracy, public life, and citizenship, had associations that made it powerful for both educated elites and the popular classes. But these associations were quite different. For educated leaders, "commonwealth" summed up the classical tradition of government responsive to citizens. For popular groups, the term conveyed a much more down-to-earth notion of "the commons," those basic public goods in which all had a stake and which all needed to help build and preserve.

Commonwealth was a term for the Greek *polis,* the Roman republic, and the Italian city states of the Renaissance. In the American colonies, it conveyed the struggles against the British monarchy for expanded rights. "Commonwealth" had early become identified with the concept of the public, the established and recognized body of citizenry. In this way it connected to the idea of republican government in which "the whole people" had voice. By the seventeenth century, commonwealth customarily meant the idea of government *of* and *by* free citizens, instead of the crown. Thus, the Parliamentary act of May 19, 1649, ending the monarchy declared "That the People of

England . . . shall henceforward be Governed as a Commonwealth and Free State." Thus, during the American Revolution commonwealth suggested a republican government—a popular alternative to the monarchy. John Adams urged that every state declare itself a commonwealth, and four eventually did so officially.

Even more important than the associations with political tradition and theory, commonwealth had power for farmers, artisans, small business, and others through its association with the idea of common (public) work. "Commonwealth" meant simply what one took care of collectively.[19]

This association drew on old traditions. In English history, deliberation by villagers about the exercise of the rights and upkeep of common lands, footpaths, farm lands, and fishing areas, as well as maintenance of common buildings like the village church, gave middle-level peasantry a constant, daily schooling in rough democracy. Sometimes village communities collaborated with lords, sometimes they engaged in bitter struggle with them. But there was customarily space for regular deliberation over commons issues. Male villagers regularly promulgated laws, sometimes in joint consultation with lords. Churches, as community centers, were especially important to the commons. Village churches provided space for multiple purposes: feasts and celebrations, public deliberation, refuge from raids, dances, marketplace, and sometimes even theater for pagan plays. As Edward Miller and John Hatcher have put it, parishioners "were called on to keep the nave in repair, the churchyard in good order, to provide many items of equipment including . . . bells for the steeple, a pyx, a Lenten veil, a font, a bier for the dead, a vessel for holy water and certain other items of equipment." Churches were supported through taxes and tithes of corn, garden produce, and livestock, as well.[20]

Traditions of the commons were transplanted to the colonies with the first European settlers of the seventeenth century. Indeed, immigrants left England and other nations in some cases partly out of distaste for the spreading practices of "engrossing," that saw the gentry seize common lands by force or purchase. New England settlers typically created a pattern of one "house lot" from one to ten acres for each family, with shares in the common lands of pasture, wood, and meadow. A separate land was set aside for the church and meeting house, often adjoining the town green, or commons, "which provided a kind of physical axis of the community and served other community functions—militia muster, farmers market, even in some places, common pasture."[21]

20 In the first settlements, most crops were grown in common fields, but the soil and weather in New England proved not to be as favorable to single-crop planting, and soon individual planting of a variety of crops became the norm. Continuing immigration into towns also created sharp political tensions: Were newcomers to get a share in the commons, for instance? Did they receive land for a household lot—the very symbol of citizenship in English society? The commons, in short, was an object of constant debate, discussion, and conversation.

These practices of collective effort to build and sustain things of value to communities expanded throughout the nineteenth century and came to include social welfare, in addition to material public works. This dynamic created the vast and rich array of formal and informal associations that observers like Alexis de Tocqueville said was most typically American. Practices of concern for the community and national welfare on broad topics involved many groups with seemingly quite different aims. For instance, the Women's Christian Temperance Union (WCTU) of the late nineteenth century sought to control the "demon rum." Yet it combined moral reform agitation with communal problem-solving efforts. Its slogan was "Do-Everything." By 1889, WCTU activities in Chicago included nurseries, Sunday schools, an industrial school, a homeless shelter, a free medical dispensary, and a lodging for poor men.[22]

These efforts often gave groups who had been excluded from public arenas a new sense of their power. As Frances Willard, the WCTU's guiding force, put it:

> Perhaps the most significant outcome of this movement was the knowledge of their own power gained by the conservative women of the Churches. They had never even seen a "woman's rights convention," and had been held aloof from the "suffragists" by fears as to their orthodoxy; but now there were women prominent in all Church cares and duties eager to clasp hands for a more aggressive work than such women had ever before dreamed of undertaking.[23]

These traditions of public work for the commons also generated a vibrant culture of public talk.

Public Talk

America overflowed with public talk. Foreign observers were constantly struck by contentious street corner debates, public disputations, political festivals, and democratic self-education movements.

John Adams, with his patrician gaze, nonetheless conveyed a confidence in such talk in a letter to his wife, Abigail, in 1776. "Time has been given for the whole People, maturely to consider the great Question of Independence and to ripen their Judgments, dissipate their Fears, and allure their Hopes, by discussing it in News Papers and Pamphletts, by debating it, in Assemblies, Conventions, Committees of Safety and In-spection, in Town and County Meetings, as well as in private Conversations."[24]

The view of the citizenry as a deliberative, talking body produced large civic education movements through the nineteenth century. Voluntary citizen organizations played a key role in public education. Public libraries created through citizen efforts, for example, were justified as "arsenals of democracy." In the early 1830s, John Holbrook's Lyceum Movement created adult learning centers in order to provide forums for citizens to discuss public affairs. By 1837, the movement included an estimated 3,000 towns. After the Civil War, the Chatauqua Assembly movement continued this legacy, eventually including 15,000 "home study circles" for discussion of public affairs. Similarly, university extension programs, adopted from England in the 1880s, were designed to promote better rural citizenship, as well as improved farming. In poor and immigrant communities, institutions like the Workmen's Circle and settlement houses educated citizens to current public issues.

More generally, public language assumed the common sense and intelligence of ordinary people and challenged the pretensions of any who spoke in arcane fashion.

Medical advice was a good illustration. "No discovery can ever be of general utility while the practice of it is kept in the hands of a few," wrote William Buchan, whose *Domestic Medicine* became a standard popular guide from the late eighteenth through the mid-nineteenth centuries. Buchan subtitled his work as "an attempt to render the Medical Art more generally useful, by showing people what is in their own power both with respect to the Prevention and Cure of Diseases." Buchan argued that "every thing valuable in the practical part of medicine is within reach of common sense." John C. Gunn's *Domestic Medicine,* published in 1830, followed in this vein. Gunn proposed that Latin words for common medicine were intended "to *astonish the people*" and aid in deception and fraud. "The more nearly we can place men on a level of equality in point of *knowledge,* the happier we would become in a society with each other, and the less danger there would be of *tyranny.*"[25]

At the same time, Americans valued common sense. Many artisans, mechanics, and others who named themselves freethinkers simultaneously held that engagement with large ideas must infuse everyday life. They believed that working people could realize democratic possibility only as they became free in their thinking from the control of unreflected convention—religious orthodoxy, traditionalism, or deference to political authority. Such convictions spawned a wide variety of workers' education movements, debating societies, and other organizations dedicated to the legacy of Thomas Paine. For instance, by the 1830s, New York had become a center of free thought activity, with organizations like the Society of Free Inquirers, the Temple of Arts, the Minerva Institution, and the Institution of Practical Education proliferating. Their vision, writes the historian, Sean Wilentz, was "a world turned upside down where men [*sic*] would truly be able to think, reflect, and act for themselves, free of aristocratic and religious tyranny: Where one would find according to a freethinkers' toast 'soldiers at the plow, kings in the mines, lawyers at the spinning genney, and priests in heaven.'"[26]

Democratic manners and common work were distinctive features of public life in nineteenth-century America. As the society changed, another aspect of the commonwealth tradition of public work also shaped the country. Commonwealth was not only a descriptive term. It also conveyed an ideal. The commonwealth was a vision of a future society of equality and justice. Its spirit had a contagious effect. It inspired a myriad of struggles against exclusions and injustices of all kinds.

* * *

Today it takes conscious, artful effort to retrieve public work and its larger meanings and resonances. The commonwealth language in recent years has provided resources to accomplish this task. The commonwealth holds within itself the labor that creates and sustains "the commons," thus making visible that work helps illustrate and substantiate the idea of commonwealth as well. It can reveal larger purposes and significance of work, by bringing to center stage the very meaning of wealth and progress. These issues are highlighted in the modern commonwealth story of Seattle's Lake Union.

A Commonwealth Retrieved

Seattle, Washington, today at first sight seems overwhelmingly oriented to the future, not the past. The airport reflects advanced technology, with cavernous spaces and automated trains. The drive into the city curves like spaghetti past the "space needle," left over from a World's Fair, and takes one into glass and steel canyons at the city's center.

But there remains an older heritage alive beneath the modern gloss. On a clear day, the stunning natural beauty of the city is augmented by an abundance of trees and public gardens filled with scotch broom, purple heather, foxglove, daffodils, rhododendron, and forsythia. Similarly, the richly textured human environment mingles old-fashioned scenes with landmarks of change. Seattle is a city of neighborhoods, many still bearing the names of original ethnic villages: Greenwood, Belltown, Ballard, and Fremont, all of which joined together at the turn of the century.

The waterfront is the city's focal point. Sailboats are everywhere alongside trawlers, ferries, and tugboats. The Pike Place Market in the city's central district has retained the sort of jumbled, crazy-quilt diversity and informality that downtown San Francisco has lost. Merchants from dozens of nationalities display wares and foods: Alex's Phillipine Cuisine; Hassan Brothers; and the Athenian, where old retired sailors from the low-income housing project across the street gather and sip coffee. There are fruit and vegetable and fish stalls selling hundreds of different goods, from garlic to Alaskan crabs.

Whatever the complexities of progress in Seattle, the city retains a balance with its older traditions that many communities have lost. How was this accomplished? Part of the answer lies in the successful efforts of Terry Pettus, a long-time newspaper man and activist who kept alive a vision of public work for "the commonwealth," long after it disappeared in the country as a whole.

In the 1920s, Terry Pettus and his wife, Berta, moved to Seattle, where Pettus became a newspaperman and well-known writer. Over the next two decades, Pettus was a leading figure in many popular movements: the fight for public utilities and rural electrification; efforts to achieve the referendum; a campaign to win industrial accident insurance and old-age pensions. At the heart of each, in his view, was the notion of the whole, the common good.

In the mid-1930s, labor unions, farmers, and neighborhood groups came together during the Great Depression in a new political movement to press their interests. Calling themselves the Washington Commonwealth Federation, they drew on older currents of radicalism. Organized by precincts, the Commonwealth Federation in the late 1930s and 1940s became the dominant force in the state Democratic Party, sending several congressmen to Washington, at times controlling the state legislature.[33]

However, in the early 1950s, the mood of the country changed sharply as charges of subversion were leveled against radicals and reformers of all kinds. Pettus, target of FBI investigations, was convicted under the Smith Act and spent six months in jail before his conviction was overturned. Once free, he decided to retire after a life-career as a journalist and activist. He wrote mystery novels. Retirement lasted a decade.

In 1933, Terry and Berta had purchased and moved into a houseboat on Seattle's Lake Union. At that time, over a thousand houseboats were moored close together along the lake near the center of town. Houseboaters paid dirt cheap rents for moorage. From the beginning, the houseboaters included an interesting mix of people. Boatyard workers, sailors, students, and bohemians mingled with retired radicals from the revolutionary union, Industrial Workers of the World. Large numbers of the city's poor, who could scarcely afford to live anywhere else, also lived in the houseboat area.

Along the shores, speakeasies and brothels were scattered through the small shacks and apartments. "It was a breeding ground for nonconformity," wrote Howard Drucker, who authored a history of the houseboats.[34]

From the beginning of the settlement by Europeans, and arguably of Indians as well, Lake Union was a "working lake." In the 1870s, barges carrying coal and lumber crossed the water, heading from the nation's interior to the rail lines on the western shore. In those years, much of the shoreline retained its natural quality. Wildlife on the waterfront was plenty. A hunter killed a cougar there in 1870.

In the first years of the great boom in immigration, which increased the city's size from 3,533 in 1880 to 237,194 in 1910, streetcars and rail lines made the lake accessible from all the surrounding villages. In the twentieth century, boat works and dry docks appeared along the shore, servicing water vessels of all kinds. Along with the expanding commercial activity came the first houseboaters.

City officials had long looked askance at the floating community as a "health hazard." At the same time, real estate developers had coveted the lakeshore. They exerted growing pressure on the city to take action. In 1962, the city administration moved vigorously to evict boaters, in order to acquire the land to erect apartment buildings and other development projects along the lakefront.

A major complaint against the houseboats in the 1960s was sewage pollution on the lake. Few knew that in fact the city of Seattle itself dumped raw sewage into Lake Union through thirteen sewer lines. The boaters' contribution was minuscule—something like one-half of 1 percent of the total. Houseboaters knew they could never win by debating percentages, or claiming "less responsibility" than others, so they turned the issue on its head. To the consternation of the city, they demanded that they be permitted to pay for sewer lines to their boats. The Floating Homes Association, the houseboaters group, held workshops on how to weld pipes and how to hook up sewer lines. In the process they found new allies, like the city's health department.

Most thought the rugged individualists of Lake Union could never be organized, but Pettus understood the power of a larger vision. "People will fight for their existence, if not for abstractions," he explained. The Floating Homes Association formed to solidify the houseboat community. But instead of banding together to fight city hall, they redefined the issue. They tied their own fate to the future of the city as a whole. "We knew we could never win if the issue was simply the survival of the houseboats," said Pettus.

Drawing on the commonwealth legacy which had shaped Pettus's politics for decades, Pettus and his neighbors described the problem in commonwealth terms. They created a broad vision of Lake Union as the commonwealth of the people of Seattle—"a gift to us from the Ice Age." Key to the strategy was connecting the heritage of the city and the lake to the idea of practical work.

They created a public conversation about control over the future in a variety of ways. As the campaign developed, houseboaters connected the idea of the lake as an environmental resource with the concept of the lake as a working lake, a lake *of* and *for* public work. Its multiple uses—recreation, commerce, residency—all were interconnected. The process of the campaign itself was diverse public work. Houseboaters sponsored tours. They led in the building of a public park. They created social events and festivals. They made alliances across the city. They made the lake, its legacy, and its symbolism come alive.

45 Citizen action had dramatic effect. By late 1963, the city, responding to the association's remarkable popular support, initiated a study that called for protection of the lake. With such a statement, the association was able to block industrial use of a large area; press the city to acquire 23 acres to create a public park; and inspire the state legislature to pass one of the nation's strongest shoreline management control acts on new development. Terry Pettus helped write the legislation.

By the early 1970s, the spirit of the houseboaters' victory energized a number of other citizen efforts. The historic Pike Place Market was saved from the developers when a local architect and friend of Pettus's, Victor Steinbrueck, framed the controversy in broad commonwealth language. He touted the market as an irreplaceable part of the city's heritage.

At the decade's end, Seattle had achieved national recognition as a pioneer in a number of neighborhood-based programs and participatory civic initiatives, most of which could trace their roots one way or another to the Lake Union fight which drew directly on the commonwealth vision that Terry Pettus reinvigorated. Even traditional establishment leaders who fought the community activists acknowledged the benefits. "Seattle had a major era of citizen participation," said James Ellis, a man sometimes called the informal leader of the city's elite. As a result, "there was an incredible flowering in the city."[35]

The houseboaters' greatest contribution was to make Lake Union take on a much larger meaning as symbol of people's work and connection, the city's diverse interests, and its future possibilities. In the process they retrieved the nineteenth-century traditions of public work and commonwealth, and also changed and adapted them for a radically different environment. This adaptive, innovative quality was the essence of the "portable democracy" that Americans created in the nineteenth century. Where people and their work went, so went the opportunity for democratic creativity. For Americans, democracy was not confined to institutional structures; rather it was something they carried with them. It became a way of life.

Such a democracy, because it was incorporated into people's identities and it was tied to the skills of their everyday work, meant that the people themselves were the ultimate producers. Portable democracy created the capacity for people to change and rebuild the commons, as well as preserve and enhance it.

50 Public work, as expressed and elaborated in the nineteenth-century tradition of the commonwealth, most simply conveyed the idea of common work on things people needed to do together. It embodied the democratic spirit of American manners and talk. And it created a culture and a wide-ranging process of citizenship education through which people sought to understand, define, and gain control over technical progress and wealth itself.

Notes

1. Quoted in Michael Kazin, *The Populist Persuasion: An American History* (New York: Basic Books, 1995), p. 9.
2. Jane Addams, *Twenty Years at Hull-House* (New York: Macmillan, 1938), p. 179.
3. Robert Wiebe, *Self-Rule: A Cultural History of American Democracy* (Chicago: The University of Chicago Press, 1995), pp. 45–46.

. . .

16. Grund, Chevalier, Tocqueville, quoted in Wood, *Radicalism,* p. 285.
17. John Michael Vlach, *By the Work of Their Hands: Studies in Afro-American Folklife* (Charlottesville: University of Virginia, 1991), p. 222. For a description of the "free spaces" in which black slaves created their own religious traditions, see for instance Sara M. Evans and Harry C. Boyte, *Free Spaces: The Roots of Democratic Change in America* (Chicago: University of Chicago Press, 1992), Chapter 2.
18. Wiebe, *Self-Rule,* pp. 104–111, summarized the literature on women's roles and their relation to democracy. See also Nancy Cott, *The Bonds of Womanhood* (New Haven: Yale University Press, 1977); Mary Ryan, *Women in Public* (Baltimore: Johns Hopkins, 1990); Sara M. Evans, *Born for Liberty: A History of Women in America* (New York: Free Press, 1989), especially Chapters 3 and 4; Evans and Boyte, *Free Spaces,* Chapter 3.
19. Historians Oscar and Mary Handlin have described the association of the word in Massachusetts with the founding of towns, churches, schools, and a variety of other institutions: "For the farmers and seamen, for the fishermen, artisans and new merchants, commonwealth . . . embodied . . . the value of common action." Oscar and Mary Handlin, *Commonwealth: A Study of the Role of Government in the American Economy, Massachusetts, 1774–1861* (Cambridge: Harvard University Press, 1969), p. 30.
20. Edward Miller and John Hatcher, *Medieval England: Rural Society and Economic Change, 1086–1348* (London: Longman, 1978), pp. 105, 106, 108–109. On traditions of open-field agriculture in England, see Tremor Rowley, ed., *The Origins of Open-Field Agriculture* (London: Croom Helm, 1981).
21. Richard Lingeman, *Small-Town America: A Narrative History, 1620 to the Present* (Boston: Houghton Mifflin, 1980), p. 29.

    Commons, as Ivan Illich has described, bears close resemblance to German terms *Almende* and *Gemeinschaft* and the Italian *gli usi civici.* Illich defines the commons as "that part of the environment which lay beyond the person's own threshold and outside his own possession, but to which, however, that person had a recognized claim of usage—not to produce commodities but to provide for the subsistence of kin. Neither wilderness nor home is commons, but that part of the environment for which customary law exacts specific forms of community respect." Illich conveys the nonprivate nature of the commons, and concepts of stake-holding and responsibility—but he neglects the public and power dimensions. See Chapters 6 and 7 and Appendix 2. Ivan Illich, *Gender* (New York: Pantheon, 1982), pp. 17–18.
22. Ruth Bordin, *Woman and Temperance: The Quest for Power and Liberty, 1873–1900* (Philadelphia: Temple University Press, 1980), p. 98.
23. Quoted from Barbara Epstein, *The Politics of Domesticity: Women, Evangelism and Temperance in Nineteenth Century America* (Middletown: Wesleyan University Press, 1981), p. 100.
24. John Adams, quoted in David Mathews, *The Promise of Democracy* (Dayton: Kettering Foundation, 1988), p. 5.
25. Paul Starr, *The Social Transformation of American Medicine* (New York: Basic Books, 1982), pp. 32–34.

26. Sean Wilentz, *Chants Democratic: New York City and the Rise of the American Working Class, 1788–1850* (New York: Oxford University Press, 1984), p. 156.

. . .

33. The quotes from Pettus are taken from interviews on March 14, 17, and 18, 1983, Seattle. Other accounts of the Seattle houseboat story are found in "Subversive?" a special documentary by John de Graaf for KCTS, aired in Seattle, September 5, 1983; and Howard Drucker, *Seattle's Unsinkable Houseboats* (Seattle: Watermark Press, 1977). For a detailed description of the Lake Union effort and other "commonwealth" stories of the seventies and eighties, see Harry C. Boyte, *Community Is Possible: Repairing America's Roots* (New York: Harper & Row, 1984).
34. Howard Drucker, *Seattle's Unsinkable Houseboats* (Seattle: Watermark Press, 1977), p. 75.
35. Steinbrueck's battle is described in detail in Alice Shorett and Murray Morgan, *The Pike Place Market: People, Politics and Produce* (Seattle: Pacific Search Press, 1982); Ellis quoted from Leonard Silk, "Seattle Looks for its Future," *New York Times*, April 22, 1983.

Exploring Texts and Contexts

For activities with icons, refer to the Guides to Analyzing Contexts for Writing and Analyzing Readings in Context.

1. Boyte and Kari argue that the work of a civil society is best conducted through public work. Think of a situation or scenario in which a group of people gathers together to make a positive change in their neighborhood or community. Identify the problem they are trying to solve and how speaking or writing might provide a way to solve the problem. Next, consider specifically what genres the group might identify as useful, and write about how these specific speaking or writing activities could help the group achieve their goals. Genre
2. This activity follows up on the preceding one. Once you have identified a situation and considered genres of speech and writing that might be useful, consider the consequences that might follow from employing these particular acts of speaking and writing in association with others. Brainstorm about what consequences you'd like your speaking and writing to have, but also consider unexpected and even unwanted consequences that might occur. How could you prevent unwanted consequences? Consequences
3. Boyte and Kari are building an argument that depends on the word *commonwealth,* which once had a vibrant meaning, but has since fallen into disuse. Summarize the way the term has been used historically by reviewing Boyte and Kari's discussion of it. If the term *commonwealth* means "taking care of the commons," identify public situations in which the term might be brought back to use. Language

Creating Texts

For activities with icons, refer to the Guides to Analyzing Contexts for Writing and Analyzing Readings in Context. For additional help with these writing projects, read the descriptions of the **Essay** and **Dialogue** in the Genre Glossary.

1. Boyte and Kari claim that an increased emphasis on public work will create "the capacity for people to change and rebuild the commons, as well as preserve and enhance it." They trace the history of the concept of public work through various historical contexts and conclude with a contemporary case study. Their argument depends in large part on the notion that individuals and individual work can change the character of our democracy. Write an argumentative essay in which you take a position on whether or not the notion of public work can help support democracy in the way that Boyte and Kari claim.
2. Imagine that a group of people wants to publicize a position about a local issue and invite response from others affected by it—for example, a group of parents concerned about school-busing arrangements. Or this group simply wants to stimulate discussion about some issue—an increase in crime in the neighborhood, for example. The group is considering how to get its message out and begin a discussion: a letter to the editor, an opinion piece in a local paper, a call to a talk radio show, a listserve, a Web page, a neighborhood meeting, or some completely new strategy. For this project you can do one of several things. Write an essay in which you describe a situation and then discuss the benefits and drawbacks of several different channels for deliberation. Or write a dialogue that captures the group's conversation on this issue. Or choose an appropriate genre and produce the message yourself. Consult the Genre Glossary for ideas.

Toward an Agenda for Social Capitalists

Robert D. Putnam

In 1995 a Harvard social scientist captured the public's imagination when he argued that the disaffection and alienation that Americans reported in polls could be traced to a decline in civic engagement. The article, written by Robert D. Putnam and published in an academic journal, bore the title "Bowling Alone," a phrase that caught on with the media. The title refers to the fact that, while bowling is as popular as ever, we are no longer bowling in leagues. Although that might seem like an odd piece of information, Putnam uses it to illustrate the fact that we no longer have as many opportunities for the lively, small-scale social interactions that a bowling league provided.

According to Putnam, these social networks are vital to making democracies work. His theory hinges on the notion of social capital—the connections among individuals and the "norms of reciprocity" and "trustworthiness" they inspire. A school newspaper, a community-service club, and senior-citizen school volunteers are all examples of social networks that increase social capital because they create opportunities for close, nonfamilial relationships and collective action. Putnam's research indicates that since 1970 opportunities to form social connections and create networks have been dwindling, as measured by declining enrollments in parent-teacher organizations, the YMCA, Little League, labor unions, hobby clubs, churches, the League of Women Voters, and many other groups that Putnam studied. As these networks shrivel, our stock of social capital is diminished, and with it mutual trust, a sense of belonging, and social institutions that run effectively.

His findings set the terms for a national debate on civic engagement. He has been profiled in *People* magazine and has appeared on talk shows. He is a popular speaker at university forums. Bill Clinton invited him to Camp David, and, more recently, Al Gore and George W. Bush have sought his advice. Putnam attributes his popularity with high-profile politicians to the political viability of this issue. In a *New York Times* interview, Putnam was quoted as saying politicians feel the need to respond to the growing concern Americans feel about their communities.

Now, in a book published five years after that original article, he takes up the charges of his critics who questioned his assumptions, his research methods, and his conclusions. Most of his book is devoted to proving that there has indeed been a decline in participation and that this social change has had significant costs. But identifying a problem, and even the source of the problem, Putnam has admitted, is just the beginning. In the concluding chapter of his book, included here, Putnam lists his suggestions for rebuilding community and increasing the stock of social capital. His agenda includes suggestions for "actionable ideas" and is organized around six areas: youth and schools; the workplace; urban and metropolitan design; religion; arts and culture; and politics and government. As is fairly common in a concluding chapter, there are numerous references to other parts of his book. Putnam moves back and forth among ideas discussed in different parts of the book, interspersing his recommendations for re-creating social capital with references both to earlier chapters in which he establishes that participation has declined and middle sections that document strategies that were effective in the past.

Connecting with the Conversation

1. What is the scope of your civic participation? Do you volunteer for social-action projects, join team sports, or participate in clubs and organizations? Describe your experience. Interview a grandparent or other relative or neighbor from an older generation. In your journal compare your experience with that of the people you interviewed. What conclusions can you draw about the nature of civic engagement today?
2. Visit the Saguaro Seminar Web site at www.ksg.harvard.edu. Find out a little about this seminar by reviewing the notes from the last meeting and reading about the participants.

"To everything there is a season, and a time for every purpose under the heaven," sang the Hebrew poet in Ecclesiastes. When Pete Seeger put that ancient maxim to folk music in the 1960s, it was, perhaps, a season for Americans to unravel fetters of intrusive togetherness. As we enter a new century, however, it is now past time to begin to reweave the fabric of our communities.

From *Bowling Alone: The Collapse and Revival of American Community.* New York: Simon and Schuster, 2000, pp. 402–414 and pp. 501–502.

At the outset of our inquiry I noted that most Americans today feel vaguely and uncomfortably disconnected. It seemed to many as the twentieth century closed, just as it did to the young Walter Lippmann at the century's opening, that "we have changed our environment more quickly than we know how to change ourselves." We tell pollsters that we wish we lived in a more civil, more trustworthy, more collectively caring community. The evidence from our inquiry shows that this longing is not simply nostalgia or "false consciousness." Americans are *right* that the bonds of our communities have withered, and we are *right* to fear that this transformation has very real costs. The challenge for us, however, as it was for our predecessors moving from the Gilded Age into the Progressive Era, is not to grieve over social change, but to guide it.

Creating (or re-creating) social capital is no simple task. It would be eased by a palpable national crisis, like war or depression or natural disaster, but for better *and* for worse, America at the dawn of the new century faces no such galvanizing crisis. The ebbing of community over the last several decades has been silent and deceptive. We notice its effects in the strained interstices of our private lives and in the degradation of our public life, but the most serious consequences are reminiscent of the old parlor puzzle: "What's missing from this picture?" Weakened social capital is manifest in the things that have vanished almost unnoticed—neighborhood parties and get-togethers with friends, the unreflective kindness of strangers, the shared pursuit of the public good rather than a solitary quest for private goods. Naming this problem is an essential first step toward confronting it, just as labeling "the environment" allowed Americans to hear the silent spring and naming what Betty Friedan called "the problem that has no name" enabled women to articulate what was wrong with their lives.

Naming our problem, however—and even gauging its dimensions, diagnosing its origins, and assessing its implications, as I have sought to do in this book—is but a preliminary to the tougher challenge. In a world irrevocably changed, a world in which most women are employed, markets global, individuals and firms mobile, entertainment electronic, technology accelerating, and major war (thankfully) absent, how can we nevertheless replenish our stocks of social capital? Like most social issues, this one has two faces—one institutional and one individual. To use the convenient market metaphor, we need to address both the *supply* of opportunities for civic engagement and the *demand* for those opportunities.

5 Just as did our predecessors in the Progressive Era, we need to create new structures and policies (public and private) to facilitate renewed civic engagement. As I shall explain in more detail in a moment, leaders and activists in every sphere of American life must seek innovative ways to respond to the eroding effectiveness of the civic institutions and practices that we inherited. At the same time we need to fortify our resolve as individuals to reconnect, for we must overcome a familiar paradox of collective action. Even if I privately would prefer a more vibrant community, I cannot accomplish that goal on my own—it's not a meeting, after all, if only I show up, and it's not a club if I'm the only member. It is tempting to retreat to private pleasures that I *can* achieve on my own. But in so doing, I make it even harder for you to solve your version of the same problem. Actions by individuals are not sufficient to restore community, but they *are* necessary.

So our challenge is to restore American community for the twenty-first century through both collective and individual initiative. I recognize the impossibility of proclaiming any panacea for our nation's problems of civic disengagement. On the other hand, because of my experience in spearheading in recent years a concerted nationwide conversation modeled on the intensive interchange among scholars and practitioners in the Progressive Era, I am optimistic that, working together, Americans today can once again be as civically creative as our Progressive forebears. These deliberations, the "Saguaro Seminar: Civic Engagement in America," brought together thinkers and doers from many diverse American communities to shape questions and seek answers.[1] The ensuing discussions have informed my suggestions in this chapter in many ways. The group's objectives have been, first, to make Americans more aware of the collective significance of the myriad minute decisions that we make daily to invest—or disinvest—in social capital and, second, to spark the civic imaginations of our fellow citizens to discover and invent new ways of connecting socially that fit our changed lives.

Figuring out in detail how to renew our stock of social capital is a task for a nation and a decade, not a single scholar, a single book, or even a single group. My intention in this chapter is modest—to identify key facets of the challenge ahead, by sketching briefly six spheres that deserve special attention from aspiring social capitalists: youth and schools; the workplace; urban and metropolitan design; religion; arts and culture; and politics and government. For each, by offering some suggestions of my own, I seek to provoke the reader's own imagination in the hope that together we can produce something even more creative and powerful.

PHILOSOPHERS FROM ARISTOTLE and Rousseau to William James and John Dewey have begun discussions of civics with the education of youth. They have pondered the essential virtues and skills and knowledge and habits of democratic citizens and how to instill them. That starting point is especially appropriate for reformers today, for the single most important cause of our current plight is a pervasive and continuing generational decline in almost all forms of civic engagement. Today's youth did not initiate the erosion of Americans' social capital—their parents did—and it is the obligation of Americans of all ages to help rekindle civic engagement among the generation that will come of age in the early years of the twenty-first century.

10 So I set before America's parents, educators, and, above all, America's young adults the following challenge: *Let us find ways to ensure that by 2010 the level of civic engagement among Americans then coming of age in all parts of our society will match that of their grandparents when they were that same age, and that at the same time bridging social capital will be substantially greater than it was in their grandparents' era.* One specific test of our success will be whether we can restore electoral turnout to that of the 1960s, but our goal must be to increase participation and deliberation in other, more substantive and fine-grained ways, too—from team sports to choirs and from organized altruism to grassroots social movements.

The means to achieve these goals in the early twenty-first century, and the new forms of connectedness that will mark our success, will almost surely be different from those of the mid-twentieth century. For this reason, success will require the sensibility and skills of Gen X and their successors, even more than of baby boomers and their elders. Nevertheless, some "old-fashioned" ideas are relevant. Take civics education, for example. We know that knowledge about public affairs and practice in everyday civic skills are prerequisites for effective participation. We know, too, that the "civics report card" issued by the U.S. Department of Education for American elementary and high school students at the end of the twentieth century was disappointing.[2] So improved civics education in school should be part of our strategy—not just "how a bill becomes a law," but "How can I participate effectively in the public life of my community?" Imagine, for example, the civic lessons that could be imparted by a teacher in South Central Los Angeles, working with students to *effect* public change that her students think is important, like getting lights for a neighborhood basketball court.

We know other strategies that will work, too. A mounting body of evidence confirms that community service programs really do strengthen the civic muscles of participants, especially if the service is meaningful, regular, and woven into the fabric of the school curriculum. Episodic service has little effect, and it is hard to imagine that baby-sitting and janitorial work—the two most frequent types of "community service" nationwide, according to one 1997 study—have much favorable effect. On the other hand, well-designed service learning programs (the emerging evidence suggests) improve civic knowledge, enhance citizen efficacy, increase social responsibility and self-esteem, teach skills of cooperation and leadership, and may even (one study suggests) reduce racism.[3] Interestingly, voluntary programs seem to work as well as mandatory ones. Volunteering in one's youth is, as we noted in chapter 7, among the strongest predictors of adult volunteering. Intergenerational mentoring, too, can serve civic ends, as in Boston's Citizen Schools program, which enables adult volunteers to work with youth on tangible after-school projects, like storywriting or Web site building.

Participation in extracurricular activities (both school linked and independent) is another proven means to increase civic and social involvement in later life. In fact, participation in high school music groups, athletic teams, service clubs, and the like is among the strongest precursors of adult participation, even when we compare demographically matched groups.[4] From a civic point of view, extracurricular activities are anything but "frills," yet funding for them was decimated during the 1980s and 1990s. Reversing that perverse development would be a good start toward our goal of youthful reengagement by 2010. Finally, we know that smaller schools encourage more active involvement in extracurricular activity than big schools—more students in smaller schools have an opportunity to play trombone or left tackle or King Lear. Smaller schools, like smaller towns, generate higher expectations for mutual reciprocity and collective action. So deconcentrating megaschools or creating smaller "schools within schools" will almost surely produce civic dividends.

Our efforts to increase social participation among youth must not be limited to schooling. Though it is not yet easy to see what the Internet-age equivalent of 4-H or settlement houses might be, we ought to bestow an annual Jane Addams Award on the Gen X'er or Gen Y'er who comes up with the best idea. What we need is not civic broccoli—good for you but unappealing—but an updated version of Scouting's ingenious combination of values and fun. I challenge those who came of age in the civically dispiriting last decade of the twentieth century to invent powerful and enticing ways of increasing civic engagement among their younger brothers and sisters who will come of age in the first decade of the twenty-first century.

15 THE CHANGING CHARACTER of work and the closely related movement of women into the paid workforce were among the most far-reaching upheavals in American society during the twentieth century. This transformation of the workplace was comparable in magnitude to the metamorphosis of America a century earlier from a nation of farms to one of factories and offices. Yet as the twenty-first century opens, American institutions, both public and private, and norms and practices within the workplace have only begun to adapt to this change. As we saw in chapter 11, this workplace revolution is implicated in the nearly simultaneous decline of social connectedness and civic involvement. So I challenge America's employers, labor leaders, public officials, and employees themselves: *Let us find ways to ensure that by 2010 America's workplace will be substantially more family-friendly and community-congenial, so that American workers will be enabled to replenish our stocks of social capital both within and outside the workplace.*

Fortunately there is some evidence that community- and family-oriented workplace practices benefit the employer as well as the employee. At least in periods of full employment, moreover, such practices become a key ingredient in recruiting and retaining a high-quality, loyal workforce. Happily, the proportion of American workers who reported some flexibility in their work schedules increased from 16 percent in 1990 to 30 percent in 1997.[5] However, many of the benefits of employment practices that encourage social capital formation—stronger families, more effective schools, safer neighborhoods, more vibrant public life—"leak" outside the firm itself, whereas all the costs stay put. This fact gives firms an incentive to underinvest in civic engagement by their employees. Conversely, workplace practices that inhibit community involvement and family connectedness produce a classic case of what economists term "negative externalities," imposing an unrequited cost on society.

In the case of environmental pollution, it is now widely accepted that tax and other financial incentives are an appropriate public response to negative externalities, reinforcing moral suasion as a means of encouraging environmentally friendly behavior. Similarly, we need to rethink how to reward firms that act responsibly toward their employees' family and community commitments and how to encourage other employers to follow their example. Many firms offer released time to employees who volunteer for community service, a valuable practice that should be extended. But volunteering is only one form of civic engagement. Public policies like the Family and Medical Leave Act of 1993 and legal requirements that employers facilitate jury service illustrate that the public interest in civic and social connectedness can justify public regulation of employment contracts. However, caring for sick loved ones is not the only family responsibility, and jury service is not the citizen's only duty, and our labor law should recognize that.

Our findings in chapter 11 point unambiguously to the civic as well as the personal dividends associated with part-time employment. For many people, we discovered, part-time work is the best of both worlds—enhancing one's exposure to broader social networks while leaving enough time to pursue those opportunities outside the workplace. We found that part-time workers are typically more involved in community activities than *either* full-time employees or people who are not employed at all. Not everyone wants a part-time job, of course, but many do, and America's public, nonprofit, and private institutions have only begun to address the challenge of restructuring work to meet that demand. The new politics of time must be high on the public agenda in the new century.

Civic engagement and social connectedness can be found inside the workplace, not only outside it. Thus our workplace agenda should also include new means of social-capital formation on the job. This is especially true with regard to bridging social capital, since the increasing diversity in the workplace is a valuable and not yet fully exploited asset for social capitalists. As we saw in chapter 5, some encouraging initiatives along these lines—teamwork, architectural restructuring, and the like—are already under way. On the other hand, other changes that we discussed there—especially the proliferation of "contingent" work—heighten the challenge of creating work-based social capital. Employers, labor unions, labor relations experts, and employees themselves need to be more creative in meeting the social connectivity needs of temps, part-timers, and independent contractors.[6] Finally, we need to challenge the notion that civic life has no part in the workplace. Why not employer-provided space and time for civic discussion groups and service clubs? Why not better protection for privacy of employees' communications?

20 As THE TWENTIETH CENTURY ENDED, Americans gradually began to recognize that the sprawling pattern of metropolitan settlement that we had built for ourselves in the preceding five decades imposes heavy personal and economic costs—pollution, congestion, and lost time. In chapter 12 we discovered that metropolitan sprawl has also damaged the social fabric of our communities. So I challenge America's urban and regional planners, developers, community organizers, and home buyers: *Let us act to ensure that by 2010 Americans will spend less time traveling and more time connecting with our neighbors than we do today, that we will live in more integrated and pedestrian-friendly areas, and that the design of our communities and the availability of public space will encourage more casual socializing with friends and neighbors.*[7] One deceptively simple objective might be this: that more of us know more of our neighbors by first name than we do today.

Urban designers, marching under the banner of "the new urbanism," have produced many creative suggestions along precisely these lines over the past decade or two.[8] Admittedly, far more time and energy have been invested so far in articulating and even implementing these ideas than in measuring their impact on community involvement. It is surely plausible that design innovations like mixed-use zoning, pedestrian-friendly street grids, and more space for public use should enhance social capital, though it is less obvious that the cosmetic details of Victorian or colonial design and the echoes of nineteenth-century public architecture typically found in new urbanist communities like Disney's Celebration, Florida, will necessarily have that effect. (The brand-new town in Easton, Ohio, includes a town center built to resemble a converted train station, although there was never any train station there.) In any event it is time to begin assessing rigorously the actual consequences of these promising initiatives.[9]

The new urbanism is an ongoing experiment to see whether our thirst for great community life outweighs our hunger for private backyards, discount megamalls, and easy parking. In the end Americans will get largely the kind of physical space we demand; if we don't really want more community, we won't get it. On the other hand, in the past segregated suburban sprawl was also powerfully shaped (often unintentionally) by public policies like highway construction, mortgage interest deduction, redlining, and concentrated public housing. As the costs of sprawl (economic and environmental as well as social) become clearer, public policies to discourage it will become more attractive, as they already have in places from Atlanta to Portland. Finally, innovative community thinkers and organizers like Harry Boyte, Ernesto Cortes, and John McKnight have devoted much effort to finding and exploiting unexpected assets in disadvantaged communities. Community Development Corporations, created in the 1970s to foster physical reconstruction of blighted neighborhoods, are now turning their attention to investing in social capital, too, and groups like the Local Initiatives Support Corporation (LISC) have had some success in that area.[10] I challenge all of us to add to that good work the objective of creating networks that bridge the racial, social, and geographic cleavages that fracture our metropolitan areas.

FAITH-BASED COMMUNITIES REMAIN such a crucial reservoir of social capital in America that it is hard to see how we could redress the erosion of the last several decades without a major religious contribution. Particularly in the public realm, Americans cherish the First Amendment strictures that have enabled us to combine unparalleled religiosity and denominational pluralism with a minimum of religious warfare. On the other hand, it is undeniable that religion has played a major role in every period of civic revival in American history. So I challenge America's clergy, lay leaders, theologians, and ordinary worshipers: *Let us spur a new, pluralistic, socially responsible "great awakening," so that by 2010 Americans will be more deeply engaged than we are today in one or another spiritual community of meaning, while at the same time becoming more tolerant of the faiths and practices of other Americans.*

In our national history, religion has contributed to social-capital creation, above all, in three dramatic and fervent "awakenings." During the Great Awakening from 1730 to 1760, revivals "explode[d] like a string of firecrackers" into "massive and continuous revival meetings . . . kept in motion by traveling preachers." The Second Great Awakening from 1800 to 1830 was an equally frothy period of engagement, in which "circuit riders" carried the new gospel from one churchless frontier settlement to another. Circuit riders formed groups of ten to twelve converts to reinforce each other's spiritual seeking until regular churches could be established. Historians debate the motivation and even the religiosity of these evangelists, but the movement inspired many to turn toward the poor, reject slavery, and found missionary and temperance societies. One notable invention was the Sunday school movement, integrating revivalism with a desire to teach literacy to those excluded from common schools, including women (black and white), factory children, and frontiersmen.[11]

25 In the previous chapter we observed a third major period of religious engagement with social issues at the end of the nineteenth century, embodied in activities like the Social Gospel movement and the Salvation Army—the so-called church of the poor that focused on the "submerged tenth" of American life, buffeted by the strains of urbanization and industrialization. The Salvation Army, "saving the world one soul at a time," was an interesting hybrid of doctrinal fundamentalism, liturgical

heterodoxy (with marching bands and "hallelujah lassies"), and progressive beliefs about helping the poor, raising the religious status of women, and ministering to white and black alike.[12]

Are there the ingredients in America at the beginning of the twenty-first century for another Great Awakening? Megachurches, to take a single example, use contemporary marketing and entertainment techniques to craft an accessible religious experience for their typically suburban, middle-class market. (Though initially focused on the white population, megachurches are increasingly attracting people of color.) While their church services, by dint of size if nothing else, often seem impersonal and theologically bland, megachurch leaders are savvy social capitalists, organizing small group activities that build personal networks and mix religion and socializing (even bowling teams!). Meanwhile, in a different portion of the religious spectrum, as we saw in chapters 4 and 9, evangelical and fundamentalist churches (along with their counterparts among Jews and other religious traditions) constitute one of the most notable exceptions to the general decline in social capital that I have traced in this book.

From a civic point of view, a new Great Awakening (if it happened) would not be an unmixed blessing. As we noted in chapters 4 and 22, proselytizing religions are better at creating bonding social capital than bridging social capital, and tolerance of unbelievers is not a virtue notably associated with fundamentalism. In our culture, if not our jurisprudence, a new Great Awakening would raise issues about the constitutional separation of church and state, as illustrated by the controversy surrounding the "charitable choice" provision of welfare reform that provides public funds for religiously linked social services. On the other hand, one can also detect signs of a broadly ecumenical and socially engaged religiosity in movements like the evangelical Call to Renewal. In addition, some of the innovations of the Gilded Age and Progressive Era, like the settlement house and the Chautauqua movement, though not narrowly religious, could inspire twenty-first century equivalents.[13]

NO SECTOR OF AMERICAN SOCIETY will have more influence on the future state of our social capital than the electronic mass media and especially the Internet. If we are to reverse the adverse trends of the last three decades in any fundamental way, the electronic entertainment and telecommunications industry must become a big part of the solution instead of a big part of the problem. So I challenge America's media moguls, journalists, and Internet gurus, along with viewers like you (and me): *Let us find ways to ensure that by 2010 Americans will spend less leisure time sitting passively alone in front of glowing screens and more time in active connection with our fellow citizens. Let us foster new forms of electronic entertainment and communication that reinforce community engagement rather than forestalling it.* The recent flurry of interest in "civic journalism" could be one strand to this strategy, if it is interpreted not as a substitute for genuine grassroots participation, but as a goad and soapbox for such participation.[14] I noted in chapter 13 that, as a technical matter, the extraordinary power of television can encourage as well as discourage civic involvement. Let us challenge those talented people who preside over America's entertainment industry to create new forms of entertainment that draw the viewer off the couch and into his community.

We saw in chapter 9 that the Internet can be used to reinforce real, face-to-face communities, not merely to displace them with a counterfeit "virtual community." Let us challenge software designers and communications technologists to heed the call of University of Michigan computer scientist Paul Resnick to make the Internet social capital-friendly and to create a Community Information Corps to encourage youthful computer professionals to use their skills to help rebuild community in America.

30 In chapter 9 I discussed several important obstacles to the use of computer-mediated communication to build social capital. Some of those obstacles, like the digital divide, can (and must) be addressed by public policy. Others, like anonymity and single strandedness, might be amenable to technological "fixes." On the other hand, computer-mediated communication also opens opportunities for hitherto unthinkable forms of democratic deliberation and community building—like citywide citizen debates about local issues or joint explorations of local history or even announcements of a local ultimate Frisbee tournament. Several early studies of well-wired communities suggest—tentatively, but hopefully—that residents who have easy access to local computer-based communication use that new tool to strengthen, not supplant, face-to-face ties with their neighbors and that some of them become more actively involved in community life, precisely as we social capitalists would wish.[15] Electronic support groups for elderly shut-ins might be useful complements to (not substitutes for) regular personal visits. The key, in my view, is to find ways in which Internet technology can reinforce rather than supplant place-based, face-to-face, enduring social networks.

To build bridging social capital requires that we transcend our social and political and professional identities to connect with people unlike ourselves. This is why team sports provide good venues for social-capital creation. Equally important and less exploited in this connection are the arts and cultural activities. Singing together (like bowling together) does not require shared ideology or shared social or ethnic provenance. For this reason, among others, I challenge America's artists, the leaders and funders of our cultural institutions, as well as ordinary Americans: *Let us find ways to ensure that by 2010 significantly more Americans will participate in (not merely consume or "appreciate") cultural activities from group dancing to songfests to community theater to rap festivals. Let us discover new ways to use the arts as a vehicle for convening diverse groups of fellow citizens.*

Art manifestly matters for its own sake, far beyond the favorable effect it can have on rebuilding American communities. Aesthetic objectives, not merely social ones, are obviously important. That said, art is especially useful in transcending conventional social barriers. Moreover, social capital is often a valuable by-product of cultural activities whose main purpose is purely artistic.

Liz Lerman's Dance Exchange has built unlikely community togetherness using community-based modern dance, bringing together, for example, unemployed shipyard workers and white-collar professionals when the closing of the Portsmouth (N.H.) shipyard strained local community bonds. The Roadside Theater Company has mustered diverse local folks in declining towns in Appalachia to celebrate their traditions and restore community confidence through dramatization of local stories and music. The Museum of the National Center for African American Artists in Boston has convened diverse groups of black Americans (Haitians, Jamaicans, Afro-Brazilians, and native African Americans) to build and then parade twenty-foot fish sculptures to the New England Aquarium. Toni Blackman's Freestyle Union in Washington, D.C., uses *ciphering,* a novel combination of hip-hop, rap poetry, and improvisational poetry slams, to attract people from all walks of life, from a Filipino break-dancer to a right-to-life Christian. The Baltimore Museum of Art urges local residents to exploit its public spaces on "Freestyle Thursdays" by inviting local choral groups and others to perform. Chicago's Gallery 37 provides apprenticeships for diverse young budding artists—rich and poor, suburban and inner city, black, white, Latino—to follow their own muses, building social connections among artist-mentors, artist-apprentices, and observers. In the Mattole Valley of northern California, David Simpson has used community theater to build bridges between loggers and environmentalists. Many of these activities produce great art, but all of them produce great bridging social capital—in some respects an even more impressive achievement.[16]

POLITICS AND GOVERNMENT is the domain where our voyage of inquiry about the state of social capital in America began, and it is where I conclude my challenges to readers who are as concerned as I am about restoring community bonds in America. Nowhere is the need to restore connectedness, trust, and civic engagement clearer than in the now often empty public forums of our democracy. So I challenge America's government officials, political consultants, politicians, and (above all) my fellow citizens: *Let us find ways to ensure that by 2010 many more Americans will participate in the public life of our communities—running for office, attending public meetings, serving on committees, campaigning in elections, and even voting.* It is perhaps foolhardy to hope that we could reverse the entire decline of the last three to four decades in ten years, but American democracy would surely feel the beneficent effects of even a partial reversal.

35 Campaign reform (above all, campaign finance reform) should be aimed at increasing the importance of social capital—and decreasing the importance of financial capital—in our elections, federal, state, and local. Since time is distributed more equally across the population than money, privileging time-based participation over check-based participation would begin to reverse the growing inequality in American politics. Government authority should be decentralized as far as possible to bring decisions to smaller, local jurisdictions, while recognizing and offsetting the potential negative effect of that decentralization on equality and redistribution. Indeed, liberals alert to the benefits of social capital should be readier to transfer governmental authority downward in exactly the same measure that compassionate conservatives should be readier to transfer resources from have to have-not communities. Decentralization of government resources and authority to neighborhood councils has worked in cities like Minneapolis, Portland, and Seattle, creating new social capital in the form of potluck dinners, community gardens, and flea markets, though deft design is needed

to be sure that the balance between bridging and bonding does not tip too far toward urban fragmentation.

Policy designers of whatever partisan persuasion should become more social capital-savvy, seeking to do minimum damage to existing stocks of social capital even as they look for opportunities to add new stocks. How about a "social-capital impact statement" for new programs, less bureaucratic and legalistic than environmental impact statements have become, but equally effective at calling attention to unanticipated consequences? For example, the greatest damage to social capital in the inner city of Indianapolis, Indiana, in the last half century was the unintended disruption of neighborhood networks when those neighborhoods were pierced by Interstate 65 in the early 1960s. The Front-Porch Alliance created by former mayor Stephen Goldsmith more than a quarter century later was a worthy effort to help restore some Indianapolis neighborhood institutions, but Goldsmith himself would be the first to say that it would have been better to avoid the damage in the first place.[17]

In all the domains of social-capital creation that I have discussed here all too briefly, social capitalists need to avoid false debates. One such debate is "top-down versus bottom-up." The roles of national and local institutions in restoring American community need to be complementary; neither alone can solve the problem. Another false debate is whether government is the problem or the solution. The accurate answer, judging from the historical record (as I argued in chapter 15), is that it can be both. Many of the most creative investments in social capital in American history—from county agents and the 4-H to community colleges and the March of Dimes—were the direct result of government policy. Government may be responsible for some small portion of the declines in social capital I have traced in this volume, and it cannot be the sole solution, but it is hard to imagine that we can meet the challenges I have set for America in 2010 without using government.

The final false debate to be avoided is whether what is needed to restore trust and community bonds in America is individual change or institutional change. Again, the honest answer is "Both." America's major civic institutions, both public and private, are somewhat antiquated a century after most of them were created, and they need to be reformed in ways that invite more active participation. Whether the specific suggestions I have made for institutional reform are persuasive or not is less important than the possibility that we may have a national debate about how to make our institutions more social capital-friendly. In the end, however, institutional reform will not work—indeed, it will not happen—unless you and I, along with our fellow citizens, resolve to become reconnected with our friends and neighbors. Henry Ward Beecher's advice a century ago to "multiply picnics" is not entirely ridiculous today. We should do this, ironically, not because it will be good for America—though it will be—but because it will be good for us.

Notes

1. The Saguaro Seminar is composed of thirty-three accomplished thinkers and doers who meet regularly to develop actionable ideas to increase Americans' connectedness to one another and to community institutions. Participants come from diverse backgrounds, professions, and parts

of the country; they have included Xavier de Souza Briggs, Bliss Browne, Kirbyjon Caldwell, John DiIulio, E. J. Dionne, Carolyn Doggett, Lewis Feldstein, Christ Gates, Stephen Goldsmith, Amy Gutmann, Henry Izumizaki, Louise Kennedy, Vanessa Kirsch, Carol Lamm, Liz Lerman, Glenn Loury, John Mascotte, Martha Minow, Mark Moore, Barack Obama, Peter Pierce, Ralph Reed, Paul Resnick, Kris Rondeau, Tom Sander, Juan Sepúlveda, Robert Sexton, Harry Spence, George Stephanopoulos, Dorothy Stoneman, Lisa Sullivan, Jim Wallis, Vin Weber, and William Julius Wilson. None bears any responsibility for my recommendations here. More information about the Saguaro Seminar can be found by contacting the Seminar staff at the John F. Kennedy School of Government, Harvard University, or at www.ksg.harvard.edu/saguaro. For a complementary compendium of recommendations for revitalizing American democracy, see Levine, *New Progressive Era.*

2. Delli Carpini and Keeter, *What Americans Know About Politics and Why It Matters;* A. D. Lutkus et al., *The NAEP 1998 Civics Report Card for the Nation* (Washington, D.C.: U.S. Department of Education, National Center for Education Statistics, 1999).

3. Fred M. Newmann and Robert A. Rutter, "The Effects of High School Community Service Programs on Students' Social Development" (Washington, D.C.: National Institute of Education, December 1983); Virginia Hodgkinson and Murray S. Weitzman, *Volunteering and Giving Among Teenagers 12 to 17 Years of Age* (Washington, D.C.: Independent Sector, 1997); Richard Battistoni, "Service Learning and Democratic Citizenship," *Theory into Practice 35* (1997): 150–156; Thomas Janoski, Mark Musick, and John Wilson, "Being Volunteered? The Impact of Social Participation and Pro-Social Attitudes on Volunteering," *Sociological Forum* 13 (September 1998): 495–519; Alan Melchior and Larry Orr, *Evaluation of National and Community Service Programs, Overview: National Evaluation of Serve-America (Subtitle B1)* (Washington, D.C.: Corporation for National Service, October 20, 1995); Alexander W. Astin and Linda J. Sax, "How Undergraduates Are Affected by Service Participation," *Journal of College Student Development* 39, no.3 (May/June 1998): 251–263; Dwight E. Giles Jr. and Janet Eyler, "The Impact of a College Community Service Laboratory on Students' Personal, Social, and Cognitive Outcomes," *Journal of Adolescence* 17 (1994): 327–339; Richard G. Niemi, Mary Hepburn, and Chris Chapman, "Community Service by High School Students: A Cure for Civic Ills?" *Political Behavior* (forthcoming, 2000) and the works cited there. "Service learning" refers to community service that is coupled to classwork, and most observers believe that it is more effective in inculcating civic habits. In 1999 about 57 percent of U.S. students in grades 6–12 participated in some form of community service, up from 49 percent in 1996; on the other hand, only slightly more than half of them (30 percent of all students) engaged in service learning. See "Youth Service-Learning and Community Service among 6th-through 12th-Grade Students in the United States, 1996 and 1999" (Washington, D.C.: National Center for Education Statistics, 1999).

4. James Youniss, Jeffrey A. McLellan, and Miranda Yates, "What We Know about Engendering Civic Identity," *American Behavioral Scientist* (March/April 1997): 620–631; Elizabeth Smith, "Extracurricular Activities and Political Participation: Exploring the Connection," paper presented at 1998 Midwestern Political Science Association, unpublished ms., 1998: Michael Hanks, "Youth, Voluntary Associations, and Political Socialization," *Social Forces* 60 (1981): 211–223; Verba, Schlozman, and Brady, *Voice and Equality,* 423–442, 449, 452; Paul Allen Beck and M. Kent Jennings. "Pathways to Participation," *American Political Science Review* 76 (1982): 94–108; David Ziblatt, "High School Extracurricular Activities and Political Socialization," *Annals of the American Academy of Political and Social Science* 361 (1965): 20–31; John Wilson and Thomas Janoski, "Contribution of Religion to Volunteer Work," *Sociology of Religion* 56 (1995): 137–152; Nicholas Zill, Christin Winquist Nord, and Laura Spencer

Loomis, "Adolescent Time Use, Risky Behavior, and Outcomes: An Analysis of National Data" (at http://aspe.os.dhhs.gov/hsp/cyp/xstimuse.htm).

5. Sandra E. Black and Lisa M. Lynch, "How to Compete: The Impact of Workplace Practices and Information Technology on Productivity" (Cambridge, Mass.: National Bureau of Economic Research working paper Series #6120, August 1997); *Report on the American Workforce* 1999, 103. More generally on issues of work, family, and community, see the publications of the Families and Work Institute at www.familiesandwork.org/.

6. One group experimenting in this area is Working Today (www. workingtoday.org).

7. For a reasoned discussion of alternatives for reducing sprawl, see Richard Moe and Carter Wilkie, *Changing Places: Rebuilding Community in the Age of Sprawl* (New York: Henry Holt, 1997).

8. For an overview, see William Fulton, *New Urbanism: Hope or Hype for American Communities?* (Cambridge, Mass.: Lincoln Institute of Land Policy, 1996). The Congress for the New Urbanism (www.cnu.org) forged a charter to which builders, architects, planners, government officials, and others subscribe.

9. For nuanced first-person impressions of Celebration, see Douglas Frantz and Catherine Collins, *Celebration, U.S.A.: Living in Disney's Brave New Town* (New York: Henry Holt, 1999), and Andrew Ross, *The Celebration Chronicles: Life, Liberty and the Pursuit of Property Value in Disney's New Town* (New York: Ballantine Books, 1999).

10. John L. McKnight and John P. Kretzmann, *Building Communities from the Inside Out: A Path Toward Finding and Mobilizing a Community's Assets* (Chicago, Ill.: ACTA Publications, 1993); Harry C. Boyte and Nancy N. Kari, *Building America: The Democratic Promise of Public Work* (Philadelphia: Temple University Press, 1996). The Texas Industrial Areas Foundation, led by Ernesto Cortes, has pioneered many effective community organizing techniques; for a useful overview, see Mark Russell Warren, *Social Capital and Community Empowerment: Religion and Political Organization in the Texas Industrial Areas Foundation* (Ph.D. diss., Harvard University Department of Sociology, 1995). On CDCs and social capital, see *Urban Problems and Community Development,* Ferguson and Dickens, eds., and Xavier de Souza Briggs and Elizabeth Mueller, *From Neighborhood to Community: Evidence on the Social Effects of Community Development* (New York: Community Development Research Center, New School for Social Research, 1997).

11. William G. McLoughlin, *Revivals, Awakenings, and Reform;* Marshall William Fishwick, *Great Awakenings: Popular Religion and Popular Culture* (New York: Haworth Press, 1995); Anne Boylan, *Sunday School: The Formation of an American Institution, 1790–1880* (New Haven, Conn.: Yale University Press, 1988); Boyer, *Urban Masses and Moral Order,* 34–53.

12. Diane Winston, *Red-Hot and Righteous: The Urban Religion of the Salvation Army* (Cambridge, Mass.: Harvard University Press, 1999).

13. In 1995 a number of evangelicals, spearheaded by Jim Wallis of Sojourners, formed an evangelical coalition spanning the political spectrum from ultra-liberal to ultra-conservative. See Jim Wallis, *Faith Works* (New York: Random House, 2000). See also Howard Husock, "Bringing Back the Settlement House," *The Public Interest* 109 (Fall 1992): 53–72.

14. Lewis A. Friedland, Jay Rosen, and Lisa Austin, *Civic Journalism: A New Approach to Citizenship* (1994) at www.cpn.org/sections/topics/journalism; Jay Rosen and Paul Taylor, *The New News v. the Old News: Press and Politics in the 1990s* (New York: Twentieth Century Fund Press, 1992); James Fallows, *Breaking the News* (New York: Vintage Books, 1997); Frank Denton and Esther Thorson, "Civic Journalism: Does It Work?" (a Special Report for the Pew Center for Civic Journalism, 1997), available at www.pewcenter.org/doingcj/research/r_doesit.html. For a

thoughtful critique, see Charlotte Grimes, "Whither the Civic Journalism Bandwagon?" Discussion Paper D-36, Joan Shorenstein Center on Press and Politics (John F. Kennedy School of Government, Harvard University: 1999).

15. Keith Hampton and Barry Wellman, "Examining Community in the Digital Neighborhood: Early Results from Canada's Wired Suburb," in *Lecture Notes in Computer Science,* Toru Ishida and Katherine Isbister, eds. (Berlin: Springer-Verlag, 2000); Andrea Kavanaugh, "The Impact of the Internet on Community: A Social Network Analysis" (Blacksburg, Va.: Blacksburg Electronic Village, Virginia Polytechnic Institute and State University, 1999); Andrew S. Patrick, "Personal and Social Impacts of Going On-Line: Lessons from the National Capital FreeNet" (Ottawa, Canada: Communications Research Center, 1997), at http://debra.dgbt.doc.ca/services-research/survey/impacts. Caution is appropriate in assessing these early returns, especially given the possibility of self-selection. More generally, see Douglas Schuler, *New Community Networks: Wired for Change* (New York: Addison-Wesley, 1996).

16. For information on some of the projects cited here, see: Liz Lerman Dance Exchange at www.danceexchange.org/lizhome.html; Roadside Theater at www.appalshop.org/rst/99rstabt.htm; Baltimore Museum of Art at www.artbma.org; Galley 37 at www.gallery37.org. See also *Opening the Door to the Entire Community: How Museums Are Using Permanent Collections to Engage Audiences* (New York: Lila Wallace Reader's Digest Fund, November 1998), available at www.wallacefunds.org/lilaframesetpub.htm.

17. On Indianapolis's Front Porch Alliance, see www.indygov.com/mayor/fpa/. On neighborhood government, see Berry, Portney, and Thomson, *The Rebirth of Urban Democracy.*

Exploring Texts and Contexts

For activities with icons, refer to the Guides to Analyzing Contexts for Writing and Analyzing Readings in Context.

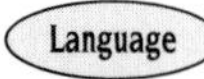

1. Describe the structure of each of the six entries in Putnam's agenda. How does he use the structure to develop his argument? How effective is his strategy?

2. In many ways, the key sphere on the agenda is the first one, aimed at youth. Putnam contends that the habit of participating, if instilled early, will continue to grow. Assess this section from your perspective. How effective do you think his suggestions will be in raising the number of young people who vote and participate in other ways?

3. Putnam writes that his suggestions are not meant to be definitive but rather to inspire his readers' imaginations to come up with other ideas. What effects has Putnam's writing had on you? Has he inspired you to envision new forms of participation? What are they? Or do you disagree with his analysis of American society? Why?

Creating Texts

For activities with icons, refer to the Guides to Analyzing Contexts for Writing and Analyzing Readings in Context. For additional help with these writing projects, read the descriptions of **Feature Story, Brochure,** and **Essay** in the Genre Glossary.

1. Write a feature article on the topic of civic participation. Use the story of a school or community project to illustrate a point about the value of social connectedness and civic participation. For help choosing a project, you might check out Putnam's "Interactive Portrait of Civic America" at www.bettertogether.org. You may even live in a locale featured on his Website. If you are familiar with one of the projects cited, you may want to use your feature story to develop your own perspective about its impact on your school or community.
2. For the school or community project you discussed in the feature article for the first writing project, design a brochure for prospective volunteers. Consider how you would encourage them to join this kind of participatory activity. How could you use visual material to persuade an audience to read and respond to your brochure? Who is your audience, and how would you distribute the brochure to them?

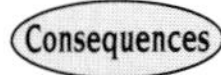

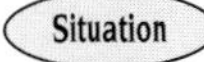

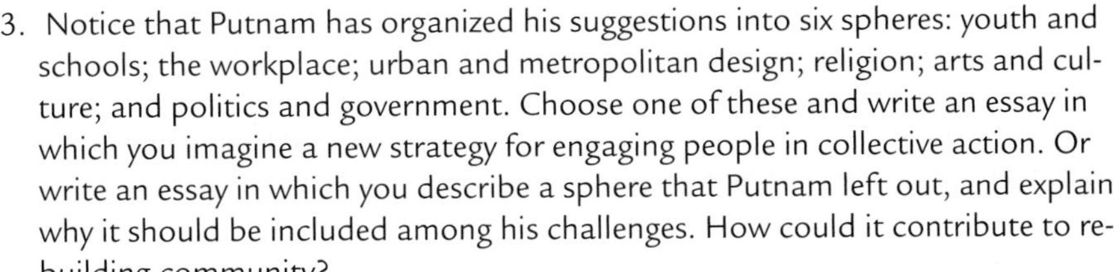

3. Notice that Putnam has organized his suggestions into six spheres: youth and schools; the workplace; urban and metropolitan design; religion; arts and culture; and politics and government. Choose one of these and write an essay in which you imagine a new strategy for engaging people in collective action. Or write an essay in which you describe a sphere that Putnam left out, and explain why it should be included among his challenges. How could it contribute to rebuilding community?

Hate Radio

Why We Need to Tune In to Limbaugh and Stern

Patricia J. Williams

In this article that appeared in *Ms.* magazine, Patricia J. Williams writes about her experiences as an African American woman making her way through her everyday routine: listening to the radio, rushing to an appointment, catching a cab. More and more, the social space she inhabits is becoming hostile and unfriendly. She hears code words like "blafrican" used to insinuate slurs about people of color; she gets out of a cab before her destination to avoid the driver's insulting stare. In an uncivil society, she is a scapegoat for all the problems of society—joblessness, poverty, and unwed mothers. It concerns her that in the wider society, she is not an individual personality but a stand-in for a dangerous and suspect group.

Williams sees a connection between the confrontational style of what she calls hate radio and her lack of a sense of community and well-being. Although the power and influence of Rush Limbaugh and Howard Stern have waned since she first wrote about them in 1995, their brand of divisive, inflammatory rhetoric is a feature of national and local political campaigns, special-interest Web sites, and radio and TV talk shows. It gains its power by appealing to individual self-interest and pitting "us" against "them."

Along the way, the facts get blurred or are misrepresented, and the solution to social problems becomes a matter of targeting a specific group for blame. Although best known for her work on race and the law, Williams has turned her keen intellect to the relationship between the way we talk to each other and our ability to solve our problems.

Williams is a professor of law at Columbia University and the author of *The Alchemy of Race and Rights* and, more recently, *Seeing a Color-Blind Future.* Her column, "Diary of a Mad Lawyer," appears in *The Nation.*

Connecting with the Conversation

1. Do you listen to Rush Limbaugh, Bob Grant, or Howard Stern? What about your friends or family? Why do they say they choose these programs in particular? In your journal, speculate on why these talk show hosts have such a large following.
2. Code words are a kind of shorthand to refer to complex concepts and ideas. For example, in the 1994 election "soccer moms" was used to refer to a group of people who were voting for Bill Clinton and also as a way of capturing the political, social, and economic issues that made him their favorite candidate. What code words have emerged from recent events? Make a brief list of any you can think of, and note whether the usage is positive or negative. In a small group, compare your lists. What conclusions can you draw about the use of code words?

Three years ago I stood at my sink, washing the dishes and listening to the radio. I was tuned to rock and roll so I could avoid thinking about the big news from the day before—George Bush had just nominated Clarence Thomas to replace Thurgood Marshall on the Supreme Court. I was squeezing a dot of lemon Joy into each of the wineglasses when I realized that two smoothly radio-cultured voices, a man's and a woman's, had replaced the music.

"I think it's a stroke of genius on the president's part," said the female voice.

"Yeah," said the male voice. "Then those blacks, those African Americans, those Negroes—hey 'Negro' is good enough for Thurgood Marshall—whatever, they can't make up their minds [what] they want to be called. I'm gonna call them Blafricans. Black Africans. Yeah, I like it. Blafricans. Then they can get all upset because now the president appointed a Blafrican."

"Yeah, well, that's the way those liberals think. It's just crazy."

5 "And then after they turn down his nomination the president can say he tried to please 'em, and then he can appoint someone with some intelligence."

Back then, this conversation seemed so horrendously unusual, so singularly hateful, that I picked up a pencil and wrote it down. I was certain that a firestorm of

From *Ms.*, March/April 1994, pp. 25–29.

protest was going to engulf the station and purge those foul radio mouths with the good clean soap of social outrage.

I am so naive. When I finally turned on the radio and rolled my dial to where everyone else had been tuned while I was busy watching Cosby reruns, it took me a while to understand that there's a firestorm all right, but not of protest. In the two and a half years since Thomas has assumed his post on the Supreme Court, the underlying assumptions of the conversation I heard as uniquely outrageous have become commonplace, popularly expressed, and louder in volume. I hear the style of that snide polemicism everywhere, among acquaintances, on the street, on television in toned-down versions. It is a crude demagoguery that makes me heartsick. I feel more and more surrounded by that point of view, the assumptions of being without intelligence, the coded epithets, the "Blafrican"-like stand-ins for "nigger," the mocking angry glee, the endless tirades filled with nonspecific, nonempirically based slurs against "these people" or "those minorities" or "feminazis" or "liberals" or "scumbags" or "pansies" or "jerks" or "sleazeballs" or "loonies" or "animals" or "foreigners."

At the same time I am not so naive as to suppose that this is something new. In clear-headed moments I realize I am not listening to the radio anymore, I am listening to a large segment of white America think aloud in ever louder resurgent thoughts that have generations of historical precedent. It's as though the radio has split open like an egg, Morton Downey, Jr.'s clones and Joe McCarthy's ghost spilling out, broken yolks, a great collective of sometimes clever, sometimes small, but uniformly threatened brains—they have all come gushing out. Just as they were about to pass into oblivion, Jack Benny and his humble black sidekick Rochester get resurrected in the ungainly bodies of Howard Stern and his faithful black henchwoman, Robin Quivers. The culture of Amos and Andy has been revived and reassembled in Bob Grant's radio minstrelry and radio newcomer Daryl Gates's sanctimonious imprecations on behalf of decent white people. And in striking imitation of Jesse Helms's nearly forgotten days as a radio host, the far Right has found its undisputed king in the personage of Rush Limbaugh—a polished demagogue with a weekly radio audience of at least 20 million, a television show that vies for ratings with the likes of Jay Leno, a newsletter with a circulation of 380,000, and two best-selling books whose combined sales are closing in on six million copies.

From Churchill to Hitler to the old Soviet Union, it's clear that radio and television have the power to change the course of history, to proselytize, and to coalesce not merely the good and the noble, but the very worst in human nature as well. Likewise, when Orson Welles made his famous radio broadcast "witnessing" the landing of a spaceship full of hostile Martians, the United States ought to have learned a lesson about the power of radio to appeal to mass instincts and incite mass hysteria. Radio remains a peculiarly powerful medium even today, its visual emptiness in a world of six trillion flashing images allowing one of the few remaining playgrounds for the aural subconscious. Perhaps its power is attributable to our need for an oral tradition after all, some conveying of stories, feelings, myths of ancestors, epics of alienation, and the need to rejoin ancestral roots, even ignorant bigoted roots. Perhaps the visual quiescence of radio is related to the popularity of E-mail or electronic networking. Only the voice is made manifest, unmasking worlds that cannot—or dare not?—be seen. Just yet. Nostalgia crystallizing into a dangerous future. The preconscious voice erupting into the expressed, the prime time.

10 What comes out of the modern radio mouth could be the *Iliad,* the *Rubaiyat,* the griot's song of our times. If indeed radio is a vessel for the American "Song of Songs," then what does it mean that a manic, adolescent Howard Stern is so popular among radio listeners, that Rush Limbaugh's wittily smooth sadism has gone the way of prime-time television, and that both vie for the number one slot on all the best-selling book lists? What to make of the stories being told by our modern radio evangelists and their tragic unloved chorus of callers? Is it really just a collapsing economy that spawns this drama of grown people sitting around scaring themselves to death with fantasies of black feminist Mexican able-bodied gay soldiers earning $100,000 a year on welfare who are so criminally depraved that Hillary Clinton or the Antichrist-of-the-moment had no choice but to invite them onto the government payroll so they can run the country? The panicky exaggeration reminds me of a child's fear. . . . *And then, and then, a huge lion jumped out of the shadows and was about to gobble me up, and I can't ever sleep again for a whole week.*

As I spin the dial on my radio, I can't help thinking that this stuff must be related to that most poignant of fiber-optic phenomena, phone sex. Aural Sex. Radio Racism with a touch of S & M. High-priest hosts with the power and run-amok ego to discipline listeners, to smack with the verbal back of the hand, to smash the button that shuts you up once and for all. "Idiot!" shouts New York City radio demagogue Bob Grant and then the sound of droning telephone emptiness, the voice of dissent dumped out some trapdoor in aural space.

As I listened to a range of such programs what struck me as the most unifying theme was not merely the specific intolerance on such hot topics as race and gender but a much more general contempt for the world, a verbal stoning of anything different. It is like some unusually violent game of "Simon Says," this mockery and shouting down of callers, this roar of incantations, the insistence on agreement.

But, ah, if you *will* but only agree, what sweet and safe reward, what soft enfolding by a stern and angry radio god. And as an added bonus, the invisible shield of an AM community, a family of fans who are Exactly Like You, to whom you can express, in anonymity, all the filthy stuff you imagine "them" doing to you. The comfort and relief of being able to ejaculate, to those who understand, about the dark imagined excess overtaking, robbing, needing to be held down and taught a good lesson, needing to put it in its place before the ravenous demon enervates all that is true and good and pure in this life.

The audience for this genre of radio flagellation is mostly young, white, and male. Two thirds of Rush Limbaugh's audience is male. According to *Time* magazine, 75 percent of Howard Stern's listeners are white men. Most of the callers have spent their lives walling themselves off from any real experience with blacks, feminists, lesbians, or gays. In this regard, it is probably true, as former Secretary of Education William Bennett says, that Rush Limbaugh "tells his audience that what you believe inside, you can talk about in the marketplace." Unfortunately, what's "inside" is then mistaken for what's outside, treated as empirical and political reality. The *National Review* extols Limbaugh's conservative leadership as no less than that of Ronald Reagan, and the Republican party provides Limbaugh with books to discuss, stories, angles, and public support. "People were afraid of censure by gay activists, feminists, environmentalists—now they are not because Rush takes them on," says Bennett.

15 U.S. history has been marked by cycles in which brands of this or that hatred come into fashion and go out, are unleashed and then restrained. If racism, homophobia, jingoism, and woman-hating have been features of national life in pretty much all of modern history, it rather begs the question to spend a lot of time wondering if right-wing radio is a symptom or a cause. For at least 400 years, prevailing attitudes in the West have considered African Americans less intelligent. Recent statistics show that 53 percent of people in the U.S. agree that blacks and Latinos are less intelligent than whites, and a majority believe that blacks are lazy, violent, welfare-dependent, and unpatriotic.

I think that what has made life more or less tolerable for "out" groups have been those moments in history when those "inside" feelings were relatively restrained. In fact, if I could believe that right-wing radio were only about idiosyncratic, singular, rough-hewn individuals thinking those inside thoughts, I'd be much more inclined to agree with Columbia University media expert Everette Dennis, who says that Stern's and Limbaugh's popularity represents the "triumph of the individual" or with *Time* magazine's bottom line that "the fact that either is seriously considered a threat . . . is more worrisome than Stern or Limbaugh will ever be." If what I were hearing had even a tad more to do with real oppressions, with real white *and* black levels of joblessness and homelessness, or with the real problems of real white men, then I wouldn't have bothered to slog my way through hours of Howard Stern's miserable obsessions.

Yet at the heart of my anxiety is the worry that Stern, Limbaugh, Grant, et al. represent the very antithesis of individualism's triumph. As the *National Review* said of Limbaugh's ascent, "It was a feat not only of the loudest voice but also of a keen political brain to round up, as Rush did, the media herd and drive them into the conservative corral." When asked about his political aspirations, Bob Grant gloated to the *Washington Post,* "I think I would make rather a good dictator."

The polemics of right-wing radio are putting nothing less than hate onto the airwaves, into the marketplace, electing it to office, teaching it in schools, and exalting it as freedom. What worries me is the increasing-to-constant commerce of retribution, control, and lashing out, fed not by fact but fantasy. What worries me is the reemergence, more powerfully than at any time since the institution of Jim Crow, of a sociocentered self that excludes "the likes of," well, me for example, from the civic circle, and that would rob me of my worth and claim and identity as a citizen. As the *Economist* rightly observes, "Mr. Limbaugh takes a mass market—white, mainly male, middle-class, ordinary America—and talks to it as an endangered minority."

I worry about this identity whose external reference is a set of beliefs, ethics, and practices that excludes, restricts, and acts in the world on me, or mine, as the perceived if not real enemy. I am acutely aware of losing *my* mythic individualism to the surface shapes of my mythic group fearsomeness as black, as female, as left wing. "I" merge not fluidly but irretrievably into a category of "them." I become a suspect self, a moving target of loathsome properties, not merely different but dangerous. And that worries me a lot.

20 What happens in my life with all this translated license, this permission to be uncivil? What happens to the social space that was supposedly at the sweet mountaintop of the civil rights movement's trail? Can I get a seat on the bus without having to be reminded that I *should* be standing? Did the civil rights movement guarantee us nothing

more than to use public accommodations while surrounded by raving lunatic bigots? "They didn't beat this idiot [Rodney King] enough," says Howard Stern.

Not long ago I had the misfortune to hail a taxicab in which the driver was listening to Howard Stern undress some woman. After some blocks, I had to get out. I was, frankly, afraid to ask the driver to turn it off—not because I was afraid of "censoring" him, which seems to be the only thing people will talk about anymore, but because the driver was stripping me too, as he leered through the rearview mirror. "Something the matter?" he demanded, as I asked him to pull over and let me out well short of my destination. (I'll spare you the full story of what happened from there—trying to get another cab, as the cabbies stopped for all the white businessmen who so much as scratched their heads near the curb; a nice young white man, seeing my plight, giving me his cab, having to thank him, he hero, me saved-but-humiliated, cabdriver pissed and surly. I fight my way to my destination, finally arriving in bad mood, militant black woman, cranky feminazi.)

When Yeltsin blared rock music at his opponents holed up in the parliament building in Moscow, in imitation of the U.S. Marines trying to torture Manuel Noriega in Panama, all I could think of was that it must be like being trapped in a crowded subway car when all the portable stereos are tuned to Bob Grant or Howard Stern. With Howard Stern's voice a tinny, screeching backdrop, with all the faces growing dreamily mean as though some soporifically evil hallucinogen were gushing into their bloodstreams, I'd start begging to surrender.

Surrender to what? Surrender to the laissez-faire resegregation that is the metaphoric significance of the hundreds of "Rush rooms" that have cropped up in restaurants around the country; rooms broadcasting Limbaugh's words, rooms for your listening pleasure, rooms where bigots can capture the purity of a Rush-only lunch counter, rooms where all those unpleasant others just "choose" not to eat? Surrender to the naughty luxury of a room in which a Ku Klux Klan meeting could take place in orderly, First Amendment fashion? Everyone's "free" to come in (and a few of you outsiders do), but mostly the undesirable nonconformists are gently repulsed away. It's a high-tech world of enhanced choice. Whites choose mostly to sit in the Rush room. Feminists, blacks, lesbians, and gays "choose" to sit elsewhere. No need to buy black votes, you just pay them not to vote; no need to insist on white-only schools, you just sell the desirability of black-only schools. Just sit back and watch it work, like those invisible shock shields that keep dogs cowering in their own backyards.

How real is the driving perception behind all the Sturm und Drang of this genre of radio-harangue—the perception that white men are an oppressed minority, with no power and no opportunity in the land that they made great? While it is true that power and opportunity are shrinking for all but the very wealthy in this country (and would that Limbaugh would take that issue on), the fact remains that white men are still this country's most privileged citizens and market actors. To give just a small example, according to the *Wall Street Journal,* blacks were the only racial group to suffer a net job loss during the 1990–91 economic downturn at the companies reporting to the Equal Employment Opportunity Commission. Whites, Latinos, and Asians, meanwhile, gained thousands of jobs. While whites gained 71,144 jobs at these companies, Latinos gained 60,040, Asians gained 55,104, and blacks lost 59,479. If every black were hired in the United States tomorrow, the numbers would not be sufficient to account for white men's expanding balloon of fear that they have been specifically dispossessed by African Americans.

25 Given deep patterns of social segregation and general ignorance of history, particularly racial history, media remain the principal source of most Americans' knowledge of each other. Media can provoke violence or induce passivity. In San Francisco, for example, a radio show on KMEL called "Street Soldiers" has taken this power as a responsibility with great consequence: "Unquestionably," writes Ken Auletta in the *New Yorker,* "the show has helped avert violence. When a Samoan teenager was slain, apparently by Filipino gang members, in a drive-by shooting, the phones lit up with calls from Samoans wanting to tell [the hosts] they would not rest until they had exacted revenge. Threats filled the air for a couple of weeks. Then the dead Samoan's father called in, and, in a poignant exchange, the father said he couldn't tolerate the thought of more young men senselessly slaughtered. There would be no retaliation, he vowed. And there was none." In contrast, we must wonder at the phenomenon of the very powerful leadership of the Republican party, from Ronald Reagan to Robert Dole to William Bennett, giving advice, counsel, and friendship to Rush Limbaugh's passionate divisiveness.

The outright denial of the material crisis at every level of U.S. society, most urgently in black inner-city neighborhoods but facing us all, is a kind of political circus, dissembling as it feeds the frustrations of the moment. We as a nation can no longer afford to deal with such crises by *imagining* an excess of bodies, of babies, of job-stealers, of welfare mothers, of overreaching immigrants, of too-powerful (Jewish, in whispers) liberal Hollywood, of lesbians and gays, of gang members ("gangsters" remain white, and no matter what the atrocity, less vilified than "gang members," who are black), of Arab terrorists, and uppity women. The reality of our social poverty far exceeds these scapegoats. This right-wing backlash resembles, in form if not substance, phenomena like anti-Semitism in Poland: there aren't but a handful of Jews left in that whole country, but the giant balloon of heated anti-Semitism flourishes apace, Jews blamed for the world's evils.

The overwhelming response to right-wing excesses in the United States has been to seek an odd sort of comfort in the fact that the First Amendment is working so well that you can't suppress this sort of thing. Look what's happened in Eastern Europe. Granted. So let's not talk about censorship or the First Amendment for the next ten minutes. But in Western Europe, where fascism is rising at an appalling rate, suppression is hardly the problem. In Eastern and Western Europe as well as the United States, we must begin to think just a little bit about the fiercely coalescing power of media to spark mistrust, to fan it into forest fires of fear and revenge. We must begin to think about the levels of national and social complacence in the face of such resolute ignorance. We must ask ourselves what the expected result is, not of censorship or suppression, but of so much encouragement, so much support, so much investment in the fashionability of hate. What future is it that we are designing with the devotion of such tremendous resources to the disgraceful propaganda of bigotry?

Exploring Texts and Contexts

For activities with icons, refer to the Guide to Analyzing Readings in Context.

1. Now that you have read Williams's article, try to answer her implied question: "Why do we need to tune in to Limbaugh and Stern?" What does she say are the consequences of ignoring these talk show hosts?

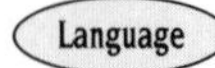

2. Williams's article critiques the polemics of right-wing radio and its argumentative style. Search through her article for all the words that she uses to describe this kind of language. Based on your review, compose a definition for this style of argument.
3. According to Williams we can no longer afford to deal with our social poverty by using scapegoats, that is, by blaming our problems on "welfare mothers" or "overreaching immigrants." What does she mean by this? What does she feel will be the social consequences? Point to specific ideas in her writing that help you understand her position.

Creating Texts

For activities with icons, refer to the Guides to Analyzing Contexts for Writing and Analzing Readings in Context. For additional help with these writing projects, read the descriptions of **Dialogue/Symposium** and **Comics** in the Genre Glossary.

1. Williams is just one of the writers in this unit concerned about the state of American public life. Robert Putnam, Harry Boyte, and Nancy Kari also voice concerns about the disintegration of civil society. Putnam associates the problems with weakening community bonds; Boyte and Kari want to resurrect the idea of the commonwealth. Conduct a symposium on the state of American public life. Invite Williams, Putnam, Boyte and Kari, and one other writer from this unit to participate. How does each of these writers assess public life? What does each writer identify as the problem or problems? What solution does each offer? According to each, what is the outlook for the future of American civil life?
2. Comics, in particular the political cartoons found in the editorial section of the paper, are a particularly useful medium to characterize the way we talk to each other in highly politicized or charged situations. Sketch an interaction between identifiable characters that uses humor to capture a particular moment in the communication process.

Symposium on Minority Journalists and the Media

Ray Suarez, Ellis Cose, Joie Chen, George de Lama, and Mark Trahant

Among the ancient Greeks, a symposium was a lively party fueled by drink, talk, and intellectual entertainment. Today's symposia keep the conversation but not the drink; their purpose is to get a group of people together to talk about a particular topic, as in this symposium on minority journalists and the media. This symposium focuses on the role of minority journalists in providing balanced coverage and diverse perspectives in the media. It aired on "Talk of the Nation," a popular call-in radio show produced by National Public Radio (NPR) and hosted by Ray Suarez for many years.

A national meeting of minority journalists, Unity '99, allowed Suarez to bring his professional interests as a journalist of color to his own radio call-in show. Suarez aired the symposium from Unity '99, at which journalists met from four organizations: the Asian American Journalists Association, the National Association of Hispanic Journalists, the National Association of Black Journalists, and the Native American Journalist Association. These organizations have recently emerged to offer support for media professionals who find themselves either the only person or one of a very few people of color in a news organization. For example, in 1978 newspapers had fewer than 4 percent people of color on their staff, but now have about 12 percent. Still, as many as 40 percent of newsrooms have no people of color.

Throughout the transcript of this live radio symposium, we can follow the participants as they respond to each other and answer questions from callers. The question posed initially by Suarez gets to the heart of civic participation: How does our shifting sense of self—say, from African American to managing editor—influence the way we do our job and the way we represent the news to our audience? As you read the transcript of the symposium, notice how the respondents bring their own experiences and perspectives to the table.

Connecting with the Conversation

1. Listen to a radio or television symposium; check the listings for C-SPAN or your local National Public Radio station. Take notes on the questions asked by the audience and how the symposium participants respond. How would you characterize the interaction between the symposium participants and the audience? In your opinion, was the topic explored fully? If not, why not? Write up your responses to these questions, and bring your notes to class.
2. For the next few days as you watch television, listen to the radio, or read the newspaper make note of minority journalists and the sorts of stories they cover. Bring your notes to class for a discussion of whether minority journalists contribute a particular perspective.

RAY SUAREZ, *host:* This is TALK OF THE NATION. I'm Ray Suarez.

We're coming to you this hour from the Seattle Convention Center where the largest-ever meeting of American journalists is under way, Unity '99. It's a meeting of the big four national minority journalists organizations, held for the first time in five years. We're back together and still arguing with our business about some of the same fundamental questions we faced back in Atlanta in 1994.

So what are we saying to the American news business? That we're as good as anyone else, but different? That we can cover our own communities better than anyone else, but cover any other community as well as anyone else? Are we somehow signaling to the people who hire that we are ethnically, personally, culturally authentic and imposing on ourselves a requirement that our newsroom colleagues have no need to bother with? And as our business becomes increasingly middle-class, increasingly well-educated, professionally secure, does this obligation to authenticity involve a kind of subterfuge that we, white-collar and increasingly mainstream, can explain a complex American experience that is, in fact, increasingly remote from our own lives, to a largely white audience? Are we trying to straddle a double life, neither one thing or the other?

Authenticity, ethnic presentation and the life of the newsroom this hour on the program. All my guests are with me here at Unity '99 in Seattle. Ellis Cose is a columnist and contributing editor for *Newsweek* and the author of "Colorblind: Seeing Beyond Race in a Race-Obsessed World." Welcome to the program.

Mr. ELLIS COSE (*Newsweek*): Thank you, Ray. Glad to be here.

5 SUAREZ: Joie Chen is an anchor and correspondent for "The World Today" at CNN. Welcome.

Ms. JOIE CHEN (CNN): Thank you, Ray.

SUAREZ: George de Lama is associate managing editor for foreign and national news at the *Chicago Tribune.* Good to have you with us.

Mr. GEORGE de LAMA (*Chicago Tribune*): Thank you, Ray.

SUAREZ: And Mark Trahant is a columnist for *The Seattle Times.*

10 Mr. MARK TRAHANT: Thank you, Ray.

SUAREZ: As always, we'll take your calls from around the country, and we'll also hear from our Unity '99 conventioneers here in the studio audience.

Ellis Cose, I wanted to start with you, since the half a million or so of our close, personal friends that are listening in other places and aren't going to be here won't make it for your panel "Is It Race or Is It Me?" What are you going to tell people who are looking for an answer to that question?

Mr. COSE: Well, I think basically—and this goes to the first point—or the first question you were asking, Ray: What are we trying to say to people? What are we trying to say to the editors? I think what we're trying to say to editors and publishers is that we are all part of the American family, that the various communities that we come from are part of either their readership or their audience, which they ought to be concerned about.

I think, though, that we as organizations—and I don't speak for an organization, but we as members of organizations—have too often focused too much on just num-

---

From "Talk of the Nation," July 8, 1999, National Public Radio.

bers, and we've had the sort of assumption that if you hire enough of us, everything's going to somehow work out and be better. And I think that's just not enough. It's just not far enough. And it really comes from the historical reasons why this movement started. I mean, it actually started because of the riots in the '60s and the Kerner Commission, which said, in effect, 'Hey, we had no clue of what was going to be happening to our country. We need some people who do.' And if we look at who populates newspapers and television stations, there are virtually no blacks, firstly, no people of color. That has to change, and it has changed, to some extent. But the next step is, OK, once it begins to change, what does all this change mean?

15 SUAREZ: I wonder if there's a trap, though, waiting in that assumption. You mentioned the pitfalls of saying, 'If you hire enough of us, things will take care of themselves.' But America, for all its remaining problems, is still a very different place for—let's take the example for black Americans—than it was in 1966. And when we say that there has to be some presence in the newsroom, and indeed, a lot of major American news organizations hired their first black editorial staff after those riots. . . .

Mr. COSE: Right.

SUAREZ: Are we presenting a uniform self to the news business as Exhibit A, in the same way that we would have in 1966? Do you have to be a representative of black culture, a representative of black America, when all you want to do is be a metro editor or a photog or just a working stiff?

Mr. COSE: Well, I mean, certainly it's a key question. And I think if we're smart, the answer to that is no, we don't say that we represent anybody but ourselves. But I think that we also recognize that, in representing ourselves, we represent all kinds of things. And let me just use a brief example. Several years ago, when I was first starting in the business, I went to *Esquire* magazine to try to get an assignment there as a free-lance writer. And I remember having this bizarre conversation with a senior editor there who looked at me sort of incredulously, at one point, and said to me, 'Well, Ellis, you know, I'm not sure how many black readers we have. I'm not sure we need someone like you writing for us.' And I, of course, was extremely angry and a bit baffled and confused because, clearly, what he was saying was that he could only see me as someone who would address a black audience.

But the larger point, you know, is that we come to this business, we as people, with all kinds of baggage and with all kinds of experiences. And it would be naive to assume that some of those experiences aren't rooted in the different treatment that we've had as different ethnic groups and as different racial groups. So inevitably, we're going to bring something different to a newsroom than someone who hasn't had those experiences. We also, as a profession, are in the knowledge business, which means that we're in the business of trying to find out as much about as many things, as many people, as many cultures, as we can. And to the extent that we increase the number of people who represent something different, whatever that difference is, we're a bit ahead. But I think you're absolutely right; no, I mean, we shouldn't be in the trap of saying, you know, 'I represent this group' or 'Someone else represents the other group.' In the final analysis, I just represent me.

SUAREZ: But, Joie Chen, the physical presence that television provides sort of forces being a symbol on some people, whether they signed up for the symbol business or not. The camera does not blink, and there you are.

20 Ms. CHEN: I think that those of us who are minorities and journalists can test that question constantly in our own lives. When I walk into a room, am I a journalist

first? Am I Asian first? When I come into the room in a professional capacity, I think I'm certainly a reporter before I'm an Asian, but I don't think you could fail to notice what I look like. I think that these questions are always going to be with you, in a way.

Recently, for example, in the Chinese Embassy bombing in Belgrade, I had someone who's actually very close to me in the newsroom say, 'Well, I saw your reporting. Were you angry about the Chinese Embassy being bombed?' And I thought, 'Was I angry about the Chinese Embassy being bombed?' Well, yeah, I mean, I do think, certainly, that it was a bad thing to accidentally bomb an embassy. Was I particularly, personally angry because I'm half ethnically Chinese? No. But apparently, there was some perception, some misperception, some understanding that perhaps I was receiving it in a way differently than a white colleague or a black colleague would.

SUAREZ: So for the record, you would have been upset if it was the Latvian Embassy that . . .

Ms. CHEN: Sure. Well, I mean, I think from a political standpoint it was a particularly bad idea for that mistake to be made. But, you know, was I personally more offended by this? No, of course not.

SUAREZ: George, the American Society of Newspaper Editors has recently and famously had to back away from a commitment it made to newsroom diversity, and has had to take a lot of heat for that. And while you might admire the honesty that comes with saying, 'Hey, we're not going to make it. Let's figure out what we can do and by when we can do it,' it is still seen as a large disappointment that it didn't happen. And you're sort of in this funny inside-outside position.

Mr. de LAMA: Well, I think justifiably so that there was a lot of heat. That's—you know, I personally was very disappointed. I think that's not good enough. I'll tell you, as an editor, one of the phrases I hate the most is, particularly when we're recruiting for a senior-level position, the phrase, 'Well, there aren't many minority candidates out there' or 'There aren't any,' I hear sometimes. And excuse me; sure, there are. You just need to know where to look. You know, this place right here in these few days is a good example. There's a lot of talent here. But I think they're well-meaning people in most of the—certainly the larger newspapers, and they mean well and the intentions are good. I personally have to admit I get very frustrated sometimes.

SUAREZ: Is the *Tribune* a different product because its staff is a different animal than it was 20 years ago? There wouldn't have been a George de Lama, a Cuban guy, being an associate managing editor 20 years ago.

Mr. de LAMA: No. As a matter of fact, I think last Saturday made 21 years for me there, and I was the second Hispanic reporter in the history of the *Tribune.* This is a 150-year-old organization. We have a couple associate managing editors, Latinos, now, and others of color as well. I like to think we're a much better newspaper in that we have many more people of different backgrounds. I agree with Ellis. We bring different things to the table as individuals. So does somebody who speaks Russian or somebody who's well-traveled or somebody who's an expert in science.

It's funny; we're all the sum of our experiences. We're the products of what we know. The thing about news is that news is what we don't know. And I think when you have more people, it's good common sense to—diversity—the question earlier, is diversity good? It's good common sense. It makes for better journalism. And that, in turn, is good business. And the last one, that's the one that gets the attention of all the nice people who run newspapers and news organizations these days.

SUAREZ: Mark Trahant, the Native American journalists, away from more formal programs like this one, can be heard to complain loudly or privately that they are sometimes the afterthoughts, even at an organizational meeting like this one, where they should be central to our thoughts. And I wonder if that's just—after a while you take that as part of the given of the territory, or whether there is a real expectation that it has to change and some anger that it hasn't quite.

30 Mr. TRAHANT: Sure. I think part of that is a phenomenon of numbers; just the sheer numbers of Native American populations in general is so much smaller that it takes it a while to catch up. I do have a specific example, though, that I was thinking about, building on the previous point on examples of how newsroom coverage could be different and improved. When the hantavirus crisis broke out in the Southwest, I was in management at *The Salt Lake Tribune,*

And two interesting things happened. One, we happen to have Navajo-speaking reporters and correspondents, interestingly enough, one of whom was co-opted by National Public Radio during the process. And the second thing was, in preparing for our coverage, I had decided that I didn't want us to cover funerals, because Navajos felt that was offensive. And to prepare my argument for the news meetings, I went and researched all the coverage of the Legionnaires' disease in Philadelphia, and could find no funeral coverage. I went into the news meeting with all of that material, saying, 'Look, here's how it was covered before.' And it was funny; I didn't even get to present it. Once I said I didn't think we should be at funerals, everyone agreed with me. So I think in a real quiet, effective way, you can change how the business covers these stories.

SUAREZ: Is it less remarkable having you around than it was when you were just starting out?

Mr. TRAHANT: Absolutely. My first mainstream—I went back and forth between tribal newspapers and mainstream papers my whole career, and my first mainstream newspaper was the *Arizona Republic.* And I think the first two years everyone thought I was going to leave. And so anytime something would happen, there would be rumors about that more than what I was doing.

SUAREZ: If you want to join the conversation, our number is (*800*) 989-8255; that's (*800*) 989-TALK.

35 We'll go first to Pasadena, California. Richard, welcome to the program.

RICHARD (*Caller*): Thank you very much. I just wanted to comment on what a racist question you're discussing here: How do journalists of a particular ethnic background influence the news? And, you know, I'm tired of Americans being split up and pitted against each other racially by programs like this and others. And I'd comment to your Asian journalist, Joie Chen, when she's deciding whether to report as an Asian or a journalist, how about being an American? It's really—you know, for myself, I'm getting really tired of it. The—if you look at the programs that are on television, if you would substitute the word 'white' in place of things like 'Miss Black College beauty contest' or 'Hispanic music awards' or 'Ebony Awards'—if you put 'white' in there, everyone would be up in arms.

And then when you get a guy like Clinton doing what he's doing and the black community is supporting him, on the Monica Lewinsky thing—Clinton is the guy that gave us NAFTA, that took the jobs away from a lot—all Americans—minorities, whites, everyone, and everybody keeps supporting him. It's time to get down to the real truth of this thing, that we're all Americans, and let's act like it.

SUAREZ: Well, Richard, I understand the point you're trying to make, but I'm wondering, when in a place where all kinds of people live and live in large numbers, if you were to walk into the newsroom of a large media organization in that metropolitan area and basically see a sea of white faces, should that be taken as a coincidence, unremarkable and not worth being remarked upon? Or is that something that—a question we shouldn't even concern ourselves with?

RICHARD: Well, I don't know where you're looking, but when I turn television on, here in the Los Angeles area, I'd say that 80 percent of the reporters on television are not white. They're other ethnic backgrounds. Connie Chung was here in LA, Tritia Toyota, etc., etc., etc. And so as far as being represented, it appears to me that they have a very high representation, and I have no prejudice. In my business, I deal with the Chinese-Americans, I deal with Korean-Americans, I deal with black Americans; I deal with people of all ethnic backgrounds. And I look at them not as minorities; I look at them as Americans. And that's how I deal with them. And can't we get back to that? Can't we do that?

SUAREZ: Yeah. I—'Can't we do that,' I think, is a better, more rational question than 'Can't we get back to that,' because back then, we didn't do that. So yeah, I. . .

RICHARD: Well, that. . .

SUAREZ: But I take your point.

RICHARD: That isn't necessarily true. When there was full employment in the United States, when the jobs were here in the United States, there was much—there was discrimination. But there was much less problems with the amount of money people were making, fighting over jobs of inequality—of quality, not inequality, but jobs of quality. And everyone got along much better. Now the jobs are gone from the country. No cars are manufactured in the United States. You look at every product you see and it's manufactured in some other country by slave labor. Incidentally, if they want a global economy, let's have a global minimum-wage law. And that's why the races are really fighting against each other, but nobody wants to address that problem.

SUAREZ: Well, I think, Richard. . .

Mr. COSE: Well, I'm not quite sure I understand all the points. I mean, at present, we have the fullest—excuse me—fullest employment economy since the 1960s. So I'm not quite clear what he's trying to say about the employment stats. But I think that what Richard has articulated, you know, is a wonderful and fantastic dream. I think the problem is grappling with the reality. If we, in fact, could all just be Americans, we wouldn't have segregated communities. We wouldn't be even able to talk about a black neighborhood or an Italian-American neighborhood or a Chinatown or any of these things, because they wouldn't exist. There would just be one community where everybody sort of lived among each other. We wouldn't be actually even able to talk about racial groups because everybody would be getting married to one another, and there wouldn't be this whole division that we have here. I think what we're sort of grappling with is, how do you deal with the reality where there are racial distinctions that are made and racial categories that exist and racialized thinking as a consequence of that?

I think that's the issue that we're talking about here, you know, not how can we just sort of close our eyes, forget that these differences exist and pretend that we're all Americans, starting from the fact that we're not sort of all at that same point and that same place.

SUAREZ: Well, Richard's comments gorgeously illustrate what, in more narrow senses, we've been saying to managements and saying to bosses and saying to owners for 40 years. But it's very hard to see it when you look back at a world and say, 'Once it was better. We shouldn't label people,' and that, in fact, a lot of the dragons are already slain. There is no problem.

Mr. COSE: Well, see—well, once, it was better, because the only world that mattered to a lot of people who were in a position to say anything was the white world.

Mr. de LAMA: I want to build on that. I think one of America's unresolved questions—and I think it's critical that we come to a conclusion on it for the next century—is the idea that I would call cultural manifest destiny, or assimilation. Can this country allow and respect cultures to be different in the next generation, and to somehow fuse that as an American value?

50 SUAREZ: So you are optimistic?

Mr. TRAHANT: Yeah. I mean, it's a slow process. I guess I look at it with a very long view. One of the ways I think this conversation started—and I mentioned it in my column today—is that in 1947, a group of all white scholars came together, the Hutchins committee, chaired by Robert Maynard Hutchins, and they talked about the notion that if America couldn't understand its constituent groups—they didn't even call it race—constituent groups, that American democracy would be fragile. And I think that's still true.

Mr. de LAMA: I agree with Ellis very much. I think there's one other point, though, as the—you've been talking about here, Ray, as minorities, increasingly, not just in newsrooms, become more the majority, the mainstream—the demographics say minorities will be the majority in this country—I think it's also incumbent on us to present other images and to erase some of the stereotypes or try to combat some of the stereotypes. For instance, in coverage of poverty, we really, when we write welfare stories, we need to seek out welfare recipients who are not African-American.

I think it's interesting, as President Clinton, in his anti-poverty swing, the White House was very conscious of symbolically having the different faces, ethnically also, and racially, of poverty over the last few days as he's gone around the country. I think by the same token, when we write about black doctors, it shouldn't only be in stories about black middle-class or black professionals. It should be quoting black doctors about osteoporosis. And I—that's something that we've heard a lot from our readers. And I think that's a good point—I mean, from our minority readers.

SUAREZ: But how do you change the habits, though, because even the minority reporters that you have in your newsroom fall into those same habits, going back to the same profs at the local universities to get a quote on science, going back to the same authorities in various fields to get a quote. I mean, we all do that, even though, supposedly, we're supposed to be more conscious about these questions.

55 Ms. CHEN: I think one of the great failures of all of the news media today is that pack mentality, I think, Ray, that you're sort of referring to, that we tend to fall on the same experts, the same voices of whatever community we think we're talking to, you know? I grew up in Chicago and I remember a time when we actually were convinced that Jesse Jackson spoke for all black people in the country, you know, that he was the voice. And if you had an issue that somehow involved African-Americans, then Jesse Jackson was the only voice. But clearly, we know today. And that is—that advancement goes back to what Richard was saying. There—what we have learned—and, I think, ultimately, that is the best of what journalism is. It is about education and what we learn and what we provide as journalists is new information, new things to learn for the communities. I think that's something that we have done, and I think that it is most effectively done when you have a lot of different voices.

It wouldn't matter if we were talking about division that were not by race. Say they were by gender, say they were by understanding of sports or of medicine or of space or whatever. Whatever our expertise is, we bring that to the table. Whatever our understanding, whatever our interests are, we bring that to the table and we broaden understanding by doing that.

SUAREZ: Yes, let's go to the floor.

Mr. HARRISON CHESTING(*ph*): Hi, Ray. My name is Harrison Chesting. I'm with KPOO Radio in San Francisco. And there's going to be a panel tomorrow, called "The Color of Film," talking about the problems people of color, particularly Asians and Latins, are having being represented—and Native Americans—in television and on the movies. And issues concerning African-Americans and other people of color in the movie business often get first reported in the ethnic media and then they get picked up by the mainstream press. In the newsrooms, do you find that there's a dilemma of: 'I know the story's out there, but if myself, as a person of color, if I don't bring it to the editors or write it up or report it myself, it won't get covered.' Or on the flip side, do you have a situation where you, as a person of color, feel, 'I don't want to be the reporter that is constantly reporting on the issues concerning people of color.' And conversely, should newspapers and media outlets do their own research and coverage of issues, rather than depending on the ethnic media to find out about these stories and just more or less rewrite it or rebroadcast it from the ethnic press?

SUAREZ: Great question.

60 Mr. COSE: Want me to take a crack at it?

SUAREZ: Sure.

Mr. COSE: The answer to the second part of it first, I think there's always going to be a function for the ethnic press. I think there's always going to be a function for specialized press. And there are, to some extent, going to be tip sheets for the so-called mainstream media, which are going to look at them and get information from them for things they don't cover as well or as consistently. And I think that function will always exist.

The more interesting question, though, I think, is the one you asked as your first question. And I just want to share, again, a brief anecdote. Several years ago, when I was in Chicago with the *Chicago Sun-Times,* which is where I began my career, for a brief time, I was asked by the editor, then a fellow named Jim Hoge, to head up a team of reporters. I was in charge of a task force of reporters who were charged with covering what—with what he considered the minority community, which meant Asian-Americans, Latinos and blacks in Chicago. And I had a small group of reporters, four reporters, to do this with. And I was given responsibility or at least the charge to do stories about everything in all sections of the paper.

I did that exercise for about six months, and we got a hell of a lot more coverage of all of those communities in the newspaper, in all sections, than we had before that. And yet, at the end of the six months, I found myself going back to Jim Hoge and saying, 'This is a bad idea,' because part of what I found was that the city editor, for instance—and these were in the days talking about Jesse Jackson and Jesse Jackson and Operation Breadbasket, dating myself a bit—you know, and he used to have this Saturday morning meeting every morning. The city editor would come to me and say, 'Well, I'm not gonna staff that, Ellis, because you're sending one of your people, right?' You know, and it became a ghettoization of the news function. What happened was that all of these other editors who otherwise you would have expected to have been responsible for this coverage sort of decided, well, they really didn't have to think about this anymore because this special minority team or team dealing with the minority community was going to think about that.

I mean, I offer that anecdote because I think that it illustrates sort of the paradox that a lot of journalists of color sometimes face and that the question are raised, which is the one, 'Yes, if you do take responsibility, personal responsibility, to make sure things get covered in your community, you probably are going to get a lot more coverage than there would otherwise. The problem with that is that it also encourages other people to think they don't have to do that.' And ideally, what you should do is be able to force other people to accept that as part of their mandate.

SUAREZ: But there, there's the trap that I began the program talking about because if journalists who belong to these organizations say, 'One of the reasons you need us in your newsrooms is because of what we bring,' then we jump salty when the editor says, 'OK, I brought you in here to bring this. Bring it.' That seems like a little bit of bait-and-switch. I sold myself as a certain bill of goods, but now I don't want to be the go-to guy on everything Latino, everything American Indian.

Mr. TRAHANT: You know, and being a columnist, you have a lot of freedom, but one of the things I try to bring to my task is to be an eagle bird, to fly as high as I can and look at the region. And part of that is bringing that experience, but it—also, an understanding of the other experiences and then trying to show how the fabric is working together or not. And that is not really—it's not an either/or. You can do both. You can—I think you learn to change the face of what you're going to cover pretty easily.

SUAREZ: Either of you want to jump in on that?

Mr. de LAMA: Well, I think, Ellis—I had a very similar experience at *The Tribune* covering Latino affairs in Chicago when I was a young reporter, but that said, I remember talking to my editors and I didn't want to be just perceived as that, as almost being professionally minority. And I think it's incumbent on minority reporters, you have to balance that. These communities need to be covered. It helps to have people who understand them, can penetrate them, can provide us with some context and insight. At the same time, you want to balance that and have the same expanded opportunities to grow up to be Carol Simpson or Ray Suarez and to be thought of as a White House correspondent or a foreign correspondent. Those are the same opportunities our colleagues have always had, so it's incumbent on reporters and editors to be able to visualize themselves and visualize your staff in these positions, to be able to project them there and provide those opportunities.

70 Ms. CHEN: And visualize how that helps your organization.

Mr. de LAMA: Absolutely. And you have to go get it because nobody's going to hand it to you, which is probably fair enough.

SUAREZ: Yeah, but how does that square with us saying, 'We have to be there because of what we bring'?

Mr. COSE: Well, I think it squares very simply, Ray. And the answer is, 'Yes, we're there because of what we're bring, but we're also there for many other reasons' and deal with complexity because that's reality.

SUAREZ: We'll go back to the floor. Yes.

75 Ms. ENUPE SINGLA(*ph*): Hi. I'm Enupe Singla. I'm a reporter with Bloomberg News and I'm a member of Asian American Journalists Association as well as the South Asian Journalists Association. And it really struck me that we're here at Unity and the presidents of all four minority organizations this year are women.

And, Joie, I'd just like you to talk about the struggles you possibly went through being a woman of color in journalism, as well as where you see the future for women in the newsroom.

Ms. CHEN: You know, actually, this is going to sound a little backward, but I'm a little bit concerned that the future of television journalism actually becomes too dominated by women. And the reason I feel this way is that I've been in a number of journalism schools recently where the population is about 80 percent female.

And my concern about this is that I suspect that this is becoming something of a girl job in the most pejorative sense, the kind of job that a pretty girl gets for a few years until she finds a wealthy husband and does this. I don't see it as of much of a commitment to journalism as I would like to, as much as I see a number of young women who are committed to being on television. That concerns me greatly.

I think that I will admit that I've come from a generation that probably had great advantage coming as a woman and a minority. I'm in recognition that that is probably the case. Certainly, I had the sense of certain discrimination. I was hired by my first news director in Charleston, South Carolina, and I remember thinking, 'Why would Charleston, South Carolina's, television stations need to have an Asian-American woman on there for their audience? What possible use would I be in their audience?' And I went to interview with him and he said—talked a lot about issues, about the news and a number of skills. And he said to me, 'You know, I was stationed in Korea and you look just like a girl I used to date.' And I recognized then and there that that was the reason I was sitting in the room. I had an advantage. It was not an advantage I particularly wanted to have. But it is the advantage that I had.

80 SUAREZ: And in a burst of self-righteous rage, you told him he could take his job and his station . . .

Ms. CHEN: No, I took the job. I took the job and made the most of it because, let me tell you what, for every disadvantage you get, there may be an advantage in it. And I'm willing to understand that there are trade-offs and some I have taken. And that happened to be one of them.

SUAREZ: Ian writes from Minneapolis, 'With the media becoming increasingly corporate, does the individual journalist or their ethnicity matter anymore? If a newscast wants a mainstream anchor, does it matter if that anchor happens to be black? I see black anchors who are only distinguishable from their peers by their skin color, not their accent, their clothing or the news they read. On the radio, everyone at the Unity meeting sounds white. Is this stealth tactics or have they sold out?' Well, Ian, I don't think you give us much choice there: Is it stealth tactics or have we sold out? I don't know if I want to choose from either of those choices, but fair enough question.

Mr. COSE: Well, let me start with a very idiosyncratic definition of news. News is what an editor finds interesting. And what you find interesting has a lot to do with who you are and where you come from. So even in this age where a few corporations seem to own most of the major communications outlets of the countries, ultimately, a lot of decisions get left up to the personal idiosyncratic proclivities of editors. And those editors—there's no way to automate that, there's no way to put that on any sort of other than individual basis. Certainly, you can allocate a certain number of—certain types of stories that you want more of and certain types you don't. But ultimately, it comes down to people and the individuals making the decisions, even in this corporate age.

I mean, this question of everyone sounding white, I'm not quite sure what sounding white is. So I won't even dare address that.

85 SUAREZ: Well, maybe you should get a tape of this show afterwards. But, Ian, by making his point in that way, I mean, he brings up the question: Can you be an unreconstructed race man? Can you be some sort of—some urban primitive, every bit of what you were and what your family has been and not learn the well-modulated tones and careful accents of the radio performer. There, I said it, performer (*pronounced PAH-former*). Excuse me—performer and hope to have a career? And/or do you submit a certain part of yourself or what you see as yourself to the needs of a wider organization that—and the needs of making a living?

Mr. TRAHANT: I think you pay attention to craft. And if your craft is radio, you learn some simple techniques to help you be better at it. The same if you're a writer, you learn things that pass on ways of telling stories that are better. It's no different than if you're a tremendous storyteller learning what works with a group in front of you.

Ms. CHEN: I think there's a really—to go after what Ian wrote about—I think that there's a really practical side to all this. I live in Atlanta, where all of the evening television newscasts, local evening television newscasts, are anchored by a white man with a black woman, all the way across the board. Now you could argue—it makes a difference, it doesn't make a difference. Well, apparently, it makes a difference (*technical difficulties*) make decisions in those four television stations, the only four television stations in that city. They made the decision that that was going to have the greatest appeal to their audience. And they all made the same decision, so maybe they're basing it on the same research. I don't know. But they've all made the same decision. They're doing it over and over again. And I think that they have the perception that that's the best thing for their business. And maybe it's the most simplistic and awful way to view it, but maybe it's the best business decision and that's how they made it.

SUAREZ: Are any of the four a younger white man paired with an older black woman?

Ms. CHEN: Well, I haven't checked their driver's license for their ages . . .

90 SUAREZ: Ah, come on, Joie.

Ms. CHEN: . . . but, no, I mean, I think that they're actually fairly balanced in age for the most part. I think in one case, the woman may be older than the man. I'm not quite sure. But none of the women are significantly younger than the man.

SUAREZ: Because that's been a very common entry ramp in television, to be Tonto to an aging Lone Ranger. And . . .

Mr. COSE: But I think part of the question in that is how much power do these respective anchors have? I mean, you know, Joie, a lot more about television than I do. But it seems there are some anchors who actually make decisions about what gets on the air, and there are other anchors who are basically faces, who read what they're given. And if you're asking whether it makes a heck of a lot of difference if the person is merely a reader, what complexion they are, it probably makes relatively little, except for the audience, if you ask . . .

Ms. CHEN: Except for the marketing question.

95 Mr. COSE: Except for the marketing question. Yeah, if you're asking something about who determines what is news, it may make a bit more of a difference. But I think it depends upon how much power that anchor has.

Mr. TRAHANT: So many of our judgments about news also are what's in the front of the book or the lead on television. I think part of where both the authenticity and how we make a difference is what's in the back of the book. I think of stuff that gets clipped out and put on refrigerators. And if that's the stuff where we can contribute so young kids can look and see, 'Hey, I'm in this newspaper, too,' that may be far more significant than anything we put on the front page over time.

Mr. de LAMA: I think the bottom line of a lot of what we've been talking about and about diversity in our coverage and so forth is if you just hold up to people images, stories, coverage of themselves and people like themselves, really, you run the risk of just—we're holding up a mirror to people. And that just reinforces preconceptions and existing values, when we're really in the business of when we're at our best of holding up a window to the world to try to bring about a little better understanding. And the world is beyond somebody's self. It's what's out there beyond them. And that's the challenge for us. And all of this diversity, we talk about it as an end, but it's not an end, it's a means also to really do our job better. And the way that people and corporations take that and instill that as a value in the corporations is, bottom line, frankly, if they think that will be better for their businesses. And that's what they'll decide it on.

Ms. CHEN: And underlying everything that we've said here is, I think, what you were saying earlier, Ellis, if the presenters, the front men, are the people of color, but the decision-making isn't, then, no, you really haven't solved any sort of issue at all. You haven't done any sort of service to your viewer or to your reader or anything else. If you're only doing it cosmetically, no, you don't change the picture at all. It really doesn't matter who it is. But I think that's one of the underlying issues of this conference and of the thinking of a number of these organizations: How do you get more people in positions of power who change coverage in not necessarily pro or con ways but diversify it, where diversity does not represent a positive or a negative, just a reality?

SUAREZ: Scott is with us now from New Castle, Indiana. Sorry I made you wait so long, Scott, but thanks for hanging on.

100 SCOTT (*Caller*): That's OK, Ray. It was worth the wait. Yeah, I'd like to address some of the—you answered a question, actually, a rebuttal from a question from the floor, Mr. Ellis answered. I think you did hit the nail right on the head there, Ray. It just seems it's never enough. You know, affirmative action is nothing more than reverse discrimination and it's not a perfect world. It's never going to be a perfect world. And it seems to me some of these people like to just form these organizations for one purpose: to find something to complain about. I think they ought to be grateful for what they have, count their blessings and say, 'Hey, you know, I've made it this far. Hey, this is great.' And let time—let fate take its course. You know, it's just—it's a cry baby country, and I'm just flooded with tears here and I have no sympathy for anyone.

SUAREZ: Well, had we just let nature take its course 20 or 30 years ago, when there was zero hiring of various ethnic minorities in many newsrooms, are you convinced that without groups to advocate for this kind of change, that it would have just (*technical difficulties*) organically?

SCOTT: I—no, I am completely for the diversification that's there. I see diversification everywhere, on all news channels. And I don't understand why there are—what the big deal is. I mean, they want more power. That seems to me—they want to be in control. Hey, I think there are a lot of people of color are CEOs in this country, of color, you know, quite a few, as a matter of fact.

SUAREZ: No, but I'm suggesting to you that one of the ways they got there for you to see them was from the cry baby culture that you were just talking about.

SCOTT: Perhaps. Perhaps it was just somebody finally waking up and saying, 'Hey, these people are equal. They're just as good as we are.' And I think that's where it's at right now. I think they're equal. Everyone is equal. And I think that's where it's at now. And I want it to stay that way, and it just seems to me they want more and more and more and more. And I think they should count their blessings and say, 'Hey, we've done a great job,' and not be so negative.

105 SUAREZ: Fair enough, Scott in New Castle, Indiana, thanks for your call. That's all the time we have for today. I want to thank everyone who called and wrote and spoke to us from the floor, and especially my guests.

Exploring Texts and Contexts

For activities with icons, refer to the Guide to Analyzing Readings in Context.

Genre

1. How is the transcript of a symposium like this one different from an essay? How does the situation in which participants talk to each other and answer questions change the way information is expressed to an audience? Characterize the differences. What are the benefits and difficulties of using a symposium to explore this topic versus using an essay?

Situation

2. During this symposium, Cose makes the following statement:

   > . . . we come to this business, we as people, with all kinds of baggage and with all kinds of experiences. And it would be naïve to assume that some of those experiences aren't rooted in the different treatment that we've had as different ethnic groups and as different racial groups. . . . We also, as a profession, are in the knowledge business, which means that we're in the business of trying to find out as much about as many things, as many people, as many cultures, as we can. (329)

   Perhaps you are in school preparing to join a particular profession or perhaps you are already working and have come back to school. To what extent and in what ways does Cose's statement apply to you? Write an essay in which you explore the relationship between your "baggage" and experiences and your professional orientation.

Creating Texts

For activities with icons, refer to the Guides to Analyzing Contexts for Writing and Analyzing Readings in Context. For additional help with these writing projects, read the description of **Dialogue/Symposium** and **Essay** in the Genre Glossary.

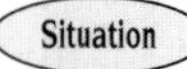

1. As a class, organize a symposium on a topic related to civic participation. Your topic might be, for example, how to get college students more actively engaged in public deliberations about issues that concern them. The class should decide collectively who will be participants—for example, a journalist or talk show host, a politician, a college administrator, a student activist, a couple of typical students, and a moderator. The class should then divide into groups, with each group responsible for researching and discussing what one of the participants would say. Typically in a symposium, after an introduction from the moderator, the participants begin by making a statement of their position, sometimes in response to a specific question from the moderator. Then, with encouragement from the moderator, the participants respond to each other's statements, which ideally should lead them into the spontaneous back-and-forth of a conversation. Ideally, too, at least some of the participants will learn something from some of the others. Each group might want to write a general description of the person it is representing

and that person's views; the person's opening statement; two or three other prepared comments on different aspects of the issue; and ideas for how the person might respond to the other participants. Then each group should choose a member to actually play that person's role, and the symposium can begin. The rest of the class can be the audience, which at some point will be invited to ask questions and make comments.

2. Drawing on the discussion in Connecting with the Conversation 2, write an essay in which you make an argument about whether minority journalists contribute a particular perspective and whether or not they should.

Redefining Disability

THE DISABILITY RAG
& ReSource
September/October 1995
$3.95
a celebration
of disability culture

Situation: Artist Robert Styles used the wheels of his motorized chair to create this image in paint on canvas, titled "Quickie," reproduced on the cover of *The Disability Rag & Resource.* What was your first reaction to this piece of art? How does the title affect your response? How does knowing about the technology used to create this work influence your reaction?

Genre: This image is both a picture of a magazine cover and a reproduction of a painting. In this way it combines two genres. How does the consideration of genre affect your response to the image? Can you think of other images that combine genres?

Language: In addition to using different forms and media, artists often experiment with different techniques to express ideas and communicate with an audience. This image was painted with the wheels of a motorized chair. How does knowing this contribute to its overall effect on you?

Consequences: Why do you think this picture was chosen as a cover for *The Disability Rag & Resource?*

During the February 2000 Superbowl, a commercial for an investment firm featured a computerized image of Christopher Reeve rising from his wheelchair, creating the illusion that the paralyzed actor was walking. Different from the kind of ads that usually air during the annual football game, it was an emotional message about the power of hope, investment in the future, and technology. But because it tapped into a broader conversation about disability, it sparked a debate that kept radio and TV personalities, commentators, politicians, and the rest of us talking for months.

In 1995 Reeve was left paralyzed from the neck down after a fall from his horse during a competition. In the face of an injury that drastically altered his life, he maintains a very public presence. He has spoken out on the need to provide more money for wheelchairs and to make buildings more accessible to the disabled. Although he continues to work hard for the disabled—as well as for a variety of other humanitarian causes such as homelessness, the endangered environment, and public funding for the arts—his goal to walk again by his fiftieth birthday in 2002 has gotten the most media attention.

While no one wants to deny Reeve his dream of walking again or underplay the role of spirit and determination in succeeding, many people, especially members of what has become known as the disability rights movement, believe that the Superbowl ad sent the wrong message. Whether the ad is "a motivating vision" as Reeve has claimed or the propagation of a dangerous myth is at the heart of the controversy. The commercial has been criticized for misrepresenting science's ability to produce miracle cures and cruelly raising the expectations of those long confined to wheelchairs. Others in the disability movement fault the ad because it plays into the myth of the "crippled hero" who is applauded for approximating normalcy. The disability rights movement advocates a sense of identity that does not depend on personal tragedy and triumph.

The debate over Reeve's Superbowl ad is just one recent moment in a national conversation that's been going on for at least twenty years. In the 1970s and 1980s, with the civil rights and women's rights movements as models, people with disabilities and their advocates began to organize to change perceptions about disability and raise public awareness about the need to improve physical access and social services for persons with disabilities. They claimed the right to become full members of society, living independently, working alongside able-bodied people, and participating in determining public policy. Many activists identified language as the key to understanding harmful perceptions about disability. Words such as "cripple" and "deformed" identify disability as a defect needing a cure or a correction and to some extent disregard the identity of the individual. They also argued that defining disability exclusively from a medical perspective focuses on the individual physical impairment while ignoring the role that larger social, economic, and political forces play in determining the quality of life for people with disabilities.

Their efforts sparked discussion in the media, attracted the attention of politicians, and eventually led to debates on the floor of the House and Senate that resulted, in 1990, in the passage of the Americans with Disabilities Act (ADA). The ADA recognized people with disabilities as a minority group, historically discriminated against and deserving the protection of the law. On a practical level, it guaranteed them equal access and opportunities in areas such as housing, transportation, and employment. But perhaps even more important, influenced by the efforts of the disability rights movement to redefine the terms of the discussion, the legislation institutionalized a change in the way we understand disability:

Its language not only mandates the removal of physical and social barriers to persons with disabilities, but it also recognizes that it is these barriers, rather than the individual impairment, that keeps people with disabilities from full participation in civic life.

Thus the discussions instigated by the disability rights movement paved the way for the passage of the ADA, which has dramatically changed the lives of people with disabilities in the United States. But in the twelve years since its passage, the conversation in the disability rights movement has shifted from the immediate practicalities needed to pass legislation back to the larger philosophical questions about the best way to participate in a culturally diverse society. Even as they continue trying to realize the full economic and political power promised by the ADA, individuals in the disability rights movement are questioning the underlying societal values and beliefs that gave rise to the medical model of disability. Newly developing disability studies programs in colleges and universities are playing a role in showing how categories such as normal and abnormal are socially constructed, defined in different ways in different societies and continually redefined within the same society. But these broader conversations, in turn, are helping to shape concrete policy, as the Supreme Court debates the legal threshold for disability status under the ADA.

The public deliberation about disability is a fascinating illustration of how important public issues get discussed, in particular of the interactions between arguments made by "special interest" groups, wide-ranging public discussions of these arguments, and the resulting debates that may take place in legislatures and courthouses. But it's more than just another illustration. Though disability may seem to be an issue that concerns only a few, stories such as Christopher Reeve's remind us that disability concerns all of us. The issue of disability pushes us to consider what it means to live in an inclusively diverse society. Thus deliberating about disability is key to making a diverse democracy work.

The Second Phase: From Disability Rights to Disability Culture

Paul K. Longmore

In "The Second Phase: From Disability Rights to Disability Culture," Paul K. Longmore writes about the disability rights movement in the United States, and in particular, about the relationship between "disability studies" programs that are newly developing within many research universities, disability culture, and disability rights activism. According to Longmore, the first phase of the disability rights movement focused on attaining equal rights. Disability rights activism in many ways set the stage for legislation such as the Americans with Disabilities Act in 1990 that made radical changes in the lives of people with disabilities. The work of the first phase reflects activists' concerns for equal access, opportunity, and inclusion in mainstream society. The second phase will entail the process of self-representation and definition, based on the values and beliefs of people with disabilities and not on the expectations and norms of the nondisabled majority.

A scholar as well as a political activist, Longmore sees a connection between the new phase of the disability rights movement and the emerging discipline of disability studies. In this article adapted from his speech, he explores how the critique and analysis of social problems can support the important work of the disability rights movement. Longmore is a history professor at San Francisco State University. He has written of his own experiences living with disability, in an opinion piece published on *The Electric Edge,* the online edition of *The Ragged Edge.*

Connecting with the Conversation

1. Have you ever heard of *The Disability Rag & Resource?* What connotations does the title suggest? Who might publish in this journal, and what kinds of things do you think they might write about? You can find it at http://www.raggededgemagazine.com/archive/index1.htm. Record your answers in your journal.
2. Have you ever belonged t o a political action group or participated in a project devoted to social change? How do you evaluate your experience? What satisfaction did you get from being part of a collective action? What frustrations did you experience? Discuss your participation with the members of your small group.

The movement of disabled Americans has entered its second phase. The first phase has been a quest for civil rights, for equal access and equal opportunity, for inclusion. The second phase is a quest for collective identity. Even as the unfinished work of the first phase continues, the task in the second phase is to explore or to create a disability culture.

This historic juncture offers a moment for reflection and assessment. It is an opportunity to consider the aims and achievements of the disability movement over the past generation and in the last few years.

In August 1985, *The Disability Rag* reported an incident that captured the essence of the disability movement's first phase:

"'It comes to a point where you can't take it any more,' said Nadine Jacobson, sounding for all the world like Rosa Parks. She and her husband Steven were arrested July 7th for refusing to move from seats in the emergency exit row of a United Airlines flight on which they were to leave Louisville after the National Federation of the Blind convention here. 'You lose some of your self-respect every time you move,' she told *Louisville Times* reporter Beth Wilson. United has a policy of not letting blind people sit in emergency exit rows, because it believes they might slow an evacuation in an emergency, though there seems to be no airline policy against serving sighted passengers in emergency exit rows as many drinks as they want for fear they might become too intoxicated to open an emergency door properly in the event of a disaster. NFB

From *The Disability Rag & Resource,* September/October 1995, pp. 3–11.

members say it's discriminatory treatment, plain and simple. The airline says it is not. The Jacobsons pleaded 'not guilty' to the charge of disorderly conduct."

Six months later, *The Rag* related that the Jacobsons had been acquitted of the charge. A half year after that, in the fall of 1986, it announced that Congress had passed the Air Carrier Assistance Act, which amended the Federal Aviation Act to prohibit discrimination against persons with disabilities in airline travel. Yet over the next three years, *The Rag* reported instances of discrimination against blind and wheelchair-riding travelers, FAA regulations that restricted the rights of disabled airline passengers, including a rule prohibiting them from sitting in exit rows, and the opposition of the NFB, the Eastern Paralyzed Veterans Association, and ADAPT to these practices and policies.

Despite the problem with its implementation, the Air Carrier Assistance Act was one of some fifty federal statutes in a quarter century of legislation that reflected a major shift in public policymaking regarding Americans with disabilities. That process began in 1968 with the Architectural Barriers Act and culminated in 1990 with the ADA. In between came such legislative high points as Section 504 and P.L. 94-142. This body of laws departed significantly from previous policies because it sought not just to provide more "help" to persons regarded as disadvantaged by disability, but rather expressed and implemented a fundamental redefinition of "disability" as a social more than a medical problem.

The new-model policies coincided with, and to a degree reflected, the emergence of disability-rights activism. Airline accessibility was only one of the issues spurring that activism. Deaf and disabled activists moved on everything from the presidency of Gallaudet University to the pervasive impact of telethons. But whatever the particular issue at hand, activists were redefining "disability" from the inside.

This activism was the political expression of an emerging consciousness among a younger generation of Americans with disabilities. A 1986 Louis Harris survey of adults with disabilities documented that generational shift in perspective. While only a minority of disabled adults over the age of 45 regarded people with disabilities as a minority group like blacks or Hispanics, 54% of those aged 18 to 44 agreed with the perspective. In addition, substantial majorities in every age bracket believed people with disabilities needed legal protection from discrimination, but the largest percentage of respondents holding that view was in the youngest age group, 18–30. Yet only one-third were aware of Section 504. It appeared that the great mass of disabled people had not yet become politically active. Their views reflected a proto-political consciousness, the emerging minority-group consciousness of a new generation.

That younger generation has spurned institutionalized definitions of "disability" and of people with disabilities. At its core, the new consciousness has repudiated the reigning medical model, which defines "disability" as physiological pathologies located within individuals. That definition necessarily prescribes particular solutions: treatments or therapies to cure those individuals or to correct their vocational or social functioning. Cure or correction has been viewed as the only possible means by which people with disabilities could achieve social acceptance and social assimilation.

Those who are not cured or corrected have been defined as marginalized by disability. They have been relegated to invalidism. This has meant not just physical dependency or institutionalization, but, most fundamentally, social invalidation.

While the medical model claims to be scientific, objective and humane, within its practice has lurked considerable ambivalence toward the people it professes to aid. In one respect, the medical model has been the institutionalized expression of societal anxieties about people who look different or function differently. It regards them as incompetent to manage their own lives, as needing professional, perhaps lifelong, supervision, perhaps even as dangerous to society.

The new disability perspective has presented a searching critique of the medical model. It has argued that by locating the *problem* in the bodies of individuals with disabilities, the medical model cannot account for, let alone combat, the bias and discrimination evident in such actions as the mistreatment and arrest of Nadine and Steven Jacobson. Indeed, disability-rights advocates have argued that the implementation of the medical model in health care, social services, education, private charity, and public policies has institutionalized prejudice and discrimination. Far from being beneficial, or even neutral, the medical model has been at the core of the problem.

In the place of the medical model, activists have substituted a sociopolitical or minority-group model of disability. "Disability," they have asserted, is primarily a socially constructed role. For the vast majority of people with disabilities, prejudice is a far greater problem than any impairment: discrimination is a bigger obstacle for them to "overcome" than any disability. The core of the problem, in the activists' view, has been historically deep-seated, socially pervasive and powerfully institutionalized oppression of disabled people.

To combat this oppression, the disability movement not only called for legal protection against discrimination, it fashioned a new idea in American civil-rights theory: the concept of equal access. Traditional rehabilitation policy defined accommodations such as architectural modifications, adaptive devices (wheelchairs, optical readers) and services (sign-language interpreters) as special benefits to those who are fundamentally dependent. Disability-rights ideology redefined them as merely different modes of functioning, and not inherently inferior.

15 Traditional civil-rights theory permitted differential treatment of minorities only as a *temporary* expedient to enable them to achieve parity. Disability rights ideology claimed reasonable accommodations as legitimately *permanent* differential treatment because they are necessary to enable disabled persons to achieve and maintain equal access.

"Access" could have been limited to physical modifications in the personal living and work environments of disabled individuals. Instead, disability activists have pressed forward a broad concept of equal access that has sought to guarantee full participation in society. To ensure equal opportunity, they have declared, equal access and reasonable accommodations must be guaranteed in law as civil rights.

To nondisabled opponents, disabled activists have not sought equal opportunities, they have demanded special treatment. Disabled people could not, the critics have complained, on the one hand, claim equal opportunity and equal social standing, and, on the other, demand "special" privileges such as accommodations and public financial aid (e.g., health insurance). Disabled people could not have it both ways. According to majority notions, equality has meant identical arrangements and treatment. It is not possible in American society to be equal and different, to be equal and disabled.

On this basic issue of the nature of equality and the means of accomplishing it, disabled activists and their nondisabled opponents have had radically different perceptions. And that difference was not new in the 1970s and '80s. It had a long history.

To take just one example, in 1949 a spokesman for the National Federation of the Blind testifying before a Congressional committee argued simultaneously for Aid to the Blind (ATB), a social-welfare program of financial assistance, and for what today would be called civil rights. The disability of blindness was a physical condition that incurred significant expenses and limitations, he argued, and therefore required societal aid. But it was also a social condition that involved discriminatory exclusion. He quoted the famous legal scholar and blind activist Jacobus ten Broek's "Bill of Rights for the Blind" to the effect that the real handicap of blindness, far surpassing its physical limitations, was "exclusion from the main channels of social and economic activity."

20 Throughout the history of disabled activism, advocates like this NFB spokesman simultaneously called for "social aid" *and* civil rights. Unlike their nondisabled opponents, they saw no contradiction in this position. It was possible in America, they implicitly proclaimed, to be equal and to require aid and accommodations, to be equal and different. Indeed, for Americans with disabilities, any other approach to equality seemed impossible.

The disability-movement critique of the medical model has also argued that the complete medicalization of people with disabilities has advanced the agenda of professional interest groups. People with disabilities have served as a source of profit, power, and status.

An estimated 1.7 million mentally, emotionally, or physically disabled Americans have been defined as "incurable" and socially incompetent and have been relegated to medical warehouses. Another ten to eleven million disabled adults, 70% of working-age adults with disabilities in the United States, are unemployed and welfare dependent, while uncounted others languish below the poverty line.

According to the disability-movement analysis, the immediate causes of this marginalization have been public policies. Health-care financing policies force disabled people into institutions and nursing homes rather than funding independent living. Income-maintenance and public health-insurance policies include "disincentives" that penalize disabled individuals for trying to work productively. Disabled adults have also been relegated to dependency because of continuing widespread inaccessibility and pervasive job-market discrimination.

But according to this analysis, the ultimate cause of their marginalization is that people with disabilities are highly profitable. For that reason, they have been kept segregated in what is virtually a separate economy of disability. That economy is dominated by nondisabled interests: vendors of over-priced products and services; practitioners who drill disabled people in imitating the "able-bodied" and deaf people in mimicking the hearing; a nursing-home industry that reaps enormous revenues from incarcerating people with disabilities.

25 Thus, concludes this analysis, millions of deaf and disabled people are held as permanent clients and patients. They are confined within a segregated economic and so-

cial system and to a socioeconomic condition of childlike dependency. Denied self-determination, they are schooled in social incompetency, and then their confinement to a socially invalidated role is justified by that incompetency. According to this critique, disabled issues are fundamentally issues of money and power.

The disability-rights movement marked a revolt against this paternalistic domination and a demand for disabled and deaf self-determination. That revolt and that demand has been at the center of the controversy over telethons. Who should have the power to define the identities of people with disabilities and to determine what it is they *really* need? Or parallel to this dispute, how could the hearing majority on the Gallaudet University board of trustees reject two qualified deaf educators to select yet another hearing president? "Who has decided what the qualifications [for president] should be?" asked Gallaudet student-government president Greg Hlibok. "Do white people speak for black people?" Hence the students' demand for a deaf majority on the board of trustees.

But the attack on the medical model has gone beyond merely questioning the motives of nondisabled interest groups. At a still deeper level, that critique has explained the relentless medicalization of people with disabilities as an attempt to resolve broader American cultural dilemmas. In a moment of intense social anxiety, it has helped reassure nondisabled people of their own wholeness as human beings, their own authenticity as Americans. It has done so by making "disability," and thus people with disabilities, the negation of full and valid American humanity.

In order for people with disabilities to be respected as worthy Americans, to be considered as whole persons or even approximations of persons, they have been instructed that they must perpetually labor to "overcome" their disabilities. They must display continuous cheerful striving toward some semblance of normality. The evidence of their moral and emotional health, of their quasi-validity as persons and citizens, has been their exhibition of the desire to become like nondisabled people. This is, of course, by definition, the very thing people with disabilities cannot become. Thus, they have been required to pursue a "normality" that must forever elude them. They have been enticed into a futile quest by having dangled before them the ever-elusive carrot of social acceptance.

Recognition that "overcoming" is rooted in nondisabled interests and values marked the culmination of the ideological development of the disability movement's first phase. And that analytical achievement prepared the way for a transition into the second phase.

30 The first phase sought to move disabled people from the margins of society to the mainstream by demanding that discrimination be outlawed and that access and accommodations be mandated. The first phase argued for social inclusion. The second phase has asserted the necessity for self-definition. While the first phase rejected the medical model of disability, the second has repudiated the nondisabled majority norms that partly gave rise to the medical model.

* * *

That repudiation of dominant values has been most obvious in the rejections of the medically proclaimed need to be cured in order to be validated. At the time of the Gallaudet student revolt, Eileen Paul, co-founder of an organization called Deaf

Pride, proclaimed, "This is a revolt against a system based on the assumption that deaf people have to become like hearing people and have to fit into the dominant hearing society."

As they spurned devaluing nondisabled definitions, deaf people and disabled people began to celebrate themselves. Coining self-affirming slogans such as "Disabled and Proud," "Deaf Pride" and "Disability Cool," they seized control of the definition of their identities. This has been not so much a series of personal choices as a collective process of reinterpreting themselves and their issues. It is a political and cultural task.

Beyond proclamations of pride, deaf and disabled people have been uncovering or formulating sets of alternative values derived from within the deaf and disabled experiences. Again, these have been collective rather than personal efforts. They involve not so much the statement of personal philosophies of life as the assertion of group perspectives and values. This is a process of deaf cultural elaboration and of disabled culture-building.

For example, some people with disabilities have been affirming the validity of values drawn from their own experience. Those values are markedly different from, and even opposed to, nondisabled majority values. They declare that they prize not self-sufficiency but self-determination, not independence but interdependence, not functional separateness but personal connection, not physical autonomy but human community. This values-formation takes disability as the starting point. It uses the disability experience as the source of values and norms.

35 The affirmation of disabled values also leads to a broad-ranging critique of nondisabled values. American culture is in the throes of an alarming and dangerous moral and social crisis, a crisis of values. The disability movement can advance a much-needed perspective on this situation. It can offer a critique of the hyperindividualistic majority norms institutionalized in the medical model and at the heart of the contemporary American crisis. That analysis needs to be made not just because majority values are impossible for people with disabilities to match up to, but more important, because they have proved destructive for everyone, disabled and nondisabled alike. They prevent real human connection and corrode authentic human community.

Another manifestation of the disability movement's analysis and critique has been the attempts over the past dozen years to develop "disability studies" within research universities. Every social movement needs sustained critical analysis of the social problems it is addressing. Such movements develop their own cadres of intellectuals and scholars who arise from the community and often connect it with academic institutions. Disability studies has been conceived as a bridge between the academy and the disability community.

But what should disability studies look like? Professor Simi Linton, a disabled scholar/activist, and her colleagues at Hunter College in New York have proposed a useful working definition of disability studies:

"Disability Studies reframes the study of disability by focusing on it as a social phenomenon, social construct, metaphor, and culture, utilizing a minority group model. It examines ideas related to disability in all forms of cultural representation throughout history, and examines the policies and practices of all societies to understand the social, rather than physical and psychological, determinants of the experience of disability. Disability Studies both emanated from and supports the Disability Rights Movement, which advocated for civil rights and self-determination. The focus shifts the emphasis away from a prevention/ treatment/remediation paradigm, to a social/cultural/political paradigm. This shift does not signify a denial of the presence of impairments, nor a rejection of the utility of intervention and treatment. Instead, Disability Studies has been developed to disentangle impairments from the myth, ideology, and stigma that influence social interaction and social policy. The scholarship challenges the idea that the economic and social status and the assigned roles of people with disabilities are inevitable outcomes of their condition."

This definition captures the fundamental features of disability studies as it has grown out of the disability-rights movement.

40 If disability studies is to serve the disability community and movement effectively, it needs to define an agenda. That project should include the following goals:

Disability studies should serve as an access ramp between the disability community and research universities. It must forge a fruitful connection between the disability community/ movement and such institutions.

The traffic of ideas and persons on that ramp should flow in both directions. It must be a two-way street. The disability perspective, the insights, experience, and expertise of people with disabilities, must inform research, producing new questions, generating new understandings.

At the same time, academic researchers can help bring new rigor to the disability-rights movement's analysis and activism. Collaboration between scholars and advocates can produce a deeper critique of disability policy and the social arrangements that affect people with disabilities and can generate a more fully elaborated ideology of "disability" and disability rights.

Complementing these endeavors, disability studies should also forge a link with disabled artists and writers. This collaboration can support the current flowering of disability arts. It will also promote disability-based cultural studies that can uncover disabled values, explain the social/cultural construction of "disability" by the majority culture, and critique dominant nondisabled values.

45 To implement this agenda, disability studies must obtain support for faculty and graduate students. That support must come in two forms: funding to pay for research and teaching, and affirmative action to recruit faculty and students with disabilities to develop disability studies. We need to build a phalanx of disabled disability-studies scholars and intellectuals.

To succeed and to remain true to its purpose, disability studies needs the active support and involvement of the disability community. Disability studies can then help advance both phases of the disability movement.

Those two phases are not separate and successive chronological periods. They are complementary aspects of the disability movement. The concept of equal access represents a politics of issues. It is the effort of Americans with disabilities to build an infrastructure of freedom and self-determination. The proclamation of disability and deaf pride and the elaboration of disability and deaf cultures express a politics of identity. It is an affirmation, a celebration of who we are, not despite disability or deafness, but precisely because of the disability and deaf experiences.

These two phases of the disability movement are reciprocal. Each is essential to the other. Together they declare who we are and where we intend to go.

Exploring Texts and Contexts

For activities with icons, refer to the Guide to Analyzing Readings in Context.

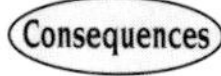

1. Longmore uses his article to review the progress of the disability movement over the last twenty years or so. In what ways has his article confirmed your ideas about disability? In what ways has he challenged your assumptions? How has your thinking been affected?

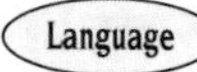

2. Longmore uses two key terms to describe the differences between the two phases of the disability movement: *disability rights* and *disability culture.* What is the difference between the words "rights" and "culture"? How do these terms contribute to Longmore's analysis? What effect does each word create?

3. Longmore's article started out as an address he delivered to a group of educators at a college conference about disability and the arts. What parts of it seem reminiscent of this other genre? How do you think the readers of Longmore's article differ from the audience for his speech? What changes do you think Longmore made in transforming his speech into a journal article? What do you think stayed the same?
4. On page 350 Longmore says that critiquing majority values will be worthwhile for disabled and nondisabled alike because many of these values are destructive. For example, he says "hyperindividualism" is at the heart of our moral and social crisis. What does he mean by hyperindividualism? Do you agree that we are in a moral and social crisis? Explain.

Creating Texts

For activities with icons, refer to the Guides to Analyzing Contexts for Writing and Analyzing Readings in Context. For additional help with these writing projects, read the descriptions of **Report** and **Essay** in the Genre Glossary.

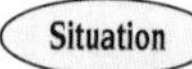

1. Longmore, speaking at a university conference on disability and the arts, describes the role of disability studies in the disability rights movement. Write a report about the disability studies program on your campus. What is its role? What impact have its courses and curriculum had on your campus culture? Do you see a relationship between the disability studies program and any changes in representations of disability on your campus? Interview instructors from the program to get their perspective on the program and what they hope to accomplish. If

your campus does not have a disability studies program, write a report on the program at another university or community college. You can find a great deal of information about programs and curricula by exploring a school's Web site.

2. Longmore observes, "American culture is in the throes of an alarming and dangerous moral and social crisis, a crisis of values." Robert Putnam also in this unit writes about the weakening fabric of American society. In an essay, compare Longmore's analysis of American society with Putnam's. To what does each writer attribute the decline in society? What does each writer suggest as a remedy? How do the various contexts of each writer shape and influence his perspective? 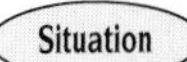

Negotiating Disability

Simi Linton

In the introduction to Simi Linton's book, *Claiming Disability: Knowledge and Identity,* Michael Bérubé tells us that when we see the study of disability as central to the humanities, we will be able to understand it as "a broad, general subject that shapes public life and public policy" (viii). Bérubé wants us to look beyond the Americans with Disabilities Act, through which Americans with disabilities are guaranteed protection from discrimination in employment, public services, and public accommodations. In this groundbreaking book, Linton argues against seeing disability solely as a medical condition. Rather, she wants us to see it as a way to establish one's identity, to articulate the ways in which a disability affects one's daily life, and to recognize the ways in which it binds one to other people with similar political and social experiences.

As a psychologist, a teacher, and a woman with a disability, Linton challenges views of disability that focus narrowly on a medical model that defines people with disabilities as inferior, broken bodies needing repair. Linton argues for an academic focus called "disability studies" that could broaden the work currently done in applied and professional courses such as special education, in which disability is often seen as pathology. Instead, disability studies should have a prominent place in the liberal arts curriculum, where academics and students can consider not only all the human variations that constitute disability but, most important, how we come to understand the meaning of those variations. Linton would like to see courses in disciplines such as history, rhetoric, art, literature, and philosophy reflect on how persons with disabilities are represented and on the social and political consequences of that representation. For example, women's studies, which often focuses on a "stigmatized social identity," could readily include a feminist analysis of how the body with a disability is stigmatized because of its difference.

In the excerpt included here, Linton focuses on what happens once students are out of college, in the workplace, or simply living their everyday lives. It is most likely, she tells us, that students will not have studied disability in the way she proposes and will face issues that challenge underlying and unexplored assumptions about disability. The scenarios Linton includes do two things: First, they describe contexts that require civic deliberation and result in important consequences for building a civil society. Second, they give us some sense of what disability studies has to offer to a comprehensive undergraduate education.

Connecting with the Conversation

1. Talk to a professional who is working in a job for which you might consider preparing. First, ask this person what things had to be learned "on the job," that is, what could not be learned in school. Then, ask specifically about disability issues. What situations or interactions have presented themselves that left your interviewee unprepared? Ask whether he or she has any advice for changes in the undergraduate curriculum or for career preparation.
2. Look through your university's undergraduate course catalogue for courses that mention the study of disability. Make notes on what you find. Also, ask your friends and fellow students to what extent disability issues are discussed in their classes. Report to the class on what you have found.

Every year increasing numbers of students, both disabled and nondisabled, are entering college from primary and secondary schools where mainstreamed classrooms are common. Future incoming students will have been part of inclusive classrooms, where not only a few high-performing physically disabled children but a spectrum of students with significant cognitive, emotional, and physical and sensory disabilities will all be part of the central, core culture of the school.

Of course, there's not going to be an instant transformation, but I do think that disabled and nondisabled students will be used to one another, and used to working together in ways that faculty have never experienced. The faculty are more likely to remember a time when disabled students and nondisabled students went to different schools, or at least different classes, took different school buses, and were usually isolated from one another in school and play. Not many will have been in colleges and universities, as the entering freshmen class of 1996 was, where more than 10 percent of the students reported having disabilities.

The students' college curriculum will also be out of step with their experience of a range of phenomena related to being disabled in late-twentieth-century America or of witnessing disability in these circumstances. Most of the students will not notice. Their high school classes will probably not have made mention of disability in any overt way. Disability is unlikely to have been employed as a perspective in their literature, current events, or biology classes. The dramatic changes in public education over the past twenty years would not have been interpreted for them. Although

From *Claiming Disability: Knowledge and Identity.* New York: New York University Press, 1998, pp. 157–183.

I hope that some mechanisms are put into place to teach young disabled people this history, to learn in substantive ways about their newly won rights, and to help them see the relationship between the personal and the political nature of the experience of disability, it is likely that that will not be consistently provided. Therefore, although both the disabled and nondisabled students coming up are likely to be more experienced, they will need the opportunity to interpret that experience within and throughout the curriculum. Otherwise, they will not understand the historical specificity of this moment, its meaning and significance, nor how to create meaningful change.

The arguments throughout this book in favor of integrating disability studies into the curriculum are not presented solely because more disabled students are entering college, or because disabled and nondisabled people will be interacting with one another in schools and in the community in ways that they never have before. The need to understand disability, and the construction of disability, clearly predates the present moment and extends beyond the boundaries of educational institutions. Moreover, as I've argued, there are epistemological reasons to debunk the primacy of medical interpretations of disability, to interpret metaphors of disability in order to bring more accurate readings to a text, to challenge the normal/abnormal dichotomies and all their manifestations, and to create theories or conduct research that is more representative, valid, and universal. Yet it would be a mistake to ignore the shifting culture of the schools and the changing student body in considering how curriculum is shaped.

5 In this chapter, rather than look inside the academic world, I turn the camera outward, toward the world that students inhabit when they leave college. Let's consider what they face and examine the reasons that a more substantive curriculum in disability studies is crucial for preparing disabled and nondisabled students for work and citizenship, including the specific preparation of disabled students to assume leadership roles in their communities, organizations, and workplaces. All of these students will meet with an array of issues that would benefit from, or are absolutely dependent on, a close disability analysis. As they leave school, or even in the course of their education, they will confront critical incidents—some taking up a few minutes, some complex and long-lasting—that will require experience in thinking about disability in a number of different domains, critical reasoning skills, and, often, a conscious well-considered sense of their own feelings about disability and disabled people. Both disabled and nondisabled students will encounter such incidents, and they will encounter them whether or not their work or community life directly involves disabled people or disability issues.

What follows are a few examples of some of these issues embedded in vignettes or case histories of persons in a job situation, or in family or community life. Imagine yourself in each situation and consider how well prepared you are to play out your role.

An Assistant Curator

You work at an art museum and are in charge of developing the written materials that accompany exhibitions. An installation of paintings by Goya is planned, and in preparation for that event you conduct research on the artist, his patronage, his subjects, and the historical period in which he worked. It occurs to you as you write the text for the audio guide, the pamphlet on the exhibit, and the commentary to be posted beside each painting that there are a number of disability themes and issues that could be explicated in these materials. You wonder if, and how, you might discuss the function of people of short stature in Goya's paintings and their function in the court of Charles IV. Should you point out the depictions of fictional monsters and the real people with anomalous bodies portrayed as monstrous? More important, should you comment on the tendency of Goya, and of viewers, to blur the distinctions between people and supernatural creatures? In other words, is it a good idea to provide an explicit disability studies reading of Goya's paintings?

You examine your old college textbook and wonder how to counter the received wisdom that the "follies and brutalities" Goya witnessed and his "increased infirmities, including deafness, combined to depress his outlook and led to his late 'dark style' " (Gardner 1970, 639). How can you, in the context of the overall mission of the exhibition, challenge the kinds of beliefs that you yourself have held, and surely other visitors to the exhibit may hold as well? Many who view the paintings will have taken the standard introductory art history course in college and read that "Goya presents with a straight face a menagerie of human grotesques who, critics have long been convinced, must not have had the intelligence to realize that the artist was caricaturing them" (637). Yet, you recognize that many visitors will be offended by that perspective, including people who have physical characteristics similar to those portrayed in Goya's paintings. They may well understand that they are being objectified and mocked in his paintings and are hoping that the accompanying materials will interpret Goya's motivation and discuss the consequence of those representations.

Now, rather than imagining that you are this curator, put yourself in the shoes of a college professor teaching future curators who will go on to write such materials. You might be a literature professor, or an art historian, biologist, ethicist, or sociologist. What is your responsibility to help students challenge ideas such as those found in Gardner's text, or to provide perspectives and information when even those covert messages are absent? If you are a psychology professor, is it logical to say that it is not your job, that the art history classes will provide the analysis of representations of disability? Instead, consider what you might say about reinforcement theory and stereotypes that might help a future curator and other students to understand how paintings or other representations may reinforce distorted views of disabled people. If you are a historian, what might you say about the function of marginal figures in the court of various kings and noblemen, and the particular role of people with anomalous bodies? You might turn to David Gerber's (1996) essay on the careers of people exhibited in freak shows to contextualize your discussion of the use of dwarfs as jesters in European courts from 1600 to 1800. If you teach art history, you might discuss the cultural history of the museum, and focus on the Musée Universel des Sourds-Muets, part of the Institute for the Deaf in France, and the Museum of Pathological Anatomy in London, which were representative of a "new direction in museology, towards the recording of the Other" (Mirzoeff 1995, 199). Such museums were indicative of a trend in the late nineteenth century that did not bring about greater exposure of disabled people's perspectives but, instead, resulted in the valorization of medical practice. In the case of the French museum, "[R]ather than promote the achievement of deaf artists, the museum sought to commemorate the modern triumph over deafness" (198).

10 If you, the assistant curator, had taken such a class, you might well ask: In preparing this exhibition, what is my obligation to consider the moral, aesthetic, intellectual, psychological, and social questions that the paintings raise? What can any professor do to ensure that a future curator will, at least, consider writing about this element of a painter's work and possess the knowledge and perspectives needed to follow through on the project if she or he chooses to?

A Personnel Director

You are the new personnel director for a midsized company. Because of a number of factors, including an outreach effort that your predecessor organized a couple of years ago, the firm has hired several people with different disabilities. You have learned that a group of them have been meeting over the past six months. They appear to be well organized and call themselves the Disability Action Group (DAG). They have requested an appointment with you, and you anticipate that they want to discuss some remaining access issues, of which you are aware. When you meet, you find that their agenda is quite different. To your surprise, they present a five-page memo concerning the in-house hostile atmosphere and the failure of some managers to provide reasonable accommodations. The memo includes the following:

- Jokes that had been circulating on interoffice e-mail include a few whose targets were people of short stature and people with mental retardation. A member of DAG had sent an e-mail message to all employees that the jokes were offensive and should stop, but they continued to circulate for several days.
- A ramp had recently been installed to make a formerly inaccessible building accessible to employees who use wheelchairs. Before that, two disabled employees scheduled to move to the building had submitted a memo to the design team with suggestions on the type of ramp needed, its ideal location, and some safety measures to consider, and had asked that a member of DAG be included in meetings to design the ramp. Despite the initiative, the team had not included a member and had ignored most of their suggestions. The ramp exited the building in a deserted area of the parking lot, next to the door where garbage is removed. When the DAG coordinator confronted the design team and the manager in charge of safety issues with the facts that the garbage smells, that rats had been spotted in the area, and that the ramp imposed isolation, she was told that there was no other way to have installed the ramp, it was built to code, and new lights would make the ramp and lot safe.
- Further, the parking spaces designated for people with disabilities had often been used by other employees. DAG took up the matter with the Security Office, which began ticketing illegally parked cars. A week later, one of the signs with the wheelchair symbol had been defaced.

- The company had held the Christmas party in a restaurant not wheelchair accessible, and whose bathrooms are not accessible. A DAG member brought this to the attention of the party planner and was told that somebody would carry him up the stairs; things were going to be fine; the location couldn't be changed because of company custom; and arrangements had already been made.
- An employee who is blind had asked for a different work station because of noise that at times drowns out her talking computer. The supervisor responded that he had already made enough adjustments for her; there was no other place available; and she should try to ignore the noise.

As you read the DAG memo, you recall that on another occasion a similar complaint had been made against the same supervisor. The charge had been dropped, but the supervisor had been warned by the Personnel Department that the company is legally and ethically bound to comply with such requests and they are to be taken seriously.

- An employee who uses a wheelchair reported that a man well known and respected in the company has been behaving in ways that she identifies as both disability and sexual harassment. When she is going down the hall he begins pushing her wheelchair without asking permission. Her statements that she prefers to push her own chair are countered by remarks such as "Don't worry. I'm glad to help you out," "Give your arms a rest; you must get tired," "I like doing it; I push all the handicapped ladies' wheelchairs at church." On a number of occasions, he has jumped in front of her and opened the door to the Women's Room in such a way that he entered the room, obviously uninvited. He has sat next to her in the cafeteria a few times, insisting on talking about her disability and asking personal questions. She has tried consistently to tell him that his presence and attentions are not welcome, but he has not been deterred.

The company is proud of its responsible social practices and has been praised by the union and consumer groups. Your predecessor had also worked to have disabled people included as a protected group in the company's affirmative action policy. You must now figure out what the company's legal and ethical obligations are, what the impact of adverse publicity might be for the company if DAG "goes public" with its complaints, and what management issues might ensue if these well-informed and disgruntled employees speak out. It will be your job to handle DAG, to communicate to the company executives the nature of the complaints, and to finesse the interpersonal tensions that may arise from the airing of these issues.

20 After confirming the complaints' legitimacy you take the file home and spend a good part of the weekend mulling matters over. It is difficult to analyze the elements of the situation and to weigh the complaints. You alternate, at one time seeing a pattern of behaviors that constitute a hostile environment—which requires a systemic response—and at another time seeing isolated incidents that are neither as virulent nor as pervasive as alleged.

The complaints raise a number of questions. Is disability harassment equivalent to sexual harassment, in either nature of coercion or in consequences for the individual being harassed? How is unwanted physical contact with the woman's wheelchair similar to or different from the kinds of unwanted bodily contact that would be considered sexual harassment? Is entering the Women's Room, seemingly to "help" with the door, a sexually menacing behavior? Is an inaccessible restaurant comparable to a club that discriminates against African Americans or doesn't allow women to become members? What type of scale can be used to weigh these differences? If someone who uses a wheelchair is willing to be carried into the restaurant and is then given a table, can the restaurant be deemed to be discriminating? Is the real issue not whether the restaurant itself is accessible but what it means symbolically, ethically, and legally for the company to persist in using it? Should the employees most affected by a ramp have the right to a say in its placement and design? Although OSHA codes and ADA codes were adhered to, the codes don't cover every contingency.

Consider the preparation the actors in this drama need in order to engage in resolving this conflict. Who are the players? You, the personnel director, have an undergraduate degree in some liberal arts field and a master's degree in business or human services. Where in your academic career would you have obtained the tools to handle this situation? A graduate course or, more likely, a workshop on the ADA and employment issues would be inadequate to ground you in the complex issues presented here. Further, such courses and workshops rarely link disability issues to sexist and racist issues that arise in the workplace. Would a similarly conceived workshop on gender issues be sufficient to understand gender equity issues in the workplace and sexual harassment? What about the employees? Where would they have gained the knowledge to analyze the inequities, to recognize one another as members of a constituency group, and to coalesce around these issues? What of the other employees implicated in the charges—where would their disability training have come from? Where would the unaccommodating supervisor, the "helpful" employee, or the autonomous design team have had the opportunity to challenge their own beliefs or take on new ideas about disability?

Also consider how understanding and resolving each of these dilemmas can have an impact on other management and personnel concerns. One can read each complaint in terms of a particular disability issue, as well as in terms of its relationship to accepted codes of behavior, power differentials among employees and their impact on individual rights, and autocratic decisions and their impact on members of a group. A well-prepared personnel director might be able to contextualize these complaints and discuss them in terms of the broader problems that all companies face but not lose sight of the specific disability issues raised.

An Architect

You are an architect in a midsize firm, in a midsize city, working on a midsize job. You are new in the firm, and this is your first solo project: a library; a small center, with an auditorium for cultural events and community meetings; and a playground. The center will be in a neglected downtown area, and the city has requested a building that will draw some attention to the area.

25 When you joined the firm, you discussed with your employers your commitment to innovative projects, particularly those that are models of integration and accommodation for people with disabilities. For the present project, you want to include a

number of features that will go beyond the requirements of the ADA, in that they will integrate access into the overall concept of the building rather than being add-ons. Although the features could be replaced with standard "handicap"-access materials without compromising the overall design, you believe that a more innovative approach could have significant symbolic, functional, and aesthetic impact, and it will be your job to convince the city to back the plan.

As you anticipate creating the desired environment, you are stymied by your lack of experience with truly integrated and accommodating buildings. You are particularly interested in creating an entrance that declares your intention: rather than the standard ramp alongside the building—which separates people who use the ramp from people who use the steps—you envisage an entrance that weaves together steps and slopes so all visitors can enter and leave the building together and interact with one another as they do so. A second innovation you are considering takes some of the features required by the ADA, such as the signs in Braille in the elevators and on office doors, and embeds them in the surface texture of the walls as part of a visual and tactile design motif. You have already consulted with two people who are blind and who have expertise in signage; they are enthusiastic. You also want railings along hall walls for people who need assistance in walking. Again, rather than the standard-issue, utilitarian ADA-approved railings, you're considering a combination of materials to produce functional equivalent railings that look and feel like decorative molding.

You are working on the playground design, in consultation with teachers from an inclusive elementary school. It will have features that promote social interaction and cognitive development. For instance, the teachers suggested play spaces that encourage children to face one another, so children with hearing impairments can watch the hearing children's lips and follow other visual cues, or where two children who use sign language can talk with each other. You want to come up with spaces for children who use wheelchairs to transfer to platforms joined by chutes and slides. You are thinking about a mapping system that will enable children who are blind to find the play areas. As with the building, you want to make the map interesting to users; something the sighted and blind children can use together.

The theater would incorporate wheelchair seating in every section, so wheelchair users are not isolated in back rows. It would also include a technical studio where subtitles for films and captions for live performance could be devised, as well as audio descriptions.

Your dilemma: the city's allocation provides for access and accommodation based on a model that complies with the ADA, not for the features you are proposing. Further, the funds for the library cover access and accommodation only for patrons, not staff and performers. You had reflexively gone along with that thinking in giving your assent when you should have kept your mind open to all concerned.

30 Your presentation includes a rationale for your design that you hope will appeal to the civic leaders and others in attendance. Will the rationale "speak" to them? For instance, you describe how the integration of the Brailled information in a stuccoed wall relief invites sighted people to look and touch, to investigate and think about Braille rather than ignore it as something not for them. In much the same way that Andy

Warhol's Campbell's soup cans or Christo's wrapping the Reichstag encourages us to think about those elements in a different way, everyday elements of life can be made more available and interesting to sighted people as well as to blind people. Even putting a sign in Braille and in print on the wall that says "Please touch" alters the environment, and suggests to sighted people that touch is an important means to access beauty, information, and ideas. These combined tactile features provide a shared experience in the same way that the step/slope combined entranceway invites ramp and stair users to travel together, and the playground spaces encourage disabled and nondisabled children to play together.

As a further example to explain your motivation, you point out how American Sign Language, long considered by the general public simply as a pragmatic solution to the "problem" of deafness, has been incorporated into staged performances as an aesthetic and communicative element. This has helped people see it as interesting and expressive. You are suggesting that a rethinking of ramps may be similarly conducive to an enlarged perspective on the active participation of disabled people. Further, you are suggesting that not much creative energy has been invested in ramps not because they are not as interesting as steps but because they are associated with disability. In saying that, you allude to the transformation in thinking about women's work and women's creative endeavors both of which have been considered of lesser merit because of their association with a devalued group.

I would like to think that architects with your commitment and expertise are graduating from universities after having been exposed to the philosophical underpinnings of such environments, and having acquired the desired technical expertise to design them. Although some degree holders may fall into that category, I don't believe that schools of architecture are consciously reshaping their curricula to prepare architects to meet these challenges.

Courses in disability studies could find a natural home in schools of architecture. For instance, a course could examine the history of spaces tailored for people with disabilities— from institutions to sheltered workshops, to the placement of special education classrooms in schools—and consider the aesthetic and ideological statements these spaces make. Another course might consider the architecture of containment and confinement, and look at institutions of all stripes, how they comment on their inhabitants and how they comment on the relationship between the inhabitants and those outside. A course in marginalized groups and marginalized spaces, cross-listed in departments of architecture, geography, urban planning, and sociology, could examine the parallels between the social status of women, of disabled people, and of members of the economic underclass, and the spaces designed for them. Texts such as Leslie Kanes Weisman's (1992) *Discrimination by Design: A Feminist Critique of the Man-Made Environment* that have been used to bring a gendered reading to architecture could be included with readings on disability to investigate the properties of the "nondisabled-made environment." Weisman points out that "gender, race, class, occupation, and other factors like age and disability collectively create distinctly different spatial experiences for people, even within the same environmental setting" (40). Her comments about the imbalance in numbers of bathrooms and toilets for women and men can be discussed in terms of the unavailability of accessible toilets for people with mobility impairments. Courses that look at disability reflectively rather than reflexively can help students think in sophisticated ways about environments that invite the participation of all people.

Program Director

For a number of years you have been the director of a service organization providing day programs to people with physical disabilities and mental retardation. The organization, which has more than one hundred employees, is working well. Donations are up, programs such as the sheltered workshop, the social activities, and the educational programs have attracted national attention because they are seen as innovative by professional groups and are well-attended.

However, the *Disability Rag,* a disability rights quarterly, publishes a scathing piece on the organization and your directorship. The writer asserts that the programs do not prepare disabled people for outside employment and do not foster independent living. Further, that you and the staff, with very few exceptions, are nondisabled; exceptions hold low-level jobs, and they have no say in how the organization is run. Moreover, the Board of Directors has never had a member who was disabled.

The writer acknowledges that many of the people who attend the programs have mental retardation and don't have the type of professional training that would prepare them for management jobs but contends that other disabled people in the community would qualify but have not been hired. Additionally, the organization could facilitate the participation of people with mental retardation in planning and decision making. The writer also criticizes the organization's fund-raising activities, such as last year's bike-a-thon, which you perceived as a huge success, for having excluded people who cannot ride bikes, and hence most program participants. Only two of the day-program participants were invited to the evening ceremony following the event. They were seated at the head table, but speakers, using only first names, told the audience how much each of them liked the day program. The participants were not given a chance to voice their opinions directly but later told the reporter simply but clearly about their discomfiture and were critical of the center and staff—comments that appeared in the article.

It is likely that you and the administrative staffers have degrees in rehabilitation or special education. You have devoted your lives to working with people with disabilities. Yet you find, when the article is discussed at the staff meeting, that your academic background and professional experience have in no way prepared you for the moral, political, and intellectual challenge the controversy presents. To compound your problem, the ombudsperson hired by you to represent participants' interests has read the article to a group and explained a number of the points to them. That group has asked to speak with you.

What might have prepared you and the staff for this moment? How might you have anticipated some of these criticisms, and what might have motivated you to change the practices long before the article appeared? Of course, agency personnel might not experience the article as a threat to conscience or practices. You all may be convinced that your intentions and behavior are exemplary and that the criticism is of a "political" nature and outside the realm of professional conduct. You may not heretofore have encountered any ideas that would challenge the benevolence and humanitarian concern that you believe guide your endeavors.

Academic programs designed to prepare students to work with disabled people have a particular responsibility to evaluate their own philosophy and their own practice with respect to the issues discussed in this vignette. For instance, college students may hear in their classes that inclusion in public education is a good thing but observe that general education and special education are separate departments in the institutions they are attending. Accordingly, they are not being prepared to work in inclusive classrooms. Some of their professors may give an occasional lecture on the importance of the ADA, and the history of discrimination and oppression of people with disabilities in this country, yet students may note that there is only one faculty member with a disability in their department, that only a few of their professors have joined a group to pressure the university to make the campus more accessible, or that a faculty member in special education refuses to provide extra time on an exam for a student who has a learning disability. These disjunctures between the overt and the covert curriculum may make it more difficult for students to integrate and act on personal and social change. Both disabled and nondisabled students may be influenced by this hidden curriculum, but the particular tragedy for disabled students is that they may internalize the message that disability leadership and equality are not that important, even, or most conspicuously, in departments of special education and rehabilitation.

Students might get a different message if they observed their department developing an explicit affirmative action policy and inclusion policy and then pressuring for university-wide adoption. If students observed a department providing disabled students with the support needed to become professionals and to assume leadership roles, they might learn more directly that it is important to perpetuate independence and leadership when they become directors of day programs. If professors conducted outreach efforts to attract disabled students and wrote grants for scholarships for disabled students, they would demonstrate to students that they value disabled people's success and participation. If the faculty refused to participate in planning conferences or research projects on disability unless disabled people are a significant portion of the team, students would learn that their teachers are willing to practice what they preach. If faculty lobbied for the participation of disabled people and of people with expertise in disability studies in college-wide curriculum projects, students might learn that disability studies is part of diversity and multicultural agendas. If departments of special education and rehabilitation offered regularly scheduled courses in disability studies, students would find an excellent site to challenge established beliefs and practices and to consider their own ideas about disability as a socially constructed category. If students saw special education and general education faculty working together on an inclusive teacher-education curriculum they might learn how to create inclusive classrooms and schools once they graduate.

You, as the program director described here, may not have realized when you hired the ombudsperson, or when you agreed to let the writer from the *Rag* visit your organization, that your decisions would precipitate this critical moment. Yet, you're sure to recognize that even if this blows over, other people could disrupt the smooth flow of events in the future. A new participant may transfer into the program from a different city. She may come from a group home with an assisted-employment program, where she worked in the community with occasional support from a job trainer who monitored her work weekly. She may have gotten used to the autonomy, freedom, and income, and may resent the newly imposed limitations. She may urge the other participants to attend an administrative meeting and speak up about problems in the center. It's also possible that an employee might oppose current practice, based on differing views about what constitutes disabled people's rights. These kinds of confrontations are the outcome of paternalistic systems that seek to "care for" disabled people rather than support integration and accommodation in the community. If service providers are perceived as arrogant or supercilious by disabled people, even if their intention is to be supportive and to facilitate growth, we need to reexamine both the structure of our institutions as well the academic preparation of people who staff them.

A Parent

You are a parent of a nondisabled young woman away at college. She calls to tell you she's bringing home a young man whom she is dating; he's "terrific, nice, smart, funny, and accomplished and has cerebral palsy." She tells you he uses a wheelchair and asks if you can get a large board he can use as a ramp to get into the house. She says his speech is sometimes hard to understand, but she'll be there and she's gotten so used to it; she understands pretty much everything.

When you hang up the phone, a flood of feelings and memories rush in. You recall sitting around the kitchen table twenty years ago with your brother and your parents, as your brother patiently explained that he was gay, that that wasn't going to change, and that he hoped that they would love him, accept him, and accept his partner. You wonder whether you will be open to accepting your daughter's partner, as you once hoped your parents would accept your brother's. You also recall that when your daughter was in kindergarten, a family moved in next door who had a disabled child named Rosie. You fought along with them to get the local school to set up an inclusive classroom that she could join. Your daughter and Rosie became friends, rode the school bus together, and attended each other's high school graduation parties. These memories and the pleasure you recall taking in your principled positions in each of these events did not prepare you for your disquiet and dismay at the prospect of your daughter's dating someone you anticipate feeling sorry for and uneasy around.

You recognize that your feelings might change once you meet him, but you also fear that they may not and that you may have to face the repercussions of being honest or of being dishonest when you see your daughter. You find yourself thinking about the same kinds of concerns your parents voiced to you about your brother, about how the rest of the family would perceive him and about how he would be an outcast in society. You realized then that these fears were a projection of your parents' personal feelings onto others, and now you find yourself running from your own feelings by attributing your own anxieties to others. You know that you are concerned about your daughter's well-being, and what you fear are her emotional and physical burdens if she marries a man with disabilities. On a deeper level you are aware that you have difficulty accepting that any man, and now you realize this man in particular, will be having sex with your daughter, and simultaneously you fear that if your daughter marries this man, she may not have children.

A question that needs to be considered here is whether any curriculum,[1] even one with a full complement of disability studies material, can alter personal feelings such as yours. If you, as the parent described here, have made efforts to reduce the ableist practices in society but draw a line when personal commitments are at stake, can we consider your reaction ableist and can curriculum change such reactions? It is a question that is asked about racist, sexist, and homophobic feelings. Are these personal feelings and behaviors amenable to change by academic means or best left to interventions aimed at individuals or at social structures? Also, are ableism, racism, sexism, and heterosexism parallel issues? If so, and curricular change is implemented to address them, would the curricula have similar form, albeit some differing content?

Of course, I can't say for certain whether you, as the parent, would or would not be aided by courses in disability studies. I suspect that such previous exposure might prepare you for this internal struggle, if only to the extent that you would have had practice thinking consciously and deliberately about disability. Obviously, much more than curricular change is needed to alter such deeply held beliefs. Therefore, those of us who are outside the experience need an education in disability as well. Anyone attempting to think about, write about, and analyze such a moment, whether in teaching philosophy, writing a movie script, reporting for a newspaper, or counseling a parent at the local family center, or anyone who can potentially shape this moment would benefit from exposure to disability studies.

What if you were the young man about to meet your girlfriend's parents? What might help you to prepare for this meeting? If you anticipate or encounter hostility, pity, disgust, mawkishness, or awkward oversolicitousness in these people whom you want to get to know, want to have like you, what would prepare you not to be defensive or to personalize the parents' response? Although, again, your self-confidence, self-awareness, and social abilities might seem to be psychological variables, I can think of a hundred ways that a course in disability history or a literature class analyzing representations of disability might make you more resilient to the parents' interpretation of you. Maybe you could have taken a general liberal arts film course with a professor who incorporated disability perspectives into its content. Perhaps the professor showed *Guess Who's Coming to Dinner?* and asked the students to write papers on various alternative versions of the film. Rather than Katherine Ross's bringing home a "Negro," she may have invited someone of a different social class, or a woman with whom she was in love, or someone with a disability. Would the parents' response have been different or the same?

What if, in addition to such courses, there had been a disabled students' center at the university, built on the concept of disability culture and run by disabled students? What if you had organized a leadership training workshop or an outward bound program, where disability pride and disability leadership skills were taught—might that not bolster your internal resilience? Would you be helped by forming friendships with other disabled people your age or older who could tell you how they had fared in social encounters? These are lessons that your family, if they are nondisabled, and your nondisabled friends may not have much experience with.

Colleges and universities have in the past refused to admit disabled women and men, something they are not now permitted to do, and they now must provide access and accommodation. Yet they incur no legal sanctions if they don't tell the truth about disability. That is up to them to decide. For each discipline or area of study there are specific truths to be told. And specific lies. A lie that literature tells can be heard in the metaphors that create analogies between disability and insentience, or evil, or ineptness. Psychology tells lies when it reifies through theory and measurement the concept of normal. Anthropology's lies are found in the construction of a culture's ideas about disability, based solely on nondisabled people's input. History tells lies when it eliminates the perspectives of disabled people, and other marginalized people, from the annals of history, or eliminates information on public figures' disabilities. Women's studies lies when it excludes disabled women's perspectives, and then proceeds to make global statements about women's feelings and experience. Education proffers the idea that disabled and nondisabled children are separate groups best taught in separate classrooms by teachers separately trained. The lies told by clinical psychology and counseling are similar: disabled people's needs and problems are sufficiently different from nondisabled people's that specialists, called rehabilitation psychologists/counselors, are needed to treat them. Sociology fabricates a center, and then creates the concept of deviance to reinforce the centrality of nondisabled people. Medicine tells lies when it reduces differences to deficits, deficiencies, or pathologies. These are among the more obvious problems.

Disability studies tells a different story. Its tenets need to be worked through every discipline and field to assess their validity and applicability to a range of intellectual, social, political, and moral questions that we as a society face. The "truths" of disability studies will be revealed as we see how compromised the answers are without this perspective.

Note

1. Many people do not go to college and will not have access to the academic curriculum I am promoting. My focus in the book has been on higher education curriculum, but I believe that elementary and secondary schools will benefit from these ideas as well. In some ways, elementary schools have been addressing disability more deliberately than higher education has done. Although there are problems with that presentation—see chapter 4—schools have still attempted, through puppets, stories, American Sign Language demonstrations, and discussions about new children who will be included in the classroom, to talk openly about disability.

References

Gardner, H. 1970. *Art through the ages.* 5th ed. New York: Harcourt, Brace and World.

Gerber, D.A. 1996. The "careers" of people in freak shows: The problem of volition and valorization. In R.G. Thomson, ed, *Freakery: Cultural spectacles of the extraordinary body,* 38–54. New York: New York University Press.

Mirzoeff, N. 1995. *Silent poetry: Deafness, sign, and visual culture in modern France.* Princeton: Princeton University Press.

Weisman, L.K. 1992. *Discrimination by design: A feminist critique of the man-made environment.* Urbana: University of Illinois Press.

Exploring Texts and Contexts

For activities with icons, refer to the Guide to Analyzing Readings in Context.

1. One of the most important aspects of the scenarios Linton offers here is the Situation ways in which they encourage civil deliberation: that is, in order to respond to unanticipated assumptions about disability, one must pay close attention to how we talk to each other. Examine the scenarios closely to see what sorts of communication situations arise. Choose at least two situations that offer opportunities for communication. Describe the two situations and offer suggestions for the participants.
2. Review the scenarios presented—assistant curator, personnel director, architect, program director, and parent—and consider which one surprised you the most and why. Examine your response and articulate what it was about the scenario that you were unable to anticipate. What assumptions might you hold that the scenario asked you to examine?
3. After completing Activity 2, in which you consider Linton's scenarios, meet in small groups and share your responses. Ask a member of your group to record your work as you explore the similarities and differences in your responses. Discuss what you can do to prepare for situations such as the ones Linton describes. Make a list of these things and share it with your class.

Creating Texts

For activities with icons, refer to the Guides to Analyzing Contexts for Writing and Analyzing Readings in Context. For additional help with these writing projects, read the descriptions of **Dialogue/Symposium** and **Essay** in the Genre Glossary.

1. Imagine that you are the program director described on pages 362–364 of Linton's scenario. You are surprised that your efforts to "care for" the disabled have been met with criticism. To rethink your approach and gain perspective on your situation, you invite several writers and activists to sit down with you, talk about the situation, offer ways to think anew about the situation, and consider changes you would like to make. Choose several people whose voices we hear in this chapter, and write a dialogue in which the participants examine the situation closely, articulate the issues, and propose possible solutions.

2. Reread the scenario about the assistant curator, in which you are writing materials to accompany an exhibition. Linton stresses how important language is in representing the images the artist Goya presents. Quoting a college textbook, she reminds us we may have been taught that Goya "presents with a straight face a menagerie of human grotesques . . . " (Gardner, quoted in Linton, p. 356). Similarly, Michael Bérubé in this chapter quotes from his college genetics textbook a description of mongoloid idiocy, now known as Down Syndrome. Bérubé argues that there is a strong connection between the way people are represented and the way they are treated. Write an essay in which you examine the consequences of people being represented in a particular way. Your essay might—but need not—focus solely on disability. Look around you, examine your everyday life, your studies, your workplace, and your family life, and choose one or more examples that allow you to explore the consequences of representation.

Life as We Know It

Michael Bérubé

In this essay about his son Jamie, Michael Bérubé writes, "There has never been a better time to be born with Down syndrome." Bérubé is referring in part to the progress in medical research that has uncovered important connections between physical development and mental ability and made it possible for Jamie to have increased intellectual potential. He is also referring to changing social policy that now makes it common practice for children like Jamie to be raised at home and receive a public education. Years ago, Jamie would have been institutionalized and presumed incapable of learning; today he enjoys the love and support of his family. The National Society for Down Syndrome, an organization that maintains a Web site to educate people about Down syndrome, advises us that "children raised at home and included in all aspects of community life can best reach their potential and function in society with a greater degree of independence."

What accounts for social policy? Bérubé points to the connection between the language we use to name a thing and how we come to understand it. People who are skeptical of the power of language often label this sensitivity to what things are called "political correctness." Bérubé approaches this issue from a different perspective. As a professor at Penn State, Bérubé is interested in both cultural studies and disability studies, fields that examine the various ways in which our culture—social, political, and economic forces—constructs reality. Here Bérubé explores the connection between the language we use to define and represent disability and the social policy that determines reality for people with disabilities. Bérubé is obviously a writer who understands and knows how to use the power of language.

Connecting with the Conversation

1. *Mainstreaming* and *inclusion* refer to the educational practices of integrating disabled students into classrooms in the regular program. Write in your journal about your experiences with these approaches to educating disabled students, or write about the experiences of a friend or relative.
2. What images of Down syndrome do you have from popular culture? Think about TV shows, books, movies, and even commercials. Are you aware of any changes in the portrayal of people with Down syndrome or other persons with disabilities? In your group discuss what impact these images from popular culture might have on your perceptions of this condition.

In my line of work I don't think very often about carbon or potassium, much less about polypeptides or transfer RNA. I teach American and African-American literature; Janet Lyon, my legal spouse and general partner, teaches modern British literature and women's studies. Nothing about our jobs requires us to be aware of the biochemical processes that made us—and, more recently, our children—into conscious beings. But in 1985–86, when Janet was pregnant with our first child, Nicholas, I would lie awake for hours, wondering how the baseball-size clump of cells in her uterus was really going to form something living, let alone something capable of thought. I knew that the physical processes that form dogs and drosophilas are more or less as intricate, on the molecular level, as those that form humans; but puppies and fruit flies don't go around asking how they got here or how (another version of the same question) DNA base-pair sequences code for various amino acids. And though humans have been amazed and puzzled by human gestation for quite a while now, it wasn't until a few nanoseconds ago (in geological time) that their wonder began to focus on the chemical minutiae that somehow differentiate living matter from "mere" matter. The fact that self-replicating molecules had eventually come up with a life-form that could actually pick apart the workings of self-replicating molecules . . . well, let's just say I found this line of thought something of a distraction. At the time, I thought that I would never again devote so much attention to such ideas. I figured the miracle of human birth, like that of humans landing on the moon, would be more routine than miracle the second time around. It wasn't.

Five years later, in September 1991, Janet was pregnant again, another fall semester was beginning, and I was up late writing. At 2:00 A.M., Janet asked when I was coming to bed. At 4:00 A.M., she asked again. "Soon," I said. "Well, you should probably stop working now," she replied," because I think I'm going into labor." At which point she presented me with an early birthday present, a watch with a second hand.

That was the first unexpected thing: James wasn't due for another two weeks. Then came more unexpected things in rapid succession.

From *Harper's Magazine,* December 1994, pp. 41–51.

Eight hours later, in the middle of labor, Janet spotted a dangerous arrhythmia on her heart monitor. The only other person in the room was an obstetrics staff nurse; Janet turned to her and barked, "That's V-tach. We need a cardiologist in here. Get a bolus of lidocaine ready, and get the crash cart." (Being an ex-cardiac-intensive-care nurse comes in handy sometimes.) Pounding on her chest and forcing herself to cough, she broke out of what was possibly a lethal heart rhythm. Labor stalled; Janet and I stared at each other for an hour. Suddenly, at a strange moment when she and I were the only people in the room, James's head presented. I hollered down the hall for help. James appeared within minutes, an unmoving baby of a deep, rich, purple hue, tangled in his umbilical cord. "He looks Downsy around the eyes," I heard. Downsy? He looks stillborn, I thought. They unwrapped the cord, cut it, gave him oxygen. Quickly, incredibly, he revived. No cry, but who cared? They gave him an Apgar score of 7, on a scale of 1 to 10. I remember feeling an immense relief. My wife was alive, my second child was alive. At the end of a teeth-grating hour during which I'd wondered if either of them would see the end of the day, Down syndrome somehow seemed like a reprieve.

5 Over the next half hour, as the nurses worked on James, and Janet and I tried to collect our thoughts, I realized I didn't know very much about Down's, other than that it meant James had an extra chromosome and would be mentally retarded. I knew I'd have some homework to do.

OVER ON HIS TABLE in the birthing room, James wasn't doing very well. He still wasn't moving, he had no sucking reflex, and he was getting bluer. It turned out that the fetal opening in his heart hadn't closed fully. You and I had the same arrangement until around the time of birth, when our heart's ventricles sealed themselves off in order to get us ready to start conducting oxygen from our lungs into our bloodstream. But James still had a hole where no hole should be, and wasn't oxygenating properly.

There was more. Along with his patent ductus arteriosus and his trisomy 21, there was laryngomalacia (floppy larynx), jaundice, polycythemia (an abnormal increase in red blood cells), torticollis, vertebral anomaly, scoliosis, hypotomia (low muscle tone), and (not least of these) feeding problems. That's a lot of text to wade through to get to your kid.

Basically, James was in danger. If he made it through the night he would still be a candidate, in the morning, for open-heart surgery *and* a tracheostomy. Because of the laryngomalacia, which isn't related to Down's, he couldn't coordinate sucking, swallowing, and breathing, and his air supply would close off if he slept on the wrong side. The vertebral problems, we learned, occur in roughly one of six kids with Down's; his first three vertebrae were malformed, his spinal cord vulnerable. And his neck muscles were abnormally tight (that's the torticollis), leaving him with a 20-degree head tilt to the left. He was being fed intravenously and had tubes not only in his arm but in his stomach as well, run neatly through his umbilical artery, still viable from the delivery. Our first Polaroid of him shows a little fleshy thing under a clear plastic basin, lost in machinery and wires. I remember thinking, it's all right that they do all this to him now because he'll never remember it. But it can't be a pleasant introduction to the world.

Within days things got better, and one anxiety after another peeled away: Jamie's duct closed, and as I entered the intensive-care unit one morning I found that the staff had erased from his chart the phone number of the emergency helicopter service that would have flown him to Peoria for heart surgery. His blood-oxygen levels reached the high 90s and stayed there, even as he was weaned from 100 percent oxygen to a level just above the atmospheric norm. A tracheoscopy (that is, a viewing of his throat with an eyepiece at the end of a tube) confirmed that he didn't need a tracheostomy. He still wasn't feeding, but he was opening an eye now and then and looking out at his brother and his parents.

10 I got hold of everything I could on genetics, reproduction, and "abnormal" human development, dusting off college textbooks I hadn't touched since before Nick was born. At one point a staff nurse was sent in to check on *our* mental health; she found us babbling about meiosis and monoploids, wondering anew that Jamie had "gotten" Down syndrome the second he became a zygote. When the nurse inadvertently left behind her notes, Janet sneaked a peek. "Parents seem to be intellectualizing," we read. "Well," Janet shrugged, "that seems accurate enough."

Of the 15 percent of pregnancies that end in miscarriage, more than half are the result of chromosomal abnormalities, and half of these are caused by trisomy—three chromosomes where two should be. Of the myriad possible genetic mistransmissions in human reproduction, excluding anomalies in the sex chromosomes, it appears that only three kinds of trisomies make it to term: people with three thirteenth chromosomes (Patau's syndrome), three eighteenth chromosomes (Edwards' syndrome), and three twenty-first chromosomes (Down syndrome). About one in four or five zygotes with Down's winds up getting born, and since Down's accounts for one of every 600 to 800 live births, it would appear that trisomy 21 happens quite often, maybe on the order of once in every 150 to 250 fertilizations. Kids with Edwards' or Patau's syndrome are born severely deformed and profoundly retarded; they normally don't live more than a few months. That's what I would expect of genetic anomaly, whatever the size of the autosome: though the twenty-first chromosome is the smallest we have, James still has extra genetic material in every single cell. You'd think the effects of such a basic transcription error would make themselves felt pretty clearly.

But what's odd about Down's is how extraordinarily subtle it can be. Mental retardation is one well-known effect, and it can sometimes be severe, but anyone who's watched Chris Burke in TV's *Life Goes On* or "Mike" in McDonald's commercials knows that the extent of such retardation can be next to negligible. The *real* story of Down's lies not in intelligence tests but in developmental delays across the board, and for the first two years of James's life the most important of these were physical rather than mental (though thanks to James I've come to see how interdependent the mental and physical really are). His muscles are weaker than those of most children his age, his nasal passages imperceptibly narrower. His tongue is slightly thicker; one ear is crinkly. His fingers would be shorter and stubbier but for the fact that his mother's are long, thin, and elegant. His face is a few degrees flatter through the middle, his nose delicate.

Down's doesn't cut all children to one mold; the relations between James's genotype and phenotype are lacy and intricate. It's sort of like what happens in Ray Bradbury's short story "A Sound of Thunder," in which a time traveler accidentally steps on a butterfly while hunting dinosaurs 65 million years ago and returns home to find that he's changed the conventions of English spelling and the outcome of the previous day's election. As he hit the age of two, James was very pleased to find himself capable of walking; by three, he had learned to say the names of colors, to count to ten, and to claim that he would *really* be turning four. Of all our genetic nondisjunctions (with the possible exception of hermaphroditism), only Down syndrome produces so nuanced, so finely articulated a variation on "normal" reproduction. James is less mobile and more susceptible to colds than his peers, but—as his grandparents have often attested—you could play with him for hours and never see anything "wrong."

And then there's a variant form of Down's, called mosaicism, which results from the failure of the chromosome to divide not *before* fertilization but immediately *after,* during the early stages of cell division. Only one in a hundred people with Down's are mosaics, but it's possible for such folks to have some normal cells and some with trisomy 21; there's something about the twenty-first, then, that produces anomalies during either meiosis *or* mitosis. Now, that's truly weird. There's also translocation, in which the twenty-first chromosome splits off and joins the fourteenth or fifteenth, producing people who can be called "carriers"; they can give birth to more translocation carriers, normal children, or translocation kids with Down's. And although everyone knows that the incidence of Down's increases with maternal age, almost no one knows that three quarters of all such children are born to mothers under thirty-five, or that fathers are genetically "responsible" for about one fifth of them. *Parents seem to be intellectualizing.* And why not?

15 THERE HAS NEVER BEEN A BETTER time than now to be born with Down syndrome—and that's really saying something, since it has recently been reported in chimpanzees and gorillas. Because our branch of the evolutionary tree split off from the apes' around 15 to 20 million years ago, these reports would seem to suggest that we've produced offspring with Down syndrome with great regularity at every point in our history as hominids—even though it's a genetic anomaly that's not transmitted hereditarily (except in extremely rare instances) and has no obvious survival value. The statistical incidence of Down's in the current human population is no less staggering: there may be 10 million people with Down's worldwide, or just about one on every other street corner.

But although *Homo sapiens* (as well as our immediate ancestors) has always experienced some difficulty dividing its chromosomes, it wasn't until 1866 that British physician J. Langdon Down diagnosed it as "mongolism" (because it produced children with almond-shaped eyes reminiscent, to at least one nineteenth-century British mind, of central Asian faces). At the time, the average life expectancy of children with Down's was under ten. And for a hundred years thereafter—during which the discovery of antibiotics lengthened the life span of Down's kids to around twenty—Down syndrome was formally known as "mongoloid idiocy."

The 1980 edition of my college genetics textbook, *The Science of Genetics: An Introduction to Heredity,* opens its segment on Down's with the words, "An important and tragic instance of trisomy in humans involves Down's syndrome, or mongoloid idiocy." It includes a picture of a "mongoloid idiot" along with a karyotype of his chromosomes and the information that most people with Down's have IQs in the low 40s.

The presentation is objective, dispassionate, and strictly "factual," as it should be. But reading it again in 1991, I began to wonder: is there a connection between the official textual representation of Down syndrome and the social policies by which people with Down's are understood and misunderstood?

You bet your life there is. Anyone who has paid attention to the "political correctness" wars on American campuses knows how stupid the academic left can be: we're always talking about language instead of reality, whining about "lookism" and "differently abled persons" instead of changing the world the way the real he-man left *used* to do. But you know, there really is a difference between calling someone "a mongoloid idiot" and calling him or her "a person with Down syndrome." There's even a difference between calling people "retarded" and calling them "delayed." Though these words may appear to mean the same damn thing when you look them up in Webster's, I remember full well from my days as an American male adolescent that I never taunted my peers by calling them "delayed." Even from those of us who were shocked at the frequency with which "homo" and "nigger" were thrown around in our fancy Catholic high school, "retard" aroused no comment, no protest. In other words, a retarded person is just a retard. But *delayed* persons will get where they're going eventually, if you'll only have some patience.

One night I said something like this to one of the leaders of what I usually think of as the other side in the academic culture wars. Being a humane fellow, he replied that although epithets like "mongoloid idiot" were undoubtedly used in a more benighted time, there have always been persons of goodwill who resisted such phraseology. A nice thought, but it just ain't so. Right through the 1970s, "mongoloid idiot" wasn't an epithet; it was a *diagnosis.* It wasn't uttered by callow, ignorant persons fearful of "difference" and central Asian eyes; it was pronounced by the best-trained medical practitioners in the world, who told families of kids with Down's that their children would never be able to dress themselves, recognize their parents, or live "meaningful" lives. Best to have the child institutionalized and tell one's friends that the baby died at birth. Only the most stubborn, intransigent, or inspired parents resisted such advice from their trusted experts. Who could reasonably expect otherwise?

20 It's impossible to say how deeply we're indebted to those parents, children, teachers, and medical personnel who insisted on treating people with Down's as if they *could* learn, as if they *could* lead "meaningful" lives. In bygone eras, parents who didn't take their children home didn't really have the "option" of doing so; you can't talk about "options" (in any substantial sense of the word) in an ideological current so strong. But in the early 1970s, some parents did bring their children home, worked with them, held them, provided them physical therapy and "special learning" environments. These parents are saints and sages. They have, in the broadest sense of the phrase, uplifted the race. In the 15-million-year history of Down syndrome, they've allowed us to believe that we're finally getting somewhere.

Of course, the phrase "mongoloid idiocy" did not cause Down syndrome any more than the word "homo" magically induces same-sex desire. But words and phrases are the devices by which we beings signify what homosexuality, or Down syndrome, or anything else, will mean. There surely were, and are, the most intimate possible relations between the language in which we spoke of Down's and the social practices by which we understood it—or refused to understand it. You don't have to be a poststructuralist or a postmodernist or a post-*anything* to get this; all you have to do is meet a parent of a child with Down syndrome. Not long ago, we lived next door to people whose youngest child had Down's. After James was born, they told us of going to the library to find out more about their baby's prospects and wading through page after page of outdated information, ignorant generalizations, and pictures of people in mental institutions, face down in their feeding trays. These parents demanded the library get some better material and throw out the garbage they had on their shelves. Was this a "politically correct" thing for them to do? Damn straight it was. That garbage has had its effects *for generations.* It may only look like words, but perhaps the fragile little neonates whose lives were thwarted and impeded by the policies and conditions of institutionalization can testify in some celestial court to the power of mere language, to the intimate links between words and social policies.

Some of my friends tell me this sounds too much like "strict social constructionism"—that is, too much like the proposition that culture is everything and biology is only what we decide to make (of) it. But although James is pretty solid proof that human biology "exists" independently of our understanding of it, every morning when he gets up, smiling and babbling to his family, I can see for myself how much of his life depends on our social practices. On one of those mornings I turned to my mother-in-law and said, "He's always so full of mischief, he's always so glad to see us—the only thought I can't face is the idea of this little guy waking up each day in a state mental hospital." To which my mother-in-law replied, "Well, Michael, if he were waking up every day in a state mental hospital, he wouldn't *be* this little guy."

As it happens, my mother-in-law doesn't subscribe to any strict social constructionist newsletters; she was just passing along what she took to be good common sense. But every so often I wonder how common that sense really is. Every ten minutes we hear that the genetic basis of something has been "discovered," and we rush madly to the newsweeklies: Disease is genetic! Homosexuality is genetic! Infidelity, addiction, obsession with mystery novels—all genetic! Such discourses, it would seem, bring out the hidden determinist in more of us than will admit it. Sure, there's a baseline sense in which our genes "determine" who we are: we can't play the tune unless the score is written down somewhere in the genome. But one does not need or require a biochemical explanation for literary taste, or voguing, or faithless lovers. In these as in all things human, including Down's, the genome is but a template for a vaster and more significant range of social and historical variation. Figuring out even the most rudimentary of relations between the genome and the immune system (something of great relevance to us wheezing asthmatics) involves so many trillions of variables that a decent answer will win you an all-expenses-paid trip to Stockholm.

I'm not saying we can eradicate Down's—or its myriad effects—simply by talking about it more nicely. I'm only saying that James's intelligence is doing better than it would in an institution, and people who try to deny this don't strike me as being among the geniuses of the species. And every time I hear some self-styled "realist" tell me that my logic licenses the kind of maniacal social engineering that produced Auschwitz, I do a reality check: the people who brought us Auschwitz weren't "social constructionists." They were eugenicists. They thought they knew the "immutable laws" of genetics and the "fixed purpose" of evolution, and they were less interested in "improving" folks like Jamie than in exterminating them. I'll take my chances with the people who believe in chance.

25 And yet there's something very seductive about the notion that Down syndrome wouldn't have been so prevalent in humans for so long without good reason. Indeed, there are days when, despite everything I know and profess, I catch myself believing that people with Down syndrome are here for a specific purpose—perhaps to teach us patience, or humility, or compassion, or mere joy. A great deal can go wrong with us in utero, but under the heading of what goes wrong, Down syndrome is among the most basic, the most fundamental, the most common, *and* the most innocuous, leavening the species with children who are somewhat slower, and usually somewhat gentler, than the rest of the human brood. It speaks to us strongly of design, if design may govern in a thing so small.

AFTER SEVENTEEN DAYS IN THE ICU, James was scheduled for release.

Slowly we got James to bottle feed. After all, for our purposes, Jamie's nasal tube, like unto a thermonuclear weapon, was there precisely so that we *wouldn't* use it. Each week a visiting nurse would set a minimum daily amount for Jamie's milk intake, and whatever he didn't get by bottle would have to go in by tube. So you can see the incentive at work here. Within a month we began to see glimpses of what James would look like sans tube. Then we stopped giving him oxygen during the night, and gradually his tiny nostrils found themselves a lot less encumbered. He still didn't have a voice, but he was clearly interested in his new home and very trusting of his parents and brother.

In the midst of that winter James began physical therapy and massages. We stretched his neck every night, and whenever we could afford it we took him to a local masseuse who played ambient music, relaxed us all, and worked on James for an hour. His physical therapist showed us how everything about James was connected to everything else: His neck, if left uncorrected, would reshape the bones of his face. The straighter his neck, the sooner he'd sit up, the sooner he'd walk. If he could handle simple solid foods with equal facility in both sides of his mouth, he could center himself more easily; and the sooner he could move around by himself, the more he'd be able to explore and learn. In other words, his eating would affect his ability to walk, and his thighs and torso would impinge upon his ability to talk. I suppose that's what it means to be an organism.

Not only did we realize the profound interdependence of human hearts and minds; we also discovered (and had to reconfigure) our relations to a vast array of social practices and institutions. "Developmental" turns out to be a buzzword for a sprawling nexus of agencies, state organizations, and human disabilities. Likewise, "special needs" isn't a euphemism; it's a very specific marker. We're learning about the differences between "mainstreaming" and "inclusion," and we'll be figuring out the Americans with Disabilities Act for the rest of our lives. Above all else, we know that James is extremely lucky to be so well provided for; when every employer is as flexible as ours, when parental leave is the law of the land, when private insurers can't drop families from the rolls because of "high risk" children, when every child can be fed, clothed, and cared for—*then* we can start talking about what kind of a choice "life" might be.

30 Because, after all he's been through, James is thriving. He's thrilled to be here and takes a visible, palpable delight in seeing his reflection in the oven door as he toddles across the kitchen, or hearing his parents address him in the voices of the *Sesame Street* regulars, or winging a Nerf ball to his brother on the couch. He knows perfectly well

when he's doing something we've never seen before, like riding his toddler bicycle down the hall into the laundry room or calling out "Georgia" and "Hawaii" as he flips through Nick's book of the fifty states. He's been a bibliophile from the moment he learned to turn pages. His current favorite is Maurice Sendak's classic *Where the Wild Things Are,* surely a Great Book by any standard; he began by identifying with Max and then, in one of those "oscillations" described by reader-response criticism and feminist film theory, switched over to identifying with the wild things themselves—roaring his terrible roar and showing his terrible claws.

He has his maternal aunts' large deep eyes, and a beautiful smile that somehow involves his whole body. He's not only an independent cuss, but he also has an attention span of about twenty minutes—eighteen minutes longer than the average American political pundit. He's blessed with a preternaturally patient, sensitive brother in Nick, who, upon hearing one of his classmates' parents gasp "Oh my God" at the news that Jamie had Down's, turned to her and said with a fine mixture of reassurance and annoyance, "He's perfectly all *right.*" Like Nick, James has a keen sense of humor; the two of them can be set agiggle by pratfalls, radical incongruities, and mere sidelong looks. He's just now old enough to be curious about what he was like as a baby: as he puts it, all he could do was go "waaah" (holding his fists to his eyes). Barring all the contingencies that can never be barred, James can expect a life span of anywhere from thirty-five to fifty-five years. For tomorrow, he can expect to see his friends at day care, to put all his shapes in his shapes box, and to sing along with Raffi as he shakes his sillies out and wiggles his waggles away.

BEFORE JAMES WAS BORN I frankly didn't think very highly of appeals to our "common humanity." I thought such appeals were well intentioned but basically inconsequential. Clearly, Muslim and Christian do not bond over their common ancestor in *Australopithecus.* Rwandan Hutu and Rwandan Tutsi do not toast to the distinctive size of their cerebral cortices. The rape of Bosnia, and Bosnian women, does not stop once Serbian soldiers realize that they too will pass from the earth.

And yet we possess one crucial characteristic: the desire to communicate, to understand, to put ourselves in some mutual, reciprocal form of contact with one another. This desire hasn't proven any better at disarming warheads than any of the weaker commonalities enumerated above, but it stands a better chance nonetheless. For among the most amazing and hopeful things about us is that we show up, from our day of birth, programmed to receive and transmit even in the most difficult circumstances; the ability to imagine mutual communicative relations is embedded in our material bodies, woven through our double-stranded fibers. Granted, it's only one variable among trillions, and it's not even "fundamentally" human—for all we know, dolphins are much better at communication than we are. And the sociohistorical variables of human communication will always be more significant and numerous than any genetic determinism can admit. All the same, it's in our software somewhere, and, better still, it's a program that teaches itself how to operate each time we use it.

Whether you want to consider reciprocal communication a constant or a variable, though, the point remains that it's a human attribute requiring other people if it's going to work. Among the talents we have, it's one we could stand to develop more fully. It's only natural: among our deepest, strongest impulses is the impulse to mutual cuing. Nothing will delight James so much as the realization that you have understood him—except the realization that he has understood *you,* and recursively understood his own understanding and yours. Perhaps I could have realized our human stake in mutual realization without James's aid; any number of other humans would have been willing to help me out. But now that I get it, I get it for good. Communication is itself self-replicating. Sign unto others as you'd have them sign unto you. Pass it on.

Exploring Texts and Contexts

For activities with icons, refer to the Guide to Analyzing Readings in Context.

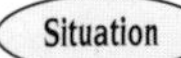

1. Bérubé is writing as a professor of literature and a parent of a child with a disability. Compare his writing with the work of Simi Linton, in this unit, who approaches the subject of disability as an educator, or with that of Paul Longmore, also in this unit, who writes as a scholar and a disability rights activist. What does Bérubé's perspective add to the conversation about disability?

2. On page 373 Bérubé says that there is a connection between social policies for people with Down syndrome and the language that is used to describe it. What concrete examples does he provide to help you think about this connection?

3. On page 370, Bérubé says, "That's a lot of text to wade through to get to your kid." What does he mean? Have you ever felt that you had to wade through a lot of text to get to something? Discuss your responses with the class.

Creating Texts

For activities with icons, refer to the Guides to Analyzing Contexts for Writing and Analyzing Readings in Context. For additional help with these writing projects, read the descriptions of **Academic Article/Research Paper** and **Essay** in the Genre Glossary.

1. In his article, Bérubé describes the representation of Down syndrome in a 1980 college genetics textbook. Write a research paper about the changes in the way Down syndrome has been portrayed during the latter part of the twentieth century. A good place to find information about contemporary depictions is The National Society for Down Syndrome web site at www.ndss.org. It maintains a list of journal articles, books, videos, and links to related sites. You may find leads on material published earlier in the 1980s or still earlier by reviewing the bibliographies of some of the books listed. In addition, try to locate previous volumes of the social science journals listed on the Web site. In your paper, speculate on the relationship between representations of Down syndrome and the social reality for people with Down's.

Genre

2. This article originally appeared in *Harper's* magazine, a journal of social commentary. Find a news article from a national or local newspaper that deals with the issue of disability. In an essay, compare the two pieces of writing. How do they differ in structure, organization, language, and design? How does the type of publication help shape and influence what Bérubé writes and how he writes it?

Media Commentary on the Americans with Disabilities Act

The word *deliberation* might make you think of lawmakers debating in a legislative chamber, jury members discussing evidence in a jury room, or executives making a decision in a boardroom. In fact, such face-to-face conversations are at the heart of a society's deliberations, but they are surrounded by a number of more indirect channels of deliberation, and ideas and decisions circulate in all directions through these channels. The pieces on disability in this chapter suggest the range of the forms and channels of deliberation that Americans use today to discuss important issues.

We might not think of personal essays as channels of deliberation, but personal testimonies can be important catalysts in deliberation because they contribute what you might call "news from the front" about experiences or perspectives unfamiliar to the general public. Perhaps more recognizable as channels of deliberation are academic studies, which provide new facts and ideas that have the authority of institutions and expertise behind them. But the indirect, non-face-to-face channel of deliberation that we probably think of first is "the media," the big local and national newspapers, magazines, television and radio stations, and now Internet sites that have considerable power because they are read or viewed by politicians, policymakers, CEOs, voters, and other people who make decisions that affect us all.

In one sense these decisions are the end of the deliberative process, but then they themselves are discussed in the media, studied by academics, and portrayed in their real-life impacts by essayists and artists, and the process continues. The next two readings show us a moment in that process. The readings are an opinion piece and an editorial that influenced the Senate debate over the Americans with Disabilities Act. These pieces appeared in one of the country's most influential newspapers, the *New York Times,* in the days preceding the debate, and several senators used ideas or information from them to support arguments for or against the ADA. As you read these articles, consider what consequences you think their writers might have intended.

Connecting with the Conversation

1. For several days, read the editorial and op ed (the page opposite the editorial page) pages of your favorite newspaper and a newspaper that you don't usually read, perhaps because it favors positions you don't agree with. What similarities and differences do you notice in the editorials, regular opinion columns, guest opinion pieces, letters to the editor, and editorial cartoons? Compare notes in a small group, and then share your findings with the class.
2. Many university and college libraries today have access to databases, such as LexisNexis, from which researchers can retrieve a wide range of materials from the mass media, including not only newspaper and magazine articles but also transcripts or summaries of stories in the electronic media. Most of these databases go back at least 15 years. Search August and September 1989—that is, just

before and after the Senate debate on the ADA—for materials, especially editorials and opinion pieces, about the Americans with Disabilities Act. Share your findings with the class.

Save Money: Help the Disabled

James S. Brady

Washington

Astonishingly, it is legal under Federal law for a restaurant to refuse to serve a mentally retarded person, for a theater to deny admission to someone with cerebral palsy, for a dry cleaner to refuse service to someone who is deaf or blind. People with disabilities—the largest minority in the U.S.—were left out of the historic Civil Rights Act of 1964. Twenty-five years later, discrimination against disabled people is still pervasive.

Congress has a chance to correct this injustice. The Americans with Disabilities Act is now before the full Senate, and President Bush and more than 200 national organizations have endorsed the bill.

As a Republican and a fiscal conservative, I am proud that this bill was developed by 15 Republicans appointed to the National Council on Disability by President Reagan. Many years ago, a Republican President, Dwight D. Eisenhower, urged that people with disabilities become taxpayers and consumers instead of being dependent upon costly Federal benefits. The Disabilities Act grows out of that conservative philosophy.

Today 66 percent of working-age adults with disabilities are unemployed and dependent on Federal subsidies. The Disabilities Act could save taxpayers billions of dollars by outlawing discrimination, putting disabled people on the job rolls and thereby reducing Government disability payments.

5 Experience has shown that no civil right has ever been secured without legislation. A law such as the Disabilities Act would insure that facilities and employers—public and private—maintain minimum standards of accessibility. The act would require installation of ramps, elevators, lifts, and other aids in new private businesses and public buildings, and on newly purchased buses and trains. And it would prohibit discrimination in private employment, public accommodations, transportation, and telecommunications.

By breaking down barriers in stores and offices, it would enable more disabled people to purchase goods and services—and thereby strengthen our national economy. By breaking down barriers in public transportation, the act would allow more people with disabilities to be employed and participate in community activities. The act would free

From The *New York Times,* August 29, 1989, p. A19.

hundreds of thousands of citizens who are virtually prisoners in their homes because of inaccessible transportation and public accommodations.

There are 37 million people in America who live with some form of disability. I never thought I would be one of them. Most people don't like to think about disability at all. But disability can happen to anyone. In fact, as our population ages and medical technology prolongs life, many more eventually will be disabled.

Since I took a bullet in the head eight years ago during the assassination attempt on Ronald Reagan, I have come to know the daily problems, frustrations, and needs of those who live with disability. I have had to learn to talk again, to read again, and to walk again. I have succeeded, and I know that everyone can learn to overcome the final obstacle to our equal inclusion in American life: prejudice toward people with disabilities.

Passage of the Americans with Disabilites Act will increase the acceptance, dignity and full participation of citizens with disabilities. We do not want pity or sympathy. All we want is the same civil rights and opportunities that all citizens have. We want fairness, acceptance and the chance to contribute fully to our nation—just like everyone else.

Blank Check for the Disabled?

New York Times Editors

With surprisingly narrow public scrutiny, Congress is moving swiftly to extend broad civil rights protection to the nation's 40 million disabled citizens. The sentiment is laudable: to bring the disabled closer to the mainstream of American society. But the legislation is vague; not even its defenders are able to calculate its benefits and costs. Those costs could be monumental. The proposal thus requires patient, unemotional examination.

That won't be easy. The bill was unanimously approved by the Senate Labor and Human Resources Committee last month, and though it still awaits hearings in four separate House committees, it commands strong bipartisan support in both House and Senate and the endorsement of President Bush. As one skeptic put it, "No politician can vote against this bill and survive."

* * *

The bill would ban discrimination in employment in all businesses with more than 15 workers. That's caused no controversy. What has is a provision requiring nearly every retail establishment, large or small, old and new—barber shops, banks, restaurants, movie theaters—to be accessible to the disabled. The legislation does not spell out how. But in many cases it would mean building ramps, widening doorways, modifying restrooms. Elevators would be required in all new buildings of more than two stories.

The bill would also require bus companies to include lifts, specially designed restrooms, and other facilities on all new buses built five to six years after enactment. The

From The *New York Times*, September 6, 1989, 1, p. A24.

bill calls for a study—after the bill is passed, not before—to determine how much this would cost the companies.

5 The bus companies are angry. Most businessmen are simply fretful and confused. That's partly because the bill's language is so vague. It says that existing facilities must make only "readily achievable" changes that won't involve "burdensome expense." Yet what do these words mean in practice? Obviously, no bill can give precise instructions to thousands of individual businesses. But several states already have laws on the books that provide business more useful guidance than the Senate bill does.

Senator Tom Harkin, Iowa Democrat, argues that "costs do not provide a basis for exemption from the basic principles in a civil rights statute." Mr. Harkin has a hearing-impaired brother and a quadriplegic nephew. He's fought honorably for the bill, and has already made compromises.

He also points out that the Federal Government now spends nearly $60 billion a year on benefits for the disabled—a sum that could shrink if the disabled had easier access to jobs and could move from welfare rolls to tax rolls. The Census Bureau reported last month that less than 25 percent of all disabled men and only 13 percent of disabled women held full-time jobs. And the earnings of those who do work average only two-thirds that of all workers.

Predictions about the bill's projected benefits are obviously speculative. Worse, nobody has even tried to speculate about its costs. But it shouldn't be impossible to provide estimates. The Office of Management and Budget has done so before in tough instances, like the costs of air bags.

Congress and the Administration now have a similar responsibility to stand back, to weigh, to calculate. No one wishes to stint on helping the disabled. It requires little legislative skill, however, to write blank checks for worthy causes with other people's money.

Exploring Texts and Contexts

For activities with icons, refer to the Guide to Analyzing Readings in Context.

1. Opinion pieces present the opinion of an identified individual, and editorials present the position of the newspaper as a whole. What type of authority does each genre thus rely on, and what are the strengths and weaknesses of these sources of authority? How well does each of these pieces use the type of authority that its genre relies on?

2. Compare the styles of these two pieces with regard to word choice, organization, rhetorical devices, and voice. Which do you find more persuasive and why?

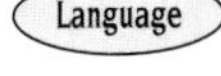

Creating Texts

For assignments with icons, refer to the Guides to Analyzing Contexts for Writing and Analyzing Readings in Context. For additional help with these writing projects, read the descriptions of **Interview** and **Academic Article/Research Paper** in the Genre Glossary.

1. Interview a local politician—for example, your U.S. Representative, state representative, mayor, or city councilperson—about how he or she responds to the media. You might ask, for example, what media sources the person reads, listens to, or watches regularly; does the person read editorials, opinion pieces, and letters to the editor, or just news stories, and which of these forms of writing is that person most likely to be influenced by; are there particular periodicals or writers that the person is more likely to listen to than others; what kinds of facts and information are likely to persuade that person; what does the person find more persuasive, articles in the media or letters from constituents; and has that person ever referred to media articles in debates over legislation or policies? Write up your interview in order to contribute to a general class discussion about how politicians are or are not influenced by the media.

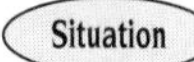

2. These two pieces are both from the *New York Times.* Using your library's mass media database (See Connecting with the Conversation Activity 2) or online indexes, search for recent articles about disability, and in particular, the Americans with Disabilities Act. Write a research-based essay in which you discuss what kinds of arguments are being made about the ADA.

The FDR Memorial

Who Speaks from the Wheelchair?

Rosemarie Garland-Thomson

Throughout the 1990s, as the Americans with Disabilities Act was changing many aspects of the public sphere and becoming part of our public discourse about disability, the disability rights movement continued to work on other issues related to disability. During the discussion about the design of the national memorial to President Franklin Delano Roosevelt, disability rights activists argued that Roosevelt should be represented in his wheelchair. Roosevelt lost the use of his legs to polio when he was 39, making it necessary for him to use a wheelchair. He learned to stand with assistance so that, as president, he was rarely seen by the public in his chair. As the memorial was being planned and designed, the prevailing view was that it should represent Roosevelt as he preferred to be seen during his lifetime. But after the memorial was dedicated in 1997, disability rights activists, arguing that this was an opportunity to change our national "story" about disability, persuaded President Clinton to support an addition to the memorial including a life-size bronze statue showing Roosevelt in his wheelchair.

As the addition was being completed, disability rights activists and disability studies scholars were asked to propose quotations to be carved into the stone near the new statue. In this article from the *Chronicle of Higher Education,* disability studies scholar and professor of English Rosemarie Garland-Thomson discusses the controversy over this inscription. The story of this controversy gives us a glimpse into how new ideas about disability might change the way we see and represent ourselves as a people.

Connecting with the Conversation

1. Have you visited public memorials in Washington, D.C., or other places? How do they "tell a story" about the person or event memorialized?
2. What do you know about our thirty-second president, Franklin Delano Roosevelt? What mental images do you have of him?

As public spaces transformed into collective stories, memorials are inherently controversial. Didactic narratives about who we are and what we believe, they span generations and vast differences in human perceptions, bringing to light all sorts of divisions in the national "we." One of those divides has occurred between a group of scholars in disability studies and the designers of the Franklin Delano Roosevelt Memorial in Washington. The five-year struggle over the collective story told by the F.D.R. memorial ended only this month, when President Clinton dedicated an addition to the memorial. The controversy—and, unfortunately, its not entirely satisfactory conclusion—tells us much about disability in American culture, about disability studies, and about ourselves.

Even before its dedication, on May 2, 1997, the memorial had splintered the national "we." The original monument consisted of four granite-walled outdoor "rooms,"

From *The Chronicle of Higher Education,* January 26, 2001. pp. B11–B12.

which narrated F.D.R.'s presidency with inscriptions of his own words and with nine bronze bas-reliefs and statues, representing scenes of his presidency, all intermingled with pools, waterfalls, and greenery.

The segment of the American "we" representing disability-rights activists and scholars in disability studies had wanted to avoid repeating the persistent stereotypes of disability—the ones that tell us that disability is a shameful personal problem relegated to the private realm of charity and medicine, but inappropriate in the public sphere.

We had wanted the memorial to tell the story of a man who was both disabled by polio and president of the United States for 12 years; to claim F.D.R. as a disabled public figure who represented not just the 15 percent of the U.S. population who have disabilities, but everyone, since we will all become disabled if we live long enough. The memorial's present and future audiences, we had argued, would consist of people whose consciousness had been transformed by civil-rights movements that included the disability-rights movement, and by legislation like the Americans with Disabilities Act, the landmark law that mandates full integration of people with disabilities into American society.

5 But the only statue that even remotely referred to F.D.R.'s disability showed him seated, covered by a cape, on a chair with small wheels barely peeking out. The threat of protests by disability activists at the memorial's dedication convinced President Clinton to seek an addition, and the designers agreed—the first time that an existing national memorial was to be changed. Maya Lin's controversial Vietnam Veterans Memorial was augmented with representational figures of soldiers, but those traditionally heroic statues only flank, rather than fundamentally change, the somber black-granite slab and the space of meditation and mourning it creates.

The bold mandate to reimagine F.D.R. as at once heroic and disabled has now been realized. A new "room" at the entrance to the present memorial contains a simple, life-size bronze statue depicting Roosevelt seated in his wheelchair, wearing his trademark rumpled suit, pince-nez, and fedora. It differs from the regal, robed, larger-than-life figure represented in the third room, where the ample cloak erases and denies the mark of his disability. The new statue witnesses the simple humanity of the great leader and registers it as the universality of disability. It also marks today's historical moment, when disability defined as a civil-rights issue is superseding disability as a medical or charitable issue.

YET THE CONTROVERSY CONTINUES, because the story that the new "room" of the F.D.R. memorial tells is still fraught with contradiction. At issue is the phrasing of the words inscribed on the granite wall behind the new statue of F.D.R. A group of us from the field of disability studies had been invited to recommend potential quotations, from which the designers were to choose an inscription. As historians and literary critics who traffic in words, we relished the chance to influence the way that people present and future would understand disability. The memorial's other inscriptions are illustrious words that enrich the story told by the spaces and the statues. F.D.R.'s eloquent verbal commitments to equality are literally set in stone, shaping the story of his presidency and of the nation itself. One powerful quotation reads, "We must scrupulously guard the civil rights and civil liberties of all citizens, whatever their background. We must remember that any oppression, any injustice, any hatred, is a wedge designed to attack our civilization." We wanted the new addition to continue the theme of equal rights that is the hallmark of both the disability-rights movement and the F.D.R. memorial.

We had a story about disability that we wanted the new room to tell. We sought to offer a quotation as crisp, powerful, and unambiguous as the bold "I hate war" chiseled into the wall above the tumbled stones that suggest the blasted buildings of World War II while creating a majestic waterfall that implies transcendence.

F.D.R.'s strategy in the Depression had been to alter the environment to meet the needs of the people. That was parallel, we reasoned, to the idea that people with disabilities need a material situation that accommodates the differences of their bodies or minds. So we looked for a quotation to convey the idea that political equality and access to the workplace for people with disabilities requires a leveling of the playing field—both literally, in the case of wheelchair users like F.D.R., and metaphorically, for those of us who need other accommodations to be fully integrated into the public sphere.

10 We also wanted to tell the story of a determined man who used a wheelchair, and whose use of it influenced the world around him. As scholars in disability studies, we examine disability as a cultural concept that shapes history, belief, art, literature, and other aspects of culture. We saw F.D.R. as someone whose disability shaped him and who, in turn, shaped his own world and the world that has come after. We looked for a quotation telling that story about disability while eschewing stereotypical stories about courageous people who overcame their disabilities or found serenity through suffering.

Enough of those oppressive narratives dominate public thought and circulate in telethons, fiction, and sentimental tracts. The F.D.R. memorial should offer up an accomplished leader, not a cheerful or chastened cripple.

To provide criteria for selecting the inscription in the new room, we suggested three themes that should be emphasized, and three that should be avoided. We sought a quotation, first of all, that would advance the idea that disability is integral to a person's character and life experience, rather than a defect to be eliminated. Second, we wanted a quotation suggesting that the experience of disability can enrich a life, foster leadership, and create a sense of community. Third, in keeping with the human scale of the statue, we searched for words hinting that F.D.R.'s disability made him an accessible—rather than a lofty—hero. In other words, we recommended that any new inscription present disability as a common, yet influential, human experience, one that can be integrated into a meaningful and full life.

Conversely, we argued that the quotation should avoid the stereotypical narrative that disability is a tragic experience to be overcome. Discrimination, more than impairment, is what people with disabilities have to surmount. Our second caveat was more complex: In keeping with our conviction that disability should be viewed as a political issue of rights and access, we intended to circumvent the idea that disability is simply a matter of having an individual impairment to contend with. Recasting social attitudes and removing environmental barriers are more important for improving the lives of people with disabilities than are their own spunk, saintliness, iron will, or the generosity of others. Third—the most subtle point to convey—we strove to dispel the pervasive attitude that disabled people warrant attention only to provide lessons or inspirations to others. We wanted to focus on how F.D.R. himself experienced disability, rather than turn him into a homily for the nondisabled that inspires pity and admiration—or gratitude that they are not themselves disabled.

Gracing the humble but commanding statue of a disabled F.D.R. with a quotation that could do all of that political and cultural work was challenging. After reviewing more than 100 possibilities, consulting with other scholars and disability activists, and, at times, disagreeing among ourselves, we offered a unanimous recommendation to the designers, trusting that they would understand and support our criteria: "We know that equality of individual ability has never existed and never will, but we do insist that equality of opportunity still must be sought." Combined with the image of a U.S. president using a wheelchair, those words sent the unequivocal message that disability is an issue of equal opportunity.

To our dismay, however, the designers and the other people advising them selected an inscription for the new room of the F.D.R. memorial that has exactly the effect we'd hoped to avoid. Disregarding our recommendation, they instead used a quotation from Eleanor Roosevelt: "Franklin's illness gave him strength and courage he had not had before. He had to think out the fundamentals of living and learn the greatest of all lessons—infinite patience and never-ending persistence." That quotation is compelling, and it even fulfills some of our criteria, because it interprets F.D.R.'s disability as a positive influence on his life. Indeed, we had offered it along with several others as a possible addition that might augment our recommended choice. But we did not want it to be the only story of disability that the memorial would tell.

Alone, Eleanor Roosevelt's words undermine disability-rights goals. To begin with, we believe that F.D.R. should speak for himself. Too often, others have spoken for and about people with disabilities. In the old way of understanding disability, people with disabilities were silenced while the authority to define them and to narrate their experience was appropriated by medical experts, service providers, or family members. Having another person speak for F.D.R. repeats the humiliating experience of being ignored that people with disabilities often endure. A quotation from his wife also reinforces the myth that F.D.R. denied his disability—especially since nowhere else in the memorial do quotations from anyone but him appear.

Even more important, to have the first two words a visitor encounters at the memorial be "Franklin's illness" presents disability in a way that doubly violates the spirit of equality. "Illness" is a synonym for impairment, a term that disability scholars and activists use to denote functional limitation. "Disability," on the other hand, is a term we use to describe the system of representation that produces discriminatory attitudes and barriers to full integration. In essence, "impairment" and "illness" are about bodily differences, whereas "disability" is about the social and political context in which our bodies operate. The distinction is much the same as the one that scholars often draw between "sex" and "gender." "Illness" locates the story of disability in hospitals and rehabilitation centers. We want the story of disability to be placed in independent-living centers. To object to "illness" is not to fault Eleanor Roosevelt for being politically incorrect; rather, it is to suggest that the way we view disability in 2001 and beyond has changed from the way it was imagined in 1949. After all, a memorial should not simply replicate the past, but use history to create a future vision.

"Franklin's illness" also personalizes rather than politicizes disability. While the quotation the designers propose is certainly moving, it tells the stereotypical, apolitical story of disability as an individual catastrophe, psychological adjustment, and moral chastening. Impairment is a private problem that an individual must overcome, not a public problem of environmental and attitudinal barriers that can be removed through legislation, policy, and education. Moreover, opening with this quotation places the F.D.R. memorial in the genre of public works intended for collective grieving—like war memorials, the AIDS Memorial Quilt, the Oklahoma City National Memorial, or plaques for sailors lost at sea.

In our debate with the designers, they asserted that their quotation would make F.D.R. "very personal, very accessible." But they confused their intent to humanize F.D.R. with personalizing his disability. The inscription that now flanks the statue encourages visitors to respond with sympathy, admiration, and charity rather than with support for equal access and integration. A more effective way to humanize F.D.R. would be to suggest that his impairment reinforced his commitment to the universal mandate for "equality of opportunity," a point to which our recommended quotation alludes.

The designers also mistakenly justified the choice of their text on aesthetic grounds. The story of "Franklin's illness" as well as of his "strength," "courage," "patience," and "persistence" would create an aesthetically differentiated and inspirational space, they argued in commenting on our recommendation. The new room was to be a "prologue." In reality, that suggests separating the personal story of disability from the political content of the memorial's other rooms. The quotation clings to the stubborn stereotypes of disability that still feel comfortable to many Americans, simply because those ideas are so easily recognizable. A wheelchair-using F.D.R., spoken about by others, is segregated within his own memorial. That denies the political work of disability-rights activists and scholars, who have sought to eliminate precisely such segregation.

MANY OF US in disability studies wish to register our dissent from the choice of the inscription for the new room of the F.D.R. memorial. Pleased as we are with the statue itself, we worry that this memorial to our first markedly disabled president ultimately replicates the segregation and privatization of disability. The inscription undermines the work of disability-rights advocates who worked so hard to make the new room a reality. It tells the story that disability is separate from politics—a personal problem rather than a public political struggle.

In the year 2001, we are on the cultural cusp of a new way to understand disability. The memorial's figures, spaces, and, particularly, its words implicitly instruct visitors in how they should imagine disability. In the controversy over the F.D.R. memorial, our evolving national narrative of disability was played out as a quarrel between aesthetics and politics. But underneath, the disagreement was a struggle between familiar old stories and bold new ones, between moving stories about personal suffering and empowering ones about social equality. While the designers of the F.D.R. memorial have laudably affirmed disability with the depiction of the president using a wheelchair, they did not succeed in rewriting the story of disability in terms that will resonate for future generations.

The addition to the F.D.R. memorial suggests two conflicting stories: yesterday's story of disability as a personal failing overcome by individual effort, and today's and tomorrow's story of disability as an issue of civil rights, integration, and diversity. Our national disability politics has come a long way since the 1930s. Shouldn't our national aesthetics now take up the challenge to transform the meaning of disability?

Exploring Texts and Contexts

For activities with icons, refer to the Guide to Analyzing Readings in Context.

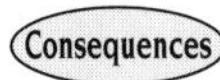

1. Like Paul Longmore, Simi Linton, and Michael Bérubé, Garland-Thomson argues for a redefinition of disability. Working in a small group, compare the new definitions for which these writers call. What perspectives does each bring to the issue of disability, and what does each hope will be the consequences of redefining disability?

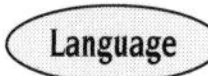

2. In a class discussion, compare the quotation proposed by the disability rights activists with the one chosen by the memorial designers. What story do you think each quote tells about disability?

Creating Texts

For assignments with icons, refer to the Guides to Analyzing Contexts for Writing and Analyzing Readings in Context. For additional help with these writing projects, refer to the descriptions of **Address** and **Essay** in the Genre Glossary.

1. Imagine that you have a sibling, cousin, or neighbor in eighth grade. This young person's class is planning a graduation visit to Washington, D.C., and they have invited a series of speakers to talk with the class about the various places they plan to visit. Knowing that you have been writing about disability, they invite you to speak about the FDR Memorial, which has become one of the most popular sites in the capital. Prepare a talk in which you give some background on Roosevelt himself, explain the controversy over the memorial, and put this controversy into the wider context of the disability rights movement. Using the Internet or your school library, find pictures that you can use to illustrate your talk.
2. The controversy over the FDR Memorial centers on the relationship between art, reality, and representation. Write an essay in which you explore the relationship between artistic freedom and integrity and the responsibilities of representation. You might want to use actual or hypothetical situations to illustrate the relationship you support. For example, you might imagine a meeting between a disability rights group and an artist commissioned to paint a mural for a new playground.

CHAPTER 11

CASE STUDY
Designing Memorials

The Case

This case study focuses on two different sets of events: the public conversations surrounding the design and construction of the Vietnam Veterans Memorial in the early 1980s and the design of the World Trade Center Memorial that began in 2003.

In 1979, a group of Vietnam veterans formed a commission to design and dedicate a memorial that came to be known as the Vietnam Veterans Memorial. The enormously positive public response to the completed memorial almost completely obscures the intense civic debate that dogged its planners for the entire length of the project. The choice of Maya Lin's V-shaped wall of polished black granite inscribed with names of the soldiers sparked a public debate that became so contentious it threatened to derail the project. The memorial was eventually funded and built but not officially dedicated until two statues were added to the site. The memorial has since become one of the most loved public sites in the country.

On September 11, 2001, Americans stood transfixed in horror and disbelief as terrorists flew airplanes into the Pentagon and the twin towers of the World Trade Center. Since that moment, and through our long, painful recovery, the conversation about how to memorialize those who died has continued. In the first edition of this book, this case study focused on the Vietnam Veterans Memorial and we also made mention of the memorial that was built to commemorate the bombing of the Alfred P. Murrah Federal Building in Oklahoma City. As we've used this case study in our classes we naturally followed the discussion about the design of the memorial to those who died in the collapse of the World Trade Center. And, indeed, much of the ongoing conversation has commented on what the public has learned from the design of the Vietnam Veterans Memorial. Thus, this case study focuses on the two memorials and the design issues they share.

The Issues

Public memorials have come to represent many things in our culture: a way to pay tribute to the victims of a tragedy, a way to create some meaning in an otherwise senseless act of violence, and a form of therapy for a bereaved community and nation. In an era when public

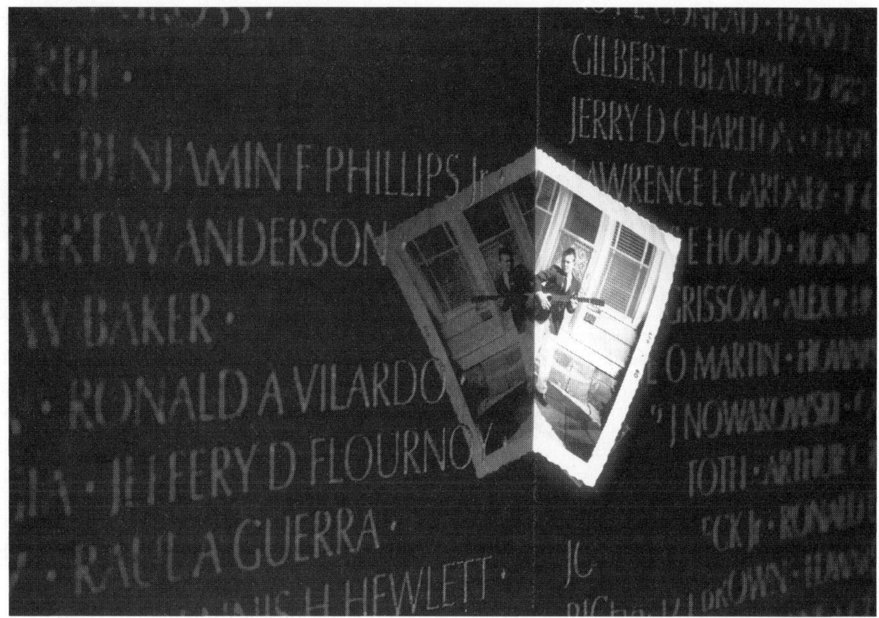

apathy is reflected in low voter turnout and declining participation in community groups, the intensity of civic engagement with public memorials is noteworthy. Both the Vietnam Veterans Memorial and the World Trade Center Memorial make a good case for thinking about the issues involved in public art controversies and the significance of these deliberations in a democratic culture. Although the issues surrounding both designs are varied and complex, they might be organized into those having to do with history, politics, art, and religion or spirituality.

History and Politics. The Vietnam War was the longest engagement in our nation's history, and it ended in defeat. An infamous photo of U.S. military and South Vietnamese government officials crowding aboard a helicopter on the roof of the U.S. Embassy to flee the advancing North Vietnamese soldiers captures the ignominy of the withdrawal. The strong feelings that Americans had about the war were reignited in the national debate about the memorial.

Although the national political debates have been intense, the politics around the design of the new World Trade Center have been more local than national. The land on which the World Trade Center was built is extremely valuable real estate and at the same time it is just a New York City neighborhood; since September 11, it has become the burial ground for those who died in the attack. None of these complications were present in the planning and design of the Vietnam Veterans Memorial, which was built on public land designated for that purpose. The design of the two memorials is influenced in different ways by the history and politics of the events being memorialized.

Art and Spirituality. Memorials must serve as a place to help visitors make peace with a loved one's death. With this single aim in mind, Maya Lin designed a simple, abstract memorial that would allow individuals to connect with their memory of someone they had lost. Her vision for the memorial grew from personal experiences but emerged as a form only after seeing the potential site. Lin's decisions to include the names of the dead in the chronological order of their deaths and to use shiny, mirror-like black granite for the monument contributed to the impact of the monument on the individuals who visited it.

In the case of the Vietnam Veterans Memorial, the history of the war influenced the political debate about the monument, just as the politics of the debate influenced the discussion of artistic issues. The abstract design, the black granite V-shaped wall, was seen by some as a critique of the war rather than an honoring of those who died. Some insisted that a realistic representation of soldiers was the best way to focus on the human lives rather than on the concept of the war. Maya Lin herself insisted that she had not intended any political comment on the war, but instead had thought about how each visitor would respond to the memorial. Lin has been proven right by the millions who have visited since the memorial opened. Every aspect of its design has had a powerful impact on its visitors. Perhaps the memorial is so well loved because Maya Lin focused on the spiritual aspects of the design. In writing her proposal, she focused on the way in which the memorial would help individuals come to terms with death itself rather than with any specifics of the war.

Our acceptance of the abstract design of the Vietnam Veterans Memorial might have made it easier for the American public to accept and appreciate this sort of abstract or highly symbolic design. And yet the question of realism—whether or not to include a realistic statue of soldiers as part of the design—has not disappeared from the debate. At least one of the design proposals for the World Trade Center Memorial included a plan for projecting changing photographs of the victims. Thus the artistic issues seem simpler and less rancorous; on the other hand the spiritual aspects seem more difficult to resolve. Because the site is not simply a memorial to the dead but is actually the burial site for many victims, the victims' families feel strongly that this fact should be recognized in the design. In addition, discussions note that the attacks themselves had a religious dimension and yet people of many religious faiths died in the attack. This circumstance has, in fact, promoted agreement that while the site should have a powerful spiritual dimension, this memorial should not include any specific religious symbols.

The following documents will help you explore in more depth these and other issues involved in the design and building of these two memorials so important to American history, civic life, and culture.

The Documents

- In early November 1980, the competition for the Vietnam Veterans Memorial Design was announced to the public. Given out as a press release, this **statement of purpose** written by **Robert Doubek,** the executive director of the Vietnam Veterans Memorial Fund, was intended to explain what the veterans hoped to accomplish by building a memorial. The founders conceived of the memorial as a way to reconcile a nation still reeling from the bitter controversy caused by the war. By building a memorial that honored their comrades but didn't make judgments about the war itself, the founders believed they could achieve a measure of public healing. As you read Doubek's explanation of the project, notice how he tries to influence the memorial's design.
- In May 1981 **Maya Lin,** then a 20-year-old undergraduate at Yale University, submitted her design for the competition as part of a project for her class in funerary art. The proposal accompanying her pastel sketch of the memorial describes her design. Presented as part of the competition submission, the **proposal** needed to account for the major criteria set out by the VVMF: The memorial must have a contemplative character and be in harmony with its surroundings; the names of all who died or remained missing must appear; and it should make no political statements about the war. Her design was chosen unanimously from 1,421 entries. Since Lin included only a sketchy illustration with her proposal, her writing must have played an important role in persuading the jury. What aspects of her writing do you think were most effective?
- As the memorial was being completed in 1982, **Maya Lin** began writing her own personal account of how the memorial was designed and constructed. But it wasn't until she published her memoir, ***Boundaries,*** in 2000 that she was able to finish writing her account of those events. As she says in the memoir, for years after the memorial was built she wanted to put the events behind her and move on with her life. Indeed, it wasn't until she saw a documentary about herself, *Maya Lin: A Strong Clear Vision,* by Frieda Lee Mock, that she was able to write again about these events. In this chapter from her memoir, she describes from her own perspective the complex series of events that unfolded throughout the early 1980s as the memorial design was being debated

and the memorial constructed. This chapter will give you a good insight into the historical, political, artistic, and spiritual issues that surrounded the design and construction of the memorial. A little over a year after Lin published her memoir, she became involved in the design of another memorial: She was asked to be one of the judges in the contest to design a memorial for the World Trade Center. As we see in the next three documents, the similarities and differences between the situations surrounding the two memorials became an important part of the conversation about the design of the memorial for the World Trade Center.

- Just days after the attacks on the World Trade Center and Pentagon, a public conversation began about how to rebuild the sites, especially the World Trade Center site, and how to memorialize these terrible events. Almost any extended discussion of how to design a memorial for the World Trade Center site eventually turns to how this situation is both similar to and different from the situation surrounding the Vietnam Veterans Memorial, as well as how we can learn from that experience. This document is an article from the July 2002 issue of the magazine *Architectural Record,* "**Memorials, Monuments, and Meaning,**" by architect **Robert Ivy**. This cover story from a magazine addressed primarily to other architects focuses on a wide range of historical, philosophical, artistic, and religious aspects of memorial design. Ivy addresses very broad questions about human nature, attitudes toward death, and spiritual beliefs, and he discusses how these questions have been played out in the discussions about both the Vietnam Veterans Memorial and the proposed World Trade Center Memorial.
- The next document was published in the *New York Times* on August 31, 2003. In **"The New Ground Zero: Finding Comfort in the Safety of Names," Michael Kimmelman** discusses the significance of including names of the dead on memorials even when, as with the Vietnam Veterans Memorial, the numbers are in the thousands. The chronological listing of names on the Vietnam Veterans memorial has become one of its most powerful features, and Kimmelman asks what we can learn from that as we contemplate possible designs for the World Trade Center Memorial.
- Throughout 2002 and 2003, as we can see in the previous two documents, discussions about the World Trade Center site and memorial took place in many different forums. In the spring of 2003, while tentative plans were being made for rebuilding on the site of the World Trade Center, a contest was announced for the design of the memorial that would be included in the site. In some ways this contest was similar to the one for the Vietnam Veterans Memorial: It was open to the public and it included the stipulation that all victims of the attacks on September 11 be recognized in the design. But in other ways it was quite different: Although anyone over 18 could potentially enter, all entrants had to pay a fee and had to enter in conjunction with a professional design team, among other fairly complicated restrictions. But what the contests had in common was the often heated discussions that the memorial design stimulated, often led by the families of those who had died. In the fall of 2003, eight finalists were announced, and pictures and descriptions of their designs began to be widely discussed around the country, but especially in New York. This document is a **transcript of a news story** that aired on **NPR's Tavis Smiley Show on December 5, 2003,** soon after the finalists were announced, and it gives a glimpse into the public debate about the emotional topic of the memorial design.

- On January 14, 2004, designers Michael Arad and Peter Walker presented their revised design, *Reflecting Absence,* in a press release. The choice of the design launched the process of bringing the memorial to reality. The final document in the case study is a **photograph of the model of the design.** We include for comparison photographs of the Vietnam Veterans Memorial (390) and the Oklahoma Murrah Building Memorial (391).

YOUR ROLE

The Vietnam Veterans Memorial and the World Trade Center Memorial make good cases for thinking about the role of memorials in our national life and culture and about the role of public discussion and debate in making important public decisions. In the first of the writing projects, we ask you to reflect on the impact of one of these memorials and to design a brochure for students planning to visit one of the memorials. In the second writing project, we ask you to write an essay in which you analyze the public discussions surrounding the building of these memorials.

1. Imagine that your school sponsors an annual trip by an interdisciplinary group of students to various important national sites. This year the group will visit either the Vietnam Veterans Memorial or the World Trade Center Memorial (you decide). You are part of a group that's been chosen to produce a brochure for the students who will be going on the trip this year. Design a brochure that gives general information and background about the memorial as well as information that would be of specific interest to students from several different disciplines, including for example history, political science, art/architecture, and philosophy/theology/religious studies. Your brochure should be visually appealing, reader friendly, and useful for this particular audience. (See **Brochure** in the Genre Glossary.)
2. Write an essay in which you discuss what U.S. society can learn about the possibilities and pitfalls of public debate from the processes surrounding the design and building of the Vietnam Veterans Memorial and the World Trade Center Memorial. What was done right and what went wrong in the public debates surrounding the design and construction of these memorials, and what can we learn from these processes for future debates about other issues of public importance? (See **Essay** in the Genre Glossary.)

FOR IMMEDIATE RELEASE

Vietnam Veterans Memorial Statement of Purpose

While debate and demonstrations raged at home, these servicemen and women underwent challenges equal to or greater than those faced in earlier wars. They experienced confusion, horror, bitterness, boredom, fear, exhaustion, and death.

In facing these ordeals, they showed the same courage, sacrifice, and devotion to duty for which Americans traditionally have honored the nation's war veterans in the past.

The unique nature of the war—with no definite fronts, with vague objectives, with unclear distinctions between ally and enemy, and with strict rules of engagement—subjected the Vietnam soldier to unimaginable pressures.

Because of inequities in the draft system, the brunt of dangerous service fell upon the young, often the socially and economically disadvantaged.

While experiences in combat areas were brutal enough in themselves, their adverse effects were multiplied by the maltreatment received by veterans upon their return home. . . .

The purpose of the Vietnam Veterans Memorial is to recognize and honor those who served and died. It will provide a symbol of acknowledgment of the courage, sacrifice, and devotion to duty of those who were among the nation's finest youth.

The Memorial will make no political statement regarding the war or its conduct. It will transcend those issues. The hope is that the creation of the Memorial will begin a healing process.

Excerpted From Jan C. Scruggs and Joel L. Swerdlow, *To Heal a Nation: The Vietnam Veterans Memorial.* New York: Harper and Row, 1985, p. 53.

Statement by Maya Ying Lin, March 1981, Presented as Part of Her Competition Submission

Walking through this park-like area, the memorial appears as a rift in the earth, a long, polished, black stone wall, emerging from and receding into the earth. Approaching the memorial, the ground slopes gently downward and the low walls merging on either side, growing out of the earth, extend and converge at a point below and ahead. Walking into this grassy site contained by the walls of the memorial we can barely make out the carved names upon the memorial's walls. These names, seemingly infinite in number, convey the sense of overwhelming numbers, while unifying these individuals into a whole.

The memorial is composed not as an unchanging monument, but as a moving composition to be understood as we move into and out of it. The passage itself is gradual; the descent to the origin slow, but it is at the origin that the memorial is to be fully understood. At the intersection of these walls, on the right side, is carved the date of the first death. It is followed by the names of those who died in the war, in chronological order. These names continue on this wall appearing to recede into the earth at the wall's end. The names resume on the left wall as the wall emerges from the earth, continuing back to the origin where the date of the last death is carved at the bottom of this wall. Thus the war's beginning and end meet; the war is 'complete,' coming full-circle, yet broken by the earth that bounds the angle's open side, and continued within the earth itself. As we turn to leave, we see these walls stretching into the distance, directing us to the Washington Monument, to the left, and the Lincoln Memorial, to the right, thus bringing the Vietnam Memorial into an historical context. We the living are brought to a concrete realization of these deaths.

Brought to a sharp awareness of such a loss, it is up to each individual to resolve or come to terms with this loss. For death is in the end a personal and private matter, and the area contained with this memorial is a quiet place, meant for personal reflection and private reckoning. The black granite walls, each two hundred feet long, and ten feet

From competition submission for the Vietnam Veterans Memorial, March, 1981.

below ground at their lowest point (gradually ascending toward ground level) effectively act as a sound barrier, yet are of such a height and length so as not to appear threatening or enclosing. The actual area is wide and shallow, allowing for a sense of privacy, and the sunlight from the memorial's southern exposure along with the grassy park surrounding and within its walls, contribute to the serenity of the area. Thus this memorial is for those who have died, and for us to remember them.

The memorial's origin is located approximately at the center of the site; its legs each extending two hundred feet towards the Washington Monument and the Lincoln Memorial. The walls, contained on one side by the earth, are ten feet below ground at their point of origin, gradually lessening in height, until they finally recede totally into the earth, at their ends. The walls are to be made of a hard, polished black granite, with the names to be carved in a simple Trajan letter. The memorial's construction involves recontouring the area within the wall's boundaries, so as to provide for an easily accessible descent, but as much of the site as possible should be left untouched. The area should remain as a park, for all to enjoy.

Vietnam Veterans Memorial

It's taken me years to be able to discuss the making of the Vietnam Veterans Memorial, partly because I needed to move past it and partly because I had forgotten the process of getting it built. I would not discuss the controversy surrounding its construction and it wasn't until I saw the documentary, *Maya Lin: A Strong Clear Vision,* that I was able to remember that time in my life. But I wrote the body of this essay just as the memorial was being completed—in the fall of 1982. Then I put it away . . . until now.

I think the most important aspect of the design of the Vietnam Veterans Memorial was that I had originally designed it for a class I was taking at Yale and not for the competition. In that sense, I had designed it for me—or, more exactly, for what I believed it should be. I never tried to second-guess a jury. And it wasn't until after I had completed the design that I decided to enter it in the competition.

The design emerged from an architectural seminar I was taking during my senior year. The initial idea of a memorial had come from a notice posted at the school announcing a competition for a Vietnam Veterans Memorial. The class, which was on funereal architecture, had spent the semester studying how people, through the built form, express their attitudes on death. As a class, we thought the memorial was an appropriate design idea for our program, so we adopted it as our final design project.

At that point, not much was known about the actual competition, so for the first half of the assignment we were left without concrete directions as to what "they" were looking for or even who "they" were. Instead, we had to determine for ourselves what a Vietnam memorial should be. Since a previous project had been to design a memorial for World War III, I had already begun to ask the simple questions: What exactly is a memorial? What should it do?

My design for a World War III memorial was a tomblike underground structure that I deliberately made to be a very futile and frustrating experience. I remember the professor of the class, Andrus Burr, coming up to me afterward, saying quite angrily, "If I had a brother who died in that war, I would never want to visit this memorial." I was somewhat puzzled that he didn't quite understand that World War III would be of such devastation that none of us

From *Boundaries* by Maya Lin. New York: Simon and Schuster, 2000.

would be around to visit any memorial, and that my design was instead a prewar commentary. In asking myself what a memorial to a third world war would be, I came up with a political statement that was meant as a deterrent.

I had studied earlier monuments and memorials while designing that memorial and I continued this research for the design of the Vietnam memorial. As I did more research on monuments, I realized most carried larger, more general messages about a leader's victory or accomplishments rather than the lives lost. In fact, at the national level, individual lives were very seldom dealt with, until you arrived at the memorials for World War I. Many of these memorials included the names of those killed. Partly it was a practical need to list those whose bodies could not be identified—since dog tags as identification had not yet been adopted and, due to the nature of the warfare, many killed were not identifiable—but I think as well the listing of names reflected a response by these designers to the horrors of World War I, to the immense loss of life.

The images of these monuments were extremely moving. They captured emotionally what I felt memorials should be: honest about the reality of war, about the loss of life in war, and about remembering those who served and especially those who died.

I made a conscious decision not to do any specific research on the Vietnam War and the political turmoil surrounding it. I felt that the politics had eclipsed the veterans, their service and their lives. I wanted to create a memorial that everyone would be able to respond to, regardless of whether one thought our country should or should not have participated in the war. The power of a name was very much with me at the time, partly because of the Memorial Rotunda at Yale. In Woolsey Hall, the walls are inscribed with the names of all the Yale alumni who have been killed in wars. I had never been able to resist touching the names cut into these marble walls, and no matter how busy or crowded the place is, a sense of quiet, a reverence, always surrounds those names. Throughout my freshman and sophomore years, the stonecutters were carving in by hand the names of those killed in the Vietnam War, and I think it left a lasting impression on me . . . the sense of the power of a name.

One memorial I came across also made a strong impression on me. It was a monument to the missing soldiers of the World War I battle of the Somme by Sir Edwin Lutyens in Thiepval, France. The monument includes more than 100,000 names of people

(continued)

who were listed as missing because, without ID tags, it was impossible to identify the dead. (The cemetery contains the bodies of 70,000 dead.) To walk past those names and realize those lost lives—the effect of that is the strength of the design. This memorial acknowledged those lives without focusing on the war or on creating a political statement of victory or loss. This apolitical approach became the essential aim of my design; I did not want to civilize war by glorifying it or by forgetting the sacrifices involved. The price of human life in war should always be clearly remembered.

But on a personal level, I wanted to focus on the nature of accepting and coming to terms with a loved one's death. Simple as it may seem, I remember feeling that accepting a person's death is the first step in being able to overcome that loss.

I felt that as a culture we were extremely youth-oriented and not willing or able to accept death or dying as a part of life. The rites of mourning, which in more primitive and older cultures were very much a part of life, have been suppressed in our modern times. In the design of the memorial, a fundamental goal was to be honest about death, since we must accept that loss in order to begin to overcome it. The pain of the loss will always be there, it will always hurt, but we must acknowledge the death in order to move on.

What then would bring back the memory of a person? A specific object or image would be limiting. A realistic sculpture would be only one interpretation of that time. I wanted something that all people could relate to on a personal level. At this time I had as yet no form, no specific artistic image.

The use of names was a way to bring back everything someone could remember about a person. The strength in a name is something that has always made me wonder at the "abstraction" of the design; the ability of a name to bring back every single memory you have of that person is far more realistic and specific and much more comprehensive than a still photograph, which captures a specific moment in time or a single event or a generalized image that may or may not be moving for all who have connections to that time.

Then someone in the class received the design program, which stated the basic philosophy of the memorial's design and also its requirements: all the names of those missing and killed (57,000) must be a part of the memorial; the design must be apolitical, harmonious with the site, and conciliatory.

These were all the thoughts that were in my mind before I went to see the site.

Without having seen it, I couldn't design the memorial, so a few of us traveled to Washington, D.C., and it was at the site that the idea for the design took shape. The site was a beautiful park surrounded by trees, with traffic and noise coming from one side—Constitution Avenue.

I had a simple impulse to cut into the earth.

I imagined taking a knife and cutting into the earth, opening it up, an initial violence and pain that in time would heal. The grass would grow back, but the initial cut would remain a pure flat surface in the earth with a polished, mirrored surface, much like the surface on a geode when you cut it and polish the edge. The need for the names to be on the memorial would become the memorial; there was no need to embellish the design further. The people and their names would allow everyone to respond and remember.

It would be an interface, between our world and the quieter, darker, more peaceful world beyond. I chose black granite in order to make the surface reflective and peaceful. I never looked at the memorial as a wall, an object, but as an edge to the earth, an opened side. The mirrored effect would double the size of the park, creating two worlds, one we are a part of and one we cannot enter. The two walls were positioned so that one pointed to the Lincoln Memorial and the other pointed to the Washington Monument. By linking these two strong symbols for the country, I wanted to create a unity between the nation's past and present.

The idea of destroying the park to create something that by its very nature should commemorate life seemed hypocritical, nor was it in my nature. I wanted my design to work with the land, to make something with the site, not to fight it or dominate it. I see my works and their relationship to the landscape as being an additive rather than a combative process.

On our return to Yale, I quickly sketched my idea up, and it almost seemed too simple, too little. I toyed with adding some large flat slabs that would appear to lead into the memorial, but they didn't belong. The image was so simple that anything added to it began to detract from it.

I always wanted the names to be chronological, to make it so that those who served and returned from the war could find their place in the memorial. I initially had the names beginning on the left side and ending on the right. In a preliminary critique, a (continued) professor asked what importance that left for the apex, and I, too, thought it was a weak point, so I changed the design for the final critique. Now the chronological sequence began and ended at the apex so that the time line would circle back to itself and close the sequence. A progression in time is memorialized. The design is not just a list of the dead. To find one name, chances are you will see the others close by, and you will see yourself reflected through them.

The memorial was designed before I decided to enter the competition. I didn't even consider that it might win. When I submitted the project, I had the greatest difficulty trying to describe it in just one page. It took longer, in fact, to write the statement that I felt was needed to accompany the required drawings than to design the memorial. The description was critical to understanding the design since the memorial worked more on an emotional level than a formal level.

Coincidentally, at the time, I was taking a course with Professor Vincent Scully, in which he just happened to focus on the same memorial I had been so moved by—the Lutyens memorial to the missing. Professor Scully described one's experience of that piece as a passage or journey through a yawning archway. As he described it, it resembled a gaping scream, which after you passed through, you were left looking out on a simple graveyard with the crosses and tombstones of the French and the English. It was a journey to an awareness of immeasurable loss, with the names of the missing carved on every surface of this immense archway.

I started writing furiously in Scully's class. I think he has always been puzzled by my connection to the Lutyens memorial. Formally the two memorials could not be more different. But for me, the experiences of these two memorials describe a similar passage to an awareness about loss.

The competition required drawings, along with the option to include a written description. As the deadline for submission approached, I created a series of simple drawings. The only thing left was to complete the essay, which I instinctively knew was the only way to get anyone to understand the design, the form of which was deceptively simple. I kept reworking and reediting the final description. I actually never quite finished it. I ended up at the last minute writing freehand directly onto the presentation boards (you can see a few misprints on the actual page), and then I sent the project in, never expecting to hear about it again.

The drawings were in soft pastels, very mysterious, very painterly, and not at all typical of architectural drawings. One of the comments made by a juror was "*He* must really know what he is doing to dare to do something so naive" (italics mine). But ultimately, I think it was the written description that convinced the jurors to select my design.

On my last day of classes my roommate, Liz Perry, came to retrieve me from one of my classes, telling me a call from Washington had come in and that it was from the *Vietnam Veterans Memorial* Fund; they needed to talk to me and would call back with a few questions about the design. When they called back, they merely said they needed to ask me a few questions and wanted to fly up to New Haven to talk to me. I was convinced that I was number 100 and they were only going to question me about drainage and other technical issues. It never occurred to me that I might have won the competition. It was still, in my mind, an exercise—as competitions customarily are for architecture students.

And even after three officers of the fund were seated in my college dorm room, explaining to me that it was the largest competition of its kind, with more than fourteen hundred entries, and Colonel Schaet, who was talking, without missing a beat calmly added that I had won (I think my roommate's face showed more emotion than mine did at the time), it still hadn't registered. I don't think it did for almost a year. Having studied the nature of competitions, especially in Washington (for instance, the FDR Memorial, still unbuilt in 1981, nearly forty years after it was first proposed, or the artwork Robert Venturi and Richard Serra collaborated on for L'Enfant Plaza, which was completely modified as it went through the required Washington design process of approvals), my attitude about unusual projects getting built in Washington was not optimistic. Partly it's my nature—I never get my hopes up—and partly I assumed the simplicity of the design, and its atypical form and color, would afford it a difficult time through the various governmental-approval agencies.

After the design had been chosen, it was subject to approval by various governmental agencies at both the conceptual and design development phases. I moved to Washington and stayed there throughout these phases. I expected the design to be debated within the design-approval agencies; I never expected the politics that constantly surrounded its development and fabrication.

(continued)

I was driven down to D.C. the day of my college graduation, and I immediately became part of an internal struggle for control of the design. I think my age made it seem apparent to some that I was too young to understand what I had done or to see it through to completion. To bring the design into reality would require that I associate with an architect of record, a qualified firm that would work with me to realize the design. I had a very difficult time convincing the fund in charge of the memorial, the VVMF, of the importance of selecting a qualified firm that had experience both in architecture and landscape-integrated solutions, and that would be sympathetic to the design.

I had gone to Cesar Pelli, then dean of Yale's School of Architecture, for the names of some firms that could handle the job. A firm by the name of Cooper-Lecky was the one he recommended, and I presented its name to the fund, unaware that the competition's adviser was the fund's choice as architect of record. I was told by the fund that this person was the architect of record, and that was that.

After a few weeks of tense and hostile negotiations (in which at one point I was warned that I would regret these actions, and that I would "come crawling back on my hands and knees"), I was finally able to convince the fund to go through a legitimate process of selecting a firm to become the architect of record. The then architecture critic for the *Washington Post,* Wolf Von Eckardt, was instrumental in pressing the fund to listen to me. But the struggle left a considerable amount of ill will and mistrust between the veterans and myself.

Through the remaining phases of the project I worked with the Cooper-Lecky architectural firm. We worked on the practical details of the design, from the addition of a safety curb to a sidewalk to the problems in inscribing the names. Many of the issues we dealt with were connected to the text and my decision to list the names chronologically. People felt it would be an inconvenience to have to search out a name in a book and then find its panel location and thought that an alphabetical listing would be more convenient—until a tally of how many Smiths had died made it clear that an alphabetical listing wouldn't be feasible. The MIA groups wanted their list of the missing separated out and listed alphabetically. I knew this would break the strength of the time line, interrupting the real-time experience of the piece, so

I fought hard to maintain the chronological listing. I ended up convincing the groups that the time in which an individual was noted as missing was the emotionally compelling time for family members. A system of noting these names with a symbol* that could be modified to signify if the veteran was later found alive or officially declared dead would appease the concerns of the MIA groups without breaking the time line. I knew the time line was key to the experience of the memorial: a returning veteran would be able to find his or her time of service when finding a friend's name.

The text of the memorial and the fact that I had left out everything except the names led to a fight as to what else needed to be said about the war. The apex is the memorial's strongest point; I argued against the addition of text at that point for fear that a politically charged statement, one that would force a specific reading, would destroy the apolitical nature of the design. Throughout this time I was very careful not to discuss my beliefs in terms of politics; I played it extremely naive about politics, instead turning the issue into a strictly aesthetic one. Text could be added, but whatever was said needed to fit in three lines—to match the height of the dates "1959" and "1975" that it would be adjacent to. The veterans approved this graphic parameter, and the statements became a simple prologue and epilogue.

The memorial is analogous to a book in many ways. Note that on the right-hand panels the pages are set ragged right and on the left they are set ragged left, creating a spine at the apex as in a book. Another issue was scale; the text type is the smallest that we had come across, less than half an inch, which is unheard of in monument type sizing. What it does is create a very intimate reading in a very public space, the difference in intimacy between reading a billboard and reading a book.

The only other issue was the polished black granite and how it should be detailed, over which I remember having a few arguments with the architects of record. The architects could not understand my choice of a reflective, highly polished black granite. One of them felt I was making a mistake and the polished surface would be "too *feminine*." Also puzzling to

---

*Each name is preceded (on the west wall) or followed (on the east wall) by one of two symbols: a diamond or a cross. The diamond denotes that the serviceman's or servicewoman's death was confirmed. The cross symbolizes those who were missing in action or prisoners at the end of the war. When a serviceperson's remains were returned, the diamond symbol is superimposed over the cross. If a serviceman or woman returns alive, a circle will be inscribed around the cross.

(continued)

them was my choice of detailing the monument as a thin veneer with barely any thickness at its top edge. They wanted to make the monument's walls read as a massive, thick stone wall, which was not my intention at all. I always saw the wall as pure surface, an interface between light and dark, where I cut the earth and polished its open edge. The wall dematerializes as a form and allows the names to become the object, a pure and reflective surface that would allow visitors the chance to see themselves with the names. I do not think I thought of the color black as a color, more as the idea of a dark mirror into a shadowed mirrored image of the space, a space we cannot enter and from which the names separate us, an interface between the world of the living and the world of the dead.

One aspect that made the project unusual was its politicized building process. For instance, the granite could not come from Canada or Sweden. Though those countries had beautiful black granites, draft evaders went to both countries, so the veterans felt that we could not consider their granites as options. (The stone finally selected came from India.) The actual building process went smoothly for the most part, and the memorial was built very close to my original intentions.

As far as all of the controversy, I really never wanted to go into it too much. The memorial's starkness, its being below grade, being black, and how much my age, gender, and race played a part in the controversy, we'll never quite know. I think it is actually a miracle that the piece ever got built. From the very beginning I often wondered, if it had not been an anonymous entry 1026 but rather an entry by Maya Lin, would I have been selected?

I remember at the very first press conference a reporter asking me if I did not find it ironic that the memorial was for the Vietnam War and that I was of Asian descent. I was so righteous in my response that my race was completely irrelevant. It took me almost nine months to ask the VVMF, in charge of building the memorial, if my race was at all an issue. It had never occurred to me that it would be, and I think they had taken all the measures they could to shield me from such comments about a "gook" designing the memorial.

I remember reading the article that appeared in the *Washington Post* referring to "An Asian Memorial for an Asian War" and I knew we were in trouble. The controversy exploded in Washington after that article. Ironically, one side attacked the design for being "too Asian," while others saw its simplicity and understatement, not as an intention to create a more

Eastern, meditative space, but as a minimalist statement which they interpreted as being non-referential and disconnected from human experience.

This left the opinion in many that the piece emanated from a series of intellectualized aesthetic decisions, which automatically pitted artist against veterans. The fact that I was from an Ivy League college, had hair down to my knees, further fueled this distrust of the design and suspicions of a hippie college liberal or aesthetic elitist forcing her art and commentary upon them.

Perhaps it was an empathetic response to the idea about war that had led me to cut open the earth—an initial violence that heals in time but leaves a memory, like a scar. But this imagery, which some detractors would later describe as "a black gash of shame and sorrow" in which the color black was called the "universal color of shame and dishonor," would prove incredibly difficult to defend. The misreading of the design as a negative political statement that in some way was meant to reflect upon the service of the veterans was in part fueled by a cultural prejudice against the color black as well as by the misreading or misinformation that led some veterans to imagine the design as a ditch or a hole. It took a prominent four-star general, Brigadier General George Price, who happened to be black, testifying before one of the countless subcommittee hearings and defending the color black, before the design could move forward.

But the distrust, the fact that no veterans had been on the jury, the unconventionality of the design and the designer, and a very radical requirement made by the Vietnam veterans to include all the names of those killed made it inevitable that the project would become controversial. I think ultimately that much of the negative response goes back to the very natural response to cover up or not acknowledge that which is painful or unpleasant. The very fact that the veterans themselves had required the listing and therefore the acknowledgment of the more than 57,000 casualties, which is a landmark in our country in terms of seeing a war via the individual lives lost, was very hard for many to face. I remember Ross Perot when he was trying to persuade the veterans that it was an inappropriate design, asking me if I truly didn't feel that the veterans would prefer a parade instead, something happy or uplifting, and I can

(continued)

remember thinking that a parade would not in the long term help them overcome the enormous trauma of the politics of that war.

I do not think I fully realized until the dedication and homecoming parade that the veterans needed both. In effect the veterans gave themselves their own homecoming. In November 1982, I was in tears watching these men welcoming themselves home after almost ten years of not being acknowledged by their country for their service, their sacrifice.

But until the memorial was built I don't think they realized that the design was experiential and cathartic, and, most importantly, designed not for me, but for them. They didn't see that the chronology of the names allowed a returning veteran the ability to find his or her own time frame on the wall and created a psychological space for them that directly focused on human response and feeling. I remember one of the veterans asking me before the wall was built what I thought people's reaction would be to it. I realized then that these veterans were willing to defend a design they really didn't quite understand. I was too afraid to tell him what I was thinking, that I knew a returning veteran would cry.

An architect once told me to look always at what was originally envisioned and try to keep it. I left Washington before ground breaking. I had to. The fund and I knew that we had to accept a compromise. The closer you watch something grow, the less able you are to notice changes in it. When I saw the site again, the granite panels were being put up and the place was frighteningly close to what I thought it should be. It terrified me. It was a strange feeling, to have had an idea that was solely yours be no longer a part of your mind but totally public, no longer yours.

Memorials, Monuments, and Meaning

Two vast and trunkless legs of stone
Stand in the desert. Near them, on the sand,
Half sunk, a shattered visage lies
And on the pedestal, these words appear:
"My name is Ozymandias, king of kings:
Look on my works, ye Mighty, and despair!"

Ozymandias
Percy Bysshe Shelley

How do we, the living, recall the dead? How do we signal the people or places that altered history? How do we institutionalize pain? How do we signify what matters to our civilization? The questions sound abstract, yet in this fractious, dangerous world, the issues confront and confound us with urgency, and architects find themselves at the center of the debate. Not all solutions are architectural, however.

Society knows that we will remember what we are reminded of; history, whether oral or written, is a structured narrative that reforms the past, interweaving memory and experience into a singular tale, says Craig Barton in his book, *Sites of Memory.* When we build for remembrance's sake, we recast history—from objects to whole cities. Barton refers to the process as "the codification of memory," an idea apparent in symbols as obvious as the great St. Louis Gateway Arch, which leaps toward Manifest Destiny and the opening of the American West. Our traditions, our prejudices, and our beliefs flow from such constructions.

Historically, remembrance has been central to architecture. For more than five thousand years, architects have made monuments to the dead, to glorious battles, and to ideas. Ironically, the earliest and grandest abide. Despite ancient social upheavals, shifts in pharaonic power, unification and dispersal of Upper and Lower Kingdoms, Hellenism, Rome, Islam, and the birth of the modern state, Khufu's monumental pyramid (ca. 2500 b.c.) still stands, a memorial to the god-king and a monument to ancient Egypt's collective genius. In death, Khufu traveled to other realms; in life, only the stones remain.

Jump to the 20th century. Spoleto Festival, 1997, outside Charleston, South Carolina. At McLeod Plantation, the landscape architect and artist Martha Schwartz hung multiple cotton sheets arrayed near the houses of former slaves. As the day progressed, the fabric scrim altered with changing light; morning and evening breezes animated each piece and changed its form. Animate, poetic, Schwartz's art installation stirred emotions within the viewer and provoked speculation in an unexpected way about slavery—both about the system itself and the contributions of slaves to material culture.

The two illustrations underscore the differentiation between two apparently similar words, monument and memorial. While linguists might debate the distinctions, fundamentally a monument comprises a designed and constructed physical object intended as a commemoration. Memorials that celebrate or grieve may take a more ephemeral form—including the strewing of flowers in memory of the deceased, such as occurred during the Memorial Day/Decoration Day movement of the 19th century or the free-form floral outpouring at the gates of Kensington Palace following the death of Princess Diana. Both involve the physical world, both involve remembrance.

While structures may house ideas, it is people who actually do the remembering, and people

(continued)

From "Memorials, Monuments, and Meaning" by Robert Ivy. *Architectural Record 190,* Issue 7 (July 2002), p. 84.

vary. The vastly differing populations comprising the early Egyptians and 20th-century museum-goers each carry the baggage of time; location; political, social, and cultural history; and religion that author James Young in *The Texture of Memory* calls "collected memory." Each person brings to the memorial experience a personal set of expectations—not a reflection of zeitgeist so much as a composite of emotion and recollected thought—that the effective memorial recalls. Those memories shift over time, much like the light at McLeod Plantation.

Evolution of meaning. Memorials shift in meaning as generations change. Time alters understanding and blurs memory; architecture remains. According to James Young (and Shelley), "Monuments that resist transformation risk losing their significance to future generations." Following the immediacy of loss, when grief has thinned or disappeared, we inevitably begin to appreciate the monument or the memorial for its more abstract qualities. Ultimately, time may blur our collective vision and we may entirely forget the events that generated the memorial, so removed from our lives or so potent has the architecture or the symbol grown. Although few persons might know the historical roots of the Arc de Triomphe as a representation of Napoleonic victories, today everyone identifies the arch with the city of Paris.

Fixed power. Monuments may be fixed or temporary. In writing about the blues (in *Blues Ideology and Afro-American Literature—A Vernacular Theory*), Houston Baker addresses stability. According to Baker, "Fixity is a function of power." He states that those who "maintain place, who decide what takes place and dictate what has taken place, are power brokers of the traditional." The rootless, the "placeless," by contrast, find other, more "fluid" ways of memorializing. To Maya Angelou, as she says in her novel *I Know Why the Caged Bird Sings,* rather than any buildings or monuments, the poetry of preachers and the blues epitomizes African-American memorial making. To Baker, the crossroads becomes the symbol where art and memory conjoin.

Thus, the Vietnam Memorial on the Mall in Washington, a fixed, evocative monument, represents the tragic consequences of war by the nation-state. By contrast, the AIDS quilt, "nomadic, portable, constantly being added to," formed a temporary installation that was spread on the same Washington soil occupied by the Vietnam Memorial. Both affected the American conscience and consciousness, through two different means. Both resonate today, although only one remains in place.

The resolution of a memorial depends on who tells the story. Monument building, like museum design, can be construed as a political act, controlling the narrative of actual events, determining the sequence of experiences, and interpreting them for subsequent generations. Digital guides and video-speak round out the story, much as guides or interpreters at historic sites like Chartres Cathedral tell us their history and thereby frame our understanding of events. Their narratives reflect controlled authorship and ownership of ideas.

In a democracy like our own, split wide open by the Internet, everyone has a say. Architecture's role becomes a "repository of our collective and individual cultural history and memory," says author Craig Barton. Reductivist in nature, architecture compresses and contains history in a single place at one time, while democratizing forces that surround us in cyberspace may call for dispersal across time and space. James Young encourages the search for the "art of public memory," a process that engages audiences in the making and the viewing, creating a dialogue that transcends the mere appearance of any memorial.

Some sites blend media to probe authenticity. In Amsterdam, at the Anne Frank House, the visitor passes by an orchestrated pathway through the actual chambers inhabited by the Frank family from 1942–1944. According to careful design, space after space reveals the mundane artifacts of daily life—toys, games, a sink—for a particular Jewish family hidden from German authorities in a high attic. By clustering around strategically placed monitors, gaggles of people from all over the world can hear Anne's own words from her diary and view the video testimony of her childhood friend or of Miep Gies, the secretary who helped keep the Frank family alive. Anne's house museum memorializes a family's struggles, and for a brief moment, brings them vividly to life.

Abstractions. How abstract should a memorial be? The response varies with the proximity to the event. Survivors of a tragedy often raise potent arguments for realistic monuments that appropriately memorialize their lost loved ones. They belong to the camp that views the memorial as a "witness and reminder," says Young. A review of recent monument making in Washington, D.C., however, raises questions about the literal. The Korean Monument, for example, depicts a squad of soldiers in bronze, but their representation, unfortunately, makes them appear lost, and the meaning of the war becomes compromised as we confront the limitations of the objects themselves. The words and spaces and elementary materials at Washington's FDR Memorial seem more potent than the sculptural figures meant to recall Depression hardship. Imagination trumps the literal.

Touch and feelings. Memory and the locus of emotions can be unlocked by the senses. Tactility, for example. How many of us have reached the Vietnam Memorial Wall to rub the names of lost friends with our own hands? Water, in particular, represents the mythic veil between the real and spiritual realms. Fire, such as the eternal flame at John Kennedy's simple grave on the Arlington hillside, or present in Hindu cremation, conjures up transformation. Moving water moves the hearing, which affects the mind: calming in a fountain, or churning as it falls with a cavernous, preternatural force in Tadao Ando's work at the Sayamaike Historical Museum near Osaka.

From Ground Zero. Since September 11, the process of memorial making has already shifted from the individual to the institution. While countless little altars, handmade signs, poems mounted to fences, and photographs once sprang up across the city—at Union Square, at Brooklyn's Promenade, at Grand Central—the fire from a thousand candles is beginning to be extinguished. Even the number of poignant obituaries of the deceased in the *New York Times* is diminishing with each week.

With the removal of the last structural column from the devastated site, we are entering a new phase, searching for an appropriate memorial for a cataclysmic event that tore at the heart of a city, took almost 3,000 lives, and wrenched New York's optimistic spirit. How will the city respond? With monument or memorial? With literal interpretation of events? With knowledge of and accommodation to change?

Victor Iannuzi, an interpersonal psychoanalyst, warns that whatever happens, we must reconcile with the meaning of the event. If not, "those meanings go underground—they go into our unconscious, where they wreak havoc." The answer will depend on who tells the story, and how responsive those in power prove to an event larger than themselves.

The New Ground Zero
Finding Comfort in the Safety of Names

Michael Kimmelman

The capitalized words printed just above these, which you may have read or maybe your eye skipped over them, are my first and last names. In the cafeteria of the building where I work, a similar name—Jay M. Kimmelsman—appears on a plaque commemorating *New York Times* employees killed during World War II. Jay M. Kimmelsman worked in the department of outgoing mail. When I pass the plaque, I think of him. I feel a connection.

What is it about a name? Its power is palpable but mysterious. Without thinking, we say we know someone when we know his name. "Do you know who that is?" "Yes, that's Jay from outgoing mail." But how much do we know? We react to names that resemble ours, or resemble the names of people we know, in the same vague way that we scour other people's family snapshots. We hunt for clues to what they tell us, often idly. We look for something of ourselves.

But names, like photographs, unless they are ours or those of our friends and family, say much less than we expect.

The competition guidelines for the memorial at ground zero require that the design "recognize each individual who was a victim" on Sept. 11, 2001, and on Feb. 26, 1993, when the World Trade Center was first attacked. It's a safe bet that many of the 5,200 submissions interpret that as some kind of list of names. By aesthetic and social consensus, names are today a kind of reflexive memorial impulse, lists of names having come almost automatically to connote "memorial," just as minimalism has come to be the presumptive sculptural style for memorial design, the monumental blank slate onto which the names can be inscribed.

During the past week the news broke that the remains of more than 1,000 of the 2,792 people who are missing from the Sept. 11 attack will be buried at the memorial. Investigators cannot identify more than 12,000 body parts—the DNA is too badly damaged—and so the remains will be dried and vacuum sealed, preserved, like ancient mummies, in white opaque pouches, in the hope that technologies of the future can decode who is who. The Lower Manhattan Development Corporation, in addition to requiring recognition of each victim, instructed entrants in the competition to include space to store remains, just in case.

So now the memorial becomes a literal cemetery, with the oldest form of human identification, names, most likely testifying to victims the newest science can't distinguish. The ethos will be different from that of the Vietnam Veterans Memorial. There are no bodies buried at the Vietnam memorial, nor any unaccounted-for remains. That memorial is a list of names, a neutral place to meditate abstractly on the war and on the dead and missing, who are elsewhere.

By the afternoon of Sept. 11, people were already taping photocopied fliers with the names and pictures of their dead or missing friends and relatives at makeshift shrines around the city: instant, homegrown demonstrations against the anonymity of mass killing.

From "The New Ground Zero: Finding Comfort in the Safety of Names" by Michael Kimmelman. *The New York Times,* Arts and Leisure, August 31, 2003. p. 1, 22.

The fliers, which were at first missing-persons posters, quickly became private memorials, reminding everybody that the people who died at the World Trade Center were not numbers but someone's husband or sister or son.

This isn't new. The impulse to name names already became commonplace with World War I. Partly, it democratized war. Foot soldiers were recognized not as nameless peons but as individuals, like the generals who sent them to die. The war had made many people cynical about everything except the doughboys in the trenches. These men emerged as the everyday heroes, if there still were any heroes, instead of the military leaders or lone Paul Revere types who had traditionally been singled out for memorials. The listing of their names reduced the distance between the recruit and the officer but also represented a tacit protest against the anonymity of modern warfare. Names both stood for the individual soldier and, correlatively, pleaded for a more humane approach to battle, which is to say they gained both literal and symbolic value.

World War I also inspired tombs of the unknown soldier. The tomb tried to reconcile two conflicting ideologies about war: the dehumanizing anonymity of death and the nobility of personal sacrifice. The unknown soldier symbolized both the masses of anonymous dead and each missing soldier, whose name we were implicitly meant to attach to the tomb.

To this morbid history, World War II contributed lists of innocent victims. Fifty years after its founding, Israel's Holocaust memorial, Yad Vashem, which in Hebrew means "a monument and a name," is still recovering the names of the Jews who died during the Holocaust, a vain and fruitful enterprise in that all the names will never be accounted for, so that the process of trying to remember cannot end.

By the time of Maya Lin's Vietnam memorial in 1982, the idea of names, engraved simply and identically—a visual equivalent to the monotone roll-call of the dead, which has also become a standard memorial ritual—achieved Platonic form, more moving for being so spare. Minimalism proved itself there as the sculptural language of the memorial sublime, combining the abstraction of the memorial's physical form with the absolute specificity of the names of every dead and missing soldier. It was the inverse of the tomb to the unknown soldier, which had become nearly obsolete, thanks to improved forensic science and record keeping, or so it seemed until Sept. 11.

Ms. Lin's memorial, which carefully took no side in the debate about Vietnam, was made out of polished black granite so that people would literally see themselves reflected in the names on the wall, a mirror of perception. The Vietnam War was an unresolved issue, but the dead and missing from that war could be listed. Names seemed morally neutral. They were a compromise in a society that could not decide where it stood. Today, it is too early to know the historical lessons of the attacks on the World Trade Towers, but the casualty list can be drawn up. A world that does not seem to agree about anything can settle on the names of the dead. Lists of names promise closure, a conflict-averse path to catharsis in an age of instant gratification and short attention spans.

But written words, as Shimon Attie, an artist of memorials, has said, are images, and images have an aesthetic component and a political one. A long list of names is, first of all, an incantatory sight, the length of the list implying the scale of the event memorialized. Seeing 57,000 names is

(continued)

not the same as seeing 168 (the number of people killed in the 1995 bombing of the Alfred P. Murrah Federal Building in Oklahoma City) or 2,792 or 6 million, by which point a list becomes almost unreadable. Numbers suggest the enormity of loss but are a dubious measure of history. Not many people died at Lexington and Concord, but what happened there changed the fate of the nation.

And names only seem morally neutral. Ms. Lin's Vietnam memorial made names the basic irreducible fact of this episode in history. Names were all that was left after the pomp and flourish of old-fashioned memorial design were stripped away. In hundreds of years, when the historical debates Ms. Lin studiously sidestepped may be forgotten, the names of the men will be what remain written in stone. Picture, for a second, that memorial without the names: a plain black tombstone, an open wound on the Washington Mall, which was how Ms. Lin imagined the design sculpturally. The message about the war would be very different.

Names animate space. They are like ghosts. We read into them. The ethnic variety of names on the Vietnam memorial summons up an image of a diverse population, a model democracy, a political portrait that belies the rifts of the culture. One nation. One family.

The Vietnam memorial is also shaped like a book. Ms. Lin purposely chose a small typeface, unheard of in monumental design, so that reading the names would seem more intimate, like scanning a printed page. The memorial is supposed to be our national story. She also listed the 57,000 names not alphabetically but chronologically according to when the soldiers died or went missing, an artistic device. Imagine all the John Smiths who died in Vietnam listed alphabetically. Now imagine that your father or son or brother or husband were one of them. Which John Smith on the wall would you touch or pin a photograph beside or leave flowers underneath?

The engraved style of these names, sans pomp and serif, is now standard. The names on the 168 chairs that, like headstones in rows, represent the dead in Oklahoma City are graphic descendants of the names on the Vietnam memorial. But names are fickle signifiers, containers for information that can be filled differently by different people, depending on what they know or think or hear about the person named. In Oklahoma City, some parents, unhappy with their sons-in-law, wanted their dead daughters' maiden names on the memorial, not their daughters' married names. Names are loaded. A list of the dead SS officers buried at Kolmeshohe cemetery in Bitburg, Germany, would have a different effect on their relatives than on Jews.

We engrave the names of donors on walls of museums and other public buildings. Your money or your life. Lists democratize veterans in battle, but they are also signs of difference. At Oklahoma City, a committee needed to be formed to decide who qualified for a list of survivors. If you were injured and went to a hospital, you would be eligible; if you went to a doctor's office, you might not be. If you lost friends and colleagues and your life was turned upside down but you had left the Murrah building for a dentist's appointment before the explosion or had stayed home sick that day, you were not a survivor, although of course you were. Just not in name.

Edward Linenthal, who wrote a book about the memorial in Oklahoma City, has described memorial hierarchies. Resolving them—who gets named and how—is, he argues, part of the process of setting history right, a service to the dead, the essence of what memorials are for. In Oklahoma City, there are the names of the dead on the chairs but also a museum, in which anyone can tell his or her story.

Ground zero may consider something similar: the museum as egalitarian bulletin board, a repository of consolations to survivors, who can decide how they want to remember their dead. Families of the firefighters who died in the World Trade Center, for example, have pleaded publicly that their dead relatives be identified as firefighters in the memorial. The families said the men lived and died as firefighters. Their ladder units were their other families. It isn't that they were greater human beings than the stockbrokers and restaurant workers who died, only that the dead men would want to be remembered as firefighters. They belonged to a community. Their names should be accompanied by F.D.N.Y., maybe even grouped separately. But then how does a list not rank the dead?

The memorial at ground zero, with its unidentified remains, will be a special kind of memorial. It is partly a tomb of the unknown victim, with the abstract language of memorial design, if it ends up being abstract, that much more in tension with the literal: in this case not just literally lists of names but parts of bodies, the corporeal and the symbolic. Many people may think about these bodies when they stand there reading the names: about their own inability to connect the remains to names, about the insufficiency of names to conjure up and stand in for the people who are lost.

What's in a name? Memorials are ultimately local, as the historian James Young has said. They are above all for the families and for a community, common ground to grieve. There are many ways to enshrine and recall the dead. Memorials can be places of contention, which keep alive history through debate. Names, foreclosing political conflicts that may be the real unhealed wounds of the event memorialized, provide instead the possibility of solace for the relatives of the victims. Strangers show up and may be overwhelmed by the sight of long lists of people they did not know, with whom they can only try to identify, just as we all greet unfamiliar names, whose meanings remain elusive.

Finally, only the families and friends of the dead can really know what those names mean.

Continuing Controversy over Construction of a Memorial at the World Trade Center Site

TONY COX, host:
In New York, a spirited dialogue is raging over what will be built on the 16 acres once occupied by the World Trade Center. Eight finalists were recently selected in a competition to design a memorial on the site. But disagreements over what ultimately should be constructed there are far from over. Our reporter Allison Keyes sorts out the controversy and its effect on some who lost loved ones.

ALLISON KEYES:
Linda McGee sits in the living room of her Bronx, New York, house and shakes her head as she talks about her twin sister, Brenda Conway, who was killed in the attacks on September 11th, 2001. She worked on the 97th floor of Tower One and vanished after the planes hit.

Ms. LINDA McGEE:
We just never really heard from her since she left for work that morning. We spent a lot of time searching and looking but nothing was ever found of her.

ALLISON KEYES:
McGee, an African-American third-grade teacher and mother of two, is still trying to come to terms with the loss of the woman she shared everything with.

Ms. McGEE:
It's very difficult and I'm still really having a very difficult time adjusting to life without her because I'm so used to doing everything with her.

KEYES:
McGee says she's been paying only scant attention to the debate raging over what will eventually be constructed on the 16-acre site, but she does have some ideas about the elements that should be included in the memorial. She's glad it will include a sacred space where families can get away from the tourists that flock to the site every day. McGee thinks there should also be a way for people to see the faces of the near 3,000 people who died.

Ms. McGEE:
I think the ones with the pictures would be great, especially—like we have a couple of nephews or even people as small children that may not, say, as they get older, really remember. At least they'll be able to see the picture.

Unidentified Woman #1:
We thought about how this is set in an urban setting and all of the buildings—a lot of the buildings that surround the site are going to be high-rises and they're going to be tall. That's how we set up our landscape.

KEYES:
Just before Thanksgiving, the eight finalists in the design competition for the World Trade Center memorial were announced with much fanfare. One, called Dual Memory, features the photos of the victims McGee and many other family members say they'd like to see at the site. The pictures would be projected onto glass panels along with a short history of each person. Another design, Suspending Memory, turns the so-called footprints where the twin towers stood into two islands in the midst of a vast tree-covered pool separated by a single bridge. But competing interests have made it difficult to decide on the final configuration of the site. For example, many firefighters, police officers and emergency workers want their names to be listed apart from the civilians who died.

From National Public Radio's Tavis Smiley Show, December 5, 2003.

Lieutenant MICHAEL MARSHALL (Vice President, Vulcan Society):
Not that our lives were worth any more than anybody else's lives, but just the fact that we were there as rescuers. People were going out; we were going in to save lives.

KEYES:
Lieutenant Michael Marshall is vice president of the Vulcan Society, an advocacy group for New York's black firefighters.

Lt. MARSHALL:
One guy that came out, survived, told me that the look on the chiefs' faces like they were sending us to our deaths, and guys still went in. And, you know, I mean, this is what we do and we know that there's—every time we go out the door there's a life risk, but, you know, I just think that we need to be listed separately.

KEYES:
Also, another advocacy organization, the Coalition for 9/11 Families, issued a report card giving the designs an F. Many in the coalition want the footprints to extend down to the original foundation, where the remains of many victims were found. Some family members, like Monica Iken, who lost her husband, Michael, in the attacks, thinks the design selection jury did a great job whittling 5,201 submissions from 63 nations down to eight.

Ms. MONICA IKEN:
All of them were significant. They reflected the key things that I was looking for: spirituality, a sense of peace, a sense of hope.

KEYES:
But other people don't think the design plans tell the real story of what happened on September 11th. That was the reaction of Ann Van Heim, who attended a recent workshop where members of the public were discussing the memorial plans.

Ms. ANN VAN HEIM (Workshop Attendee):
Some of these—I mean, they are beautiful and very innovative and all that, but if you went there and you knew nothing of what happened that day, you would learn nothing of what happened that day. You would not know that a plane hit into the towers and they collapsed.

KEYES:
Rick Bell, executive director of the New York chapter of the American Association of Architects, agrees. He's part of a coalition of designers and planners who've sent a letter to the design jury criticizing the finalists. Bell thinks there's room in the memorial for some of the steel left standing when the towers collapsed.

Mr. RICK BELL:
People who did that clearance were able to save those fragments, and the expectation was that those fragments would come back in some manner.

KEYES:
Most of that steel was recycled but the Port Authority of New York and New Jersey, which owns the site, still has a few pieces of it. Some say the spirit of the memorial designs continues a trend which began in 1981 with the Vietnam Veterans Memorial for Washington's National Mall. Max Page is an associate professor of architecture at the University of Massachusetts.

Professor MAX PAGE:
What we see here is actually a continuation, I think, of the abstract design of memorials that Maya Lin pioneered. In other words, it is an effort to not try to picture the single hero but rather to make a space that will be open to a lot of different people's viewpoints and will be evocative to a lot of different people.

KEYES:
Kevin Rampe, president of the Lower Manhattan Development Corporation, says the bottom line is that the final de-

(continued)

sign for the memorial will likely be different from any of the finalists' proposals.

Mr. KEVIN RAMPE:
There's probably a high chance that the ultimately selected memorial will be different from any of the eight that we see out there right now because of the changes that will occur in response to the jury's concerns, the jury's consideration.

KEYES:
The LMDC is overseeing the site's redevelopment. Rampe says the design guidelines for the master plan for the 16-acre site, which will determine the size and look of the office buildings that will surround the memorial, are also being revised. But Linda McGee says she's less worried about what the finished site should look like than she is about getting through the holidays without her twin sister, Brenda Conway.

Ms. McGEE:
But a lot of my emphasis really isn't on the design as far as it is trying to get on with my life, you know, just trying to find what is normal now without her.

KEYES:
For the TAVIS SMILEY show, I'm Allison Keyes in New York.

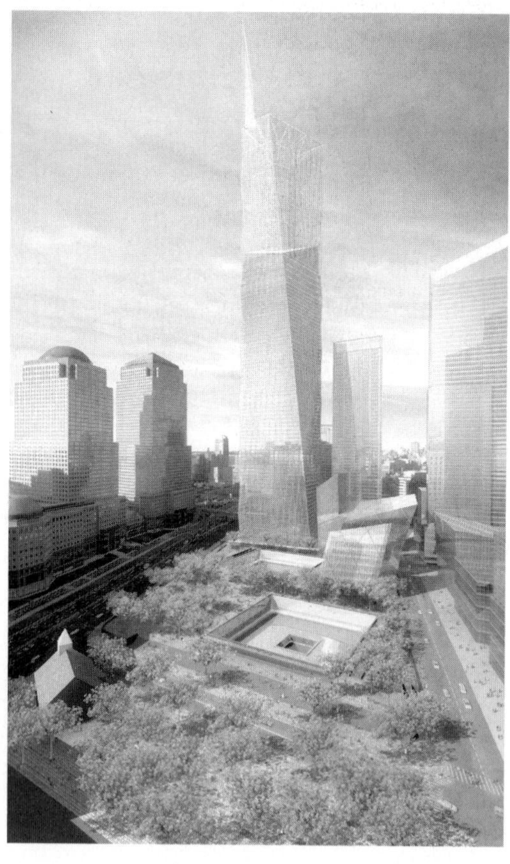

UNIT V

Adapting to the Changing Economy

If one thing unites our conversations about the global economy and the changing workplace, it is McDonald's. Vying with Disney as the most visible and despised symbol of American consumer culture, McDonald's is the target of protests whenever it opens a restaurant overseas. For many Americans, though, the most damning argument against McDonald's comes from the American workplace. Even in the economic optimism of the late 1990s, many worried that too many jobs were only "McJobs": low skill, low wage, low benefits jobs that kept people employed but outside the American dream. Yet McDonald's continues to be the restaurant of choice for millions here and abroad. The appeal of McDonald's may go beyond the satisfaction of individual consumer cravings. Journalist Thomas Friedman pointed out in 1999 that no two countries with McDonald's franchises had gone to war with each other since their McDonald's opened. Though he has since modified this claim, his larger point is that participation in the global economy promotes international cooperation. The way we feel about McDonald's—and about globalization—may have much to do with how we see ourselves in the American workplace, the American economy, the global economy, and global culture. What is your reaction to this photograph?

CHAPTER 12

Living in the Global Economy

Situation: You might be able to guess from his clothes and hair that this man is an Orthodox Jew. He is standing at the Western Wall in the Old City of Jerusalem, also called the Wailing Wall. With this information, can you guess what he is doing?

Genre: Do you think this is a family snapshot, a news photo, or a work of photographic art? Could it belong to more than one genre?

Language: How do the dark and light shapes "compose" this picture? How do the man's posture and facial expression "speak" to us?

Consequences: How do you respond to the picture? How do you think your own background influences your response? And how has your response changed as you've learned more about the photo?

In Millau, France, Jose Bove, a French sheep farmer, vandalized a McDonald's in a violent protest against "Americanization" or, as some call it, "globalization." Bove, whose sheep produce the milk to make Roquefort cheese, was caught in a transnational tug of war. McDonald's uses beef from the United States, but France refused to import the beef unless it was labeled as to its hormone content. In retaliation, the United States added a 100 percent tax on Roquefort cheese and other similar French specialty items. Bove claims that organizations such as the World Trade Organization are behind a push for genetically engineered food produced by multinational corporations and against small-time, all-natural farmers. As a result of the tax increase, Bove would be unable to sell his all-natural cheeses in an export market. Stories like this abound, illustrating the confusion and anger many feel about the movement of money and jobs around the globe and the effects on individuals.

Americans are divided about the benefits of globalization. On the one hand international borders are open for trade, and American companies are competitive. However, Americans feel a gnawing anxiety that what's good for large corporations and the macroeconomy is not good for the average worker or consumer, whether American, French, Thai, or Chinese. Since the passage of the North American Free Trade Agreement (NAFTA) in 1993, Americans have been reluctant to support other trade initiatives that might jeopardize their jobs. In a recent *Business Week*/Harris Poll, between 63 percent and 68 percent of Americans said that globalization was good for consumers, good for American companies, and good for the U.S. economy. But 77 percent of the respondents felt that preventing the loss of U.S. jobs should be a major priority in developing other trade agreements. Respondents felt just as strongly about protecting the environment as preventing competition from countries that treat workers unfairly.

We have seen this complex reaction to globalization in the case of college students who realized that sweatshop workers in third-world countries probably make their favorite college-brand tee shirts. They have taken an activist role in pressing corporations in the apparel industry to come clean about the working conditions under which those garments are made. This criticism emerged while companies such as Nike were establishing themselves in the global marketplace, sponsoring highly publicized contests, games, and events around the world, and making enormous profits. The astounding success of Nike and other transnational corporations is tempered by cries of foul play from concerned consumers. College students began to demand that companies such as Nike, Reebok, and Liz Claiborne agree to a monitoring plan and disclose the location of their factories. Student groups also want to see codes of conduct written and adhered to and a formula for a living wage instituted. The governments of countries where these garments are made, such as Mexico, Guatemala, Thailand, and Indonesia, are worried that if they have to raise the standard of pay, they will be pricing their workers out of the market, and corporations will go elsewhere.

The paradox of globalization offers competing stories of winners and losers. Globalization clearly benefits large corporations by creating markets and keeping prices low. It also allows developing countries new opportunities for training and production. The downside is felt keenly by individuals, whose stories we hear again and again, stories about lost jobs, intolerable workplace conditions, and unfair labor practices.

Mr. Order Meets Mr. Chaos:

A Debate Between Robert Wright and Robert Kaplan

This debate appeared in the journal *Foreign Policy* during the spring of 2001. Think back to that season and that year; the twin towers of the World Trade Center still marked the Lower Manhattan skyline. Although much of the news and even everyday dinner conversation across America concerned globalization, jobs, and the economy, most people had no idea that terrorism would strike or how central these two buildings were to our conversations about these topics. So even though this debate appeared before the terrorist attacks of September 11, 2001, it creates a framework for thinking about globalization as captured in the title, "Mr. Order Meets Mr. Chaos." Many of the issues the article discusses here taken on renewed urgency since 2001.

In this debate Robert Wright, who plays the role of "Mr. Order," presents a perspective that emerges from his recent book, *Nonzero: The Logic of Human Destiny.* He argues that we will make the world a better place going forward if we learn from the lessons of history. History is not, as he says, "just one damn thing after another, it's a process with direction; it has an arrow." Wright has a formula for thinking about the direction of history that he takes from game theory. He asks us to think about who wins and who loses in any given situation. In tennis, Wright explains, a point for you is good but at the same time it is bad for your opponent. In the context of globalization, quite the opposite is true, the sweatshirt you bought is good for you but he argues it is also good for the person in a developing country who made it. This situation, in which economic factors create an unlikely relationship, illustrate a non-zero-sum relationship, in which both parties can win. The possibility for nonzero relationships, Wright argues, contributes to a vision of potential order as we move into the future global context.

Robert Kaplan takes up his role in this debate as "Mr. Chaos." In this debate and in his recent book, *The Coming Anarchy: Shattering the Dreams of the Post Cold War,* Kaplan attempts to jolt us out of any dreamy, optimistic hopes we might have for the future of modern societies around the globe. He provokes us through the use of "constructive pessimism," the idea that by imagining the worst we may be able to prevent it. The worst-case scenarios that Kaplan presents result from the growing divide between parts of the world that enjoy prosperity and parts of the world that are burdened by environmental scarcity, disease, climate change, and rapid urbanization. In Kaplan's view, democracy—which is often seen as the solution to all these problems—doesn't offer a quick fix, but may offer support to struggling nations over a longer period of time. Kaplan's dire prognostications are meant to get us thinking. And they do.

Connecting with the Conversation

1. Try to explain the difference between zero-sum games and non-zero-sum games from the explanation given in this introduction. Think of some situations from your personal experience in which either a zero-sum game or a non-zero-sum game seemed to be at work. For instance, consider examples from sports or video games. What about circumstances such as classroom discussion, test-taking, or group projects?
2. Read two sections of the newspaper, the international section and either the local or business section. What evidence do you find about issues of wealth or poverty, work or joblessness, peaceful governance or unstable political situations? See if you can draw any connections between what is happening locally with what is happening globally.
3. Robert Kaplan introduces the idea of "constructive pessimism," which he says means imagining the worst thing that could happen so that you can prepare for it. Consider what this notion could mean in your own life. How might you employ this sort of thinking about your job, your school, or your family?

My Minivan and World Peace

Robert Wright

Anyone who knows me would be surprised to find me cast as an optimist, but when you're juxtaposed with Robert Kaplan, it's not hard to come off looking pretty chipper and upbeat about the world.

What is the basis for my relative optimism? My prescription and diagnosis are built upon the notion of the non-zero-sum game, which is a reference to game theory. A zero-sum game is what you see in an athletic event like tennis: Every point in the match is good for one player and bad for the other. So the fates of the players are inversely correlated. In a non-zero-sum game, the fortunes can be positively correlated; the outcome can be win-win or lose-lose, depending on how competitors play the game. And, in fact, in a tennis doubles match the players on the same team have a highly non-zero-sum relationship because they'll both win or they'll both lose.

Nowadays we're all embedded in lots of non-zero-sum relationships that we really don't even think about. For instance, when I bought my Honda minivan I was in a non-zero-sum relationship with workers in various countries. The deal was I paid a tiny bit of their wages and they built me a car. It is characteristic of globalization that it embeds us in these non-zero-sum relationships. It makes our fates more correlated

Foreign Policy no. 124, May/June 2001, p. 51–60.

with the fates of people at great distances. It's a subtle process that we usually don't think about, but every once in a while this correlation of fortunes becomes glaringly evident, as was the case with the Asian crisis when we realized that a financial downturn can instantly spread around the world; or when a virus spreads across the Internet and you realize that computer users on different continents are all vulnerable, their fates are correlated.

In theory, as globalization makes relations among nations more and more non-zero-sum, you would expect to see more in the way of institutionalized cooperation to address these problems. That is not a pathbreaking insight. For some time now, political scientists have been talking about the growing interdependence of nations and the growing logic behind cooperation. But I believe that this process is now moving so fast that, much sooner than most people expect, we're going to reach a system of institutionalized cooperation among nations that is so thorough it qualifies as world governance. I don't mean world government, a single centralized authority. I imagine a looser mix of global and regional organizations. But still I'm imagining some very significant sacrifices of national sovereignty to supranational bodies. We've already seen a little of this surrender of national sovereignty with the World Trade Organization, and I would argue there was a little bit of surrender (a well-advised surrender) when 174 nations signed the Chemical Weapons Convention.

5 I fully expect this trend toward global governance to continue, although I'm much more confident about it happening in the long run than in the short run. The zone of non-zero-sumness has been expanding for a very long time: You can go back to the Stone Age when the most complex polity on earth was a hunter-gatherer village and chart the evolution to the level of the chiefdom—a multivillage polity—and then to the level of the ancient state, and then to the system of modern nation-states, and so on. The key element that has driven the evolution of social complexity and of governance to higher levels is technology. Sometimes it is information technology, as when the invention of writing often accompanied the evolution of the first ancient states. Sometimes it is transportation technology and sometimes, ironically enough, it is weapons technology. Weapons technologies can make relations much more non-zero-sum—certainly nuclear weapons make war a very non-zero-sum endeavor in the sense of making it a lose-lose game, wherein the object of the game is never to play. Nuclear weapons thus strengthen the argument for a system of collective security pursued through some supranational institution such as the United Nations.

We don't know in detail what the future of technological evolution will be, but we have a pretty good idea. Information technologies will continue to evolve and enmesh people in webs of transactions, interactions, and interdependence. Weapons technologies will evolve, but perhaps more important, the information about how to build very lethal weapons of mass destruction will likely be accessible to more and more people. Thus, almost all nations share a common interest in controlling the development and use of these weapons. Technological evolution will continue doing what it has done for the broad sweep of history, which is expanding the realm of non-zero-sumness, making the fates of peoples and nations more correlated, and in the process driving governance to a higher level, to the global level.

That the fates of the world's people have grown more and more correlated over time is not by itself especially good news. As you may have noticed, many examples of non-zero-sum dynamics are actually negative-sum games, lose-lose games, where the object of the game is to break even. Global warming is an example of such a negative-sum game—where we just want to fend off the bad outcome—that I think calls for institutionalized cooperation and some real, if small, sacrifice of national sovereignty.

So when I argue that history features more and more of this non-zero-sumness, that statement isn't by itself good or bad, it just is. It's just something we have to reckon with. But there is one feature of the direction of human history that is at least mildly upbeat, in some ways redeeming. It's what I call the expanding moral compass. Philosopher Peter Singer has written about this. If you go back to ancient Greece, there was a time when members of one Greek city-state considered members of another Greek city-state literally subhuman. They would slaughter and pillage without any compunction whatsoever. Then the Greeks underwent a process of enlightenment and they decided that actually other Greeks are humans, too. It's just the Persians who aren't humans. (Okay, it was limited progress, but it was progress.) And today I think we've made more progress, especially in economically developed nations. I think almost everyone in such countries would say that people everywhere, regardless of race, creed, or color, deserve at least minimal respect.

If you ask why that has happened, I argue that it gets back to this basic dynamic of history, this growth of non-zero-sumness. If you look at Greece at the time of their limited enlightenment, relations were growing more non-zero-sum among Greek city-states because they were fighting a war together against the Persians. They needed each other more, they were in the same boat, and to cooperate they had to accord each other at least minimal respect. And if you ask why an ethos of moral universalism now prevails in economically advanced, globally integrated nations, I would say it's the same answer. If you ask me why don't I think it's a good idea to bomb the Japanese, I'd say, "For one thing, because they built my minivan." I'm proud to say I have some more high-minded reasons as well, but I do think this basic, concrete interdependence forces people to accord one another at least minimal respect, to think a little about the welfare of people halfway around the world. I expect this dynamic to grow and persist in the future because in a world where disease can spread across borders in no time at all, it's in the interest of Americans to worry about the health of people in Africa or Asia. In a world where terrorists can wield unprecedentedly lethal technologies, it's in the interests of Americans to worry about political grievances before they fester to the point of terrorism. One feature of a globalized society is that disaster can happen at the global level, so we're now in this process where either we grasp the moral and political implications of this increasingly shared fate we have with other people or very bad things will happen.

The modern world is in many ways a disoriented and disturbing place. Things are changing very fast, but I think if you look at the broad sweep of the past it offers a way to orient ourselves. History is not just one damn thing after another, it's a process with a direction; it has an arrow. And I think if we use that arrow to orient ourselves then I would predict that the coming decades will not be characterized by chaos.

Hope for the Best, Expect the Worst

Robert Kaplan

Well, Bob, while you've been looking ahead to discern the broad, cosmic sweep of history, I've been looking ahead just 10 or 15 years in terms of foreign policy—which is often most effective when it's conceived of in light of worst-case scenarios, in the hope that those scenarios don't occur. I should remind you that constructive pessimism is profoundly in the American tradition. It's the basis for the U.S. Constitution. If you read *The Federalist Papers,* you can see that Americans have become a country of optimists over 225 years precisely because we've had the good fortune of having our systems of government founded by pessimists. The French Revolution conversely was founded on optimism, on the belief that elites could engineer positive results from above, and it devolved into the guillotine and Napoleon's dictatorship. Alexander Hamilton, whom I consider the greatest of the Founding Fathers, said don't think there will be fewer wars in the world simply because there will be more democracies. In *Federalist Number Six* he said there are as many wars from commercial motives as from territorial aggrandizement. So it is in that spirit of *The Federalist Papers* that I'm going to present a scenario about what worries me over the next 10 or 15 years.

I wrote in 1994 that even as part of the globe was moving toward economic prosperity, another part—containing much of the population—was marching in another direction due to issues such as demography, resource scarcity, and disease. So let me tell you how I see things now, seven years later. The European colonialists did a lot of terrible things, but they did bring a certain degree of order to much of sub-Saharan Africa, South Asia, and Central Asia. That colonial grid work of states started dissolving in the 1990s when we saw the weakening or outright collapse of several marginal places. I use the term "marginal" not because their well-being wasn't important, but because they had low populations, their economies were small, and they didn't really affect the region around them all that much. Somalia, Sierra Leone, Tajikistan, Haiti, and Rwanda were not core regional states in any sense, but look at how they disrupted the international community.

I believe that, for a number of reasons, we're going to see the weakening, dilution, and perhaps even crackup of larger, more complex, modern societies in the next 10 or 15 years in places such as Nigeria, Ivory Coast, and Pakistan. And we're going to see severe crises in countries like Brazil and India. This dissolution of the colonial grid work is going to create the kind of crises where there will be no intervention scenarios, or the intervention scenarios will be far worse than they were in Bosnia or Sierra Leone. The problem is not that these places have particularly bad governments. They're coping as best as any could. The reasons are far more complex and intractable.

First of all, these societies are modernizing. Although history teaches us that modern democratic institutions provide stability, history also reveals that the process of creating and developing modern democratic institutions is very destabilizing. As free-market democracies develop, more and more people are brought into the political process. And all of these people are full of yearning, ambitions, and demands that governing institutions very often cannot keep pace with. So things start to break down here and there. It is economic growth that typically fuels political upheavals, not poverty.

The other challenge to the stability of the nation-state is demography. You hear a lot about how the world population is aging, but that's over the long term and throughout the world as a whole [see "The Population Implosion," *Foreign Policy,* March/April 2001]. But when you look ahead at just 20 or 30 countries over the next 10 or 20 years, you see dramatic rises in the youth population (what demographers call "youth bulges"). When you watch your television and you see unrest or rioting in Indonesia, Ivory Coast, Gaza, and the West Bank, what's similar about all of them? All of the violence is typically conducted by young men, ages 15 to 29, who are unemployed and frustrated. The sector of the young male population within this age group is going to grow dramatically in the countries that already have tremendous unrest and are already on the edge. In other words, the places that will have a population pyramid that is bottom-heavy with the youngest members of society are the ones that can least afford it.

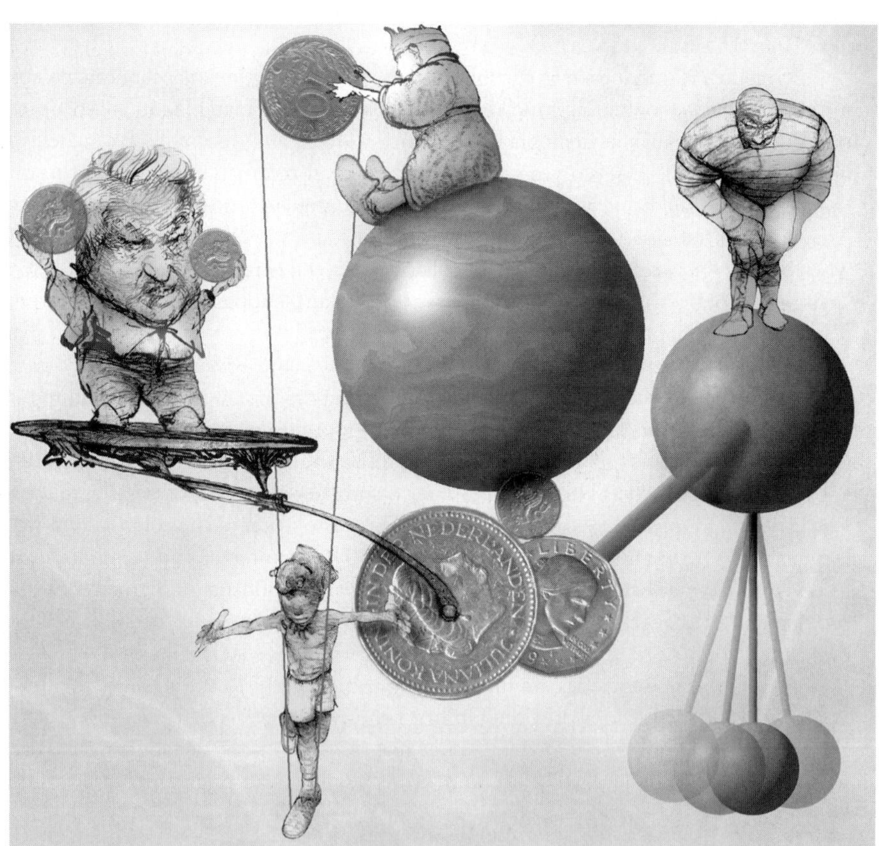

And if that isn't enough, you've got urbanization. The 21st century is going to be the first century in world history when more than half of humanity will live in cities. Even sub-Saharan Africa is almost 50 percent urban. Urban societies are much more challenging to govern than rural societies. In rural societies people can grow their own food, so they are less susceptible to price increases for basic commodities. Rural societies don't require the complex infrastructure of sewage, potable water, electricity, and other things that urban societies have. Urbanization widens the scope of error for leaders in the developing world while simultaneously narrowing the scope for success. It is harder to satisfy an urban population than a rural population, especially when that population is growing in such leaps and bounds that governing institutions simply cannot keep pace.

Then you have resource scarcity, particularly water. I spent the summer in a small village in Portugal where we only had running water about eight hours a week. We had to drive about half a mile to a local fountain to fill pitchers of water. Anyone who has not gone without water has no idea what it's like not to be able to flush your toilet or take a bath. There's been a drought for the last four years across a swath of South Asia from Afghanistan, Pakistan, and into India. Dams are low, so there is not enough water for drinking or generating electricity. So in these hot cities of the subcontinent you have less and less air conditioning in the summer. This kind of stuff doesn't necessarily cause political crises, but it's all part of the background noise that aggravates existing crises. This frustration worsens ethnic tension and makes social divides harder to resolve. In short, people get angry. There was a spate of riots in Karachi, Pakistan, not long ago that was preceded by an extended period when there was very little electricity due to water shortages.

Then there's the issue of climate change. Let's just say for the sake of argument that this whole global warming issue has been exaggerated, that it really doesn't exist, that it's not going to be a problem. Well, even if you factor out global warming, the normal climatic variations of the earth during the next few decades will still ensure devastating floods and other upheavals because, for the first time in world history, you have hundreds of millions of human beings living in environmentally fragile terrain—where perhaps human beings were never meant to live at all. So even without global warming you're going to have natural events that can spark political upheaval.

And finally, the other factor that's going to spark serious institutional crises in a lot of states is democracy. Everyone wants to be democratic, no use denying it. But democracy tends to emerge best when it emerges last. It should be the capstone to all other types of development, when you already have middle classes that pay income taxes, when you already have institutions run by literate bureaucrats, when the major issues of a society (such as territorial borders) are all resolved and you already have a functioning polity. Then, and only then, can a society cope with weak minority governments. Then, and only then, can democracy unleash a nation's full potential. Right now, we're seeing democracy evolve in many places around the earth accompanied by unemployment and inflation rates every bit as dire as Germany in the 1930s, when Hitler emerged under democratic conditions, and in Italy, when Mussolini came to power in the early 1920s. I'm not arguing against democracy, but I believe democracy will be another destabilizing factor.

10 If it seems like I'm deliberately cultivating a sense of the tragic it's because that's how you avoid tragedy in the first place. Remember that Klemens von Metternich was so brilliant in creating a post-Napoleonic order that Europe saw decades of peace and prosperity—so much so that politicians in France and England lost their sense of the tragic. All they saw ahead were optimistic scenarios and, as such, they stumbled and miscalculated their way into World War I. Take my concern in that spirit.

In the Long Run, We're All Interdependent

Robert Wright responds.

Well Bob, I'm actually something of a fan of pessimism myself. I think it focuses us on the problems that need our attention. I find it particularly heartening that your books have a sizable American readership, since that suggests that Americans increasingly realize their fates are intertwined with the fates of people around the world. But I don't want to overdo the pessimism. And in particular I don't want to make it sound like globalization and its attendant technological fluctuations are part of some kind of uniformly bad force. I'm actually something of a cheerleader for globalization. It has problems, but I think on balance it's a good thing.

You said that the world was increasingly dividing into two parts, echoing the common refrain that globalization exacerbates income inequality worldwide. But that conclusion actually depends on how you examine the data. If you look at the number of rich versus poor nations, then you can certainly make that argument. But if you look at the total number of people in the world, ignoring where the borders fall, then what's happening in absolute terms is that there are fewer poor people than there used to be. And even in relative terms, it's far from clear that income inequality is growing, and a number of people have argued that the income gap is actually shrinking worldwide. It turns out that many of the world's poor people are concentrated in a few very large countries (like China and India) that have seen more progress than some of the smaller countries (notably those in Africa). But even in Africa, globalization has seen a kind of vindication: The countries that have seen the most economic advancement are the ones that are most open to trade and investment.

Another virtue of globalization is that it is basically an antiwar activity. I think as peoples and nations become more economically intertwined, war becomes more of a lose-lose kind of non-zero-sum game that it doesn't make sense to play. There still are wars in the world, but there is a very interesting feature of the modern world that is insufficiently noted: We increasingly think of wars between nations as something that poor countries do. Nobody expects any of the most economically advanced nations to go to war with one another, which represents a real shift of mind-set. If you look back at most of history it was really standard procedure for the most powerful polities to go to war with one another. Nowadays, most interstate fighting breaks out in parts of the world that could be termed "underglobalized" areas. I don't mean that pejoratively. It's not their fault that they're underglobalized. There are various quirks of history or geographical circumstance that explain why some parts of the world have advanced faster economically than others. But the fact is that wars are mostly a threat in the poorest parts of the world.

Now, when you get to subnational conflict, war within nations, I agree, Bob, that's a problem that may grow more serious. You argue that conflict is often exacerbated by economic development. I'd add another way in which modernization has given rise to intranational conflict, and that is through the propagation of information technology. As I suggested earlier, information technology has certain globalizing effects, but it also has fragmenting effects because whenever you lower the cost of communication you make it easier for small groups with meager resources to organize. It's no coincidence that the Protestant Reformation roughly coincided with the invention of the printing press. After Martin Luther had tacked up his 95 Theses, printers took it upon themselves to start printing them in various cities. That is how Luther first organized the masses, because printing was suddenly so cheap.

You're seeing the same thing in the modern world thanks to the Internet. Inevitably, information technology is going to empower separatist groups such as Muslims in the west of China and Basques in Spain. But, in the long run, you can imagine this secessionist frenzy working itself out, because as some of these subnational groups choose to drop out of nations they can at the same time cement themselves into supranational bodies. In fact, the Quebec separatists have said they plan to join the North American Free Trade Agreement (NAFTA) as soon as they get out of Canada, and I would expect that European separatist groups would be strongly tempted to join the European Union. So, I certainly agree that globalization presents us with all kinds of short-term difficulties, but I do still think it's a process that is fundamentally beneficial and will lead to a new equilibrium in the long run.

Passion Play

Robert Kaplan responds.

Bob, let me draw some distinctions here, just in the spirit of argument. You tend to put a lot of emphasis on the ability of people to make good, rational choices. But if you think that people are always going to behave according to their best, rational self-interest, read *Mein Kampf.* As Hamilton said, "the passions of men will not conform to the dictates of reason and justice, without constraint." The U.S. Constitution was established to slyly organize and control our passions. I'm not convinced that we're going to act any more rationally than we have in the past. It is true that there is a movement toward world governance, but a single, unifying thread is not necessarily a good thing. For instance, the European Union could readily devolve into a benign bureaucratic despotism that will ignore the interests of the lower middle classes. I think the nationalist movements popping up throughout Europe are already a reaction to this benign bureaucratic despotism from Brussels. If there is to be world governance, it has to be a kind that doesn't only appeal to the elites.

And those who feel marginalized have resources at their disposal that go way beyond the Internet. The Industrial Revolution was about bigness—big aircraft carriers, tanks, and railway grids—so that only large states could take advantage of the power the Industrial Revolution had to offer. But when you're talking about cyberwarfare, biological weapons, and this whole new gamut of weaponry in the post-Industrial Revolution, when you live in a world where just a telephone jack and a petri dish give you power, then it's not just large nations that can benefit. Nonstate actors who feel shut out can also magnify their power through this new technology. Power relationships are going to be more complex than ever. You were right when you said that technology drives history, but it doesn't necessarily do so in an orderly manner.

As for the moral universalism that you mention, I think we have to be a bit careful because the West is now using the term "global community" in the way we used to use the term "free world." We're trying to define the whole world in terms of our own moral outlook and what we want. There may be other powers and other cultures that have dif-

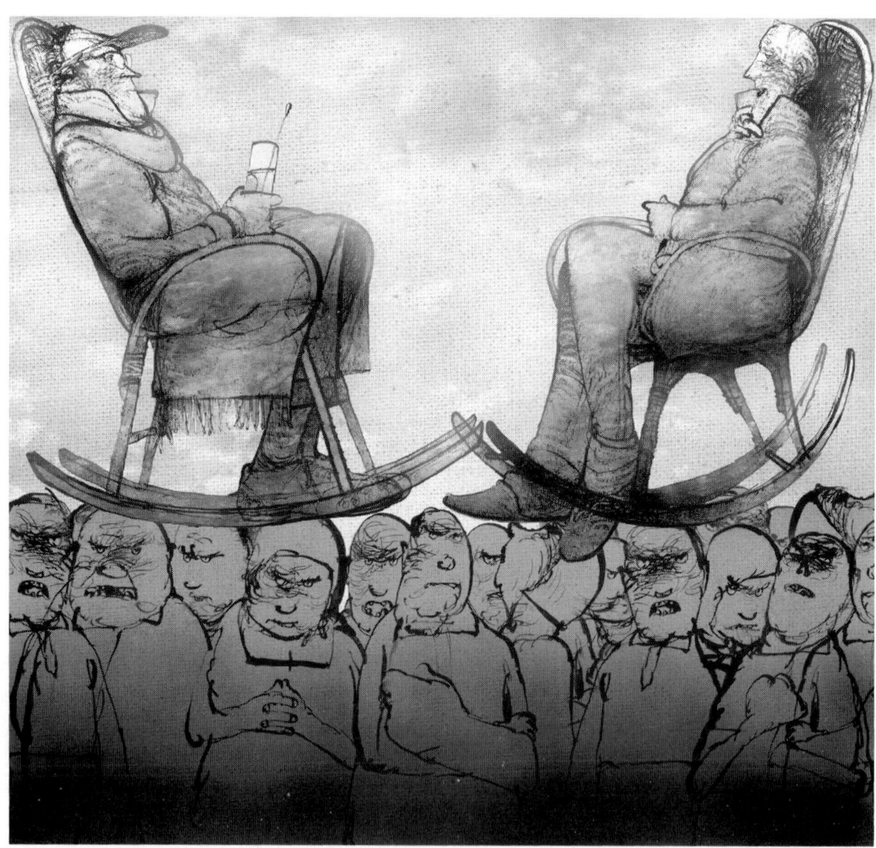

ferent views of how the world should be organized, so we have to be careful not to sound triumphalist. And although inequality might be decreasing, I believe the most significant form of inequality is not what we see between the United States and sub-Saharan Africa, but the income gap you see between the wealthy coastal community and poor interior of a place such as Ghana. The biggest divides are between these globalized communities within the poorest countries—with their own electricity generators, their own water wells, and their own private security guards—that are hooked up to the world economy and surrounded by people with whom they have less and less in common.

You're right Bob, history is not one damn thing after another, but neither is it on a direct, predetermined course à la Karl Marx. The philosopher who captures it all best is Charles de Montesquieu who, in *The Spirit of the Laws,* sees the course of history as just a gradual improvement, punctuated with a lot of ups and downs.

5 But, lest I sound too contrarian, allow me to point out that I've been concentrating on the zero-sum games that occur within your vast non-zero-sum game. So, in that sense, there is no contradiction between us.

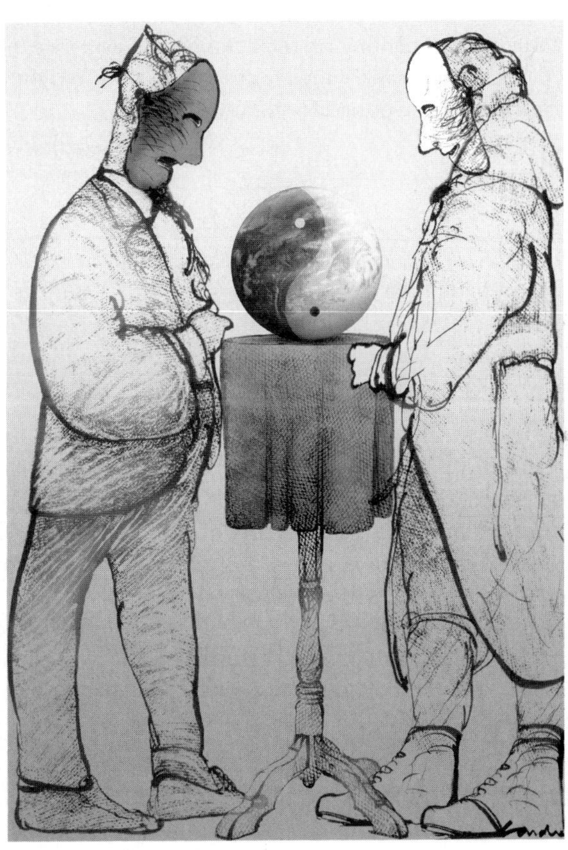

Exploring Texts and Contexts

For activities with icons, refer to the Guides to Analyzing Contexts for Writing and Analyzing Readings in Context.

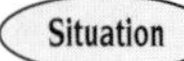

1. What sort of journal is *Foreign Policy?* Visit the Web site at www.foreignpolicy.com. Explore the Web site: take note of what topics are discussed, what links are included, what sorts of documents are either included or pointed to on the Web site. Search the sites of other magazines such as the *Wilson Quarterly,* or *The Economist.* Again, consider what issues are being discussed, what examples are used as illustrations, what sort of features or links these Web sites offer.

2. Much of this discussion about globalization, the politics of the world stage, and economic well-being involves a very specific vocabulary. List ten words used by Wright and ten words used by Kaplan. Using a dictionary and an encyclopedia, write a few sentences to explain their meaning.
3. Review the arguments presented in each side of this debate. Using a highlighter, mark each of Wright's and Kaplan's claims—some will be major claims and some will be subclaims—then list the evidence they provide. Since each knows that the other debater will be commenting on their claims and evidence, how do they prepare for each other's objections? How, for example, does Wright anticipate and refute Kaplan's focus on the possibility for anarchy?

Creating Texts

For activities with icons, refer to the Guides to Analyzing Contexts for Writing and Analyzing Readings in Context. For additional help with these writing projects, read the descriptions of **Comics, Cover letter/Reflective Letter,** and **Address/Speech** in the Genre Glossary.

1. Design a comic to illustrate the consequences of a particular point made in these debates. Ask yourself, "So What?" and design a comic that will illustrate the answer to that question. The provocative title for this debate may provoke visual images that capture the conundrum, or puzzle, of globalization. Create a situation in which two characters exchange words about a situation that concerns the global economy. Consider various options for what that situation might be; try to work with a relatively current topic that others in your class will recognize. When you've completed the comic, compose a reflective essay that explains the choices you made and tells something about what you hope your audience will take away from your graphic text.
2. Write a speech that you will deliver to a lunchtime meeting of a current-events club that you belong to. Choose a side of this debate that you feel comfortable supporting. If you completed Activity 3 from Connecting with the Conversation,

use it here to plan your speech. Use the logic of that writer—either Kaplan or Wright—to interpret recent events at some location in the world. You might consider a situation here in the United States. Or you might explore the war initiated by the United States to topple the regime of Saddam Hussein. Consider the arguments made for either possible world order or possible anarchy. As you plan and write, remember that a speech is delivered orally, which makes it more difficult for your audience to follow. Be sure to include enough cues so that your listener can follow your talk. Remember, too, that, personal anecdotes and lively examples will make your speech more effective.

A Passage to India

The Case of Bangalore

William Wolman and Anne Colamosca

William Wolman and Anne Colamosca took for their chapter the title of E. M. Forster's novel, *A Passage to India,* about the difficult interpersonal relationships between the English and Indians during Britain's colonial rule. The reference to Forster's novel is an attempt to ask what the new transnational relationships will mean for India—will India once again be subject to colonial rule, or will it come into its own as an equal player in the global context? Bangalore, a city set high on a plateau in Southern India, provides a case study that points to success for Indian workers in the newly developing global software industry. But Wolman and Colamosca include the story of Bangalore in their recent book, *The Judas Economy: The Triumph of Capital and the Betrayal of Work,* to help make their argument that the United States' unbridled embrace of global capitalism will result in diminished opportunities for American workers.

Wolman is the chief economist for *Business Week* magazine, and Colamosca writes on the economy for a variety of national publications. They wrote *The Judas Economy* out of their concern for the direction our pro-market economy is taking. In a pro-market economy, decisions are based on who has something to sell and who has money to buy it. Thus, in a global economy, where new markets are springing up around the world, a computer programmer can do his or her job from Bangalore, India, as well as from Mountainview, California. Workers can work anywhere, and particular workers are no longer the linchpin in a company's success.

Wolman and Colamosca define the worker as anyone who earns a living through "muscles, brains, or wit." The authors contrast workers with capitalists, or "people who earn their living primarily from the ownership of *assets.*" It is the enormous wealth generated through retirement and pension funds, stocks and bonds, and real estate that generates the capital that may now endanger one's ability to earn a living through work. Whereas in times past, the capitalist system might have been seen as the partner of work, it is now a traitor, Wolman and Colamosca claim, caring only for producing more capital and not more jobs. Both authors have been strong supporters of capitalism but are now concerned that the free-market system is out of balance, having swung too far and allowed the flow of capital too much power. They tell the cautionary tale of Bangalore to illustrate that our country's information elite—high-level technology workers—are in danger of losing their jobs in the global rush to create capital.

Connecting with the Conversation

1. Talk to students in an introductory economics course. Ask them to tell you what economics is and what sorts of questions economists try to answer. Take a look at an economics textbook, and see what it says about macroeconomics in particular. Pool your information with others in a small group and report back to the class.
2. Go to a newsstand or to the browsing room at your library, and look at several popular news magazines such as *Time, Newsweek, Business Week,* or *The Economist.* See what they have to say about the global economy or the American workforce. What issues are discussed? Make note of the vocabulary used to discuss these issues. Look up terms you do not understand. Prepare an informal report for the class on what you have found.

In his exuberant, much-celebrated novel *The Moor's Last Sigh,* Salman Rushdie portrays the deep idiosyncracies of one family, the da Gama-Zogoiby clan, to illustrate the fate of modern India. Rushdie uses a canvas of surreal images—a stuffed bulldog containing the soul of Jawaharlal Nehru; a group of variously shaped Indian actors parroting Lenin's speeches in a dozen Indian dialects (comic opera efforts at importing the Russian Revolution); a torched spice grove in southern Kerala State strewn with the crucified bodies of those rumored to have belonged to India's Home Rule movement; a mysterious painting invested with the secrets of the past; and "Mother India" herself, the dazzling, brash, unsentimental artist, Aurora—to tell his story. Rushdie's saga is strewn with buffoons, fools, and seers, characters playing out the literature of magical realism who depict India's many follies and missed opportunities.

In some ways, the beautiful, chaotic, electricity-short city of Bangalore, sitting three thousand feet above the rest of southern India on a plateau deep in the interior, could almost be a page out of Rushdie's novel. But in contrast to the Moor's environs, it is very much a place where "the players" have somehow managed to win out, and the exuberance of quick fortunes being made through space-age megadeals are staged in spaces adjacent to noisy harangues over large sacks of grain being transferred from one bullock cart to another, as they have been for hundreds of years. It is in this often enchanted Indian city, still unknown to most of the Western world, that

From *The Judas Economy: The Triumph of Capital and the Betrayal of Work,* Boston: Addison Wesley, 1997, pp. 87–105, excerpted.

thousands upon thousands of Indian computer scientists work long days and nights in head-to-head competition with their American counterparts. Ironically, Robert Reich, secretary of labor in the first Clinton administration, has insisted that duplicating what he calls "symbolic-analytic" zones outside the United States is almost impossible. He has said,

> While specific inventions and insights emanating from them traverse the globe in seconds, the cumulative, shared learning on which such ideas are based is far less portable. Other nations may try, with varying degrees of success, to create a Hollywood, or . . . a Silicon Valley. But to do so requires more than money. Each of these symbolic-analytic zones represents a complex of institutions and skills which have evolved over time. To contrive exactly the right balance is no easy task.

Apparently Reich has not visited Bangalore, for although it will indeed take time to set up such an environment, that south Indian city does in fact contain a more than healthy embryo that exhibits the exact balance that Reich is talking about.

5 For in a kind of high-tech magical realism that defies all the odds, Bangalore has quietly put together all the ingredients of a broad frontal attack on American hegemony on the frontier of the information revolution, software. India's software industry, which barely existed ten years ago, notched up sales of more than $1.2 billion in 1995 and has been growing at over 40 percent a year. Unlike many other Indian industries, it is already highly competitive internationally.

India's Elite Workers Have Arrived

Workers in India, and particularly Bangalore, could easily give American workers stiff competition in the coming decade. India has managed to become a growing power in software maintenance even though no more than 150,000 computers were sold in the country in 1995. And Indian companies have already won awards for the excellence of the new software they have produced, even though in 1995 less than .5 percent of all the software sold in the world was produced in India. These are small numbers to be sure, but they point to the newness of Indian technology, rather than to its weakness. And enormous opportunities will exist as long as India retains its huge cost advantage and continues to graduate some twenty thousand software-literate engineers from its technical institutes each year. Ironically, the educational foundations for India's software industry takeoff were laid by decades of socialist government emphasis on free university education for Indians from all social classes. Although education was not mandatory, and unfortunately many poor Indians living in villages and large cities kept their children at home, through education the forty-four-year socialist-style government still managed to produce a middle class of about 120 million people, by far the largest educated class of Indians the country had ever known.

Middle-class Indians have begun to work with an army of formidable expatriate Indian professionals now hitting midlife who were of a generation that began leaving India in the late 1960s for the United States and Europe. For middle-class technology success stories, American journalists have concentrated mostly on the Japanese and Chinese. It has usually been India's spiritual emissaries, gurus in particular, who have garnered the most media attention in the United States. But it would be a mistake to ignore Indians, many of whom have worked as top mathematicians, technologists, doctors, and increasingly bankers not only in India but throughout the industrialized world. There were more than a quarter of a million Indian physicians, scientists, engineers, managers, administrators, and people in similar high-level occupations living in other countries in the 1990s.

More and more, both local and expatriate populations are working in tandem, bent on creating their own economic miracle, so as to move India alongside its counterparts in the rest of Asia. "The mid-1990s has been a time when most Indians I know believe very strongly that India's time has finally come as a nation," says Vijay Kumar, a Wharton School graduate who helps oversee Coopers and Lybrand's operations in India. Over the last three years, Kumar has begun spending about half his time in India as a business adviser, helping businesses grow. "It is much more satisfying personally to be involved with helping people get jobs in India rather than watching the annihilation of reengineering going on in the American workplace," says Kumar.

"There is no doubt that Indians in the current generation have become more creative than they were twenty-five years ago when I was starting out," he says. "Indians have always had a reputation for being rather rigid in their thinking. That may have been true in the past because Indian teaching methods depended mainly on memorization instead of intellectual give-and-take. Now, however, as the Indian bureaucracy continues to be peeled back, schools are encouraging professors to be more freewheeling in terms of seminars and vigorous class discussions. For example, the Indian Institute of Technology and its various schools throughout India are currently turning out top-notch engineers and computer scientists who are also increasingly creative.

10 "The Indian software business has grown between 40 and 50 percent a year. But it is only in the last twelve months that there has been a large effort by this dynamic industry to actually *create* software products. It probably won't be long before several of these companies come up with some great innovative products. And there will, of course, be a built-in cost advantage for many years to come. Venture capitalists in the United States are just beginning to really understand this market and are beginning to pour real money into Indian software companies. One of these, a company called Mastek, recently went public on NASDAQ in early January 1997. In addition, large U.S. companies such as Northern Telecom and Motorola with subsidiaries in Bangalore are also involved in developing software, in addition to handling all of the software maintenance work that the Indian companies also do. General Electric currently produces medical equipment in Bangalore, taking advantage of the large population of Bangaloreans with engineering and scientific training to manage company projects."

Many like Kumar originally went abroad because there was no dynamic economic base in their own country. They often left home after getting first-rate undergraduate degrees in India for free. Once abroad they were supported by deep networks, or safety nets, of uncles, aunts, village relationships, university mates who automatically opened up their homes to any Indian "friend" in the United States who got off an airplane. These networks put a high premium on education and formed a strong protective shield for those who had gone far from home. Now this successful immigrant population has started to go back to India, putting its financial backing, knowledge, and networks on several continents to work not only in Bangalore but also in places like Hyderabad, Pune, and Delhi and teaming up with entrepreneurs who have stayed at home to put the infrastructure in place for the high-tech revolution.

Flourishing Bangalore

The seeding for India to be a winner in the great software mind game is already visible in the yeasty capital of Karnataka State. Ranked by *Time* magazine in August 1995 as the fastest growing city in Asia, some say in the entire world, Bangalore is already inhabited by a first-class twenty-first-century scientific workforce of software engineers, research scientists, and medical workers. But it would be wrong to think of Bangalore as another Silicon Valley, or the equivalent of the Route 128 area outside Boston. You would come much closer if you imagined another emerging software center—Manhattan (minus its skyscrapers)—as a psychological metaphor for Bangalore. First of all, for Manhattan's hordes of pampered purebred dogs, substitute throngs of skinny, benevolent-looking sacred cows decked out with bright blue painted horns parading through the middle of Broadway traffic. Next mix in the insanity of New York traffic with zooming auto-rickshaws, motorbikes, and large platoons of new automobiles with newly licensed young drivers, creating a traffic free-for-all on potholed roads that would frighten even the most daredevil Manhattan cab driver.

For a long time some of India's most prolific writers, musicians, and artists have been Bangalore residents. But more recently, through the late 1980s and in the 1990s, the city has attracted a growing platoon of moviemakers, television producers, and graphic designers. Like Manhattan, Bangalore is also a major national center for medical research. Recently many southern Indian doctors trained in the United States and Europe have been lured back home, and they are equipping Bangalore's medical centers with some of the most sophisticated technology in the world.

All these talents live side by side in a moving kaleidoscope of heat, dust, pollution, sprawling high-tech industrial parks, an occasional squealing pig, the monumental three-hundred-year-old Mysore Palace up the road studded with sapphires, diamonds, and emeralds; women who carry cement mix in their proud headdresses at local construction sites; busy monkeys darting in and out of traffic a few miles from the center of town; mud and grass slums; a zany-looking violin-shaped music center; overworked electrical generators that produce spotty power; flickering phone connections; towering posters of movie-star lotharios; entrepreneurs with great technological vision.

15 On top of all this, a German horticulturist named Krumbigal, Bangalore's official gardener during the early part of the twentieth century, covered the city's broad avenues and rambling parks with lush blossoming trees—jacaranda, tabebuia, cassia, gulmohar, and acacia and lush cascades of bougainvillea. Bangalore became famous for its prosperous Indian contractors who first designed the large airy homes called bungalows for rich British officers, who liked to retire to the relatively cooler climate of this area. Indeed, a whole group of service workers—traders, tailors, shoemakers, tobacconists, and liquor vendors—grew up in the area, making Bangalore a Raj strong-hold for more than a century and a half. It is still a great city for upscale shopping.

Jawaharlal Nehru, India's first prime minister (1947–1964), had a radically different vision for Bangalore. Calling Bangalore India's "city of the future," in the late 1940s Nehru sought to turn it into India's intellectual capital. It would be a place, said Nehru, where scientists could get away from India's overwhelming masses and produce ideas and programs that would guide the new democracy's ambitious plans to achieve economic and military self-reliance. The city had already established a group of engineering colleges as far back as 1860. Under Nehru, New Delhi lavishly subsidized Bangalore's civilian science and technology infrastructure as well as India's advanced military and space research facilities. As a result, Bangalore and its environs today boasts three universities, fourteen engineering colleges, forty-seven polytechnic schools, and a plethora of research institutes devoted to science, health, aeronautics and space, food and agriculture, and the environment. Public sector giants such as Hindustan Aeronautics, Bharat Electronics, Indian Telephone Industries, Hindustan Machine Tools, and the Indian Space Research Organization, which develops and launches satellites for civilian purposes, are all located in the Bangalore area.

Yet neither the Raj, Nehru, nor the early south Indian scientists themselves could possibly have imagined that their city would become a software capital of Asia, doing more software business than either Israel or Singapore. Recently the Bangalorean software industry has been aping what happened in Manhattan—moving some offices into the center of the city. But for the moment, the many major facilities are located a few miles outside of downtown Bangalore in a barren-looking area dotted with squatter camps and meandering cows. Electronics City, as it is called, houses software companies in what appear from the outside to be nondescript two- or three-storey buildings set not far away from one another.

Since there are no visible restaurants or stores nearby, workers at Electronic City take all their breaks at the so-called office "campuses," which on the inside look very much indeed like their Silicon Valley, California, counterparts. At Infosys, for example, software engineers in their twenties and thirties obsess over their computer screens, chat by the coffee machine, or shoot baskets in the company gym to break up long, long work days. Often workers are picked up and delivered to and from their homes by company buses, fed company-subsidized meals, and in some cases provided with company housing. But they are not mere company drones used only to jack up corporate profits. Like many of his U.S. counterparts, their boss, N. R. Narayana Murthi, has instituted a comprehensive stock option system that has turned a handful of top staffers into millionaires and made most of the staff at Infosys at least financially comfortable.

It takes an intellectually open environment and an entrepreneurial edge to produce the kind of place that Bangalore is fast becoming. And it takes leadership, which the Bangalore software industry has in abundance. The industry has been nurtured and led by visionaries such as Murthi, who set up his own company, Infosys, more than a decade ago, and his friend and colleague, N. Varadan, a government technology expert who makes it his business to facilitate deals between Bangalore and the West. Murthi is sometimes thought of as India's Bill Gates, but he is somewhat older and more philosophical. Unlike most of India's bureaucracy, officials like Varadan are not bureaucrats' bureaucrats, but entrepreneurs' bureaucrats, totally committed to making the private sector go. Because of their deep commitment to an Indian technological nationalism, these remarkable leaders represent a huge psychological contrast to American CEOs, who don't much care about where their employees come from. Men like Varadan and Murthi care a lot about young Indian head workers and their role in the global economy, because these workers prefigure India's role in the twenty-first century.

The Software Business in Bangalore

20 Like Steve Jobs and Bill Gates, Murthi started his software company with a few hundred dollars and no big financial backers. His company came into existence in Pune, about 120 miles south of Bombay. But as the organization grew, Murthi decided to move to Bangalore, because, as he said, "This city offered better living conditions for professionals. And professionals are our most important raw material in the software business." The surrounding area also offered better opportunities for education.

Murthi works very closely with Varadan, the veteran south Indian visionary who is in charge of the industrial park that houses many of Bangalore's largest firms, including Infosys. The government-owned, but autonomous, institution that Varadan represents helps export Indian software to other countries and helps to keep jobs flowing into his industrial park. Another of Varadan's major jobs is to communicate constantly with New Delhi ministers so that the problems encountered in the fast-moving software industry can be resolved quickly, a monumental job that Varadan has worked very hard at, considering the government's legendary glacial pace. By all accounts, the first hundred days of Prime Minister Rao's government brought the largest number of reforms. As one insider put it, "Many in the New Delhi bureaucracy had no idea how serious Rao's reforms were. Many things went through before the old establishment realized all that had happened." According to a number of Bangaloreans, the pace of change slowed down tremendously after the initial hundred days, and after the old bureaucracy bore down on the prime minister's reformers.

Varadan's job also includes helping out young entrepreneurs who want to set up small companies but don't have much capital. "The Software Technology Parks of India provide space and marketing support at bargain prices. They also do training and anticipate new areas that will make us continually competitive in the global market; it's a multifaceted society," says Varadan. "We are proud of what we are doing. We think we are going in the right direction. There are many Indian companies doing joint ventures."

Indeed, the 1996 decision by Silicon Graphics, perhaps the most sophisticated major software company in the world, to erect a facility in Bangalore was governed by the company's belief that the city is ideally suited to develop computer applications in the field of high-tech medicine.

Recently, a new investment park called Information Technology Park, financed with money from Singapore and located not that far away from Electronics City, has attracted thousands of overseas inquiries about commercial space. Like most other parks growing up around Bangalore, it will have its own power, sewage, and satellite communications systems. One hundred and thirty other industrial parks have been started in other locations in India, but Bangalore is still considered the center of software activity.

25 Fortunately for Bangalore, it does not have to ship its wares to the developed world by way of India's antiquated transportation system, its abysmal roads, or even count on

its erratic telephone system. The costs of ocean transport or of airfreight are largely irrelevant to Bangalore's software industry. Instead, companies commune with the developed world using the digitized satellite communications system run by Varadan's agency, which works in much the same way as do the international financial markets. And because moving the south Indian city's output to the rest of the world is so cheap, it represents a new threat to workers in the developed world, who, in the past, have been afforded protection by the high cost of transporting bulky goods into their markets, and the impossibility of swiftly moving the mountains of data needed to run businesses.

Bangalore's software gurus fret over the slow pace at which the New Delhi bureaucrats approve new projects. But Indian technologists like Varadan are well aware that two developments are on their side: the growing use of the Internet as a way of speeding the flow of information, and the corporate trend toward controlling the cost and production of information through outsourcing could create enormous benefits for facilities that can handle information at low cost. Indian businesspeople are aware that the recent development of new universal programming languages such as Java and the use of the Internet for internal communications within corporations—the so-called Intranet—will only serve to enhance India's competitive edge. And though they know that capital-starved India cannot readily replicate the expensive wired and cabled infrastructure of the developed world's information and communications industries, they realize that Indians can create a streamlined information highway of their own based on satellites and cellular phones.

It is the software industry more than any other that has started to free up and use Indian talent in a dynamic way. "There has been a very high frustration level for a long time," says Kumar. "People are bursting to do intelligent jobs." Some Americans coming to India for the first time are in awe of the energy level of the people they meet. "We came here to give demonstrations of a simple industrial cleaning machine used in hospitals and office buildings that we make back in Minnesota," says one recently converted Bangalore enthusiast from the Midwest. "We had two hundred people show up for our seminar. They asked every technical question they could. Some were so sophisticated we didn't know how to answer, and we stayed an hour longer than usual because the audience was so fascinated. It was kind of mind-boggling." Even something as simple as a cleaning machine catches fire. But software is obviously king in Bangalore.

The Power of India's Growing Middle Class and Elite Workers

The strong positive impression that the Indian middle classes and elite workers make on businessmen from the industrialized world is new and important. An anecdote well known by many in India's emerging middle class is of a top executive of the Caterpillar Corporation who during a negotiation in the 1960s tossed a cigarette lighter across a conference table and said condescendingly, "When you guys can make one of these things, let me know about it." That kind of behavior, as middle-class Indians quickly point out, is unimaginable now.

Representative of the city's well-prepared elite is the couple we met for dinner our first night in Bangalore. Kumar's colleague in Bangalore, D. Ashok (everyone calls him Dash), who works as a software specialist, and his wife, Revathy Ashok, who is financial controller for AMP, India, an American electronics firm, took us to an elegant restaurant in a garden setting. Dash immediately began talking about his position in the world of information processing technology. "I spent a year in New York," he said, "which was one of the most important years of my professional life. I wanted to test myself against the Americans, and I found out that I came out very well indeed. It was a great boost to my confidence." Significantly, neither Dash nor his wife had been educated abroad. Both were products of India's homegrown elite universities.

30 Like most Bangaloreans, the Ashoks wanted to discuss the limits to growth imposed by the city's present infrastructure—bad roads; growing pollution from auto and truck exhausts; a telephone system that, although highly efficient in the middle of the city, reaches to the new industrial parks only with difficulty; the shortage of south Indian power and the resulting blackouts everyday in the morning and afternoon; a constant inflow from nearby villages in southern India of entire families who want to raise their own living standards by getting jobs in this new cyberspace capital.

But there is another infrastructure in Bangalore that the Bill Gateses and Andy Groves of the world are buying at an incredibly low price, and it partially explains why every big name, not just in software, but in the entire computer industry, is moving facilities into Bangalore. As our dinner conversation with the Ashoks proceeded, it gradually became apparent to us why Bangalore had become a magnet for high-tech firms trying to combine topflight work with low costs. For what American corporations are getting in India today is not only high-quality global professional talent, but also a family social network that supports workers at an extremely low cost. The Indian middle class can still rely on family to take care of elderly grandparents and children with working mothers. This built-in social infrastructure is an attraction for Western companies tired of the demands of family in the United States—demands that limit workers' availability and make U.S. workers more expensive to employ. Ironically, the very social fabric that draws multinational corporate employers like a magnet to the East has, to a large degree, been unravelled by these same companies through worker transfers and long working hours.

For instance, Dash and Revathy Ashok, the parents of two children, ages seven and thirteen, each has a driver supplied by their companies as well as a secretary. There is a governess, a family cook, a gardener, and more important, a set of intelligent, well-educated grandparents who live with their married children. Usually it is the paternal grandparents who look after the children during the many long hours that the professional pair work and travel. A dollar buys a lot in India. In round figures for the software industry, it currently costs about one third as much in India to do what is done in the United States—even with the thousands of miles of distance.

It's not just foreign corporations but Indian expatriates themselves who are becoming aware of these favorable economics. As Revathy says, "Many of our friends from graduate school who went abroad fifteen years ago are now coming home to India to work. They have found that they can maintain a much higher standard of living here, as we do, than they can by staying in the United States." Even families living on lower incomes can rely on Indian entrepreneurship to help them through their chores. Laundry men walk up and down the streets of Bangalore and other cities setting up ironing boards and pressing clothes on the sidewalk for a few rupees.

India's middle classes experience none of the job anxiety that has unhinged many of their American counterparts. "If you are well-educated, work hard, and know what you are doing, there is no chance in today's India that you will not have security in this exploding job market. There are so many opportunities to pursue." This is the assessment of Revathy Ashok. The thought of packaging and repackaging themselves as human portfolios, of never achieving real job permanence, is unthinkable among today's upper- and middle-class Bangaloreans. Instead they talk of the almost limitless opportunities that are now occurring. Kumar, who has spent thirty years straddled between the United States and India, sees a reversal of attitudes. "In the United States the anxiety level is higher than it's ever been, and in India, despite the many problems, people are extremely bullish, and they feel that the twenty-first century belongs to India. This," adds Kumar, "is without exception, whether you talk to professionals, or an average Indian on the street. And it was not so five or ten years ago. It's the way it was in the 1950s and 1960s in the United States."

The long-term impact of the emergence of a high-morale middle class in what will be the most populous country in the world early in the next millennium cannot be underestimated. Indian businessmen talk endlessly of the frustration they feel because of the huge successes achieved by their counterparts in less populous countries such as Singapore or Taiwan or Hong Kong or South Korea. And they seem highly motivated to eclipse the elites of those countries, whom they regard as fringe players in the long run.

Indeed, the power of the middle class to influence its work and living environment is far greater in Asia than in Europe or North America. In Taiwan, Indonesia, Malaysia, and even the Philippines society bends more swiftly and surely to the will of the technological elite. These are societies in the process of raising a new middle class to new highs, just as surely as during the Industrial Revolution, when steel managers, textile masters, and mine operators dominated industrialized societies. It is the world of the middle class on the move. And this is only the beginning.

The Implications of Corporate Outsourcing and the Transfer of Technology

America's elite workforce in the data processing and software programming fields probably will face strong competition from Indian mind workers if we take the rapid growth of the software industry in Bangalore seriously. This elite workforce could soon easily face the same kind of competition that led to the decline of America's high-wage workforce in traditional industries such as steel and automaking. And it is to a realistic analysis of its impact on the prospects for the American worker elites that we now turn.

So far it's the move of global corporations into Bangalore that has caught the world's attention, particularly decisions in 1995 and 1996 of such leading-edge software companies as Silicon Graphics to open facilities there, focusing on medical applications. Bangalore became a software center very recently, and so far most of what is done there is relatively unsophisticated. Most of the work done in Bangalore currently is maintenance of software systems for major U.S. corporations, so Bangalore's software business is nestled toward the bottom of the world's high-tech information industry, for now. The facilities set up in Bangalore by U.S. corporations are meant to take advantage of low costs for software system maintenance, as well as the indigenous Indian software companies. There is another advantage. Bangalore also thrives on a clock that runs some ten hours ahead of America's eastern standard time. "When an American goes to sleep we wake up," says Murthi. "If AT&T has a computer snag at night with its system, our engineers try to get the problem solved by the time AT&T goes back to work at nine A.M. the next day. We e-mail them the work. This is the way we use this time difference to our advantage."

Murthi's clients include many American blue-chip companies including AT&T, Nordstrom, Citibank, and General Electric. Infosys does many "fixed-price projects"—tailoring software tasks to the needs of a particular company at a fixed price and setting up customized systems. At first there are usually on-site meetings with new clients and Infosys staff in the United States, but as the relationship becomes more long term, communications are often shifted exclusively to videoconferencing between Bangalore and New York, or any other location.

Infosys does a good job, according to clients. As one Citibank computer specialist puts it, "The only disadvantage with any of these Indian software companies is working with people who are so far away. But we lay out an incredible amount of detail so they can do the job, and they seem to thrive on this kind of orderliness and strong direction." Citibank also has about two hundred software engineers on its own internal staff, along with a core of Indians in the top ranks of management.

American workers are currently threatened by corporate outsourcing and the globalization of work, and the more so since companies like Murthi's are so competent in performing the software maintenance work. There is no question that leading-edge work in the software business is still concentrated in the United States and the other industrialized countries and is likely to remain so for some time to come. But like almost every other industry, the software industry creates a chain of ancillary activities that are less intellectually demanding but closely related to the basic product. To take one obvious case, this kind of chain is present in the auto industry, where the production of a new vehicle automatically sets in motion huge requirements for secondary industries, maintaining cars, fixing them when they break down, servicing them with gasoline. It has frequently been estimated that one in every ten jobs in the United States has been created by the invention of the automobile. It is true, of course, that many of these jobs, mainly in parts production and in the production of cars themselves, have migrated abroad, but many of them are necessarily located in the United States. There is simply no way that a car can be transmitted to India for overnight repair.

Yet no such protections exist in an industry where the product, information, is digitized and moves between locations at almost the speed of light. That software and data processing problems can be solved anywhere and then transmitted almost instantly to a client company across the globe explains the breathtaking growth rate of Banglore's software industry. It is why Bangalore represents a template of what is to come in any era whose central feature is a stream of output that can be moved around at minimal cost. It is why Bangalore has caught the eye of those concerned with the future of the software industry.

Bangalore also offers general insights into what is probably the most important threat posed by the spread of the free market to those who earn their living from work in the United States: outsourcing and the transfer of technology. In the days when the market economy was limited to the Eurocentric world and Japan, and when business only trusted ethnic Europeans with complex tasks, there were relatively limited opportunities for companies in any industry to transfer technology abroad. As a consequence, companies' ability to take advantage of low-cost workers to produce the supporting products and systems spawned by leading-edge technology was limited. So these less sophisticated products tended to be produced within the developed world. There was no way that Bangalore could have developed a software industry of any significance before India's trade liberalization. And the same is roughly true of the period before such countries as China, Malaysia, or Indonesia turned outward. But as these countries gradually, if fitfully, merge into the global market economy, fewer and fewer such barriers exist.

India will not be content until its software industry moves firmly onto the leading edge, by producing products and programs of its own, rather than merely servicing programs and systems developed in the advanced countries. That is why the most serious long-term threat to U.S. software workers is the coming thrust by indigenous Indian companies, such as Murthi's Infosys. As these businesses succeed in introducing their own products, they will threaten not only the information revolution's lower-tier workers, but the information elite themselves.

Exploring Texts and Contexts

For activities with icons, refer to the Guide to Analyzing Readings in Context.

Situation

1. Talk to someone who has recently graduated from college, someone who is employed in a high-tech industry, a faculty member, a neighbor, or a relative. Summarize Wolman and Colamosca's story of Bangalore, and ask them what they think about this case. Does the person agree or disagree with the authors' claim that success in Bangalore will harm U.S. workers? How do you think the background of the person you spoke with influenced his or her views?

Language

2. Reread the first few paragraphs to "A Passage to India: The Case of Bangalore." Pay close attention to the authors' use of language. How would you characterize it? What do you suppose they mean by "a kind of high-tech magical realism"? How have the authors used their language choices to help bring you into the city they are writing about?
3. Take another look at the authors' description of Dash and Revathy Ashok's family life (443). Compare their life to that of a family you know of in the United States in which both parents work. What conclusions can you draw about the effects of the global economy on families? Discuss the differences that the cultural context makes in the lives of workers and families.

Creating Texts

For activities with icons, refer to the Guides to Analyzing Contexts for Writing and Analyzing Readings in Context. For additional help with these writing projects, read the descriptions of **Dialogue/Symposium** and **Essay** in the Genre Glossary.

1. Write a dialogue among several authors you have read in this book, focusing on the role of women in the workforce. Wolman and Colamosca and Chan Lean Heng present quite different views of women in the workplace. Consider how these authors characterize work. Consider, too, how the presence of women in the workplace might change it. Choose one or more speakers in the "Man's Place" symposium as well. You can also join the conversation and bring your own experience to the discussion as well.
2. Write an essay in which you discuss the effect of the global economy on family life. You may want to consider family life as it is described in Bangalore. Examine changes in your own family looking back several generations, and consider how it has been affected by changes in the economy.

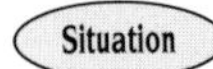

Becoming a Knowledge Worker

Robert Reich

Robert Reich is a political economist, a writer, a Rhodes Scholar, and a lawyer. He has been a professor at Harvard University's John F. Kennedy School of Government, and currently he is a professor of social and economic policy at Brandeis University. He has written over a dozen books that have influenced the way we see our society and our economy. *The Work of Nations: Preparing Ourselves for 21st Century Capitalism* was published in 1992 at about the same time Reich was appointed Secretary of Labor during the Clinton administration. It reflects his career-long interest in figuring out how government can intervene to promote economic growth. His most recent book, *I'll Be Short: Essentials for a Decent Working Society,* encourages everyone to get involved in building an economy that works for all citizens.

The *Work of Nations* offers a visionary plan for sustaining the United States' economic status as it gets drawn into the web of global capitalism. In the introduction to his book, Reich describes the global economy of the future:

> There will no longer be national economies, at least as we have come to understand that concept. All that will remain rooted within national borders are the people who comprise a nation. Each nation's primary assets will be its citizens' skills and insights. Each nation's primary political task will be to cope with the centrifugal forces of the global economy which tear at the ties binding citizens

together—bestowing ever greater wealth on the most skilled and insightful, while consigning the less skilled to a declining standard of living. (3)

Our connections to each other as workers, Reich argues, will exist in the context of a global web rather than in the context of our national boundaries. In the portion of *The Work of Nations* included here, Reich offers a new way to think about how we will see work in this global context and what the best training might be for successful participation in the global economy. Those who engage in routine tasks, such as data processing, can do their job from any place in the world. Reich argues that we must focus on educating an elite worker called the knowledge worker, or symbolic analyst, who will be at the center of the global web. Any efforts to improve our economy should be based on educating our youth as knowledge workers skilled at problem solving and collaboration.

Connecting with the Conversation

1. Write in your journal about a time when you worked either alone or in a team, either in or outside of school, on solving a problem. Write an account of the process you went through. Consider how well prepared you are to work with others in teams or to work in a problem-solving mode.
2. Go to the Department of Labor Web site at www.dol.gov. Take a look around in the site and see what kinds of resources and information it has. You might also compare this sites to one not sponsored by the government, www.2030.org.

The usual discussion about the future of the American economy focuses on topics like the competitiveness of General Motors, or of the American automobile industry, or, more broadly, of American manufacturing, or, more broadly still, of the American economy. But, as has been observed, these categories are becoming irrelevant. They assume the continued existence of an American economy in which jobs associated with a particular firm, industry, or sector are somehow connected within the borders of the nation, so that American workers face a common fate; and a common enemy as well: The battlefields of world trade pit our corporations and our workers unambiguously against theirs.

No longer. In the emerging international economy, few American companies and American industries compete against foreign companies and industries—if by *American* we mean where the work is done and the value is added. Becoming more typical is the global web, perhaps headquartered in and receiving much of its financial capital from the United States, but with research, design, and production facilities spread over Japan, Europe, and North America; additional production facilities in Southeast Asia and Latin America; marketing and distribution centers on every continent; and

---

Excerpted from *The Work of Nations: Preparing Ourselves for 21st Century Capitalism.* New York: Vintage Books, 1992, pp. 171–233.

lenders and investors in Taiwan, Japan, and West Germany as well as the United States. This ecumenical company competes with similarly ecumenical companies headquartered in other nations. Battle lines no longer correspond with national borders.

So, when an "American" company like General Motors shows healthy profits, this is good news for its strategic brokers in Detroit and its American investors. It is also good news for other GM executives worldwide and for GM's global employees, subcontractors, and investors. But it is not necessarily good news for a lot of routine assembly-line workers in Detroit, because there are not likely to be many of them left in Detroit, or anywhere else in America. Nor is it necessarily good news for the few Americans who are still working on assembly lines in the United States, who increasingly receive their paychecks from corporations based in Tokyo or Bonn.

The point is that Americans are becoming part of an international labor market, encompassing Asia, Africa, Latin America, Western Europe, and, increasingly, Eastern Europe and the Soviet Union. The competitiveness of Americans in this global market is coming to depend, not on the fortunes of any American corporation or on American industry, but on the functions that Americans perform—the value they add—within the global economy. Other nations are undergoing precisely the same transformation, some more slowly than the United States, but all participating in essentially the same transnational trend. Barriers to cross-border flows of knowledge, money, and tangible products are crumbling; groups of people in every nation are joining global webs. In a very few years, there will be virtually no way to distinguish one national economy from another except by the exchange rates of their currencies—and even this distinction may be on the wane.

5 Americans thus confront global competition ever more directly, unmediated by national institutions. As we discard vestigial notions of the competitiveness of American corporations, American industry, and the American economy, and recast them in terms of the competitiveness of the American work force, it becomes apparent that successes or failures will not be shared equally by all our citizens.

Some Americans, whose contributions to the global economy are more highly valued in world markets, will succeed, while others, whose contributions are deemed far less valuable, fail. GM's American executives may become more competitive even as GM's American production workers become less so, because the functions performed by the former group are more highly valued in the world market than those of the latter. So when we speak of the "competitiveness" of Americans in general, we are talking only about how much the world is prepared to spend, *on average,* for services performed by Americans. Some Americans may command much higher rewards; others, far lower. No longer are Americans rising or falling together, as if in one large national boat. We are, increasingly, in different, smaller boats.

IN ORDER TO SEE in greater detail what is happening to American jobs and to understand why the economic fates of Americans are beginning to diverge, it is first necessary to view the work that Americans do in terms of categories that reflect their real competitive positions in the global economy.

Official data about American jobs are organized by categories that are not very helpful in this regard. The U.S. Bureau of the Census began inquiring about American jobs in 1820, and developed a systematic way of categorizing them in 1870. Beginning in 1943, the Census came up with a way of dividing these categories into different levels of "social-economic status," depending upon, among other things, the prestige and income associated with each job. In order to determine the appropriate groupings, the Census first divided all American jobs into either business class or working class—the same two overarching categories the Lynns had devised for their study of Middletown—and then divided each of these, in turn, into subcategories.[1] In 1950, the Census added the category of "service workers" and called the resulting scheme America's "Major Occupational Groups," which it has remained ever since. All subsequent surveys have been based on this same set of categories. Thus, even by 1990, in the eyes of the Census, you were either in a "managerial and professional specialty," in a "technical, sales, and administrative support" role, in a "service occupation," an "operator, fabricator, and laborer," or in a "transportation and material moving" occupation.

This set of classifications made sense when the economy was focused on high-volume, standardized production, in which almost every job fit into, or around, the core American corporation, and when status and income depended on one's ranking in the standard corporate bureaucracy. But these categories have little bearing upon the competitive positions of Americans worldwide, now that America's core corporations are transforming into finely spun global webs. Someone whose job falls officially into a "technical" or "sales" subcategory may, in fact, be among the best-paid and most influential people in such a web. To understand the real competitive positions of Americans in the global economy, it is necessary to devise new categories.[2]

10 Essentially, three broad categories of work are emerging, corresponding to the three different competitive positions in which Americans find themselves. The same three categories are taking shape in other nations. Call them *routine production services, in-person services,* and *symbolic-analytic services.*

Routine production services entail the kinds of repetitive tasks performed by the old foot soldiers of American capitalism in the high-volume enterprise. They are done over and over—one step in a sequence of steps for producing finished products tradeable in world commerce. Although often thought of as traditional blue-collar jobs, they also include routine supervisory jobs performed by low- and mid-level managers—foremen, line managers, clerical supervisors, and section chiefs—involving repetitive checks on subordinates' work and the enforcement of standard operating procedures.

Routine production services are found in many places within a modern economy apart from older, heavy industries (which, like elderly citizens, have been given the more delicate, and less terminal, appellation: "mature"). They are found even amid the glitter and glitz of high technology. Few tasks are more tedious and repetitive, for example, than stuffing computer circuit boards or devising routine coding for computer software programs.

Indeed, contrary to prophets of the "information age" who buoyantly predicted an abundance of high-paying jobs even for people with the most basic of skills, the sobering truth is that many information-processing jobs fit easily into this category. The foot soldiers of the information economy are hordes of data processors stationed in "back offices" at computer terminals linked to worldwide information banks. They routinely enter data into computers or take it out again—records of credit card purchases and payments, credit reports, checks that have cleared, customer accounts, customer correspondence, payroll, hospital billings, patient records, medical claims, court decisions, subscriber lists, personnel, library catalogues, and so forth. The "information revolution" may have rendered some of us more productive, but it has also produced huge piles of raw data which must be processed in much the same monotonous way that assembly-line workers and, before them, textile workers processed piles of other raw materials.

Routine producers typically work in the company of many other people who do the same thing, usually within large enclosed spaces. They are guided on the job by standard procedures and codified rules, and even their overseers are overseen, in turn, by people who routinely monitor—often with the aid of computers—how much they do and how accurately they do it. Their wages are based either on the amount of time they put in or on the amount of work they do.

15 Routine producers usually must be able to read and to perform simple computations. But their cardinal virtues are reliability, loyalty, and the capacity to take direction. Thus does a standard American education, based on the traditional premises of American education, normally suffice.

By 1990, routine production work comprised about one-quarter of the jobs performed by Americans, and the number was declining. Those who dealt with metal were mostly white and male; those who dealt with fabrics, circuit boards, or information were mostly black or Hispanic, and female; their supervisors, white males.[3]

In-person services, the second kind of work that Americans do, also entail simple and repetitive tasks. And like routine production services, the pay of in-person servers is a function of hours worked or amount of work performed; they are closely supervised (as are their supervisors), and they need not have acquired much education (at most, a high school diploma, or its equivalent, and some vocational training).

The big difference between in-person servers and routine producers is that *these* services must be provided person-to-person, and thus are not sold worldwide. (In-person servers might, of course, work for global corporations. Two examples: In 1988, Britain's Blue Arrow PLC acquired Manpower Inc., which provides custodial services throughout the United States. Meanwhile, Denmark's ISS-AS already employed over 16,000 Americans to clean office buildings in most major American cities.) In-person servers are in direct contact with the ultimate beneficiaries of their work; their immediate objects are specific customers rather than streams of metal, fabric, or data. In-person servers work alone or in small teams. Included in this category are retail sales workers, waiters and waitresses, hotel workers, janitors, cashiers, hospital attendants and orderlies, nursing-home aides, child-care workers, house cleaners, home health-care aides, taxi drivers, secretaries, hairdressers, auto mechanics, sellers of residential real estate, flight attendants, physical therapists, and—among the fastest-growing of all—security guards.

In-person servers are supposed to be as punctual, reliable, and tractable as routine production workers. But many in-person servers share one additional requirement: They must also have a pleasant demeanor. They must smile and exude confidence and good cheer, even when they feel morose. They must be courteous and helpful, even to the most obnoxious of patrons. Above all, they must make others feel happy and at ease. It should come as no surprise that, traditionally, most in-person servers have been women. The cultural stereotype of women as nurturers—as mommies—has opened countless in-person service jobs to them.[4]

20 By 1990, in-person services accounted for about 30 percent of the jobs performed by Americans, and their numbers were growing rapidly. For example, Beverly Enterprises, a single nursing-home chain operating throughout the United States, employed about the same number of Americans as the entire Chrysler Corporation (115,174 and 116,250, respectively)—although most Americans were far more knowledgeable about the latter, including the opinions of its chairman. In the United States during the 1980s, well over 3 million *new* in-person service jobs were created in fast-food outlets, bars, and restaurants. This was more than the *total* number of routine production jobs still existing in America by the end of the decade in the automobile, steelmaking, and textile industries combined.[5]

Symbolic-analytic services, the third job category, include all the problem-solving, problem-identifying, and strategic-brokering activities we have examined in previous chapters. Like routine production services (but *unlike* in-person services), symbolic-analytic services can be traded worldwide and thus must compete with foreign providers even in the American market. But they do not enter world commerce as standardized things. Traded instead are the manipulations of symbols—data, words, oral and visual representations.

Included in this category are the problem-solving, problem-identifying, and strategic brokering of many people who call themselves research scientists, design engineers, software engineers, civil engineers, biotechnology engineers, sound engineers, public relations executives, investment bankers, lawyers, real estate developers, and even a few creative accountants. Also included is much of the work done by management consultants, financial consultants, tax consultants, energy consultants, agricultural consultants, armaments consultants, architectural consultants, management information specialists, organization development specialists, strategic planners, corporate headhunters, and systems analysts. Also: advertising executives and marketing strategists, art directors, architects, cinematographers, film editors, production designers, publishers, writers and editors, journalists, musicians, television and film producers, and even university professors.

Symbolic analysts solve, identify, and broker problems by manipulating symbols. They simplify reality into abstract images that can be rearranged, juggled, experimented with, communicated to other specialists, and then, eventually, transformed back into reality. The manipulations are done with analytic tools, sharpened by experience. The tools may be mathematical algorithms, legal arguments, financial gimmicks, scientific principles, psychological insights about how to persuade or to amuse, systems of induction or deduction, or any other set of techniques for doing conceptual puzzles.

Some of these manipulations reveal how to more efficiently deploy resources or shift financial assets, or otherwise save time and energy. Other manipulations yield new inventions—technological marvels, innovative legal arguments, new advertising ploys for convincing people that certain amusements have become life necessities. Still other manipulations—of sounds, words, pictures—serve to entertain their recipients, or cause them to reflect more deeply on their lives or on the human condition. Others grab money from people too slow or naïve to protect themselves by manipulating in response.

25 Like routine producers, symbolic analysts rarely come into direct contact with the ultimate beneficiaries of their work. But other aspects of their work life are quite differ-

ent from that experienced by routine producers. Symbolic analysts often have partners or associates rather than bosses or supervisors. Their incomes may vary from time to time, but are not directly related to how much time they put in or the quantity of work they put out. Income depends, rather, on the quality, originality, cleverness, and, occasionally, speed with which they solve, identify, or broker new problems. Their careers are not linear or hierarchical; they rarely proceed along well-defined paths to progressively higher levels of responsibility and income. In fact, symbolic analysts may take on vast responsibilities and command inordinate wealth at rather young ages. Correspondingly, they may lose authority and income if they are no longer able to innovate by building on their cumulative experience, even if they are quite senior.

Symbolic analysts often work alone or in small teams, which may be connected to larger organizations, including worldwide webs. Teamwork is often critical. Since neither problems nor solutions can be defined in advance, frequent and informal conversations help ensure that insights and discoveries are put to their best uses and subjected to quick, critical evaluation.[6]

When not conversing with their teammates, symbolic analysts sit before computer terminals—examining words and numbers, moving them, altering them, trying out new words and numbers, formulating and testing hypotheses, designing or strategizing. They also spend long hours in meetings or on the telephone, and even longer hours in jet planes and hotels—advising, making presentations, giving briefings, doing deals. Periodically, they issue reports, plans, designs, drafts, memoranda, layouts, renderings, scripts, or projections—which, in turn, precipitate more meetings to clarify what has been proposed and to get agreement on how it will be implemented, by whom, and for how much money. Final production is often the easiest part. The bulk of the time and cost (and, thus, real value) comes in conceptualizing the problem, devising a solution, and planning its execution.

Most symbolic analysts have graduated from four-year colleges or universities; many have graduate degrees as well. The vast majority are white males, but the proportion of white females is growing, and there is a small, but slowly increasing, number of blacks and Hispanics among them. All told, symbolic analysis currently accounts for no more than 20 percent of American jobs. The proportion of American workers who fit this category has increased substantially since the 1950s (by my calculation, no more than 8 percent of American workers could be classified as symbolic analysts at midcentury), but the pace slowed considerably in the 1980s—even though certain symbolic-analytic jobs, like law and investment banking, mushroomed. . . .

AMERICANS LOVE TO get worked up over American education. Everyone has views on education because it is one of the few fields in which everyone can claim to have had some direct experience. Those with the strongest views tend to be those on whom the experience has had the least lasting effect. The truly educated person understands how multifaceted are the goals of education in a free society, and how complex are the means.

30 Recall that America's educational system at midcentury fit nicely into the prevailing structure of high-volume production within which its young products were to be employed. American schools mirrored the national economy, with a standard assembly-line curriculum divided neatly into subjects, taught in predictable units of

time, arranged sequentially by grade, and controlled by standardized tests intended to weed out defective units and return them for reworking.

By the last decade of the twentieth century, although the economy had changed dramatically, the form and function of the American educational system remained roughly the same. But now a palpable sense of crisis surrounded the nation's schools, featuring daily lamentations in the media about how terrible they had become. The fact, however, was that most schools had not changed for the worse; they simply had not changed for the better. Early in his presidential campaign, George Bush bestowed upon himself the anticipatory title of "Education President." But, although he continued to so style himself after his election, the title's meaning remained elusive, since Bush did not want to spend any more federal money on education and urged instead that the nation's schools fix themselves. Some people who called themselves educational "reformers" suggested that the standard curriculum should become even more uniform across the nation and that standardized tests should be still more determinative of what was poured into young heads as they moved along the school conveyor belt. (Of course, standardized tests remained, as before, a highly accurate method for measuring little more than the ability of children to take standardized tests.) Popular books contained lists of facts that every educated person should know. Remarkably often in American life, when the need for change is most urgent, the demands grow most insistent that we go "back to basics."

The truth is that while the vast majority of American children are still subjected to a standardized education designed for a standardized economy, a small fraction are not. By the 1990s, the *average* American child was ill equipped to compete in the high-value global economy, but within that average was a wide variation. American children as a whole are behind their counterparts in Canada, Japan, Sweden, and Britain in mathematical proficiency, science, and geography.[7] Fully 17 percent of American seventeen-year-olds are functionally illiterate.[8] Some American children receive almost no education, and many more get a poor one. But some American children—no more than 15 to 20 percent—are being perfectly prepared for a lifetime of symbolic-analytic work.

The formal education of the budding symbolic analyst follows a common pattern. Some of these young people attend elite private schools, followed by the most selective universities and prestigious graduate schools; a majority spend childhood within highquality suburban public schools where they are tracked through advanced courses in the company of other similarly fortunate symbolic-analytic offspring,[9] and thence to good four-year colleges. But their experiences are similar: Their parents are interested and involved in their education. Their teachers and professors are attentive to their academic needs. They have access to state-of-the-art science laboratories, interactive computers and video systems in the classroom, language laboratories, and high-tech school libraries. Their classes are relatively small; their peers are intellectually stimulating. Their parents take them to museums and cultural events, expose them to foreign travel, and give them music lessons. At home are educational books, educational toys, educational videotapes, microscopes, telescopes, and personal computers replete with the latest educational software. Should the children fall behind in their studies, they are delivered to private tutors. Should they develop a physical ailment that impedes their learning, they immediately receive good medical care.

The argument here is not that America's formal system to training its future symbolic analysts is flawless. There is room for improvement. European and Japanese secondary students routinely outperform even top American students in mathematics and science. Overall, however, no other society prepares its most fortunate young people as well for lifetimes of creative problem-solving, problem-identifying, and strategic brokering. America's best four-year colleges and universities are the best in the world (as evidenced by the number of foreign students who flock to them);[10] the college track programs of the secondary schools that prepare students for them are equally exceptional. In Japan, it has been the other way around: The shortcomings of Japanese universities and the uninspiring fare offered by Japanese secondary schools have been widely noted. Japan's greatest educational success has been to ensure that even its slowest learners achieve a relatively high level of proficiency.[11]

35 THE UNDERLYING CONTENT of America's symbolic-analytic curriculum is not generally addressed openly in suburban PTA meetings, nor disclosed in college catalogues. Yet its characteristics and purposes are understood implicitly by teachers, professors, and symbolic-analytic parents.

Budding symbolic analysts learn to read, write, and do calculations, of course, but such basic skills are developed and focused in particular ways. They often accumulate a large number of facts along the way, yet these facts are not central to their education; they will live their adult lives in a world in which most facts learned years before (even including some historical ones) will have changed or have been reinterpreted. In any event, whatever data they need will be available to them at the touch of a computer key.

More important, these fortunate children learn how to conceptualize problems and solutions. The formal education of an incipient symbolic analyst thus entails refining four basic skills: *abstraction, system thinking, experimentation,* and *collaboration.*[12]

Consider, first, the capacity for abstraction. The real world is nothing but a vast jumble of noises, shapes, colors, smells, and textures—essentially meaningless until the human mind imposes some order upon them. The capacity for abstraction—for discovering patterns and meanings—is, of course, the very essence of symbolic analysis, in which reality must be simplified so that it can be understood and manipulated in new ways. The symbolic analyst wields equations, formulae, analogies, models, constructs, categories, and metaphors in order to create possibilities for reinterpreting, and then rearranging, the chaos of data that are already swirling around us. Huge gobs of disorganized information can thus be integrated and assimilated to reveal new solutions, problems, and choices. Every innovative scientist, lawyer, engineer, designer, management consultant, screenwriter, or advertiser is continuously searching for new ways to represent reality which will be more compelling or revealing than the old. Their tools may vary, but the abstract processes of shaping raw data into workable, often original patterns are much the same.

For most children in the United States and around the world, formal education entails just the opposite kind of learning. Rather than construct meanings for themselves, meanings are imposed upon them. What is to be learned is prepackaged into lesson plans, lectures, and textbooks. Reality has already been simplified; the obedient student has only to commit it to memory. An efficient educational process, it is assumed, imparts knowledge much as an efficient factory installs parts on an assembly line. Regardless of what is conveyed, the underlying lesson is that it is someone else's responsibility to interpret and give meaning to the swirl of data, events, and sensations that surround us. This lesson can only retard students' ability to thrive in a world brimming with possibilities for discovery.

America's most fortunate students escape such spoon-feeding, however. On the advanced tracks of the nation's best primary and secondary schools, and in the seminar rooms and laboratories of America's best universities, the curriculum is fluid and interactive. Instead of emphasizing the transmission of information, the focus is on judgment and interpretation. The student is taught to get *behind* the data—to ask why certain facts have been selected, why they are assumed to be important, how they were deduced, and how they might be contradicted. The student learns to examine reality from many angles, in different lights, and thus to visualize new possibilities and choices. The symbolic-analytic mind is trained to be skeptical, curious, and creative.

SYSTEM THINKING CARRIES abstraction a step further. Seeing reality as a system of causes and consequences comes naturally to a small baby who learns that a glass of milk hurled onto a hardwood floor will shatter, its contents splashing over anyone in the vicinity, and that such an event—though momentarily quite amusing—is sure to incur a strong reaction from the adult in charge. More refined forms of system thinking come less naturally. Our tendency in later life is often to view reality as a series of static snapshots—here a market, there a technology, here an environmental hazard, there a political movement. Relationships among such phenomena are left unprobed. Most formal education perpetuates this compartmental fallacy, offering up facts and figures in bite-sized units of "history," "geography," "mathematics," and "biology," as if each were distinct and unrelated to the others. This may be an efficient system for conveying bits of data, but not for instilling wisdom. What the student really learns is that the world is made up of discrete components, each capable of being substantially understood in isolation.

To discover new opportunities, however, one must be capable of seeing the whole, and of understanding the processes by which parts of reality are linked together. In the real world, issues rarely emerge predefined and neatly separable. The symbolic analyst must constantly try to discern larger causes, consequences, and relationships. What looks like a simple problem susceptible to a standard solution may turn out to be a symptom of a more fundamental problem, sure to pop up elsewhere in a different form. By solving the basic problem, the symbolic analyst can add substantial value. The invention of a quickly biodegradable plastic eliminates many of the problems of designing safe landfills; a computerized workstation for the home solves the myriad problems of rush-hour traffic.

The education of the symbolic analyst emphasizes system thinking. Rather than teach students how to solve a problem that is presented to them, they are taught to examine why the problem arises and how it is connected to other problems. Learning how to travel from one place to another by following a prescribed route is one thing; learning the entire terrain so that you can find shortcuts to wherever you may want to go is quite another. Instead of assuming that problems and their solutions are generated by others (as they were under high-volume, standardized production), students are taught that problems can usually be redefined according to where you look in a broad system of forces, variables, and outcomes, and that unexpected relationships and potential solutions can be discovered by examining this larger terrain.

In order to learn the higher forms of abstraction and system thinking, one must learn to experiment. Small children spend most of their waking hours experimenting. Their tests are random and repetitive, but through trial and error they increase their capacity to create order out of a bewildering collage of sensations and to comprehend causes and consequences. More advanced forms of experimentation also entail many false starts, often resulting in frustration, disappointment, and even fear. Exploring a city on your own rather than following a prescribed tour may take you far afield—you may even get lost, for a time. But there is no better way to learn the layout or to see the city from many different points of view. Thus are symbolic analysts continuously experimenting. The cinematographer tries out a new technique for shooting scenes; the design engineer tries out a new material for fabricating engine parts. The habits and methods of experimentation are critical in the new economy, where technologies, tastes, and markets are in constant flux.

45 But most formal schooling (both in the United States and elsewhere) has little to do with experimentation. The tour through history or geography or science typically has a fixed route, beginning at the start of the textbook or the series of lectures and ending at its conclusion. Students have almost no opportunity to explore the terrain for themselves. Self-guided exploration is, after all, an inefficient means of covering ground that "must" be covered.

And yet in the best classes of the nation's best schools and universities, the emphasis is quite different. Rather than being led along a prescribed path, students are equipped with a set of tools for finding their own way. The focus is on experimental techniques: holding certain parts of reality constant while varying others in order to better understand causes and consequences; systematically exploring a range of possibilities and outcomes and noting relevant similarities and differences; making thoughtful guesses and intuitive leaps and then testing them against previous assumptions. Most important, students are taught to accept responsibility for their own continuing learning. (Japan's schools, it should be noted, are weakest in this dimension.)

Finally, there is the capacity to collaborate. As has been noted, symbolic analysts typically work in teams—sharing problems and solutions in a somewhat more sophisticated version of a child's play group. The play of symbolic analysts may appear undirected, but it is often the only way to discover problems and solutions that are not known to be discoverable in advance. Symbolic analysts also spend much of their time communicating concepts—through oral presentations, reports, designs, memoranda, layouts, scripts, and projections—and then seeking a consensus to go forward with the plan.

Learning to collaborate, communicate abstract concepts, and achieve a consensus are not usually emphasized within formal education, however. To the contrary, within most classrooms in the United States and in other nations, the overriding objective is to achieve quiet and solitary performance of specialized tasks. No talking! No passing of notes! No giving one another help! Here again, the rationale is efficiency and the presumed importance of evaluating individual performance. Group tasks are not as easily monitored or controlled as is individual work. It is thus harder to determine whether a particular student has mastered the specified material.

Yet in America's best classrooms, again, the emphasis has shifted. Instead of individual achievement and competition, the focus is on group learning. Students learn to articulate, clarify, and then restate for one another how they identify and find answers. They learn how to seek and accept criticism from peers, solicit help, and give credit to others. They also learn to negotiate—to explain their own needs, to discern what others need and view things from others' perspectives, and to discover mutually beneficial resolutions. This is an ideal preparation for lifetimes of symbolic-analytic teamwork.

Again, the claim here is not that America's schools and colleges are doing their jobs adequately. The argument is narrower: That our best schools and universities are providing a small subset of America's young with excellent basic training in the techniques essential to symbolic analysis. When supplemented by interested and engaged parents, good health care, visits to museums and symphonies, occasional foreign travel, home computers, books, and all the other cultural and educational paraphernalia that symbolic-analytic parents are delighted to shower on their progeny, the education of this fortunate minority is an exceptionally good preparation for the world that awaits.

Notes

1. See Alba M. Edwards, *U.S. Census of Population, 1940: Comparative Occupation Statistics, 1870–1940* (Washington, D.C.: U.S. Government Printing Office, 1943).
2. Because much of the information about the American work force must be gleaned from the old categories, however, the only way to discover who fits into which new category is to decompose the government's data into the smallest subcategories in which they are collected, then reorder the subcategories according to which new functional group they appear to belong in. For a similar methodology, see Steven A. Sass, "The U.S. Professional Sector: 1950 to 1988," *New England Economic Review,* January–February 1990, pp. 37–55.
3. For an illuminating discussion of routine jobs in a high-technology industry, see D. O'Connor, "Women Workers in the Changing International Division of Labor in Microelectronics," in L. Benerici and C. Stimpson (eds.), *Women, Households, and the Economy* (New Brunswick, N.J.: Rutgers University Press, 1987).
4. On this point, see Arlie Russell Hochschild, *The Managed Heart: The Commercialization of Human Feeling* (Berkeley: University of California Press, 1983).
5. U.S. Department of Commerce, Bureau of Labor Statistics, various issues.
6. The physical environments in which symbolic analysts work are substantially different from those in which routine producers or in-person servers work. Symbolic analysts usually labor within spaces that are quiet and tastefully decorated. Soft lights, wall-to-wall carpeting, beige and puce colors are preferred. Such calm surroundings typically are encased within tall steel-and-glass buildings or within long, low, postmodernist structures carved into hillsides and encircled by expanses of well-manicured lawn.
7. A dismally large number of surveys have charted the relative backwardness of the average American student. For a sample, see "U.S. Students Near the Foot of the Class," *Science,* March 1988, p. 1237.

8. *National Assessment of Educational Progress,* various issues.
9. On the tracking system, see Jeanne Oakes, *Keeping Track: How Schools Structure Inequality* (New Haven: Yale University Press, 1985).
10. In fact, university education is one of the few remaining industries in which the United States retains a consistently positive trade balance. As a university teacher, I continuously "export" my lectures and seminars to the rest of the world by virtue of the fact that over a third of my graduate students are foreign nationals.
11. See Merry White, *The Japanese Educational Challenge* (New York: Free Press 1987); Thomas Rohlen, *Japan's High Schools* (Berkeley: University of California Press, 1983); W. Jacobson et al., *Analyses and Comparisons of Science Curricula in Japan and the United States* (New York: Teachers College of Columbia University, International Association for the Evaluation of Educational Achievement, 1986).
12. Suggestions for further reading about these skills, and how formal education can enhance them, can be found at the end of this book in "A Note on Additional Sources."

Exploring Texts and Contexts

For activities with icons, refer to the Guide to Analyzing Readings in Context.

1. Reich names four key activities engaged in by knowledge workers. They are abstraction, system thinking, experimentation, and collaboration. Describe these activities and illustrate them using your own experiences with them. Comment also on whether you have engaged in these activities in or outside of school.
2. Look through your newspaper's job section, and apply Reich's three job categories to the advertisements you see. Are the ads looking for routine production services, in-person services, or symbolic-analytic services? What do you make of the kinds of jobs you find listed? Do Reich's categories seem to work, or would you change them?
3. Review Reich's definition of in-person services (451). Read Ehrenreich's first-person narrative of her experience entering the workforce in which she leaves her comfortable life and plunges "into the low wage workforce" (499). How does the difference in genre change your understanding of low-wage work? How do the contexts of the two pieces differ? Genre

Creating Texts

For activities with icons, refer to the Guides to Analyzing Contexts for Writing and Analyzing Readings in Context. For additional help with these writing projects, read the descriptions of **Address/Speech, Interview,** and **Essay** in the Genre Glossary.

1. You have been invited back to your elementary school to speak at a teacher's institute day that has been especially set aside for reconsidering the school's 

broadest curricular aims. Prepare an address that you will deliver to the principal, teachers, and staff on the role of elementary education in preparing us for further education and for work. Reflect on your own education since elementary school, how useful it was, and how it might have been different. Consider also what your prospects are for participating in the global economy and how we should be thinking of education for the twenty-first century.

Situation

2. Interview someone who is older than you and who has been in the workforce for many years—long enough to have seen the restructuring that resulted in the loss of jobs when companies first began to open plants overseas. Develop questions that probe that person's expectations about a life of work and what it would bring. Ask about what sort of education was needed at that time. What sort of jobs were anticipated? What was the economic climate at that time? How has it changed? Then in an essay, using the information from the interview and Reich's material, trace how the context for work has changed over the last 30 years.

Women on the Global Assembly Line

Chan Lean Heng

Global education has long been a matter of professional interest among educators, government officials, and other kinds of experts. The piece included here was part of a collection that grew out of an international conference on adult education held in Cape Town, South Africa, in 1995. The specific aims of the conference were to include perspectives not typically represented in such discussions and to focus on the particular educational needs of women. Although most discussion about global education focuses on preparing people for the technological economy or simply for participation in the global economy, this conference focused on the human needs of workers whose living and working conditions have been determined by the needs of the global economy.

Chan Lean Heng is a lecturer in social work at the Universiti Putra in Malaysia. In her piece she explores the conditions of women factory workers in her country. Although she points out that these women are generally thought to be working in factories—rather than, say, in office jobs—because of their poor grades in school, her concern is not so much with education itself as with the need for programs to help workers deal with the emotional impact of their working conditions. Although much of this piece is written in academic language, Heng brings in other voices that add startling perspectives. Early in the piece she quotes a Malaysian government brochure designed to attract foreign companies to build factories in Malaysia, and the language of the brochure reveals rather strikingly, if unconsciously, how these workers are seen by their own government and by the foreign companies that employ them. Later in the piece Heng quotes the women themselves talking about their experiences at work and at home. As you read the piece, notice the different effects of these different voices: the government brochure, the speech of the factory workers, and the academic expert analyzing their experiences. How do they all contribute to the overall effect of the piece?

Connecting with the Conversation

1. When you buy clothes, do you try to find out where they were made, and does this influence your decision about what to buy? Share your experiences and ideas with the other members of a small group.
2. Have you ever had a job in which you felt mistreated? What were the circumstances, in what way did you feel mistreated, and what did you do? Write an account of your experience.

Towards the end of the 1960s many of the developing Asian countries shifted their strategy of economic development to export-oriented industrialization (EOI) to provide a new engine of growth to their economies. This coincided with the industrial redeployment of labour-intensive manufacturing industries from the high-wage advanced capitalist countries to the relatively low-wage production sites in the South. These shifts brought an unprecedented rural–urban migration and employment of female labour. The phenomenal expansion of these off-shore activities and the integration of women into the global production systems were the most dramatic developments in these countries in the 1970s.

A corollary to these developments is the suffering of women recruited as labour for these factories. To woo foreign investment, host governments set up free trade zones (FTZs) and offer foreign-owned transnational corporations (TNCs) the advantage of fiscal incentives, tariff exemptions, market opportunities, subsidized land and infrastructure, less restrictive regulations and cheap, 'disciplined' labour. In many countries, even labour enactments have been amended to meet the demands of these off-shore industries.

It is well known that the growth of TNCs and FTZs is based on the exploitation of cheap and docile female labour.[1] This is blatantly illustrated through the investment promotion campaigns of host governments. In a brochure the Malaysian government says: 'The manual dexterity of the Oriental female is famous the world over. Her hands are small and she works with extreme care. Who, therefore, could be better qualified by nature and inheritance to contribute to the efficiency of a production line than the Oriental girl?'

This chapter describes the experiences of women on the global assembly lines. In particular, it tells of the lived experiences of emotional subordination of Malaysian

---

From *Globalization, Adult Education and Training: Impacts and Issues.* Edited by Shirley Walters. London: Zed Books, 1997, pp. 79–86.

women workers. It argues for the importance of addressing these experiences and reconstructing subjectivities in and as educational work with women workers.

Malaysian Women Factory Workers

5 Malaysian women workers, like other global assembly-line operators, work in tedious, repetitive, menial tasks as non-unionized, unskilled shift-workers. They are subjected daily to rigid discipline, pressure, verbal abuse, and intimidation from supervisors and male coworkers. Their work environments are both hazardous and stressful. In fact, gender relations at work are a common source of subordination and work-related stress for the women. Corporate welfare activities, apart from obstructing and negating the development of gender- and worker-consciousness, reinforce feminine stereotypes and prejudices.

The way in which women have been integrated into the global industrial workforce makes them most vulnerable to technological, economic, and industrial change. They are the first to lose their jobs in times of recession. For example, during the 1985 recession in Penang, Malaysia, when Mostek retrenched 1,500 workers, the government told the workers not to be choosy about jobs because 'there were people who could not even find a job'. They were further told to '*balik kampung* [return to the village] . . . *tanam jagung* [plant corn] . . .' even though government officials knew that the women did not have the necessary skills as they had been working in the factories for many years. At the time, the acting Chief Minister made a public call for workers to be self-reliant. He said, 'Those who can write can earn money as freelance journalists, and those with electrical skills should open up small electrical businesses!'[2]

Malaysian women factory workers are also at the bottom of the social hierarchy. In general, it is understood that factory girls are the ones who obtained poor grades in their public examinations, often stigmatized as 'stupid girls who failed the exams'.[3] Hence the stereotype of academic failure is associated with factory work. Many factory women are still ashamed to acknowledge openly that they are production operators. A monthly-paid office job from eight to five o'clock is still regarded as of higher status, even though the take-home pay may be much less. Most factory workers are ashamed of their job and aspire to office jobs.

They are also regarded as immoral and sexually promiscuous. They are silent victims of abuse, derogation, and sexual harassment. They are made to feel responsible for and shamed by the harassment inflicted on them. Such incidents are endured in silence and accompanied by feelings of inferiority because of the shame and blame they bring. Since the establishment of the FTZs they have been ridiculed with labels such as *Minah Karan* (meaning 'hot stuff') or *jual murah* (cheap stuff). Most of the women workers are migrants from rural areas, first-generation industrial workers to the city. Many of the host community residents are very suspicious and hostile towards them.

For many of the women workers, the endurance of this humiliation is one of the most degrading experiences of factory life, a stigma which many of them recount bitterly. The social injury, brought about by society's definition of them, has been and still remains a factor in their feelings of inferiority and shame. Like other Malaysian and Asian women in general, they are socialized into accepting patriarchal values and practices. They are expected to be respectful and obedient to male authority and domination. Cultural and religious norms demand their unquestioned subservience.

10 After well over twenty years of industrial development, numerous changes have taken place, even improvements in the material conditions and economic standing of the women. However, certain subjective experiences remain much the same, in particular the prevailing experiences of subordination and denigration by men.

Talking Pain

In order to convey the women's emotional sufferings, I present direct words from women shared during educational workshops which I have held with them:

> People look down on us. They see us with only one eye. Society looks disparagingly at us. They say factory girls are cheap. They fall for any man in the street. . . . All this talk makes us feel inferior. Even when they are not saying anything I can feel their belittlement from the way they gawk at us.
>
> Young men whistle as we alight from the factory bus: 'Look, they go day and night like prostitutes.' How to retaliate? You know what kind of characters they are! All creeps! If I retaliate back they may bring their gang to tackle us—we have to use this road everyday. We just pretend not to hear.
>
> Even my own family feel embarrassed with my factory job. I avoid my neighbour so as not to be asked insinuating questions. One day she asked: 'You came back almost at midnight yesterday and left again so early this morning. What do you actually do?' All I could say was work . . . I felt ashamed, defensive, actually disgusted . . . I am not what she may be thinking.
>
> 15 We are petrified all the time. You can literally see some jerking when shouted at, stammering and shivering. You can imagine the kind of tension we work in. I do not know any more how to think, only anticipating when I will be shouted at.
>
> It is very difficult to tell anyone about hurts from your own family. Outsiders cannot know how it hurts. Five years ago, in my first annual leave, I had a quarrel with my brother. He hit my niece over the head for playing in the sun. I tried to stop him but he only shouted at me, 'Who are you to control me? Is this what the factory has taught you?' My mother, instead of appeasing us, reproached me. Such is the fate of girls in Indian families. This brother is much younger than me. Yet I have to obey him and get his approval for everything since my father's death. Maybe if I were an office clerk I would have a better say.
>
> My husband derides me until I am not worth a cent. Not only does he prevent me from participating in neighbourhood activities, he tells others that I am a stupid useless woman, that anything I do will bring chaos. . . . How not to feel mad but if I retaliate I am no longer a good wife! More ammunition for him to run me down. Better to ignore him than invite more attacks.

The Effects of Emotional Subordination

Daily experiences of emotional subordination generate feelings of shame, guilt, inadequacy, self-doubt, and inferiority. The cumulative effect of these experiences is to ingrain a deep sense of helplessness, fear, ineptitude, and incapacity. Minds become blank and dulled over time, as the women I worked with narrated. Their emotions and reactions numbed, inhibiting the potential of development. Devaluations are not only dehumanizing and demeaning. They disable and maim confidence and self-esteem. They affect not only how the women feel about themselves but also their self-image and sense of their capacities—their subjectivities and agency.

Subjectivity constitutes the individual's sense of self, thoughts, emotions, modes of understanding the world; the sense of individuality, uniqueness, identity and continuity; and the reflexive awareness of these things.[4] It refers to the conscious and unconscious thoughts and emotions of the individual, her sense of self, and her ways of understanding her relation to the world.[5]

Subjectivity is a dynamic analytical concept to understand the silenced dimensions of internalized intimations of subordination, and its effects upon the various aspects of the person. Because of its contradictory and continual nature,[6] the concept also provides a framework for change, for reconstitution. Hence, the problematic potential of reconstructing existing subjectivities that are paralysing.

Experience, feelings and subjectivity are inextricably linked. Subjectivity embodies lived experiences and experienced feelings. Experienced realities and their effects construct subjectivity, and at the same time subjectivity structures the person's psyche and sense of agency. As much as subjectivity is being constructed by experiences inflicted by others which impact on the self, it is also self-constructing and open to redefinition. The resultant subjectivity can regulate or constrain the agency and autonomy of the person, as in the case of psychological oppression and the intimations of emotional subordination.

Subjectivities are not fixed and immutable. They are constantly being reconstituted in discourse each time we think or speak.[7] Thus they are open to reinforcement or revision and reinterpretation. Usher noted that subjectivity can be reconstructed through practical and discursive encounter and engagement.[8] Subjects can recreate themselves in discourses which are oppositional to currently dominant discourses. Thus subjectivities can be sites for contestation and reconstitution for the recovery of an authentic self-reconstructed subjectivity through self-definition. It is such an understanding that allows the possibility of reconstitution from the devastating effects arising from emotional subordination of the individuals concerned.

Reconstructing Subjectivities

Emotional sufferings and their effects, when unprocessed and repressed, are disabling. In the situation of women on the global assembly line, we have seen how, through the case of Malaysian women factory workers, they have been subjected to constant denigration. They have internalized the various negative definitions, stereotyping and abuses at great personal emotional cost and incapacitation. A process which allows the reconstruction of a woman's experience from her own standpoint, in which a new subject position is reconstituted to see anew and make sense of her situation, a situation which makes her the subject rather than the cause of the contradictions and pain she is experiencing, is fundamental to consciousness-raising.

The debilitating effects of internalized oppression, commonly depicted as powerlessness and learned helplessness, have been a core concern of the women's movement.[9]

The problematic potential of lived experiences of subordination as a source of oppositional knowledge, has been the revolutionary core of feminist transformation.[10] Feminist practice emphasizes the need to address the emotional welfare of women, whether in feminist therapy,[11] in organizing,[12] in popular education[13] or programmes for women's empowerment.[14]

25 Various approaches have been experimented with, to facilitate the healing and recovery from experienced injuries and reconstitute women's subjectivities.[15] Storytelling-sharing has been used extensively and effectively as a tool for consciousness-raising and mobilization in the women's and indigenous movements.[16]

Consciousness-raising is practised as a healing and recovery process which begins with renaming reality according to personal standpoints and experienced realities. This involves rejecting names and definitions that are not grounded directly in one's own experience, but because they have been adopted, have the effect of containing, controlling, and constructing what one is or what one does.

Women's consciousness-raising groups have been a means for overcoming some of these psychological obstacles,[17] exploring feelings as a 'critical way of knowing' or 'inner knowing', the source of true knowledge of the world for women living in a society that denies the value of their perceptions.[18] Collective discussion of personal problems, often previously assumed to be the result of personal inadequacies, leads to a recognition that what have been experienced as personal failings are socially produced contradictions and inflections shared by many women in similar situations. The power of redefining and naming feelings and experiences from one's own standpoint has been proven to be powerful in helping to change perceptions and subjectivities. This process of discovery and recovery leads to a reinterpretation of one's experience and self-definition instead of allowing the self to be constructed by others.

Within feminist discourse, voice, and speech are metaphors for women's self-definitions,[19] countervailing the constructions of others. Indeed, moving from silence to voice has been shown to reclaim what has been denied and dismissed. It is to assert opposition to the dominant discourse. It is an act of profound personal and political significance, reinstating the suppressed or submerged knowledge and subject of the marginalized.[20]

I have used story-telling-sharing as education in small groups to evoke repressed voices for reconstructing subjectivities:[21] the recollection and articulation of feelings and thoughts associated with experienced subordination for the purpose of recovery, self-definition, and self-reconstitution. Narration of lived experiences of anguish and pain, which the women who had been victimized had suppressed, was encouraged. In this informal conversational mode, connections, new meanings, and understandings emerge through listening, questioning, and reflecting on each other's stories, and it is this process that contributes to the recovery of the women's authentic realities as they themselves have experienced them.

In Conclusion

30 Education for women workers on the global assembly lines must address the material–objective conditions as well as the subjective–affective dimensions. Most often educational work with women workers tends to focus only on their objective–material

conditions related to employment and their class position as worker. It is essential that silenced experiences of emotional subordination, powerlessness, and inferiority are taken on board in and as educational work. Educational methodologies and strategies of action that can unpack, challenge, and reconstitute women's sufferings of subordination and their subordinated position are vital. It is essential to address conscious and unconscious thoughts, unexpressed feelings and emotions that make up their sense of themselves, their relation to the world and their inability to act. Although emotional suffering is only one dimension of women's subordination, it is a critical aspect.

Although the focus has been on Malaysian women workers, addressing internalized effects of subordination and reconstructing subjectivities to facilitate women's recovery from hidden injuries of subjugation does not apply only to women workers in Malaysia. This aspect of educational work is essential to any other subordinated group whose voice and sense of self are muted, especially women toiling in other industrial zones. Given the impact and trend in global capitalist industrial development, many more millions of women will no doubt join the global assembly lines and will continue to need this kind of educational support.

Notes

1. Froebel, Heinrichs and Kreye 1980; Elson and Pearson 1981; Lim 1983.
2. Lochhead 1988.
3. Ackerman 1984.
4. Usher 1989.
5. Weedon 1987.
6. Weedon 1987.
7. Weedon 1987.
8. Usher 1989.
9. Steinem 1992.
10. Lourde 1984.
11. Krzowski and Land 1988.
12. Dominelli and McLeod 1989.
13. PERG 1992.
14. Gutierrez 1990.
15. Barry 1989; Collins 1990; Davies 1992.
16. Christ 1979; Buker 1987.
17. Butler and Wintram 1991.
18. Weiler 1991.
19. Collins 1990.
20. Daly 1978; Christ 1979; Rich 1975.
21. Chan 1996.

References

Ackerman, S. (1984) 'The Impact of Industrialisation on the Social Role of Rural Malay Women', in Hing Ai Yun *et al.* (eds), *Women in Malaysia,* Pelanduk Publications, Kuala Lumpur.

Barry, K. (1989) 'Biography and the Search for Women's Subjectivity', *Women's Studies International Forum,* Vol. 12, No. 6.

Buker, E. (1987) 'Storytelling Power: Personal Narratives and Political Analysis', *Women and Politics,* Vol. 7, No. 3.

Butler, S. and Wintram, C. (1991) *Feminist Groupwork,* Sage Publications, London.

Chan, L.H. (1996) 'Talking Pain: Educational Work with "Factory Women" in Malaysia', in Walters, S. and Manicom, L., *Gender in Popular Education,* Zed Books, London and CACE Publications, Bellville.

Christ, C. (1979) 'Spiritual Quest and Women's Experience', in Christ, C. and Plaskow, J. (eds), *Woman Spirit Rising: A Feminist Reader in Religion,* Harper & Row, San Francisco.

Collins, P.H. (1990) *Black Feminist Thought:. Knowledge, Consciousness and the Politics of Empowerment,* Unwin, London.

Daly, M. (1978) *Gyn/Ecology: The Metaethics of Radical Feminism,* Beacon Press, Boston.

Davies, B. (1992) 'Women's Subjectivity and Feminist Stories', in Ellis, C. and Flaherty, M. (eds), *Investigating Subjectivity: Research on Lived Experience,* Sage Publications, London.

Dominelli, L. and Mcleod, E. (1989) *Feminist Social Work,* Macmillan, London.

Elson, D. and Pearson, R. (1981) 'The Subordination of Women and the Internationalisation of Production', in Young, K., Walkowitz, C. and McCullagh, R. (eds), *Of Marriage and the Market: Women's Subordination in International Perspective,* Case Books, London.

Froebel, F., Heinrichs, J. and Kreye, O. (1980) *The New International Division of Labour: Structural Unemployment in Industrialised Countries and Industrialisation in Developing Countries,* Cambridge University Press, Cambridge.

Gutierrez, L. (1990) 'Working with Women of Color: An Empowerment Perspective', *Social Work,* March.

Krzowski, S. and Land, P. (1988) *In Our Experience: Workshops at the Women's Therapy Centre,* The Women's Press, London.

Lim, L. (1983) 'Capitalism, Imperialism and Patriarchy: The Dilemma of Third World Workers in Multinational Factories', in Nash, J. and Fernandez, K. (eds), *Women, Men and the International Division of Labour,* State University of New York Press, Albany, NY.

Lochhead, J. (1988) 'Retrenchment in a Malaysian Free Trade Zone', in Heyzer, N. (ed.), *Daughters in Industry,* Asia Pacific and Development Centre, Kuala Lumpur.

Lourde, A. (1984) *Sister Outsider,* Crossing Press, Trumansburg, NY.

PERG (1992) *Women Educating to End Violence Against Women,* Popular Education Research Group, Toronto.

Rich, A. (1975) 'For a Sister', in *Poems: Selected and New (1950–1974),* W.W. Norton, New York.

Steinem, G. (1992) *Revolution From Within: A Book of Self-Esteem,* Little, Brown, London.

Usher, R. (1989) 'Locating Experience in Language: Towards a Poststructuralist Theory of Experience', *Adult Education Quarterly,* Vol. 40, No. 1.

Weedon, C. (1987) *Feminist Practice and Poststructuralist Theory,* Basil Blackwell, Oxford.

Weiler, K. (1991) 'Freire and a Feminist Pedagogy of Difference', *Harvard Educational Review,* Vol. 16, No. 4.

Exploring Texts and Contexts

For activities with icons, refer to the Guide to Analyzing Readings in Context.

1. This article is divided into five parts, including the introductory section. Working in a small group, write a brief summary of each section, and then discuss with the class as a whole how the five parts relate to each other and how they work together. What would you say is the overall thesis of this piece, and how does each part relate to the thesis?

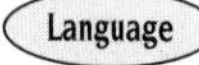

2. The language of this article, especially the last three sections, is somewhat specialized and academic, which might make the article difficult to read. The best way to handle this is to put difficult sentences into your own words. For example, put the following sentence—or others that you find difficult—into your own words, drawing first on your own vocabulary, word-analysis skills, and context clues, then consulting classmates, and finally using the dictionary or other written sources: "Subjectivity is a dynamic analytical concept to understand the silenced dimensions of internalized intimations of subordination, and its effects upon the various aspects of the person" (464). Why do you think Heng uses such language? What does she gain and lose by writing sentences like this one?
3. Heng makes three related claims in this article: that female factory workers in Malaysia are mistreated by bosses, co-workers, people in the community, and family members; that this treatment has a harmful effect on their sense of identity; and that consciousness raising can help them deal with their situation. What evidence does she offer to support these claims?

Consequences

4. The panel discussion called "A Man's Place," included in Chapter 13, discusses the role of women in the economy. Their focus is on American women, but what might the women quoted in Heng's article have to say to American women; what would they add to this symposium? Consider, for example, that while Nike's focus on selling shoes to American women athletes benefited American women, some social critics have pointed out that it was at the expense of the many women workers who were mistreated in Nike factories around the world. Should American women consumers take these issues into account when they shop? What might the consequences of this be?

Creating Texts

For assignments with icons, refer to the Guides to Analyzing Contexts for Writing and Analyzing Readings in Context. For additional help with these writing projects, read the descriptions of **Essay** and **Codes/Guidelines** in the Genre Glossary.

1. Many of the writers in this book, including Heng, Goleman, and Ehrenreich, as well as several of the writers in the case study in Chapter 14, discuss the emotional dimensions of work, though each approaches the question from a somewhat different perspective. Write an essay in which you address the following questions, drawing on information and ideas from any of these sources as well as your own experiences and observations: How important is emotional well-being in the workplace, what kinds of things affect it, and, if you do think it is important, what should be done to help ensure it?
2. The primary purpose of Heng's piece, like that of other academic articles, is to extend the discussion of issues and ideas. People who make practical decisions related to these issues might read or hear about such work and be influenced by it, and in this way academic research and writing can have an important impact on practical situations. But academic researchers and writers can get involved more directly in such situations; they may be asked, for example, to do research or advise businesses or other organizations whose work is related to their area of expertise. Imagine that Heng has been asked to join a group of Malaysian business leaders, politicians, policymakers, and academics to draw up guidelines for businesses in Malaysia on the treatment of women factory workers. The guidelines will cover wages, benefits, training, working conditions, and interpersonal relations. Heng has been asked to draft the section on interpersonal relations, which will include an introduction that explains to managers relevant social and cultural factors in the lives of women factory workers; guidelines on how to treat them with respect; and suggestions on services that should be offered to them. Use ideas and information from her article and your own knowledge and insights about workplace interpersonal relations to draft Heng's section of the guidelines.

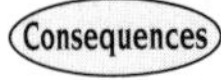

CHAPTER 13

Adapting to the Changing Workplace

Situation: What is the person in this photo doing? In what context do you think the photo was taken? What other kinds of photos might be grouped with this one?

Genre: In what situations might a photo like this be used?

Language: How does the photographer's position determine what you see in the photo?

Consequences: If the purpose of this photo is to convince you of something, what might that be?

What could be more important to a college student than knowing what jobs will be available in five or ten years? But such projections are notoriously difficult to make. Just within the last ten years, for example, the number of jobs requiring computer skills has fluctuated tremendously.

Guidance counselors, curriculum planners, business training specialists, and academics interested in long-range employment trends often turn to the Bureau of Labor Statistics to help them make projections. In their 2000–2001 *Occupational Outlook Handbook,* the Bureau reports that the largest increase in occupational growth is in the service-oriented job categories and that projections for the ten fastest-growing job categories reflect the needs of a service-oriented information economy.

One common reaction to changing workplace expectations is demand for new education and training programs. But these demands come at a time when the relationship between education and jobs is not all that clear. When measured by amount of educational preparation needed, the jobs are clustered around opposite ends of a continuum. According to information published by the Bureau, four of the job categories on the fastest-growing list require a four-year degree: computer engineer, systems analyst, database administrator, and physician's assistant. The remaining jobs require an associate's degree or on-the-job training only. A surprising number of the jobs on the list are auxiliary in nature, defined in terms of the support, assistance, or aid they provide.

The uncertainty about the relationship of jobs to education is compounded by the uncertainty of workforce predictions in general. Although most forecasts emphasize high-tech jobs, a statistic frequently reported is that Microsoft, the most high-profile company in the new, technological economy, employs only 23,000 people, whereas General Motors, the giant of the old, industrial economy, still employs 250,000. Although at one time it was the old-economy, industrial jobs that were most likely to move overseas, today it is the high-tech jobs that are the most likely to be moved to countries where there are well-educated workers willing to work for lower wages.

The changing nature of the workplace is accelerating the uneven distribution of income. Robert Reich, a public intellectual and one of the writers in this unit, observes in the foreword to his book *The Work of Nations,* "Each nation's primary political task will be to cope with the centrifugal forces of the global economy which tear at the ties binding citizens together—bestowing ever greater wealth on the most skilled and insightful, while

The 10 Fastest-growing Occupations, 1998–2008
(Numbers in thousands of jobs)

	Employment			Change
Occupation	**1998**	**2008**	**Number**	**Percentage**
Computer engineers	299	622	323	108
Computer-support specialists	429	869	439	102
Systems analysts	617	1194	577	94
Database administrators	87	155	67	77
Desktop-publishing specialists	26	44	19	73
Paralegals and legal assistants	136	220	84	62
Personal-care and home-health aides	746	1179	433	58
Medical assistants	252	398	146	58
Social and human-services assistants	268	410	141	53
Physician's assistants	66	98	32	48

Source: Bureau of Labor Statistics News Release, Nov. 30, 1999.

consigning the less skilled to a declining standard of living" (3). How widening economic inequality will affect social relations is of particular concern in a democratic society. The promise of upward social mobility has always been a fundamental tenet of our national identity. Because an unregulated free-market economy is not working for some Americans, they are becoming increasingly disillusioned as they work harder, retrain, and follow migrating jobs with relatively few gains in income, while another segment of society is growing fabulously wealthy. Diminishing expectations for future generations may disrupt the way many Americans have come to define themselves.

And it seems that for both the "winners" and the "losers" in this economy, the competitive nature of the new workplace requires longer hours on the job and more time spent away from family and community. Experts from a wide range of fields including economists, psychologists, and sociologists are beginning to wonder whether evidence of increasingly maladjusted and needy children is a sign that the changing nature of work is having a detrimental effect on family life and community institutions. As increasing numbers of women enter the workforce and the number of two-job families grows, we will continue to grapple with the relationship between workplace commitments and the needs of our families and communities.

Adapting to the changing workplace isn't something that applies only to recent college grads and people in the process of reevaluating their careers. For all of us, the changing economy will require imaginative transformations in the way we educate ourselves, work, raise our families, and relate to neighbors in our communities. These changes can be exciting as well as frightening, but they require us, as individuals and as a nation, to think carefully about the kind of world we want for ourselves, our children, and our grandchildren.

For This We Sent You To College?

Robyn Meredith

After paying $10,000 a year or more for college, you are washing cars as part of your job, and your parents are understandably upset. Through a series of profiles, Robyn Meredith introduces us to several recent college graduates, some entering high-tech industries with excellent salaries and some who feel they are underemployed. Even in a growing economy, labor-market analysts tell us that service jobs are on the rise and that high-end jobs are moving to other parts of the world. Others argue that young people finishing college are more likely to find temporary work or work at lower salaries than they'd hoped.

However, talk about jobs is not the only focus in this ongoing conversation about adapting to the changing workplace. Meredith's article assumes that college is about work, and one of the two letters to the editors written in response to the article questions that assumption, asking what we mean by work. Broader questions of what college and work mean are hardly hinted at in this feature story that appeared on graduation weekend in the Money and Business section of the *New York Times.* Some argue that the broader purpose of a college education is to prepare students to contribute to a vital civic life and that work, too, should be thought of as contributing to one's civic responsibilities. These enduring questions, however, are sometimes placed in the background at graduation time when families celebrate this momentous transition.

Connecting with the Conversation

1. Visit your college's career center and talk to its staff. Ask about how students with a general liberal arts education develop a career focus. Report to the class on what you find.
2. Search your library's online resources for articles in the popular press on a liberal education. Consider what constitutes a good undergraduate education.

As sure as the promise of a spring day, millions of proud parents have been descending lately on the nation's campuses, snapping pictures of their daughters and sons collecting college diplomas.

Parents and students alike have been preparing for this moment for decades, before many parents took out second mortgages and the typical graduate piled up $12,300 in debt to help cover bills for tuition, room and board that average $10,000 a year. Now it is time for that steep investment, as much as $130,000 in the case of some elite private schools, to return dividends.

There is plenty of good news for those receiving undergraduate degrees this year, but with just enough caveats to keep some people on edge.

Over all, the job market for the 1.2 million graduates this year is the strongest in memory, partly because companies, in their aggressive downsizing drives of recent years, may have laid off too many workers of their parents' generation.

5 Many Ivy League graduates and those with degrees in highly marketable areas like business administration and computer science can expect plenty of job offers at high pay. And the nation's highest-profile student, Chelsea Clinton, is unlikely to find herself behind a counter waiting on customers when she graduates from Stanford, where she will be a freshman this fall. In contrast, those with weak grades and little patience for job searches may struggle to find work, as they always do.

But just how good is it for the rest of the army that is resolutely marching out of the classrooms and into the real world?

It turns out to be pretty good indeed for a broad swath of the newly minted grads. Many had the luxury of choosing among several job offers months before commencement exercises began. And starting salaries are, for the most part, higher than they were last year.

But even in such upbeat times, the jobs can be far from glamorous. For instance, Rachel D. Gunderson is busy making sure there is enough dirt on the shelves of Target

From the *New York Times,* June 8, 1997, Money and Business section pp. 10–11. Also two letters to the editor, which appeared in subsequent issues, by Peter A. Benoliel and Peter Vergano.

A. William D. Lucy, *Southwest Missouri State University, rents out vehicles for* Enterprise Rent-a-Car (5,000 *graduates hired; starting pay from* $22,000 *to* $30,000). **B.** Linda C. Roman, *University of* Florida, *develops packaging for* Kraft *cottage cheese and dips* (85 *graduates hired; starting pay from* $21,000 *to* $42,000). **C.** *Rachel* D. *Gunderson, University of* Wisconsin, *orders potting soil for* Target *stores* (1,150 *hired by* Target's *parent,* Dayton Hudson; *starting pay from* $30,000 *to* $34,000). **D.** Malane Rogers, *University of* Arkansas, *creates reports for clients of* Andersen Consulting (4,200 *hired; starting pay from* $31,000 *to* $45,000).

stores. After graduating from the University of Wisconsin, she landed a job ordering potting soil for the chain. Linda C. Roman, of the University of Florida, has signed on at Kraft Foods to improve the packaging for cottage cheese and sour cream.

In fact, many new graduates are fast learning a lesson that their predecessors have had to accept over the decades: they have landed at the bottom of the workaday ladder, with plenty of dues to pay before they step up to the next rung.

Rebecca E. Johnson, a University of Michigan graduate and merchant trainee for Dayton's in Minneapolis, helps select the ties sold by the department store chain.

After Douglas M. Fischer left the University of Minnesota, he was put in charge of buying stationery for Target Stores. His orders on one recent day came to $350,000.

10 And for a growing number of graduates, that ladder isn't even the one that they—or their long-suffering parents—originally had in mind. For them, it is not always clear why an expensive education was needed.

"None of my friends ever told me about the carwashing part," said Julie A. Schenk, 22, who turned down two other offers to work as a management trainee at Enterprise Rent-a-Car after graduating in December from the University of Dayton.

Ms. Schenk, whose major was communications management, isn't the only one washing cars—5,000 members of the Class of 1997 are expected to sign up with Enterprise, where cleaning is just one of the dues-paying chores.

Others have taken similar training jobs at department store chains, where they wait on customers.

That can leave some parents horrified that their children don't have more to show for all the financial sacrifices.

15 "It is like sticker shock," said Kevin J. Nutter, the career services director at the University of Minnesota in Minneapolis. The problem for people in this group isn't that they won't find work, "but that they may not find what they think is good work," Mr. Nutter said.

That is because the number of service-sector jobs has grown as the number of management positions has shrunk, he said. At the same time, so many people are now graduating from college that a degree no longer carries the cachet that it did even a generation ago.

If the experience of recent graduating classes is any guide, many in this year's crop will quickly grow dissatisfied. Members of the Class of 1994 at the University of Illinois at Urbana-Champaign, for example, were asked a year after they graduated whether their college training was being put to good use.

"Almost 40 percent considered themselves underemployed," nearly double the percentage of recent years, said David S. Bechtel, director of the university's career services center.

But there is little complaining so far from the new graduates.

20 "I had a lot of friends who were working for Enterprise, and they all spoke highly of it," said Ms. Schenk, who said she was not disappointed in her job, despite being surprised by some of her duties.

Others who have crossed over to the working world in recent months are also making do or even flourishing.

Following are four tales from the trenches that offer hope and guidance to those just now trading in their diplomas, caps and gowns for briefcases and business suits.

Rental Clerks

Joining a Fraternity with 12-Hour Days

Few parents who squirrel away money for years to pay college bills picture their children hanging up a hard-won diploma behind a rental car counter, but about 10,000 moms and dads will watch it happen this year.

Indeed, Enterprise Rent-a-Car is probably hiring more members of this year's graduating class than any other company. The 5,000 graduates scheduled to join Enterprise will be paid $22,000 to $30,000, depending on where they live, and all will start out behind the counters of the company's 3,000 branches around the country.

25 Most graduates who join Enterprise—along with their parents—must first get over the idea of working for a car rental company.

"Recruiting is tough," said Andrew C. Taylor, president and chief executive of Enterprise, based in St. Louis. Some of those who accept jobs have a hard time breaking the news to their families. "What do you think their parents' reaction might be?" Mr. Taylor asked.

Still, satisfied Enterprise hires said they found the jobs refreshing because the company is so entrepreneurial, offering responsibility and a chance to move up quickly.

Mr. Taylor's company tends to hire men and women who are a lot like him—friendly, clean-cut and active at college in fraternities or sororities or team sports. Oh, and they must not be too proud to clean cars from time to time, either.

"The management of this business started behind a rent-a-car counter," Mr. Taylor said, telling how he recently pitched in to vacuum a car during a visit to a busy Enterprise branch.

30 Consider William D. Lucy, 25, who was a member of Delta Chi and played intramural volleyball and flag football at Southwest Missouri State University in Springfield. He graduated last year with a 3.2 grade-point average, with a major in marketing and a minor in management.

"I did not go to college thinking I wanted to rent cars," Mr. Lucy acknowledged. Instead, "I saw myself going into business."

The affable Mr. Lucy, who likes to grasp your shoulder when he shakes your hand, had several sales jobs to choose from, but Enterprise looked the best to him. Since starting in March in St. Louis, Mr. Lucy has been working 12-hour days, what passes for normal at Enterprise, starting at 7:15 each morning. He pins a gold name tag—just plain "Bill"—on his gray suit and greets customers as they walk in the door.

He rents cars during the morning and evening rushes—including driving to pick up customers at their homes or offices, Enterprise's trademark service touch. In between, he calls body shops on behalf of renters whose cars were crumpled in accidents. When the mechanics take longer than promised, he calls the renters' insurance companies to arrange for extensions of Enterprise rentals. Once a week, Mr. Lucy spends part of the day delivering pizza or doughnuts to mechanics at nearby repair shops and secretaries at local offices, trying to win business for Enterprise with his company's equivalent of taking a client to lunch.

Now, Mr. Lucy sees himself as the businessman he always wanted to be. "I'm wearing a suit every day," he said with a proud smile.

35 About 25 percent of Enterprise's trainees will grow dissatisfied and leave the company within six months. Most of those who remain will have a chance to apply for a promotion within a year. Those who make the grade get raises, are named assistant managers and have their salaries tied to the performance of their branches.

If Mr. Lucy does well, he could turn out like Cory A. Phillips, 26, a 1992 graduate of Columbia College in Columbia, Mo., who joined Enterprise 14 months ago and has already been promoted twice.

"If you prove yourself, you don't have to worry about spending two years before you become a manager," said Mr. Phillips, now a branch manager in St. Louis. The training means that all managers learn the business from the bottom up and have a financial interest in seeing it succeed, he said.

Mr. Taylor, the chief executive, said he thought of his company "as a confederation of small businesses run by entrepreneurs."

The strategy seems to have worked: Enterprise now has 31,200 domestic employees but just 1,000 at its corporate headquarters, with 700 of those responsible for keeping the company's computer network up and running. The privately held company has grown 25 percent a year for 11 years, and now has the largest fleet in the rental car business. It avoids airport business, concentrating instead on the so-called replacement niche, providing rentals for customers whose cars are being repaired or who just need an extra set of wheels for a while.

40 Mr. Taylor, a business major who graduated from the University of Denver, was social chairman of his fraternity, Tau Kappa Epsilon. Things haven't changed all that much he said with a smile, in the three decades since he graduated.

"You see," he said, "I'm the social chairman of a very large company."

Packaging Developer

Trading the Stage for Live Culture

Linda C. Roman started her college career as a theater major who made ends meet by working as a waitress. "Every once in a while I see someone on TV I waited tables with," she said.

But Ms. Roman, too, has left waitressing behind for a full-time job in culture—in "live cultures," that is, the kind that produce sour cream, cottage cheese and chip dips.

After changing her major to chemical engineering, Ms. Roman was offered a job in Glenview, Ill., at Kraft Foods, which is owned by Philip Morris and is the country's largest packaged-food company. She helps develop the packaging for 126 varieties of Kraft products, chief among them Breakstone's sour cream, Light 'n Lively cottage cheese and Kraft creamy onion dip.

45 Kraft plans to hire 85 new graduates like Ms. Roman this year to help sell more Jell-O, Stove Top Stuffing, Maxwell House coffee, Kool-Aid, Toblerone chocolate bars and Cheez Whiz spread, paying salaries of $21,000 to $42,000. Thousands of similar entry-level jobs will be filled at companies like General Mills, Nabisco and Frito-Lay; Procter & Gamble will hire more than 700.

When Ms. Roman, 31, graduated last August from the University of Florida in Gainesville with a grade-point average of 3.75, she had long since sewn up the job at Kraft; its offer was one of five that came her way. So in the weeks after graduation, she took the time to portray the Wicked Witch in a children's play before moving to the Chicago suburbs last September to begin at Kraft.

There, she works in her cubicle or in a lab, and has so far visited five of the six factories where her sour creams, dips and cottage cheeses are made, making sure the plastic tubs and boxes work properly and helping to develop better packaging for future products. In the lab, she measures and tests the packages, checking, for instance, that when a customer opens a lid, it peels off smoothly and doesn't tear. "I love the consumer end," she said.

She didn't expect to. Ms. Roman recalls her negative reaction when she came upon Kraft at a college recruiting fair. "When I first saw Kraft, I didn't want to work for them," she said. She thought that serious chemical engineers worked for oil and chemical corporations, she said, not a company best known for macaroni and cheese.

Kraft's competitors face similar hurdles. A glossy brochure distributed by Procter & Gamble at recruitment fairs shows young employees standing proudly next to their wares: Metamucil, Sure deodorant and Charmin toilet paper.

50 Still, one irresistible force lured plenty of candidates to the Kraft recruiting booth on campus. "They had free food," Ms. Roman said with a shrug. After a summer internship in which she helped develop apple-cinammon-flavored cream cheese, she discovered that she liked applying what she learned in the classroom to the real world of supermarket shelves.

Being an actress might be more glamorous, but her father, Kenneth Roman, said he used to worry about her plans to make a living on stage. "Two out of a thousand make it," he said.

Now, Mr. Roman says he feels his daughter has a secure future. "I really had no idea that she would go into engineering," Mr. Roman said. "I feel very proud."

Indeed, his daughter is among those that Kraft found through its college recruitment program. Kraft focuses its recruiting efforts on a short list of large colleges and universities where it previously had success: Ohio State, Wisconsin, Penn State, Purdue, Howard, Florida and Michigan State, along with Illinois and Northwestern—schools that are relatively near its headquarters in Northfield, Ill.

Kraft weeds out some students in short, on-campus interviews, then brings the rest to Chicago for further screening. Students check into a hotel the night before their interview to find duffel bags full of—what else?—Kraft food. With the economy booming, recruiters try to decide quickly whom to hire.

55 "If you wait to make an offer," said Karen Y. Vaughn, a senior human resources manager at Kraft, "the good students are gone."

New Blood

Number of 1997 college graduates each company is planning to hire this year.

Enterprise Rent-a-Car	5,000
Andersen Consulting	4,200
Lockheed	2,040
Price Waterhouse	1,500
General Electric	1,300
*Dayton Hudson**	1,150
Motorola	1,000
Procter & Gamble	700
Osco Drugs (American Stores)	600
Caterpillar	400
Amoco	200
Ameritech	150
Chrysler	160
Hyatt	150
Kraft†	65

*Owns Target Stores.
†Owned by Philip Morris.
Source: Listed companies

Merchandise Analysts

From Shirt Buying to Dirt Buying

Deep inside a building in downtown Minneapolis, past the rows of cubicles watched over by a giant Winnie the Pooh and dozens of other stuffed animals, beyond the spot where the furry animals give way to plants lining the offices, is the desk of Rachel D. Gunderson, 22.

Ms. Gunderson, a graduate of the University of Wisconsin at Madison, is one of the newest merchandise analysts at the headquarters of Target, the discount-store chain.

"I'm in charge of soil," Ms. Gunderson said. As in potting soil. Target sells about 20 different bags, and it falls on Ms. Gunderson to make sure there is enough on the shelves of the chain's 750 stores nationwide.

Buying dirt for Target is typical of the entry-level responsibilities that thousands of this year's graduates will soon assume. The Dayton Hudson Corporation, based in Minneapolis, owns Target, Mervyn's and three department store chains: Dayton's, Hudson's and Marshall Field's. The company plans to hire 1,150 graduates this year at starting pay of $30,000 to $34,000. Dayton Hudson's competitors—including the May Department Stores, Neiman Marcus, J.C. Penney, Kmart and Federated Department Stores—together hire thousands more.

Ms. Gunderson, who graduated with a 3.0 grade-point average in December, started her job in mid-April. A journalism major who specialized in marketing and had a minor in business, she turned down an offer from Andersen Consulting and instead took this 8-to-5 job, which came with 12 weeks of training.

Ms. Gunderson inherited the potting-soil responsibilities from her designated mentor. She is learning how to send electronic orders to Target's suppliers, how to use spreadsheets to show soil sales histories and how to project how many bags of dirt Target will need on hand when an ad for potting soil appears.

Jacqueline T. Punch, central human resources director for Dayton Hudson, said competition for high-quality graduates was fierce. "There is definitely a sense that they can be very selective," Ms. Punch said. "The last two years it has really become more difficult."

Still, Dayton Hudson hires only 5 to 7 percent of the students it talks to, so the competition goes both ways.

The entry-level merchandising jobs go fast. "This job is like the most sought-after position" at the Carlson School of Management of the University of Minnesota, said another new Target merchandise analyst, Douglas M. Fischer, 23.

65 After graduating in March with an accounting major and a 3.0 grade-point average, Mr. Fischer was put in charge of buying stationery at Target. His best day so far came when he pushed a button on his computer to order $350,000 worth of paper and envelopes.

Across the street, Rebecca E. Johnson, 23, who graduated from the University of Michigan with an art history degree and a 3.4 grade-point average, is a merchant trainee for Dayton's. Her job is to help select the men's shirts and ties for the department store chain.

By the time Ms. Johnson, Ms. Gunderson and Mr. Fischer hand their shirt buying, dirt-buying and stationery-buying responsibilities to the graduates of 1998, they could be well on their way to solid futures at Dayton Hudson. Within five years, successful new hires earn $45,000 to $70,000 as full-fledged buyers, Ms. Punch said.

Technical Assistants

Helping Hands for Various Clients

Andersen Consulting is a ubiquitous name at college career fairs. More than 150,000 seniors—about 13 percent of the nation's graduating class—sent their résumés to the company this year. About 4,200 will be hired by Andersen Consulting, the management and technical consulting arm of Andersen Worldwide.

So what do all those new hires do? Think of Andersen Consulting as a giant temporary firm, only with far better pay (starting salaries are $31,000 to $45,000) and more challenging assignments than those of, say, Kelly Services or Manpower Inc.

70 Many Fortune 500 companies depend on Andersen Consulting to send teams of energetic, well-educated workers to complete short-term tasks or complicated grunt work—like making various computer systems talk to one another—for which they don't want to hire their own staff.

Companies also use Andersen for more traditional management consulting jobs—to guide strategic planning, for instance—but Andersen hires mostly M.B.A.'s for those spots.

The Dallas office is one of 23 nationwide for Andersen Consulting, but only a small percentage of its employees in the region work in the tidy offices on the 54th floor of a glass skyscraper downtown. Most report to the offices of Andersen clients in the area for a few weeks or months, then move to another project at a different client.

Malane Rogers, 23, is a good example. She graduated from the University of Arkansas in December with a degree in industrial engineering and a 2.9 grade-point average. She started at Andersen in February, and travels each morning to the Dallas office of Texas Instruments.

Her task is to pull detailed financial data from Texas Instruments' huge mainframe computers and fashion them into easy-to-read reports for company executives. When a vice president wants to check quarterly revenues in a certain region, Ms. Rogers finds the needles in the data haystack.

College on the Up and Up - and Up

DESPITE CLIMBING COSTS...

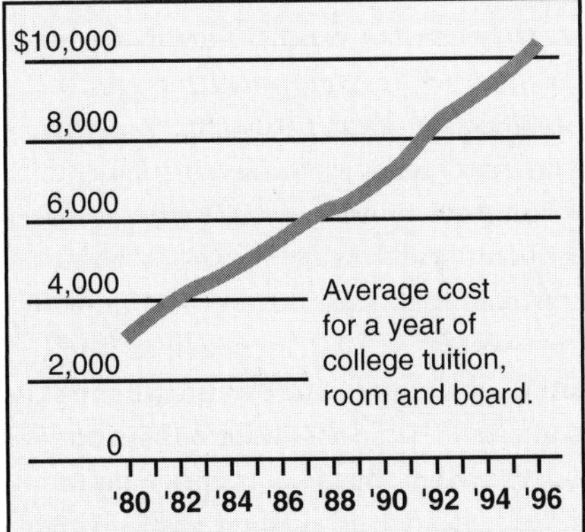

...GRADUATING CLASSES GROW...

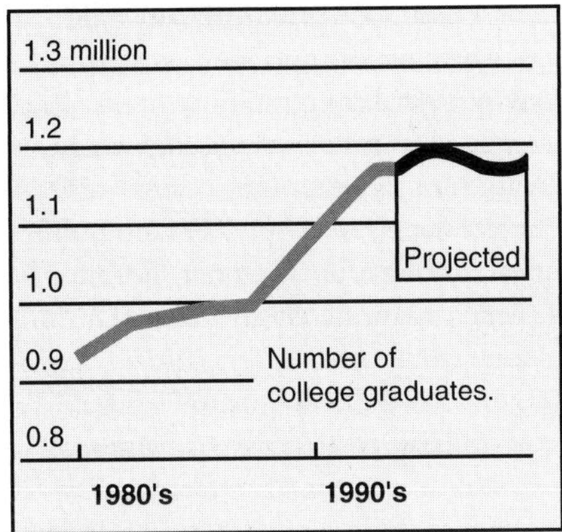

...AND STUDENTS ACQUIRE MORE DEBT

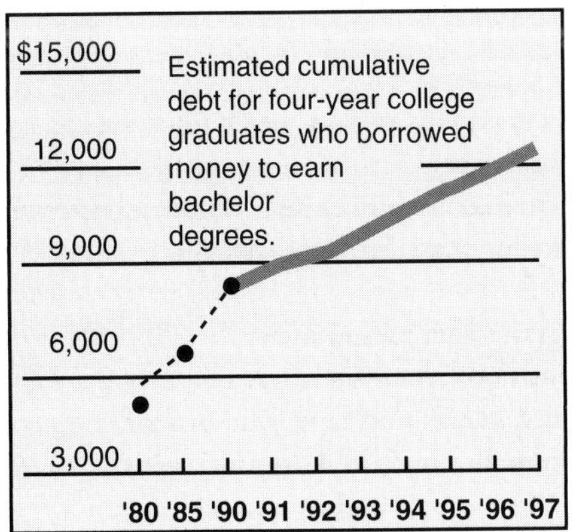

75 Well before she graduated, Ms. Rogers had four other job offers, and would have had more had she not tightly limited her interviewing to companies in which she was keenly interested.

Thousands of graduates like Ms. Rogers are hired by Andersen and its brethren in the consulting field—Price Waterhouse and Ernst & Young's consulting arms, as well as computer consulting firms like Electronic Data Systems. The Big Six accounting firms—including Andersen Consulting's sister company, Andersen Accounting—hire still more thousands for traditional accounting jobs.

Kim K. Dodson, 23, turned down 11 other offers to sign on at Andersen Consulting. She graduated from Texas A & M with a 3.4 grade-point average, having majored in business analysis, and started work in February. She wears a gold Aggie ring—a popular accessory in Andersen's Dallas office—with her business suit. For the last six weeks, she has been driving to the Fort Worth offices of Burlington Resources, an oil and gas company, to help program its computers.

Also working on Burlington's new computer codes is Nichole A. Inloes, 22, a December graduate of Texas A & M with a major in marketing. She programs Burlington's computers to cut checks automatically for energy royalties.

She is glad she chose Andersen over the other company that offered her a job: Enterprise Rent-a-Car.

80 Her father, Gerald T. Inloes of San Antonio, said he was looking forward, now that the college expenses were past, to resuming the family's trips to the beach at Corpus Christi and an annual vacation in Las Vegas, luxuries the Inloes had been doing without.

Still, the financial sacrifice was worth it. "I don't regret it for a second," Mr. Inloes said. "I am just so proud of her."

LETTERS

Education, Not Glamour

To the Editor:

"For This We Sent You to College?" (June 8) showed that there are a lot of jobs out there for a college graduate, although they may fall below expectations in regard to glamour and remuneration.

But what should we expect from our institutions of higher learning, and what is our collective notion of "work"? The article reflected today's notions of job-centered pursuits and expectations for education. Two important visions, however, have been lost. The first is how education prepares students for undertaking a fulfilling vocation, for assuming citizenship and experiencing life in many dimensions. The second is that vocation is a "calling" that leads to a career.

We are probably witnessing a third generation of students and parents who look to the college or university experience as a place to attain vocational training. Such training has a very important place in our educational system, but it doesn't belong in our institutions of higher learning. They should be dedicated to training an individual's mind and opening intellectual and spiritual horizons. Impractical? Not in the least. Liberally educated graduates without specific vocationally centered courses could perform the jobs described in the article with the utmost competency and panache. Furthermore, these graduates would have greater potential to move on to higher levels of responsibility (perhaps glamour?) than those who graduated with specific, vocationally centered degrees.

Much of the problem relates to parents' and students' expectations of job training and job procurement. Don't we have a far greater obligation to young people who spend four years at an institution of higher learning than merely to train them for a specific job or an expertise that probably will soon be outdated?

So we come back to the title of the article, "For This We Sent You To College?" For graduates, "This" should be a whole life in its complexity, challenges and richness.

Peter A. Benoliel
Conshohocken, Pa., June 13
The writer is the retired chairman of Quaker Chemical Corporation.

To the Editor:

There are at least three lessons in all the data about today's job market for college graduates:

First, parents do not complain when their child graduates into a job paying \$30,000 to \$40,000 a year, considering that four years earlier, that child's skills were worth only \$5 an hour.

Second, most universities have niche programs that place essentially 100 percent of their graduates in high-paying professional positions. A recent graduate of the packaging science department at Clemson University, for example, will be one of the new hires at Kraft Foods, working in the same area mentioned in the article.

A third lesson is that professional positions compel interest. The challenge of competition, of making a difference, is what makes a position interesting, not the often false facade of glamour.

Peter J. Vergano
Clemson, S.C., June 9
The writer is a professor of packaging science at Clemson University.

Exploring Texts and Contexts

For activities with icons, refer to the Guide to Analyzing Readings in Context.

1. Read the two letters to the editor that respond to Meredith's article, and consider who wrote them and how their experience might have contributed to their point of view. Show this article to several people you know: an older person, perhaps a parent; someone from work; or a friend, and ask them what they make of it. From what other perspectives do people respond to this article? Consider, too, that this article appeared in 1997. Has the situation for workers changed since then? 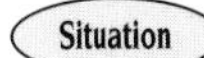

2. This article focuses on the moment of graduation—the elation of both parents and their children at this time of transition. But let's look ahead one or two years and think about the nature of the workplace. In Chapter 9, Robert Putnam argues for increasing social capital in many areas of our lives. Regarding the workplace, he says, "Let us find way s to ensure that . . . America's workplace will be substantially more family-friendly and community-congenial . . ." (309). Consider what features of the workplace might change for these young workers. How might their jobs become more "family friendly" and "community congenial"? Is this a good thing? Why or why not?
3. Examine the photos, captions, tables, and the general layout of this article. How does the visual arrangement contribute to its message? What other kinds of data might you have included? Language

Creating Texts

For activities with icons, refer to the Guides to Analyzing Contexts for Writing and Analyzing Readings in Context. For additional help with these writing projects, read the descriptions of **Feature Story/Profile** and **Letter to the Editor** in the Genre Glossary.

1. W rite a feature story or profile of several recent college graduates. You will want to tell a compelling story as well as offer some insightful analysis. The point you

make could be quite different from Meredith's and will depend, in part, on how you choose your subjects and what lessons can be learned from their experiences.

2. Write a letter to the editor in response to this article. Remember to state Meredith's position before you elaborate on your own response. You may want to integrate into your response a perspective from other readings—perhaps Robert Reich's focus on the knowledge worker or Boyle and Kari's argument for public work. Or you may want to focus on your own experience or those of friends and acquaintances.

What Makes a Leader?

Daniel P. Goleman

Unlike other writers in this unit who question the structure of jobs or the role of society in creating meaningful work environments, Daniel Goleman focuses on the inner life of the individual. His views about the relationship between leadership skills and success in the changing workplace are set out in his 1998 book, *Working with Emotional Intelligence*. Goleman's argument is that it takes more than cognitive ability or technical training to succeed in today's global workplace; the most successful people also have a high degree of emotional intelligence.

Goleman is a Harvard-trained psychologist and former *New York Times* science writer who is now co-chairman of the Consortium for Research on Emotional Intelligence in Organizations. As a society we traditionally rely on measures of cognitive ability, for example the kind of analytical skills measured by IQ tests, to predict success. Goleman's writing suggests there is another way to be smart. In *Emotional Intelligence,* the book that preceded *Working with Emotional Intelligence,* he drew on the research of two psychologists, John D. Mayer and Peter Salovey, who studied the role of emotions in the workings of the brain, in order to challenge the notion that IQ is the exclusive measure of potential.

According to Goleman, one big difference between IQ and emotional intelligence is that emotional intelligence can be learned. When his book was first published, it was marketed as an educational tool, and he was interested in working with educators to put emotional intelligence into the school curriculum. Although neither Mayer nor Salovey supports the claims Goleman makes about the benefits of emotional intelligence, Goleman's ideas about effectiveness and personal development resonated with the business community. Business leaders quickly picked up on emotional intelligence as a way to gain a competitive edge. In this essay from the *Harvard Business Review,* Goleman argues that emotional intelligence is a strong indicator of leadership potential.

Connecting with the Conversation

1. Look up the consortium on the Internet at www.eiconsortium.org. Write about the overall goals and aims of this consulting group. What are your initial impressions of the kind of work this Web site is interested in?
2. Identify several people you think of as leaders. These people need not be national figures; list any family or friends you know who exhibit leadership skills. Think about the leadership ability of these people and see whether you can draw any conclusions about the qualities that make up a leader. Working in a small group, compare your conclusions. In addition to personal qualities, are there external elements that contributed to their leadership abilities?

Every businessperson knows a story about a highly intelligent, highly skilled executive who was promoted into a leadership position only to fail at the job. And they also know a story about someone with solid—but not extraordinary—intellectual abilities and technical skills who was promoted into a similar position and then soared.

Such anecdotes support the widespread belief that identifying individuals with the "right stuff" to be leaders is more art than science. After all, the personal styles of superb leaders vary: some leaders are subdued and analytical; others shout their manifestos from the mountaintops. And just as important, different situations call for different types of leadership. Most mergers need a sensitive negotiator at the helm, whereas many turnarounds require a more forceful authority.

I have found however, that the most effective leaders are alike in one crucial way: they all have a high degree of what has come to be known as *emotional intelligence*. It's not that IQ and technical skills are irrelevant. They do matter, but mainly as "threshold capabilities"; that is, they are the entry-level requirements for executive positions. But my research, along with other recent studies, clearly shows that emotional intelligence is the sine qua non of leadership. Without it, a person can have the best training in the world, an incisive, analytical mind, and an endless supply of smart ideas, but he still won't make a great leader.

In the course of the past year, my colleagues and I have focused on how emotional intelligence operates at work. We have examined the relationship between emotional intelligence and effective performance, especially in leaders. And we have observed how emotional intelligence shows itself on the job. How can you tell if someone has high emotional intelligence, for example, and how can you recognize it in yourself? In the following pages, we'll explore these questions, taking each of the components of emotional intelligence—self-awareness, self-regulation, motivation, empathy, and social skill—in turn.

Evaluating Emotional Intelligence

5 Most large companies today have employed trained psychologists to develop what are known as "competency models" to aid them in identifying, training, and promoting likely stars in the leadership firmament. The psychologists have also developed such models for lower-level positions. And in recent years, I have analyzed competency models from 188 companies, most of which were large and global and included the likes of Lucent Technologies, British Airways, and Credit Suisse.

In carrying out this work, my objective was to determine which personal capabilities drove outstanding performance within these organizations, and to what degree they did so. I grouped capabilities into three categories: purely technical skills like accounting and business planning; cognitive abilities like analytical reasoning; and competencies demonstrating emotional intelligence such as the ability to work with others and effectiveness in leading change.

To create some of the competency models, psychologists asked senior managers at the companies to identify the capabilities that typified the organization's most outstanding leaders. To create other models, the psychologists used objective criteria such as a division's profitability to differentiate the star performers at senior levels within their organizations from the average ones. Those individuals were then extensively interviewed and tested, and their capabilities were compared. This process resulted in the creation of lists of ingredients for highly effective leaders. The lists ranged in length from 7 to 15 items and included such ingredients as initiative and strategic vision.

When I analyzed all this data, I found dramatic results. To be sure, intellect was a driver of outstanding performance. Cognitive skills such as big-picture thinking and long-term vision were particularly important. But when I calculated the ratio of technical skills, IQ, and emotional intelligence as ingredients of excellent performance, emotional intelligence proved to be twice as important as the others for jobs at all levels.

Moreover, my analysis showed that emotional intelligence played an increasingly important role at the highest levels of the company, where differences in technical skills are of negligible importance. In other words, the higher the rank of a person considered to be a star performer, the more emotional intelligence capabilities showed up as the reason for his or her effectiveness. When I compared star performers with average ones in senior leadership positions, nearly 90% of the difference in their profiles was attributable to emotional intelligence factors rather than cognitive abilities.

10 Other researchers have confirmed that emotional intelligence not only distinguishes outstanding leaders but can also be linked to strong performance. The findings of the late David McClelland, the renowned researcher in human and organizational behavior, are a good example. In a 1996 study of a global food and beverage company, McClelland found that when senior managers had a critical mass of emotional intelligence capabilities, their divisions outperformed yearly earnings goals by 20%. Meanwhile, division leaders without that critical mass underperformed by almost the same amount. McClelland's findings, interestingly, held as true in the company's U.S. divisions as in its divisions in Asia and Europe.

In short, the numbers are beginning to tell us a persuasive story about the link between a company's success and the emotional intelligence of its leaders. And just as important, research is also demonstrating that people can, if they take the right approach, develop their emotional intelligence.

Self-Awareness

Self-awareness is the first component of emotional intelligence—which makes sense when one considers that the Delphic oracle gave the advice to "know thyself" thousands of years ago. Self-awareness means having a deep understanding of one's emotions, strengths, weaknesses, needs, and drives. People with strong self-awareness are neither overly critical nor unrealistically hopeful. Rather, they are honest—with themselves and with others.

People who have a high degree of self-awareness recognize how their feelings affect them, other people, and their job performance. Thus a self-aware person who knows that tight deadlines bring out the worst in him plans his time carefully and gets his work done well in advance. Another person with high self-awareness will be able to work with a demanding client. She will understand the client's impact on her moods and the deeper reasons for her frustration. "Their trivial demands take us away from the real work that needs to be done," she might explain. And she will go one step further and turn her anger into something constructive.

Self-awareness extends to a person's understanding of his or her values and goals. Someone who is highly self-aware knows where he is headed and why; so, for example, he will be able to be firm in turning down a job offer that is tempting financially but does not fit with his principles or long-term goals. A person who lacks self-awareness is apt to make decisions that bring on inner turmoil by treading on buried values. "The money looked good so I signed on," someone might say two years into a job, "but the work means so little to me that I'm constantly bored." The decisions of self-aware people mesh with their values; consequently, they often find work to be energizing.

15 How can one recognize self-awareness? First and foremost, it shows itself as candor and an ability to assess oneself realistically. People with high self-awareness are able to speak accurately and openly—although not necessarily effusively or confessionally—about their emotions and the impact they have on their work. For instance, one manager I know of was skeptical about a new personal-shopper service that her company, a major department-store chain, was about to introduce. Without prompting from her team or her boss, she offered them an explanation: "It's hard for me to get behind the rollout of this service," she admitted, "because I really wanted to run the project, but I wasn't selected. Bear with me while I deal with that." The manager did indeed examine her feelings; a week later, she was supporting the project fully.

Such self-knowledge often shows itself in the hiring process. Ask a candidate to describe a time he got carried away by his feelings and did something he later regretted. Self-aware candidates will be frank in admitting to failure—and will often tell their tales with a smile. One of the hallmarks of self-awareness is a self-deprecating sense of humor.

Self-awareness can also be identified during performance reviews. Self-aware people know—and are comfortable talking about—their limitations and strengths, and they often demonstrate a thirst for constructive criticism. By contrast, people with low self-awareness interpret the message that they need to improve as a threat or a sign of failure.

The Five Components of EI

	Definition	**Hallmarks**
Self-awareness	the ability to recognize and understand your moods, emotions and drives, as well as their effect on others	self-confidence realistic self-assessment self-deprecating sense of humor
Self-regulation	the ability to control or redirect disruptive impulses and moods the propensity to suspend judgment—to think before acting	trustworthiness and integrity comfort with ambiguity openness to change
Motivation	a passion to work for reasons that go beyond money or status a propensity to pursue goals with energy and persistence	strong drive to achieve optimism, even in the face of failure organizational commitment
Empathy	the ability to understand the emotional makeup of other people skill in treating people according to their emotional reactions	expertise in building and retaining talent cross-cultural sensitivity service to clients and customers
Social skill	proficiency in managing relationships and building networks an ability to find common ground and build rapport	effectiveness in leading change persuasiveness expertise in building and leading teams

Self-aware people can also be recognized by their self-confidence. They have a firm grasp of their capabilities and are less likely to set themselves up to fail by, for example, overstretching on assignments. They know, too, when to ask for help. And the risks they take on the job are calculated. They won't ask for a challenge that they know they can't handle alone. They'll play to their strengths.

Consider the actions of a mid-level employee who was invited to sit in on a strategy meeting with her company's top executives. Although she was the most junior person in the room, she did not sit there quietly, listening in awestruck or fearful silence. She knew she had a head for clear logic and the skill to present ideas persuasively, and she offered cogent suggestions about the company's strategy. At the same time, her self-awareness stopped her from wandering into territory where she knew she was weak.

Despite the value of having self-aware people in the workplace, my research indicates that senior executives don't often give self-awareness the credit it deserves when they look for potential leaders. Many executives mistake candor about feelings for "wimpiness" and fail to give due respect to employees who openly acknowledge their shortcomings. Such people are too readily dismissed as "not tough enough" to lead others.

In fact, the opposite is true. In the first place, people generally admire and respect candor. Further, leaders are constantly required to make judgment calls that require a candid assessment of capabilities—their own and those of others. Do we have the management expertise to acquire a competitor? For ages, people have debated if leaders are born or made. So too goes the debate about emotional intelligence. Are people born with certain levels of empathy, for example, or do they acquire empathy as a result of life's experiences? The answer is both. Scientific inquiry strongly suggests that there is a genetic component to emotional intelligence. Psychological and developmental research indicates that nurture plays a role as well. How much of each perhaps will never be known, but research and practice clearly demonstrate that emotional intelligence can be learned.

One thing is certain: emotional intelligence increases with age. There is an old-fashioned word for the phenomenon: maturity. Yet even with maturity, some people still need training to enhance their emotional intelligence. Unfortunately, far too many training programs that intend to build leadership skills—including emotional intelligence—are a waste of time and money. The problem is simple: they focus on the wrong part of the brain.

Emotional intelligence is born largely in the neurotransmitters of the brain's limbic system, which governs feelings, impulses, and drives. Research indicates that the limbic system learns best through motivation, extended practice, and feedback. Compare this with the kind of learning that goes on in the neocortex, which governs analytical and technical ability. The neocortex grasps concepts and logic. It is the part of the brain that figures out how to use a computer or make a sales call by reading a book. Not surprisingly—but mistakenly—it is also the part of the brain targeted by most training programs aimed at enhancing emotional intelligence. When such programs take, in effect, a neocortical approach, my research with the Consortium for Research on Emotional Intelligence in Organizations has shown they can even have a *negative* impact on people's job performance.

To enhance emotional intelligence, organizations must refocus their training to include the limbic system. They must help people break old behavioral habits and establish new ones. That not only takes much more time than conventional training programs, it also requires an individualized approach.

25 Imagine an executive who is thought to be low on empathy by her colleagues. Part of that deficit shows itself as an inability to listen; she interrupts people and doesn't pay close attention to what they're saying. To fix the problem, the executive needs to be motivated to change, and then she needs practice and feedback from others in the company. A colleague or coach could be tapped to let the executive know when she has been observed failing to listen. She would then have to replay the incident and give a better response; that is, demonstrate her ability to absorb what others are saying. And the executive could be directed to observe certain executives who listen well and to mimic their behavior.

With persistence and practice, such a process can lead to lasting results. I know one Wall Street executive who sought to improve his empathy—specifically his ability to read people's reactions and see their perspectives. Before beginning his quest, the executive's subordinates were terrified of working with him. People even went so far as to hide bad news from him. Naturally, he was shocked when finally confronted with these facts. He went home and told his family—but they only confirmed what he had heard at work. When their opinions on any given subject did not mesh with his, they, too, were frightened of him.

Enlisting the help of a coach, the executive went to work to heighten his empathy through practice and feedback. His first step was to take a vacation to a foreign country where he did not speak the language. While there, he monitored his reactions to the unfamiliar and his openness to people who were different from him. When he returned home, humbled by his week abroad, the executive asked his coach to shadow him for parts of the day, several times a week, in order to critique how he treated people with new or different perspectives. At the same time, he consciously used on-the-job interactions as opportunities to practice "hearing" ideas that differed from his. Finally, the executive had himself videotaped in meetings and asked those who worked for and with him to critique his ability to acknowledge and understand the feelings of others. It took several months, but the executive's emotional intelligence did ultimately rise, and the improvement was reflected in his overall performance on the job.

It's important to emphasize that building one's emotional intelligence cannot—will not—happen without sincere desire and concerted effort. A brief seminar won't help; nor can one buy a how-to manual. It is much harder to learn to empathize—to internalize empathy as a natural response to people—than it is to become adept at regression analysis. But it can be done. "Nothing great was ever achieved without enthusiasm," wrote Ralph Waldo Emerson. If your goal is to become a real leader, these words can serve as a guidepost in your efforts to develop high emotional intelligence.

Can we launch a new product within six months? People who assess themselves honestly—that is, self-aware people—are well-suited to do the same for the organizations they run.

Self-Regulation

30 Biological impulses drive our emotions. We cannot do away with them—but we can do much to manage them. Self-regulation, which is like an ongoing inner conversation, is the component of emotional intelligence that frees us from being prisoners of our feelings. People engaged in such a conversation feel bad moods and emotional impulses just as everyone else does, but they find ways to control them and even to channel them in useful ways.

Imagine an executive who has just watched a team of his employees present a botched analysis to the company's board of directors. In the gloom that follows, the executive might find himself tempted to pound on the table in anger or kick over a chair. He could leap up and scream at the group. Or he might maintain a grim silence, glaring at everyone before stalking off.

But if he had a gift for self-regulation, he would choose a different approach. He would pick his words carefully, acknowledging the team's poor performance without rushing to any hasty judgment. He would then step back to consider the reasons for the failure. Are they personal—a lack of effort? Are there any mitigating factors? What was his role in the debacle? After considering these questions, he would call the team together, lay out the incident's consequences, and offer his feelings about it. He would then present his analysis of the problem and a well-considered solution.

Why does self-regulation matter so much for leaders? First of all, people who are in control of their feelings and impulses—that is, people who are reasonable—are able to create an environment of trust and fairness. In such an environment, politics and infighting are sharply reduced and productivity is high. Talented people flock to the organization and aren't tempted to leave. And self-regulation has a trickle-down effect. No one wants to be known as a hothead when the boss is known for her calm approach. Fewer bad moods at the top mean fewer throughout the organization.

Second, self-regulation is important for competitive reasons. Everyone knows that business today is rife with ambiguity and change. Companies merge and break apart regularly. Technology transforms work at a dizzying pace. People who have mastered their emotions are able to roll with the changes. When a new change program is announced, they don't panic, instead, they are able to suspend judgement, seek out information, and listen to executives explain the new program. As the initiative moves forward, they are able to move with it.

Sometimes they even lead the way. Consider the case of a manager at a large manufacturing company. Like her colleagues, she had used a certain software program for five years. The program drove how she collected and reported data and how she thought about the company's strategy. One day, senior executives announced that a new program was to be installed that would radically change how information was gathered and assessed within the organization. While many people in the company complained bitterly about how disruptive the change would be, the manager mulled over the reasons for the new program and was convinced of its potential to improve performance. She eagerly attended training sessions—some of her colleagues refused to do so—and was eventually promoted to run several divisions, in part because she used the new technology so effectively.

I want to push the importance of self-regulation to leadership even further and make the case that it enhances integrity, which is not only a personal virtue but also an organizational strength. Many of the bad things that happen in companies are a function of impulsive behavior. People rarely plan to exaggerate profits, pad expense accounts, dip into the till, or abuse power for selfish ends. Instead, an opportunity presents itself, and people with low impulse control just say yes.

By contrast, consider the behavior of the senior executive at a large food company. The executive was scrupulously honest in his negotiations with local distributors. He would routinely lay out his cost structure in detail, thereby giving the distributors a realistic understanding of the company's pricing. This approach meant the executive couldn't always drive a hard bargain. Now, on occasion, he felt the urge to increase profits by withholding information about the company's costs. But he challenged that impulse—he saw that it made more sense in the long run to counteract it. His emotional self-regulation paid off in strong, lasting relationships with distributors that benefited the company more than any short-term financial gains would have.

The signs of emotional self-regulation, therefore, are not hard to miss: a propensity for reflection and thoughtfulness; comfort with ambiguity and change; and integrity—an ability to say no to impulsive urges.

Like self-awareness, self-regulation often does not get its due. People who can master their emotions are sometimes seen as cold fish—their considered responses are taken as a lack of passion. People with fiery temperaments are frequently thought of as "classic" leaders—their outbursts are considered hallmarks of charisma and power.

But when such people make it to the top, their impulsiveness often works against them. In my research, extreme displays of negative emotion have never emerged as a driver of good leadership.

Motivation

40 If there is one trait that virtually all effective leaders have, it is motivation. They are driven to achieve beyond expectations—their own and everyone else's. The key word here is *achieve.* Plenty of people are motivated by external factors such as a big salary or the status that comes from having an impressive title or being part of a prestigious company. By contrast, those with leadership potential are motivated by a deeply embedded desire to achieve for the sake of achievement.

If you are looking for leaders, how can you identify people who are motivated by the drive to achieve rather than by external rewards? The first sign is a passion for the work itself—such people seek out creative challenges, love to learn, and take great pride in a job well done. They also display an unflagging energy to do things better. People with such energy often seem restless with the status quo. They are persistent with their questions about why things are done one way rather than another; they are eager to explore new approaches to their work.

A cosmetics company manager, for example, was frustrated that he had to wait two weeks to get sales results from people in the field. He finally tracked down an automated phone system that would beep each of his salespeople at 5 p.m. every day. An automated message then prompted them to punch in their numbers—how many calls and sales they had made that day. The system shortened the feedback time on sales results from weeks to hours.

That story illustrates two other common traits of people who are driven to achieve. They are forever raising the performance bar, and they like to keep score. Take the performance bar first. During performance reviews, people with high levels of motivation might ask to be "stretched" by their superiors. Of course, an employee who combines self-awareness with internal motivation will recognize her limits—but she won't settle for objectives that seem too easy to fulfill.

And it follows naturally that people who are driven to do better also want a way of tracking progress—their own, their team's, and their company's. Whereas people with low achievement motivation are often fuzzy about results, those with high achievement motivation often keep score by tracking such hard measures as profitability or market share. I know of a money manager who starts and ends his day on the internet, gauging the performance of his stock fund against four industry-set benchmarks.

45 Interestingly, people with high motivation remain optimistic even when the score is against them. In such cases, self-regulation combines with achievement motivation to overcome the frustration and depression that come after a setback or failure. Take the case of an another portfolio manager at a large investment company. After several successful years, her fund tumbled for three consecutive quarters, leading three large institutional clients to shift their business elsewhere.

Some executives would have blamed the nosedive on circumstances outside their control; others might have seen the setback as evidence of personal failure. This portfolio manager, however, saw an opportunity to prove she could lead a turnaround. Two years later, when she was promoted to a very senior level in the company, she described the experience as "the best thing that ever happened to me; I learned so much from it."

Executives trying to recognize high levels of achievement motivation in their people can look for one last piece of evidence: commitment to the organization. When people love their job for the work itself, they often feel committed to the organizations that make that work possible. Committed employees are likely to stay with an organization even when they are pursued by headhunters waving money.

It's not difficult to understand how and why a motivation to achieve translates into strong leadership. If you set the performance bar high for yourself, you will do the same for the organization when you are in a position to do so. Likewise, a drive to surpass goals and an interest in keeping score can be contagious. Leaders with these traits can often build a team of managers around them with the same traits. And of course, optimism and organizational commitment are fundamental to leadership—just try to imagine running a company without them.

Empathy

Of all the dimensions of emotional intelligence, empathy is the most easily recognized. We have all felt the empathy of a sensitive teacher or friend; we have all been struck by its absence in an unfeeling coach or boss. But when it comes to business, we rarely hear people praised, let alone rewarded, for their empathy. The very word seems unbusinesslike, out of place amid the tough realities of the marketplace.

50 But empathy doesn't mean a kind of "I'm okay, you're okay" mushiness. For a leader, that is, it doesn't mean adopting other people's emotions as one's own and trying to please everybody. That would be a nightmare—it would make action impossible. Rather, empathy means thoughtfully considering employees' feelings—along with other factors—in the process of making intelligent decisions.

For an example of empathy in action, consider what happened when two giant brokerage companies merged creating redundant jobs in all their divisions. One division manager called his people together and gave a gloomy speech that emphasized the number of people who would soon be fired. The manager of another division gave his people a different kind of speech. He was upfront about his own worry and confusion, and he promised to keep people informed and to treat everyone fairly.

The difference between these two managers was empathy. The first manager was too worried about his own fate to consider the feelings of his anxiety-stricken colleagues. The second knew intuitively what his people were feeling, and he acknowledged their fears with his words. Is it any surprise that the first manager saw his division sink as many demoralized people, especially the most talented, departed? By contrast, the second manager continued to be a strong leader, his best people stayed, and his division remained as productive as ever.

Empathy is particularly important today as a component of leadership for at least three reasons: the increasing use of teams; the rapid pace of globalization; and the growing need to retain talent.

Consider the challenge of leading a team. As anyone who has ever been a part of one can attest, teams are cauldrons of bubbling emotions. They are often charged with reaching a consensus—hard enough with two people and much more difficult as the numbers increase. Even in groups with as few as four or five members, alliances form and clashing agendas get set. A team's leader must be able to sense and understand the viewpoints of everyone around the table.

55 That's exactly what a marketing manager at a large information technology company was able to do when she was appointed to lead a troubled team. The group was in turmoil, overloaded by work and missing deadlines. Tensions were high among the members. Tinkering with procedures was not enough to bring the group together and make it an effective part of the company.

So the manager took several steps. In a series of one-on-one sessions, she took the time to listen to everyone in the group—what was frustrating them, how they rated their colleagues, whether they felt they had been ignored. And then she directed the team in a way that brought it together: she encouraged people to speak more openly about their frustrations, and she helped people raise constructive complaints during meetings. In short, her empathy allowed her to understand her team's emotional makeup. The result was not just heightened collaboration among members but also added business, as the team was called on for help by a wider range of internal clients.

Globalization is another reason for the rising importance of empathy for business leaders. Cross-cultural dialogue can easily lead to miscues and misunderstandings. Empathy is an antidote. People who have it are attuned to subtleties in body language; they can hear the message beneath the words being spoken. Beyond that, they have a deep understanding of the existence and importance of cultural and ethnic differences.

Consider the case of an American consultant whose team had just pitched a project to a potential Japanese client. In its dealings with Americans, the team was accustomed to being bombarded with questions after such a proposal, but this time it was greeted with a long silence. Other members of the team, taking the silence as disapproval, were ready to pack and leave. The lead consultant gestured them to stop. Although he was not particularly familiar with Japanese culture, he read the client's face and posture and sensed not rejection but interest—even deep consideration. He was right: when the client finally spoke, it was to give the consulting firm the job.

Finally, empathy plays a key role in the retention of talent, particularly in today's information economy. Leaders have always needed empathy to develop and keep good people, but today the stakes are higher. When good people leave, they take the company's knowledge with them.

60 That's where coaching and mentoring come in. It has repeatedly been shown that coaching and mentoring pay off not just in better performance but also in increased job satisfaction and decreased turnover. But what makes coaching and mentoring work best is the nature of the relationship. Outstanding coaches and mentors get inside the heads of the people they are helping. They sense how to give effective feedback. They know when to push for better performance and when to hold back. In the way they motivate their protégés, they demonstrate empathy in action.

In what is probably sounding like a refrain, let me repeat that empathy doesn't get much respect in business. People wonder how leaders can make hard decisions if they are "feeling" for all the people who will be affected. But leaders with empathy do more than sympathize with people around them: they use their knowledge to improve their companies in subtle but important ways.

Social Skill

The first three components of emotional intelligence are all self-management skills. The last two, empathy and social skill, concern a person's ability to manage relationships with others. As a component of emotional intelligence, social skill is not as simple as it sounds. It's not just a matter of friendliness, although people with high levels of social skill are rarely mean-spirited. Social skill, rather, is friendliness with a purpose: moving people in the direction you desire, whether that's agreement on a new marketing strategy or enthusiasm about a new product.

Socially skilled people tend to have a wide circle of acquaintances, and they have a knack for finding common ground with people of all kinds—a knack for building rapport. That doesn't mean they socialize continually; it means they work according to the assumption that nothing important gets done alone. Such people have a network in place when the time for action comes.

Social skill is the culmination of the other dimensions of emotional intelligence. People tend to be very effective at managing relationships when they can understand and control their own emotions and can empathize with the feelings of others. Even motivation contributes to social skill. Remember that people who are driven to achieve tend to be optimistic, even in the face of setbacks or failure. When people are upbeat, their "glow" is cast upon conversations and other social encounters. They are popular, and for good reason.

65 Because it is the outcome of the other dimensions of emotional intelligence, social skill is recognizable on the job in many ways that will by now sound familiar. Socially skilled people, for instance, are adept at managing teams—that's their empathy at work. Likewise, they are expert persuaders—a manifestation of self-awareness, self-regulation, and empathy combined. Given those skills, good persuaders know when to make an emotional plea, for instance, and when an appeal to reason will work better. And motivation when publicly visible, makes such people excellent collaborators; their passion for the work spreads to others, and they are driven to find solutions.

But sometimes social skill shows itself in ways the other emotional intelligence components do not. For instance, socially skilled people may at times appear not to be working while at work. They seem to be idly schmoozing—chatting in the hallways with colleagues or joking around with people who are not even connected to their "real" jobs. Socially skilled people, however, don't think it makes sense to arbitrarily limit the scope of their relationships. They build bonds widely because they know that in these fluid times, they may need help someday from people they are just getting to know today.

For example, consider the case of an executive in the strategy department of a global computer manufacturer. By 1993, he was convinced that the company's future lay with the Internet. Over the course of the next year, he found kindred spirits and used his social skill to stitch together a virtual community that cut across levels, divisions, and nations. He then used this de facto team to put up a corporate Web site, among the first by a major company. And, on his own initiative, with no budget or formal status, he signed up the company to participate in an annual Internet industry convention. Calling on his allies and persuading various divisions to donate funds, he recruited more than 50 people from a dozen different units to represent the company at the convention.

Management took notice within a year of the conference, the executive's team formed the basis for the company's first internet division and he was formally put in charge of it. To get there, the executive had ignored conventional boundaries forging and maintaining connections with people in every corner of the organization.

Is social skill considered a key leadership capability in most companies? The answer is yes, especially when compared with the other components of emotional intelligence. People seem to know intuitively that leaders need to manage relationships effectively; no leader is an island. After all, the leader's task is to get work done through other people and social skill makes that possible. A leader who cannot express her empathy may as well not have it at all. And a leader's motivation will be useless if he cannot communicate his passion to the organization. Social skill allows leaders to put their emotional intelligence to work.

70 IT WOULD BE FOOLISH to assert that good-old-fashioned IQ and technical ability are not important ingredients in strong leadership. But the recipe would not be complete without emotional intelligence. It was once thought that the components of emotional intelligence were "nice to have" in business leaders. But now we know that, for the sake of performance, these are ingredients that leaders "need to have."

It is fortunate, then, that emotional intelligence can be learned. The process is not easy. It takes time and, most of all, commitment. But the benefits that come from having a well-developed emotional intelligence, both for the individual and for the organization, make it worth the effort.

Exploring Texts Contexts

For activities with icons, refer to the Guide to Analyzing Readings in Context.

1. According to Goleman, why is it important to have emotional intelligence? How does he describe the way EI will affect businesses and corporations in the global economy?

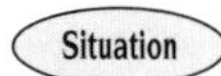

2. How does Goleman define success? In addition to rereading Goleman, you might want to revisit his consortium web site for clues. How do Goleman's assumptions about success compare to those of the other writers in this unit?

3. Both Goleman and Robert Reich, also in this unit, discuss retraining and education as a way to prepare for the globalization of the economy. Reich identifies four basic skills necessary to a symbolic analyst: abstraction, system thinking, experimentation, and collaboration. Goleman claims cognitive abilities alone will not suffice and that emotional intelligence is a factor in attaining a position at the highest levels of any organization. Compare Goleman's components of emotional intelligence with Reich's list of basic skills. How do the two writers differ in their assessment of the qualities necessary to compete in the global economy?

Creating Texts

For activities with icons, refer to the Guides to Analyzing Contexts for Writing and Analyzing Readings in Context. For additional help with these writing projects, read the descriptions of **Interview** and **Business Letter/Memo** in the Genre Glossary.

1. To gain another perspective on leadership, interview someone who works in a leadership capacity in a company you are familiar with or in a workplace related to the field you are studying. During the interview, ask the person to respond to the qualities and characteristics Goleman lists. Based on the information gleaned from your interview, your personal experience, and conversations with your classmates on this subject, write an essay in which you reconsider Goleman's ideas. Decide whether Goleman's list is accurate and complete. What is the relationship between effective leadership and the nature of a particular business or workplace? Do you agree with Goleman that it is possible to acquire qualities that make people effective leaders?
2. Daniel Goleman offers his training for employees in a variety of settings. Imagine that you brought up Goleman's approach during a discussion about communication difficulties among employees. The personnel director running the meeting suggested that you write a persuasive letter to her that she could bring to her boss. Compose a letter in which you describe Goleman's program, the need you see for it in your unit, and the possible benefits, as well as an estimate of the cost of the training.

Nickel-and-Dimed

On (Not) Getting by in America

Barbara Ehrenreich

There is a long history in journalism of investigative stories in which the reporter goes "undercover" in order to enter and report on an unfamiliar world. Reporters have used this method to write stories about mental hospitals, prisons, street gangs, homeless communities, and other institutions or aspects of life that are usually hidden from or somehow strange to most readers of the stories and to the reporters themselves. This is essentially what Barbara Ehrenreich does in this piece, though with one important difference. The world she enters and writes about—low-wage service work—is not really hidden from Ehrenreich's audience, the readers of *Harper's* magazine; they probably see such workers all the time.

But Ehrenreich is most interested in revealing something that she assumes *is* hidden to her readers: how these workers support themselves and their families on such jobs, where they live, how they get to and from work, whether they have health insurance, and how they feel about their work and lives. And she wants to reveal this for a reason: She is concerned about the long-term impact of welfare reform, the changes to the welfare system passed in 1995 that set limits on the length of time single women with dependent children can receive welfare benefits, encouraging these women to find jobs to support themselves and their children. Ehrenreich is concerned that although this may sound good—who could object to the idea of people taking responsibility for the support of themselves and their children?—the reality of the American workplace and economy makes it very difficult for people with dependent children and few skills to make an income that they can live on.

Over the past 30 years, Ehrenreich has developed into a writer who often makes her readers uncomfortable and sometimes impatient. When she began writing in the early 1970s, her typical audience was young baby boomers who shared her liberal-to-radical leftwing perspective. But as her audience aged, settled down, and started to earn money, and as the country in general seemed to grow more prosperous, the issues that Ehrenreich continued to write about—the growing gap between rich and poor, the anxieties of the middle class, the conditions of life for those left behind by the nation's general prosperity—were often issues that her well-educated and generally well-off readers might prefer not to think about. But Ehrenreich's witty style and the rich detail with which she describes the worlds she enters keep her readers engaged. Thus, though Ehrenreich presents this piece as an argument against welfare reform, the funny and gripping stories she tells stand on their own. This piece was published in *Harper's* magazine, but later appeared in her book of the same name, published in May 2001 by Metropolitan Books.

Connecting with the Conversation

1. Many of us have had some experience working in low-wage service jobs—including waiting tables, working in fast-food restaurants, and doing housekeeping, maintenance, and many retail jobs—but often, especially when we are young, we don't think of these jobs as lifetime occupations. Have you ever had a job like this? How did you feel about it? How would you have felt if you had thought of it as a lifelong occupation? Write about your experiences and perceptions.
2. With the class divided into groups, each group should search a section of the Sunday want ads, looking at job ads in waiting tables, fast food, and housekeeping. Make note of the average hourly wages, benefits, and hours. Do any of the ads mention drug testing as a condition of employment? Each group should report its findings to the class, and then discuss with the class as a whole the implications of the overall findings.

3. Search your library's article database for articles by Ehrenreich. What kinds of topics does she write about, and in what kinds of periodicals does she publish? Given where she usually publishes, how would you characterize her target audience, and do you consider yourself a member of this audience?

At the beginning of June 1998 I leave behind everything that normally soothes the ego and sustains the body—home, career, companion, reputation, ATM card—for a plunge into the low-wage workforce. There, I become another, occupationally much diminished "Barbara Ehrenreich"—depicted on job-application forms as a divorced homemaker whose sole work experience consists of housekeeping in a few private homes. I am terrified, at the beginning, of being unmasked for what I am: a middle-class journalist setting out to explore the world that welfare mothers are entering, at the rate of approximately 50,000 a month, as welfare reform kicks in. Happily, though, my fears turn out to be entirely unwarranted: during a month of poverty and toil, my name goes unnoticed and for the most part unuttered. In this parallel universe where my father never got out of the mines and I never got through college, I am "baby," "honey," "blondie," and, most commonly, "girl."

My first task is to find a place to live. I figure that if I can earn $7 an hour—which, from the want ads, seems doable—I can afford to spend $500 on rent, or maybe, with severe economies, $600. In the Key West area, where I live, this pretty much confines me to flophouses and trailer homes—like the one, a pleasing fifteen-minute drive from town, that has no air-conditioning, no screens, no fans, no television, and, by way of diversion, only the challenge of evading the landlord's Doberman pinscher. The big problem with this place, though, is the rent, which at $675 a month is well beyond my reach. All right, Key West is expensive. But so is New York City, or the Bay Area, or Jackson Hole, or Telluride, or Boston, or any other place where tourists and the wealthy compete for living space with the people who clean their toilets and fry their hash browns.[1] Still, it is a shock to realize that "trailer trash" has become, for me, a demographic category to aspire to.

So I decide to make the common trade-off between affordability and convenience, and go for a $500-a-month efficiency thirty miles up a two-lane highway from the employment opportunities of Key West, meaning forty-five minutes if there's no road construction and I don't get caught behind some sun-dazed Canadian tourists. I hate the drive, along a roadside studded with white crosses commemorating the more effective head-on collisions, but it's a sweet little place—a cabin, more or less, set in the swampy back yard of the converted mobile home where my landlord, an affable TV repairman, lives with his bartender girlfriend. Anthropologically speaking, a bustling trailer park would be preferable, but here I have a gleaming white floor and a firm mattress, and the few resident bugs are easily vanquished.

Besides, I am not doing this for the anthropology. My aim is nothing so mistily subjective as to "experience poverty" or find out how it "really feels" to be a long-term

From *Harper's Magazine,* January 1999, pp. 37–49, excerpted.

low-wage worker. I've had enough unchosen encounters with poverty and the world of low-wage work to know it's not a place you want to visit for touristic purposes; it just smells too much like fear. And with all my real-life assets—bank account, IRA, health insurance, multiroom home—waiting indulgently in the background, I am, of course, thoroughly insulated from the terrors that afflict the genuinely poor.

5 No, this is a purely objective, scientific sort of mission. The humanitarian rationale for welfare reform—as opposed to the more punitive and stingy impulses that may actually have motivated it—is that work will lift poor women out of poverty while simultaneously inflating their self-esteem and hence their future value in the labor market. Thus, whatever the hassles involved in finding child care, transportation, etc., the transition from welfare to work will end happily, in greater prosperity for all. Now there are many problems with this comforting prediction, such as the fact that the economy will inevitably undergo a downturn, eliminating many jobs. Even without a downturn, the influx of a million former welfare recipients into the low-wage labor market could depress wages by as much as 11.9 percent, according to the Economic Policy Institute (EPI) in Washington, D.C.

But is it really possible to make a living on the kinds of jobs currently available to unskilled people? Mathematically, the answer is no, as can be shown by taking $6 to $7 an hour, perhaps subtracting a dollar or two an hour for child care, multiplying by 160 hours a month, and comparing the result to the prevailing rents. According to the National Coalition for the Homeless, for example, in 1998 it took, on average nationwide, an hourly wage of $8.89 to afford a one-bedroom apartment, and the Preamble Center for Public Policy estimates that the odds against a typical welfare recipient's landing a job at such a "living wage" are about 97 to 1. If these numbers are right, low-wage work is not a solution to poverty and possibly not even to homelessness.

It may seem excessive to put this proposition to an experimental test. As certain family members keep unhelpfully reminding me, the viability of low-wage work could be tested, after a fashion, without ever leaving my study. I could just pay myself $7 an hour for eight hours a day, charge myself for room and board, and total up the numbers after a month. Why leave the people and work that I love? But I am an experimental scientist by training. In that business, you don't just sit at a desk and theorize; you plunge into the everyday chaos of nature, where surprises lurk in the most mundane measurements. Maybe, when I got into it, I would discover some hidden economies in the world of the low-wage worker. After all, if 30 percent of the workforce toils for less than $8 an hour, according to the EPI, they may have found some tricks as yet unknown to me. Maybe—who knows?—I would even be able to detect in myself the bracing psychological effects of getting out of the house, as promised by the welfare wonks at places like the Heritage Foundation. Or, on the other hand, maybe there would be unexpected costs—physical, mental, or financial—to throw off all my calculations. Ideally, I should do this with two small children in tow, that being the welfare average, but mine are grown and no one is willing to lend me theirs for a month-long vacation in penury. So this is not the perfect experiment, just a test of the best possible case: an unencumbered woman, smart and even strong, attempting to live more or less off the land.

ON THE MORNING of my first full day of job searching, I take a red pen to the want ads, which are auspiciously numerous. Everyone in Key West's booming "hospitality industry" seems to be looking for someone like me—trainable, flexible, and with suitably humble expectations as to pay. I know I possess certain traits that might be advantageous—I'm white and, I like to think, well-spoken and poised—but I decide on two rules: One, I cannot use any skills derived from my education or usual work—not that there are a lot of want ads for satirical essayists anyway. Two, I have to take the best-paid job that is offered me and of course do my best to hold it; no Marxist rants or sneaking off to read novels in the ladies' room. In addition, I rule out various occupations for one reason or another: Hotel front-desk clerk, for example, which to my surprise is regarded as unskilled and pays around $7 an hour, gets eliminated because it involves standing in one spot for eight hours a day. Waitressing is similarly something I'd like to avoid, because I remember it leaving me bone tired when I was eighteen, and I'm decades of varicosities and back pain beyond that now. Telemarketing, one of the first refuges of the suddenly indigent, can be dismissed on grounds of personality. This leaves certain supermarket jobs, such as deli clerk, or housekeeping in Key West's thousands of hotel and guest rooms. Housekeeping is especially appealing, for reasons both atavistic and practical: it's what my mother did before I came along, and it can't be too different from what I've been doing part-time, in my own home, all my life.

So I put on what I take to be a respectful-looking outfit of ironed Bermuda shorts and scooped-neck T-shirt and set out for a tour of the local hotels and supermarkets. Best Western, Econo Lodge, and HoJo's all let me fill out application forms, and these are, to my relief, interested in little more than whether I am a legal resident of the United States and have committed any felonies. My next stop is Winn-Dixie, the supermarket, which turns out to have a particularly onerous application process, featuring a fifteen-minute "interview" by computer since, apparently, no human on the premises is deemed capable of representing the corporate point of view. I am conducted to a large room decorated with posters illustrating how to look "professional" (it helps to be white and, if female, permed) and warning of the slick promises that union organizers might try to tempt me with. The interview is multiple choice: Do I have anything, such as child-care problems, that might make it hard for me to get to work on time? Do I think safety on the job is the responsibility of management? Then, popping up cunningly out of the blue: How many dollars' worth of stolen goods have I purchased in the last year? Would I turn in a fellow employee if I caught him stealing? Finally, "Are you an honest person?"

10 Apparently, I ace the interview, because I am told that all I have to do is show up in some doctor's office tomorrow for a urine test. This seems to be a fairly general rule: if you want to stack Cheerio boxes or vacuum hotel rooms in chemically fascist America, you have to be willing to squat down and pee in front of some health worker (who has no doubt had to do the same thing herself). The wages Winn-Dixie is offering—$6 and a couple of dimes to start with—are not enough, I decide, to compensate for this indignity.[2]

I lunch at Wendy's, where $4.99 gets you unlimited refills at the Mexican part of the Superbar, a comforting surfeit of refried beans and "cheese sauce." A teenage employee, seeing me studying the want ads, kindly offers me an application form, which I fill out, though here, too, the pay is just $6 and change an hour. Then it's off for a round of the locally owned inns and guest-houses. At "The Palms," let's call it, a bouncy manager actually takes me around to see the rooms and meet the existing housekeepers, who, I note with satisfaction, look pretty much like me—faded ex-hippie types in shorts with long hair pulled back in braids. Mostly, though, no one speaks to me or even looks at me except to proffer an application form. At my last stop, a palatial B&B, I wait twenty minutes to meet "Max," only to be told that there are no jobs now but there should be one soon, since "nobody lasts more than a couple weeks." (Because none of the people I talked to knew I was a reporter, I have changed their names to protect their privacy and, in some cases perhaps, their jobs.)

Three days go by like this, and, to my chagrin, no one out of the approximately twenty places I've applied calls me for an interview. I had been vain enough to worry about coming across as too educated for the jobs I sought, but no one even seems interested in finding out how overqualified I am. Only later will I realize that the want ads are not a reliable measure of the actual jobs available at any particular time. They are, as I should have guessed from Max's comment, the employers' insurance policy against the relentless turnover of the low-wage workforce. Most of the big hotels run ads almost continually, just to build a supply of applicants to replace the current workers as they drift away or are fired, so finding a job is just a matter of being at the right place at the right time and flexible enough to take whatever is being offered that day. This finally happens to me at one of the big discount hotel chains, where I go, as usual, for housekeeping and am sent, instead, to try out as a waitress at the attached "family restaurant," a dismal spot with a counter and about thirty tables that looks out on a parking garage and features such tempting fare as "Pollish [sic] sausage and BBQ sauce" on 95-degree days. Phillip, the dapper young West Indian who introduces himself as the manager, interviews me with about as much enthusiasm as if he were a clerk processing me for Medicare, the principal questions being what shifts can I work and when can I start. I mutter something about being woefully out of practice as a waitress, but he's already on to the uniform: I'm to show up tomorrow wearing black slacks and black shoes; he'll provide the rust-colored polo shirt with HEARTHSIDE embroidered on it, though I might want to wear my own shirt to get to work, ha ha. At the word "tomorrow," something between fear and indignation rises in my chest. I want to say, "Thank you for your time, sir, but this is just an experiment, you know, not my actual life."

So BEGINS MY CAREER at the Hearthside, I shall call it, one small profit center within a global discount hotel chain, where for two weeks I work from 2:00 till 10:00 P.M. for $2.43 an hour plus tips.[3] In some futile bid for gentility, the management has barred employees from using the front door, so my first day I enter through the kitchen, where a red-faced man with shoulder-length blond hair is throwing frozen steaks against the wall and yelling, "Fuck this shit!" "That's just Jack," explains Gail, the wiry middle-aged waitress who is assigned to train me. "He's on the rag again"—a condition occasioned, in this instance, by the fact that the cook on the morning shift had forgotten to thaw out the steaks. For the next eight hours, I run after the agile Gail, absorbing bits of instruction along with fragments of personal tragedy. All food must be trayed, and the reason she's so tired today is that she woke up in a cold sweat thinking of her boyfriend, who killed himself recently in an upstate prison. No refills on lemonade. And the reason he was in prison is that a few DUIs caught up with him, that's all, could have happened to anyone. Carry the creamers to the table in a monkey bowl, never in your hand. And after he was gone she spent several months living in her truck, peeing in a plastic pee bottle and reading by candlelight at night, but you can't live in a truck in the summer, since you need to have the windows down, which means anything can get in, from mosquitoes on up.

At least Gail puts to rest any fears I had of appearing overqualified. From the first day on, I find that of all the things I have left behind, such as home and identity, what I miss the most is competence. Not that I have ever felt utterly competent in the writing business, in which one day's success augurs nothing at all for the next. But in my writing life, I at least have some notion of procedure: do the research, make the outline, rough out a draft, etc. As a server, though, I am beset by requests like bees: more iced tea here, ketchup over there, a to-go box for table fourteen, and where are the high chairs, anyway? Of the twenty-seven tables, up to six are usually mine at any time, though on slow afternoons or if Gail is off, I sometimes have the whole place to myself. There is the touch-screen computer-ordering system to master, which is, I suppose, meant to minimize server-cook contact, but in practice requires constant verbal fine-tuning: "That's gravy on the mashed, okay? None on the meatloaf," and so forth—while the cook scowls as if I were inventing these refinements just to torment him. Plus, something I had forgotten in the years since I was eighteen: about a third of a server's job is "side work" that's invisible to customers—sweeping, scrubbing, slicing, refilling, and restocking. If it isn't all done, every little bit of it, you're going to face the 6:00 P.M. dinner rush defenseless and probably go down in flames. I screw up dozens of times at the beginning, sustained in my shame entirely by Gail's support—"It's okay, baby, everyone does that sometime"—because, to my total surprise and despite the scientific detachment I am doing my best to maintain, I care.

15 The whole thing would be a lot easier if I could just skate through it as Lily Tomlin in one of her waitress skits, but I was raised by the absurd Booker T. Washingtonian precept that says: If you're going to do something, do it well. In fact, "well" isn't good enough by half. Do it better than anyone has ever done it before. Or so said my father, who must have known what he was talking about because he managed to pull himself, and us with him, up from the mile-deep copper mines of Butte to the leafy suburbs of the Northeast, ascending from boilermakers to martinis before booze beat out ambition. As in most endeavors I have encountered in my life, doing it "better than anyone" is not a reasonable goal. Still, when I wake up at 4:00 A.M. in my own cold sweat, I am not thinking about the writing deadlines I'm neglecting; I'm thinking about the table whose order I screwed up so that one of the boys didn't get his kiddie meal until the rest of the family had moved on to their Key Lime pies. That's the other powerful motivation I hadn't expected—the customers, or "patients," as I can't help thinking of them on account of the mysterious vulnerability that seems to have left them temporarily unable to feed themselves. After a few days at the Hearthside, I feel the service ethic kick in like a shot of oxytocin, the nurturance hormone. The plurality of my customers are hard-working locals—truck drivers, construction workers, even housekeepers from the attached hotel—and I want them to have the closest to a "fine dining" experience that the grubby circumstances will allow. No "you guys" for me; everyone over twelve is "sir" or "ma'am." I ply them with iced tea and coffee refills; I return, mid-meal, to inquire how everything is; I doll up their salads with chopped raw mushrooms, summer squash slices, or whatever bits of produce I can find that have survived their sojourn in the cold-storage room mold-free.

There is Benny, for example, a short, tight-muscled sewer repairman, who cannot even think of eating until he has absorbed a half hour of air-conditioning and ice water. We chat about hyperthermia and electrolytes until he is ready to order some finicky combination like soup of the day, garden salad, and a side of grits. There are the German tourists who are so touched by my pidgin "Willkommen" and "Ist alles gut?" that they actually tip. (Europeans, spoiled by their trade-union-ridden, high-wage welfare states, generally do not know that they are supposed to tip. Some restaurants, the Hearthside included, allow servers to "grat" their foreign customers, or add a tip to the bill. Since this amount is added before the customers have a chance to tip or not tip, the practice amounts to an automatic penalty for imperfect English.) There are the two dirt-smudged lesbians, just off their construction shift, who are impressed enough by my suave handling of the fly in the piña colada that they take the time to praise me to Stu, the assistant manager. There's Sam, the kindly retired cop, who has to plug up his tracheotomy hole with one finger in order to force the cigarette smoke into his lungs.

Sometimes I play with the fantasy that I am a princess who, in penance for some tiny transgression, has undertaken to feed each of her subjects by hand. But the non-princesses working with me are just as indulgent, even when this means flouting management rules—concerning, for example, the number of croutons that can go on a salad (six). "Put on all you want," Gail whispers, "as long as Stu isn't looking." She dips into her own tip money to buy biscuits and gravy for an out-of-work mechanic who's used up all his money on dental surgery, inspiring me to pick up the tab for his milk and pie. Maybe the same high levels of agape can be found throughout the "hospitality industry." I remember the poster decorating one of the apartments I looked at, which said "If you seek happiness for yourself you will never find it. Only when you seek happiness for others will it come to you," or words to that effect—an odd sentiment, it seemed to me at the time, to find in the dank one-room basement apartment of a bellhop at the Best Western. At the Hearthside, we utilize whatever bits of autonomy we have to ply our customers with the illicit calories that signal our love. It is our job as servers to assemble the salads and desserts, pouring the dressings and squirting the whipped cream. We also control the number of butter patties our customers get and the amount of sour cream on their baked potatoes. So if you wonder why Americans are so obese, consider the fact that waitresses both express their humanity and earn their tips through the covert distribution of fats.

Ten days into it, this is beginning to look like a livable lifestyle. I like Gail, who is "looking at fifty" but moves so fast she can alight in one place and then another without apparently being anywhere between them. I clown around with Lionel, the teenage Haitian busboy, and catch a few fragments of conversation with Joan, the svelte fortyish hostess and militant feminist who is the only one of us who dares to tell Jack to shut the fuck up. I even warm up to Jack when, on a slow night and to make up for a particularly unwarranted attack on my abilities, or so I imagine, he tells me about his glory days as a young man at "coronary school"—or do you say "culinary"?—in Brooklyn, where he dated a knock-out Puerto Rican chick and learned everything there is to know about food. I finish up at 10:00 or 10:30, depending on how much side work I've been able to get done during the shift, and cruise home to the tapes I snatched up at random when I left my real home—Marianne Faithfull, Tracy Chapman, Enigma, King Sunny Ade, the Violent Femmes—just drained enough for the music to set my cranium resonating but hardly dead. Midnight snack is Wheat Thins and Monterey Jack, accompanied by cheap white wine on ice and whatever AMC has to offer. To bed by 1:30 or 2:00, up at 9:00 or 10:00, read for an hour while my uniform whirls around in the landlord's washing machine, and then it's another eight hours spent following Mao's central instruction, as laid out in the Little Red Book, which was: Serve the people.

I COULD DRIFT ALONG like this, in some dreamy proletarian idyll, except for two things. One is management. If I have kept this subject on the margins thus far it is because I still flinch to think that I spent all those weeks under the surveillance of men (and later women) whose job it was to monitor my behavior for signs of sloth, theft, drug abuse, or worse. Not that managers and especially "assistant managers" in low-wage settings like this are exactly the class enemy. In the restaurant business, they are mostly former cooks or servers, still capable of pinch-hitting in the kitchen or on the floor, just as in hotels they are likely to be former clerks, and paid a salary of only about $400 a week. But everyone knows they have crossed over to the other side, which is, crudely put, corporate as opposed to human. Cooks want to prepare tasty meals; servers want to serve them graciously; but managers are there for only one reason—to make sure that money is made for some theoretical entity that exists far away in Chicago or New York, if a corporation can be said to have a physical existence at all. Reflecting on her career, Gail tells me ruefully that she had sworn, years ago, never to work for a corporation again. "They don't cut you no slack. You give and you give, and they take."

20 Managers can sit—for hours at a time if they want—but it's their job to see that no one else ever does, even when there's nothing to do, and this is why, for servers, slow times can be as exhausting as rushes. You start dragging out each little chore, because if the manager on duty catches you in an idle moment, he will give you something far nastier to do. So I wipe, I clean, I consolidate ketchup bottles and recheck the cheesecake supply, even tour the tables to make sure the customer evaluation forms are all standing perkily in their places—wondering all the time how many calories I burn in these strictly theatrical exercises. When, on a particularly dead afternoon, Stu finds me glancing at a *USA Today* a customer has left behind, he assigns me to vacuum the entire floor with the broken vacuum cleaner that has a handle only two feet long, and the only way to do that without incurring orthopedic damage is to proceed from spot to spot on your knees.

On my first Friday at the Hearthside there is a "mandatory meeting for all restaurant employees," which I attend, eager for insight into our overall marketing strategy and the niche (your basic Ohio cuisine with a tropical twist?) we aim to inhabit. But there is no "we" at this meeting. Phillip, our top manager except for an occasional "consultant" sent out by corporate headquarters, opens it with a sneer: "The break room—it's disgusting. Butts in the ashtrays, newspapers lying around, crumbs." This windowless little room, which also houses the time clock for the entire hotel, is where we stash our bags and civilian clothes and take our half-hour meal breaks. But a break room is not a right, he tells us. It can be taken away. We should also know that the lockers in the break room and whatever is in them can be searched at any time. Then comes gossip; there has been gossip; gossip (which seems to mean employees talking among themselves) must stop. Off-duty employees are henceforth barred from eating at the restaurant, because "other servers gather around them and gossip." When Phillip has exhausted his agenda of rebukes, Joan complains about the condition of the ladies' room and I throw in my two bits about the vacuum cleaner. But I don't see any backup coming from my fellow servers, each of whom has subsided into her own personal funk; Gail, my role model, stares sorrowfully at a point six inches from her nose. The meeting ends when Andy, one of the cooks, gets up, muttering about breaking up his day off for this almighty bullshit.

Just four days later we are suddenly summoned into the kitchen at 3:30 P.M., even though there are live tables on the floor. We all—about ten of us—stand around Phillip, who announces grimly that there has been a report of some "drug activity" on the night shift and that, as a result, we are now to be a "drug-free" workplace, meaning that all new hires will be tested, as will possibly current employees on a random basis. I am glad that this part of the kitchen is so dark, because I find myself blushing as hard as if I had been caught toking up in the ladies' room myself: I haven't been treated this way—lined up in the corridor, threatened with locker searches, peppered with carelessly aimed accusations—since junior high school. Back on the floor, Joan cracks, "Next they'll be telling us we can't have sex on the job." When I ask Stu what happened to inspire the crackdown, he just mutters about "management decisions" and takes the opportunity to upbraid Gail and me for being too generous with the rolls. From now on there's to be only one per customer, and it goes out with the dinner, not with the salad. He's also been riding the cooks, prompting Andy to come out of the kitchen and observe—with the serenity of a man whose customary implement is a butcher knife—that "Stu has a death wish today."

Later in the evening, the gossip crystallizes around the theory that Stu is himself the drug culprit, that he uses the restaurant phone to order up marijuana and sends one of the late servers out to fetch it for him. The server was caught, and she may have ratted Stu out or at least said enough to cast some suspicion on him, thus accounting for his pissy behavior. Who knows? Lionel, the busboy, entertains us for the rest of the shift by standing just behind Stu's back and sucking deliriously on an imaginary joint.

The other problem, in addition to the less-than-nurturing management style, is that this job shows no sign of being financially viable. You might imagine, from a comfortable distance, that people who live, year in and year out, on $6 to $10 an hour have discovered some survival stratagems unknown to the middle class. But no. It's not hard to get my coworkers to talk about their living situations, because housing, in almost every case, is the principal source of disruption in their lives, the first thing they fill you in on when they arrive for their shifts. After a week, I have compiled the following survey:

25 • Gail is sharing a room in a well-known downtown flophouse for which she and a roommate pay about $250 a week. Her roommate, a male friend, has begun hitting on her, driving her nuts, but the rent would be impossible alone.

- Claude, the Haitian cook, is desperate to get out of the two-room apartment he shares with his girlfriend and two other, unrelated, people. As far as I can determine, the other Haitian men (most of whom only speak Creole) live in similarly crowded situations.
- Annette, a twenty-year-old server who is six months pregnant and has been abandoned by her boyfriend, lives with her mother, a postal clerk.

- Marianne and her boyfriend are paying $170 a week for a one-person trailer.
- Jack, who is, at $10 an hour, the wealthiest of us, lives in the trailer he owns, paying only the $400-a-month lot fee.

30 • The other white cook, Andy, lives on his dry-docked boat, which, as far as I can tell from his loving descriptions, can't be more than twenty feet long. He offers to take me out on it, once it's repaired, but the offer comes with inquiries as to my marital status, so I do not follow up on it.

- Tina and her husband are paying $60 a night for a double room in a Days Inn. This is because they have no car and the Days Inn is within walking distance of the Hearthside. When Marianne, one of the breakfast servers, is tossed out of her trailer for subletting (which is against the trailer-park rules), she leaves her boyfriend and moves in with Tina and her husband.
- Joan, who had fooled me with her numerous and tasteful outfits (hostesses wear their own clothes), lives in a van she parks behind a shopping center at night and showers in Tina's motel room. The clothes are from thrift shops.[4]

IT STRIKES ME, IN my middle-class solipsism, that there is gross improvidence in some of these arrangements. When Gail and I are wrapping silverware in napkins—the only task for which we are permitted to sit—she tells me she is thinking of escaping from her roommate by moving into the Days Inn herself. I am astounded: How can she even think of paying between $40 and $60 a day? But if I was afraid of sounding like a social worker, I come out just sounding like a fool. She squints at me in disbelief, "And where am I supposed to get a month's rent and a month's deposit for an apartment?" I'd been feeling pretty smug about my $500 efficiency, but of course it was made possible only by the $1,300 I had allotted myself for start-up costs when I began my low-wage life: $1,000 for the first month's rent and deposit, $100 for initial groceries and cash in my pocket, $200 stuffed away for emergencies. In poverty, as in certain propositions in physics, starting conditions are everything.

There are no secret economies that nourish the poor; on the contrary, there are a host of special costs. If you can't put up the two months' rent you need to secure an apartment, you end up paying through the nose for a room by the week. If you have only a room, with a hot plate at best, you can't save by cooking up huge lentil stews that can be frozen for the week ahead. You eat fast food, or the hot dogs and styrofoam cups of soup that can be microwaved in a convenience store. If you have no money for health insurance—and the Hearthside's niggardly plan kicks in only after three months—you go without routine care or prescription drugs and end up paying the price. Gail, for example, was fine until she ran out of money for estrogen pills. She is supposed to be on the company plan by now, but they claim to have lost her application form and need to begin the paperwork all over again. So she spends $9 per migraine pill to control the headaches she wouldn't have, she insists, if her estrogen supplements were covered. Similarly, Marianne's boyfriend lost his job as a roofer because he missed so much time after getting a cut on his foot for which he couldn't afford the prescribed antibiotic.

35 My own situation, when I sit down to assess it after two weeks of work, would not be much better if this were my actual life. The seductive thing about waitressing is that you

don't have to wait for payday to feel a few bills in your pocket, and my tips usually cover meals and gas, plus something left over to stuff into the kitchen drawer I use as a bank. But as the tourist business slows in the summer heat, I sometimes leave work with only $20 in tips (the gross is higher, but servers share about 15 percent of their tips with the bus-boys and bartenders). With wages included, this amounts to about the minimum wage of $5.15 an hour. Although the sum in the drawer is piling up, at the present rate of accumulation it will be more than a hundred dollars short of my rent when the end of the month comes around. Nor can I see any expenses to cut. True, I haven't gone the lentil-stew route yet, but that's because I don't have a large cooking pot, pot holders, or a ladle to stir with (which cost about $30 at Kmart, less at thrift stores), not to mention onions, carrots, and the indispensable bay leaf. I do make my lunch almost every day—usually some slow-burning, high-protein combo like frozen chicken patties with melted cheese on top and canned pinto beans on the side. Dinner is at the Hearthside, which offers its employees a choice of BLT, fish sandwich, or hamburger for only $2. The burger lasts longest, especially if it's heaped with gut-puckering jalapeños, but by midnight my stomach is growling again.

So unless I want to start using my car as a residence, I have to find a second, or alternative, job. I call all the hotels where I filled out housekeeping applications weeks ago—the Hyatt, Holiday Inn, Econo Lodge, HoJo's, Best Western, plus a half dozen or so locally run guesthouses. Nothing. Then I start making the rounds again, wasting whole mornings waiting for some assistant manager to show up, even dipping into places so creepy that the front-desk clerk greets you from behind bulletproof glass and sells pints of liquor over the counter. But either someone has exposed my real-life housekeeping habits—which are, shall we say, mellow—or I am at the wrong end of some infallible ethnic equation: most, but by no means all, of the working housekeepers I see on my job searches are African Americans, Spanish-speaking, or immigrants from the Central European post-Communist world, whereas servers are almost invariably white and monolingually English-speaking. When I finally get a positive response, I have been identified once again as server material. Jerry's, which is part of a well-known national family restaurant chain and physically attached here to another budget hotel chain, is ready to use me at once. The prospect is both exciting and terrifying, because, with about the same number of tables and counter seats, Jerry's attracts three or four times the volume of customers as the gloomy old Hearthside.

I START OUT WITH the beautiful, heroic idea of handling the two jobs at once, and for two days I almost do it: the breakfast/lunch shift at Jerry's, which goes till 2:00, arriving at the Hearthside at 2:10, and attempting to hold out until 10:00. In the ten minutes between jobs, I pick up a spicy chicken sandwich at the Wendy's drive-through window, gobble it down in the car, and change from khaki slacks to black, from Hawaiian to rust polo. There is a problem, though. When during the 3:00 to 4:00 P.M. dead time I finally sit down to wrap silver, my flesh seems to bond to the seat. I try to refuel with a purloined cup of soup, as I've seen Gail and Joan do dozens of times, but a manager catches me and hisses "No eating!" though there's not a customer around to be offended by the sight of food making contact with a server's lips. So I tell Gail I'm going to quit, and she hugs me and says she might just follow me to Jerry's herself.

But the chances of this are minuscule. She has left the flophouse and her annoying roommate and is back to living in her beat-up old truck. But guess what? she reports to me excitedly later that evening: Phillip has given her permission to park overnight in the hotel parking lot, as long as she keeps out of sight, and the parking lot should be totally safe, since it's patrolled by a hotel security guard! With the Hearthside offering benefits like that, how could anyone think of leaving?

True, I take occasional breaks from this life, going home now and then to catch up on e-mail and for conjugal visits (though I am careful to "pay" for anything I eat there), seeing *The Truman Show* with friends and letting them buy my ticket. And I still have those what-am-I-doing-here moments at work, when I get so homesick for the printed word that I obsessively reread the six-page menu. But as the days go by, my old life is beginning to look exceedingly strange. The e-mails and phone messages addressed to my former self come from a distant race of people with exotic concerns and far too much time on their hands. The neighborly market I used to cruise for produce now looks forbiddingly like a Manhattan yuppie emporium. And when I sit down one morning in my real home to pay bills from my past life, I am dazzled at the two- and three-figure sums owed to outfits like Club BodyTech and Amazon.com.

40 MANAGEMENT AT JERRY'S is generally calmer and more "professional" than at the Hearthside, with two exceptions. One is Joy, a plump, blowsy woman in her early thirties, who once kindly devoted several minutes to instructing me in the correct one-handed method of carrying trays but whose moods change disconcertingly from shift to shift and even within one. Then there's B.J., a.k.a. B.J.-the-bitch, whose contribution is to stand by the kitchen counter and yell, "Nita, your order's up, move it!" or, "Barbara, didn't you see you've got another table out there? Come on, girl!" Among other things, she is hated for having replaced the whipped-cream squirt cans with big plastic whipped-cream-filled baggies that have to be squeezed with both hands—because, reportedly, she saw or thought she saw employees trying to inhale the propellant gas from the squirt cans, in the hope that it might be nitrous oxide. On my third night, she pulls me aside abruptly and brings her face so close that it looks as if she's planning to butt me with her forehead. But instead of saying, "You're fired," she says, "You're doing fine." The only trouble is I'm spending time chatting with customers: "That's how they're getting you." Furthermore I am letting them "run me," which means harassment by sequential demands: you bring the ketchup and they decide they want extra Thousand Island; you bring that and they announce they now need a side of fries; and so on into distraction. Finally she tells me not to take her wrong. She tries to say things in a nice way, but you get into a mode, you know, because everything has to move so fast.[5]

I mumble thanks for the advice, feeling like I've just been stripped naked by the crazed enforcer of some ancient sumptuary law: No chatting for you, girl. No fancy service ethic allowed for the serfs. Chatting with customers is for the beautiful young college-educated servers in the downtown carpaccio joints, the kids who can make $70 to $100 a night. What had I been thinking? My job is to move orders from tables to kitchen and then trays from kitchen to tables. Customers are, in fact, the major obstacle to the smooth transformation of information into food and food into money—they are, in short, the enemy. And the painful thing is that I'm beginning to see it this way myself. There are the traditional asshole types—frat boys who down multiple Buds and then make a fuss because the steaks are so emaciated and the fries so sparse—as well as the variously impaired—due to age, diabetes, or literacy issues—who require patient nutritional counseling.

I make friends, over time, with the other "girls" who work my shift: Nita, the tattooed twenty-something who taunts us by going around saying brightly, "Have we started making money yet?" Ellen, whose teenage son cooks on the graveyard shift and who once managed a restaurant in Massachusetts but won't try out for management here because she prefers being a "common worker" and not "ordering people around." Easy-going fiftyish Lucy, with the raucous laugh, who limps toward the end of the shift because of something that has gone wrong with her leg, the exact nature of which cannot be determined without health insurance. We talk about the usual girl things—men, children, and the sinister allure of Jerry's chocolate peanut-butter cream pie—though no one, I notice, ever brings up anything potentially expensive, like shopping or movies. As at the Hearthside, the only recreation ever referred to is partying, which requires little more than some beer, a joint, and a few close friends. Still, no one here is homeless, or cops to it anyway, thanks usually to a working husband or boyfriend. All in all, we form a reliable mutual-support group: If one of us is feeling sick or overwhelmed, another one will "bev" a table or even carry trays for her. If one of us is off sneaking a cigarette or a pee,[6] the others will do their best to conceal her absence from the enforcers of corporate rationality.

But my saving human connection—my oxytocin receptor, as it were—George, the nineteen-year-old, fresh-off-the-boat Czech dishwasher. We get to talking when he asks me, tortuously, how much cigarettes cost at Jerry's. I do my best to explain that they cost over a dollar more here than at a regular store and suggest that he just take one from the half-filled packs that are always lying around on the break table. But that would be unthinkable. Except for the one tiny earring signaling his allegiance to some vaguely alternative point of view, George is a perfect straight arrow—crew-cut, hardworking, and hungry for eye contact. "Czech Republic," I ask, "or Slovakia?" and he seems delighted that I know the difference. "Václav Havel," I try. "Velvet Revolution, Frank Zappa?" "Yes, yes, 1989," he says, and I realize we are talking about history.

My project is to teach George English. "How are you today, George?" I say at the start of each shift. "I am good, and how are you today, Barbara?" I learn that he is not paid by Jerry's but by the "agent" who shipped him over—$5 an hour, with the agent getting the dollar or so difference between that and what Jerry's pays dishwashers. I learn also that he shares an apartment with a crowd of other Czech "dishers," as he calls them, and that he cannot sleep until one of them goes off for his shift, leaving a vacant bed. We are having one of our ESL sessions late one afternoon when B.J. catches us at it and orders "Joseph" to take up the rubber mats on the floor near the dishwashing sinks and mop underneath. "I thought your name was George," I say loud enough for B.J. to hear as she strides off back to the counter. Is she embarrassed? Maybe a little, because she greets me back at the counter with "George, Joseph—there are so many of them!" I say nothing, neither nodding nor smiling, and for this I am punished later when I think I am ready to go and she announces that I need to roll fifty more sets of silverware and isn't it time I mixed up a fresh four-gallon batch of blue-cheese dressing? May you grow old in this place, B.J., is the curse I beam out at her when I am finally permitted to leave. May the syrup spills glue your feet to the floor.

45 I make the decision to move closer to Key West. First, because of the drive. Second and third, also because of the drive: gas is eating up $4 to $5 a day, and although Jerry's is as high-volume as you can get, the tips average only 10 percent, and not just for a newbie like me. Between the base pay of $2.15 an hour and the obligation to share tips with the busboys and dishwashers, we're averaging only about $7.50 an hour. Then there is the $30 I had to spend on the regulation tan slacks worn by Jerry's servers—a setback it could take weeks to absorb. (I had combed the town's two downscale department stores hoping for something cheaper but decided in the end that these marked-down Dockers, originally $49, were more likely to survive a daily washing.) Of my fellow servers, everyone who lacks a working husband or boyfriend seems to have a second job: Nita does something at a computer eight hours a day; another welds. Without the forty-five-minute commute, I can picture myself working two jobs and having the time to shower between them.

So I take the $500 deposit I have coming from my landlord, the $400 I have earned toward the next month's rent, plus the $200 reserved for emergencies, and use the $1,100 to pay the rent and deposit on trailer number 46 in the Overseas Trailer Park, a mile from the cluster of budget hotels that constitute Key West's version of an industrial park. Number 46 is about eight feet in width and shaped like a barbell inside, with a narrow region—because of the sink and the stove—separating the bedroom from what might optimistically be called the "living" area, with its two-person table and half-sized couch. The bathroom is so small my knees rub against the shower stall when I sit on the toilet, and you can't just leap out of the bed, you have to climb down to the foot of it in order to find a patch of floor space to stand on. Outside, I am within a few yards of a liquor store, a bar that advertises "free beer tomorrow," a convenience store, and a Burger King—but no supermarket or, alas, laundromat. By reputation, the Overseas park is a nest of crime and crack, and I am hoping at least for some vibrant, multicultural street life. But desolation rules night and day, except for a thin stream of pedestrian traffic heading for their jobs at the Sheraton or 7-Eleven. There are not exactly people here but what amounts to canned labor, being preserved from the heat between shifts.

In line with my reduced living conditions, a new form of ugliness arises at Jerry's. First we are confronted—via an announcement on the computers through which we input orders—with the new rule that the hotel bar is henceforth off-limits to restaurant employees. The culprit, I learn through the grapevine, is the ultra-efficient gal who trained me—another trailer-home dweller and a mother of three. Something had set her off one morning, so she slipped out for a nip and returned to the floor impaired. This mostly hurts Ellen, whose habit it is to free her hair from its rubber band and drop by the bar for a couple of Zins before heading home at the end of the shift, but all of us feel the chill. Then the next day, when I go for straws, for the first time I find the dry-storage room locked. Ted, the portly assistant manager who opens it for me, explains that he caught one of the dishwashers attempting to steal something, and, unfortunately, the miscreant will be with us until a replacement can be found—hence the locked door. I neglect to ask what he had been trying to steal, but Ted tells me who he is—the kid with the buzz cut and the earring. You know, he's back there right now.

I wish I could say I rushed back and confronted George to get his side of the story. I wish I could say I stood up to Ted and insisted that George be given a translator and allowed to defend himself, or announced that I'd find a lawyer who'd handle the case pro bono. The mystery to me is that there's not much worth stealing in the dry-storage room, at least not in any fenceable quantity: "Is Gyorgi here, and am having 200—maybe 250—ketchup packets. What do you say?" My guess is that he had taken—if he had taken anything at all—some Saltines or a can of cherry-pie mix, and that the motive for taking it was hunger.

So why didn't I intervene? Certainly not because I was held back by the kind of moral paralysis that can pass as journalistic objectivity. On the contrary, something new—something loathsome and servile—had infected me, along with the kitchen odors that I could still sniff on my bra when I finally undressed at night. In real life I am moderately brave, but plenty of brave people shed their courage in concentration camps, and maybe something similar goes on in the infinitely more congenial milieu of the low-wage American workplace. Maybe, in a month or two more at Jerry's, I might have regained my crusading spirit. Then again, in a month or two I might have turned into a different person altogether—say, the kind of person who would have turned George in. But this is not something I am slated to find out.

50 I can do this two-job thing, is my theory, if I can drink enough caffeine and avoid getting distracted by George's ever more obvious suffering.[7] The first few days after being caught he seemed not to understand the trouble he was in, and our chirpy little conversations had continued. But the last couple of shifts he's been listless and unshaven, and tonight he looks like the ghost we all know him to be, with dark half-moons hanging from his eyes. At one point, when I am briefly immobilized by the task of filling little paper cups with sour cream for baked potatoes, he comes over and looks as if he'd like to explore the limits of our shared vocabulary, but I am called to the floor for a table. I resolve to give him all my tips that night and to hell with the experiment in low-wage money management. At eight, Ellen and I grab a snack together standing at the mephitic end of the kitchen counter, but I can only manage two or three mozzarella sticks and lunch had been a mere handful of McNuggets. I am not tired at all, I assure myself, though it may be that there is simply no more "I" left to do the tiredness monitoring. What I would see, if I were more alert to the situation, is that the forces of destruction are already massing against me. There is only one cook on duty, a young man named Jesus ("Hay-Sue," that is) and he is new to the job. And there is Joy, who shows up to take over in the middle of the shift, wearing high heels and a long, clingy white dress and fuming as if she'd just been stood up in some cocktail bar.

Then it comes, the perfect storm. Four of my tables fill up at once. Four tables is nothing for me now, but only so long as they are obligingly staggered. As I bev table 27, tables 25, 28, and 24 are watching enviously. As I bev 25, 24 glowers because their bevs haven't even been ordered. Twenty-eight is four yuppyish types, meaning everything on the side and agonizing instructions as to the chicken Caesars. Twenty-five is a middle-aged black couple, who complain, with some justice, that the iced tea isn't fresh and the tabletop is sticky. But table 24 is the meteorological event of the century: ten British tourists who seem to have made the decision to absorb the American experience entirely by mouth. Here everyone has at least two drinks—iced tea and milk shake, Michelob and water (with lemon slice, please)—and a huge promiscuous orgy of breakfast specials, mozz sticks, chicken strips, quesadillas; burgers with cheese and without, sides of hash browns with cheddar, with onions, with gravy, seasoned fries, plain fries, banana splits. Poor Jesus! Poor me! Because when I arrive with their first tray of food—after three prior trips just to refill bevs—Princess Di refuses to eat her chicken strips with her pancake-and-sausage special, since, as she now reveals, the strips were meant to be an appetizer. Maybe the others would have accepted their meals, but Di, who is deep into her third Michelob, insists that everything else go back while they work on their "starters." Meanwhile, the yuppies are waving me down for more decaf and the black couple looks ready to summon the NAACP.

Much of what happened next is lost in the fog of war. Jesus starts going under. The little printer on the counter in front of him is spewing out orders faster than he can rip them off, much less produce the meals. Even the invincible Ellen is ashen from stress. I bring table 24 their reheated main courses, which they immediately reject as either too cold or fossilized by the microwave. When I return to the kitchen with their trays (three trays in three trips), Joy confronts me with arms akimbo: "What is this?" She means the food—the plates of rejected pancakes, hash browns in assorted flavors, toasts, burgers, sausages, eggs. "Uh, scrambled with cheddar," I try, "and that's . . ." "NO," she screams in my face. "Is it a traditional, a super-scramble, an eye-opener?" I pretend to study my check for a clue, but entropy has been up to its tricks, not only on the plates but in my head, and I have to admit that the original order is beyond reconstruction. "You don't know an eye-opener from a traditional?" she demands in outrage. All I know, in fact, is that my legs have lost interest in the current venture and have announced their intention to fold. I am saved by a yuppie (mercifully not one of mine) who chooses this moment to charge into the kitchen to bellow that his food is twenty-five minutes late. Joy screams at him to get the hell out of her kitchen, please, and then turns on Jesus in a fury, hurling an empty tray across the room for emphasis.

I leave. I don't walk out, I just leave. I don't finish my side work or pick up my credit-card tips, if any, at the cash register or, of course, ask Joy's permission to go. And the surprising thing is that you *can* walk out without permission, that the door opens, that the thick tropical night air parts to let me pass, that my car is still parked where I left it. There is no vindication in this exit, no fuck-you surge of relief, just an overwhelming, dank sense of failure pressing down on me and the entire parking lot. I had gone into this venture in the spirit of science, to test a mathematical proposition, but somewhere along the line, in the tunnel vision imposed by long shifts and relentless concentration, it became a test of myself, and clearly I have failed. Not only had I flamed out as a housekeeper/server, I had even forgotten to give George my tips, and, for reasons perhaps best known to hardworking, generous people like Gail and Ellen, this hurts. I don't cry, but I am in a position to realize, for the first time in many years, that the tear ducts are still there, and still capable of doing their job.

WHEN I MOVED out of the trailer park, I gave the key to number 46 to Gail and arranged for my deposit to be transferred to her. She told me that Joan is still living in her van and that Stu had been fired from the Hearthside. I never found out what happened to George.

55 In one month, I had earned approximately $1,040 and spent $517 on food, gas, toiletries, laundry, phone, and utilities. If I had remained in my $500 efficiency, I would have been able to pay the rent and have $22 left over (which is $78 less than the cash I had in my pocket at the start of the month). During this time I bought no clothing except for the required slacks and no prescription drugs or medical care (I did

finally buy some vitamin B to compensate for the lack of vegetables in my diet). Perhaps I could have saved a little on food if I had gotten to a supermarket more often, instead of convenience stores, but it should be noted that I lost almost four pounds in four weeks, on a diet weighted heavily toward burgers and fries.

How former welfare recipients and single mothers will (and do) survive in the low-wage workforce, I cannot imagine. Maybe they will figure out how to condense their lives—including child-raising, laundry, romance, and meals—into the couple of hours between full-time jobs. Maybe they will take up residence in their vehicles, if they have one. All I know is that I couldn't hold two jobs and I couldn't make enough money to live on with one. And I had advantages unthinkable to many of the long-term poor—health, stamina, a working car, and no children to care for and support. Certainly nothing in my experience contradicts the conclusion of Kathryn Edin and Laura Lein, in their recent book *Making Ends Meet: How Single Mothers Survive Welfare and Low-Wage Work,* that low-wage work actually involves more hardship and deprivation than life at the mercy of the welfare state. In the coming months and years, economic conditions for the working poor are bound to worsen, even without the almost inevitable recession. As mentioned earlier, the influx of former welfare recipients into the low-skilled workforce will have a depressing effect on both wages and the number of jobs available. A general economic downturn will only enhance these effects, and the working poor will of course be facing it without the slight, but nonetheless often saving, protection of welfare as a backup.

The thinking behind welfare reform was that even the humblest jobs are morally uplifting and psychologically buoying. In reality they are likely to be fraught with insult and stress. But I did discover one redeeming feature of the most abject low-wage work—the camaraderie of people who are, in almost all cases, far too smart and funny and caring for the work they do and the wages they're paid. The hope, of course, is that someday these people will come to know what they're worth, and take appropriate action.

Notes

1. According to the Department of Housing and Urban Development, the "fair-market rent" for an efficiency is $551 here in Monroe County, Florida. A comparable rent in the five boroughs of New York City is $704; in San Francisco, $713; and in the heart of Silicon Valley, $808. The fair-market rent for an area is defined as the amount that would be needed to pay rent plus utilities for "privately owned, decent, safe, and sanitary rental housing of a modest (non-luxury) nature with suitable amenities."
2. According to the *Monthly Labor Review* (November 1996), 28 percent of work sites surveyed in the service industry conduct drug tests (corporate workplaces have much higher rates), and the incidence of testing has risen markedly since the Eighties. The rate of testing is highest in the South (56 percent of work sites polled), with the Midwest in second place (50 percent). The drug most likely to be detected—marijuana, which can be detected in urine for weeks—is also the most innocuous, while heroin and cocaine are generally undetectable three days after use. Prospective employees sometimes try to cheat the tests by consuming excessive amounts of liquids and taking diuretics and even masking substances available through the Internet.
3. According to the Fair Labor Standards Act, employers are not required to pay "tipped employees," such as restaurant servers, more than $2.13 an hour in direct wages. However, if the sum

of tips plus $2.13 an hour falls below the minimum wage, or $5.15 an hour, the employer is required to make up the difference. This fact was not mentioned by managers or otherwise publicized at either of the restaurants where I worked.

4. I could find no statistics on the number of employed people living in cars or vans, but according to the National Coalition for the Homeless's 1997 report "Myths and Facts About Homelessness," nearly one in five homeless people (in twenty-nine cities across the nation) is employed in a full- or part-time job.

5. In *Workers in a Lean World: Unions in the International Economy* (Verso, 1997), Kim Moody cites studies finding an increase in stress-related workplace injuries and illness between the mid-1980s and the early 1990s. He argues that rising stress levels reflect a new system of "management by stress," in which workers in a variety of industries are being squeezed to extract maximum productivity, to the detriment of their health.

6. Until April 1998, there was no federally mandated right to bathroom breaks. According to Marc Linder and Ingrid Nygaard, authors of *Void Where Prohibited: Rest Breaks and the Right to Urinate on Company Time* (Cornell University Press, 1997), "The right to rest and void at work is not high on the list of social or political causes supported by professional or executive employees, who enjoy personal workplace liberties that millions of factory workers can only daydream about. . . . While we were dismayed to discover that workers lacked an acknowledged legal right to void at work, (the workers) were amazed by outsiders' naive belief that their employers would permit them to perform this basic bodily function when necessary. . . . A factory worker, not allowed a break for six-hour stretches, voided into pads worn inside her uniform; and a kindergarten teacher in a school without aides had to take all twenty children with her to the bathroom and line them up outside the stall door when she voided."

7. In 1996, the number of persons holding two or more jobs averaged 7.8 million, or 6.2 percent of the workforce. It was about the same rate for men and for women (6.1 versus 6.2), though the kinds of jobs differ by gender. About two thirds of multiple jobholders work one job full-time and the other part-time. Only a heroic minority—4 percent of men and 2 percent of women—work two full-time jobs simultaneously. (From John F. Stinson Jr., "New Data on Multiple Jobholding Available from the CPS," in the *Monthly Labor Review,* March 1997.)

Exploring Texts and Contexts

For activities with icons, refer to the Guide to Analyzing Readings in Context.

1. Compare Ehrenreich's vision of work in America with that of other writers in this book, such as Robert Reich, Boyte and Kari, and Robyn Meredith. How might the different contexts and genres of these pieces contribute to the different views they present of the American workplace? 

2. In her article in Chapter 12, Chan Lean Heng argues that consciousness-raising discussions would help Malyasian factory workers cope with the emotional stresses of their jobs. Would Heng's recommendations make a difference for the workers Ehrenreich describes? 

3. In Connecting with the Conversation Activity 3, what did you conclude about Ehrenreich's target audience? Do you think the people she describes in this piece 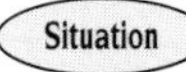

are members of that audience? How do you think audience considerations influenced the way Ehrenreich wrote this piece?

Creating Texts

For assignments with icons, refer to the Guides to Analyzing Contexts for Writing and Analyzing Readings in Context. For additional help with these writing projects, read the descriptions of **Essay** and **Academic Article/Research Paper** in the Genre Glossary.

1. Write an essay in which you describe a good or bad experience you've had in the workplace. Ehrenreich's piece is in many ways like a personal essay, but she makes it clear that it is more than a description of a personal experience; her larger goal is to get people to think about the lives and working conditions of the working poor and in particular the long-term consequences of welfare reform. Ehrenreich hopes that her piece will show people that it's not as easy as policymakers would like us to believe for single mothers with few job skills to support themselves. Think of your essay in terms of the kinds of consequences you would like it to have; what larger point about work, the economy, employers, and employees would you like to make?

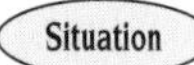

2. Although Ehrenreich's piece is structured primarily like a personal essay, with narrative, dialogue, and description intertwined with commentary, she also includes footnotes with additional facts and information about sources. Choose one of the issues that Ehrenreich raises—for example, the effects of welfare reform on former welfare recipients, homelessness among the working poor, drug testing in the workplace, the rights of workers to breaks and amenities, the numbers of workers working more than one job, or other issues that you identify—and write a short research paper on this topic. You might use Ehrenreich's footnotes as hints to get you started, but you should also use your online and library research skills to find other relevant and up-to-date sources. Discuss with your teacher whether the paper should be a report or a research-based argument. Include a brief note at the end about the new perspective your research adds to Ehrenreich's story and argument.

A Man's Place

Victoria de Grazia, Claudia Goldin, Jacqueline Jones, Juliet B. Schor, Marta Tienda, William Julius Wilson, and moderator Michael Weinstein

This panel discussion which appeared in the *New York Times Magazine,* examines the transformations in women's lives that took place during the course of the twentieth century. In "A Man's Place," experts from a variety of academic fields including economics, sociology, and history assess the changing economic circumstances of women during the last hundred years.

One way of measuring women's economic gains of the last hundred years is by looking at the numbers. In the United States, the proportion of women in the workforce has been increasing steadily since the 1920s; by 2008 women are projected to make up 48 percent of the workforce. Although statistics differ on the issue of wage equity, almost no one disagrees that the wage gap is narrowing and according to some statistics the pay for men and women of equal education and experience is virtually equal.

Yet the workplace that the women's rights movement envisioned is far from a reality. Technological innovation and increased productivity once promised a 20-hour workweek and the possibility of job sharing. However, the fast pace and competition of the global economy have actually increased the number of hours in the workweek for both men and women. Although men are spending more time rearing children and participating in the housework, women still put in twice as many hours caring for the family and doing household chores. In the discussion that follows, the panelists examine present-day work issues and family concerns in light of women's role in the economy.

Connecting with the Conversation

1. Write about the difference in economic circumstances between your mother and her mother. If you are female, write about the way your situation differs from either your mother's or your grandmother's. If you are male, describe any differences you see between male and female economic circumstances in your family.
2. Review several newspapers for articles and editorials on work, women, and the economy. What sorts of issues are being discussed? Discuss your impressions in your class or online.

When the subject is women's economic progress, it's easy to get lost in the controversies of the moment. So the *New York Times Magazine* convened six experts to consider how that progress has played out over a longer stretch of history. They began by examining the transformation in the lives of working women, then looked at the power of women as consumers and finally appraised how well (or poorly) the economy has adapted to women's needs and desires.

The conversation was moderated by Michael Weinstein, an economist who writes the Economic Scene column in the *Times*. The panelists:

Victoria de Grazia, professor of history at Columbia University and author of "The Sex of Things: Gender and Consumption in Historical Perspective."

Claudia Goldin, professor of economics at Harvard University and author of "Understanding the Gender Gap: An Economic History of American Women."

5 *Jacqueline Jones,* Truman professor of history at Brandeis University and author of "American Work: Four Centuries of Black and White Labor."

From the *New York Times Magazine,* May 16, 1999, pp. 48, 64–68, 73–74.

Juliet B. Schor, economics lecturer at Harvard and author of "The Overspent American: Why We Want What We Don't Need."

Marta Tienda, professor of sociology and public affairs at Princeton University and author of "The Hispanic Population of the United States."

William Julius Wilson, Geyser University professor at Harvard and author of "The Bridge Over the Racial Divide: Rising Inequality and Coalition Politics."

A Woman's Place Is in the Workplace

MICHAEL WEINSTEIN: How far have women come over the past century or so? How would the economic circumstances of, say, a 20-year-old woman living in the United States 100 years ago be different from her counterpart's today?

10 CLAUDIA GOLDIN: Typically, she would have spent a lot of time working alongside and learning from her mother. One of the profound changes in the 20th century was the movement of young women from being "at home" to being "at school." I'm referring to the large movement of young women first to high school and then to college. In terms of working outside the home, if you were a young woman in rural America and had gone to school beyond eighth grade, you would probably have become a teacher for a while. In cities, we would find the women described by the Progressives as the pitiable young factory women—those of O. Henry's New York stories—about half of whom worked for piece rates. By the 1920's, young women would be working in retail sales and in offices.

VICTORIA DE GRAZIA: One of the biggest changes in women's lives is their capacity to control their fertility. Efficient contraception was almost unimaginable 100 years ago. The risk of pregnancy, not to mention the hardship of childbearing, enormously determined how women lived.

MARTA TIENDA: There is also the issue of how family arrangements constrained women. Even as recently as 15 or 20 years ago in the Southwest, the idea of women moving out of the parental household and living alone was unacceptable.

GOLDIN: But women did move out of the parental household, and their stories gave rise to the literature of Dreiser and O. Henry. They wrote about the young women who moved off the farm into the boarding houses that filled New York City and Chicago. Carroll Wright, the great early-20th-century labor statistician, studied the young women who lived alone and worked in manufacturing and who, to him, faced an increased risk of becoming prostitutes.

JACQUELINE JONES: One of the dramatic changes in the last 100 years is that most white women—I'm uncomfortable limiting this discussion to white women—today believe, and rightly so, that they'll probably work for wages after marriage.

15 WILLIAM JULIUS WILSON: Let me shift the focus to black women. Noncollege black women had very little chance during the first half of this century to take a job other than as a domestic servant. After 1960, demand increased for clerical and service workers. Black women were able to take those positions, so much so that by 1980, only a small percentage of black women were domestic household servants. But, ironically, just as blacks and Hispanics started to move into those clerical positions, changing

demand began to reduce opportunities as bank tellers, typists and so on. Now, folks who don't have college degrees face a new challenge because the areas that were opening up are starting to close. Yet it's far better than it was.

GOLDIN: Let's talk about occupations 100 years ago. You could hardly find an occupation in which both men and women did the same job. Many industries excluded women, perhaps because they were unionized or because they involved work in dirty and hot places like iron foundries and steel mills, or in disgusting places like slaughterhouses. Being part of the labor force was not considered progress for much of our history. Progress was having enough money to liberate your wife from the dirty, disgusting work of the factory, so she didn't have to be at risk of sexual advances and injury. The aim was not to preserve a patriarchal system but to create a better family life, a kinder life for women.

WEINSTEIN: Victoria, did you want to say more about family structure?

DE GRAZIA: A century ago, the role of women's unpaid household labor in maintaining the family was simply huge. Take into account the primitive equipment. Consider the difficulties of carrying provisions from the market. Think of the time involved in cooking, which meant getting coal or hauling wood. But even with new equipment, there has still been more "work for mother," as standards of hygiene and nutrition and the quality of caring for children have been raised. That suggests the question: has there been real progress or only a change in how women work in the household?

JONES: Can I add a couple of points about changes? One is that 100 years ago, women played very small roles in labor leadership and in fact, there were very few unions composed of women. Today, obviously, women are in the forefront of union organizing because of the shift in the economy and the importance of the service sector in particular. Another point is that 100 years ago, modern jobs went only to whites. The conventional wisdom said African-Americans should not work machines.

20 TIENDA: If you just compare white and minority women between 1960 and the early 1970's, the occupational distribution of black and white women converged. But since 1980, the trend has reversed. Asian women, with their higher college-completion rates, have benefited from the increased demand for skilled labor, but black and Hispanic women have fallen back.

GOLDIN: Many people think that the late 1960's, with the revival of feminism, was also the beginning of women's increase in labor-force participation. That is not the case. Among married women, labor-force participation rates rose 10 percentage points per decade for each 10-year period from 1940 to 1990. So today, the rates are over 70 percent for all women age 25 to 64, and a little over 80 percent for women who have bachelor's degrees, rates that are rapidly approaching those of men.

JULIET SCHOR: That's misleading. You don't want to give people the impression that 100 years ago women weren't working. They were not *officially* in the labor force.

GOLDIN: Let's go beyond labor-force participation rates and look at what has happened to earnings. The mantra in the 60's was 59 cents on the dollar—that was the button many of us wore then, meaning that for every dollar the average man earned, a woman earned 59 cents. It stayed that way through the 1970's. Then, suddenly, it began to zoom so that now, women are earning more like 70 to 75 cents to the male dollar, even 80 to 85 cents when corrected. For young people with college degrees, there's virtual parity. Meanwhile, who's doing the work at home? Here you won't find numbers that make us feel good. In a 1968 survey, husbands claimed to work on average 125 hours a year in housework, not including various child-care tasks. That amounts to a little more than two hours a week. By 1991, husbands claimed to do more than three times that amount—about seven hours a week. But wives in 1968 did nearly 39 hours per week and in 1991 did about 25 hours. In other words, there has been some narrowing, but only some.

The question is: Have women come a long way in the 20th century? The answer is unequivocally yes. They have enormously narrowed the gap in labor-force participation rates and in earnings. Occupational segregation has also decreased and so have hours of housework, enhancing the ability of college-graduate women, for example, to do the ultimate—combine career with family. Of course, there are lots of qualifications. Few women actually achieve both career and family. Women now become doctors at nearly the same rate as men, but they become family physicians, not surgeons.

25 TIENDA: The progress cited by Claudia has been uneven. Labor-force participation of Puerto Ricans has actually declined over a 20-year period. Participation of black women has not kept pace with whites.

GOLDIN: Yet despite the qualifications, women have come a long way. They have gained independence, dignity, respect, greater bargaining power at home, freedom, ability to socialize and have a life apart from family—I think that's extraordinarily important—and of course, the ability to divorce.

Women's Consumption: Might or Myth?

WEINSTEIN: We've been talking exclusively about women at work or home. But how about their role as consumers?

GOLDIN: A role we love.

WEINSTEIN: Is it not true that the more women earn in their own right, the more discretionary income they control, the more the economy will bend toward their needs and tastes? And is consumerism a trap or a route toward further liberation?

30 SCHOR: Much of what women used to do was buy for their family. Mrs. Consumer felt that she, in effect, brought income into the household by saving money through smart purchasing.

DE GRAZIA: The identification of women with consumption has been, as in the 19th century, in part metaphoric. Anything fickle was identified with women, and consumption habits were fickle; therefore, women were consumers. Then, as families' disposable income rose, advertising and other media exaggerated the sexual division of roles: men were producers, women consumers. The image that consumption is natural to women has, rightly, been very much contested by feminists.

JONES: I think all this talk about women as consumers loses sight of the fact that about 14 percent of households are poor. In Boston, the self-sufficiency index for a single head of household and two kids is nearly $40,000 a year, about three times the official poverty level. Yes, she has enough money to buy cosmetics, but not enough to fit the stereotype of women who wield a great deal of economic power. She's buying the necessities for her family.

DE GRAZIA: The question comes down to whether massively increased private consumption gives women choices, whether it empowers women in particular. That would be to say that consumption is a mainly female activity, that the more women consume, the more they make choices, the more power they have to make the economic world go round. This argument has to be unpacked. Consumption means many things. There is social consumption, meaning the significant public expenditure on goods such as Social Security, education, health care and other goods that we need to be effective private consumers. Women have not been able to play a very organized role in shaping the allocations of government budgets on these kinds of consumption. Indeed, with the recent attacks on social programs, one can speak of a lessening of women's role in shaping consumption. As for private consumption, the realm of discretionary spending of women in families is really very small. The media highlight the spending habits of the young, the beautiful and the very rich. The important point is that there is no sign, statistically, that women have significant powers when viewed against this entire range of consumption.

JONES: I find the idea of consumer as an agent of social change to be oxymoronic. The way consumption is practiced in this country is a deeply conservative force. I look at mass advertising, the engine that drives consumption, and the message that comes across is divisive and mean-spirited: You will look young, you will look pretty, you will attract a man, you will outdo your neighbor. These impulses will not lead to radical change, but in fact will keep people stuck in a past that's based on the power of physical appearance and the power of gender.

Detours on the Mommy Track

35 WEINSTEIN: Let's move on to our third question: How has the economic system accommodated women who want to pursue a career as they rear their children?

GOLDIN: By my calculations, less than 20 percent of college-graduate women born between 1944 and 1954 actually achieved both career and family by their early 40's.

SCHOR: We are at an unusual moment in history, in which the idea of a nonpatriarchal society—the idea of equality—has made tremendous inroads. The idea that men and women should have egalitarian marriages and share parenting and housework is a vast departure. That we are asking these questions indicates a tremendous revolution in the last 30 years.

WEINSTEIN: Are there groups that the revolution has skipped?

TIENDA: Many immigrant groups. The Latino and Asian populations are two of the most traditional groups, where the women's movement still lags behind.

40 JONES: Here's a good example of the unevenness of development. Take an upper-middle-class suburban couple, where both the husband and wife have high levels of education. We find these women worked when they first got their degrees, and when the kids started to come, they decided to stay home. The husband becomes the sole breadwinner. She's taking care of the house and the kids and she's dependent on him for the money to run the household, and I think with that economic dependence comes the real vulnerability. The household might be at the vanguard in socioeconomic status, but I think in certain respects, it's very traditional.

WEINSTEIN: Is there a barrier society needs to dismantle, or are these decisions worked out well within the family?

SCHOR: The major barrier is the structure of jobs. We have not been able to make good jobs compatible with child-rearing roles. The labor market is inflexible.

TIENDA: Because we rely on other women to take care of our children, two women can enter the labor force for every one that takes on a new job. When women go to work, we buy child-care services, more takeout food and other services, all of which are driving economic growth in a profound way. It also means that we are fueling stratification. But there are real costs, studied by psychologists, to children who have limited exposure to their parents.

WILSON: You know, Marta, I was thinking not only about the cost to children along the lines you're pointing out, but when you look at the low-income families we are now pushing into labor markets, there's no basic support. Employers are just waiting to fire them if they don't show up for work consistently on time. We don't realize how difficult it is for mothers who do not have basic child-care support. When their child gets sick and the mother stays at home to care for the child, the next thing you know, her job is in jeopardy. This increases stress on the mothers, threatening their interaction with their kids.

45 DE GRAZIA: Either our criteria for judging progress are too narrow or we are too focused on our own culture. If the convergence of male/female labor-participation rates is the standard, then we would have to recognize the achievement in the former Soviet bloc, where women were medical doctors and engineers, not to mention tractor drivers. Juliet has written amply on the lack of leisure in the U.S. If leisure is regarded as a kind of restoration, of community life and family life, rather than the opportunity to work or spend more, then we would have to look at European social-democratic experiences as models. What does it mean to society when child care is inadequate, as it is in ours? Insofar as we have decent services, they are privatized and discriminate against women in lower income classes.

WEINSTEIN: Roll the tape forward 20 to 40 years. Can you imagine these gender differences disappearing?

JONES: You start in the home where things have not changed that much. There is still "women's work." And until that whole notion disappears, until child care and the drudge work are shared equally by men, all else is secondary. What happens in the home conditions what women do in the workplace and the constraints they face. We're not sitting around talking about whether *men* can combine work and family.

GOLDIN: The playing field is most unlevel inside the home. Let me throw this back another generation. It's the young son who should be taught to wash the dishes and to make his bed and his sister's bed. He needs to be taught to work in the home and to treat that work as respectful, dignified and communal. Until that's done, we will continue to reproduce generations of good men and women who attempt to go on the same path as equals in the labor market, yet who diverge when they enter the front door.

WILSON: It seems to me that we should try to talk about generating ongoing national dialogues. This should become a major public issue that would be discussed in the media, taken up by the President and other leaders. That way we can increase our consciousness as well as our conscience about these things. If we just lay back and hope some evolutionary process will work itself out, we could be in the 22nd century before significant changes take place.

50 DE GRAZIA: I am skeptical that single families have the power to socialize their offspring to do away with gender inequality in the home, much less the workplace. Too many social trends undermine them.

SCHOR: A big part of women's problem is they entered a male economy, a male work culture, an economy structured to meet the situations of men. Until the workplace changes to accommodate the fact that we are now a society in which men and women participate full time, we will not achieve the goal of equality.

WILSON: I fight pessimism all the time. But I'm going to be a little bit optimistic here. I have in mind a coalition: whites, African-Americans, Hispanics, Asians, Native Americans who will start to demand a serious national debate on the need for social and family supports to mute or cushion the effects of economic changes. We're beginning to see some of that already with increasing talk of child care. And there's research to suggest that if you can reduce child-care costs, it can increase women's labor-force participation, improve the types of jobs they could get and could ultimately result in a reduction in gender inequality. So I'm going to put on my optimistic hat and say I think that the eventual development of this progressive coalition will have many positive effects, including reduction of gender inequality.

Exploring Texts and Contexts

For activities with icons, refer to the Guides to Analyzing Contexts for Writing and Analyzing Readings in Context.

1. The panel brings together people who have a variety of perspectives on women's issues. What is the moderator's role in a panel discussion? Chart the interactions the moderator has with members of the panel. Does the moderator shape and influence the discussion? From the comments made by the moderator, what can you infer about his ideas and beliefs? Explain. Genre
2. On page 522 William Julius Wilson calls for a national dialogue to address work and family issues. How does his idea of change differ from that of fellow panel member Claudia Goldin? According to each, what change is needed and how will it be effected?
3. This piece is a transcript of a face-to-face conversation. Does it sound like a conversation? What might the editors have changed to prepare it for publication? Language

Creating Texts

For activities with icons, refer to the Guides to Analyzing Contexts for Writing and Analyzing Readings in Context. For additional help with these writing projects, read the descriptions of **Dialogue/Symposium** and **Academic Article/Research Paper** in the Genre Glossary.

1. This panel discussion ranges over several topics, the changing economic circumstances of women, the power of women as consumers, and how well the economy meets the needs and desires of women. What areas could you add to the discussion? Drawing on both your own experience and the ideas you developed Situation

from working with the texts in this unit, choose another issue to add to the discussion. What do you think each panelist would say about this issue? Create a dialogue in which each panelist contributes at least once to the conversation. Create a part for yourself or make yourself the moderator.

2. Panel member de Grazia suggests we might learn something about solving the economic problems facing women and families today by finding out what other countries and societies are doing to support their families. Choose one of the issues raised in the discussion, for example child-care services, the structure of jobs, the lack of leisure time, or another issue, and write a short research paper on how another country or culture approaches that problem. Investigate online as well as print sources, making sure your research is up-to-date. In your paper explore how American society might be affected by seeing the issue from another perspective.

CHAPTER 14

CASE STUDY

Advocating for Temporary Workers

The Case

Temporary workers are the fastest-growing segment of our labor force. In fact, many believe that the growth of temporary, or contingent, labor is changing the nature of work. Our traditional notion of work means one employer for a number of years; benefits such as health insurance, contributions to a retirement fund, paid vacations, and sick days; and gradually moving up through the ranks of the company. But companies are increasingly reluctant to hire permanent employees, which means paying benefits and risking having to pay unemployment. Increasingly, workers are employed by companies such as Manpower, Inc., or Kelly Services, who act as intermediaries, supplying temporary help to corporations.

Temporary-help companies argue that they provide a service not only to businesses but also to workers who may not want or need permanent, full-time jobs. In fact, these companies often claim to be offering part-time workers the ability to lead what they call a flexible lifestyle. But temporary workers often do not see the situation this way, experiencing flexibility as uncertainty and instability. Karen Ford, featured in a news article included in this case study, fills in the details of a temporary worker's life—no sick leave, no personal days, and no retirement benefits. If workers complain or attempt to join an organization to fight for their rights, they are often fired. Recently, however, law suits and advocacy groups have called attention to the plight of the temporary worker and the unfair labor practices that surround them.

The Issues

Manpower, Inc., is the largest provide of "staffing services" in the United States. What they call staffing services is, to others, called "contingent labor," a term that has been used increasingly to describe workers and their relationship to their employers. This term can cover a variety of tenuous employer–employee relationships such as temporary-help agency workers, who are paid by a temporary-help company; independent contractors, who are freelance workers, whether self-employed or salaried; and on-call workers who are called to

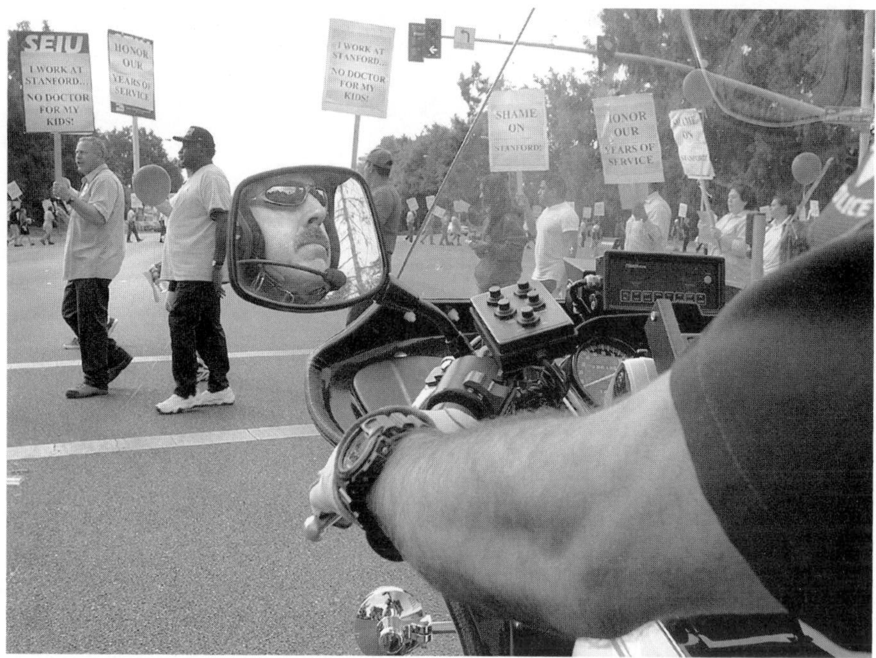

work as needed. According to the Bureau of Labor Statistics, contingent work is frequently characterized by lower pay and few benefits. Some analysts claim that the contingent work force accounts for 25 percent of the total workforce and compare this workforce to a "just in time" inventory—workers are employed only when they are needed.

Many see this rapid growth in contingent labor as a direct consequence of global competition, which instigated corporate restructuring. In the mid-seventies after steady growth in corporate income and profits, corporations experienced unprecedented international competition. By the mid-1980s families were spending large amounts of their disposable cash on imported goods, and corporations were struggling to resuscitate their shrinking profits. Corporations began a process of restructuring by firing workers to cut costs, a response that came to be known as *downsizing.* Even after the economy recovered, workers who were fired were not rehired as permanent workers. One manager of a temporary-help company explained in an interview why employers continue to hire temporary workers: "They [Employers] can keep their costs, especially fringe costs, down with the use of temps. In short, the major reason for growth has to do with maintaining a lean payroll . . . to avoid overstaffing."[1] Even in a robust economy, employers are anxious about the possibility of another economic downturn that may leave them responsible for the salaries of more employees than the company can support.

---

[1]Robert E. Parker. *Flesh Peddlers and Warm Bodies: The Temporary Help Industry and Its Workers.* New Brunswick, N.J.: Rutgers University Press, 1994.

Characteristics of Temporary and Permanent Workers in 1993[a]

	Temp Workers	Perm Workers
Average age	35.6	37.7
Male	39%	52%
White	77%	85%
Less than high school	10%	14%
High school graduate	35%	34%
Started college	35%	28%
College graduate or more	20%	24%
Married, spouse present	41%	58%
Voluntarily part-time	14%	14%
Part-time for economic reasons	20%	5%
Average usual hours per week	34.6	38.5
Average # of weeks unemployed in previous year[b]	4.8	1.4
Average # of weeks out of labor force in the previous year[b]	9.9	2.9
Average hourly wage rate	$8.47	$11.70
Private health insurance[b]	57%	79%

Source: Lewis Segal and Daniel Sullivan. *The Growth of Temporary Services Work.* Working Paper Serices (WP-96-26) Chicago: Federal Reserve Bank of Chicago, 1996.

[a]1993 outgoing rotations of the Current Population Survey unless otherwise noted.

[b]March Current Population Survey's pooled from 1989 to 1993.

The temporary segment of the contingent labor pool continues to grow rapidly. In each of the last few years, the growth in workers supplied by the temporary-services industry was about the same as the total work force of some of the largest employers in the United States—AT&T, Ford, and General Electric.The table on the following page compares key characteristics of temporary workers (those paid hourly) with those of permanent workers. Temporary workers differ sharply from permanent workers in several ways: Most are women (61 percent); one-quarter of all temporary workers are minorities compared with only 15 percent of permanent workers; fewer are married and living with their spouse; temporaries work fewer hours per week and were off the job for longer periods during the previous year; temporary workers earned less per hour; and fewer have health insurance.

While it is true that more women than men are temporary workers, the table does not support the industry's claim that it is providing a gateway for housewives, students, and highly independent individuals to enter the labor force in a flexible and creative way. On the one hand, 35 percent of temporary workers have started college, suggesting that they may be using temporary work to help pay for college expenses. But, because temporary and permanent workers have achieved about the same educational level, we know that their education is not holding them back from greater job security. Only 14 percent are voluntarily part-time, suggesting that they have not chosen this work because of a need for flexibility. The data also suggest that the 20 percent who take on temporary work for economic reasons do so because they must work and cannot find full-time employment. Other data from the Bureau of Labor Statistics indicate that 57 percent of temporary workers would prefer a traditional work relationship with an employer.[2]

In the 1960s, Kelly Services, then called "Kelly Girl," focused on attracting suburban housewives to the world of work. Today, however, we can no longer assume that the temporary workforce is made up of married women with young children who are supplementing a male breadwinner's salary. In 1975 a male breadwinner headed 44 percent of all families with children compared to 20 percent in 1994. In a recent analysis two economists who look closely at the policy implications of the growth of contingent labor argue that, although temporary work might once have been supplemental income, female single parents who now take up temporary work often rely on welfare benefits to supplement the low wages obtained from contingent work.[3] As welfare reform continues, moving people increasingly into low-paying, part-time work, temporary workers are less likely to be able to support themselves and their families. This shift from temporary work used to supplement a male breadwinner's income to work used to supplement welfare income signals what has come to be called a restructuring of labor.

The increasing use of contingent labor is found in universities as well as in corporate settings and in particular in first-year writing classes. The *Chronicle of Higher Education* reported that the use of part-time faculty has nearly doubled since 1970. In 1997 about 31 percent of the faculty was employed part-time at four-year colleges and universities, but about 66 percent of the faculty at state two-year colleges were employed part-time. Discussions about this trend follow the larger discussion about contingent labor. Some say this excessive reliance on part-time faculty is in response to larger numbers of students, but Richard Moser, of the American Association of University Professors, likens the trend to a "corporatization of higher education" in which economic concerns override academic ones. He reminds us, too, that the only way to protect workers' rights is through unionization.[4] Universities, like corporations, struggle with difficult decisions about how to balance their many commitments to their employees as well as to students.

During the era of corporate restructuring, one of the key tactics used to cut the cost of labor was what businesses referred to as "union avoidance" or, as others called it, "zapping

---

[2]Labor Force Statistics for the Current Population Survey. *Employed Workers with Alternative Work Arrangements by Their Preference for a Traditional Work Arrangement,* February 1999. http://www.bls.gov/news.release/conemp.t11.htm. (April 24, 2000).

[3]Roberta Spalter-Roth and Heidi Hartmann. "Gauging the Consequences for Gender Relations, Pay Equity, and the Public Purse." In Kathleen Barker and Kathleen Christensen, *Contingent Work: American Employment Relations in Transition.* Ithaca, N.Y.: Cornell University Press, 1998, p. 71, 94–95.

[4]Courtney Leatherman. "Part-Timers Continue to Replace Full-Timers on College Faculties." *Chronicle of Higher Education,* January 28, 2000.

labor."[5] Currently, because temporary workers are hired by a third-party agency and can be easily fired and because of the multiemployer doctrine of the National Labor Relations Board (which considers as a bargaining unit all the temporary workers at a company), they find it hard to organize to advocate for their own rights. The recent emergence of advocacy groups, lawsuits on behalf of temporary workers, and federal legislation is responding to the rapid growth of temporary workers. Two national organizations have recently launched web sites that will help you follow these issues and gather more information. The National Alliance for Fair Employment (www.fairjobs.org) brings together organizations concerned with a wide range of nonstandard work situations. Another organization, The 2030 Center (www.2030.org), is a public-policy organization that advocates for the economic interests of young workers, those between 20 and 30 years old, but it also refers to the year 2030, for its significance in the economic future of today's younger generations.

The Documents

- **Merrill Goozner,** in his front-page article from the *Chicago Tribune,* **"Longtime Temps Want Some Perks,"** reports on the situation of "permatemps," temp workers who have been with a company for over six months. Who is this worker's employer—the temporary agency or the firm where she works temporarily? Recently lawyers have argued on behalf of permatemps that even though the workers may find their jobs through a temporary agency, the firm where they work is, in fact, a "common-law" employer. This front-page news article explains the complex relationship between employer and employee. Consider how Goozner creates a context by including a variety of types of information. Examine whom he quotes and where he gets his statistics. Consider also who his audience is and how he is attempting to convince them of his perspective.
- Lawsuits are one way to help redefine employer-employee relationships, but they often take a long time to be resolved while workers need immediate help with what has become a dire situation for many. In **"A Leg Up for the Lowly Temp"** by **Aaron Bernstein,** which appeared in *Business Week,* Bernstein reports that a number of advocacy support services have recently emerged in response to growing concern about the fate of temporary workers. Amy Dean, working with the AFL-CIO, formed a support group to help get health-care benefits for members, and she has also started a temporary agency that provides training and benefits. Another group, the Temp Workers Alliance, focuses on getting temporary agencies to agree to a code of conduct.
- **"The Temp Workers Alliance's Consumer Guide to 'Best Practices' Temp Agencies,"** written and published by **Barry Peterson** and the **Temp Workers Alliance,** has received much notice in the media for the immediate and practical support it provides for temp workers. It includes a variety of documents. The **mission statement,**

---

[5] Bennett Harrison and Barry Bluestone. *The Great U-Turn: Corporate Restructuring and the Polarizing of America.* New York: Basic Books, 1988, 1990, p. 51.

Purpose of Temp Task Force, explains the support group's goals. A reader who is considering temp work will want to read the **guidelines,** Considering the Temp Option. A **list** called "Ethics for Temporary Workers" enumerates the temp worker's responsibilities. The guide also provides a **summary** of the state and federal laws relevant to temp workers. A **survey** allows temp workers to report on their experiences. One of the most important documents included in this guide is aimed at the temp agency; the Principles of Fair Conduct for Temporary Employment Agencies provides a **code of conduct** that asks agencies to grade themselves and agree to accept a common set of fair practices. Notice how each section of the guide serves a different purpose and is shaped in the genre that best suits that purpose.

- **Brian Hassett's "The Temp Survival Guide: How to Prosper as an Economic Nomad of the Nineties"** boldly proclaims on the back cover that the author hasn't had a real job in 15 years. The upbeat, unfailingly positive tone is characteristic of the advice book genre. One sharp difference between this guide—we include the first chapter—and Peterson's consumer guide described earlier is the underlying assumption that you, as an individual, hold the key to your own success. Compare how these two guides present very different perspectives or contexts for understanding the temp worker's position. How would you evaluate the message that each offers to readers, and how does the genre support that message?
- If you have something to say, one way to make yourself seen and heard is by creating a Web-based 'zine.[6] That's what **Jeff Kelly** did under the pen name of "Keffo" when, in the mid-nineties, he began a **'zine** called *Temp Slave!* Kelly wanted to respond vociferously to his own situation and offer support to others who found themselves, often suddenly, members of the "disposable workforce." The new genre, the Web-based 'zine, which evolved in response to new technology as well as unmet needs, offered Kelly and others an opportunity to articulate their fight against the isolation, anomie, and ignominy that temp workers experience. In 1997 Kelly published a compilation of stories and cartoons in ***The Best of Temp Slave!*** How do these stories and cartoons add to our growing understanding of temporary workers?

YOUR ROLE

You may have held temporary positions or know someone who works as a temp. This case study focuses on how advocacy groups have sprung up to defend the rights of temporary workers. We ask you to consider your position on this issue. It is one that may affect you personally but that has also generated local and national conversation. It is also the subject of much academic research. The value of creating a case study including documents that vary by all of the key elements in this book–situation, genre, language, and consequences–is that you can see what a difference writing makes in shaping the issue, and thus in improving the situation temporary workers find them-

[6]For a rich compilation of recent Web-based 'zines, see http://www.zinebook.com. This source offers search capabilities, advice on starting 'zines, interviews, comics, and reviews of notable 'zines.

selves in. In the following activities, we ask you to enter the conversation. The first activity asks you to role-play an activist response to the issues of the case study. The material you develop could indeed be used, should you become involved in this issue. The second activity asks you to reflect on the experience of being a temp worker. In both assignments we ask you to take your place in this important ongoing conversation.

1. You're working as a temp—perhaps as an office assistant—while you are in school. You are particularly concerned because although this sort of part-time, temporary job suits you well, you notice that many others at your workplace are out of school and cannot find full-time jobs in their area of expertise. You see a flier on the table in the employees' lunch area that invites you to come to a meeting for a newly forming advocacy group for temporary employees. At the meeting, the organizer asks for volunteers for various aspects of their effort. You are already a member of a student organization that focuses on future employment opportunities in your field, (for example, Future Electrical Engineers, or Teachers, or Lawyers, etc.). You decide to write a speech in which you inform other college students of your perspective on temporary work and the way it may affect you and others who plan to obtain a full-time job after completing school. (See **Address/Speech** in the Genre Glossary.)
2. Use the documents in the case study as well as your own experiences to write a personal essay describing the experience of being a temp worker. If you have worked part-time, you might rely on your own experience, or you may want to interview others. If you have an interest in part-time work, you could apply to several temporary agencies and take the series of tests they use to evaluate skills. Talk to them about your possibilities for part- and full-time employment. Consider focusing on a particular industry or a particular group of workers. Consider, too, as you write, how the situation and genre of the materials in this case study contribute to the way the temporary worker is portrayed. (See **Essay** in the Genre Glossary.)

Longtime Temps Want Some Perks
Now Some Are Suing Companies for Benefits

Merrill Goozner

Washington Bureau

WASHINGTON—This week, Karen Ford celebrates her sixth anniversary as an almost-IBM employee.

Though the receptionist works a 40-hour week at the computer giant's office tower in downtown Chicago, the company does not pay for her health insurance and provides no retirement benefits.

She gets no sick days or personal days and does not get paid for holidays such as the day after Thanksgiving or Christmas like the other IBM employees, although she does have a limited benefits package through her temporary agency.

During IBM's celebration of "Bring Your Child to Work" day, the 42-year-old Ford was allowed to bring in her son, but he couldn't participate in the special activities set up for the children of regular IBM employees. He had to remain at her workstation all day.

"It was just mean," she said.

There are dozens of workers like Ford at IBM who receive their paychecks from Manpower Inc., the nation's largest temporary agency. Like Ford, many have been there for years.

"We utilize contract talent in a wide variety of fields and typically for a specific period of time," said Peter McLaughlin, a spokesman for IBM.

Corporate managers and academic researchers have developed several names for such workers: non-core staff, the flexible workforce, contingent employees. But to a growing number of temporary workers, their deflated status has a less flattering title: permatemps.

Now, the permatemps are rebelling. A growing number are filing suits to get benefits from their semipermanent employers. A major ruling against Microsoft last month may trigger a rush to the courthouse, although some previous rulings have gone against temporary workers.

Even the government is taking notice. Last October, in what could turn into a major test of employee rights, the Labor Department filed suit against media giant Time Warner Inc. for denying benefits to its temporary employees. And, on Capitol Hill, Rep. Lane Evans (D-Ill.) is readying legislation that would give comparable benefits to workers who have been at a firm for six months, no matter who writes their paycheck.

"Contingent work has gone too far," said Barry Peterson, a career counselor who has set up a monthly support group for temporary workers in Bergen County, N.J. "It sets up two classes or workers where one group can't get into the core workforce with benefits, training and upward mobility. That's not in the best long-term interests of either employee or the business . . . which loses skills and institutional memory."

According to a recent Labor Department survey, more than half of the nation's 1.3 million workers employed by temporary help agencies in 1997 had been on their current job assignments for more than six months.

Nearly a quarter of all temps had been at their current place of employment for more than a year. Temporary employment has grown by 10 percent since 1995, or more than three times faster than the growth in traditional employment.

Once limited to office help and construction day labor,

(continued)

From the *Chicago Tribune*, June 22, 1999, pp. 1 and 14.

Many temporary positions not so short-lived

Temporary work is one of the nation's fastest-growing job categories. Although a 1997 Labor Department survey revealed that over half of the country's temporary employees had been on their job more than six months, most did not receive the benefits permanent employees did.

Number of temporary-worker registrations
These numbers are higher than the total number of temporary workers because many workers register with more than one temporary agency.

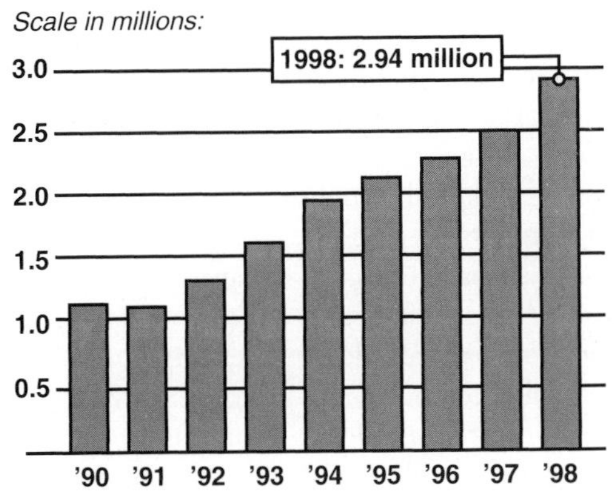

Sources: National Association of Temporary and Staffing Services, Monthly Labor Review, *Chicago Tribune.*

Tenure
Time in current job for 1.3 million temporary workers:

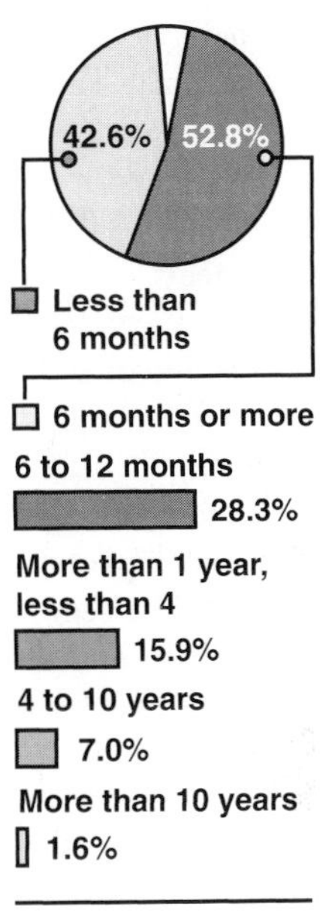

Tenure unavailable 4.6%

temporary staffing now exists in virtually every industry. The practice has become especially common in education, entertainment and publishing, and among computer software firms. Among occupations, postsecondary teachers, administrative support workers and receptionists have the highest levels of contingency.

For employers, the benefits are immediate and fall directly to the bottom line. Temporary workers are brought in when workloads are high and let go when they are not. For many firms like IBM, it is a way to replace permanent workers who have a full range of benefits, with similarly skilled workers who have a much less generous package.

Because they do not have to pay the large administrative and benefits costs of hiring full-time workers, they can pay the temporary help agency a substantial premium over the hourly wage to procure the necessary workers.

Despite the booming economy and widespread fears of labor shortages, growth at temporary staffing agencies shows no sign of letting up. The 1,600 firms belonging to the National Association of Temporary & Staffing Services added 300,000 workers to their rolls last year, bringing total daily registration to 2.9 million (higher than the Labor Department figure because many such temporary workers register with more than one agency). Industry revenue grew 16.7 percent over 1997, to $58.7 billion, with clerical and

(continued)

industrial workers accounting for three-quarters of the total, according to the association.

"Most companies cite meeting peak work demands as the most important reason for using temporary help services" said association spokesman Tim Brogan. "And the workers enjoy the flexibility of choosing among a variety of diverse and challenging assignments."

Surveys of temporary workers tell a less sanguine story. Only 45 percent of the temporary workers surveyed had health insurance, and that was almost always because a spouse had coverage. Just 2.5 percent reported any form of retirement plan. Some temporary agencies do offer access to limited benefits packages for workers who remain with the agency for a limited period of time.

And as far as attitudes were concerned, the Labor Department survey found that 35 percent of temporary workers complained that temporary work was all they could find; another 18 percent hoped their temporary job would lead to full-time employment with the firm where they had been placed. "It's problematic when people really need the benefits and don't have a spouse to fall back on," said Harry Holzer, chief economist at the Labor Department.

The agency's Advisory Council on Employee Welfare and Pension Benefits Plans recently launched a study of how contingent work affects employee benefits, and plans on issuing recommendations later this year.

Among major firms, Microsoft Inc. has faced the longest-running battle with its army of temporary workers. A group of Microsoft's longtime temps filed suit in 1992 because they did not receive the same benefits as regular employees. The software giant employs an estimated 10,000 software testers, Web designers, graphic artists and technical writers through temporary agencies. Many of them have been employed at Microsoft for years.

"Microsoft pays top dollar to people with computer programming and software development skills," said David West, an attorney who helped file the original suit and now runs the Center for a Changing Workforce in Redmond, Wash. "But people without a computer science background, who are in essence people with liberal arts backgrounds, are treated like second-class citizens."

Last month, a panel of the 9th Circuit Court of Appeals in San Francisco ruled that Microsoft's permatemps were in fact common-law employees of Microsoft and not employees of the temporary agency that cut their paychecks. That would make them eligible for all regular Microsoft benefits. Microsoft immediately appealed the ruling.

Earlier this month, hospital workers in California's Santa Clara County sued the county government for denying them benefits. Nearly a thousand of 3,500 orderlies, nurses aides and rehabilitation counselors at Valley Medical Center have been classified as temporary, even though many of them have been employed by the hospital for years.

Not all court cases are going temporary workers' way. The 10th Circuit in Kansas City ruled last year that newspaper carriers for the Kansas City Star were not eligible for benefits because they had signed waivers when they became independent contractors for the newspaper. The court ruled the waiver foreclosed their right to equal treatment on benefits even if they proved their common-law employee status.

In the Time Warner case, the Labor Department sued on behalf of "hundreds of employees" denied benefits because they were either independent contractors or hired through a temporary agency. "The test under ERISA [the Employment Retirement Income Security Act of 1974] is, who is the common-law employer?" said Sherman Kaplan, deputy solicitor at the department. "If

(continued)

the client of the leasing company is calling all the shots, then they are the employer under ERISA." Time Warner is contesting the suit.

Rep. Evans plans to introduce a "protection for temporaries in the workplace" bill in Congress in the next several weeks. The bill would define a common-law employee of a firm as any worker who puts in 1,000 hours per year (about six months) at that place of employment, even if a temporary help agency actually writes the paycheck. The legislation would also prohibit discrimination against common-law employees in benefit plans.

"We're asking for equal coverage for these workers, that they be treated in a fair manner, which is not occurring at this point," Evans said. He first became interested in the issue several years ago when part-time workers at Rock Island Arsenal complained about not receiving the same benefits as full-time employees.

The industry is already gearing up to fight the bill. "This would be a major change in the voluntary structure of U.S. benefits policy," said Edward Lenz, general counsel for the National Association of Temporary & Staffing Services. "It is in effect a mandated benefit."

A Leg Up for the Lowly Temp

Advocates are Lobbying for Better Benefits and an Employers' Code of Conduct

Aaron Bernstein

You'll get an earful if you ask Thomas Sullivan what it's like to be a temp. Two people working side by side at exactly the same job may get different paychecks if they were hired by separate temp agencies, says the Quincy (Mass.) resident, who usually temps in telephone-call centers. One agency made it clear, he says, that a client company didn't want him because he's too old (Sullivan is in his mid-40s). When another agency tried to prevent him from collecting unemployment benefits by saying he had quit a job when, in fact, he had been laid off, Sullivan got legal help from the Campaign on Contingent Work, a Boston advocacy group. "As a temp, you have no security or rights," says Sullivan. "They can dump you for anything, and they don't even need a reason."

In recent years, more than a dozen advocacy groups have sprung up around the country to help people such as Sullivan. They point out that the 8 million-plus employees who move in and out of temp work every year get paid less than full-timers, lack health care and other benefits, and often fall through the cracks in labor and employment law.

Good Timing. The groups are experimenting with various approaches. Some offer legal aid and job counseling. Others are lobbying cities and states to pass laws that would help temps with everything from benefits coverage to unemployment insurance, which in many states excludes temps. A San Jose (Calif.) group even started a nonprofit temp agency that plans to forgo profits to subsidize job training and health care for members.

Now, these groups aim to tackle the issue nationwide. In March, several dozen leaders formed a loose coalition that plans to push for federal and state laws to help such "nonstandard" workers, who do everything from clerical work to light manufacturing. Their effort may be well-timed, with today's tight labor markets giving contingent workers more leverage.

The group also is planning a campaign later this year for a code of conduct for the temp industry. It will follow a code adopted in 1997 by the Temp Workers Alliance in northern New Jersey. The idea is similar to codes drawn up in the apparel industry to deal with sweatshops. Essentially, advocacy groups hope to pressure the industry to police itself by agreeing to a common set of principles. "We're trying to create new models for the next generation of employee organizations to represent temps and other contingent workers," says Amy Dean, head of the San Jose arm of the AFLCIO, which started the nonprofit temp agency.

The move isn't likely to sit well with the temp industry, which has resisted the New Jersey effort. "We don't feel that as an industry we need to have a government or any other entity acting as a watchdog," says Edward A. Lenz, general counsel of the National Association of Temporary & Staffing Services (NATSS), an industry trade group.

The groups have been moved to action by phenomenal growth. Nearly 3 million workers hold temp jobs on a given day, double the number in the early 1990s, according

(continued)

From *Business Week,* June 21, 1999, pp. 102–103.

to the NATSS. But turnover is more than 400% a year, largely because three-quarters of temps find permanent posts. As a result, some 8.5 million workers, more than 6% of the workforce, spent at least part of 1998 temping, the NATSS estimates.

While many temps like the flexibility temping offers, they earn only $329 a week on average, 35% less than regular workers, according to the Bureau of Labor Statistics. Only 7% of temps get health-care insurance from their employer, and just 4% get a pension.

Temp groups claim that abusive and even illegal working conditions are widespread. No hard data exist, but NATSS officials concede that abuses occur. They argue that most are committed by small agencies, not such giants as Manpower Inc. or Olsten Staffing Services.

One of the few surveys found big complaints from temps. In 1994, a South Carolina community group called the Carolina Alliance for Fair Employment (CAFE) paid some two dozen temps for a week to detail problems they had encountered. They said that agencies tell temps to take jobs they're not trained for and don't provide that training. Agencies also don't give written notice of what the wage will be, put temps in unsafe working conditions, and often place them based on race, age, or sex. The group tried to implement a code of conduct based on the findings but gave up after agencies refused to comply, says Charles Taylor, CAFE's head.

The New Jersey Temp Workers Alliance picked up CAFE's code idea and gave it a consumer-oriented approach. It drew up 24 "Principles of Fair Conduct" and invited all 500 temp agencies in the state to sign in 1997. The NATSS mounted vigorous opposition. "Their credibility is suspect to us because they operate under the auspices of the AFL-CIO," says the NATSS' Lenz. Barrie A. Peterson, an Alliance founder, says the local AFL-CIO, the United Way, and Republican-dominated Bergen County all contribute to his group's budget.

Still, 32 New Jersey agencies have endorsed the Alliance's principles so far. The group publishes a *Consumer Reports*-style review that lists agencies using "best practices." "I agreed because it sounded like they're trying to keep the industry legitimate," says Alan Baker, owner of Horizon Personnel Inc., a small agency in Parsippany, N.J.

The San Jose group decided to go even further and create a model agency. It's part of an ambitious three-year project by the San Jose AFL-CIO to help temps and other contingent workers. The AFL-CIO's Dean, director of the project, has raised $1 million from private foundations. She formed a temp group called Together@Work, which began accepting dues-paying members in January.

Dean also started the non-profit agency called Solutions@Work to help temps find good jobs.

Focusing on low-wage clerical jobs in Silicon Valley, the agency has placed a dozen temps since it opened early this year. It formed a link with a local community college, where it offers members free classes in computer skills and word processing. One temp, Mireya Soltero, spent seven months getting training and finishing a high school equivalency diploma. That helped her qualify for a data-entry job at M&M Home Medical Co., a private company in Sunnyvale, Calif. "I asked my boss for a permanent job, and [now] he's looking for something for me," says Soltero, who started in late April.

Premium Price. M&M was willing to pay Soltero $10 an hour, more than what other

(continued)

local agencies charge, because of her prior training. "We've hired two temps from them, and they'll be our first choice, because other agencies don't bring us the caliber of people we need," says Bob Burnett, M&M's operations director.

Solutions@Work also is negotiating with health-care providers for a group rate, says Dean. Eventually, if the agency grows fast enough, it hopes to tap the markup other agencies take as profit and return it to members so they can buy coverage.

Of all the ranks of temps, says the NATSS, about one-third choose temp jobs for the flexibility. The rest, however, say they want a permanent job. Advocacy groups may not achieve that goal. But today's booming economy is giving temps and their defenders a window of opportunity for making their concerns something more than just a temporary concern.

CONSUMER GUIDE

to "BEST PRACTICES" Temp Agencies

Volume 8 ✧ OCTOBER 2000

Newly expanded—aided by Central Jersey Job Developers Association and Cape May–Atlantic Legal Services—to cover all of New Jersey

IN THIS ISSUE

Purpose/Temp Workers Alliance	> 1
Considering the Temp Option	> 2
Stats on Temp Career Charts	(Inserts)
"Best Practices" Agencies	>3–8
177 Reports on 82 other Agencies	>9
Tips for Handling Problems	>10
"Share Your Experiences" (report forms)	>11
Temp Workers: *Know the Law*	>12–15
Ethics for Temporary Workers	>16
Tips for Employer/Client Firms	>17–20
Other Sources of Information	>21
"Principles of Fair Conduct" for Temporary Employment Agencies	>22–24

Temp Workers Alliance meets:

"First Tuesday" of each month from 5:30 to 7 P.M.
Oct. 10> Nov. 7> Dec. 5> Jan. 2> Etc.
at United Labor Agency–214 State Street, Room 201
Hackensack, NJ (201) 489-7476 {Refreshments}
Website–<www.member.tripod.com/tempguide>
E-mail~Wib88@bergen.org

PURPOSE OF TEMP TASK FORCE

*** Publishers of this Guide ***

To build toward real solutions to the problems faced by temp workers, we conduct research, disseminate information, educate the public, provide direct assistance when possible, advocate for higher standards and collaborate with any groups sharing our goals.

Our initial strategy since 1997, is to provide job seekers with information on "best practices" temp agencies so they can make informed choices. In doing so we are forming strategic alliances with those agencies as a means of protecting workers' rights in this rapidly growing industry.

By attending the ***Temp Workers Alliance,*** you can share experiences with other temps. By consulting our *Black Book* of over 175 reports on temp agencies, you can learn something of how the agencies ("Best Practices" or not) treat workers and learn what assignments they have available.

"TWA" **NEEDS YOUR INPUT**

- ✔ Share your experiences
- ✔ Help monitor Temp Agencies
- ✔ Build an organization to advance our goals
- ✔ Publish Newsletter

"TWA" **INVITES OTHERS**

- ✔ Temp agencies listed or seeking to be included in future consumer guides
- ✔ Client firms looking for info on temp firms
- ✔ Career Counselors

Source: Temp Workers Alliance, 214 State Road, Room 201, Hackensack, New Jersey.

CONSIDERING THE TEMP OPTION

FACTORS MAKING TEMPING VIABLE:

- You need immediate income.
- You want to gain exposure to different work environments.
- You are covered under someone else's health insurance (or go to one of the few agencies offering affordable insurance).
- You do not feel physically or emotionally capable of sustained work.
- You prefer to work off and on, or you travel regularly.
- You need a regular job and can find a temp agency and assignments which are truly "temp to perm" within your time frame.
- You're not such a good self-promoter and need a Counselor to line up work for you.

FACTORS MITIGATING AGAINST TEMPING:

- You need the time for a job search.
- You need health insurance coverage provided by employer.
- Your comfort with changing environments and supervisors is limited.
- You enjoy/need being a full member of a work team.
- Your family responsibilities vary (less flexibility in hours exists in a succession of temp assignments).
- You have no car/Drivers License.

We have identified a growing number of agencies following "Best Practices" in how they deal with you, the job seeker. By studying this Guide you will better negotiate the complexities of temping.

Call 201-489-7476 to receive a four-page "Guide to Temporary Employment," published in 1996 by the Unemployment Coalition of North Jersey.

ETHICS
For Temporary Workers

1. a. Understand the potential assignment length before commiting. Bring up any schedule conflicts.

   b. Once commitment has been made to start an assignment, a minimum of 2 working days notice must be given if you cannot start the assignment.

   c. Give 1 week notice if the position becomes permanent or you take another job.

   d. Never walk off the assignment without talking to your agency coordinator.

2. On the first day of your assignment, arrive 15 minutes before your scheduled time to start. Dress professionally.

3. Be positive *always*—remember that attitude is 50% of a great assignment. You are representing yourself as well as the agency.

4. Coordinators, not client firm must be contacted by 8 A.M. regarding any illnesses, lateness or car problems that prevent you from being at work on time.

5. Do not use company phone for personal use—limit personal calls to emergencies.

6. If you have completed your tasks, offer to assist others in your department. Be flexible—you are on assignment to *assist the client firm.* If the assignment is over, call the temp agency *the next day* as required by Unemployment Insurance regulations to maintain your rights and request another assignment.

7. Employment interviews should be scheduled in the AM or late afternoon—not in the middle of the day unless during a lunch break. Agency and client firm staffing managers must be notified one day in advance of the interview date.

8. You must provide information on hours worked promptly as requested.

9. You must contact the agency immediately if your job functions change or if you are asked to report to a different department or manager from the original assignment.

10. When available, you *should* come in to the agency and update your computer skills on software training system.

11. It is improper to leave an assignment prematurely for a pay increase offered by another agency on the same or different assignment. This is disruptive to the client company and to the assignment.

TEMP WORKERS
Know the Law!

WHAT YOU NEED TO KNOW ABOUT EMPLOYMENT LAW............

As a working person in New Jersey, you are protected by a range of workplace laws. This pamphlet will tell you about employment laws which protect your rights, and what to do if they are violated. It will tell you about both laws that apply to all workers in New Jersey and those that apply only to temps. If you believe that a temp agency or client firm has broken the law, contact us.

YOUR LEGAL STATUS

Every person who works for another person is an employee at will. This means that either the employee or the employer is free to end the employment relationship at any time and for any reason. A worker can quit a job whenever she/he chooses; a worker can be fired for a good reason or for no reason at all. This is the basic status of workers, including temp workers.

But employment at will has been modified in some ways. When an employee receives a handbook or letter or other documents describing the terms of her employment, there may be a contract governing the employment. Verbal promises can also create a contract. The contract governs the employment, not the employment at will relationship. Every contract includes what are called the implied covenants (promises) of good faith and fair dealing. This means that you cannot be fired without good cause, and the employer cannot arbitrarily change other terms and conditions of your employment. It is therefore important that you keep all of the materials which are given to you by the temp agency when you registered for work, and that you make a written record of any promises your employer makes to you. These documents are your contract of employment with the temp agency; make sure you keep them.

The New Jersey state legislature and United States Congress have also enacted laws which protect employees and change employment at will. These laws assure you a safe workplace and guarantee that you will be paid at least minimum wage and overtime in a timely fashion. The law also protects you from firing or discrimination because of:

- race, religion (creed), color, nationality/national origin/ancestry
- age
- sex or marital status
- affectional or sexual orientation
- organizing a union or joining groups like the Temporary Worker Alliance
- disability
- whistleblowing (complaining about unlawful workplace activities publicly)

Laws that protect workers are harder to enforce when it comes to temp workers. Temps are technically employed by the temp agency, not by the client firm. Even though temps go to work at the office of the client firm, and are told what to do and how to do it by the client firm, temps are paid employees of the temp agency, not the client firm. And it's understood that every temp job can end at any time; it's temporary. So even if an assignment is cut short illegally, a client firm or temp agency can claim that they simply no longer need the temp. But there are some provisions of law which an employer cannot evade.

Know the Law!.... <continued>

CONSUMER FRAUD

The *New Jersey Consumer Fraud Act* requires temp agencies to give workers copies of all signed documents. It also prohibits bait and switch routines, false advertising, and other fraud. If you are sent on an assignment and it turns out the pay or the conditions of employment are not what you were told, or if you are sent on a temp-to-perm assignment and it turns out to be only temporary, or if you register with a temp agency because of a newspaper advertisement which promises temp-to-perm, and the promise proves false, the agency may have broken the *Consumer Fraud Act*.

New Jersey law licenses temporary agencies to provide workers for a firm's temporary, excess, or special workload. We believe it is a common and growing fraud to place temp workers in permanent jobs without ever converting them to regular employees. Employers do this in order to avoid the cost of benefits. This exploitative practice, so-called perma-temping, is expedited by contracts between temp agencies and client firms that often include on-site supervisors from the temp agency. The employer hires temps and then replaces them every six months or so, even if they do a good job.

If a job is in truth a permanent job, every time a temp is replaced in that job, that temp has been wrongfully discharged. And both the temp agency and the client firm have violated the *Consumer Fraud Act*. If you have been victimized by this practice, and you would like to do something about it, contact us. We intend to stop this abuse.

UNEMPLOYMENT INSURANCE

The Unemployment Compensation Law covers all employees in N.J., including temps. When your job assignment ends, if the temp agency doesn't have a new assignment, they are required to provide you with info about how to apply for unemployment insurance (U.I.). If your temp agency does not provide you with this information, you should complain to the Dept. of Labor/Div. of Unemployment (609-292-7860). You should also contact us, the ***Temporary Workers Alliance*** (TWA).

U.I. is important to everybody, but it is vital to temps. Temps often have downtime between assignments, a week or so after an assignment ends and before the next one starts. During these weeks, temps can and should apply for and receive U.I. And if you're stuck temping because you don't have the skills employers are looking for, you may be able to get training and improve those skills while you collect. If you are stuck temping because you don't have the skills employers are looking for, or if you want to start a career, you may be able to get job training while you collect benefits.

But U.I. has special rules that apply only to temps, and you must be careful to follow them. Temp agencies try to keep temps from collecting U.I. They do this because every temp agency has a kind of a bank account with U.I. and your unemployment check draws down on that account. When the account gets too low, then the temp agency's taxes go up. So if you file a claim which draws on their account, a temp agency will try to get you back to work quickly.

The first rule is the most important when your temp job ends, ***contact your agency*** before the end of the next business day. If you don't, you won't be able to collect U.I. When you contact the temp agency, they may offer you a job. You must take the job offered to you if it's the kind of work that you have been doing for the agency and has a starting date anytime within the next month. The same kind of work means the job they offer must be at about the same pay, during about the same hours, and at about the same commuting distance. If you refuse to accept a similar job, you won't be able to collect U.I. But if you have a week or most of a week without work, make sure you apply for U.I.

If you signed an agreement with the temp agency in which you said that you would take a job for $9/hr. and would work the late shift, then you have to take any job that fits the description in that agreement. If you refuse to accept a job which has the salary, hours and commute that you agreed to, you won't be able to collect U.I. Remember: when you register with a temp agency, be careful what you agree to. The agreement can be used to prevent you from collecting U.I. and force you to take jobs you don't want. When a temp agency asks you to put a starting salary in writing, put down an amount that is on the high side. And don't agree to work any hours you don't want to work, or travel any distance you don't really want to travel.

To keep you from collecting U.I. the temp agency might try to offer you any job at all, even if it is for only a few days, even if the pay is very low or even if it is far away or on the night shift. Remember, the temp agency wants to get you off unemployment as quickly as possible, and offering you a job, any job, will help them to do that. Even if you are offered a job that difffers from the one you've been doing or the kind of work you agreed in writing you would do, you can refuse to take it and should not be bounced off U.I.

Regional U I Managers, Marianne Waysek, North (973)916-2667 and William Baxter, Central (609)292-8879 can answer questions. If you have a problem with your unemployment insurance, or if your temp agency starts offering you lousy jobs and you are not sure if you have to take them, call the ***Temporary Workers Alliance.*** We can tell you what your rights are, how to appeal, and we can accompany you to the appeal.

DISCRIMINATION

Title VII of the *Civil Rights Act of 1964* creates a cause of action for employment discrimination based on race, color, religion, sex and national origin. The *New Jersey Law Against Discrimination* (LAD) prohibits discrimination in employment because of race, creed, color, national origin, ancestry, age, marital status, affectional or sexual orientation (homosexuality; bisexuality), familial status or sex. These laws apply to temp workers.

Depending upon the circumstances, either the temp agency, or the client firm, or both will be considered the temp's employer. If you believe that you have been discriminated against for any reason, you may either file a complaint with the *NJ Division of Civil Rights* or file a lawsuit.

In some cases, the LAD and Title VII provide for attorney fees, so you may be able to find a lawyer to take the case without cost to you. But remember: time limits are short for filing charges and the procedure involving federal and state laws and regulations is complicated. Consult an attorney quickly if you are victimized.

DISCRIMINATION BECAUSE OF AGE

The federal *Age Discrimination in Employment Act* and the *New Jersey Law Against Discrimination* protect people over 40 from discrimination because of age. It is against these laws to fail to hire or to fire someone because of their age.

It is also against the law to pay someone less, or to provide worse terms or conditions of employment because of age. It is against the law for a temp agency to do any of these, or to classify or refuse to refer someone for employment because of their age.

EQUAL PAY FOR MEN AND WOMEN

Under New Jersey and federal law, men and women must receive the same pay if they do the same work. This law provides recovery of the full amount of the difference between your salary and that of your coworker where the difference is a result of discrimination based on sex, plus the same amount as damages. Since temp workers are covered by the *Consumer Fraud Act*, this amount may be tripled. There is provision for attorney's fees and costs of suit, so if you believe that you are or have been discriminated against in your pay because of your sex, you should be able to find an attorney to represent you without cost to you.

Know the Law!....<continued>

DISCRIMINATION BECAUSE OF DISABILITY

The *New Jersey Law Against Discrimination* (LAD) and the *Americans with Disabilities Act* (ADA) protect disabled people. Disabled means either a physical or a psychological disability. These laws also protect those who have an association with a disabled person, such as a parent who takes care of a disabled child. The LAD also specifically prohibits employment discrimination because of genetic information, for refusing to submit genetic information or a typical hereditary or blood trait.

The ADA and LAD require employers to provide reasonable accommodations to protect the rights of individuals with disabilities (or associated with a disabled individual) in all aspects of employment. Employment includes the application process, hiring, wages and benefits. Medical examinations and questions about your medical history are highly regulated. If you are asked to take a medical examination, or if you are asked questions about your medical history apart from requirements of a particular assignment, your rights have been violated.

MINIMUM WAGE AND OVERTIME

The provisions of the federal and state wage and hour laws apply to most workers. With a few exceptions, for example trainees or people who normally receive tips, all workers must be paid at least the federal minimum wage. The minimum wage is $5.15 per hour.

If you work more than 40 hours per week for a single employer, you must be paid time and one-half for each hour beyond 40 hours. Temps must also be paid overtime if they work more than 40 hours for one temp agency, even if they work at several different client firms.

If a temp works for several different client firms, then overtime is calculated by taking an average of all hours worked at all the various rates of pay. Once the average hourly pay for the week is computed, that average rate is multiplied times one and one-half for each hour over forty. If you work only a portion of a hour, you must be paid for that time.

Workers earning $600 a week or less must be paid at least twice a month. If you are fired, quit, laid off or cannot work because of a labor dispute, you must be paid all wages owed to you no later that the usual payday for those wages. Your employer may not hold back any part of your pay without cause. If your employer disputes some part of your pay, she/he is still obligated to pay you, on your regular pay-day, any amount that is not in dispute.

If your employer (either the temp agency or the client firm) breaks any of these laws, you can file a lawsuit in either state or federal court. The laws provide for damages, costs and attorney fees, so you should be able to find a lawyer to take the case without cost to you. . . . and the *Consumer Fraud Act* may triple the amount of money that you were not paid.

You can reach us at:

Temporary Workers Alliance

214 State Street, Room 201
Hackensack, NJ 07601

Phone: (201) 489-7476

Fax: (201) 342-0608

E-mail: Wib&@bergen.org

A good resource is:

"The Employer/Employee Relationship in the Contemporary Workplace"—John J. Sarno, Employers Association of NJ, 1997, 20 pp. for $19.95 or call (973)239-8600.

SHARE YOUR TEMP EXPERIENCES

If you can't attend one of our monthly gatherings, we would especially like to hear from you. This helps everyone by noting patterns and identifying both growing opportunities and concerns.

***Please* mail to:**

****Task Force on Temporary Work, 214 State St., Rm. 201 - Hackensack, NJ 07601**
or Fax to: (201) 342-0608

Temp agency__________________________________ Town_________________________
Approximate time frame with this agency_____________________
Describe the application process____

____

Were you asked questions regarding personal medical/disability information? Yes____ No____
If Yes []—on application form
[]—during 1st. interview
[]—when a specific job offer discussed

Staff qualities and responsiveness____
Types of tests given and training offered____

____

Time till first assignment_______________________________
Duration of assignment(s)_______________________________
Type of work____
Typical of available assignments?____
Note type & name of client firm____
Salary per hour, promised/given $_______ /$_______ Benefits promised/given______________
Was agency responsive if questions arose or you sought permanent, benefited employment? ____

____

Did this agency offer the opportunity to apply for (after proving yourself for 90 days) conversion to perm position at a client firm?
If Yes []—during first interview
[]—when specific job offer
Did conversion occur? Yes_____ No_____

*Comments: (*Please be specific with both agency and client firm—use additional sheets if needed*)
Positive: ____

____

Negative: ____

____

Date of Report___________________________
Name (Optional)_______________________________________ Telephone:_____________________

**The Temp Task Force Monitoring Committee is available to assist you.
It is composed of a Temp Worker, a *pro-bono labor* attorney, a Career Counselor and a listed Temp Agency manager. If you have a concern or problem and wish them to contact in confidence, please check box ❐

Principles of Fair Conduct For Temporary Employment Agencies

ADVERTISING/INFORMATION

1] Advertisements and information given temporary workers accurately describe in writing the position[s] and benefits. ___IN PLACE ___WILL ADD

TREATMENT BY THE AGENCY

2] All applicants and employees are treated courteously, with dignity and respect. Qualified counselor informs applicants if they lack the necessary qualifications and advises them of ways to improve their skills and qualifications. ___IN PLACE ___WILL ADD

3] Applicants are not asked about family income, health, marital status or other inappropriate or illegal questions. ___IN PLACE ___WILL ADD

4] Applicants are not given or refused assignments based on gender, race, age, national origin, religion, sexual orientation, size or physical ability. ___IN PLACE ___WILL ADD

5] Applicants have copies of all documents, including signed applications/ agreements. ___IN PLACE ___WILL ADD

JOB DESCRIPTION

6] The agency provides a written job description before each new assignment detailing:
> the name of the supervisor and place to report
> the hours, days, wages, holiday schedule and anticipated duration
> task to be performed and any training required ___IN PLACE ___WILL ADD

7] Any changes will be reflected in an updated agreement. ___IN PLACE ___WILL ADD

8] Once assignment is made, the temporary agency makes sure that actual duties match job descriptions and responds promptly to any inquiries or problems. ___IN PLACE ___WILL ADD

ORIENTATION AND TRAINING

9] Adequate on-site orientation and training are provided for each assignment. ___IN PLACE ___WILL ADD

10] If the job calls for safety equipment, the temporary worker receives comparable equipment to that of permanent employees at the same job site. ___IN PLACE ___WILL ADD

11] The agency does not require workers to pay for safety equipment, test or training required for an assignment nor deduct such costs from their pay. ___IN PLACE ___WILL ADD

12] The agency provides workers information about state and federal employment laws and what to do if they experience discrimination or a health and safety violation at a client company. The agency makes clear its responsibility to act on behalf of the worker in such an instance. ___IN PLACE ___WILL ADD

<CONTINUED NEXT PAGE>

<"Principles" continued>

BENEFITS

13] The agency provides group rate health insurance, vacation and holidays to workers after 90 days, with clear disclosure of hours and premium requirements, and percentage of eligible temps who actually use insurance. ___In Place ___Will Add

MOVING TO PERMANENT JOBS

14] The agency does not require temp workers to register with only one agency or prohibit temp workers from accepting a job directly with a client company. ___In Place ___Will Add

15] The agency will not require client companies to pay an additional fee for hiring a temporary employee as a permanent employee. ___In Place ___Will Add

16] The agency will make known the percentage of long-term placements and rate of conversion to permanent jobs, including at specific clients. ___In Place ___Will Add

17] The agency allows time off for interviews, provides references promptly on request and won't discriminate in assignments for temps looking for permanent work. ___In Place ___Will Add

TURNING DOWN ASSIGNMENTS/UNEMPLOYMENT

18] The agency will not use a different standard for contesting unemployment than for direct hires. At minimum, the agency does not deny appropriate assignments, place a person on the "ineligible" list or oppose a request for unemployment because the worker has:

> filed for workers' compensation or unemployment insurance
> complained about bad working conditions
> needed to take leave for health or family reasons
> declined an assignment due to:
- travel time/distance
- insufficient notice
- hours incompatible with available child care arrangements
- dangerous working conditions or exposure to hazardous materials
- too short an assignment
- experience with discriminatory or disrespectful treatment at that worksite
- pay lower than currently earned
- refusal to serve as a replacement worker during a strike ___In Place ___Will Add

NOTICE/PENALTIES

19] While encouraging advance notice wherever possible, the agency does not fine workers who leave an assignment without written notice or who are unable to give advance notice for missing a day's work. ___In Place ___Will Add

20] The agency requests that client firms give written notification if the assignment is going to last less time than the worker was originally told. If the job is to be extended beyond the anticipated duration, the worker may decline without reprisal. ___In Place ___Will Add

<CONTINUED NEXT PAGE>

RELATIONSHIP TO UNIONS

21] When a union contract is in effect at a client, the worker may join in accordance with the collective bargaining agreement and union by-laws. The agency does not supply "new" temps to avoid this provision. ___IN PLACE ___WILL ADD

22] If a union organizing effort is underway under National Labor Board regulations, the temporary agency takes a neutral position. ___IN PLACE ___WILL ADD

WORKING WITH WELFARE-TO-WORK PARTICIPANTS

23] The agency will not help displace existing workers with welfare participants and will pay wages and benefits comparable to those of other temps in similar jobs. ___IN PLACE ___WILL ADD

24] Agency will make public contracts, placement, pay and retention figures. ___IN PLACE ___WILL ADD

Name of Agency________________________ NJ Registration________________

Telephone____________________ Person Filling Out Form____________________

The Temp Survival Guide

HOW TO PROSPER
AS AN ECONOMIC NOMAD
OF THE NINETIES

Brian Hassett

~A Tempting Life~

Perhaps one of the first questions you have to ask yourself is: "Do I really want to work all that much?" If the answer is "No," you're well on your way to becoming a successful temp.

True Story Department

I remember one night hanging out earning $24 an hour to make small talk with some lawyers at one of America's most prestigious law firms, and all of them were lamenting what they'd done with their lives. They had these huge law school debts, they weren't making diddlysquat in their first years as lawyers, and they were having to work eighty-hour weeks just to stay with the firm. One of them said to me, "I'll bet you're making the most per hour of any of us," and they all laughed until we figured it out, and I was.

Survival in the Post-Employment Age

Technology is changing our economic world like speed dial channel-surfing. We're flying through changes in seconds that used to evolve over centuries, and it's only getting faster. The era of "forty years and a watch" died with Rockwell, and I'll bet there's even some of you who aren't sure who Rockwell was.

Whether you're being forced into temping by an economic downturn, or you're looking to supplement your current income, or you're an artist or student who needs part-time funds to fund the full-time dream, temping will change your life. It's fun, flexible, lucrative, empowering, experience-building, skill-enhancing, cash-flowing, plus →

(continued)

From *The Temp Survival Guide,* Citadel Press/Carol Publishing Group, 1997, pp. 3–11.

Temps Are Cool

Temps answer to no one. We're like the nomadic circus workers of the Wild West, the Woody Guthrie train hoppers, the woolly menace Dennis Hoppers, the secret spies who slip under cover of the night. People don't even know our names. We don't ever have to be anywhere, or do anything, and that's the way things are going to stay.

Temping will expand the flight pattern of your migrations. No longer will you be walking the same road to the same factory to work with the same people until the lights go out. As an autonomous free human at the crest of the millennium, you're in a world of geographic freedom where laptops and cellphones are taking you places your grandparents couldn't even imagine. And now your skills are about to take you even further!

Tuition-Free College

Every temping assignment is like a trip to the United Nations, a Berkeley philosophy class, or an M.I.T. computer lab. It's an opportunity to meet and work with people from the widest spectrum of our communities. In fact, one of temping's greatest rewards is the rainbow collage of cultures you're exposed to. Each day you have an eight-hour time frame to explore your new universe. You can use this tuition-free seminar in life to understand the Haitian mother's troubles with her two teenage boys, or ask the Born Again how you can get to heaven if you've already sinned and plan to again, or the Egyptian if she considers herself black or white, or the computer guy about the fastest way to the root of your program.

Temping is a paid college education, except every day's a field trip and there's no homework! You get to take an extended safari through the fields of human interaction, constantly testing and improving yourself as you go. For the rest of your life you can practice getting along with people until you get really good at it. You can master the old Make-This-Person-My-Best-Friend-in-the-Whole-World-Before-Noon routine. You can treat each day like a new test of your computer skills. Or your secretarial skills. Or whatever quality you want to improve each day. And did I mention the pay?

Stop Worrying About Money

The part about not knowing where you're going to be tomorrow or whether you'll get work next week scares some people. First of all, you'll get work, I guarantee it. Follow these easy-to-read instructions and I'll make you rich or at least give you the confidence to find your bliss career, or help you live more and work less—so stop worrying about money. You'll have plenty. In fact, if you want, you can make more than you ever have in your life, so chill out. It isn't the money, but what you'll discover along the way that makes this so interesting.

(continued)

SURFING GENERAL'S WARNING: Lots of people aren't cut out for surfing the waves of uncertainty, and I don't want to suggest that you dive in unless you're okay with letting them take you. If you want to have a safe and particular view of the ocean, stay on the shore and homestead some beachfront—there's nothing wrong with it. It's safe, it's steady, and you can string up some party lanterns.

This is really the quandary you're facing:

What am I going to do with my life?

You're wasting valuable time thinking, "I'm completely screwed up, aren't I? Look how low I've sunk! I'm actually reading a book about *How to Be a Temp.* What's next? *How to Miss a Bus?*"

So-called "average" people retiring today have worked in 4.7 different jobs in their lifetime, according to the Office of Randomly Selected Numbers—but now you can do that in a week! Assuming we get only one shot at life, wouldn't it be better to have done more than 4.7 different things by the end of it?

Most people feel scared to leave their regular job for a variety of financial and psychological reasons. One of the most common is "If I sit in this chair long enough, eventually I'll be promoted and be able to sit in a more comfortable chair and hate my life a little less."

Temping keeps the future open. You can move when you don't like the neighbors. You can stay home and work on your own projects, or go to the park when nobody's there—any time of the year. You work when you want and don't when you don't. *You're a temp!*

The Most Lucrative Jobs-Search Program in the World

Besides everything else, temping is also the most lucrative job-search program in the world. In fact, all sorts of studies of employment patterns have found that people get higher-paying jobs after first working as a temp. So, not only does it pay you to look for a job, but you'll get a bigger paycheck when you're hired!

Later on I'll include an entire chapter on going full-time, but the essence of it is that temping switches the balance of power in the salary negotiations. You're no longer hat-in-hand hoping for any kind of a job, but rather confidently employed by various temp agencies and making more money than you ever have in your life, so this new potential employer better be offering something pretty special to lure you away from where you're already quite happy, thank you. In fact, one of the causes of the boom in the temping business has been the failure rate of employment-hiring practices.

The story goes something like this:

(continued)

The Temporary Times

Today: Sunny and Warm 50¢

New York—Back in the old days when a beetle was just an insect, a business would hang a help wanted sign in its window, or if there were a lot of jobs they'd go hog-wild and take out an ad in the local paper. The people who applied were mostly what they seemed and probably knew somebody who knew the boss, and if they didn't smell too much like beer at the time, they got the job. Then the beetles became the Beatles and the whole world went to pot, so to speak. Inventions were patented, industries grew, leisure time became Big Time, and with the globalization of television, people became stupider.

This didn't become a problem until we actually had to go to work the next day and the poor employers had the unenviable task of hiring the TV Generation. Even as they became more careful in the selection process they still ended up with a roomful of Ralphs and Potsies. The only thing they could do was to try to make the testing process more thorough, perhaps follow up on a reference now and again, and have several people involved in the decision-making. Except it still turned out after only a few short weeks that the TV nobs they hired couldn't spell their vegetables and thought Murphy Brown was a real person.

And thus, the temporary world was born!

Know What You're Working Into

If you've ever had a job, chances are the impression you had at the interview bore little resemblance to your daily reality. As a temp, you get to actually do the job and make your decision after having worked there. Imagine if they let you move into a house before you decided to buy. Or you got to wake up with your date the next morning before first going to bed with him. That's why temping's so great: You get paid for having breakfast instead of getting screwed at night.

Now, rather than spending your days getting all gussied up and trudging from interview to interview following phony ads while losing money on parking, lunch, and clothes—you get *paid* to go in to a company that needs extra help, so you can interview *them* for a change. And at the same time you'll be collecting contacts, expanding your résumé, and learning new skills. You are suddenly freed up to float above the employment surface to see where your piece fits in the giant jigsaw puzzle of life.

Tell your agencies you're interested in specific fields so while they're keeping you working at rent-paying assignments they can also be looking to place you in your dream job. Registering with the right agency can catapult you over the wall into the middle of the profession you seek. Once you're inside it's up to you to hustle the gig (at which point, turn to the "Landing a Job in a Day" chapter).

By working somewhere, you're distinguishing yourself from the stack of resumés in the pile because not only will the company know who you are, they'll have the chance to evaluate you

(continued)

on the job. And you have the chance to shine. They see you, you see them, and whether you mate for life or it's a one-day stand, you still get paid for the time you're there. Plus you're spending the day on the inside of your profession where the bulk of the jobs are created and filled.

If a job, like an apartment, makes it into the classified ad pages, there's probably something wrong with it. I've gone on plenty of temp assignments at prestigious companies you'd think from their reputation were really nice, but once you got on the inside they were petty or dirty or stodgy or cheap. If you only saw their personnel office when you interviewed, you might have ended up working there. As a temp, you'll never have to go on another unpaid job interview again.

Living When Other People Aren't

One of the best areas to specialize in is off-hours work. This is a huge benefit of the temping biz that rarely gets mentioned, so it's a good candidate for your own personal capitalization.

Regular Joannie

Commutes twice a day on crowded roadways or trains, then runs her errands after work in the crowded store before it closes, then goes to the crowded park on Saturday with everybody else in the world who's trying to get away from it all, so by Saturday night she just gives up and gets bombed, then wakes up Sunday morning and joins a TV ministry in Florida.

You and Me

We sleep in and do whatever we want all day, including shopping when the stores and streets are empty, or having the museums and parks to ourselves all day long. If we feel like it, maybe around 4 P.M. we can call in for work, then while everybody else is clogging the other side of the road leaving work, we cut over to the empty lane and arrive at a place where everyone is already pooped from slogging through a full day's flogging—but we're arriving with the joy of being alive and just in time to make those extra dineros at the evening rate. After a little cushy nighttime work including a free three-course meal and being sent home in a car with enough leftovers to feed a family of four, we stay up as late as we want doing whatever we want until sunrise because we have nowhere to be tomorrow, such as work.

Sex and Where to Get It

Let's face it, one of the safest places to meet that special person is on the job. Everyone's putting their best foot forward, even shy people can find excuses to talk to people they like, and you all get off around happy hour.

By taking jobs in different positions in different parts of town, you quickly begin to see which ones offer the best type of people in your preferred demographic.

You know how you're always thinking about the same few prospects where you work now? And you keep coming back to: your first and second choices are taken, and three and four aren't even really worth talking about. Then you run through the rest of the possibilities and you're down to the Fed-Ex guy, or the girl in the elevator last week. No wonder!

(continued)

How about this: Every day, for the rest of your life, you get to go to a different almost foreign location with a bunch of new people, except they're all from your hometown, and they're actually quite a lot like you, and you go there for eight, ten, twelve hours at a time, mingle, maybe have a little lunch, chat on the phone, meet over coffee, share a desk, share a job, share the sidewalk at the end of the day 'n' date in the sunset dusk as you walk together from the mirror and glass palace into the twilight's last gleaming. How much would you pay for this kind of romantic adventure? $100? $200?

What if we paid *you,* that's right, YOU, to go on this dating spree! Don Pardo, tell her what she's won! "All right, Dave: You'll be taking home the financial security through regular temping to keep yourself independent, beautiful, and free, well into the new millennium. Plus, you'll receive a lifetime supply of cute prospects *who've got a job* parading past your desk like models on a runway until you take your pick!"

Yes, that's right! In the Dream Come True, Am I Reading This Right? Wait a Minute, I Think I'm Getting It Department:

Go to your phone right now. Dial 1-800-MyAgent and they'll have you wrapped in a bun warmer faster than you can say Calvin Klein.

Actors and Writers Alert

One last thing for you actors, writers, and artists that's even more profitable than the rates: on each assignment you're stationed smack dab in the middle of other people's lives for a day and get to study all different kinds of characters, and then leave! It's like being a taxi driver or a waiter or something, except for the high pay I may have mentioned and the fact you're sitting in front of a computer.

There you are, quietly writing your novel, memoir, or screenplay, minding your own business and appearing to be working so that after a few minutes the other people around you don't even know you're there and begin going about their very strange business. And people are extremely weird if left to their own devices, believe me.

You get to study successful executive bosses and how they got that way, or the most efficient secretaries and how they do their work. In fact, I've learned every desk organizing trick in the entire world (and you'll find most of them in chapter 8).

Back when you first started at the job you're currently at, you probably learned ways of doing things from the people there—from accomplishing their goals to ordering a delivery. Wouldn't you be better off if you got to work with and observe *thousands* of people a year rather than the ten or twenty who work in one place? As a professional temp, you're actually paid each day to add new colorful characters to an ever-expanding palette.

But enough of this. Let's start making money.

CHRISTIAN ANGST

Unemployed? Why bother yourself with the stress that accompanies looking for a job when you can rely on your friendly neighborhood *Job Placement Service!*

Yes, highly-skilled career counselors are standing by right now, ready to lend you their wisdom and experience which will lead you to the new high-paying career of your dreams!
That's right, I can get you a job that pays ten thousand dollars a year!
Great! And you say your fee is only eleven thousand?

Looking to change your career entirely? It's no problem when you trust your future to caring, sensitive job placement personnel who are specially trained to discover talent inside of you that you didn't even know you had!
Good news...I can get you a job for minimum wage as a fry cook!
Wow! I *knew* that college diploma would come in handy some day!

Remember...When you rely on the services of your nearest Job Placement Service, you get the job while they do all the work!

From *Best of Temp Slave!* Edited by Jeff Kelly. Garrett County Press, 1997.

CHRISTIAN ANGST

From *Best of Temp Slave!* Edited by Jeff Kelly. Garrett County Press, 1997.

My Last Temp Job?

Trevor Rigler

I was a Kelly Girl. It sounds pretty strange to say it now, but I really was a Kelly Girl. It happened during my last semester of college. I was hoping to gain some professional experience and earn some money as well. Everyone in the know told me to go with Kelly. They said Kelly would take care of me and look after my best interests.

I made an appointment and went in to find out about my future with Kelly. The ultra friendly Kelly Bosses encouraged me to take numerous software, typing and grammar tests to find out what sort of wonderful assignments I'd be eligible for. Of course I scored well on these tests. I watched exciting videos detailing my responsibilities and rights as a Kelly Girl. I was ready for any challenge Kelly could sling my way.

A call finally came one blustery January afternoon. It was a Kelly Boss: "Mr. Rigler, it says on your application that you once worked in a copy store . . . ?"

"That's correct," I replied in my most business-like tone.

"And it says that you are good at binding, collating, and that sort of thing . . . ?"

"Of course," I chirped, my bosom full. "I am quite familiar with those procedures."

"Well, that's just great because we have a job lined up for you," she said, almost as excited as I was. "Tomorrow, show up at the —— firm at 8 A.M. Mr. —— will explain your assignment when you get there.

The next day just couldn't come fast enough. I sprung [sic] weightlessly from my futon and rushed to the shower. I imagined what my coworkers would be like. Would they like me? Would they laugh at my jokes? Would they go for an after work Fresca with me? My head swimmed [sic] with possibilities. I quickly shaved, slathered on some deodorant and got dressed.

The bus arrived right on time as usual. I bounded aboard to get out of the steady drizzle and found a seat next to a kindly old man with a flatulence problem. Even his rank, intestinal stinkiness couldn't put a damper on my glowing mood.

Mr. —— met me in the front office of what turned out to be a large building. The room was adorned with the taxidermied heads of dead animals. I followed him through the building to a cavernous room, where he handed me a piece of paper and pen. "You need to sign this," he said, matter of factly.

When I started to read the paper, he seemed confused, perhaps a little annoyed, but the Kelly videos had admonished me to read carefully any document I was supposed to sign.

The piece of paper said that as a trained temp, contract-labor employee, I would receive a wage that was technically lower than minimum wage. The document went on to claim that should the company be unhappy with the quality of my work at the end of my one week period, they could legally refuse to pay me one red cent.

"C'mon, just sign it," Mr. —— persisted, "It's just for our records. We can't pay you unless you sign it."

I just knew that Kelly wouldn't send me on any sort of questionable assignment, so I put my doubts behind me and signed the paper. He folded the paper and gestured to a row of tables at which sat 3 or 4 employees. "Take a seat over there next to that stack of paper."

(continued)

From *Best of Temp Slave!* Edited by Jeff Kelly. Garrett County Press, 1997, pp 65–69.

I quickly seated myself and looked up at him, beaming. Mr. —— picked up an odd-shaped piece of paper from the stack, bent it in a few places, then glued it with a strange tool. He placed the completed object, a folder, to my right. "Got it?" he asked, somewhat sarcastically.

"You mean, this is what I'll be doing for this assignment? No binding, collating, or that kind of thing?" I asked, incredulous.

"This is it. Time to get started. Lunch is at 12:30." He walked off.

I decided to take stock of my surroundings. The room was actually a warehouse, no, a factory. A paper-products factory, where all sorts of things are made from paper. There was loud machinery and strange smells that made me a little queasy. It was then I noticed the music—loud country and western tunes were played over the PA, occasionally interrupted by announcements from the nasal voiced receptionist I had seen up front.

Shaken, I thought I would try and do a few folders. I folded one up and was about to put it on top of the one Mr. —— had done, when I heard someone say, "Nope, that ain't right." I looked over and saw a middle-aged polyesterclad woman. She seemed to enjoy the work and took great pride in it. There was a tall stack of completed folders in front of her. "You better do it right if ya wanna stay 'round here f'long," she offered. I pretended not to hear and continued. The Kelly videos had said to never engage in office gossip.

Five or six folders later, my head began to ache. I felt so confused. Why would Kelly send me on such a strange assignment? Was it some kind of test to find out how loyal I was? I tried to carry on. The insightful woman to my left began to sing along to the country music. I winced.

Fifteen folders later, I began to feel somewhat nauseous. The chemical smell burned my nasal passages and my hands were throbbing and sticky with glue. My skin looked horribly pale in the artificial lighting of the factory. My doubts resurfaced. I thought of the battery of high-end tests I had performed so well on and the promises of good jobs, great jobs even, made by the all-knowing Kelly Bosses. I simply was not the right person for this particular assignment. Why, the day before, I had turned in a research assignment about middle-high German love poetry. I was intelligent, well-versed in political thought, and a darn good speller to boot. What had gone wrong? What had I done to deserve this? How had I raised Kelly's ire? I had to find out.

When I stood up and backed away from the table, no one seemed to notice. Mr.—was several feet away. I walked directly to him. He looked up, surprised, and began to say something but I cut him off. "There's been a mistake. This isn't the right assignment for me. I'm sorry but I just can't do this." He said something sternly, but I only nodded absently and turned away from him. As I walked my pace quickened.

Soon I was out in the rain. Luckily the Kelly office was only a few blocks away. I trotted toward it, still believing I was the victim of a simple mistake, a mistake that would be worked out by the time I arrived at the House of Kelly. I walked in the Kelly office breathless. The Kelly Boss who had arranged my assignment saw me and motioned me over, hanging up the phone. She was angry. "What happened? Mr. —— said you just walked off the job! What was so wrong that you had to put us all in such a bad position?"

I slowly explained the situation at the paper factory, the smells, the sounds, the "pay contract," the nature of the job itself, everything. When I was finished, I felt relieved.

(continued)

My Kelly Boss wasn't buying it. "There was nothing wrong with that assignment. We picked it for you because we wanted to see how versatile you were. I don't think we'll be able to give you anything better if you can't make do with what we give you."

Suddenly, my confusion was replaced with anger! Who was this woman? Did Kelly approve of what she was doing? I didn't think so. "Look, if those are the types of assignments you're going to send me on, you can just forget it. Find some other fool." With that I turned and left. Everyone in the Kelly office, including some new Kelly inductees, stared at me as I hurried out.

It took a few weeks before I realized that Kelly would never vindicate me. Perhaps Kelly no longer had control of the business, like some figurehead monarch. I gave up on Kelly and thought about getting a job with the (gasp) IRS. My life had reached a new low. My friends couldn't console me, no matter how many times they put on nuns' habits and played Twister to the music of Englebert Humperdink. My lover gave up trying to arouse me with her East-European-Gymnast-Tours-A-Corn-Processing-Plant routine.

One Friday afternoon, as I sat reorganizing my collection of Kelly brochures, the telephone rang. I let the answering machine pick it up. At first I didn't believe my ears, but it was a Kelly Boss! I snatched the phone and shouted, "Hello? Hello? I'm Here! I'm ready to work—honest!"

The voice at the other end of the line was curt and business-like, "Listen, we have an assignment here that needs doing and the woman who normally does it had to go out of town. There's no one else around who can do this on such short notice, so I figured I'd give you another chance, even if you don't deserve it."

Instantly my old skepticism returned. "So . . . what's the job?"

"Okay, all you have to do is go to an office downtown, listen to the bids people make for some state road projects, write down what you hear, then call a lady in New Jersey and give her the results. Can you do that?"

"Of course. I'm amply qualified for such work. Now, may I inquire as to the rate of pay?" I wasn't screwing around this time.

"For about 30 minutes of work you'll get paid $20. Take it or leave it."

I bummed a ride downtown from a friend and glided up the steps to the bidding office, the invisible hand of Kelly guiding me along the way.

A Genre Glossary

The following glossary describes key features of the genres you will find in this book. The concept of *genre* refers to the way a text's content and form are shaped by the situation in which it occurs. When you watch television, you know whether a particular show aims to be comic or dramatic or even a comic takeoff on a dramatic genre. When you read an epic poem, a lease, or anything else, you know—from common sense and experience—what to expect. Genres provide a kind of social agreement between writers and readers.

Each Genre Glossary entry briefly describes the situations, purposes, forms, content, and language and design choices typically associated with that genre. These descriptions can help you in two ways. As you read, they can help you figure out what genre a reading belongs to and how the reading follows or breaks the conventions of that genre. As you write, they can help you think about what genres you might use in a given situation and what readers typically expect from those genres. Then it is up to you to decide which genre to use and to what extent you will meet those expectations.

Academic Article/Research Paper

(Also referred to as academic essay, paper, study, or research report)

Situation/Purpose This entry describes two genres different in many ways but with much in common: articles written by professors and other professionals and published in disciplinary or professional journals or as chapters in books, and research papers written by students as course assignments.

Academic articles are written by professors and other professionals in order to contribute new ideas, arguments, or research findings to their field. Typically they write about a topic that they have specialized in and may have written about before. Some academics and other professionals, especially in the sciences and social sciences, collaborate with others in research or writing or both. But even scholars who work alone are always working within a complex context that includes their own previous work and that of others both past and present. In fact, a hallmark of academic writing is that it is part of an ongoing conversation in which people interested in the same ideas or problems share information and ideas, argue with each other, and try to work together to solve problems and make progress.

Research papers usually have a double purpose: to learn about a topic and to learn about the values and conventions of academic research and writing. Thus, although students are usually writing about a topic that is new to them, teachers often try to create a situation like the ones in which academic articles are written, providing readings and preparatory assignments that give students a context in which to research and make a claim about a topic. Academic articles are usually written to an audience of peers. Students' research paper topics, especially in upper-level courses, may develop into professional interests.

Teachers may sometimes encourage students to publish their papers—with the Internet there are many more opportunities—or deliver them at student conferences, in which case they cross a genre boundary and become academic articles. But in most cases teachers and students see research papers as apprentice work in which students learn the subject matter, ideas, and methods of a discipline and have an opportunity to share their ideas at least with their teachers and sometimes with others as well.

Content/Form Despite these differences in situation and purpose, academic articles and research papers have much in common in terms of content and form. Academic articles are often longer, are usually read in their published form, and often begin with an abstract followed by a series of key words to help readers search related topics. Beyond this, there are many similarities.

Both academic articles and research papers conduct an inquiry, and in doing so they make a claim about a problem or issue. This claim is sometimes directly stated in a sentence or two in the introduction, usually after some kind of contextualizing discussion. This direct statement of the claim is often called the thesis statement, especially if the article or paper presents an original argument as opposed to a report of research findings. As part of the introduction or immediately after it, the writer often shows how the claim relates to what others have said; if this is done in an extended or formal way, it is sometimes referred to as a review of the literature. Whether or not the claim is stated directly in the introduction, it is developed and supported in the body of the paper with various kinds of analysis, arguments, and evidence. The analysis and argument are the writer's original interpretations of the evidence or positions on the issue. Evidence might include, depending on the field, research data, descriptions of observations or case studies, quotations from analyzed texts, and references to various authorities in the form of quotations, paraphrases, and summaries. There usually is some kind of conclusion, in which the writer draws together different strands of the discussion to make a synthesizing observation, sums up the main points, reiterates the thesis statement, or makes suggestions about future research. In most of these characteristics, the academic article and research paper overlap with the essay as a genre; see the description of **Essay** in this glossary.

What distinguishes academic articles and research papers from other kinds of essays is the use of formalized documentation conventions to indicate the sources of the evidence presented. The most common conventions for documentation involve the use of parenthetical references and lists of works cited; some fields still use footnotes or endnotes and a bibliography. These conventions are more than just formalities to avoid plagiarism; they are an important way of expressing that academic writing is an ongoing, collaborative effort in which one writer builds on or challenges the work of earlier writers.

The format of articles and papers may differ according to the field. In the sciences, writers may make heavy use of headings to mark sections, which may be organized according to a predetermined structure, and they often include charts and other kinds of graphics. Articles and papers in the humanities may be much more loosely organized and may include no graphics or section markers of any kind, although headings are becoming common even in the humanities. Both professional academics and students sometimes publish their papers on the Internet, and in that case they may use hypertext, allowing readers to follow a particular thread of argument or information through related links.

Language/Design Both academic articles and research papers usually use formal, impersonal language intended to convey unbiased judgment, though in some fields and courses a more informal, personal style is acceptable. Academic articles and research papers may also use specialized language related to the field or issue. This specialized language is an important aspect of academic writing but can cause difficulties.

Academic articles usually use special terminology related to the issue or to disciplinary methods; references to people and ideas familiar to those in the discipline; and quotations, paraphrases, and summaries from sources related to the issue. Some readers see this specialized language as an attempt to make the writers sound important or to confuse outsiders, but writers who use specialized language argue that it captures particular meanings important to the discipline or to the writer's particular argument. Some academic writers, especially if they are writing books aimed at a wider audience, might use a less-specialized language; others, especially if they are publishing in journals likely to be read only by other people in the field, use the highly specialized language that they know their readers expect, understand, and respect.

Research papers, often assigned in college classes, draw ideas and information from academic articles, and students are often encouraged to see themselves as engaging in conversation with the writers of these articles. Students may thus adopt in their research papers the specialized language of these academic articles but may feel awkward putting their own ideas into this language; they may also feel awkward putting new and complex ideas into their own words. Using direct quotations, paraphrases, and summaries from sources is particularly challenging because their use depends on fully understanding the material and being able to integrate the language into the discussion. This struggle, however, is a necessary stage in the process through which a practicing writer develops a language that expresses his or her own thinking but also allows the writer to engage in conversation with experts in the field.

(For an example of this genre, see page 67.)

Address/Speech

Situation/Purpose Speeches, also called addresses, are used in a variety of public and private ceremonial occasions including political rallies, dedication and awards ceremonies, religious services, business and educational situations, and weddings, funerals, and graduations. Depending on the situation, the purpose may be to persuade, motivate, celebrate, commemorate, entertain, or instruct.

Content/Form A speech often opens with comments about the specific occasion, remarks to focus the audience's attention and set the tone of the speech, and a statement or foreshadowing of the main idea to be developed. The body of the speech develops this idea with arguments, facts and statistics, and various kinds of examples, including personal anecdotes, depending on the situation and purpose. Speakers must consider how illustrations, pertinent stories, examples, and epigrams can add interest. For example, in commencement addresses, speakers often include personal anecdotes about their education and subsequent use of things they learned in school. Most speeches close with a statement meant to leave the audience reflecting on the topic and the occasion.

Language/Design The tone must of course be appropriate to the occasion. The tone can range, even within a single speech, from casual and humorous to formal and even elevated. Speakers must carefully balance seriousness, demanded by the occasion, with humor, to keep the speech from being dull.

Advice Book/Article

Situation/Purpose Books and articles giving advice are generally written to help people solve problems that are perceived to be widespread. They usually offer solutions that individuals can implement on their own without other outside assistance. More generally, they respond to a desire for self-improvement and for specific and easy-to-follow guidelines on how to achieve it. They cover a wide range of topics including diet, fitness and health, finding a mate, marital success, child rearing, business and financial success, ways to write well, and ways to stop procrastinating. Advice books are often marketed along with, or through, audio- and videotapes, seminars, and even TV specials. Advice articles usually appear in women's magazines, teen magazines, increasingly in men's magazines, and magazines related to health, fitness, and parenting.

Content/Form Writers of advice books and articles often present a philosophy or analysis related to the problem, but the heart of the book is usually the specific advice. The advice is usually broken into short, very readable sections of prose, usually with liberal use of headings, lists, and other formatting devices, and often with pictures or graphs. The writer usually enumerates aspects and consequences of the relevant problem, qualities to be cultivated, goals to be reached, and steps that must be taken. These lists are usually long enough to be useful but short enough to be manageable. Writers often present themselves as mavericks, going against the standard beliefs about the problem and how to solve it. Advice books and articles often include personal anecdotes and testimony from the writer and others who have succeeded by following the advice.

Language/Design The tone of the language is positive and upbeat. The diction and sentence structures are meant to be accessible to most readers. Sometimes the usage is colloquial.

(For an example of this genre, see page 550.)

Brochure

Situation/Purpose A brochure's purpose is to promote an idea, distribute information, or market a product. Although we often think of a brochure as a triple-folded sheet of paper. There are as many approaches to designing brochures as you can imagine. For instance, when you purchase a cell phone, the pocket guide describing its use is a brochure. The glossy sales inserts from department stores that accompany your Sunday newspaper are also brochures. A brochure offers an opportunity to illustrate something, explain how a product works, argue that some action be taken, detail a company's accomplishments, or describe an organization and its services. Sometimes it is the only representation of that product and service because readers may not be able to obtain further information. Often, to develop a brochure, a designer is called in to assist. A brochure may dazzle you with its color and design, but these elements must work with the writing to create a document that is meant to persuade or inform an audience.

Content/Form The content and form of a brochure are extremely flexible, but the key is to communicate through a synthesis of visual and textual information. A brochure uses imaginative techniques to express its message, techniques that combine language, color, shape, texture, and form. For example, a corporation might develop an annual report using a form very much like a children's book: bright colors, bold graphic images, a glossy cover, and text arranged like a story, all designed to suggest a particular reality. Or a low-budget brochure for a school might make creative use of a variety of typefaces to illustrate visually a contrast between the chaotic thoughts of students studying a poorly conceptualized curriculum versus the clear, sharp, interwoven thoughts of students attending the school described in the brochure. These brochures are designed to offer a clear and coherent representation of the service or product, usually through a strong visual argument.

Language/Design The rule in designing brochures is "Show, don't tell." Sometimes this is done through examples but can also be achieved through the brochure's physical design, through shapes, size, and use of color, and even through pop-up or pull-tab additions. The particular type or quality of paper also influences decisions about design. Brochures can be designed and produced with a simple word processor, but most often a designer will rely on software such as QuarkXPress, Adobe Photoshop, or Adobe Illustrator.

(For an example of this genre, see page 269.)

Business Letter/Memo

Situation/Purpose Although much workplace communication takes place on the phone, through e-mail, or face to face, a great deal of it still takes the form of letters and memos. There are many purposes for business letters and memos, but most fall into one of four categories, according to whether the basic purpose is to inform or to request and according to whether the reader will perceive the message as routine or nonroutine, positive/neutral or negative. Thus the four categories might be labeled routine announcements, routine requests, nonroutine requests (often called persuasive messages), and negative announcements, (often called bad-news messages). But keep in mind that some kinds of messages (for example, thank-you notes or notes of congratulation) do not fit into any of these categories; that most messages have some elements of both informing and requesting; and that the line between routine and nonroutine can be fuzzy. Letters are generally used for external correspondence, though they might also be used for very nonroutine internal correspondence. Memos are generally used for internal correspondence, though they might be used for very routine external correspondence.

Content/Form The kind of information included in a letter or memo obviously depends on the purpose of the message and the specific information depends on the situation. But, in general, use only the most relevant and/or persuasive information. Business correspondence in the United States generally does not include much personal information or many personal remarks, although business correspondence in other cultures often does.

Although letters and memos have different formats (memos do not include internal addresses; letters usually do not include a subject line, though occasionally they do), the overall structure of the message can be the same for letters and memos. In general, the first paragraph should be fairly brief; it either provides a lead-in to the main point or states the main point. The middle paragraphs develop the different points or aspects of the message in some sort of logical order and are generally of medium length. The last paragraph is generally fairly brief, indicates what, if anything, will or should happen next, and includes a polite closing. Although both letters and memos can be of any length, we generally think of memos as shorter and letters as longer. In general, both should be kept to one page if possible.

Language/Design Letters are generally personal (addressed to a single person) but are also usually formal in tone; memos are usually impersonal (addressed to many people) and can be more informal in tone. But the language of both generally follows these principles:

clarity: specific and precise but simple; formal but not pretentious or jargony

conciseness: as brief as possible

coherence: hangs together and flows smoothly

courtesy: reader-focus, positive emphasis, good manners

correctness: no errors in sentence structure, grammar, or punctuation

Business letters and memos should be carefully revised, edited, and proofread, using spelling and grammar checkers.

Codes/Guidelines

Situation/Purpose Codes of conduct, sometimes also called guidelines, are increasingly common in the workplace because they set the standard for employee conduct by establishing guidelines. These codes both protect the employer from unacceptable employee behavior and inform the employee of employer expectations. Some businesses allow employees to contribute to the development of the codes, thus creating a forum for communication between employees and management. These codes are different from procedural manuals such as employee handbooks; they will not tell you how to do a specific job but will help you make general workplace decisions. These codes also serve a public-relations function by announcing the company's principles and standards to its clients and customers. A code of conduct can play a role in inducting new employees into the company's philosophy and can offer guidance to employees when they are confronted with difficult choices while performing their duties. If the code is to play a role in the day-to-day life of the business, it should reflect the particular circumstances and characteristics of the organization and must be adaptable enough to remain relevant as the economic climate changes.

Content/Form Codes are usually divided into numbered sections. They usually begin with a brief description of the company and a statement of its mission and values, setting the context for the guidelines that follow. Middle sections may cover general principles of behavior such as honesty, loyalty, and commitment to excellence, as well as more specific rules relevant to the particular environment of the company. Codes should spell out the kinds of behavior rewarded in the workplace and the kinds of behavior not accepted, and ideally both reasons and consequences should be explained. A good code will strike a balance between spelling out specific rules and advocating employees' use of sound judgment and ethics.

Language/Design The tone of a code of conduct is usually formal, even stern, in order to convey the seriousness of the guidelines. Beyond that, the language follows rules for writing in the workplace with its demands for brevity and standard edited English usage and mechanics.

(For an example of this genre, see pages 540–547.)

Comics

Situation/Purpose Comics are a form of visual communication that include everything from the comic strips and books that young people collect to the increasingly popular graphic novels aimed at adult audiences. In addition, as more and more people become accustomed to learning visually, comics have become another way to present complex and technical information such as that found in instruction manuals for loading a digital camera or scanning images into a computer. In this respect, comics can be instructional as well as entertaining. Comics depend on the particular arrangement of the pictures and words to communicate the stories and ideas and are meant to be read in a sequence.

Content/Form Although comics are often thought of as a simple form of communication, they are really quite complex and require a literate audience. The narrative action proceeds in segments called panels or frames that draw on the reading conventions of the Western world and are meant to be read from left to right and top to bottom. Since space is limited, the artist/writer has to make a series of judgments about what to include and depends on the reader to fill in the gaps. For example, the shape of a human head might be used to indicate a human figure, or the profile of a person with her hands on a steering wheel to create the impression of driving a car. The space between the frames also serves a purpose; it requires the reader to supply the transitions between the frames. In this way, comics require a high level of interaction on the part of the reader. Artists introduce comics in a variety of ways; however, one common way is to include a full-page scene—called a splash page—to set the stage. The writer/artist can impact the reading process to some extent by experimenting with framing devices to achieve different effects. Notice the framing devices in the comics in your favorite newspaper or comic book. The size and shape of the frame may convey important information about narrative action or atmosphere. For example, a series of progressively smaller frames conveys a quickening pace of action, while lengthening the shape of a frame can indicate slowly passing time. Sharp lines around the frame can imply a sense of urgency or horror.

Language/Design In comics, the writer and artist are often the same person. Comics are a highly visual medium; the artistry of the images is often the first thing that captures the reader's attention. Many comics rely on images alone. But more often there is a balance between pictures and words. Often the words support the pictures, but at other times the effect is created by the contrast between word and image. Because comics are a static print medium, conveying things such as mood, sound, and motion presents a particular challenge. Visual clues such as speed lines or even footprints create the effect of motion. The characters' facial expressions and exaggerated gestures help create the mood and depict emotions. Sound can be implied through word balloons. The lines around the balloons indicate the words the characters are saying as well as those they are only thinking. Comics appear in both black-and-white and color. Often the colors are the primary colors, which are easily printed in newspapers.

(For an example of this genre, see page 556.)

Cover Letter/Reflective Essay

Situation/Purpose A cover letter is any letter that accompanies and explains another document or artifact. The most common use of cover letters is to accompany and introduce a résumé as part of a job application; for a description of this type of cover letter, see **Resume/Cover Letter** in this glossary. But cover letters may accompany a wide range of other kinds of documents. Teachers may ask students to write a cover letter, note, or reflective essay to accompany an assignment or set of assignments, explaining how the assignment(s) was completed, why certain choices were made, and what was learned. For example, an assignment that asks you to reshape material from one genre into another might ask you to include a cover letter in which you discuss what you learned about the nature of and differences between the two genres. The goal is to have you think about how you work as a writer and how the text works as a piece of writing.

Content/Form Cover letters and reflective essays of this type are typically fairly short. The necessary content is usually specified in the assignment and typically includes a discussion of what was written, a description of the writing process, a discussion of the situation that surrounded the writing, and reflection on insights gained from the assignment. They can be formatted as an informal note or a formal letter, with date, greeting ("Dear . . ."), body, closing ("Yours truly," etc.), and signature, and optionally the writer's address and that of the receiver. Typically they are about one or two pages in length, including a paragraph for each topic that the assignment asks you to address, with optional introductory and concluding paragraphs. The teacher will be looking for a frank, thoughtful discussion that refers to specific aspects of the text, its context, or the writing process. Students should use cover letters as an opportunity to gain insight into their own writing and writing in general.

Language/Design The language might be more personal than in the assignment itself since you might be discussing habits, perceptions, and insights related to your own writing. But it should still follow the principles of academic style in terms of diction and the correctness of sentence structure, grammar, and mechanics.

Dialogue/Symposium/Debate

(This description is adapted from William A. Covino's *Forms of Wondering.*)

Situation/Purpose Symposia and debates often occur in public contexts. You may have seen a roundtable discussion on television or heard one on a radio show. Political candidates often defend their platforms through a process of public debates: A symposium offers an opportunity for conversations that explore different perspectives. A debate, on the other hand, highlights the opposing viewpoints of two or more participants who argue through persuasive technique and through the presentation of evidence. The term *dialogue* can mean many different things, but as we use it here, a dialogue is an intellectual exercise in which a writer creates a hypothetical conversation in order to explore different perspectives on an issue; the Platonic dialogues are probably the best-known examples.

In writing classes, teachers often use dialogues to encourage students to explore different points of view, perhaps the points of view of different readings in the course. A related genre is the symposium, which may be either the transcript of a conversation or a set of written exchanges. In both real symposia and imagined dialogues, different points of views are expressed, but in an imagined dialogue the writer has intentionally created these different points of view in order to explore an issue. Ideally, each perspective should be fairly represented.

Content/Form An imagined dialogue resembles a transcript of a real conversation, but it is in fact more carefully constructed. There may be about four or five characters, representing different points of view, usually specific real or imaginary people. Ideally, each character speaks about the same number of times and in mainly paragraph-length comments, though these may be interspersed with shorter comments. Each comment is carefully planned to express the character's views and to respond to the other characters' comments. If the characters are real people, the comments should accurately reflect their actual opinions and attitudes. It is acceptable but not necessary to use exact quotes from writings by these people. When exact words are used, they should be enclosed in quotation marks. When the characters are imaginary, their comments should express consistent opinions and attitudes. Characters should make compelling arguments supported by convincing evidence. They should be consistent but show a willingness to change their views, if that is what the character would do. Comments should demonstrate an understanding of the participants positions. The responses as a whole should make interesting connections among the perspectives.

Language/Design Each response should be written in the persona of the real or imaginary person. They should be written in the first person and should use the words and sentence structures that the character would use.

(For an example of a symposium, see page 516.)

Essay

Situation/Purpose There are many kinds of essays, from personal narrative or reflective essays that are similar to fiction and even poetry, to impersonal expository essays that are similar to reports and proposals. You may write many kinds of essays in your life, and each might seem very different. But all essays develop a main idea by making connections between related ideas and experiences, whether it is a five-paragraph essay with three examples supporting a stated thesis or a many-page essay interweaving complex ideas and references to develop an implied thesis.

The most common, broadly defined purpose of an essay is for the writer to explore, and allow the reader to explore, ideas and the relationships between ideas. But this broadly defined purpose can be embodied in a variety of situations, each of which will shape the writer's purpose in a particular way. For example, a student might write an essay to analyze the ideas covered in the course or to make connections between the course ideas and the student's personal experience. A public figure might write an essay for a magazine or newspaper in order to persuade an audience about an issue of public concern. In fact, when a persuasive essay is used in this way, we might call it an **Opinion Piece, Column,** or **Commentary** (see page 578). A novelist or a journalist might write an essay to explore and share with the reader a personal experience and give the reader insight into similar experiences. A professional in any field might write an essay to inform other members of the profession of ideas or discoveries important to the field. In all of these cases, the writing might be called an essay, but in each case the content, form, and language will be different.

Content/Form While literary writing usually involves description and narration, and professional, scientific, or workplace writing usually involves the exposition of facts and ideas, essays tend to include a combination of description, narration, and exposition, with the emphasis depending on the particular purpose and situation. What we often call the personal, informal, or literary essay might be mostly narrative, description, and even dialogue, interspersed or framed with expository comments. Such essays are often written by students or by professional writers in literary magazines. What we often call formal, academic, analytic, argumentative, or persuasive essays give more space to exposition—presentation of information or explanation of ideas—but allow for some narrative or description that illustrates or illuminates the exposition. Such essays might be written about public, professional, or academic issues, by students as well as professionals. At the extremes, an essay might be all narrative/description or all impersonal exposition, but for most essays the essential feature is the combination, which allows the reader and the writer to share an experience and contemplate ideas related to it.

Thus there is no single template for essays, which might have almost any overall shape. But typically the first paragraphs draw the reader into the topic of the essay in a way that is appropriate to the situation and subject. Students often begin an essay as if they are directly addressing the teacher in response to a question. But a convention of essays is that any reader should feel invited into and addressed by the essay, which is why the introduction usually does not begin with a thesis statement but rather with something designed to interest the reader in the topic and lead into a statement of the thesis or otherwise point toward the thesis. The middle paragraphs—which can be of almost any number, from one to dozens, and of varying lengths, averaging about five to ten sentences—develop the topic in a logical or associative way, using transitions to clarify connections; these paragraphs may interweave narration/description and exposition. The final paragraphs reiterate important connections between ideas and point these ideas to the world outside the essay. All essays should have a thesis, which simply means that all essays should have a point that the writer wants to convey to the reader. The thesis, whether simple or complex, may be stated outright in the essay—often toward the end of the introduction or toward the beginning of the conclusion—or implied. But if the thesis is not stated outright, it must be implied strongly and clearly enough that the reader could state it.

Language/Design Depending on the type of essay, the language may be poetic, intimate, concrete, and informal, or highly formal, abstract, objective, or anywhere in between. But wherever the essay is on this spectrum, the language must be clear. It can be informal but should not be imprecise; it can be formal but should not be obscure or full of jargon.

Personal, informal, and literary essays are often written throughout in the first person; the writer's personal and individual voice is absolutely essential to the experience of the essay. Academic, journalistic, and other kinds of persuasive essays may intersperse first-person and third-person discussions; the effect is often to move in and out between close, personal perspectives and wider, more impersonal perspectives. The most formal, objective, and scientific essays typically do not use the first person at all; the writer aims to efface him- or herself and give the impression that the subject matter is simply presenting itself without the medium of a particular writer.

As this description suggests, there are many different kinds of essays, and the boundaries between them are not always clear. For essays specifically characterized by the documented use of sources and usually written in an academic context, see the Academic Article/Research Paper (p. 561). For brief, reflective essays that—typically in school situations—accompany an assignment or set of assignments, see the Cover Letter/Reflective Essay (p. 568). For argumentative or persuasive essays on current issues published in newspapers and magazines, see Opinion Piece/Commentary (p. 578).

In the following section we describe some of the key features of two broadly defined and different kinds of essays, the personal, informal, or literary essay, and the argumentative, analytical, or persuasive essay.

Personal/Informal/Literary Essay

Situation/Purpose The key characteristic of personal, informal, or literary essays is that the focus or emphasis is on the writer's experience or perspective. While analytical, argumentative, or persuasive essays may take their authority from evidence, logic, or methodology, personal essays take their authority from a combination of the significance of the personal experience and the power of the essay's language, and they are usually written to offer a personal perspective or testimony about some phenomenon or situation. Personal essays often appear in the front or back pages of magazines or journals or the "op-ed," page of newspapers, kept separate from more academic, professional, or journalistic writing, but the writers of such essays may include experts writing from a personal rather than an "expert" perspective; professional writers using the power of their language skills to evoke a situation or frame a concept; and ordinary people who want to offer a personal perspective on an issue. These ordinary people may be very skilled writers, but even if they are not, if they have a relevant, interesting experience or perspective to share, their essay may have a strong impact. This may be why teachers often ask students to write personal essays, typically asking them to describe a personal experience and draw some kind of conclusion from it or to comment on a situation or phenomenon, drawing on their personal experience to do so. But although such assignments recognize that anyone has the potential to write a good personal essay, they may not recognize that such essays are more complex and more difficult to write than they may seem at first, for reasons we will see below.

Content/Form Personal essays almost always contain some kind of first-person narrative—a story told from the perspective of the writer and in which the writer usually has a part—and some essays may be almost all narrative and thus may seem to many readers to be almost indistinguishable from short (fictional) stories. But what characterizes most personal essays is an interweaving of narrative and descriptive passages with what we might call expository or discussion passages. An essay might simply begin with a personal anecdote and then go on to make connections between this experience and some larger issues, or it might be a complex interweaving of narrative and commentary in which the narrative gives rise to discussion, the discussion gives rise to further narratives, and so on. But in any case almost all personal essays draw on personal experiences to illuminate, comment on, or testify about larger issues or phenomena, and almost all use some combination of literary techniques and expository strategies to create texts that allow readers to both share an experience and understand its larger significance.

Language/Design The language of personal essays is usually somewhat informal and intimate rather than formal or "professional," and it is often highly descriptive, vivid, and idiosyncratic, often making use of figurative language—images and metaphors, for example—and sometimes using dialogue or otherwise incorporating other voices. But the writer's own individual and recognizable voice is the strongest presence in the essay, determining the overall tone of the essay and synthesizing the other voices that might be incorporated.

(For an example of this genre, see page 43.)

Argumentative/Analytical/Persuasive Essay

Situation/Purpose While the emphasis in a personal essay is on the writer's experiences and perspective, the emphasis in an argumentative, analytical, or persuasive essay is on the subject matter and the audience. In a personal essay, the writer reaches inside and draws upon personal experiences in order to share insights with readers; while some personal essays are written in response to ongoing conversations, many personal essays might be said to start new conversations and even to create new audiences. In an argumentative, analytical, or persuasive essay, the writer joins an ongoing conversation in order to state a claim to a targeted audience or persuade that audience to take some action. Such essays are used by academics and other professionals to share ideas and make arguments about issues of professional or disciplinary concern, as well as by public figures or even private citizens to make arguments about issues of public concern. The assumption in a personal or literary essay is often that the writer can speak to anyone, either because the topic is of broad human interest or because the writer's style gives the text an esthetic value apart from its topic and arguments. The premise of an argumentative, analytical, or persuasive essay is that the writer is addressing a particular audience for a particular purpose, and the essay is framed by the expectations of this audience and driven by this purpose.

Content/Form An argumentative, analytical, or persuasive essay usually adheres to generic essay form in a somewhat more disciplined way than the typical personal essay. The introductory section is more likely to state the thesis explicitly, often toward the end of the section. The body paragraphs are more likely to be organized according to some identifiable logic rather than associatively, and the essay is more likely to make use of clear transitional devices. The conclusion is more likely to clearly reiterate the thesis and perhaps to call for further discussion, investigation, or specific action. But perhaps what most distinguishes this type of essay in terms of content and form is the way that it presents its claims or makes its arguments. While a personal essay may make a claim obliquely, indirectly, or by inference, an argumentative, analytical, or persuasive essay usually develops its claims or arguments in very explicit ways, and these all have to do with the important role of the audience in such essays. Because the argument is directed to a specific audience for a specific and fairly immediate purpose, the audience plays an active part in the essay itself. First, as we've already seen, the thesis is usually stated or at least strongly implied in the introduction. Then the body of the essay is developed with the concerns and needs of the audience in mind. The audience might include both those who agree and those who disagree with the claim or argument of the essay, but the disagreers play a more defining role in the essay. Thus, such essays often proceed by first taking into account the arguments or objections to the essay's claims; the paragraphs immediately following the introduction often include a discussion of the issue or question from the perspective of the "other side." Bringing the other side into the essay is a way of both acknowledging the other side and taking control of it by framing and defining it in one's own terms. This is usually followed by, in some cases, an acknowledgment of the legitimacy or force of some aspects of the other side's arguments or view of the situation, then, in most cases, by some kind of rebuttal of the other side's arguments or claims. The rebuttal can take the form of both showing what is wrong or weak in the argument or claim of the other side and presenting arguments and evidence for one's own side. The issue of arguments and evidence is crucial and complex because the arguments and evidence must be defined and presented with a particular audience and situation in mind; what is convincing and even acceptable as an argument and evidence for one audience in one situation may not be acceptable in another. Thus, whereas the content and form of a personal essay may be shaped primarily by the writer's experiences and perceptions, the content and organization of an argumentative, analytical, or persuasive essay are shaped largely by the expectations of a particular audience in a particular situation.

Language/Design At one end of the spectrum, in some literary or personal essays, the writer's individual "voice" is the most forceful source of authority in the essay; and at the other end of the spectrum the writer might try to efface his or her voice so that the argument or evidence seems to present itself directly to the audience without the intervention of a writer. In most argumentative, analytical, or persuasive essays, the voice of the writer is crucial but not in the same ways as in a personal or literary essay. In personal essays, the writer's experience or the esthetic appeal of the writing is crucial; what's crucial in argumentative, analytical, or persuasive essays is the writer's professional, disciplinary, or other kind of expert authority, and of course this must be communicated in a particular situation and to a particular audience. Thus the language of such essays must be not simply generically formal but authoritative to a particular audience. This may involve using a specialized vocabulary, sometimes called *jargon,* though in most situations clarity is valued more than specialized precision.

(For an example of this genre, see page 382.)

Feature Story/Profile

Situation/Purpose Feature stories are a regular part of newspapers and magazines, sometimes placed near a related news story or in a special "features" section. Feature stories are a cross between a news story and a work of literature. They usually relate events in the news but do not so much report facts as try to share with the reader an experience related to the news event. Profiles can be either a special kind of feature story or part of a longer feature story. While a feature may present a situation in a broad focus, a profile usually focuses narrowly on a specific person, place, or thing, describing it in evocative detail or telling a compelling story about it. Writers might use a profile of a specific person or group of people in order to characterize a social, economic, or political trend.

Content/Form Feature writers must tell a good story as well as provide an insightful analysis. The organization can be more complex than a news story, for example, which is typically organized as an inverted pyramid. Profiles include information from interviews, personal stories, and quotes from the people interviewed. Writers interweave these elements with narration about and description of the subject. The stories of the people profiled are arranged to support the writer's particular analysis. But, because the main purpose of a profile is to characterize a phenomenon rather than to simply tell a good story, a keen interpretation of the situation is necessary. Charts, tables, and graphs may be included to document the validity of the writer's analysis. Special layouts, often photographs, provide another dimension to the story.

Language/Design Word choice and quotations help evoke an image. Profiles are often characterized by the use of the third person, although the profile is primarily a subjective account of a societal, cultural, or economic phenomenon.

(For an example of this genre, see page 472.)

Interview

Situation/Purpose People conduct interviews in order to find out information or different perspectives on a topic and to make the information and perspectives known to others. Common interview subjects are politicians, experts of various kinds, athletes, authors, musicians, artists, and other celebrities. In this textbook you will conduct interviews with others to find out information or learn their perspectives on the issues you're exploring. For example, if you want to learn about marketing strategies in the fashion industry, you might interview someone who works in the industry. If you want to learn different perspectives on the question of whether graffiti is art or vandalism, you might interview a museum curator, a graffiti artist, other kinds of artists, a city official, and someone whose garage door has been tagged.

Content/Form The content of an interview consists of the writer's questions about the topic, the subject's responses, and sometimes other discussion by the writer, for example introductory background or additional information. Interviews usually take the form of questions from the interviewer followed by the subject's response, which may be very brief or quite long. Sometimes interviews take the form of an article in which the subject's responses are woven into the writer's discussion of the topic; sometimes an interview may be only a small part of a longer piece of writing. But keep in mind that the final written version is rarely just a transcript of the interview; rather, the writer has selected and shaped the material to focus on the topic and achieve the desired effect.

The interviewer must carefully plan the questions ahead of time in order to cover all the necessary ground but must also be flexible enough to follow the subject's train of thought and ask good follow-up questions. Interviewers develop strategies for establishing a rapport with their subjects—putting them at ease and getting them to open up—for example by beginning with easy questions or sharing their own views on the topic. Some interviewers like to use tape recorders—with the subject's permission—in order to preserve the subject's exact words; others prefer to take notes. Interviewers typically avoid yes or no questions such as "Do you agree that all graffiti is art?" Rather, they try to draw the subject out by using open-ended questions beginning with phrases like "Tell me about . . . " or "Describe for me. . . . " For example, interviewers will often ask the subject to describe a typical day or specific event.

Language/Design One of the reasons people love to read interviews is that they can hear the subject speak in his or her own voice. Rather than reading someone else's summary or paraphrase, they can read the subject's exact words, which help provide a mental picture of what the subject is like. Thus, in writing up an interview, it is important to use as many of the subject's own words as possible, making sure that the subject is quoted exactly. At the same time, it is important to present the subject's words in such a way that they are not taken out of context and do not misrepresent the subject's intentions.

Letter to the Editor

Situation/Purpose Most newspapers and magazines publish letters from readers, which are usually written in response to an article, column, editorial, or another letter that has appeared in that newspaper or magazine or to issues and events in the news. Letters are usually published on a special page near the beginning of a magazine or on the editorial page of a newspaper. Although they are usually called *letters to the editor,* they are actually aimed more at other readers or the author of an article. Letters to the editor are the most traditional way for ordinary people to communicate their ideas to the public. And although talk radio and the Internet now provide other ways for people to communicate ideas, letters to the editor are still popular. People write letters to the editor when they feel strongly about something or when they feel an issue has not been addressed in the forum they are writing to. The purpose is usually to disagree or agree with a previously published position, to correct a statement of fact, or to add supporting information or ideas to an ongoing discussion.

Content/Form Letters to the editor are subject to screening and editing. This means that a letter is more likely to get published if it meets expectations about form and content. Letters are usually about recently published articles or events and topics currently in the news. They should be as brief as possible while still developing a position convincingly. They usually begin by identifying the topic and/or the article being responded to and briefly stating the writer's position. The position is then developed as concisely but persuasively as possible, making reference to opposing positions when necessary. The ending should be pithy or thought-provoking. Most large newspapers and magazines get more letters than they can publish, so they look for letters that contain very well-argued positions, perspectives that have not been presented before, new information, interesting anecdotes, or humor. Editors usually want to confirm that the letter is authentic and accurate. Most editors will not publish anonymous letters or letters whose authorship has not been confirmed.

Language/Design There is a range of acceptable tones in letters to the editor, from serious, formal, and polite through lightly humorous to angry and sarcastic. But whatever the tone, the language must be clear enough for the average reader of that publication and not offensive or profane, at least not in mainstream publications. The tone and language should follow that used in other letters to that publication but should also express the writer's individuality. Usually letters are edited, but editors might avoid letters that have too many errors; if errors slip by, the writer may feel embarrassed when the letter is published.

(For an example of this genre, see page 278.)

Manifesto

Situation/Purpose A manifesto is a public declaration aimed at changing a social situation. Closely tied to a current, often political situation, the manifesto presents an argument that distinguishes itself as a call to action. Writers compose a manifesto to instigate an immediate and often consequential response. A manifesto is intended to change the course of history, shining a light on previously ignored or misunderstood situations. Not only does a manifesto attempt to explain the past or justify future actions, it also attempts to redefine the situation in which these actions occur. The root of the word, *manifest,* suggests that it makes obvious the previously submerged aspects of the situation. Originally, manifestos were proclamations issued, or at least sanctioned, by a head of state, but they have evolved into a genre that anyone can take up. Most often manifestos represent the concerns of a group rather than the thinking of an individual. The best known manifesto, The Communist Manifesto, by Marx and Engels, was written not only to convince workers of the viability of socialism but also to suggest that revolution was a possible consequence of this new understanding. More recently you may have heard of the years-long hunt for the criminal known as the Unabomber, Theodore Kaczynski, whose essay, "Industrial Society and Its Future," was labeled a manifesto by the press. An even more recent and quite different example can be found in a recent book titled *The Cluetrain Manifesto: The End of Business as Usual,* which proclaims that the Internet is turning business upside down and offers a new way to look at business in the information age.

Content/Form The manifesto is an excellent example of how a genre evolves. Having begun as a proclamation by heads of state, it has been adapted for use in a variety of situations, changing its form in each of these new contexts. Overall, though, manifestos typically begin with an introduction offering a general statement about the problem or situation and proceed through a series of short paragraphs or questions and answers that convince readers of the initial proposition's truth. All of the various possibilities for persuasion exist: emotional appeals, a carefully developed series of logical propositions, a series of definitions or even an extended metaphor that tells a story in a new way. Whatever form the manifesto takes, it aims to bring the reader to a new vision and a readiness to act.

Language/Design The language of a manifesto is formal and carefully crafted but incisive, using strong language to startle or shock its readers with a newly unveiled revelation. For example, the Communist Manifesto begins as follows: "A spectre is haunting Europe—the spectre of communism. All the powers of old Europe have entered into a holy alliance to exorcise this spectre" (Marx and Engels, 1848). Marx used an evocative choice of words to set the stage with an "old" Europe that sees communism as a strange and unholy apparition that must be banished. From this beginning he continued to develop his argument for his particular explanation of capitalism and how it should change.

(For an example of this genre, see page 189.)

Online Posts

Situation/Purpose Many teachers now use electronic communication in the classroom to allow students to carry on discussions online, just as people outside the classroom use blogs, listservs, bulletin boards, and MOOs or MUDs. Most of the electronic writing assignments in this textbook involve listservs or online threaded discussions. Listservs allow people to send a message simultaneously to all members of a group. Chatrooms, bulletin boards, and threaded discussion forums allow for the development of a conversation online, which all participants can read as it develops. Unlike other electronic discussion groups, online discussions in a classroom are limited to the students in the class, although discussions can be continued outside the class period.

Content/Form Although students are often tempted to use online discussions to chat about personal matters, teachers generally want them to be reserved for discussion of ideas and issues that come up in class, just as in a face-to-face class discussion. It is important to remember that everyone on the listserv, including the teacher, will read the message. The interaction proceeds at a different pace than a face-to-face discussion; there is time for reflection before you respond. Online posts usually conform to the standards of other informal writing activities in this book, for example, a journal entry. If you have kept a journal for a class, you have an idea of the requirements of such informal writing. Generally, the quality of the ideas takes precedence over demands for correctness. Depending on the assignment, you may be asked to reply to a specific question or raise a question relating to the class. You may use your online posts to respond to a specific text or be asked to participate in the discussion of a broader issue.

Language/Design Although online posts are considered an informal type of writing, they should be well crafted and thoughtful. Although the tone can be informal, as in a face-to-face discussion, writers should attempt to use the terminology of the texts being discussed. Online discussions give students a chance to practice using course- or issue-related terminology before they write more formal papers on the topic. Since many people read online posts, the language should not be offensive, personal, or embarrassing. It's a good idea to reread a comment before you post it.

Opinion Piece/Commentary

Situation/Purpose Opinion pieces and commentaries are an important part of a democratic society. They allow ordinary citizens and public figures to exchange ideas about important public issues. Thus most newspapers and other periodicals devote regular space to these commentaries in a section known as the opinion page or op-ed page. Some of these pieces are regular columns written by local or syndicated columnists while others are written by guest contributors; writers may be private individuals but are usually professional journalists or public figures. Local newspapers, campus newspapers, 'zines, and some online publications might publish the opinions of writers with fewer credentials than are customarily required by national publications. This kind of commentary can address a range of topics. Opinion pieces are meant to be persuasive; the writer wants to convince others to adopt a particular position or, at the very least, consider the issue from a new perspective. Opinion pieces allow the writer to develop a position more extensively than does a related form, the **Letter to the Editor,** which is another form for expressing personal views.

Content/Form An opinion piece is essentially a short argumentative essay. (See **Argumentative Essay** for description.) Usually an opinion piece begins by referring to the context of an ongoing debate or some specific recent event, which leads the reader into the argument.

Many systems have been developed for writing arguments. A commonly used one involves making a claim and supporting the claim with evidence. An important step that writers often leave out is establishing the connection between the claim and the evidence; this connection is called the *warrant.* For example, if a writer wants to argue in support of a civic project for youth, the writer's claim is that getting youth interested in a community project like painting a graffiti mural will increase their commitment to the community and reduce the chances that they will vandalize public property. The writer would offer as evidence the fact that similar projects have had these results in other communities. The writer's warrant for using this evidence, which may or may not be stated in the argument, is that using data from similar projects is a reasonable way to make decisions about a present project. But effective arguments do not simply present one side; readers who disagree may simply say, "Well, that sounds good, but the writer hasn't considered this." An argument is more effective when it takes this opposing position into account and responds to it in some way: the *rebuttal.* For example, a writer might acknowledge that the project will cost a lot of money or that such a project will simply encourage more graffiti. After fairly presenting these perspectives, the writer might respond that the money for the project is a fraction of the cost of removing graffiti from city property and that similar projects have in fact resulted in a reduction of graffiti. But developing a logical appeal may not be enough. The writer can also use emotional appeals, for example appealing to the readers' sympathy for the community's youth or invoking the esthetic value of the mural.

An opinion piece may conclude in many different ways—summaries, restatements of the thesis—but however it ends, it should leave the feeling that the writer has considered both sides fairly and chosen the most reasonable position.

Language/Design Opinion columns usually use the first person. The overall tone and specific word choice reflect the writer's own style as well as the nature of the publication. In this textbook you will find examples of opinion pieces that use a wide variety of writing styles.

(For an example of this genre, see page 412.)

Proposal

Situation/Purpose In business, the professions, and other areas of public life, people are constantly exchanging goods, services, and money. This exchange is regulated partly by the complex mechanisms of supply and demand. But a special mechanism for the distribution of scarce resources or scarce opportunities is the proposal. When people in the workplace need to persuade an outside agency to give them money or other resources, or if they want to be chosen to provide a product or service, they write a proposal. Sometimes proposals are written in response to Requests for Proposal, or RFPs, which are circulated by agencies with resources to distribute and by companies or agencies who need a product or service. Sometimes proposals are used within a company to persuade someone to do something, usually to make a change or solve a problem of some sort, although in this situation they may be called recommendation reports.

Content/Form Proposals are basically organized as a problem/solution discussion. The problem section usually includes detailed descriptions, sets of facts, and statistics. The solution section includes analyses and recommendations. Since the proposal is used to make important decisions and will become part of a permanent record, the information should be as accurate as possible, based on reliable sources or research methods. When outside sources are used, they should be documented, using a standard documentation system, such as the MLA or APA system. When original research is involved, the research process should be carefully described.

Proposals can vary in length from a single page to hundreds of pages. The form of a typical proposal usually moves from description of a problem to presentation of a solution. A typical proposal will have most of the following elements in roughly this order:

Explain the purpose and scope of the proposal.

Describe and give some background on the situation or problem.

Suggest why the reader needs what you are proposing.

Present and analyze possible alternative solutions.

Explain why your proposal is the best solution.

Describe how your proposal would be implemented, including itemizing the costs.

Ask the reader to take some specific action.

Because proposals are meant to be as reader-friendly as possible, they usually include more elaborate formatting than other kinds of writing: headings, often accompanied by a numbering system; bullets; typographical and spacing variations; graphics are typical.

Language/Design The language is generally formal, impersonal, objective, or even scientific. It may include many technical terms, if necessary, but otherwise should be as clear, concise, and jargon-free as possible. As with other workplace or academic writing, it should avoid errors in sentence structure, grammar, and mechanics.

(For an example of this genre, see page 396.)

Report

Situation/Purpose The report is a common, varied, and flexible genre used in all kinds of situations—school, workplace, and other kinds of organizations—in which information must be recorded and communicated. Reports are usually written either to record information for bureaucratic, legal, medical, or scientific reasons or to give decision makers the information they need to make decisions. A student might use a report to record an activity or research findings.

Content/Form Since their purpose is usually to record or present information, reports usually include detailed descriptions, sets of facts, and statistics. They often also include analyses of this information and sometimes recommendations based on the information. Since the report may become part of a permanent record or may influence decisions, the information should be as accurate as possible, based on reliable sources or research methods. When outside sources are used, they should be documented, using a standard documentation system, such as the MLA or APA system. When original research is involved, the research process should be carefully described. Information that is relevant to the report but too extensive to fit smoothly into the body of the report can be included in appendices attached to the end of the report.

Reports vary in form and length. A report usually follows some variation on the following pattern:

Introductory section that might include the purpose of the report, possibly a brief statement of the overall conclusion or recommendation, or background information.

Body section that might include additional background, a detailed description of a situation or problem, a discussion of research parameters and methods, an analysis of alternatives, arguments to support a recommendation, a description of procedures or implementation steps, or a discussion of benefits and drawbacks; it might also include graphics.

Concluding section that might include a summary, a recommendation, or some other kind of concluding statement.

Because reports are meant to be as reader-friendly as possible and because they convey a lot of information, they usually include more elaborate formatting than other kinds of writing: headings, often accompanied by a numbering system; bullets; typographical and spacing variations; graphics are typical.

Language/Design The language is generally formal, impersonal, objective, or even scientific. It may include many technical terms, if necessary, but otherwise should be as clear, concise, and jargon-free as possible. As with other workplace or academic writing, it should avoid errors in sentence structure, grammar, and mechanics.

Resume/Cover Letter

Situation/Purpose At some point in their lives, most people will apply for a job and for most jobs this will include submitting a resume and cover letter. A resume is a document that includes information about a person's education, job history, job-related skills and credentials, and contact information. Usually when people submit a resume as part of a job application, they submit it with a cover letter—a letter focused specifically on one particular job.

Content/Form Resumes usually follow a fairly standard template, with name, address, phone number, and e-mail address at the top, followed by headed sections for Objectives (the kind of job being sought), Education, Job Experience or Employment History, and Skills and/or Credentials. Many also include names and contact information for people that can give references, though some resumes simply say "References available upon request." Some resumes include personal information about age and marital status, though many do not. Most people's resumes are one page, but people with long and complex careers and qualifications may have multiple-page resumes. The section on Job Experience or Employment is usually the longest and includes a list of jobs that the person has had, usually in chronological order beginning with the most recent, and specific details about responsibilities and accomplishments for each job.

Cover letters are also usually a page long and rarely more than two pages, even for people with long and complex careers, and they typically follow some variation on this format: The first paragraph identifies the job being applied for and usually how the applicant knows about the job, for example from a newspaper ad, a school placement office, or a personal contact. This paragraph may end with a brief overall statement about the applicant's interest in and/or suitability for the job. The content and order of the middle two or three paragraphs depends on the type of job and the applicant's background, but typical arrangements include a paragraph on education, training, and credentials; a paragraph on relevant job experiences; and a paragraph on accomplishments, other qualifications, and interests; or one paragraph on education and job experiences and one paragraph on why the applicant is particularly suited for this job or company. The final paragraph usually includes information on how the applicant can be contacted and a strong statement of interest in discussing the job further.

Sample resumes and cover letters can be found in many books or online sites, and word processing programs often include a variety of templates for both resumes and cover letters. These are very useful in helping you understand the reader's expectations, but avoid following these models and templates too closely, especially in terms of specific wording; remember that since many other people applying for the same job may also use these models and templates, employers may see the exact same sentence dozens or hundreds of time. The key to a successful resume and cover letter is to find the delicate balance between meeting the reader's expectations, which may be fairly narrow and even rigid, and creating a picture of yourself as a uniquely qualified individual.

Language/Design The language of a cover letter should have the characteristics of any business letter: sentences should be clear and concise; word choice should be precise and relatively formal; there should be no errors in grammar, punctuation, or mechanics; and connections between sentences and paragraphs should be clear. The layout on the page should be simple and clean, and the formatting should be fairly simple; for example, use the same type face and font size throughout. It's acceptable to put some information—for example, a list of accomplishments or skills—in the form of a bulleted list rather than a traditional paragraph, but don't rely too heavily on bulleted lists in your cover letter; the majority of the letter should be in the form of connected prose.

The formatting for a resume can be more complex and creative, with headings for categories of information like education, employment history, and skills, and bulleted lists for individual items within these categories. But, again, keep the overall layout as simple and clean as possible. Published samples and templates are generally good models for formatting. The language of a resume should also be clear, correct, and relatively formal, though resumes can make more use of phrases in bulleted lists rather than complete sentences in connected prose.

For both resumes and cover letters, use spell check and grammar check, proofread carefully, have someone else proofread carefully, and then proofread again yourself.

(For an example of a resume and cover letter, see pages 56–57.)

Review

Situation/Purpose Reviews are written in response to books, films, plays, restaurants, musical and dance performances, art exhibits, and architecture. Perhaps it is more useful to distinguish reviews by purpose, for example, scholarly reviews written for professional journals, media reviews written by professional writers, and unsolicited reviews written by the general public and published on the Internet. In the first instance, practitioners in specific disciplines assess the contribution of a text or performance to the field as a whole; media reviewers—often writing on short deadlines—give their readers the first public response to new entertainment; and customer reviews give people a forum to share their opinions about a particular book or exhibit. Part of a professional reviewer's responsibility is to discover fresh talent and original work as well as to cover work by prominent artists. It is worth nothing that a review brings a certain amount of notoriety and attention to a subject. Lack of critical attention often prevents less well-established writers or artists from getting the kind of public notice that would give them an audience. A reviewer has a certain amount of power in determining who and what gets the exposure so crucial to finding an audience.

Content/Form Reviews take much of their interest from the works they describe, but reviews are themselves written texts and, as such, should be able to stand on their own as well-organized, interesting pieces of writing. Reviews differ from reports in that they provide a critical analysis. Even an informal review submitted to an Internet bookseller will not be published online if it does not include some discussion of how and why the opinion is formed. Generally, reviews include a description of the text, exhibit, or performance; an analysis of how well it accomplishes its purpose; and an evaluation of the contribution of the work. Within that framework is much room for variation. Reviewers must include enough information for their readers to understand what they are talking about, but the description should be pointed and not include too much information. Reviews customarily include full bibliographic information. The description should provide a context to help readers understand something about the author, artist, and so on; explain why the work was written or produced; and tell something about the particular framework or approach used. The review should address the strengths and weaknesses of the text in terms of its purpose, its comprehensiveness, and its style. Examples or specific quotes help illustrate this information and enhance the reviewer's credibility. Reviewers also evaluate the worth of the work by comparing it to other works of its kind and determining what new ground it has broken or what new perspective it has added to a field.

Language/Design Language may vary depending on who is reviewing, what is being reviewed, and where the review will be published. The overall tone and specific word choice reflect the writer's individual style as well as the nature of the publication. Language may range from casual and hip to formal and academic. Consider whether or not to use the first person. Since the entire review is your opinion, it is not necessary to preface your observations with "I think" or "I believe." Most commonly the first person is reserved to describe the experience of reading or viewing rather than introducing an opinion. For example, "I sat in stunned silence with the rest of the audience after the 20-minute soliloquy." Reviewers usually use the present tense when writing about the text or the author and the past tense when discussing the subject of the book, for example, "This documentary focuses mainly on the alternative rock scene of the 1980s but pays scant attention to rap music, although rap actually contributed more to the reshaping of popular culture while alternative music mainly influenced other musicians."

(For an example of this genre, see page 90.)

Web Page

Situation/Purpose Anyone from a kid to a corporation can have a Web page, and it's likely that in the future more people and institutions will use Web pages to communicate in a variety of ways for a variety of purposes. Students at all levels make Web pages as class projects; business people and professionals have work-related Web pages; and ordinary people have Web pages to express opinions, circulate information, and find others who share their interests. Businesses and other institutions of all sizes use Web pages to sell or otherwise promote their products and services. Individuals might have one Web page that they keep updated throughout their life, they might have several for different aspects of their life, or they might create short-term ones for specific purposes. If you are creating a Web page for a class, the purpose may be just to learn how to do it, and in that case your page may simply be an introduction to yourself. Inside or outside of class, Web pages may also have a variety of specific purposes—to make connections around interests, communicate ideas, promote causes, and publicize events. Part of the purpose of a Web page is to attract people to visit and then read the page, but the primary purpose is to inform, persuade, entertain, surprise, and/or challenge those who visit and stay.

Content/Form The content includes background and current information that may be personal, institutional, or issue oriented, depending on the purpose. A Web "page" is usually in fact multiple pages, and hypertext allows readers to move quickly from one page to another in order to follow a thread of information. Hyperlinks allow readers to follow a thread of information to other sites on the Web. Often Web pages include a place for interaction between the owner and the reader or between readers. A great attraction of Web pages is that they combine words, color graphics, and even sound; and the graphics may include designs, drawings, photos, and even animated elements. The choice and arrangement of the elements should be appropriate to the purpose and intended audience. The text and graphics should interact in interesting ways, but the purpose of each element and the relationships between the elements should be clear.

Language/Design Sometimes the language is very plain and straightforward. even formal; often it is playful, casual, and personal; occasionally it is in-your-face, even offensive. As with the elements of content and form, the language should thoughtfully reflect purpose and audience.

(For an example of this genre, see page 52.)

Credits

Text Credits

Adams, Adrian and Paul McKibben, "Sampling Without Permission Is Theft" as appeared in *Billboard* (Commentary), March 5, 1994. Reprinted by permission of Billboard and its authors.

Babbitt, Milton, "Purple Politics—Individuality Surrendered for Preservation," from Insight Section, *San Antonio Express-News*, August 17, 1997. Copyright © 1997 San Antonio Express-News. Reprinted by permission.

Barrett, Andrea, "Why We Go," *The New York Times Magazine*, June 6, 1999, pp. 77–79. Copyright © 1999 by Andrea Barrett. Reprinted by permission of The Wendy Weil Agency, Inc.

Bernstein, Nell, "Goin Gangsta, Choosin' Cholita" *San Jose Mercury News*, November 13, 1994. Reprinted by permission of Nell Bernstein.

Bernstein, Aaron, "A Leg for the Lowly Temp." Reprinted from June 21, 1999 issue of *Business Week* by special permission, copyright © 1999 by The McGraw-Hill Companies, Inc.

Bérubé, Michael, from "Life as We Know It" as appeared in *Harper's Magazine*, December 1994. Reprinted by permission of Michael Berúbé.

Boyd, Todd, from *Am I Black Enough for You? Popular Culture from the 'Hood and Beyond*. Indiana University Press, 1997. Reprinted by permission of the publisher.

Boyte, Harry C. and Nancy N, Kari, from *Building America: The Democratic Promise of Public Work*, by Harry C. Boyte and Nancy N. Kari. Reprinted by permission of Temple University Press. © 1996 by Temple University. All Rights Reserved.

Brady, James, "Save Money: Help the Disabled," *New York Times*, August 29, 1989. Copyright © 1989 by The New York Times Co. Reprinted by permission.

Chappell, Mary Lil, "FOCUS: Viva el Color!" from Editorial Section, *San Antonio Express-News*, August 10, 1997. Copyright © 1997 San Antonio Express-News. Reprinted by permission.

Chiem, Phat X., "Taggers Spray Over Vandal Image," *Chicago Tribune*, September 12, 1996. Copyright © 1996 Chicago Tribune. Reprinted by permission of The Chicago Tribune.

Cisneros, Sandra, "Purple Politics—Our Tejano History Has Become Invisible," Copyright © 1997 by Sandra Cisneros. First published in *San Antonio Express-News*, August 17, 1997. Copyright © 1997 San Antonio Express-News. Reprinted by permission of Susan Bergholz Literary Services, NY. All rights reserved.

City of San Antonio, "Historic Districts of San Antonio: Neighbors in History." From a brochure funded in part by the National Park Service, U.S. Department of the Interior, as administered by the Texas Historical Commission and the City of San Antonio.

Cox, Tony. From Tavis Smiley Show "Continuing Controversy Over Construction of a Memorial at the World Trade Center Site" by Tony Cox, National Public Radio, December 5, 2003. Copyright © NPR 2003. Any unauthorized duplication is strictly prohibited.

Crawford, Margaret, "Mi Casa Es Su Casa" in *Assemblage* 24 August, 1994, pp. 12–19. Reprinted by permission of Margaret Crawford.

Durke, Martha, "Real Issue Behind Purple House Is Tolerance," *San Antonio Express-News*, August 12, 1997. Copyright © 1997 San Antonio Express-News. Reprinted by permission.

Ehrenreich, Barbara, "Nickel and Dimed: On (Not) Getting By in America" as appeared in *Harper's Magazine*, January 1999. Copyright © 1999 by Barbara Ehrenreich. Reprinted by permission of International Creative Management, Inc.

Freeman, Hayden, "Your Turn" ("Cisneros Put Your Cart Before the Horse") from Editorial Section, *San Antonio Express-News*, August 23, 1997. Copyright © 1997 San Antonio Express-News. Reprinted by permission.

Garland-Thomson, Rosemarie, "The FDR Memorial: Who Speaks from the Wheelchair?" as appeared in *The Chronicle of Higher Education*. Reprinted by permission of Rosemarie Garland-Thomson.

Goleman, Daniel. Reprinted with permission of *Harvard Business Review* from "What Makes a Leader" by Daniel Goleman, *Harvard Business Review*, November-December, 1998. Copyright © 1998 by the President and Fellows of Harvard College. All Rights Reserved.

Greenberg, Mike, "Purple Debate Reaches Commission, "*San Antonio Express-News*, August 7, 1997. Copyright © 1997 San Antonio Express-News. Reprinted by permission.

Goozner, Merrill, "Longtime Temps Want Some Perks," *Chicago Tribune*, June 22, 1999. Copyright © 1999 Chicago Tribune. Reprinted with permission of The Chicago Tribune.

Haar, Sharon and Christopher Reed, from "Coming Home: A Postscript on Postmodernism" from *Not at Home: The Suppression of Domesticity in Modern Art and Architecture* edited by Christopher Reed. Copyright © 1996 by Sharon Haar and Christopher Reed. Reprinted by permission of the publisher, Thames & Hudson.

Harrington, Richard. "On the Beat: U2's Double Trouble" by Richard Harrington, *Washington Post*, December 18, 1991. Copyright © 1991 by the Washington Post, reprinted with permission.

Hassett, Brian from *The Temp Survival Guide: How to Prosper as an Economic Nomad of the Nineties.* Copyright © 1997 by Brian Hassett. All rights reserved. Reprinted by permission of Citadel Press/Kensington Publishing Corp. http://www.kensingtonbooks.com.

Heng, Chan Lean, "Women on the Global Assembly Line" from *Globalization, Adult Education and Training: Impacts and Issues*, Shirley Walters, editor. Zed Books, 1998. Reprinted by permission of Zed Books, Ltd.

Hewson, Paul, Dave Evans, Adam Clayton and Larry Mullen, "I Still Haven't Found What I'm Looking For." Copyright © 1987 Universal-Polygram International Publishing, Inc. All rights reserved. Used by permission.

Island Records Ltd. et al. vs. SST Records et al., United States District Court, Central District of California, Case No. CV 91-4735AAH, September 1991.

Ivy, Robert, "Memorials, Monuments, and Meaning" by Robert Ivy, *Architectural Record*, July 2002, Vol. 190 Issue 7, p. 84. Reprinted by permission.

Kimmelman, Michael. "The New Ground Zero: Finding Comfort in the Safety of Names" by Michael Kimmelman from *The New York Times*, Sunday, August 31, 2003. Copyright © 2003 by The New York Times Co. Reprinted by permission.

Kitaj, R. B., from *First Diasporist Manifesto* by R. B. Kitaj. Copyright © 1989. Reprinted by permission of Thames & Hudson.

Klinghoffer, David, "The Heart of the Matter." Reprinted with the permission of The Free Press, a Division of Simon & Schuster Adult Publishing Group, from *The Lord Will Gather Men: My Journey to Jewish Orthodoxy* by David Klinghoffer. Copyright © 1998 by David Klinghoffer. All rights reserved.

Ledbetter, James, "Imitation of Life" from *Vibe* (Fall 1992). Reprinted with permission of the author.

Lin, Maya Ying. "Statement by Maya Ying Lin" from the competition submission for the Vietnam Veterans Memorial, March, 1981. Reprinted by permission of Maya Lin.

Lin, Maya Ying. "Vietnam Veterans Memorial." Reprinted with the permission of Simon & Schuster Adult Publishing Group, from *Boundaries* by Maya Lin. Copyright © 2000 by Maya Lin. All rights reserved.

Linton, Simi, from "Applications" in *Claiming Disability: Knowledge and Identity*. Copyright © 1998. Reprinted by permission of New York University Press.

Longmore, Paul K., "The Second Phase: From Disability Rights to Disability Culture" as appeared in *The Disability Rag and Resource*, September/October 1995. Reprinted by permission of Paul K. Longmore.

Madden, Shane, "A Portfolio of Self Representations" by Shane Madden. Reprinted by permission of the author.

McDowell, Edwin, "A Noted 'Hispanic' Novelist Proves to be Someone Else" in *The New York Times*, July 22, 1984. Copyright © 1984 by The New York Times Co. Reprinted by permission.

Meredith, Robyn, "For This We Sent You to College?" in *The New York Times*, June 9, 1997. Copyright © 1997 by The New York Times Co. Reprinted by permission.

Negativland, "U2 Negativland: The Case from Our Side" Press Release, November 10, 1991. Reprinted by permission of Negativland, P.O. Box 7218, Olympia, Washington 98502, http://www.negativland.com.

Negativland, "In Fair Use Debate, Art Must Come First," *Billboard* (Commentary), December 25, 1993. Reprinted by permission of Billboard and Negativland, P.O. Box 7218, Olympia, Washington 98502, www.negativland.com.

New York Times Editors, "Blank Check for the Disabled?" *New York Times*, September 6, 1989. Copyright © 1989 by The New York Times Co. Reprinted by permission.

Norris, Michele and Lisa McRee, "The Purple House," transcript from *ABC Good Morning America*, July 15, 1998. Copyright © 1998 American Broadcasting

Companies, Inc. All rights reserved. Reprinted with permission and courtesy of ABC News.

Pollan, Michael, "The Triumph of Burbopolis" as appeared in *The New York Times Magazine*, April 9, 2000. Reprinted by permission of Michael Pollan.

Putnam, Robert D., "Towards An Agenda for Social Capitalists." Reprinted with the permission of Simon & Schuster Adult Publishing Group, from *Bowling Alone: The Collapse and Revival of American Community* by Robert D. Putnam. Copyright © 2000 by Robert D. Putnam. All rights reserved.

Quammen, David, "Review of *Famous All Over Town*" from *The New York Times,* April 24, 1983. Copyright © 1983 by The New York Times Co. Reprinted by permission.

Reich, Robert, "Becoming a Knowledge Worker" from *The Work of Nations.* Copyright © 1991 by Robert B. Reich. Reprinted by permission of Alfred B. Knopf, a division of Random House, Inc.

Rigler, Trevor, "My Last Temp Job" from *Best of Temp Slave,* Jeff Kelly, ed. Garrett County Press, 1997. Reprinted with permission of the publisher.

Rodriguez, Richard, "Late Victorians: San Francisco, AIDS, and the Homosexual Stereotype" as appeared in *Harper's Magazine,* October 1990. Copyright © 1990 by Richard Rodriguez. Reprinted by permission of Georges Borchardt, Inc., for the author.

RTMARK, Press Release "RTMARK Finds Bucks For Beck Rip-off," February 17, 1998, http://www.rtmark.com. Reprinted by permission of ®TMark, Inc.

Rybczynski, Witold, "Comfort and Well Being" from *Home: A Short History of an Idea.* Copyright © 1986 by Witold Rybczynski. Used by permission of Viking Penguin, a division of Penguin Putnam, Inc.

Samiljan, Tom. "Building a Desktop Computer" by Tom Samiljan from *Rolling Stone,* June 9, 2000. Copyright © Rolling Stone LLC 2000. All Rights Reserved. Reprinted by Permission.

Santiago, Danny. Reprinted with the permission of Simon & Schuster Adult Publishing Group, from *Famous All Over Town* by Danny Santiago. Copyright © 1983 by Danny Santiago. All rights reserved.

Santiago, Esmeralda, "Skin" as appeared in *Body,* Sharon Sloan Fiffer and Steve Fiffer, editors. An Avon Book, 1999. Reprinted by permission of Esmeralda Santiago.

Salas, Berenice, "Delicious Culture in a Pushcart" by Berenice Salas. Reprinted by permission.

Scruggs, Jan C. and Joel L. Swerdlow, from *To Heal a Nation.* Copyright © 1985 by Jan C. Scruggs and Joel L. Swerdlow. Reprinted by permission of the authors.

Spiegler, Marc, "Marketing Street Culture: Bringing Hip-Hop Style to the Mainstream." Originally published in *American Demographics,* November, 1996. Updated by the author, November 2000. Reprinted by permission of Marc Spiegler.

Stallcup, Charles, "Your Turn" ("Reader Overdosed on 'Cisneros Edition'") from Editorial Section, *San Antonio Express-News,* November 23, 1997. Copyright © 1997 San Antonio Express-News. Reprinted by permission.

Suarez, Ray, with Ellis Cose, Joie Chem, George de Lama, and Mark Trahant, from transcript "Race Diversity in the Media" (Hour 2). Copyright © Copyright NPR ® 1999. The news report by Ray Suarez was originally broadcast on National Public Radio's "Talk of the Nation®" on July 8, 1999, and is used with the permission of National Public Radio, Inc. Any unauthorized duplication is strictly prohibited.

Taulbert, Clifton L., "Bright Boy from the Delta" from *Watching Our Crops Come In.* Copyright © 1997 by Clifton L. Taulbert. Used by permission of Viking Penguin, a division of Penguin Putnam, Inc.

Temporary Workers Alliance, from *Consumer Guide to "Best Practices" Temp Agencies,* Volume 8, October 2000. Reprinted by permission.

Tuan, Yi-Fu, from *Escapism,* pp. 5–11, 17–27, 205–207. Copyright © 1998. Reprinted by permission of Johns Hopkins University Press.

Turkle, Sherry. Reprinted and edited with the permission of Simon & Schuster Adult Publishing Group, from *Life On the Screen: Identity in the Age of the Internet* by Sherry Turkle. Copyright © 1995 by Sherry Turkle. All rights reserved.

Weinstein, Michael, "A Man's Place" in *The New York Times,* May 16, 1999. Copyright © 1999 by The New York Times Co. Reprinted by permission.

Wied, Nancy de, "Cisneros Put Cart Before the Horse," *San Antonio Express-News,* August 23, 1997. Copyright © 1997 San Antonio Express-News. Reprinted by permission.

Williams, Patricia, "Hate Radio" from *Ms.* Magazine, March/April 1994. Reprinted by permission of *Ms.* Magazine. Copyright © 1994.

Wolman, William. From *The Judas Economy* by William Wolman. Copyright © 1997 by William Wolman and Anne Colamosca. Reprinted by permission of Perseus Books PLC, a member of Perseus Books, L.L.C.

Wright, Robert and Robert Kaplan, "Mr. Order Meets Mr. Chaos" (Debate) by Robert Wright and Robert Kaplan, from *Foreign Policy*, May/June 2001. Copyright © 2001, Copyright Clearance Center, Inc.

Yerkes, Susan, "King William Seeing Red Over Purple," *San Antonio Express-News*, July 26, 1997. Copyright © 1997 San Antonio Express-News. Reprinted by permission.

Yerkes, Susan, "Now We Know Why It's Called Purple Passion," *San Antonio Express-News*, July 30, 1997. Copyright © 1997 San Antonio Express-News. Reprinted by permission.

Photo Credits

Page 6: Tribune Photo by Jose M. Ororio; **39L:** Van Gogh's Chair by Vincent Van Gogh. © National Gallery, London, NG3862; **39R:** © R.B. Kitaj, courtesy, Marlborough Gallery, New York; **96:** Richard Fremont/Getty Images; **167:** Douglas Kirkland/Corbis; **175:** Joel W. Rogers/Corbis; **194 (all):** Photographs from the collection of Clifton L. Taulbert, reprinted from Watching Our Crops Come In published by Viking, copyrights Clifton L. Taulbert 1997; **205:** Faith Ringold © 1983; **221:** Ezra Stoller/Esto; **225:** Ezra Stoller/Esto; **227:** Angelica Pozo © 1991. Photograph by Howard T. Agriesti; **228:** Yong Soon Min; **228:** Yong Soon Min; **229:** Stuart Netsky; **287:** Conversation Piece by Juan Munoz. Hirshhorn Museum and Sculpture Garden, Smithsonian Institution, Museum Purchase, 1995. Photo by Lee Stalsworth; **390:** Philip Gould/Corbis; **419:** David Turnley/Corbis; **421:** Menahem Kahana/AFP/Corbis; **421:** Menahem Kahana/AFP/Getty Images; **470:** Bill Stover/NYT Pictures; **474 (top, left):** Bill Stover/NYT Pictures; **474 (top right):** Lloyd DeGrane; **474 (bottom left):** Steve Woit; **474 (bottom, right):** Mark Perlstein; **475 (right):** Steve Woit; **556:** © 1994 Terry Everton; **557:** ©1993 Terry Everton.

Index

Academic article, 561
Adams, Adrian and Paul McKibbens, "Sampling Without Permission Is Theft," 160
Address, 562
Advice book, 563
Arguments, writing, 33
Aristotle, 2
Article, 563
Assimilation, 2
Audience, 2
Authenticity, 2

Babbitt, Milton, "Purple Politics—Individuality Surrendered for Preservation," 283
Barrett, Andrea, "Why We Go," 171
"Becoming a Knowledge Worker" (Reich), 447
Bernstein, Aaron, "A Leg Up for the Lowly Temp," 536
Bernstein, Nell, "Goin' Gangsta, Choosin' Cholita," 97
Bérubé, Michael, "Life as We Know It," 368
"Blank Check for the Disabled?" (*New York Times*), 380
Boyd, Todd, "Representin' the Real," 58
Boyte, Harry C., and Nancy N. Kari, "The New Democracy," 291
Brady, James S., "Save Money: Help the Disabled," 379
Brainstorming, 18
"Bright Boy from the Delta" (Taulbert), 193
Brochures, 35, 564
"Build a Desktop Studio" (Samiljan), 162
Business letter, 565

Chappell, Mary Lil, "Viva el Color!" 278
Chicago Tribune, 5, 37
Chiem, Phat X., "Taggers Spray Over Vandal Image," 5–7, 18–19
"Christian Angst" (Kelly), 556, 557
"Cisneros Put Cart before the Horse" (de Wied), 278
Cisneros, Sandra, "Purple Politics—Our Tejano History Has Become Invisible," 280
Civic dialogues, 2, 3
Codes, 566
Collaborating with others, 35–38
Collaborative teams, 37–38
"Comfort and Well-Being" (Rybczynski), 207
Comics, 35, 567
"Coming Home" (Haar and Reed), 219
Commentary, 578
Consequences, 3
  analyzing contexts for writing, 17
  analyzing readings in context, 14–15
  defined, 8–9
  in reading the graffiti article, 10
  in writing scenarios, 11–12
"Consumer Guide to the 'Best Practices' Temp Agencies," 539
"Continuing Controversy over Construction of a Memorial at the World Trade Center Site" (National Public Radio), 416
Conversations, 7
  defined, 1–3
Cover letter, 568, 582
Crawford, Margaret, and Adobe LA, "Mi Casa es Su Casa," 243
Cultural change, 2
Cultural conversations, 2, 3

de Wied, Nancy, "Cisneros Put Cart before the Horse," 278
Debate, 569
"Delicious Culture in a Pushcart" (Salas), 18–23
Dialogues, 2, 569
Diversity, 2
Drafting the writing project, 18, 30–31
Duke, Martha, "Real Issue Behind Purple Is Tolerance," 278

Editing the writing project, 33
Editorials, 2
Ehrenreich, Barbara, "Nickel-and-Dimed: On (Not) Getting by in America," 497

Elbow, Peter, *Writing Without Teachers,* 30
Electronic mediums, 35
E-mail discussions, 18
Essays, 2, 570
analytical essay, 573
argumentative essay, 573
informal essay, 572
literary essay, 572
personal essay, 572
persuasive essay, 573
Evaluating sources, 28

"Famous All Over Town," review of, (Quammen), 90
"Famous All Over Town" (Santiago), 82
"FDR Memorial: Who Speaks from the Wheelchair?, The" (Garland-Thomson), 382
Feature story, 574
Feedback, 18
"First Diasporist Manifesto," (Kitaj), 189
"For This We Sent You to College?" (Meredith), 472
Freeman, Hayden, "Go Ahead and Name Paper after Purple House," 279

Garland-Thomson, Rosemarie, "The FDR Memorial: Who Speaks from the Wheelchair?" 382
Genre, 3, 9
analyzing contexts for writing, 16
analyzing readings in context, 13
defined, 8
in reading the graffiti article, 9
in writing scenarios, 11
Genre Glossary, 561
"Go Ahead and Name Paper after Purple House" (Freeman), 279
"Goin' Gangsta, Choosin' Cholita" (Bernstein), 97
Goleman, Daniel P., "What Makes a Leader?" 484
Goozner, Merrill, "Longtime Temps Want Some Perks," 532
Grant proposal genre, 18
Greenberg, Mike, "Purple Debate Reaches Commission—Cisneros Agrees to Work with City Staff on Mutually Acceptable Color Scheme," 277
Guide to Analyzing Contexts for Writing, 15–17, 29, 30, 32
Guide to Analyzing Readings in Context, 12–15
Guidelines, 566

Haar, Sharon, and Christopher Reed, "Coming Home," 219
Handouts for presentations, 37
Harrington, Richard, "U2's Double Trouble," 138
Hassett, Brian, "The Temp Survival Guide," 550
"Hate Radio: Why We Need to Tune In to Limbaugh and Stern" (Williams), 319
"Heart of the Matter, The" (Klinghoffer), 121
Heng, Chan Lean, "Women on the Global Assembly Line," 460
"Hope for the Best, Expect the Worst" (Kaplan), 427

"I Still Haven't Found What I'm Looking For" (U2), 137
Idea development, 30
"Identity in the Age of the Internet" (Turkle), 67
"Imitation of Life" (Ledbetter), 115
"In Fair Use Debate, Art Must Come First" (Negativland), 158
Integrating material from other texts, 34–35
Internet, 18, 25, 27–28
Interview, 575
Interviewing experts, 25
"In the Long Run, We're All Interdependent" (Wright), 430
Introduction, writing project, 32
Island Records/Warner-Chappell Lawsuit, excerpts from, 140
Ivy, Robert, "Memorials, Monuments, and Meaning," 409

Kaplan, Robert
"Hope for the Best, Expect the Worst," 427
"Passion Play," 431
Kelly, Jeff, "Christian Angst," 556, 557
Kimmelman, Michael, "The New Ground Zero: Finding Comfort in the Safety of Names," 412
"King William Seeing Red over Purple" (Yerkes), 275
Kitaj, R.B., "First Diasporist Manifesto," 189
Klinghoffer, David, "The Heart of the Matter," 121

Language, 3, 8
analyzing contexts for writing, 16–17
analyzing readings in context, 14
defined, 8
in reading the graffiti article, 10
in writing scenarios, 11, 33
"Late Victorians: San Francisco, AIDS, and the Homosexual Stereotype" (Rodriguez), 249
Ledbetter, James, "Imitation of Life," 115
"Leg Up for the Lowly Temp, A" (Bernstein), 536
Letter to the editor, 576
Library research, 18, 27–28
"Life as We Know It" (Bérubé), 368
Lin, Maya Ying
"Statement by Maya Lin, March 1981," 396
"Vietnam Veterans Memorial," 398
Linton, Simi, "Negotiating Disability," 353
Longmore, Paul K., "The Second Phase: From Disability Rights to Disability Culture," 344

"Longtime Temps Want Some Perks" (Goozner), 532

Madden, Shane, "A Portfolio of Self Representations," 50
Manifesto, 577
"Man's Place, A" (de Grazia, Golden, Jones, Schor, Tienda, Wilson, and Weinstein), 516
"Marketing Street Culture: Bringing Hip-Hop Style to the Mainstream" (Spiegler), 104
McDowell, Edwin "A Noted 'Hispanic' Novelist Proves to Be Someone Else," 91
Mechanics of writing, 33
Media, 24–25
"Media Commentary on the Americans with Disabilities Act," 378
Memo, 565
"Memorials, Monuments, and Meaning" (Ivy), 409
Meredith, Robyn, "For This We Sent You to College?" 472
"Mi Casa es Su Casa" (Crawford and Adobe LA), 243
"Mr. Order Meets Mr. Chaos," 423
Multiculturalism, 2
Multiple-author teams, 36–37
"My Minivan and World Peace" (Wright), 424

National Public Radio, "Continuing Controversy over Construction of a Memorial at the World Trade Center Site," 416
"Nature and Culture" (Tuan), 177
Negativland
  "In Fair Use Debate, Art Must Come First," 158
  "U2/Negativland: The Case from Our Side," 147
"Negotiating Disability" (Linton), 353
"New Democracy, The" (Boyte and Kari), 291
"New Ground Zero: Finding Comfort in the Safety of Names, The" (Kimmelman), 412
Newspaper articles, 2
New York Times, "Blank Check for the Disabled?" 380
"Nickel-and-Dimed: On (Not) Getting by in America" (Ehrenreich), 497
Norris, Michele, and Lisa McRee, "The Purple House: Coat of Paint Causes Cultural War in San Antonio," 285
"Noted 'Hispanic' Novelist Proves to Be Someone Else, A" (McDowell), 91
"Now We Know Why It's Called Purple Passion" (Yerkes), 276

Online posts, 578
Online research, 18, 25, 27–28
Opinion piece, 578
Oral class presentation, 37
Outlining the draft, 31, 33

Paraphrasing material from other texts, 34
"Passage to India: The Case of Bangalore, A" (Wolman and Anne Colamosca), 435
"Passion Play" (Kaplan), 431
Peer review worksheet, 31–32
Personal experiences, 24
Plagiarism, 34–35
Planning the writing project, 18
Pollan, Michael, "The Triumph of Burbopolis," 234
"Portfolio of Self Representations, A" (Madden), 50
Profile, 574
Proposal, 580
"Purple Debate Reaches Commission—Cisneros Agrees to Work with City Staff on Mutually Acceptable Color Scheme" (Greenberg), 277
"Purple House: Coat of Paint Causes Cultural War in San Antonio, The" (Norris and McRee), 285
"Purple Politics—Individuality Surrendered for Preservation" (Babbitt), 283
"Purple Politics—Our Tejano History Has Become Invisible" (Cisneros), 280
Purpose for writing, 29
Putnam, Robert D., "Toward an Agenda for Social Capitalists," 304

Quammen, David, Review of "Famous All Over Town," 90
Quoting material from other texts, 34

"Reader Overdosed on 'Cisneros edition'" (Stallcup), 279
Reading strategies, 3, 24–28
  comparing with other texts, 26–27
  consequences of the text, 26
  discussions in the media, 24–25
  evaluating sources, 28
  genre of the text, 26
  interviewing experts, 25
  language of the text, 26
  related personal experiences, 24
  searching library and Internet for related texts, 25, 27–28
  situation of the writer, 25
  visiting a real or electronic bookstore, 28
"Real Issue Behind Purple Is Tolerance" (Duke), 278
Reflecting on the project, 30
Reflective essay, 568
Reich, Robert, "Becoming a Knowledge Worker," 447
Report, 581
"Representin' the Real" (Boyd), 58
Researching the project, 18
Research paper, 561
Resume, 582
Review, 583
Revising the writing project, 18, 31–33
Rhetorical concepts, 2–3, 7
Rigler, Trevor, "My Last Temp Job?" 558

Rodriguez, Richard, 2
"Late Victorians: San Francisco, AIDS, and the Homosexual Stereotype," 249
RTMARK, "RTMARK Finds Bucks for Beck Rip-Off," 164
Rybczynski, Witold, "Comfort and Well-Being," 207

Salas, Berenice, "Delicious Culture in a Pushcart," 18–23
Samiljan, Tom, "Build a Desktop Studio," 162
"Sampling Without Permission Is Theft" (Adams and McKibbins), 160
San Antonio, city of, "Understanding the Preservation Process," 269
Santiago, Danny, "Famous All Over Town," 82
Santiago, Esmeralda, "Skin," 43
"Save Money: Help the Disabled" (Brady), 379
"Second Phase: From Disability Rights to Disability Culture, The" (Longmore), 344
Sense of place, 2
Situation, 3, 9
analyzing contexts for writing, 15
analyzing readings in context, 12–13
defined, 7
in reading the graffiti article, 9
for writing, 29
in writing scenarios, 11
"Skin" (Santiago), 43
Speech, 562
Spiegler, Marc, "Marketing Street Culture: Bringing Hip-Hop Style to the Mainstream," 104
Spoken communication, 1–2
Stallcup, Charles, "Reader Overdosed on 'Cisneros edition'," 279
"Statement by Maya Lin, March 1981" (Lin), 396
Suarez, Ray, Ellis Close, Joie Chen, George de Lama, and Mark Trahant, "Symposium on Minority Journalists and the Media," 327
Summarizing material from other texts, 34
Surface errors, 33
Symposium, 569
"Symposium on Minority Journalists and the Media" Suarez, Close, Chen, de Lama, and Trahant), 327

"Taggers Spray Over Vandal Image" (Chiem), 5–7, 18–19
Taulbert, Clifton L., "Bright Boy from the Delta," 193
"Temp Survival Guide, The" (Hassett), 550
Thesis-driven writing, 33
Time frame for drafting the project, 30
"Toward an Agenda for Social Capitalists" (Putnam), 304
"Triumph of Burbopolis, The" (Pollan), 234
Tuan, Yi-Fu, "Nature and Culture," 177
Turkle, Sherry, "Identity in the Age of the Internet," 67

"Understanding the Preservation Process" (City of San Antonio), 269
"United States Copyright Act of 1976," 154
"U2's Double Trouble" (Harrington), 138
U2, "I Still Haven't Found What I'm Looking For," 137
"U2/Negativland: The Case from Our Side," (Negativland), 147

Universities, 2

"Vietnam Veterans Memorial Statement of Purpose," 395
"Vietnam Veterans Memorial" (Lin), 398
Visual texts, 35
"Viva el Color!" (Chappel), 278

Web pages, 35, 584
"What Makes a Leader?" (Goleman), 484
"Why We Go" (Barrett), 171
Williams, Patricia J., "Hate Radio: Why We Need to Tune In to Limbaugh and Stern," 319
Wolman, William, and Anne Colamosca, "A Passage to India: The Case of Bangalore," 435
"Women on the Global Assembly Line" (Heng), 460
Wright, Robert
"In the Long Run, We're All Interdependent," 430
"My Minivan and World Peace," 424
Writing arguments, 33
Writing process, 29
Writing strategies, 3, 29–38
collaborating with others, 35–38
drafting, 30–31
editing, 33
integrating material from other texts, 34–35
planning, 29–30
revising, 31–33
situation and purpose for writing, 29
visual texts, 35
writing process, 29
Writing teams, 35–38
Writing Without Teachers (Elbow), 30
Written communication, 1–2

Yerkes, Susan
"King William Seeing Red over Purple," 275
"Now We Know Why It's Called Purple Passion," 276